FORENSIC TOXICOLOGY

PUBLISHED AND FORTHCOMING TITLES IN THE *ADVANCED FORENSIC SCIENCE SERIES*

Published

Forensic Fingerprints
Firearm and Toolmark Examination and Identification
Forensic Biology
Forensic Chemistry
Professional Issues in Forensic Science
Materials Analysis in Forensic Science
Forensic Pathology
Forensic Anthropology
Forensic Engineering
Behavioral Analysis
Forensic Toxicology

Forthcoming

Digital and Document Examination

FORENSIC TOXICOLOGY

Advanced Forensic Science Series

Edited by

MAX M. HOUCK, PhD, FRSC

Managing Director, Forensic & Intelligence Services, LLC, St. Petersburg, FL, USA

ACADEMIC PRESS

An imprint of Elsevier

Academic Press is an imprint of Elsevier
125 London Wall, London EC2Y 5AS, United Kingdom
525 B Street, Suite 1800, San Diego, CA 92101-4495, United States
50 Hampshire Street, 5th Floor, Cambridge, MA 02139, United States
The Boulevard, Langford Lane, Kidlington, Oxford OX5 1GB, United Kingdom

Notices
Knowledge and best practice in this field are constantly changing. As new research and experience broaden our understanding, changes in research methods, professional practices, or medical treatment may become necessary.

Practitioners and researchers must always rely on their own experience and knowledge in evaluating and using any information, methods, compounds, or experiments described herein. In using such information or methods they should be mindful of their own safety and the safety of others, including parties for whom they have a professional responsibility.

To the fullest extent of the law, neither the Publisher nor the authors, contributors, or editors, assume any liability for any injury and/or damage to persons or property as a matter of products liability, negligence or otherwise, or from any use or operation of any methods, products, instructions, or ideas contained in the material herein.

Library of Congress Cataloging-in-Publication Data
A catalog record for this book is available from the Library of Congress

British Library Cataloguing-in-Publication Data
A catalogue record for this book is available from the British Library

ISBN: 978-0-12-800746-4
ISSN: 2352-6238

For information on all Academic Press publications visit our website at
https://www.elsevier.com/books-and-journals

Working together
to grow libraries in
developing countries

www.elsevier.com • www.bookaid.org

Publisher: Mica Haley
Acquisition Editor: Elizabeth Brown
Editorial Project Manager: Pat Gonzalez
Senior Production Project Manager: Priya Kumaraguruparan
Designer: Matthew Limbert

Typeset by TNQ Books and Journals

CONTENTS

SENIOR EDITOR: BIOGRAPHY

Max M. Houck is an internationally recognized forensic expert with research interests in anthropology, trace evidence, education, and the fundamentals of forensic science, both as a science and as an enterprise. He has worked in the private sector, the public sector (at the regional and federal levels), and academia. Dr. Houck has published in a wide variety of areas in the field, in books, book chapters, and peer-reviewed journals. His casework includes the Branch Davidian Investigation, the September 11 attacks on the Pentagon, the D.B. Cooper case, the US Embassy bombings in Africa, and the West Memphis Three case. He served for 6 years as the Chair of the Forensic Science Educational Program Accreditation Commission (FEPAC). Dr. Houck is a founding coeditor of the journal *Forensic Science Policy and Management*, with Jay Siegel; he has also coauthored a major textbook with Siegel, *Fundamentals of Forensic Science*. In 2012, Dr. Houck was in the top 1% of connected professionals on LinkedIn. Dr. Houck is currently the Managing Director of Forensic & Intelligences Services, LLC, St. Petersburg, FL. Dr. Houck is the Director of the Forensic Studies & Justice program at University of South Florida St. Petersburg.

LIST OF CONTRIBUTORS

J Beyer
Monash University, Southbank, VIC, Australia

M Breadmore
University of Tasmania, Hobart, TAS, Australia

H Buchannan
University of Strathclyde, Glasgow, UK

E Burton
Greater Manchester Police Forensic Services Branch, Manchester, UK

F Busetti
Curtin University of Technology, Perth, WA, Australia

B-L Chang
Department of Health, Taipei, Taiwan

W-C Cheng
Government Laboratory, Hong Kong Special Administrative Region

F Crispino
Université du Québec à Trois-Rivières, Trois-Rivières, QC, Canada

OH Drummer
Monash University, Southbank, VIC, Australia

J Epstein
Widener University School of Law, Wilmington, DE, USA

PD Felgate
Forensic Science Centre, Adelaide, SA, Australia

DS Fisher
King's College Hospital NHS Foundation Trust, London, UK

RJ Flanagan
King's College Hospital NHS Foundation Trust, London, UK

S Fu
University of Technology Sydney, Broadway, NSW, Australia

D Gerostamoulos
Monash University, Southbank, VIC, Australia

JV Goodpaster
Indiana University Purdue University Indianapolis, Indianapolis, IN, USA

R Guijt
University of Tasmania, Hobart, TAS, Australia

MM Houck
Consolidated Forensic Laboratory, Washington, DC, USA

M-C Huang
Department of Health, Taipei, Taiwan

GR Jones
Alberta Medical Examiners Office, Edmonton, AB, Canada

C Jurado
National Institute of Toxicology and Forensic Sciences, Sevilla, Spain

DH Kaye
Penn State School of Law, University Park, PA, USA

P Kintz
X-Pertise Consulting, Oberhausbergen, France

S-A Legrand
Ghent University, Ghent, Belgium

CE Lenehan
Flinders University, Adelaide, SA, Australia

SW Lewis
Curtin University, Perth, WA, Australia

CH Liao
Department of Health, Taipei, Taiwan

KF Lim
Deakin University, Burwood, VIC, Australia

RH Liu
University of Alabama, Birmingham, AL, USA

A Mendlein
Indiana University Purdue University Indianapolis, Indianapolis, IN, USA

C-S Ng
Government Laboratory, Hong Kong Special Administrative Region

N NicDaéid
University of Strathclyde, Glasgow, UK

JP Pascali
University of Verona, Verona, Italy

A Polettini
University of Verona, Verona, Italy

N-L Poon
Government Laboratory, Hong Kong Special Administrative Region

K Ramsey
Greater Manchester Police Forensic Services Branch, Manchester, UK

LP Raymon
NOVA Southeastern College of Osteopathic Medicine, Fort Lauderdale, FL, USA

L Rivier
Laurent Rivier Scientific Consulting, Lausanne, Switzerland

KA Savage
University of Strathclyde, Glasgow, UK

B Saw
Australian Federal Police, Canberra, ACT, Australia

WM Schneck
Spokane, WA, USA

KS Scott
Arcadia University, Glenside, PA, USA

N Scudder
Australian Federal Police, Canberra, ACT, Australia

A Shallan
University of Tasmania, Hobart, TAS, Australia

G Skopp
University Hospital, Heidelberg, Germany

E Stauffer
Commissariat d'identification judiciaire, Police cantonale Fribourg, Fribourg, Switzerland

N Stojanovska
University of Technology Sydney, Broadway, NSW, Australia

A Stowell
Environmental Science and Research Limited, Porirua, New Zealand

L Swann
University of Western Australia, Crawley, WA, Australia

C Szkudlarek
Indiana University Purdue University Indianapolis, Indianapolis, IN, USA

F Tagliaro
University of Verona, Verona, Italy

SC Turfus
Victorian Institute of Forensic Medicine, Southbank, VIC, Australia

A Verstraete
Ghent University, Ghent, Belgium

Ted Vosk
Criminal Defense Law Firm, Kirkland, WA, USA

R Wennig
Université du Luxembourg-Campus Limpertsberg, Avenue de la Faïencerie, Luxembourg

JG Wigmore
Toronto, ON, Canada

FOREWORD

> "The best thing for being sad," replied Merlin, beginning to puff and blow, "is to learn something. That's the only thing that never fails. You may grow old and trembling in your anatomies, you may lie awake at night listening to the disorder of your veins, you may miss your only love, you may see the world about you devastated by evil lunatics, or know your honor trampled in the sewers of baser minds. There is only one thing for it then — to learn. Learn why the world wags and what wags it. That is the only thing which the mind can never exhaust, never alienate, never be tortured by, never fear or distrust, and never dream of regretting. Learning is the only thing for you. Look what a lot of things there are to learn." —T.H. White, *The Once and Future King*.

Forensic science has much to learn. The breadth of the discipline alone should render any reasonably learned person dizzy with expectations—insects, explosives, liver functions, DNA, firearms, textiles, adhesives, skeletons…the list goes on forever. That is because anything, truly *anything*, can become evidence, from a single fiber to an entire ocean liner. Forensic science does not lack for specialized knowledge (some might stay too specialized) but what it is wanting is knowledge that is comprehensive, integrated, and foundational. Introductions to forensic science abound and many highly specialized texts are also available but a gap exists between the two: A bridge from novice to practitioner. As the 2009 NRC report noted,

> Forensic science examiners need to understand the principles, practices, and contexts of scientific methodology, as well as the distinctive features of their specialty. Ideally, training should move beyond apprentice-like transmittal of practices to education based on scientifically valid principles. NRC (2009, pp. 26—27).

The *Advanced Forensic Sciences Series* seeks to fill that gap. It is a unique source, combining entries from the world's leading specialists who contributed to the second edition of the award-winning *Encyclopedia of Forensic Sciences* and organizing them by topic into a series of volumes that are philosophically grounded yet professionally specialized. The series is composed of 12 volumes that cover the breadth of forensic science:

1. Professional Issues
2. Biology
3. Chemistry
4. Fingerprints
5. Firearms
6. Materials Analysis
7. Pathology
8. Anthropology

9. Engineering
10. Behavioral
11. Digital and Document Examination
12. Forensic Toxicology

Each volume contains sections common to all forensic sciences, such as professionalism, ethics, health and safety, and court testimony, and sections relevant to the topics in that particular subdiscipline. Pedagogy is included, providing review questions, discussion questions, the latest references in additional readings, and key words. Thus, each volume is suitable as a technical reference, an advanced textbook, or a training adjunct.

The *Advanced Forensic Science Series* provides expert information, useful teaching tools, and a ready source for instruction, research, and practice. I hope, like learning, it is the only thing for you.

M.M. Houck, PhD
Series Editor

Reference

National Research Council, 2009. Strengthening Forensic Science in the U.S.: A Path Forward. National Academies of Science, Washington, D.C.

PREFACE

Much is made of fingerprints being over 100 years old as a forensic method, but toxicology is over 200 years old (in its current recognizable form), thus being unquestionably the first forensic discipline. Toxicology's array of techniques sprouted from the work of Paracelsus[1] who coined the phrase "All things are poisonous and nothing is without poison; only the dose makes a thing not poisonous."

Modern toxicology truly began with the work of Orfila in the early 1800s but received a perceptual boost during the "Golden Age of Poisoning" in Victorian England.[2] Poisoning was a popular means of killing because poisons were readily available and easy to obtain. Used in myriad products, from fly paper to cosmetics (yes, cosmetics!), nearly anyone had access to lethal amounts of cyanide, strychnine, and arsenic. Cyanide and strychnine, while remarkably effective, left easy to determine clues as to their use. Arsenic, however, was the Prince of Poisons; at one point in France, arsenic was called *poudre de succession*, or "inheritance powder." Comparatively difficult to detect, arsenic is a tasteless, odorless chemical. The effects of arsenic could be mistaken for food poisoning or other illness, which made criminal intent harder to trace. Arsenic was so popular as a poison; a law was passed in 1851, the Arsenic Act, which legislated tight restrictions on its sale and required arsenic to be colored blue, making its use more apparent.

Dyeing notwithstanding, as an "invisible killer," poison casts a somewhat more fearful shadow than other approaches to homicide. Toxicology's ability to make the absent—and unseen—killer present is the pinnacle of what forensic science purports to do. From poisoning others to poisoning oneself, the role of modern forensic toxicology also identifies not only drugs of abuse but also the fatal consequences of their overuse.

Further, unlike most forensic disciplines, toxicology has an intermediary that breaks down or confounds its attempts to identify the poison or drug: The body. Toxicologists rarely see the drug in the body (possibly, however, through stomach contents) and must discern its presence and identity through its proxy data, called metabolites, of the body's attempts to break the substance down and process it. For example, heroin is broken down into morphine in the body, which is then further broken down into other by-products. This makes the toxicologist's hunt more complicated and requires not only extensive knowledge of drugs but also the body's effects on them. Related information from the crime scene (such as paraphernalia or prescription bottles) or the body (such as needle marks or other signs) can be crucial in narrowing down the possible suspected chemicals.

---

[1] His real name was Theophrastus Phillipus Auroleus Bombastus von Hohenheim (1493−1541); he worked under the name Paracelsus because he felt his work superseded that of the Roman Celsius. The original phrase is *Alle Dinge sind Gift und nichts ist ohne Gift; allein die Dosis macht, dass ein Ding kein Gift ist.*
[2] The Romans could have given the Victorians a run for their money in the poisoning game: As early as 331 BC, poisonings occurred in food or drinks at the dinner table or banquets. The Roman Emperor Nero was infamous for poisoning family members to remove political rivals. *Bon appetite!*

Section 1. Introduction

Toxicologists tend to be abstracted from their source materials. They receive vials and tubes that are samples drawn from the bodies of other people by hospital or morgue technicians. If one is squeamish (and why would you go into forensic science if you were?), then this might seem to be a good feature of the job. Plus, it does help to keep the toxicologist neutral and objective. However, it can also be a detriment because the human aspect of the case, along with potentially relevant information, might be ignored. While too much of this type of information can lead to cognitive biases, some amount is necessary to sort and prioritize evidence.

In the case of toxicology, some "traces" are truly invisible. Drugs and their metabolites cannot be seen in blood or urine and must be identified by highly technical means. The samples are real body fluids or tissues, but the "evidence" the toxicologist is seeking seems more elusive. Remember that the drugs themselves are almost never seen in the samples because the body has broken the compounds down into components and metabolites. The presence of the drug must be inferred, much as an animal's presence inferred from its tracks in the soil.

Principles of Forensic Science

F Crispino, Université du Québec à Trois-Rivières, Trois-Rivières, QC, Canada
MM Houck, Consolidated Forensic Laboratory, Washington, DC, USA

Glossary

Abduction Syllogism in which one premise is certain whereas the other one is only probable, generally presented as the best explanation to the former. Hence, abduction is a type of reasoning in which we know the law and the effect, and we attempt to infer the cause.

Deduction Process of reasoning, which moves from the general to the specific, and in which a conclusion follows necessarily from the stated premises. Hence, deduction is a type of reasoning in which, knowing the cause and the law, we infer the effect.

Forensic intelligence Understanding on how traces can be collected from the scene, processed, and interpreted within a holistic intelligence-led policing strategy.

Heuristic Process of reasoning by rules that are only loosely defined, generally by trial and error.

Holistic Emphasizing the importance of the whole and the interdependence of its parts.

Induction Process of deriving general principles from particular facts or instances, i.e., of reasoning that moves from the specific to the general. Hence, induction is a type of reasoning in which, knowing the cause and the effect (or a series of causes and effects), we attempt to infer the law by which the effects follow the cause.

Linkage blindness Organizational or investigative failure to recognize a common pattern shared on different cases.

Science The intellectual and practical activity encompassing the systematic study of the structure and behavior of the physical and natural world through observation and experiment. It is also defined as a systematically organized body of knowledge on a particular subject.

Given that it identifies and collects objects at crime scenes and then treats them as evidence, forensic science could appear at first glance to be only a pragmatic set of various disciplines, with practitioners adapting and developing tools and technologies to help the triers of fact (juries or judges) interpret information gained from the people, places, and things involved in a crime. The view could be—and has been—held that forensic science has no philosophic or fundamental unity and is merely the application of knowledge generated by other sciences. Indeed, many working forensic scientists regard themselves mainly as chemists, biologists, scientists, or technicians, and rarely as practitioners of a homogeneous body of knowledge with common fundamental principles.

Even the 2009 National Academy of Sciences National Research Council Report failed to recognize such a concept, certainly blurred by a semantic gap in the terminology itself of field practitioners, who confuse words such as "forensic science(s)," "criminalistic(s)," "criminology," "technical police," "scientific police," and so on, and generally restrict the scientific debate on analytical techniques and methods. An independent definition of forensic science, apart from its legal aspects, would support its scientific status and return the expert to his or her domain as scientist and interpreter of his analyses and results to assist the lay person.

What Is Forensic Science?

In its broadest sense, forensic science describes the utility of the sciences as they pertain to legal matters, to include many disciplines, such as chemistry, biology, pathology, anthropology, toxicology, and engineering, among others. ("Forensic" comes from the Latin root *forum*, the central place of the city where disputes and debates were made public to be solved, hence, defining the law of the city. Forensic generally means of or applied to the law.) The word "criminalistics" was adopted to describe the discipline directed toward the "recognition, identification, individualization, and evaluation of physical evidence by application of the natural sciences to law-science matters." ("Kriminalistik" was coined in the late nineteenth century by Hans Gross, a researcher in criminal law and procedure to define his methodology of classifying investigative, tactical, and evidential information to be learned by magistrates at law schools to solve crimes and help convict criminals.) In the scheme as it currently stands, criminalistics is part of forensic science; the word is a regionalism and is not universally applied as defined. Difficulties in differentiating the concepts certainly invited the definition of criminalistics as the "science of individualization," isolating this specific epistemologically problematic core from the other scientific disciplines. Individualization, the concept of determining the sole source of an item, enthroned a linear process—identification or classification onto individualization—losing sight of the holistic, variable contribution of all types of evidence. Assessing the circumstances surrounding a crime, where the challenge is to integrate and organize the data in order to reconstruct a case or propose alternative propositions for events under examination, requires multiple types of evidence, some of which may be quite nuanced in their interpretation. This is also true in the use of so-called forensic intelligence, which feeds investigative, police, or security needs, where one of the main reasons for failures is linkage blindness. Nevertheless, it seems that the essence of the forensic daily practice is hardly captured within the present definitions of both terms.

Forensic science reconstructs—in the broadest sense—past criminal events through the analysis of the physical remnants of those activities (evidence); the results of those analyses and their expert interpretation establish relationships between people, places, and objects relevant to those events. It produces these results and interpretations through logical inferences, induction, abduction, and deduction, all of which frame the hypothetico-deductive method; investigative heuristics also play a role. Translating scientific information into legal information is a particular domain of forensic science; other sciences must (or at least should) communicate their findings to the public, but forensic science is often required by law to communicate their findings to public courts. Indeed, as the Daubert Hearing stated, "[s]cientific conclusions are subject to perpetual revision as law must resolve disputes finally and quickly." This doubly difficult requirement of communicating to the public and to the law necessitates that forensic scientists should be better communicators of their work and their results. Scientific inferences are not necessarily legal proofs, and the forensic scientist must recognize that legal decisions based, in part, on their scientific work may not accord with their expert knowledge. Moreover, scientists must think in probabilities to explain evidence given possible causes, while jurists must deal in terms of belief beyond reasonable doubt. As Inman and Rudin state, "Because we [the scientists] provide results and information to parties who lack the expertise to independently understand their meaning and implications, it is up to us to furnish an accurate and complete interpretation of our results. If we do not do this, our conclusions are at best incomplete, at worst potentially misleading."

The Trace as the Basic Unit of Forensic Science

The basic unit of forensic science is the trace, the physical remnant of the past criminal activity. Traces are, by their very nature, semiotic: They represent something more than merely themselves; they are signifiers or signs for the items or events that are its source. A fiber is not the sweater it came from, a fingerprint is not the fingertip, soot in the trachea is not the victim choking from a fire, blood droplets are not the violence against the victim, but they all point to their origin (source and activity) to a greater or lesser degree of specificity. Thus, the trace is a type of proxy data, that is, an indicator of a related phenomenon but not the phenomenon itself. Traces come from the natural and manufactured items that surround us in our daily lives. Traces are, in essence, the raw material available at a crime scene, which becomes forensic intelligence or knowledge. Everyday items and their traces become evidence through their involvement in criminal activities; the activities add meaning to their existing status as goods in the world; a fireplace poker is transformed into "the murder weapon" by its use as such. The meaning added should also take into account the context of the case, the circumstances under which the criminal activities occurred, boarding the trier of fact mandate.

Traces become evidence when they are recognized, accepted as relevant (if blurred) to the past event under investigation, and collected for forensic purposes. Confusing trace, sign, and evidence can obscure the very process of trace "discovery," which lies at the root of its interpretation. Evidence begins with detection by observation, which is possible because of the available knowledge of the investigator or scientist; unrecognized traces go undiscovered and do not become evidence. When the investigator's or scientist's senses are extended through instrumental sensitivity, either at the scene or in the laboratory, the amount of potential evidence considerably increased. Microscopes, alternate light sources, instrumental sensitivity, and detection limits create increases in the number of traces that can be recognized and collected. More evidence, and more evidence types, inevitably led to increases in the complexity not only of the search for traces but also to their interpretation. Feeding back into this system is the awareness of new (micro)traces that changed the search methods at scenes and in laboratories, with yet more evidence being potentially available.

Traces are ancillary to their originating process; they are a by-product of the source activity, an accidental vestige of their criminal creation. To be useful in the determination of associations, traces whose ultimate sources are unknown must be compared with samples from a known source. Comparison is the very heart of the forensic science process; the method is essentially a diagnostic one, beginning with Georges Cuvier, and is employed by many science practitioners, including medical professionals. (Including, interestingly, Arthur Conan Doyle, a medical doctor and author, whose Sherlock Holmes character references Cuvier's method in *The Five Orange Pips*.) Questioned traces, or items, may have a provenance (a known location at the time of their discovery), but this is not their originating source; a few examples may help:

Trace (questioned)	Source (known)
Fiber on victim	Sweater
Gunshot residue	Ammunition discharge
Blood droplet	Body
Tool marks in door jamb	Pry bar used to open door
Shoeprint in soil	Shoe from suspect
Fingerprint on glass	Finger from suspect

The collection of properly representative known samples is crucial to accurate forensic analyses and comparisons. Known samples can be selected through a variety of legitimate schemes, including random, portion, and judgment, and must be selected with great care. Thus, traces are accidental and known samples are intentional.

Some of the consequences of what has been discussed so far induce the capacities and limitations of a forensic investigation based on trace analysis. A micro- to nanolevel existence allows forensic scientists to plan physical and chemical characteristics in their identifications and comparisons with other similar data. This allows forensic science to be as methodologically flexible as its objects of study require. Because time is asymmetric and each criminal action is unique, the forensic investigation and analysis in any one case is wedded, to a certain degree, to that case with no ambition to issue general laws about that event ("In all instances of John Davis being physically assaulted with a baseball bat …"). Inferences must be drawn with explicit uncertainty statements; the inferences should be revised when new data affect the traces' relevancy. Therefore, the search for traces is a recursive heuristic process taking into account the environment of the case at hand, appealing to the imagination, expertise, and competency of the investigator or scientist to propose explicative hypotheses.

Two Native Principles

With this framework, two principles can be thought of as the main native principles that support and frame philosophically forensic science. In this context, principles are understood as universal theoretical statements settled at the beginning of a deduction, which cannot be deduced from any other statement in the considered system, and give coherence to the area of study. They provide the grounds from which other truths can be derived and define a paradigm, that is, a general epistemological viewpoint, a new concept to see the natural world, issued from an empiricist corroborated tradition, accepted by the community of practitioners in the field. Ultimately, this paradigm can even pilot the perception itself.

Although similar but nonequivalent versions are used in other disciplines, Locard's exchange principle exists as the central tenant of forensic science. The principle that bears his name was never uttered as such by Locard, but its universal statement of "every contact leaves a trace" stands as a universally accepted shorthand phrasing. Locard's principle embraces all forms of contact, from biological to chemical to physical and even digital traces and extends the usual perception of forensic science beyond dealing only with physical vestiges.

One of its corollaries is that trace deposition is continual and not reversible. Increases in the number of contacts, the types of evidence involved, and cross-transfers (A–B and B–A) also increase the complexity of determining the relevance of traces in short duration and temporally close actions.

Even the potentially fallacious rubric of "absence of evidence is not evidence of absence" leads to extended discussions on the very nature of proof, or provable, that aims to be definitive, notwithstanding the explanations for the practical aspects of the concept (lack of sensitivity, obscuring of the relevant traces, human weakness, actual absence, etc.). Applying Locard's principle needs to address three levels. First is the physical level that deals with ease of transfer, retention, persistence, and affinity of materials, which could better support the exchange of traces from one source to another. Second is the situational or contextual level, which is the knowledge of circumstances and environments surrounding criminal events and sets the matrix for detection, identification, and proximate significance of any evidence. Third is the intelligence level that covers the knowledge about criminal behavior in single events or series, specific problems related to current trends in criminal behavior, and communication between relevant entities (police, scientists, attorneys, etc.); these components help the investigator in the field to focus on more meaningful traces that might otherwise go undetected.

The second, and more debated, principle is Kirk's individuality principle; again, Kirk did not state this as such beyond saying that criminalistics is the science of individualization. In its strongest form, it posits that each object in the universe can be placed demonstratively into a set with one and only one member: Itself. It therefore asserts the universal statement, "every object in our universe is unique." Philosophers such as Wittgenstein have argued that without defined rules or limits, terms such as "the same" or "different" are essentially meaningless. There is little question that all things are unique—two identical things can still be numerically differentiated—but the core question is, can they be distinguished at the resolution of detection applied? Simply saying "all things are unique" is not useful forensically. For example, each fingerprint left by the same finger is unique, but to be useful, each print must also be able to be traced back to its source finger. Uniqueness is therefore necessary to claim individualization, but not

sufficient. Thus, it is the degree of association that matters, how similar, how different these two things being compared are. Referring to Cole, "What distinguishes … objects is not 'uniqueness'; it is their diagnosticity: our ability to assign traces of these objects to their correct source with a certain degree of specificity under certain parameters of detection and under certain rules governing such assignments," or as Osterburg stated, "to approach [individualization] as closely as the present state of science allows." Statistics, typically, is required to accurately communicate levels of comparison that are reproducible. In fact, Kirk noted that individualization was not absolute. ("On the witness stand, the criminalist must be willing to admit that *absolute identity is impossible to establish*. … The inept or biased witness may readily testify to an identity, or to a type of identity, that does not actually exist. This can come about because of his confusion as to the nature of identity, his inability to evaluate the results of his observations, or because his general technical deficiencies preclude meaningful results" (Kirk, 1953; emphasis added).)

Nonnative Principles

Numerous guiding principles from other sciences apply centrally to forensic science, several of which come from geology, a cognate historical science to forensic science. That these principles come not from forensic science but from other sciences should not imply that they are somehow less important than Locard's or Kirk's notions. The first, and in many ways the most important, of the external principles is that of uniformitarianism. The principle, proposed by James Hutton, popularized by Charles Lyell, and coined by William Whewell, states that natural phenomena do not change in scope, intensity, or effect with time. Paraphrased as "the present is the key to the past," the principle implies that a volcano that erupts today acts in the same way as volcanoes did 200 or 200 million years ago and, thus, allows geologists to interpret proxy data from past events through current effects. Likewise, in forensic science, bullets test fired in the laboratory today do not change in scope, intensity, or effect from bullets fired during the commission of a crime 2 days, 2 weeks, or 2 years previously. The same is true of any analysis in forensic science that requires a replication or reconstruction of processes in play during the crime's commission. Uniformitarianism offers a level of objectivity to historical sciences by posing hypotheses or relationships generally and then developing tests with respect to particular cases.

Three additional principles from geology hold as applicable to forensic science. They are as follows:

- *Superposition*: In a physical distribution, older materials are below younger materials unless a subsequent action alters this arrangement.

- *Lateral continuity*: Disassociated but similar layers can be assumed to be from the same depositional period.
- *Chronology*: It refers to the notion of absolute dates in a quantitative mode (such as "10:12 a.m." or "1670–1702") and relative dates in a relational mode (i.e., older or younger).

These three principles are attributed to Nicolaus Steno but were also formalized and applied by William Smith. A forensic example of applying the principle of superposition would be the packing of different soils in a tire tread, the most recent being the outermost. A good case of lateral continuity would be the cross-transfer of fibers in an assault, given that the chances of independent transfer and persistence prior to the time of the incident would be improbable. An example of absolute chronology in forensic science would be the simple example of a purchase receipt from a retail store with a time/date stamp on it. Examples of relative chronology abound but could range from the *terminus post quem* of a product no longer made to something hotter or colder than it should be.

See also: **Foundations:** Forensic Intelligence; History of Forensic Sciences; Overview and Meaning of Identification/Individualization; Semiotics, Heuristics, and Inferences Used by Forensic Scientists; Statistical Interpretation of Evidence: Bayesian Analysis; The Frequentist Approach to Forensic Evidence Interpretation; **Foundations/Fundamentals:** Measurement Uncertainty; **Pattern Evidence/Fingerprints (Dactyloscopy):** Friction Ridge Print Examination—Interpretation and the Comparative Method.

Further Reading

Cole, S.A., 2009. Forensics without uniqueness, conclusions without individualization: the new epistemology of forensic identification. Law, Probability and Risk 8, 233–255.

Crispino, F., 2006. Le principe de Locard est-il scientifique? Ou analyse de la scientificité des principes fondamentaux de la criminalistique. Editions Universitaires Européennes No. 523, Sarrebrücken, Germany. ISBN:978-613-1-50482-2(2010).

Crispino, F., 2008. Nature and place of crime scene management within forensic sciences. Science and Justice 48 (1), 24–28.

Dulong, R., 2004. La rationalité spécifique de la police technique. Revue internationale de criminologie et de police technique 3 (4), 259–270.

Egger, S.A., 1984. A working definition of serial murder and the reduction of linkage blindness. Journal of Police Science and Administration 12, 348–355.

Giamalas, D.M., 2000. Criminalistics. In: Siegel, J.A., Saukko, P.J., Knupfer, G.C. (Eds.), Encyclopedia of Forensic Sciences. Academic Press, London, pp. 471–477.

Good, G. (Ed.), 1998. Sciences of the Earth, vol. 1. Garland Publishing, New York.

Houck, M.M., 2010. An Investigation into the Foundational Principles of Forensic Science. PhD Thesis. Curtin University of Technology, Perth.

Inman, N., Rudin, K., 2001. Principles and Practice of Criminalistics: The Profession of Forensic Science. CRC Press, Boca Raton, FL, pp. 269–270.

Kirk, P.L., 1953. Crime Investigation: Physical Evidence and the Police Laboratory. Interscience, New York, p. 10.

Kirk, P.L., 1963. The ontogeny of criminalistics. Journal of Criminal Law, Criminology and Police Science 54, 235–238.

Kuhn, T., 1970. La structure des révolutions scientifiques. Flammarion, Paris.

Kwan, Q.Y., 1976. Inference of Identity of Source. PhD Thesis. Berkeley University, Berkeley.

Mann, M., 2002. The value of multiple proxies. Science 297, 1481–1482.

Masterman, M., 1970. The nature of a paradigm. In: Lakatos, I., Musgrave, A. (Eds.), Criticism and the Growth of Experimental Knowledge. Cambridge University Press, Cambridge, pp. 59–86.

Moriarty, J.C., Saks, M.J., 2006. Forensic Science: Grand Goals, Tragic Flaws, and Judicial Gatekeeping. Research Paper No. 06-19. University of Akron Legal Studies.

National Research Council Committee, 2009. Identifying the Needs of the Forensic Science Community, Strengthening Forensic Science in the United States: A Path Forward. National Academy of Sciences Report. National Academy Press, Washington, DC.

Osterburg, J.W., 1968. What problems must criminalistics solve. Journal of Criminal Law, Criminology and Police Science 59 (3), 431.

Schuliar, Y., 2009. La coordination scientifique dans les investigations criminelles. Proposition d'organisation, aspects éthiques ou de la nécessité d'un nouveau métier. PhD Thesis, Université Paris Descartes, Paris. Université de Lausanne, Lausanne.

Sober, E., 2009. Absence of evidence and evidence of absence: evidential transitivity in connection with fossils, fishing, fine-tuning, and firing squads. Philosophical Studies 143, 63–90.

Stephens, C., 2011. A Bayesian approach to absent evidence reasoning. Informal Logic 31 (1), 56–65.

US Supreme Court No. 92–102, 1993. William Daubert, et al., Petitioners v Merrell Dow Pharmaceuticals, Inc. Certiorari to the US Court of Appeals for the Ninth Circuit. Argued 30 March 1993. Decided 28 June 1993.

Wittgenstein, L., 1922. Tractacus Logico-Philosophicus. Gallimard Tel 311, Paris.

Relevant Websites

http://www.all-about-forensic-science.com—All-About-Forensic-Science.COM, Definition of Forensic Science.

http://www.forensic-evidence.com—Forensic-Evidence.com.

http://library.thinkquest.org—Oracle ThinkQuest—What is Forensics?.

Forensic Classification of Evidence

MM Houck, Consolidated Forensic Laboratory, Washington, DC, USA

Glossary

Set Any group of real or imagined objects.
Taxonomy The science of identifying and naming species with the intent of arranging them into a classification.

Taxon (pl. taxa) A group of one or more organisms grouped and ranked according to a set of qualitative and quantitative characteristics; a type of set.

Introduction

Evidence is accidental: Items are transformed into evidence by their involvement in a crime regardless of their source or mode of production. By becoming evidence, their normal meaning is enhanced and expanded. Evidence is initially categorized much as the real world; that is, based on the taxonomy created by manufacturers. Forensic science adds to this classification to further enhance or clarify the meaning of evidence relevant to the goals and procedures of the discipline.

Methods of Classification

Set Theory

Any collection of objects, real or imagined, is a set; set theory is the branch of mathematics that studies these collections. Basic set theory involves categorization and organization of the objects, sometimes using diagrams, and involves elementary operations such as set union and set intersection. Advanced topics, including cardinality, are standard in undergraduate mathematics courses. All classification schemes are based on set theory, to a greater or lesser degree.

The notion of "set" is undefined; the objects described as constituting a set create the definition. The objects in a set are called the members or elements of that set. Objects belong to a set; sets consist of their members. The members of a set may be real or imagined; they do not need to be present to be a member of that set. Membership criteria for a set should be definite and accountable. The set, "All people in this room are over 5'5" tall," is a well-defined, if currently unknown, set—the height of the people in the room would have to be measured to accurately populate the set. If the definition is vague then that collection may not be considered a set. For example, is "q" the same as "Q"? If the set is "The 26 letters of the English alphabet," then they are the same member; if the set is, "The 52 upper-case and lower-case letters of the English alphabet," then they are two separate members.

Sets may be finite or infinite; a set with only one member is called a single or a singleton set. Two sets are identical if and only if they have exactly the same members. The cardinality of a set is the number of members within it, written |A| for set A. A set X is a subset of set Y if and only if every member of X is also a member of Y; for example, the set of all Philips head screwdrivers is a subset of the set of all screwdrivers. Forensic scientists would term this a "subclass," but that is a terminological and not a conceptual difference. Two more concepts are required for the remainder of our discussion. The union of X and Y is a set whose members are only the members of X, Y, or both. Thus, if X were (1, 2, 3) and Y were (2, 3, 4) then the union of X and Y, written $X \cup Y$, would contain (1, 2, 3, 4). Finally, the intersection of two sets contains only the members of both X and Y. In the previous example, the intersection of X and Y would be (2, 3), written $X \cap Y$.

Taxonomy

Natural items, such as animals, plants, or minerals, often occur as evidence. These items are classified according to schemes used in other sciences such as biology, botany, or geology. It is incumbent on the forensic scientist to be knowledgeable about the classification of naturally occurring items.

In biology, taxonomy, the practice and science of classification, refers to a formalized system for ordering and grouping things, typically living things using the Linnaean method. The taxa (the units of a taxonomic system; singular "taxon") are sufficiently fixed so as to provide a structure for classifying living things. Taxa are arranged typically in a hierarchical structure to show their relatedness (a phylogeny). In such a hierarchical relationship, the subtype has by definition the same constraints as the supertype plus one or more additional constraints. For example, "macaque" is a subtype of "monkey," so any macaque is also a monkey, but not every monkey is a macaque, and an animal needs to satisfy more constraints to be a macaque than to be a monkey. In the Linnaean method of classification, the scientific name of each species is formed by the combination of two words, the genus name ("generic" name), which is always capitalized, and a second word identifying the species within that genus. Species names (genus species) are either italicized or underlined, for example, *Homo sapiens* (humans), *Sus scrofa* (pigs), *Canis familiaris* (domesticated dogs), and *Rattus rattus* (rats).

The term "systematics" is sometimes used synonymously with "taxonomy" and may be confused with "scientific classification." However, taxonomy is properly the describing, identifying, classifying, and naming of organisms, while "classification" is focused on placing organisms within groups that show their relationships to other organisms. Systematics alone deals specifically with relationships through time, requiring recognition of the fossil record when dealing with the systematics of organisms. Systematics uses taxonomy as a primary tool in understanding organisms, as nothing about the organism's relationships with other living things can be understood without it first being properly studied and described in sufficient detail to identify and classify it correctly.

In geology, rocks are generally classified based on their chemical and mineral composition, the process by which they were formed and by the texture of their particles. Rocks are classified as igneous (formed by cooled molten magma), sedimentary (formed by deposition and compaction of materials), or metamorphic (formed through intense changes in pressure and temperature). These three classes of rocks are further subdivided into many other sets; often, the categories' definitions are not rigid, and the qualities of a rock may grade it from one class to another. The terminology of rocks and minerals, rather than describing a state, describes identifiable points along a gradient.

Manufacturing

Manufactured evidence is initially categorized by the in-house or market-specific system created by one or more manufacturers. Manufacturers of economic goods create their classifications through product identity or analytical methods. Set methods of production ensure a quality product fit for purpose and sale; the classification is based on the markets involved, the orientation of the company production methods, and the supply chain. Explicit rules exist on categories recognized by manufacturers and consumers, as either models or brands. Materials flow downstream, from raw material sources through to a manufacturing level. Raw materials are transformed into intermediate products, also referred to as components or parts. These are assembled on the next level to form products. The products are shipped to distribution centers and from there on to retailers and customers.

Forensic Approaches to Classification

The supply network of raw materials, intermediate steps, production methods, intended consumer end use, and actual end use all contribute to the characteristics available for forensic taxonomic classification. While the forensic taxonomies are unique to that discipline, they are based on the production taxonomies used in manufacturing. These characteristics form the basis for statements of significance, that is, the relative abundance or rarity of any one particular item in a criminal context. Some objects are common but have a short-entrance horizon (e.g., iPods), but are essentially identical at the outset while others are common with long-entrance horizons (denim blue jeans) but have a high variance (regular, stone washed, acid washed, etc.). It is in the best interest of forensic scientists to understand the fundamental manufacturing processes of the items that routinely become evidence. This understanding can form the basis for statistical significance statements in courts and may provide the foundations for a more quantitative approach to testimony.

Forensic analytical methods create augmented taxonomies because the discipline uses different sets of methods and forensic scientists have different goals. Their taxonomies are based on manufactured traits, but also aftermarket qualities, and intended end use, but also "as used." The "as-used" traits are those imparted to the item after purchase through either normal or criminal use. Forensic science has developed a set of rules through which the taxonomies are explicated. For example, forensic scientists are interested in the size, shape, and distribution of delustrants, microscopic grains of rutile titanium dioxide incorporated into a fiber to reduce its luster. The manufacturer has included delustrant in the fiber at a certain rate and percentage with no concern for shape or distribution (but size may be relevant). The forensic science taxonomy is based on manufacturing taxonomy but is extended by incidental characteristics that help us distinguish otherwise similar objects.

Natural, manufacturing, and forensic classifications lead to evidentiary significance because they break the world down into intelligible classes of objects related to criminal acts. Forensic science has developed an enhanced appreciation for discernment between otherwise similar objects but has yet to explicate these hierarchies to their benefit.

Class Level Information

Identification is the examination of the chemical and physical properties of an object and using them to categorize it as a member of a set. What the object is made of, its color, mass, size, and many other characteristics are used to identify an object and help refine that object's identity. Analyzing a white powder and concluding that it is cocaine is an example of identification; determining that a small translucent chip is bottle glass or yellow fibrous material and determining that they are dog hairs are also examples of identification. Most of the identifications are inherently hierarchical, such as classification systems themselves: In the last example, the fibrous nature of the objects restricts the following possible categories:

- Hairs
- Animal hairs
- Guard hairs
- Dog hairs
- German shepherd hairs

As the process of identification of evidence becomes more specific, it permits the analyst to classify the evidence into successively smaller classes of objects. It may not be necessary to classify the evidence beyond dog hairs if human hairs are being looked for. Multiple items can be classified differently, depending on what questions are asked. For example, the objects in **Figure 1** could be classified into "fruit" and "non-fruit," "sports related" and "non-sports-related," or "organic" and "inorganic."

Sharing a class identity may indicate two objects that come from a common source. Because forensic science reveals and describes the relationships among people, places, and things involved in criminal activities, this commonality of relationship may be critical to a successful investigation. Commonality can show interactions, limitations in points of origin, and increased significance of relationships. What is meant by a "common source" depends on the material in question, the mode of production, and the specificity of the examinations used to classify the object. For example, the "common source" for an automotive paint chip could be the following:

- the manufacturer (to distinguish it from other similar paints),

- the factory (to determine where it was made),
- the batch or lot of production (to distinguish it from other batches at the same factory),
- all the vehicles painted with that color paint, or
- the vehicle painted with that color paint involved in the crime in question.

All of these options, and they are not exhaustive, could be the goal in an investigation of determining whether two objects had a "common source."

Uniqueness and Individualization

If an object can be classified into a set with only one member (itself), it can be said to be unique. An individualized object is associated with one, and only one, source: It is unique. Uniqueness is based on two assumptions. The first assumption is that all things are unique in space and, thus, their properties are nonoverlapping. The assumption of uniqueness of space is considered axiomatic and, therefore, an inherently non-provable proposition for numerous reasons. The population size of "all things that might be evidence" is simply too large to account. In addition, conclusive evidence is not readily available in typical forensic investigations. Because of this, as Schum notes, statistics are required:

> Such evidence, if it existed, would make necessary a particular hypothesis or possible conclusion being entertained. In lieu of such perfection, we often make use of masses of inconclusive evidence having additional properties: The evidence is incomplete on matters relevant to our conclusions, and it comes to us from sources (including our own observations) that are, for various reasons, not completely credible. Thus, inferences from such evidence can only be probabilistic in nature (Schum, 1994, p. 2).

Figure 1 A range of objects may be classified in a variety of ways, depending on the question being asked. For example, given the objects in this figure, the sets would differ if the question was, "What is edible?" rather than "What is sporting equipment?".

A statistical analysis is therefore warranted when uncertainty, of either accounting or veracity, exists. If an absolutely certain answer to a problem could be reached, statistical methods would not be required. Most evidence exists at the class level, and although each item involved in a crime is considered unique, it still belongs to a larger class. In reality, the majority of forensic science works at a class level of resolution. Indeed, even DNA, the argued "gold standard" of forensic science, operates with classes and statistics.

It has been argued that the concept of uniqueness is necessary but not sufficient to support claims of individualization. If it is accepted that uniqueness is axiomatic, then

> What matters is whether we have analytical tools necessary to discern the characteristics that *distinguish* one object from all others or, in the forensic context, distinguish *traces* made by each object from traces made by every other object … Every object is presumably unique at the scale of manufacture. The question is whether objects are distinguishable at the scale of detection. Since all objects in the universe are in some respects "the same" and in other respects "different" from all other objects in the universe, according to Wittgenstein, what really matters is not uniqueness but rather what rules we articulate by which we will make determinations of "sameness" and "difference" (Cole, 2009, pp. 242–243).

Although things may be numerically unique at the point of *production*, this does not help to distinguish between otherwise similar objects at the point of *detection* or *interpretation*. This is where forensic science adds value to the investigative and legal processes.

Relationships and Context

The relationships between the people, places, and things involved in crimes are central to deciding what items to examine and how to interpret the results. For example, if a sexual assault occurs and the perpetrator and victim are strangers, more evidence may be relevant than if they live together or are sexual partners. Strangers are not expected to have ever met previously and, therefore, would have not transferred evidence before the crime. People who live together would have some opportunities to transfer certain types of evidence (e.g., head hairs and carpet fibers from the living room) but not others (semen or vaginal secretions). Spouses or sexual partners, being the most intimate relationship of the three examples, would share a good deal of more information (**Figure 2**).

Stranger-on-stranger crimes beg the question of coincidental associations, that is, two things that previously have never been in contact with each other have items on them, which are analytically indistinguishable at a certain class level. Attorneys in cross-examination may ask, "Yes, but could not [insert evidence type here] really have come from anywhere? Are not [generic class level evidence] very common?" It has been proven for a wide variety of evidence that coincidental matches are extremely rare. The enormous variety of mass-produced goods, consumer choices, economic factors, biological and natural diversity, and other traits create a nearly infinite combination of comparable characteristics for the items involved in any one situation.

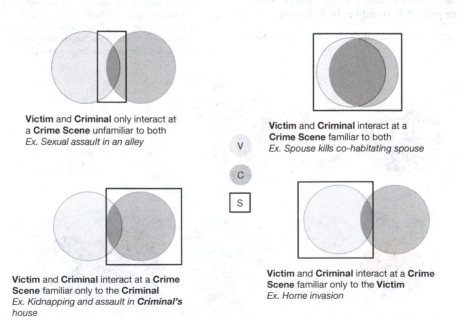

Victim and **Criminal** only interact at a **Crime Scene** unfamiliar to both
Ex. Sexual assault in an alley

Victim and **Criminal** interact at a **Crime Scene** familiar to both
Ex. Spouse kills co-habitating spouse

V
C
S

Victim and **Criminal** interact at a **Crime Scene** familiar only to the **Criminal**
*Ex. Kidnapping and assault in **Criminal's** house*

Victim and **Criminal** interact at a **Crime Scene** familiar only to the **Victim**
Ex. Home invasion

Figure 2   The relationships between suspect, victim, and scene influence what evidence is collected and what its significance is.

See also: **Foundations:** Evidence/Classification; Statistical Interpretation of Evidence: Bayesian Analysis; The Frequentist Approach to Forensic Evidence Interpretation.

Further Reading

Cole, S., 2009. Forensics without uniqueness, conclusion without individualization: the new epistemology of forensic identification. Law, Probability, and Risk 8 (3), 233–255.

Devlin, K., 1993. The Joy of Sets. Springer, Berlin.
Haq, T., Roche, G., Parker, B., 1978. Theoretical field concepts in forensic science. 1. Application to recognition and retrieval of physical evidence. Journal of Forensic Sciences 23 (1), 212–217.
Houck, M.M., 2006. Production Taxonomies as the Foundation of Forensic Significance. European Academy of Forensic Sciences, Helsinki, Finland.
Johnson, P., 1972. A History of Set Theory. Weber & Schmidt, New York.
Kwan, Q.Y., 1977. Inference of Identity of Source. PhD Thesis. University of California.
Schum, D.A., 1994. Evidential Foundations of Probabilistic Reasoning. John Wiley & Sons, New York.
Thornton, J., 1986. Ensembles of class characteristics in physical evidence examination. Journal of Forensic Sciences 31 (2), 501–503.
Underhill, P., 2000. Why We Buy: The Science of Shopping. Simon & Schuster, New York.

Interpretation/The Comparative Method

MM Houck, Consolidated Forensic Laboratory, Washington, DC, USA

Glossary

Alignable differences Differences that are connected to the hierarchical system of relatedness of two or more things.

Analogous trait A characteristic that is similar between two things, which is not present in the last common ancestor or precedent of the group under comparison.

Analogy A cognitive process that transfers information or meaning from one subject (the analog or source) to another subject (the target).

Diagnosticity The degree to which traits classify an object.

Homologous trait A characteristic shared by a common ancestor or precedent.

Nonalignable differences Differences with no correspondence at all between the source and the target.

Introduction

Analogy, and its more specific relative comparison, is a central component of human cognition. Analogy is the process behind identification of places, objects, and people and plays a significant role in many human mental operations, such as problem solving, decisions, perception, memory, and communication. Some researchers, including Hofstadter, have even argued that cognition is analogy. Likewise, the cognitive process of analogy and the method of comparison lie at the heart of the forensic sciences. The ability to compare is predicated on some sort of classification (more properly, a taxonomy) that results in classes, groups, or sets.

Aristotle is considered the first to approach comparison as a way to arrange the world. His attempt to codify the process raised, however, an intractable problem that would only be addressed later: the classification of living things. Comparison, by itself, is a minimal technique, at best. A classification system—a taxonomy—is a prerequisite to a fuller comparative methodology. Comparative anatomy, one of the earliest formal applications of the method, goes beyond mere representation (mere comparison, that is) to explain the nature and properties of each animal.

The French naturalist Pierre Belon (1517–1564) compared the skeletal structures of birds to humans in his book *L'Histoire de la Nature des Oiseaux* (*History of the Nature of Birds*, 1555; **Figure 1**), and, along with the Flemish naturalist Andreas Vesalius (1514–1564), was one of the first naturalists to explicitly apply the comparative method in biology. Georges Cuvier (1769–1832) was the first to use comparative anatomy and taxonomy as a tool, not an end in itself, in his studies of animals and fossils. Cuvier was frustrated that biological phenomena could not be reconfigured into experimental conditions that would allow controlled testing, a difficulty common to many sciences (e.g., see Diamond). The intimate integration of a living organism's physiology with its anatomy created obstacles in teasing out and relating function to structure: Once an organism was dead and prepared for dissection, its function had ceased, thus confounding the relationship of form to function. Cuvier considered that careful examinations and the interrelating of structures between specimens might also prove to be useful in revealing principles of observation and comparison. Perhaps the original scientist-as-detective, Cuvier, used scattered, fractured bits of information to reconstruct the prehistory of the Earth and its animals. In a 1798 paper, Cuvier wrote on his realization of the form and function of bones as it relates to the overall identifiable anatomy of an animal, leading to the recognition of the creature from which the bone originated:

> This assertion will not seem at all astonishing if one recalls that in the living state all the bones are assembled in a kind of framework; that the place occupied by each is easy to recognize; and that by the number and position of their articulating facets one can judge the number and direction of the bones that were attached to them. This is because the number, direction, and shape of the bones that compose each part of an animal's body are always in a necessary relation to all the other parts, in such a way that—up to a point—one can infer the whole from any one of them, and vice versa. (Rudwick, 1998, p. 36)

This has been called "Cuvier's Principle of Correlation of Parts" and is a central tenet in biology and paleontology. It is

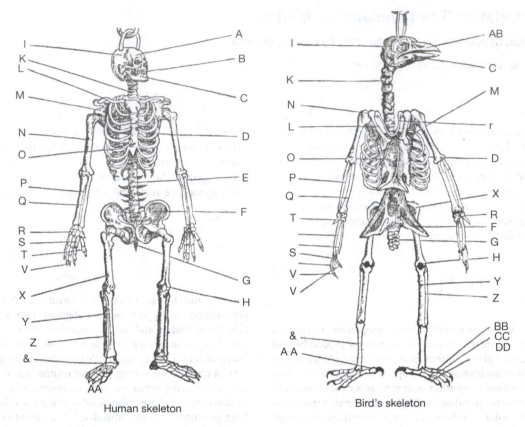

Figure 1 A drawing from Pierre Belon's 1555 book, *History of the Nature of Birds*, comparing the skeletal anatomy of birds to humans, which is one of the first books using the science of comparative anatomy. Source: Wikimedia Commons, open source.

important to note that Cuvier claimed to be able to *identify* an animal taxonomically from a single bone, but not completely *reconstruct* it, as the above quote might imply. The reconstruction would only be possible with a sufficient number of bones representing the animal in question. The comparative method has been a successful cornerstone of science ever since, with new or emerging sciences, such as ecology, moving from the purely observational or descriptive approach to that of comparison through experimental or analytical methods.

A short discussion of terms in biology will help clarify concepts used in biological comparisons. The concept of homology, the same structure under every variety of form found in different animals, is the organizing foundation for comparative anatomy. Animals share homologous traits because they also share a common ancestor with the same or related trait. By contrast, analogous traits are similarities found in organisms that were not present in the last common ancestor of the group under comparison; that is, the traits evolved separately. The canonical example of the difference between homologous and analogous traits is the wings of birds and

bats: They are homologous as forearms but analogous as wings; the latter structures evolved their functions separately. A homologous trait is termed a homolog. In biology, evolution and natural selection formed the system within which these relationships developed and were maintained, homogenized, or differentiated.

In manufacturing, other external and internal constraints form the basis for homologous and analogous traits through design, function, form, and costs. Design follows from the product's intended end use, aesthetic concerns, and cost limitations. The function and form of an object tend to correlate and variances in design cluster around necessary and sufficient criteria. In **Figure 2**, for example, although the hammer heads, opposite sides, handles, materials, weight, shape, and components all vary, they are nonetheless identifiable as hammers. If **Figure 2** were finches, as Darwin studied in the Galapagos in his historic voyage with the *Beagle*, the base process of taxonomy would be the same but the criteria and foundations—the history and causes—would obviously vary because of the vastly different processes that produce hammers and finches.

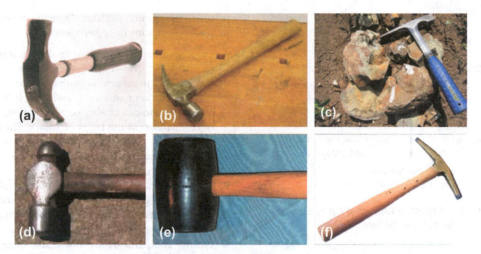

Figure 2 Hammers. All of the objects (A–F) are recognizable as hammers even though their components vary. (A) Claw hammer; (B) framing hammer; (C) geological hammer; (D) ball-peen hammer; (E) rubber mallet; and (F) upholstery hammer. Source: Wikimedia Commons, open source.

Broadly speaking, the supply chains and distribution networks of material goods are like the phylogenetic trees based on evolutionary descent. Regardless of whether the items are biological or manufactured, the independence of traits should not be assumed. Comparative studies that do not control for historical relationships through phylogeny or supply chains may imply spurious relationships (coincidences). Forensic science is unique in its use of the comparative method to reconstruct past criminal events and sourcing of evidence, either biological or manufactured (in essence, reverse engineering to a level of distribution or manufacturing resolution).

Analogy and Comparison within a Forensic Process

Analogy is a cognitive process that transfers information or meaning from one subject (the analog or *source*) to another subject (the *target*); it thus implies at least two things: situations or events. The source is considered to be the more complete and more complex of the two and the target is thus less informative and incomplete in some way. The incompleteness may be due to any of several factors, alone or combined, such as damage, fracture, deterioration, or size. The elements or traits—including their relationships, such as evolutionary or supply chains—between the source and the target are mapped or aligned in a comparison. The mapping is done from what is usually the more familiar area of experience and more complete repository of information, the source, to the typically more problematic target.

Salience of the elements or traits is of prime importance: There are an innumerable number of arbitrary differences in either elements or relations that could be considered but are not useful given the question at hand ("Are both items smaller than the Empire State Building? Are they redder than a fire truck?"). Ultimately, analogy is a process to communicate that the two comparators (the source and the target) have *some* relationship in common despite any arbitrary differences. Some notion of possible or hypothetical connection must exist for the comparison to be made. As a forensic example, consider trace debris removed from the clothing of a suspect and the body of a victim: Although there may be no physical evidence (hairs, fibers, glass, soil, etc.) in common, the suspect's clothing and the victim's body have, at least prima facie, a common *relationship* (the victim is the victim and the suspect is a person of interest in the crime) until proven otherwise. Thus, common relations, not common objects, are essential to analogy and comparison.

The comparison process as a method makes several assumptions. First, the space in which the comparators are mapped is assumed to be Euclidean. Second, the method embeds the comparators in a "space of minimum dimensionality" (Tversky) based on all observed salient similarities. Each object, a, is detailed and described by a set of elements or traits, A. Any observed similarities between a and another object b, denoted as $s(a, b)$, are expressed as a function of the salient traits they are determined to have in common. The comparison and any observed familiarity can be expressed as a function of three arguments (**Figure 3**):

- $A \cap B$, the features shared by a and b
- $A–B$, the features of a that are not shared by b
- $B–A$, the features of b that are not shared by a

Psychological studies show that people tend to pay more attention to the target (the comparator with less information)

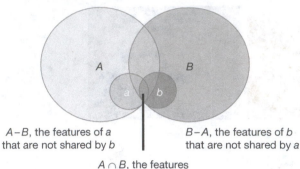

A−B, the features of *a*
that are not shared by *b*

B−A, the features of *b*
that are not shared by *a*

A ∩ B, the features
shared by *a* and *b*

Figure 3   A comparison of observed familiarities can be expressed as a function of three arguments, visualized here.

than to the source. In forensic science, this means that analysts would pay more attention to the samples from the crime scene or actors than to the known samples collected. This is true even though the known has more salience because arguably it has more information and a documented provenance than the questioned sample. For example, a toy ship is quite similar to a real ship because most of the main features of the real ship are expressed in the toy (otherwise it might not be recognized as a simulacrum of its referent). A real ship, however, is not as similar to the toy ship because many of the features of a real ship are not expressed in the toy (due to function, scale, or safety, among other factors). The reason for paying more attention to the target is, first and foremost, to determine if there is sufficiency of salient information in the target for the comparative process to occur (see Vanderkolk for a discussion on this).

The main determinant of feature salience for comparative purposes is the degree to which they classify an object, that is, their diagnosticity. A feature that serves as the basis to reassign an object from one class to another class with fewer members is more salient than one that does not. Salience is hierarchical and is based on how many members of a class share that feature; the goal is thus to place an object, by successive comparative features, into classes with increasingly fewer members. Salience of a feature, therefore, should increase inversely with the number of members of a class into which it places an object; A ∩ B increases and may be thought of as an expression of diagnosticity. A comparative process that does not maximize diagnosticity or exploit features that do so will have low forensic utility.

The Comparative Method within Forensic Science

The comparative method involves the aligning of the relational structures between one or more targets (items of questioned source; Qs) and one or more sources (items of known

provenance or source; Ks). This alignment, to work as a method, has three constraints or requirements:

- The alignment has to be *structurally consistent*, that is, it has to observe a one-to-one correspondence between the comparators in an argumentative structure that is the same between the comparisons (*parallel connectivity*). One point of comparison can be aligned with at most one other point of comparison in the target or source. Similarly, matching relationships must have matching arguments to support them (the reason for the proposed relationship cannot be based on an unrelated argument).
- The comparison has to involve *common relations* but does not have to involve common object descriptions. All the evidence that came from the crime scene, for example, need not have originated from only one source.
- Finally, comparisons are not made merely between the objects at hand but also include all of the higher order "constraining relations" that they may share (*systematicity*). In biology, this would relate to the evolutionary and genetic connections; for manufactured materials, this would be the design factors and the supply chain of raw materials and intermediate processes that lead to a finished consumer good. The deeper the relational history, the more higher order classes that two objects share, the stronger the relationship they share, and, therefore, the greater is the chance of a shared origin. This obviates the significance of coincidental matches between otherwise similar but unrelated objects: A series of coincidences between two objects are not a salient relationship, no matter how many of them exist. Type I and type II errors stem from these coincidences.

A comparison results in a type of cross-mapping of analogous traits or phenomena that have differential relational roles in two situations (e.g., victim's clothing and crime scene). A systematic mapping between source and target is a natural method for differentiating potentially ambiguous relationships. This relates to the classification of the target and source, the identification of traits or features each has that place them in one or more sets (classes) of items. The cross-mapping is of these traits within a class. Once a source has been aligned to a target, *candidate inferences*, based on the source, can be projected onto the target, such as a shared source or history. A handgun with blood on it, for example, can be compared to a bullet removed from a victim (through test firings of similar ammunition) and determined to have been the source (to some degree of certainty) of the bullet while the blood can be tested through DNA typing with the victim's known sample and be shown to have the victim as its source (again, to some degree of certainty); the fact that the victim's blood is on the handgun indicates a shared history of occurrence (lateral contemporaneity).

Comparison is selective. The requirement of systematicity is predicated on the idea that classes or sets are flexible and hierarchical. Higher order connections predict lower order relations, and commonalities that are not a part of the aligned system of relationships are considered inconsequential: A blue shoe and a blue car have little in common other than the stated color category; likewise, the fact that the source shoe and the target print might have the same kind of outsole design recedes in importance to the fact than none of the individual traits on the sole appears in the print. Differences that are connected to the hierarchical system of relatedness are called *alignable differences*; those differences with no correspondence at all between the source and the target are called *nonalignable differences*. Alignable differences are more meaningful and salient than nonalignable ones because they exist within the same relationship system making them more relevant to each other. The strange conclusion this observation leads to is that there should be more meaningful differences for comparators that are very similar (*toy train–real train*) than for ones that are less similar (*toy train–toy ship*) because the more similar comparators will have or be derived within more common systems of relationships and will have more alignable differences. As an example, consider all the possible differences for the pair *automobile–truck* and for the pair *duck–baseball*. More alignable differences could be found for the first pair than the second: After a few differences ("You don't play sports with a duck. You don't hunt baseballs."), the list seems pointless because the two are not aligned. The details that could be elicited by comparing *automobile* with *truck*, however, could go on for some time, depending on the level of detail desired. Most sets of comparators in the world are dissimilar (which is why forensic comparisons tend to be stronger in exclusion than inclusion) and this "nonconsideration" heuristic makes sense given humans' cognitive load: "Intuitively, it is when a pair of items is similar that their differences are likely to be important"

(Genter and Markman). Psychological experiments support this statement, and it seems to be an integral part of human cognition. Related to this idea is Wittgenstein's proposal 5.5303 in his work *Tractatus logico-philosophicus*: "Roughly speaking, to say of two things that they are identical is nonsense, and to say of one thing that it is identical with itself is to say nothing at all." This points to the need for a statistical evaluation of the *strength* of a comparison, either inclusive or exclusive.

> *See also:* **Foundations:** Forensic Intelligence; Overview and Meaning of Identification/Individualization; Semiotics, Heuristics, and Inferences Used by Forensic Scientists.

Further Reading

Diamond, J., Robinson, J.A. (Eds.), 2010. Natural Experiments of History. Cambridge University Press, Cambridge, MA.

Gentner, D., Markman, A.B., 1997. Structure mapping in analogy and similarity. American Psychologist 52 (1), 45–56.

Hofstadter, D., 2001. Analogy as the core of cognition. In: Gentner, D., Holyoak, K., Kokinov, B. (Eds.), The Analogical Mind: Perspectives from Cognitive Science. MIT Press/Bradford Book, Cambridge, MA, pp. 499–538.

Markman, A.B., Genter, D., 2000. Structure mapping in the comparison process. American Journal of Psychology 113 (4), 501–538.

Pellegrin, P., 1986. Aristotle's Classification of Living Things. University of California Press, Berkeley, CA.

Rudwick, M., 1997. Georges Cuvier, Fossil Bones, and Geological Catastrophes. University of Chicago Press, Chicago.

Tversky, A., 1977. Features of similarity. Psychological Review 84, 327–352.

Vanderkolk, J., 2009. Forensic Comparative Science. Academic Press, New York.

Wittgenstein, L., 1922. Tractatus Logico-Philosophicus. Translated by C. K. Ogden (1922), prepared with assistance from G. (E. Moore, F. P. Ramsey, and Wittgenstein). Routledge, London.

Toxicology: History

R Wennig, Université du Luxembourg-Campus Limpertsberg, Avenue de la Faïencerie, Luxembourg

Abbreviations

CNS	Central nervous system
DFSA	Drug-facilitated sexual assault
GABA	γ-Aminobutyric acid, the main inhibitory neurotransmitter in human central nervous system, regulating neuronal excitability and muscle tone
GHB	γ-Hydroxybutyric acid is naturally occurring in human CNS in small amounts and is considered as an illicit drug (liquid ecstasy) in many countries
UV	Ultraviolet

Glossary

Cytochrome P450 (CYP 450) A superfamily of enzymes, some polymorphically expressed, catalyzing oxidation of organic substances including xenobiotics involved in drug metabolism and bioactivation.

G-Protein-coupled receptor kinases (GRKs) Enzymes that regulate guanine-protein-coupled receptor activity by phosphorylating their intracellular parts after release and activation of associated G-proteins as mediators of tolerance via up- and downregulation.

Pharmacogenomics/toxicogenomics Deals with the influence of genetic variation on xenobiotic response in humans by correlating gene expression or single-nucleotide polymorphisms with a drug's efficacy or xenobiotic toxicity.

Xenobiotics Substances found in humans that are not normally produced or expected to be present, or substances present in much higher concentrations than are usual.

Introduction

From Antiquity to the sixteenth century, it was difficult or even impossible to perform an autopsy and prove poisoning. Proof was made by gossip, the circumstances, for example, discoloration of the corpse, suspect poisons found, confession, or by torturing the alleged culprit. Progress in toxicological analysis had to wait until the nineteenth century—a transition period of medical mindset between natural philosophy and natural sciences. Many famous criminal poisoning cases were milestones in toxicology, contributed to its progress, and can be used as a source of information for the interpretation of toxicological results. At court trials, experts had to make great efforts, as their analytical results and interpretations were challenged by lawyers, prosecutors, magistrates, and counter-experts. Modern analytical toxicology has made expert opinions less hazardous. Even if

"experts' battles" did not always increase the toxicologist's reputation, the progress of science occurred. Experts became more aware of the limited performance of analytical toxicology, with the aim to give better evidence to judicial authorities. Before the twentieth century, homicidal poisoning was far more popular than it is today, even though there are many more poisons available now.

Poisons were difficult to detect before 1800, and the legislation was inadequate to assist investigators in proving that a crime was committed. In response to many criminal cases, forensic toxicology developed, making detection increasingly more likely, and the sale of poisons became better controlled through strong legislation. Victims remained the same over the years: unwanted husbands, wives or lovers, illegitimate babies, children, rivals, employers, and individuals killed for monetary gain, but mostly cases were concerned with family disputes.

Important Historical Milestones

Since approximately 50000 BC, humanity was aware of the difference between some safe and unsafe plants, animals, or minerals probably as a result of their experiences including mishaps. Mythology, philosophy, folklore, shamanism, and religious rituals rather than science with observation, experiments, and theories guided beliefs and knowledge.

Antiquity Middle Ages and Renaissance

Since the Sumerians (3500–2000 BC), knowledge about poisons had improved only slowly until the eighteenth century.

In 1302, Bartolomeo da Varignana (1255–1321) performed the first autopsy in Bologna to investigate a poisoning case, according to a decision in 1209 by Pope Innocent III (1160–1216) and that by Gregory IX (1145/1170–1241) in 1234 to anchor medicolegal expert opinion in the *Corpus Iuris Canonici*, in case of death of a suspect.

In 1538, Paracelsus (1493–1541) formulated a fundamental statement *Dosis sola facit venenum*, a cited version in Latin from the eighteenth century but originally written in old German: *Alle Ding' sind Gift, nichts ohn' Gift, allein die Dosis macht dass ein Ding kein Gift ist.*

Evolution from the Eighteenth to the Twenty-First Century

In 1758, a Paracelsus similar statement *Alimenta a toxis, uti medicamenta a venenis, non natura sed dosis distinguit* was formulated by Carolus Linnaeus (1707–1778).

In the Mary Blandy (1720–1752) criminal case, in which the accused was charged of poisoning her father Francis from Henley-on-Thames in a trial at Oxford in 1752, the first known chemical test ever for arsenic detection was performed by medical examiner Anthony Addington (1713–1790) from Reading. This test looking primitive by today's standards was innovative in the eighteenth century. Addington heated a white powder found on a victim's pan and noticed the same garlic odor and whitish smoke as that of similarly treated arsenic.

A more reliable arsenic detection and quantification method was published in 1836 by James Marsh (1789–1846).

A systematic approach to toxicity and detection of poisons was outlined by Mateo José Bonaventura Orfila (1787–1853) in his most famous textbook *Traité des poisons tirés du règne minéral, végétal et animal ou toxicologie générale* published in 1814. He was the first who considered detecting mineral poisons in the so-called "second route" of administration and elimination. Few years later, in 1839, Orfila used Marsh's method for the detection of As in the famous Lafarge trial in France. Orfila's work was continued in the United Kingdom, notably by his students Robert Christison (1797–1882) at Edinburgh University and Alfred Swaine Taylor (1806–1880) at Guy's Hospital, London, and in Sweden by Jöns Jacob Berzelius (1779–1848) at Karolinska Institute, Stockholm. Other toxicologists, notably Thomas Stevenson (1838–1908), followed Orfila's work at Guy's Hospital and became involved in many famous trials for criminal poisoning.

In 1838, a separation scheme for inorganic cations using H_2S was proposed by Carl Remigius Fresenius (1818–1897), and in 1841, Hugo Emil Reinsch (1809–1884) used a copper wire in acidic solutions to detect Hg, As, Bi, and Sb in biological samples by forming a gray deposit (as As_2Cu_5). A screening method for mineral poisons in a biological material was proposed in 1845 by Carl Remigius Fresenius (1818–1897) and in 1847 by Lambert Heinrich von Babo (1818–1899).

Jean-Servais Stas (1813–1891) was the first to perform the isolation of alkaloids, notably nicotine, from biological specimens by solvent extraction using diethyl ether after deproteination with ethanol.

In 1859, Robert Bunsen (1811–1899) and Gustaf Kirchhoff (1824–1887) discovered flame emission spectrometry for mineral elements. Detection of white phosphorus was published in 1855 by Eilhard Mitscherlich (1794–1863).

In 1856, Friedrich Julius Otto (1809–1870) proposed a modification of Stas' method to a systematic method for the extraction of nonvolatile acidic and basic compounds.

From 1830 onward, subsequent tests for alkaloid identification were developed, either precipitation tests or color tests with more or less specific and sensitive reagents, some of which are still used today. Before these chemical tests became available, toxicologist had to use the typical odors or bitter taste of many poisons to identify them.

The first ever reported precipitation test for alkaloids by Ferdinand Ludwig Winckler (1801–1868) in 1830 used $HgCl_2$ and KI solutions, modified later and became the Mayer reagent (1863), the De Vrij test (1854), the Merck test (1855), the Julius Nessler test, and so on. Analogous reagents came up as the Wagner reagent (1866), the Marme reagent (1866), and the Draggendorff reagent (1866). Other color tests were developed, notably the Erdmann test (1861), the Fröhde test (1866), the Pellagri test, the Vitali test (1880), the Mandelin test (1884), the Marquis test (1896), and the Mecke test (1899), for general detection of alkaloids and nitrogenous bases or for some specific chemical drug families.

Francesco Selmi (1817–1881) was the first to doubt the reliability of color reactions for forensic toxicological purposes, because of interference with physiological components of various organs, such as ptomaines generated by postmortem degradation. Other tests were developed later, notably the Paul Ehrlich reagent, also known as the van Urk reagent, to detect lysergic acid diethylamide (LSD) and other indolalkylamine hallucinogens and the Bratton–Marshall test (1939) for the quantification of sulfonamides. Later, this method was adapted for amino-group-containing parathion metabolites (known as Averell–Norris reaction) and for benzodiazepine derivatives by Harald Schütz; the Schiff (1834–1915) test was adapted for the detection of aldehydes; the Fujiwara test was adapted to detect chloroform; and the Dille–Koppanyi reagent was modified by Zwikker for barbiturate detection (1934). In the 1950s, the Forrest test and the ferric chloride/perchloric acid/nitric acid reagent test were introduced for the presumptive testing of imipraminic antidepressants or +phenothiazines. In the 1960s, the Duquenois–Levine reagent as well as Fast Blue salt B was used for presumptive testing of cannabinoids and the Scott test was used for cocaine testing in 1973.

In 1931, Fritz Feigl proposed an important textbook on spot tests. Several tests using precipitation reagents with subsequent microscopic examination of the obtained crystals, or if solid compounds could be isolated by extraction, recrystallization, and subsequent melting point determination according to Kofler (1891–1951), can be performed. Pure liquids could be identified by their refractive indices.

When no chemical test was available, physiological tests were applied, notably the tetanic spasms in frogs (1856) for strychnine detection, the mydriasis test of cat eyes described by Friedlieb Ferdinand Runge (1795–1867) for atropine detection, the taste test giving peculiar numbness of the tongue with aconitine, the Straub-Hermann mouse tail test for morphine given by subcutaneous administration producing a characteristic S-shaped dorsiflexion of a mouse tail, and the asystole test observed in 1856 on isolated frog heart by Rudolf Böhm (1844–1926) and Claude Bernard (1813–1878) for digitalis detection.

Biological assays using the vinegar fly *Drosophila melanogaster* to screen for some insecticides in body tissues were proposed in the 1960s.

In 1924, Louis Lewin (1850–1929), considered as the father of psychopharmacology, published a pharmacological classification of psychotropic drugs and several papers on hallucinogenic plants.

Salting out of organ material with ammonium sulfate was proposed by L.C. Nickolls in 1937 and with sodium tungstate was proposed by Paul Valov in 1946.

Microdiffusion methods to detect cyanides, carbon monoxide, and so on, were proposed in 1947 by Edward J. Conway (1894–1965).

From 1920 onward, important discoveries in molecular pharmacology, such as neurotransmitters, second messengers, and signaling proteins, were made, allowing progress in understanding action mechanisms of psychotropic substances. In line with this, acetylcholine was discovered by Otto Loewi (1873–1961). Noradrenaline (norepinephedrine) was discovered by Ulf von Euler (1905–1983) in 1946, and its metabolism extensively studied by Julius Axelrod (1912–2004). In 1948, Maurice M. Rapport, Arda Green (1899–1958), and Irvine H. Page (1901–1991) discovered a vasoconstrictor substance serotonin, aka 5-hydroxtryptamine or 5HT, in blood serum with a broad range of physiological roles. Discovery of dopamine in 1957 by Arvid Carlsson (1923–2008) led to the development of new antidepressant drugs. In 1950, Eugene Roberts (1920–2016) and Jorge Awapara (1918–2005)

independently reported the discovery of γ-aminobutyric acid (GABA) in mammalian central nervous system. After several years of research, Ernst Florey (1927–1997) proposed in 1957 that GABA would be an inhibitory neurotransmitter.

Cyclic adenosine monophosphate was isolated in 1956 by Earl W. Sutherland Jr. (1915–1974). Alfred G. Gilman pioneered in the domain of G-protein-coupled receptor kinases. Moreover, an important step was the discovery of opioid receptors by Eric Simon et al., followed by the discovery of opioid neuropeptides in 1974 by two independent investigators: John Hughes, Hans Kosterlitz et al. isolated enkephalins from a pig brain and Rabi Simantov and Solomon H. Snyder isolated endorphins from calf brain.

In 1957, Jean Delay (1907–1987) and Pierre Deniker (1917–1998) published a new useful pharmacological classification of psychotropic drugs.

Evolution of Drugs and Poisons

Since Antiquity, humans have known that plants of the nightshades family have mind-altering properties and used them as hexing herbs associated with witchcraft, notably *Atropa belladonna*, *Mandragora officinarum*, *Datura stramonium*, *Brugmansia* spp., and *Hyoscyamus niger*.

Ethanol is one of the oldest known and remains by far the most frequently used recreational substances. The first benzodiazepine discovered by Leo Sternbach (1908–2005) in 1957 was launched as LIBRIUM and introduced as "a tranquilizer that relieves tension without causing apathy," followed in 1963 by diazepam VALIUM, and many other tranquilizers later.

Amphetamines and Designer Drugs

In 1887, Lazar Edeleanu (1861–1941) synthesized amphetamine, and methamphetamine was first synthesized from ephedrine in 1893 by Nagai Nagayoshi (1844–1929) and later in 1919 by Akira Ogata (1887–1978).

3,4-Methylenedioxymethamphetamine was first synthesized in 1912 by Anton Köllisch (1888–1916) at Merck Co (Darmstadt). In the mid-1970s, Alexander Shulgin (b1925) synthesized some 200 structural analogs with even more potent activities and studied their psychotropic effects on students. His book *PIHKAL*, an acronym for *Phenethyl Amines I have known and loved*, gives detailed recipes for clandestine laboratories. Later, hundreds of so-called designer drugs, which are structurally related to existing illicit drugs, appeared on the street scene especially via massive Internet sale called legal highs, mostly labeled as ecstasy, until they were also scheduled. In 1997, by European Council decision, the European Monitoring Centre for Drugs and Drug Addiction (EMCDDA) based in Lisbon and Europol were charged with setting up an early warning system to monitor emerging new synthetic psychoactive drugs and to provide rapid information and risk assessment on the same to its member states.

Cocaine

For over 1000 years, native Latin Americans used *Erythroxylon coca* as a stimulant and as an anesthetic during trepanation. Cocaine was first isolated by Friedrich Gaedcke in 1855. The first synthesis and molecular structure elucidation was made by Richard Willstätter in 1898. In 1863, Angelo Mariani (1838–1914) marketed a wine treated with coca leaves, which was called Vin Mariani. Cocaine was introduced for clinical use in 1884 as a local anesthetic in Germany.

LSD

In the Middle Ages, human poisoning due to rye bread consumption was rather common in Europe, generating epidemics controversially linked to ergot poisoning, notably Saint Anthony's fire, the dancing procession of prayers in Echternach/Luxembourg to honor Saint Willibrord (658–739), and the hysterical behavior of young women accused of witchcraft in colonial Massachusetts in 1692, resulting in the Salem witch trials. LSD was synthesized in 1938 by Albert Hoffmann and its psychedelic properties were discovered in 1943. Dr. Timothy Leary was the most prominent pro-LSD researcher in the United States in the 1950s and 1960s.

Opioids

In 1804, Friedrich Wilhelm Sertürner (1783–1841) isolated morphine, the alkaloid, in a pure state from *Papaver somniferum*. The invention in 1850 of the hypodermic syringe by Charles Pravaz (1791–1853) and Alexander Wood (1817–1884) allowed IV administration of narcotic analgesics. Heroin was discovered in 1874 by Charles Alder Wright (1844–1894), synthesized in 1897 by Felix Hofmann (1868–1946) at Bayer Leverkusen, and marketed or advertised as a "nonaddictive morphine substitute in 1899," but the users' rates of dependence on heroin soon became one of the highest. Many other opiates and opioids have been launched over the years.

γ-Hydroxybutyric acid

Synthesis of γ-hydroxybutyric acid (GHB) was first reported in 1874 by Alexander Mikhaylov Zaytsev (1841–1910), but the first major pharmacological research was conducted by Henri Laborit by studying neurotransmitter GABA in the early 1960s. Legitimate medical uses declined rapidly because of its use in drug-facilitated sexual assault (DFSA) and its abuse potential.

Recent Developments in Analytical Methods

Since the 1960s, there has been tremendous progress in analytical toxicology due to the development of new extraction techniques and the mushrooming evolution of chromatographic, spectrographic, and immunoassay technologies.

Extraction techniques were improved from simple liquid solvent extraction to solid-phase extraction introduced in 1949; and solid-phase microextraction and supercritical fluid extraction coupled with supercritical fluid chromatography were followed and rationally adapted to be performed by robots. Thin layer chromatography pioneered by Egon Stahl (1924–1986) and Dieter Waldi, gas chromatography pioneered by James and Martin, and high-performance liquid chromatography pioneered by Csaba Horvath (1930–2004) developed in the end of 1960s are the most performing separation technologies. Starting from Goldbaum's spectrophotometric method for barbiturates, spectrometric methods made great progress. Another revolution in analytical toxicology was pioneered by Ryhage's et al. with the application of gas chromatography coupled with mass spectrometry to toxicology, further developed by many others. Interpretation of mass spectra was made easier by the availability of spectra libraries such as the consecutive editions of the Pfleger, Maurer, and Weber Libraries in 1985, first in book format containing some 1500 mass spectra of drugs, toxicants, and metabolites, later in 1987 as software for mass spectrometry instruments, updated in 2011 with nearly 9000 mass spectra.

The emergence of immunoassays for insulin in the 1950s and subsequent development of immunoassays for drugs-of-abuse testing was followed by an automatization to run series of many specimens. Lab-on-a-chip integrates one or several laboratory functions on a single small chip, allowing the handling of <1 pl volume, for example, a biochip array technology that allows multianalyte drug screening. The knowledge of drug and poison biotransformations to allow correct interpretation of toxicological results, taking into account pharmacogenomics and toxicogenomics, as genotyping and phenotyping studies have shown inheritable mutations in drug-metabolizing enzymes, notably some cytochromes P450, was also improved.

Alternative Matrices

Since the 1990s, alternative matrices such as hair, saliva, sweat, nails, and meconium besides the classical blood and urine have become available for forensic purposes. Hair analysis is increasingly being used to detect the presence of a large number of illicit drugs, environmental pollutants, and a minor metabolite ethyl glucuronide in alcohol to detect chronic ethanol intake.

Drug-Facilitated Crime

Owing to sensitivity improvement in analytical technologies, enormous progress has been made to convict offenders in drug-facilitated crime such as DFSA where, for example, benzodi-azepines or GHB is used as a date rape drug.

Drugs and Driving

Driving under the influence of drugs, having been recognized in most countries since the beginning of the 1990s, is a serious road safety issue now. Ethanol remains by far the biggest problem, but cannabis and opioids are also commonly detected drugs. Adequate legislation is not yet in place in all countries to properly detect and convict drug-impaired drivers. In some countries, debates continue on whether to enact zero tolerance or legal tolerance limits for selected drugs.

Famous Poisoning Cases

Famous Criminal Poisoning Cases from the Fifteenth to the Seventeenth Century

The Italian School of Poisoners was most famous for poisoners such as the Borgias in the fifteenth century, and in France, a similar situation was observed with the Parisian School of Poisoners starting with Cathérine de Médicis (1519–1589). She was married to King Henri II in 1533 and is alleged to have transferred the knowledge on poisons in France to Italy. Later, in the seventeenth century under Louis XIV (1638–1715), the so-called *Affaire des Poisons* occurred from 1670 to 1682.

Famous Criminal Poisoning Cases from the Nineteenth to the Twenty-First Century

To illustrate the evolution of poisoning, six famous cases are outlined below.

Dr. Edme S. Castaing case 1823

In 1823, Dr Edme S. Castaing (1796–1823), for need of funds, poisoned two of his friends and patients called Ballet Brothers with morphine in Paris. At that moment, morphine was not detectable in the viscera. Scientists involved in this case were, among others, René TH Laennec (1781–1826), François Magendie (1783–1855), Louis-Nicolas Vauquelin (1763–1829), and Mateo JB Orfila (1787–1853). The poisoner was finally sentenced to death by guillotine.

Hannah Russel case 1826

Hannah Russel from Burwash, Sussex, with the complicity of her lodger Daniel Leney was suspected to have poisoned her husband with arsenic. At autopsy, a local surgeon named Thomas Evans had found arsenic. A controversial dispute on inconclusive evidence between Gideon Mantell (1790–1852)

(famous discoverer in 1825 of the first dinosaur iguanodon fossil in Sussex), and Sir Robert Christison (1797–1882), and Alfred Swain Taylor (1806–1880) took place. Leney was executed, but Hannah was pardoned.

Dr. George Henry Lamson case 1881

Morphine-addicted G. H. Lamson used aconite to murder his handicapped brother-in-law Percy Malcolm John. Aconite was dissimilated in Dundee raisin cake, in order to secure an inheritance. Lamson had learned about aconite—as a medical student mate of Robert Christison—that it was undetectable, but forensic science had improved since Lamson's student days. The medical/toxicological experts in court were, among others, Thomas Stevenson (1838–1908) from Guy's Hospital, August Dupré (1835–1907) from Westminster Hospital, and Walter N. Hartley who plotted the first UV (ultraviolet) Spectrum in 1881. At that trial, the criminal defense was evoked for the first time ptomaine poisoning and falsely positive alkaloid tests according to Fransesco Selmi (1817–1881). At the end of the trial in Old Bailey Court in London, Lamson was hanged in 1882.

Affaire Marie Besnard 1949

Marie Bernard was accused of poisoning 11 persons including her husband with arsenic because of a hypothetical love affair with German war prisoner Alfred Dietz in Loudun/Vienne, France. A great number of toxicologists/pathologists, notably Georges Béroud, from Marseille Crime Laboratory charged with the first autopsy, who improperly used the Marsh and Cribier methods for As detection; Louis Truffert (b1910); Henri Griffon (1904–1990) using a neutron activation method, René Piédelièvre (1891–1975), René Truhaut (1909–1994), Emile Kohn-Abrest (1880–1963); René Fabre (1889–1966); Roger Le Breton (1914–1997); Léon Dérobert (1910–1980); Fréderic Joliot-Curie (1900–1958), and Jean Keilling, Georges Schuster, Henri Ollivier, Marcel Le Peintre as counter-experts, discussed about this case for over 12 years. In a first judgment in 1952 at Poitiers Criminal Court, she was sentenced to prison, but finally in 1961 she was found not guilty at Bordeaux Appeal Court.

Christa A. Lehmann case 1954

In Worms, Germany, Lehman poisoned her husband, father-in-law, her girlfriend, and a dog, Flocky, instead of targeted girl-friend's mother with parathion in chocolate candies. At the trial, Kurt Wagner (1905–1965), Hans-Joachim Wagner (b1924–2014), Alfred "Meister" Brahm-Vogelsanger, Hans Kaiser, Theo Haag, Georg Schmidt (1923–2010), and Wolfgang Schwerd (b1924) were in charge of the case: At the end of the trial, she was sentenced to life in prison. After this case, a critical discussion on the forensic significance of Averell–Norris reaction in the identification of metabolite *p*-nitrophenol from parathion was triggered. As a result of this case, a decrease in parathion suicides among individuals in the state of postwar Germany was observed.

Kenneth Barlow case 1957

Barlow, a male nurse from Bradford, UK, was accused of poisoning his wife Elizabeth with insulin in an abortion tentative. A. S. Curry (1925–2007) and his crew—"The Harrogate People"—testified. Barlow was sentenced to lifetime in prison and released, after serving 26 years, still maintaining his innocence.

See also: **Toxicology:** Behavioral Toxicology; Drug Screening in Sport; Herbal Medicines and Phytopharmaceuticals—Contaminations; Herbal Psychoactive Substances; Interpretation of Results; Pharmacology and Mechanism of Action of Drugs; **Toxicology/Drugs of Abuse:** Drugs in Hair.

Further Reading

Emsley, J., 2005. The Elements of Murder. A History of Poison. University Press, Oxford.

Emsley, J., 2008. Molecules of Murder. Criminal Molecules and Classic Cases. RSC Publishing, Cambridge, MA.

Jones, A.W., 2010. Perspectives in Drug Discovery – A Collection of Essays on the History and Development of Pharmaceutical Substances. Rättsmedicinalverket, Linköping, Sweden.

Müller, R.K., 2003. Forensiche toxikologie. In: Madea, B., Brinkmann, B. (Eds.), Handbuch Gerichtliche Medizin, Band II. Springer Verlag, Berlin-Heidelberg, pp. 6–13.

Niyogy, S.K., 1981. In: Cravey, R.H., Baselt, R.C. (Eds.), Introduction to Forensic Toxicology. Biomedical Publications, Davis, CA.

Thorwald, J., 1976. Das Jahrhundert der Detektive Band II Handbuch für Giftmörder. Droemer-Knaur Verlag, München-Zürich.

Trestrail III, J., 2007. Criminal Poisoning. Humana Press, Totowa, NJ.

Watson, K., 2004. Poisoned Lives. English Poisoners and Their Victims. Hambledon and London, London.

Relevant Website

http://toxipedia.org – Milestones of Toxicology.

Toxicology: Overview and Applications

OH Drummer, Monash University, Southbank, VIC, Australia

Glossary

Analytical toxicology The use of analytical methods to detect substances.

Confirmation test The second test or the test that unequivocally identifies a substance.

Exhibit Applies to both specimens and physical items such as tablets and syringes.

Forensic toxicology Application of toxicology to meet the needs of the courts.

Quality assurance A process that checks the reliability of a laboratory to conduct its work.

Receptor Specific recognition site in tissues that is usually functionally connected to a physiological response.

Screening test The initial test that suggests the presence of a substance or class of substances.

Toxicology The science of poisons.

Introduction

Toxicology when used in a forensic capacity involves the analysis of specimens and other exhibits for chemical substances in cases involving an investigation that has the potential to go before a court of enquiry. This distinction to an ordinary analytical toxicologist is important, since a conventional toxicologist is mainly concerned with the detection of substances and may not understand the specific medicolegal requirements in forensic cases.

These chemical substances cover a wide variety of drugs and poisons and require the use of a variety of analytical techniques. These techniques, when used together, are able to provide sufficient coverage of possible substances to exclude relevant drugs and poisons, and when a substance(s) is detected, the analytical proof is sufficient to meet the needs of the law.

This chapter outlines the applications of this discipline, the techniques used, and how they are best applied and monitored in forensic cases.

Applications of Forensic Toxicology

Forensic toxicology has a number of applications. It plays an essential role in death investigations by providing investigators with information on whether the use of substances is relevant to the cause and manner of death. The request to perform "toxicology" may be based on information on the possible use of chemical substances (including prescribed drugs), or it may simply be requested to exclude the involvement of substances that either have a bearing on the cause of death or may have affected the behavior of the person. The latter is most important in the investigation of vehicular crashes, where substance use may have affected the ability to drive safely and therefore contributed to the event. In some cases, a suspected use of psychoactive drugs, particularly alcohol and the common drugs of abuse (amphetamines, cocaine, cannabis, benzodiazepines, etc.), in a murder is commonly encountered. While these drugs may not have caused the death, their presence indicates the use of drugs (and perhaps other substances) either for health reasons and/or for recreational purpose. In many cases, abuse of drugs leads to significant behavioral changes that can lead to criminal acts or expose them to increased vulnerability to be a victim of a crime.

Toxicology testing is also important in victims of crime or in persons apprehended for a crime. Drugs may have been given by the assailant to reduce consciousness of the victim, as in rape cases. These drugs include the benzodiazepines and related sedatives and hypnotics (e.g., alprazolam and zolpidem) and gamma hydroxybyrate (GHB). Toxicology also establishes if any drug was used by the victim that may have affected consciousness or behavior. Defendants arrested shortly after allegedly committing a violent crime may be under the influence of drugs. It is vital, therefore, that toxicology testing is conducted (on relevant specimens) to establish the extent of drug use, since allegations of drug use and its effect on intent or clinical state may be raised in legal proceedings.

Forensic toxicology is also used in employment drug testing and in human performance testing. The former category relates to the detection of drugs of abuse in persons in a place of employment, prior to being hired by an employer, or even a person in detention, such as the one in a prison. Human performance testing relates to the detection of drugs that might have increased (usually) performance in athletic events. This may even apply to animals, such as horses, and jockeys that ride them. Specimens used in these cases are usually urine, although hair can be used to provide a longer window of detection.

Initial Tests and Confirmation

The foremost goal in forensic toxicology is the need to provide unequivocal proof of the presence of a substance(s). The use of conventional techniques that do not provide proof of structure (e.g., gas chromatography, GC; thin-layer chromatography; and high-performance liquid chromatography, HPLC) would not normally be sufficient to provide unequivocal proof of the presence of a chemical substance when used alone. Two or more independent tests are normally required, or the use of a more powerful analytical test, such as mass spectrometry (MS), is expected. Because of the need to perform a rigorous analysis, the analytical schema is often broken up into two steps. The identification stage is termed the screening or initial test, while the second analytical test is the confirmation process. The confirmation process often also provides a quantitative measure of how much substance was present in the sample or else a separate test is required to quantify the amount of substance present in the specimen. In all processes, it is important that no significant analytical inconsistency appears, or else a result may be invalidated (**Figure 1**).

For example, in the identification of codeine in a blood specimen, an immunoassay positive to opiates is expected to be positive for codeine in the confirmation assay. The apparent detection of a drug in one analytical assay but not in another means that the drug is not confirmed, provided that both assays are capable of detecting this drug. **Table 1** provides a listing of common techniques used in screening and confirmation assays.

While MS is the preferred technique for confirmation of drugs and poisons, some substances display poor mass spectral definition. Compounds with base ions at mass/charge ratios of <100, or with common ions with ratios such as m/z 105, and with little or no ions in the higher mass range are not recommended for confirmation by MS alone. Derivatization of a functional group to produce improved mass spectral properties can often be successful. Common derivatives include perflouroalkyl esters, trimethyl silyl ethers, and so on. Alternatively, reliance on other chromatographic procedures can provide adequate confirmation. It is important when using any chromatographic procedure (e.g., HPLC and GC) that the retention time of the substance being identified matches with that of an authentic standard. Criteria exist for retention time variability and for acceptance of mass spectral information.

Some apparent analytical inconsistencies may provide important forensic information. For example, if a result for

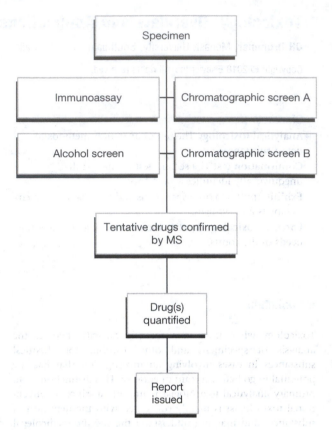

Figure 1   Schema showing identification, confirmation, and quantification processes in forensic toxicology.

Table 1   Screening and confirmation techniques

Screening tests	Confirmation tests
Immunoassays (various) Spectroscopy (UV, F, etc.)	MS (LC, GC, CE) including tandem MS TOFMS and other forms of high-resolution MS
HPLC (UV, F, ECD, CD) GC (FID, NPD, TD) TOFMS and other forms of high-resolution MS CE (UV, F) AAS, colorimetric tests	Second chromatographic test AAS and ICP-MS

AAS, atomic absorption spectroscopy; *CD*, conductivity detection; *CE*, capillary electrophoresis; *DAD*, photodiode array detector; *ECD*, electrochemical detection; *F*, fluorescence; *FID*, flame ionization detector; *GC*, gas chromatography; *HPLC*, high-performance liquid chromatography; *ICP-MS*, inductively coupled plasma MS; *MS*, mass spectroscopy; *NPD*, nitrogen phosphorous detector; *TD*, thermionic detector; *UV*, ultraviolet; *TOF*, time of flight.

opiates is negative in urine, but positive in blood, it is possible that heroin was administered shortly before death (heroin is rapidly metabolized to 6-acetylmorphine and morphine), and therefore metabolites had not yet been excreted. This situation is often found in heroin users dying from an acute sudden death in which substantial urinary excretion has not yet occurred.

Common Drugs and Poisons

The most common drugs and poisons are clearly the initial targets of any forensic toxicological analysis, particularly if no specific information is available to direct the investigation. The most common substances can be categorized as fitting into four classes, for example, alcohol (ethanol), illicit drugs, licit (ethical) drugs, and the nondrug poisons.

The most common substances detected in forensic toxicology laboratories are shown in **Table 2**. The types of substances are likely to be similar throughout developed countries, although significant regional variations can occur depending on the local availability of drugs. Herbal remedies are widely available; in some situations, these can be dangerous if mixed with pharmaceutical or illicit drugs and, in some cases, drugs are illegally added to enhance the effects of the preparation.

Table 2 Most common drugs of interest in forensic toxicology

Ethanol (alcohol)[a]

Amphetamines	Amphetamine, methamphetamine, MDMA, MDA, MDEA, etc.
Analgesics and anti-inflammatories	Acetaminophen (paracetamol), salicylate, NSAIDs, etc.
Anticonvulsants	Carbamazepine, lamotrigine, phenytoin, valproate, etc.
Antidepressants	(es)Citalopram, fluoxetine, venlafaxine, paroxetine, amitriptyline, etc.
Antipsychotics	Olanzapine, haloperidol, clozapine, etc.
Benzodiazepines	Alprazolam, clonazepam, diazepam, temazepam, oxazepam, etc.
Cannabis	Δ^9-Tetrahydrocannabinol and metabolites
Cocaine and metabolites	
Opiates	Morphine, heroin, codeine, hydromorphone, oxycodone, etc.
Opioids[b]	Methadone, meperidine, fentanyl, etc.
Muscle relaxants	Carisoprodol, dantrolene, orphenadrine, etc.
Other hypnotics	Zolpidem, zopiclone, etc.

MDA, 3,4-methylenedioxy-amphetamine; *MDEA*, 3,4-methylenedioxy-ethylamphetamine; *MDMA*, 3,4-methylenedioxy-methamphetamine; *NSAID*, nonsteroidal anti-inflammatory drugs such as ibuprofen, naproxen, etc.; *THC*, Δ^9-Tetrahydrocannabinol.
[a]This list is alphabetical after ethanol. There will be substantial variation in the incidence of these substances from one jurisdiction to another. Only the more common examples of each drug type are included as examples.
[b]These are synthetic drugs acting like the opiate drugs.

Alcohol is the most frequent detection in many countries and, when detected, it can play an important role in any investigation because of its ability to depress the central nervous system (CNS). At best, alcohol will modify behavior, causing disinhibition and possible aggression; at worst, it can cause death, either by itself or in combination with another substance.

Illicit drugs most commonly include amphetamines, cocaine, cannabis, heroin, and other opiates/opioids. In some jurisdictions, GHB, ketamine, phencyclidine, and fentanyl are available as illicit substances. Designer drugs based on existing illicit drugs are increasingly becoming available. These have included analogs of amphetamine and methamphetamine, often branded as ecstasy (3,4-methylenedioxy-methamphetamine, 3,4-methylenedioxy-ethylamphetamine, etc.), but now include a variety of other synthetic substances. Those that mimic the action of tetrahydrocannabinol (THC) have been given names such as Spice and Kronic. A series of stimulants that act like the amphetamines include piperazines, phenethylamines, 4-substituted amphetamines, β-keto-amphetamines, 2,5-dimethoxyamphetamines, pyrrolidino-phenones, and analogs of cathinone (derived from Khat) that include mephedrone.

It should be borne in mind that some illicit drugs also have medical uses in some countries. Cocaine is used in some forms of facial and nasal surgery, (dex)amphetamine is used to treat narcolepsy and attention deficit syndrome, and cannabis (as the active form THC and other cannabinoids) is used (among other indications) to reduce nausea following chemotherapy. Benzodiazepines are widely prescribed to relieve anxiety and induce sleep among other indications but are also widely abused, often with the illicit substances.

Ethical drugs include the whole range of prescription and over-the-counter drugs used in the treatment of minor to major ailments. Those of most interest include the antidepressants, antipsychotic drugs, narcotic analgesics and other forms of pain relievers, and anticonvulsants. Since these drugs are widely prescribed, they are by far the most commonly encountered drugs in toxicology. Each country will have its own list of registered drugs; hence, laboratories will need to consider these as a matter of priority over other members of a particular class available elsewhere. From time to time, laboratories will be required to consider drugs that are not legally available in their countries because of illicit supplies or supplies through tourists visiting their country.

The nondrug poisons most commonly include organo-phosphates and other pesticides, carbon monoxide and hydrogen cyanide derived from burning materials in fires, cyanide salts, and volatile substances (petrol, natural gas, kerosene, etc.). Other poisons include the metals and their salts (arsenic, mercury, thallium, etc.), plant-derived poisons (hyoscine from belladonna species, coniine from hemlock, etc.), strychnine, and toxins such as venoms. Performance-

Table 3 Most common (nondrug) poisons of interest in forensic toxicology

Alcohols (other than legal ethanol; e.g., methanol)[a]
Aliphatic hydrocarbons (methane, LPG, butane, and petroleum products)
Aromatic hydrocarbons (toluene, xylene, etc.)
Carbon monoxide (from automobile exhausts and fires)
Cyanide (as salt or derived from burning fuels forming hydrogen cyanide)
Ethylene glycol
Inorganics (salts of arsenic, lead, mercury, thallium, etc.)
Pesticides (chlorpyrifos, carbofuran, aldicarb, etc.)
Other agricultural chemicals (paraquat, diquat, 2,4-D, glyphosate, etc.)
Plant-derived poisons (scopolamine, digoxin-like glycosides, etc.)
Potassium (from legal preparations often as chloride)
Solvents (toluene, chloroform, ethers, etc.)
Strychnine and other rodenticides
Warfarin and other anticoagulants (e.g., brodifacoum)

2,4-D, 2,4-dichlorophenoxyacetic acid; *LPG*, liquid petroleum gas.
[a]This list is alphabetical. There will be substantial variation in the incidence of these substances from one jurisdiction to another. Only the more common examples of each are included as examples.

enhancing drugs such as the anabolic steroids may also be considered in some instances. Clearly, this list is potentially unending, although some chemicals are more readily available to certain occupational groups than others and are dependent on national regulations within countries. The most common poisons are shown in **Table 3**. Clearly, the distribution of unusual substances will vary from country to country.

Scope of Testing Protocols

As the previous sections indicate, cases may involve a variety of ethical and illicit drugs or unusual poisons. Worldwide experience also shows that forensic cases often involve more than one drug substance. A survey of drug-related deaths shows that three or more drugs are present in > 70% of cases. High rates of multiple drug use are also found in perpetrators and victims of violent crimes, suicides, and often also in accidents and road crashes.

It is also well known by forensic toxicologists that the information provided to the laboratory concerning possible drug use may not accord with what is actually detected. It is therefore strongly recommended that laboratories provide a systematic approach to their toxicology cases and include as wide a range of common ethical and illicit drugs as feasible. This approach is termed systematic toxicological analysis. A laboratory using this approach would normally include a range of screening methods often incorporating both chromatographic and immunological techniques. Drug classes such as alcohol, analgesics, opioid and nonopioid narcotics, amphetamines, antidepressants, benzodiazepines,

barbiturates, cannabis, cocaine, antipsychotic drugs, and other CNS depressant drugs would be included.

The incorporation of a reasonably complete range of drugs in any testing protocol is important, since many of these drugs are mood altering and can therefore affect behavior, as well as affect the health status of an individual. Persons using benzodiazepines, for example, will be further affected by cocaine, amphetamine use, and use of other CNS depressant drugs. The toxic concentrations of drugs are also influenced by the presence of other potential toxic drugs. For example, the fatal dose of heroin is affected by the concomitant use of alcohol and other CNS depressant drugs.

Specimens

It is essential that the relevant specimens are taken whenever possible, since recollection is rarely possible. In living persons, drugs and their metabolites will often not persist for more than several hours to days. The preferred specimens collected in forensic toxicology will of course depend on the nature of the case. In general, a blood specimen is a minimum requirement, although specimens such as urine can be useful for laboratories as a screening specimen and to check for the use of drugs two or more days prior to sampling.

Hair can provide even longer memory of drug intake, lasting up to several months, depending on the length of hair. Drugs are usually incorporated into the growing root matrix and are detected analytically as a band in the hair shaft when it externalizes from the skin. This process can therefore provide a history of when exposure to a drug or poison has occurred. Most drugs and poisons are incorporated into hair, although the extent will depend on the physiochemical properties of the substance. Basic drugs are often found in higher concentrations than acidic drugs, and invariably the parent drug is present rather than metabolites. For example, cocaine and the heroin metabolite 6-acetylmorphine are more likely to be found in the hair of cocaine and heroin users than their corresponding metabolites found in blood and urine (benzoylecgonine and morphine). Unfortunately, some drug will be absorbed into the hair from skin secretions adjacent to the hair follicles and may even be incorporated from external contamination. Care and treatment of hair, through processes such as washing and use of dyes and bleaches, will also affect the concentration of the drug in hair. Consequently, any interpretation of drug content in hair needs to factor these considerations.

Courts and other legal processes usually require proof that the laboratory has taken all reasonable precautions against unwanted tampering or alteration of the evidence. This applies to specimens and to physical exhibits used by the laboratory in their toxicology investigations. Consequently, it is essential that the correct identifying details are recorded on the exhibit or specimen container, and an adequate record is kept of persons in possession of the exhibit(s). Alternatively, when couriers are used to transport exhibits, then the exhibit must be adequately sealed to prevent unauthorized tampering.

General Techniques

The range of techniques available for detection of drugs in the specimens collected for postmortem is essentially identical to those collected. These range from commercial kit-based immunoassays to instrumental separation techniques such as HPLC, GC, and capillary electrophoresis. MS is the definitive technique used to establish proof of structure of an unknown substance and is usually linked to either a GC or an HPLC. High-resolution MS, sometimes known as time-of-flight MS, is also increasingly being used to identify substances on the basis of their accurate molecular weight.

The use of appropriate extraction techniques is critical to all analytical methods. Three main types of extractions are used: liquid–liquid, solid-phase, and direct injection. Traditionally, liquid techniques, in which a blood or urine specimen is treated with a buffer of an appropriate pH followed by a solvent capable of partitioning the drug out of the matrix, have been favored. Solvents used include ethyl acetate, toluene, hexane, various alcohols, and butyl chloride, and mixtures thereof. The solvent is then isolated from the mixture and either cleaned up by another extraction process or evaporated to dryness.

Solid-phase techniques, particularly using mixed-phase supports, are commonly used in that they offer the ability to extract substances of widely deferring polarity more readily than liquid–liquid techniques. Often, less solvent is used, or a simple hydroalcoholic system can be employed, rather than potentially volatile or inflammable solvents.

Direct injection into either GC or HPLC instruments bypasses the extraction step and can offer a very rapid analytical process. In GC, solid-phase microextraction is most commonly used, while HPLC tends to require use of precolumns that are backflushed with the use of column-switching valves.

Quality Assurance and Validation

An essential part of any form of toxicological testing is validation and the conduct of quality assurance. It is important that the method used is appropriately validated, that is, it has been shown to accurately and precisely detect the substance(s) detectable, that there is little or no interference (from other drugs and from the matrix) with the specimens used, and that a useful detection limit has been established. Moreover, it is essential that the method is rugged and will allow any suitably trained analyst to conduct the procedure and achieve the same results as those achieved by another analyst. To achieve these

aims, it is necessary to trial the method in the laboratory over several assays with varying specimen quality before claiming that a full validation has been conducted.

It is recommended to include internal quality controls with each batch of samples to enable an internal check of the reliability of each assay. These controls contain known drugs at known concentrations. Suitable acceptance criteria are required for these controls before results of unknown cases can be accepted and released to a client. Acceptance criteria vary depending on the analyte and application. For example, blood alcohol estimations have acceptance criteria of <5%, while postmortem blood procedures may be at 15%.

An important feature of analytical assays in forensic toxicology is the use of internal standards. These are drugs of similar chemical and physical characteristics as the drug(s) being analyzed and, when added at the start of the extraction procedure, they provide an ability to negate the effects of variable or low recoveries from the matrix. Hence, even when recoveries are low, the ratios of the analyte and drug are essentially the same as those for situations of higher recovery. An ideal recovery marker is when the internal standard is a deuterated analog of the analyte. When deuterated internal standards are used, it may not be necessary to match the calibration standards with the same matrix as the unknown samples. It is important, however, that absolute recoveries are reasonable, that is, at least over 30%. This ensures less variability between samples and optimizes the detection limit.

From time to time, it will be important to run unknown samples prepared by another laboratory, or a person not directly involved in laboratory work, to establish proficiency. These are known as proficiency programs or quality assurance programs. These trials are often conducted with many other laboratories conducting similar work and provide an independent assessment of the proficiency of the laboratory to detect (and quantify) specific drugs. The performance of the laboratory should be regularly assessed from these results, and any corrective action should be implemented, if appropriate. This process provides a measure of continuous improvement, an essential characteristic of any laboratory.

There are a number of collaborative programs available throughout the world. The College of American Pathologists (CAP) organizes an excellent series of proficiency programs in forensic toxicology.

The International Association of Forensic Toxicologists (TIAFT) and the American Society of Forensic Toxicology (SOFT) provide guidelines on the conduct of analytical assays and on quality assurance of assays.

Estimation of Dose

A common request from legal counsel and police is to estimate a dose from a blood or tissue concentration. This may relate to determining likely intent from an ingestion (or injection) or simply to rationalize the circumstances to specific amounts of drugs used.

While some practitioners attempt to calculate a dose, in reality, there are so many variables that can affect this estimation that it is not possible except in the rarest of circumstances. At best, a dose range may be estimated, but it must take into account unabsorbed drug, bioavailability, excreted drug, large variations from person to person in terms of the pharmacokinetics, possible accumulative effects of repeated doses, gender, age, and, in death investigations, the likely possibility of postmortem processes affecting the concentration of the substance.

Occasionally, it may be possible to compare blood (and tissue) concentrations to other cases in which doses were known by measuring the body burden in several tissues including muscle and fat. Analysis of gastric and intestinal drug content will assist in this process and may also provide information on the route and time of ingestion.

Interpretation of Toxicological Results

Interpretation of any toxicological result is complex. Consideration must be given to the circumstances of the case and, in particular, to the significance that may be drawn from the toxicology. For example, the finding of a drug in potentially toxic concentrations in a person killed by a gunshot wound to the head cannot reasonably lead to the conclusion that drugs caused the death. On the other hand, the absence of an obvious anatomical cause of death will lead investigators to consider the role of any substance detected in the analyses. Considerations must include the chronicity of drug use, the age of the person, the health of the person (presence of heart, liver, kidney disease, etc.), the use of multiple substances, and even genetic factors that may lead to altered metabolism.

Court Testimony

Forensic toxicologists and other analysts called in to give evidence in court should consider that much of their technical evidence is beyond the ready comprehension of lay people in juries, legal counsel, and judges. Restricting their evidence to understandable language and simple concepts is highly recommended.

A further problem relates to an assumption often made by legal counsel (and other parties) that a toxicological investigation was exhaustive and all drugs and poisons were tested for. Most toxicology performed is restricted to a few analytical tests for a range of "common drugs and poisons" unless the client (e.g., a pathologist or police officer) has made a request to examine for (additional) specific chemicals. Analysts

should make courts aware of the actual testing conducted and provide a list of substances incorporated in the investigation. Importantly, advice on any limitations applied to the interpretation of the analytical results, such as poor quality specimens, postmortem artifacts, and so on, should be provided. Above all, toxicologists must restrict their evidence to those areas in which they claim expertise. Testifying beyond their expertise or, worse, so as to favor one side in a case can lead to incorrect or misleading evidence and damage the reputation of the expert.

> See also: **Toxicology:** Herbal Medicines and Phytopharmaceuticals – Contaminations; Herbal Psychoactive Substances; Interpretation of Results; Methods of Analysis – Confirmatory Testing; Methods of Analysis – Initial Testing; Postmortem Specimens; Postmortem Toxicology: Artifacts; **Toxicology/Drugs of Abuse:** Drugs in Hair; Postmortem Blood; Urine.

Further Reading

Baselt, R.H. (Ed.), 2008. Disposition of Toxic Drugs and Chemicals in Man, eighth ed. Year Book Medical Publishers Inc, Chicago, IL.

Drummer, O.H., 2000. The Forensic Pharmacology of Drugs of Abuse. Arnold, London.

Drummer, O.H., 2007. Post-mortem toxicology. Forensic Science International 165, 199–203.

Drummer, O.H., 2010. Forensic toxicology. EXS 100, 579–603.

Jones, A.W., Kugelberg, F.C., Holmgren, A., Ahlner, J., 2011. Drug poisoning deaths in Sweden show a predominance of ethanol in mono- intoxications, adverse drug-alcohol interactions and poly-drug use. Forensic Science International 206, 43–51.

Karch, S. (Ed.), 2009. Pathology of Drug Abuse. CRC Press, Boca Raton, FL, 709 pp.

Maurer, H.H., 2010. Perspectives of liquid chromatography coupled to low- and high-resolution mass spectrometry for screening, identification, and quantification of drugs in clinical and forensic toxicology. Therapeutic Drug Monitoring 32, 324–327.

Moffatt, A.C., Osselton, D., Widdop, B., Watts, J. (Eds.), 2011. Clarke's Isolation and Identification of Drugs, fourth ed. The Pharmaceutical Press, London.

Peters, F.T., 2011. Recent advances of liquid chromatography-(tandem) mass spectrometry in clinical and forensic toxicology. Clinical Biochemistry 44, 54–65.

Peters, F.T., Martinez-Ramirez, J.A., 2010. Analytical toxicology of emerging drugs of abuse. Therapeutic Drug Monitoring 32, 32–39.

Relevant Websites

http://www.aacc.org—American Association for Clinical Chemistry.
http://www.abft.org—American Board of Forensic Toxicology.
http://www.facta.org.au —Forensic and Clinical Toxicology Association Inc.
http://www.iatdmct.org—International Association of Therapeutic Drug Monitoring and Clinical Toxicology.
http://www.soft-tox.org—The Society of Forensic Toxicologists, Inc.
http://www.tiaft.org—The International Association of Forensic Toxicologists.

Key Terms

Alternative matrices, Analogy, Analytical toxicology, Classification, Comparison, Confirmation tests, Crime, Drug-facilitated crime, Drugs and driving, Drugs and poisons, Epistemology, Evidence, Famous criminal poisoning cases, Forensic, Forensic toxicology, History, Initial tests, Kirk, Locard, Method, Methods of analysis, Paradigm, Postmortem toxicology, Quality assurance, Recent developments, Science, Set, Taxon, Taxonomy, Validation.

Review Questions

1. If the "basic unit of forensic science is the trace," how do toxicology samples fit within this conceptual framework? What would they be a "physical remnant" of?
2. What are the three levels that Locard's principle needs to address?
3. Besides Locard's principle, what else do Crispino and Houck consider to be a "native" forensic principle?
4. What are the nonnative principles that forensic science uses? Give an example of each one in action.
5. What is the difference between uniqueness and individualization?
6. What does the Latin version of Paracelsus' statement *Alimenta a toxis, uti medicamenta a venenis, non natura sed dosis distinguit* mean?
7. Who was Orfila?
8. Who discovered flame emission spectrometry for mineral elements and when?
9. What is one of the oldest known and most frequently used recreational substances?
10. What drug comes from *Erythroxylon coca*?
11. When was LSD synthesized?
12. List at least three matrices for toxicological analysis.
13. What does "GHB" stand for?
14. If a drug is detected in one analytical assay but not in another, is the presence of the drug confirmed?
15. Do illicit drugs have legitimate medical uses?
16. Three or more drugs are involved in what percentage of cases?
17. Which type of drugs are typically found in higher concentrations, acidic or basic?
18. What is validation?
19. What does CAP stand for?
20. What are TIAFT and SOFT?

Discussion Questions

1. What is the difference between toxicology and drug analysis? Why is toxicology more complicated than drug analysis? What does drug analysis have to deal with that toxicology does not? What about the reverse?
2. What is the difference between antemortem and postmortem toxicology (besides the status of the patient)? Think matrices, sampling, methods (and sampling methods), questions posed, and hypotheses.
3. Why might a decedent's medical records be important for a toxicologist to have? What role could medical care have?
4. Why might a case involving a decedent who was visiting the toxicologist's country differ from one involving a citizen? Why might the toxicologist want to know?
5. Kirk is quoted as saying, "On the witness stand, the criminalist must be willing to admit that *absolute identity is impossible to establish*. … The inept or biased witness may readily testify to an identity, or to a type of identity, that does not actually exist." What are the implications for the interpretation of forensic evidence if absolute identity is impossible to establish? If forensic scientists cannot speak of absolute identity, what can they use? Can a toxicologist "absolutely identify" a drug or compound by its break-down products?

Additional Readings

Cave, D.M., Kingston, R., 2016. 20 Hair Testing in Forensic Toxicology. Forensic Toxicology: Drug Use and Misuse, p. 411.

Cosbey, S., Elliott, S., Paterson, S., 2017. The United Kingdom and Ireland Association of Forensic Toxicologists; establishing best practice for professional training & development in forensic toxicology. Science & Justice 57 (1), 63–71.

Emsley, J., 2006. The Elements of Murder: A History of Poison. Oxford University Press.

Lemos, N.P., 2016. 19 Nail Analysis in Forensic Toxicology. Forensic Toxicology: Drug Use and Misuse, p. 400.

Oberacher, H., Arnhard, K., 2016. Current status of non-targeted liquid chromatography-tandem mass spectrometry in forensic toxicology. TrAC Trends in Analytical Chemistry 84, 94–105.

Section 2. Methods

Toxicology is one of the most, if not actually the most, complicated and technologically driven forensic disciplines. The capitalization of a toxicology laboratory is a hefty financial investment and the maintenance on all those high-priced instruments is also a significant ongoing cost. But, like most forensic laboratories, people make up the highest percentage of the annual budget. Those instruments do not run themselves, after all. Despite the emphasis in this section on instrumentation and methods, never forget that it is people that lie at the heart of a toxicology laboratory.

Capillary Electrophoresis: Basic Principles

A Shallan, R Guijt, and M Breadmore, University of Tasmania, Hobart, TAS, Australia

Abbreviations

BGE	Background electrolyte
C	Concentration of the component in the sample solution
CE	Capillary electrophoresis
D_m	Diffusion coefficient of the analyte
DNA	Deoxyribonucleic acid
E	Applied electric field
ε	Dielectric constant of the medium
EC	Electrochromatography
ECD	Electrochemical detection
ESI	Electrospray ionization
EKC	Electrophoretic chromatography
EOF	Electroosmotic flow
FASS	Field-amplified sample stacking
GC	Gas chromatography
HPLC	High-performance liquid chromatography
H_{th}	Height equivalent to the theoretical plates
IEF	Isoelectric focusing
ITP	Isotachophoresis
L_d	Capillary length from injection to detector
LIF	Laser-induced fluorescence
L_{tot}	Total capillary length
MALDI	Matrix-assisted laser desorption/ionization
μ_{app}	Apparent mobility
MEEKC	Microemulsion electrokinetic chromatography
MEKC	Micellar electrokinetic chromatography
μ_{EOF}	Electroosmotic mobility
μ_{ep}	Electrophoretic mobility
MS	Mass spectrometric
µTAS	Micro-total analysis system
m/z	Mass-to-charge ratio
N	Number of theoretical plates
OHP	Outer Helmholtz plane
Δp	Pressure difference
Q	Injection quantity
q	Charge
r_i	Radius of the ion
r_d	Capillary inner diameter
η	Solution viscosity
SDS-PAGE	Sodium dodecyl sulfate-polyacrylamide gel electrophoresis
SE	Sieving electrophoresis
SiO^-	Silanoate group
SiOH	Silanol group
t	Migration time
t_{inj}	Injection time
UV	Ultra-violet

V	Applied voltage	$w_{1/2}$	Temporal peak width at half-height
ν_i	Velocity of an ion	ζ	Zeta potential
ν_{inj}	Injection volume	ZE	Zone electrophoresis

Glossary

Capillary electrophoresis Electrophoresis in a circular tube with an internal diameter less than 100 μm.
Electroosmotic flow (EOF) Flow of solvent through movement of ions held near a charged surface in an electric field.
Electrophoresis Movement of ions in an electric field.

Electrophoretic mobility Constant that defines the speed and direction of movement of ion.
Joule heating Heat generated from movement of ions in an electric field during electrophoresis.
Microchip electrophoresis Electrophoresis in a micrometer channel sealed in a flat planar substrate.

Introduction

Capillary electrophoresis (CE) is one of the most powerful liquid phase separation techniques. Evolving about 30 years ago out of the traditional electrophoretic techniques, such as slab gel electrophoresis, it became a rapid alternative to high-performance liquid chromatography (HPLC) and gas chromatography (GC). The reasons for this were many and varied: high speed, high efficiency, different selectivity, and the ability to sample small volumes. There was much hype and promise and while it has not replaced HPLC and GC as was touted in the early days, it is nevertheless the method of choice in a number of key areas that are of particular relevance to forensic science that are discussed in the following chapter.

At its most basic level, electrophoresis is the movement of ionic species in conductive media under an applied electric field. Although much of the fundamental understanding of electrophoresis comes from around the 1900s with the pioneering work of Kohlraulsch, the first demonstration of electrophoresis as a separation technique dates back to the 1930s, with the elegant moving boundary experiments of Tiselius on the separation of human serum. The separation was performed in a glass U-tube, with an internal rectangular cross section of 3 mm × 25 mm. However, the large scale of the tube led to excessive heat production, which resulted in poor resolution. To counteract this, a solid support, such as paper, starch gel, agarose, cellulose acetate, and polyacrylamide gel, was used, and, of course, spawned the development of sodium dodecyl sulfate-polyacrylamide gel electrophoresis . When combined with isoelectric focusing (IEF), this created a 2D system that has been the cornerstone of proteomic studies (the separation and differential expression of proteins within a sample) for the last three decades. In the late 1970s, a different approach to overcoming the heat issue was presented in Europe by Hjerten in which narrow diameter tubes were used. Independently in North America, Jorgenson and Lukacs did the same thing, although on a much smaller scale using micron-sized fused silica capillaries developed for capillary GC, and it is this format that is implemented around the world today and is most well known for being the platform for sequencing DNA. The most recent significant advancement in the field of electrophoresis has been its implementation in planar microchips in the early 1990s. This has taken separations that used to require hours in gels to tens of minutes in capillaries to tens of seconds in microchips. Many of the concepts discussed here for capillaries are equally applicable to microchips (**Table 1**).

Table 1   Milestones in capillary electrophoresis development

Year	Achievement
1937	Moving boundary electrophoresis; Tiselius
1952	Paper electrophoresis; Consden
1955	Starch gel electrophoresis; Oliver Smithies
1961	Isoelectric focusing; Svensson
1970	Capillary isotachophoresis; Everaerts
1979	Defining CE experiments; Mikkers
1981	Capillary electrophoresis; Jörgenson and Lukacs
1984	Micellar electrokinetic chromatography; Terabe
1985	Capillary isoelectric focusing; Hjertén
1992	Microchip electrophoresis, Manz

For more complete details of the history of electrophoresis, the reader is referred to the texts listed in the "Further Reading" section.

Fundamentals of Capillary Electrophoresis

As mentioned above, the basic premise of an electrophoretic separation is that different charged species will move at a different velocity and can thus be separated. While correct on a conceptual level, the truth is that it is far more complex, as there exists a complex interplay between the analyte ions, the capillary surface, and additives placed in the electrolyte.

Electrophoretic Mobilities

The electrophoretic mobility of an ion (μ_{ep}) can be described in terms of physical parameters when the electrical force is equal to frictional force:

$$\mu_{ep} = \frac{q}{6\pi\eta r_i} \qquad [1]$$

where q is the charge, η is the viscosity, and r_i is the radius of the ion. From this equation comes the notion that the speed at which an ion moves is related to its charge to size ratio ($q{:}r_i$). Practically, it is more useful to consider this as the charge to shape ratio, as it is the shape created by the solvated ions that really governs the frictional force and influences the mobility. It should also be obvious from this equation that the sign of the charge, that is, whether the ion is an anion or a cation, will influence the direction in which the ion moves and thus anions and cations will move in different directions. Their simultaneous separation would be nontrivial if it were not for the very important and crucial phenomena of electroosmosis.

Electroosmosis and the Electroosmotic Flow

Electroosmosis is observed when an electric field is applied to a conductive solution in a capillary that has fixed charges on its interior wall. In a fused silica capillary, which is the most commonly used in CE, the inner surface contains ionizable silanol groups (SiOH) that have pk_a values from 4 to 6. At pH values greater than 4, SiOH ionize giving the anionic form, silanoate, and thus the surface has a negative charge. This attracts positively charged cations from the bulk solution forming a double layer with positive charge density that decreases exponentially as the distance from the wall increases. A potential difference very close to the wall will be created and this is called the zeta potential. As shown in **Figure 1**, the innermost layer close to the capillary surface is essentially static and is termed the inner Helmholtz or Stern layer, and the second layer is more diffuse and is termed the outer Helmholtz plane. Upon application of an electric field, cations in the

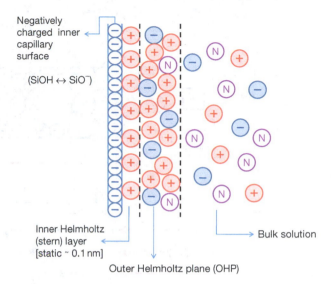

Figure 1   Electric double layer in fused silica capillaries.

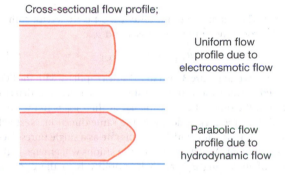

Figure 2   Uniform flow profile in capillary electrophoresis.

second more diffuse layer migrate in the direction of the cathode; in doing so, they drag associated solvent molecules along with them thus giving rise to the electroosmotic flow (EOF). The force propelling the liquid originates at the charged surface and this causes the flow to move in a "plug"-like fashion in contrast to the parabolic profile observed when pressure is used to pump liquid (**Figure 2**). It is this difference in flow profile that is one of the main reasons for the high efficiencies that can be obtained by electrophoresis.

One of the most important implications of having EOF is that it will physically move the liquid through the capillary and the electrophoretic separation is superimposed on top of this flow. This EOF or bulk flow acts as a pumping mechanism to propel all molecules (cationic, neutral, and anionic) toward the detector with separation ultimately being determined by differences in electrophoretic migration of the individual

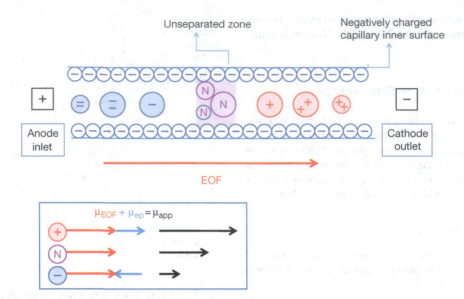

Figure 3   Migration of solutes in capillary electrophoresis.

analyte. The net apparent mobility (μ_{app}) is the vector sum of the electroosmotic mobility (μ_{EOF}) and μ_{ep}:

$$\mu_{app} = \mu_{ep} + \mu_{EOF} \quad [2]$$

As shown in **Figure 3**, in a fused silica capillary with the EOF directed toward the cathode, cations will reach the detector fastest in the order of decreasing μ_{ep} as their μ_{ep} is in the same direction as the μ_{EOF} is acting in the same direction. Next will be neutral molecules, which will migrate as a single unresolved peak with the EOF. After the EOF, the anions will emerge in the order of increasing μ_{ep}, as their mobility is in the opposite direction to the EOF. It is important to note that anions with a μ_{ep} greater than μ_{EOF} will never reach the detector and will migrate out through the inlet of the capillary.

The velocity of an ion (v_i) can be given by the following equation:

$$v_i = \mu_{app}E = (\mu_{ep} + \mu_{eo})E \quad [3]$$

where E is the applied electric field (V m^{-1}) and is simply a function of the applied voltage (in V) and the total capillary length (L_{tot}, in m):

$$E = \frac{V}{L_{tot}} \quad [4]$$

Calculation of μ_{app} can be achieved directly from the electropherogram from the following equation:

$$\mu_{app} = \frac{L_d L_t}{tV} \quad [5]$$

where L_d is the length of the capillary to the detector (in m) and t is the migration time of the analyte (in s).

Similar to the equation for the μ_{ep}, the μ_{EOF} is given by the following equation:

$$\mu_{EOF} = \frac{\varepsilon \zeta}{\eta} \quad [6]$$

where ε is the dielectric constant of the medium, ζ is the zeta potential, and η is the solution viscosity. It follows from this equation that magnitude and direction of the EOF will be proportional to the zeta potential. The zeta potential is largely dependent on the electrostatic nature of the surface, and this is an important factor to consider when performing electrophoretic separations in microchips, which are now more commonly made in plastic via mass replication techniques. What is less obvious from eqn [4] is that it can also be affected by a number of factors such as pH, ionic strength, temperature, the electric field, and the presence of some additives. For example, with increased ionic strength there is more double layer compression and hence a decreased zeta potential, and a reduced EOF is obtained. Using eqn [3] and using the migration time of a neutral marker, such as acetone, thiourea, and pure water, it is possible to calculate μ_{EOF}. It is then simple to calculate the value of μ_{ep} for each ion using eqn [2]. Values of μ_{ep} are now frequently tabulated, with the most easily accessible values obtained from the electronic database of the simulation software PeakMaster or Simul.

Electroosmotic flow Control

While the EOF can be beneficial for performing some separations, good control of the EOF is required to achieve the best results. The quickest and most efficient separations are usually obtained in a co-EOF mode in which the EOF is in the direction of ion mobility of interest, while the best resolution is obtained in a counter-EOF mode in which the EOF is in the opposite direction to the mobility of the ions. In addition, electrophoretic separation modes such as IEF and capillary sieving electrophoresis (CSE) often require reduction of EOF.

Controlling the magnitude of the EOF in a fused silica capillary can be achieved by simply varying the pH. At low pH, the SiOH are protonated and there is very little EOF. At a pH > 8, these same groups are completely ionized giving rise to a strong EOF toward the cathode. More stable and repeatable EOF is most easily achieved through capillary wall modifications, either permanent or dynamic. Permanent wall modification through covalent attachment is achieved through silylation followed by deactivation with a suitable functional group, polyacrylamide, polyethylene glycol, or polysaccharides, and a number of these are commercially available. An even simpler approach relies on dynamic modification of the surface by addition of an appropriate modifier to the background electrolyte (BGE). The modifier interacts with the capillary wall and in this way affects the EOF. Addition of anionic (or cationic) surfactants may increase (or decrease) the EOF. In addition, neutral hydrophilic polymers that adsorb to the capillary wall through hydrophobic interactions will decrease EOF by shielding surface charge and increasing viscosity. The downside of using a dynamic coating is that there is potential interaction with the analytes, which may be undesirable in some instances. To overcome this, there has been considerable research over the past decade on the formation of semipermanent capillary coatings created through the use of double-tailed surfactants or through the use of multiple layers of alternating charged polyelectrolytes. These are attractive because the capillary may need to be recoated between separations, or only once a day, and they ensure that the same exposed surface is obtained irrespective of the material allowing the same surface chemistry to be used in plastic and glass microchips and improving intercapillary and interchip repeatability.

Background Electrolytes

The composition of the electrolytes inside the capillary is typically what defines the mode of separation that occurs and the order in which peaks move past the detector. The solution chemistry requirements for the mode of separation are discussed in more detail below, but within each separation mode, variation of the composition will change the selectivity. Taking zone electrophoresis, for example, the exact composition of the electrolyte will influence the sensitivity, resolution, and separation time, as depicted in **Figure 4**. For example, changing the pH of the electrolyte will change the net charge of weak acids

and bases, which will impact upon the μ_{ep} leading to a change in resolution and separation time. pH may also change the surface charge and zeta potential of the capillary thus changing the EOF, which will also impact upon the same criteria. Changing the pH of the electrolyte will also change the ionic strength, which will impact on both μ_{ep} and EOF, thus also influencing the separation. Similarly, adding an organic solvent such as methanol will change the solvation of the ions and the viscosity of the electrolyte, which will again influence mobility and EOF.

The complexity of electrophoresis can often be daunting to the electrophoresis newcomer, but there are a number of general principles and conditions that can be used to rapidly identify the feasibility of a specific separation, which can then be further refined as necessary. Phosphate buffers at pH 2 and 7, and borate at pH 9, at a concentration of 10–50 mM are suitable electrolytes to start with as they provide a reasonable ionic strength and have excellent transmission properties for UV–vis detection. For mass spectrometric (MS) detection, 1 M formic acid and acetic acid provide low pH options, while at high pH, 10–100 mM ammonium acetate/formate is the most popular option, while conductivity detection typically uses 20–50 mM HIS/MES buffer. It can also be simpler when starting to perform separations in a co-EOF manner or in a suppressed EOF environment. Unmodified fused silica capillaries are good for cations and for anions at low pH where the EOF is suppressed. If a high pH is required for anion separations, then reversing the EOF is easily done by incorporating a cationic surfactant (such as CTAB) into the electrolyte or by coating the capillary as discussed above. If the analytes are neutral, then a suitable additive such as sodium dodecyl sulfate must be added to perform an electrokinetic chromatography separation.

Once conditions for a basic separation have been established, there are then a myriad of electrolyte additives that can be used to enhance the separation in one way or another. This may be simply changing the type of salts used in the electrolyte (through, for example, differences in ion-association interaction), changing the solvent (organic solvents and mixed solvents can provide uniquely different selectivity), and the addition of additives to alter charge or size through secondary equilibria, and various combinations of these. It is this ability to vary the position of a peak within a separation and to adjust the conditions to manipulate the system to achieve the desired outcome that is one of the reasons that electrophoresis is such a powerful separation technique. The other is the high efficiency.

Maximizing Efficiency

It is misleading to discuss theoretical plates in electrophoresis; nevertheless, it is a convenient concept to describe analyte peak shape and for comparison with other separation techniques. Efficiency is described by the number of theoretical plates and

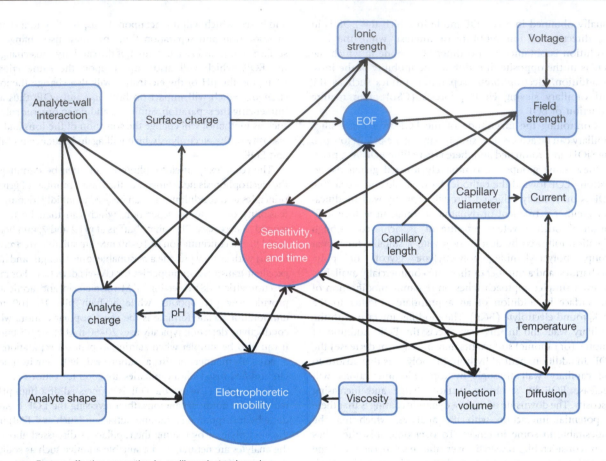

Figure 4 Factors affecting separation in capillary electrophoresis.

is related to the height equivalent to the theoretical plates (H_{th}) by the following equation:

$$N = \frac{L_d}{H_{th}} \tag{7}$$

where L_d is the effective length of the capillary. The theoretical plate number can be determined directly from an electropherogram by the following equation:

$$N = 5.54 \left(\frac{t}{w_{1/2}}\right)^2 = \mu_{app} \times \frac{V}{2D_m} \tag{8}$$

where t is the migration time, $w_{1/2}$ is temporal peak width at half-height, and D_m is the diffusion coefficient of the analyte.

CE has much higher efficiencies than can be achieved by HPLC, with typical plate numbers from 100, 000 to 500, 000 plates/m. This is primarily because CE does not have many of the sources of inefficiency that HPLC does and because of the flat plug-like profile of the EOF. Ideally in CE the zone dispersion is only due to longitudinal diffusion. In reality,

inherent in all electrophoretic separations is electromigration dispersion. This arises when there is a difference in μ_{ep} of the analyte and the electrolyte coion (**Figure 5**). If the analyte ion has a higher μ_{ep} than that of the electrolyte coion then the peak will be fronting, if μ_{ep} is equal then the peak will be symmetrical, and if the analyte has a lower μ_{ep} then the peak will be tailed. Electromigration dispersion can be decreased by matching the mobilities of the buffer constituent to the sample mobility or by maintaining a running buffer concentration approximately two orders of magnitude higher than that of the sample.

During any electrophoretic separation, heat will be generated. The temperature increase depends on the power and is determined by the capillary dimensions, conductivity of the buffer, and the applied voltage. If the heat is not dissipated efficiently, temperature gradients can develop across the capillary with ions in the center of the capillary having a higher μ_{ep} than those at the capillary wall and band broadening will be observed. This can be a significant issue when performing separations in plastic microchips that have a lower thermal

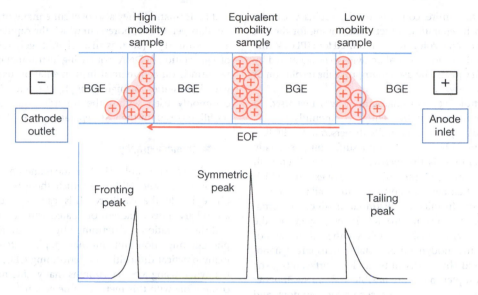

Figure 5   Peak distortions due to differences in mobilities between sample and background electrolyte .

conductivity than glass and cannot dissipate the heat as effectively. There are a number of methods that indicate excessive heat generation and possible temperature gradients. These phenomena may be indicated if efficiency is reduced as the voltage is increased. In addition, a disproportionate increase in current with voltage, Ohm's law, indicates temperature gradients. Measures to control Joule heating may include reducing the capillary inner diameter, active temperature control, or the use of low-mobility buffers that contain large, minimally charged ions, such as Tris, borate, and histidine.

One other major source of band broadening in CE is that of wall interaction. Depending on the extent of interaction, peak tailing and even total adsorption of the solute can occur. The primary causes of adsorption to the fused silica walls are electrostatic interactions between charged analytes and the charged wall and hydrophobic interactions. Significant adsorptive effects have been observed especially for large peptides and proteins, and it is imperative to minimize these to obtain highly efficient separations. The use of zwitterionic buffer systems and pH and ionic strength extremes can be useful for overcoming these issues, but the most prominent approach is to modify the capillary wall to limit solute adsorption.

Modes of Separation in Electrophoresis

One of the highly attractive features of electrophoresis is the ability to perform a number of different types of separations through simple variation of the capillary and electrolyte chemistry. These can be classified into several separation modes, each possessing its characteristic separation mechanism. These can be implemented in both capillaries (abbreviated with a c at the front) and microchips (abbreviated with an m at the front) with the same level of ease.

Zone Electrophoresis

Zone electrophoresis (ZE) is the most widely used mode. It is fundamentally the simplest form of CE, mainly because the capillary is only filled with buffer. Separation occurs because solutes migrate in discrete zones and at different velocities and are separated solely based on differences in μ_{ep}. Both anionic and cationic solutes can be separated simultaneously by ZE due to EOF (**Figure 3**). However, some analytes cannot be separated by this classical version of electrophoresis because they are neutral or they may not differ significantly in μ_{ep}.

Electrophoretic Chromatography

To allow the separation of neutral compounds, an additive is added to the electrolyte, which forms a dispersed phase moving at a different velocity with which the analytes interact. To achieve separation, either the analytes or this secondary phase should be charged. One of the main attractions of EKC is the simplicity with which the system can be varied. The nature of the additive governs the type of interaction while the concentration controls the capacity, thereby providing considerable scope for optimization. This has several advantages over chromatography, notably that neutral species migrate between the EOF and the additive and thus there is no infinite migration time, and that the entire contents of the capillary can be removed after each separation rather than waiting for the last peak to emerge from the column as is required for HPLC. While initially developed to allow neutral analytes to be separated by electrophoresis, it can also be used to improve the resolution of charged analytes.

Micellar electrokinetic chromatography was first used to demonstrate the separation of neutral compounds by CE, where the secondary phase is a micelle dispersed in the BGE. A potential problem with the use of ionic surfactants, especially at high concentrations, is the increase in current. Even with narrow bore capillaries (25–50 μm), the use of extremely high electric fields is often avoided and efficient capillary thermostating is necessary. In microemulsion electrokinetic chromatography, a microemulsion droplet is employed as the dispersed phase. Microemulsion droplets, either oil-in-water or water-in-oil, are thermodynamically stable transparent nanodroplets stabilized by surfactants and cosurfactants. The microemulsion droplets are more flexible and can swell better than micelles, providing a wider separation window and a higher resolution. However, preparation of the microemulsion can be complicated and time-consuming and not all microemulsions have suitable stability.

Chiral electrokinetic chromatography allows the separation of enantiomers by using a chiral selector as an additive. Charged and neutral cyclodextrins, macrocyclic antibiotics, crown ethers, chiral metal complexes, and chiral surfactants have all been used to form dynamic diastereomeric complexes that can be separated. This is a particularly powerful application of CE, as the type and concentration of chiral selector can be easily changed to optimize the separation of a specific enantiomeric pair at a much lower cost than can be achieved by HPLC and GC. The ability to separate enantiomers is of particular importance in some forensic applications, where one enantiomer is legally allowed while the other is not. Examples include the isomers of 3-methoxy-*N*-methylmorphinan, propoxyphene, norpseudoephedrine, and cocaine, as well as compounds in which there is a more significant physicoactive response from one isomer over the other, for example, with amphetamines. These types of applications (and others) are discussed in more detail elsewhere in the book.

Sieving Electrophoresis

Sieving electrophoresis involves the addition of a sieving medium to the BGE. The separation is based on differences in size and shape of the charged analytes and is particularly useful for the separation of large biological molecules such as proteins and DNA. Most commonly used today are solutions of water-soluble polymers (such as linear polyacrylamide or LPA) that form an entangled network through which the analytes migrate. These have a low viscosity and can be replaced between each separation thus providing improved repeatability

and performance. They also overcame many of the issues with capillary gel electrophoresis in which the capillary is filled with a cross-linked gel (such as an acrylamide gel). CSE was the basis of a generation of DNA sequencing instrumentation and can be performed on commercial instrumentation featuring 96 individual capillaries for high-throughput sequencing and is most commonly used within the forensic community for DNA profiling based on the CSE separation of PCR-amplified STRs.

Electrochromatography

Electrochromatography (EC), as the name implies, is a combination of CE and HPLC in which there is a heterogeneous phase inside the capillary. This can be achieved through a capillary, filled, packed, or coated with a stationary phase, and the migration is determined by a combination of electrophoretic migration and chromatographic retention. There are many practical difficulties in performing CEC, but it is attractive when using MS detection as many EKC methods are not compatible with this method of detection.

Isoelectric Focusing

IEF is an electrophoretic technique for the separation of amphoteric analytes according to their isoelectric point (pI) by the application of an electric field along a pH gradient formed in a capillary. In contrast to most modes of electrophoresis, the whole capillary is filled with a mixture of sample and ampholyte mixture, and each analyte is focused at its pI. It is a high-resolution technique and can be used to separate proteins that differ by 0.005 pI units and less. The protein zones remain narrow because a protein which enters a zone of different pH will become charged and migrate back.

Isotachophoresis

Isotachophoresis (ITP) involves the injection of the sample between a leading electrolyte and terminating electrolyte. When the voltage is applied, the analytes that have a μ_{ep} bracketed by the leader and terminator form zones in order of decreasing mobility, with the length of the zone proportional to the concentration of that analyte. ITP is particularly powerful for trace analysis, as low abundant components have their concentration adjusted up to the steady-state ITP plateau concentration defined by the composition of the leading electrolyte.

Instrumentation and Sample Handling

All the modes of electrophoresis mentioned above can be performed in essentially the same instrumentation in capillaries and microchips, but there are some differences in hardware between the two platforms. A schematic for CE is shown in **Figure 6**. The closed circuit is composed of a high-voltage power supply

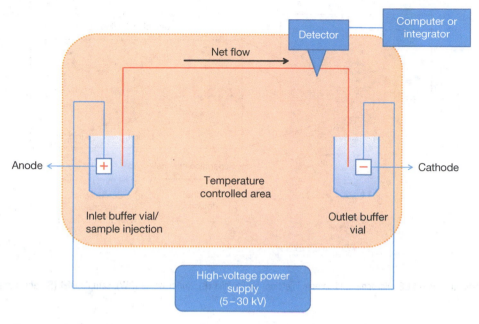

Figure 6 Basic capillary electrophoresis instrumentation.

(5–30 kV), two electrodes, two buffer reservoirs, and the separation capillary (typically 25–75 μm i.d.). A sample is introduced into the capillary from one end by pressure, vacuum, or by voltage. A detector is used to monitor the separated analytes through a window made on the capillary wall.

The capillary column is a key element of the CE separation. Fused silica is by far the most frequently used material, although columns made of Teflon and other plastic materials can also be used. The widespread use of fused silica is due to its intrinsic properties, which include good optical transparency making absorbance detection easily feasible over a wide range of UV and visible wavelengths. Fused silica is also easy to manufacture into capillaries with diameters of a few micrometers.

The sample can be introduced into the capillary in two common ways in CE. In hydrodynamic injection, a pressure difference between the inlet and outlet is applied to move the sample into the capillary. The injection volume (v_{inj}) can be calculated by the following equation:

$$v_{inj} = \frac{\Delta p \pi r_d^4 t_{inj}}{8 \eta L_{tot}}$$ [9]

where Δp is the pressure difference, r_d is the capillary inner diameter, t_{inj} is the injection time, and η is the viscosity of the buffer. With hydrodynamic injection, the quantity of the sample loaded is nearly independent of the sample matrix.

In electrokinetic injection, a voltage is applied across the capillary and solutes enter the capillary due to μ_{ep} and μ_{EOF}.

The injection quantity (Q) of a component can be given by the following equation:

$$Q = \frac{(\mu_{ep} + \mu_{eo}) \pi r_d^2 V t_{inj} C}{L_{tot}}$$ [10]

where c is the concentration of the component in the sample solution. Variations in conductivity, which can be due to matrix effects such as a large quantity of an undetected ion such as sodium or chloride, result in differences in voltage drop across the sample and hence the quantity loaded. Owing to these phenomena, electrokinetic injection is generally not as reproducible as its hydrodynamic counterpart, but this can be easily corrected with the use of an internal standard.

Instrumentation for microelectrophoresis is slightly different (**Figure 7**). The power supply is typically smaller, from 3 to 10 kV; there are four reservoirs on the microchip, three of which house buffer with the sample in the other. Injection is performed at the intersection of two microchannels interconnected in a "cross" and so far, fluorescence detection is the most common form of detection. The chip material has significant implications on the separation and can be either glass or plastic, with the latter preferred due to the ability to produce them quickly and cheaply in commercially viable quantities.

Sample Concentration

One of the major limitations of electrophoresis is its high limits of detection. This arises from the small dimensions of

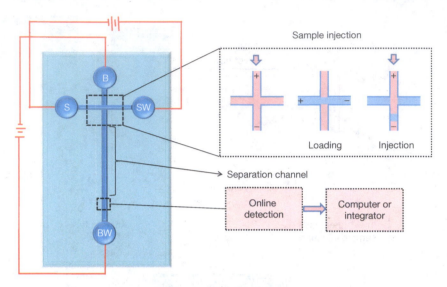

Figure 7   Schematic diagram of CE microchip and sample injection; buffer inlet (B), buffer waste (BW), sample inlet (S), and sample waste (SW).

the capillary and microchip, which limit both the volume of the sample that can be injected and the optical path length when spectrophotometric detection is used. In general, the injected sample plug is usually 1% of the total separation length to maintain high efficiency. This translates to injection volumes of approximately 0.5–50 nl. It is possible to inject more than this, but the analytes must be concentrated or stacked to preserve separation efficiency and avoid over-loading. A number of online approaches have been developed to address this issue and are based on either chromatography through integration with solid-phase and liquid-phase extraction or electrophoresis through changes in analyte velocity. Electrophoretic methods are far simpler to implement than those based on chromatography, and a number of powerful methods have been developed, which are collectively known as stacking. Field-amplified sample stacking is the simplest method for online preconcentration as it is induced by injecting the sample dissolved in a sample that has conductivity at least ten times lower than that of the BGE. This causes a higher electric field strength to fall over the sample and the ions migrating through a low-conductivity solution into a high-conductivity BGE to slow down at the boundary of the two solutions and "stack" into a narrow zone. There are a large number of variants based on large volumes and exploitation of ITP and IEF phenomena. These approaches can all improve detection limits by 100–1000. An alternative approach developed for EKC, called sweeping, relies on the accumulation of the analytes by the additive as it moves through the sample. This has been shown to be suit-able for both charged and neutral solutes and can improve detection limits by 100–1000. When these strategies are

employed with electrokinetic injection, then it is possible to improve detection limits by 1, 000, 000-fold.

Detection Methods

There are several detection methods available with the most common compared in **Table 2**. These can be either performed on-capillary or end-capillary. On-capillary (and on-chip) detection involves detection of the analytes as they migrate through the capillary/microchannel, and is typically performed with either spectrophotometry or contactless conductivity detection. End-capillary detection is performed on the effluent of the capillary, which is focused or collected into the detector and is required for some forms of detection, such as mass spectrometry. On-capillary detection such as this reduces peak distortion and loss of resolution that can be observed in end-capillary methods.

Spectrophotometric methods

Spectrophotometric detection is achieved by monitoring the change in light induced by the target analytes as they migrate through a detector. When performed on-capillary, however, sensitivity is limited by the small capillary internal diameter, which defines the path length. UV–vis absorption is the most widely used detection method in capillaries as it is cheap and has wide applicability and most commercial instruments now come equipped with diode array detectors allowing monitoring at multiple wavelengths and the collection of full spectra. It is not widespread in microchips primarily due to the significant UV absorbance of many microchip materials and the difficulty in obtaining long path lengths.

Table 2 Common detection methods for capillary and microchip electrophoresis

Method	Mass detection limit (mol)	Concentration detection limit $(M)^a$	Advantages/disadvantages
UV–vis absorption	10^{-13} to 10^{-15}	10^{-5} to 10^{-8}	• Universal • Diode array offers spectral information • Not common in microchips
Laser-induced fluorescence	10^{-18} to 10^{-20}	10^{-14} to 10^{-16}	• Extremely sensitive • Usually requires sample derivatization • Expensive
Amperometry	10^{-18} to 10^{-19}	10^{-10} to 10^{-11}	• Sensitive • Selective but useful only for electroactive analyses • Requires special electronics and integrated detection electrodes
Conductivity	10^{-15} to 10^{-16}	10^{-7} to 10^{-8}	• Universal • Simple when implemented in contactless mode
Mass spectrometry	10^{-16} to 10^{-17}	10^{-8}–10^{-9}	• Sensitive and offers structural information • Interface to MS nontrivial
Indirect UV, fluorescence, amperometry	10–100 times less than direct method	–	• Universal • Lower sensitivity than direct methods

Source: Ewing, A.G., Wallingford, R.A., Olefirowicz, T.M., 1989. Capillary electrophoresis. Analytical Chemistry 61, 292A–303A.

The problem of low sensitivity can be partially solved through the use of laser-induced fluorescence. Detection limits as low as 10^{-14} to 10^{-18} mol have been reported; however, the major drawback is that most analytes do not fluoresce well and must be derivatized with fluorescent reagents first to improve sensitivity. This has been most widely implemented in microchips.

Mass spectrophotometric detection

MS detection is the most powerful detection technique and is becoming increasingly important in forensics for the absolute identification of components and its ability to differentiate overlapping peaks with distinct mass-to-charge ratio. It can be interfaced off-line with matrix-assisted laser desorption/ionization; however, it is far more common to interface online with electrospray ionization. Interfacing CE to MS is much more difficult than LC due to the smaller volume of effluent and also the need to maintain a stable electric circuit for electrophoresis, and highly sensitive and robust interfaces are required before this detection technique will become widespread. Microchips can be interfaced directly to the MS, but there are even more significant issues than with capillaries.

Electrochemical detection

Electrochemical detection (ECD) can be carried out in either on-capillary or end-capillary. It can be classified into amperometry, conductimetry, and potentiometry according to operation principles. Amperometry is the most sensitive, but it is only responsive to electroactive analytes. For conductivity detection, a major consideration is selection of the appropriate BGE to maintain conductivity differences between the BGE and the analytes. At the same time, mobility differences between the analyte ions and coions in the BGE should be minimal to obtain symmetric peaks. The development of noncontact contactless conductivity detection has seen recent growth in this form of detection. It is interesting to note that due to the ability to easily integrate electrodes in microchips, ECD is actually easier to implement in microchips than in capillaries.

Future Directions

Electrophoresis in the capillary format is nearly 30 years old, whereas in microchips it is nearly 20 years old. However, there are still a number of issues that have yet to be resolved. There is no doubt that there will be a continued drive toward the microchip platform, particularly through the integration of sampling handling to make a so-called "micro-Total Analysis System". Many of these have already begun to appear with the biggest market being that in the field of DNA analysis, and there are already numerous microchip systems describing the integration of extraction, amplification, and separation in a single microchip. But these devices are highly complex and far from routine use, and considerable development needs to occur before these will become widespread. It is also necessary to note that many of the issues that have limited the applicability of CE, such as sensitivity and repeatability, are even more problematic in microchips, and these have yet to be resolved. Finally, interfacing both capillaries and microchips with MS does need to have a robust, sensitive, and reliable solution, and while there has been significant development in this area, there is still as yet no commercially reliable interface that can match the sensitivity and performance achieved with liquid chromatography–mass spectrometry.

See also: **Biology/DNA:** Short Tandem Repeats; **Biology/DNA/ Methods/Analytical Techniques:** Capillary Electrophoresis in Forensic Genetics; **Methods:** Capillary Electrophoresis in Forensic Biology; Capillary Electrophoresis in Forensic Chemistry.

Further Reading

Breadmore, M.C., 2007. Recent advances in enhancing the sensitivity of electro-phoresis and electrochromatography in capillaries and microchips. Electrophoresis 28 (1–2), 254–281.

Consden, R., Stanier, W.M., 1952. Ionophoresis of sugars on paper and some applications to the analysis of protein polysaccharide complexes. Nature 169, 783–785.

Cruces-Blanco, C., Garciá-Campaña, A.M., 2011. Capillary electrophoresis for the analysis of drugs of abuse in biological specimens of forensic interest. Trends in Analytical Chemistry. http://dx.doi.org/10.1016/j.trac.2011.06.019.

Everaerts, F.M., ThPEM, V., 1970. Isotachophoresis. Electrophoretic analysis in capillaries. Journal of Chromatography 53 (2), 315–328.

Ewing, A.G., Wallingford, R.A., Olefirowicz, T.M., 1989. Capillary electrophoresis. Analytical Chemistry 61, 292A–303A.

Harrison, D.J., Manz, A., Fan, Z., Lüdi, H., Widmer, H.M., 1992. Capillary electro-phoresis and sample injection systems integrated on a planar glass chip. Analytical Chemistry 64 (17), 1926–1932.

Hjertén, S., M-d, Z., 1985. Adaptation of the equipment for high-performance elec-trophoresis to isoelectric focusing. Journal of Chromatography 346, 265–270.

Issaq, H.J., 2002. Thirty-five years of capillary electrophoresis: advances and perspectives. Journal of Liquid Chromatography and Related Technologies 25 (8), 1153–1170.

Jorgenson, J.W., Lukacs, K.D., 1981. Zone electrophoresis in open-tubular glass capillaries. Analytical Chemistry 53 (8), 1298–1302.

Klampfl, C.W., 2009. CE with MS detection: a rapidly developing hyphenated tech-nique. Electrophoresis 30 (Suppl. 1), S83–S91.

Landers, J.P. (Ed.), 2008. Handbook of Capillary and Microchip Electrophoresis and Associated Microtechniques. CRC Press, Boca Raton, FL.

Lucy, C.A., MacDonald, A.M., Gulcev, M.D., 2008. Non-covalent capillary coatings for protein separations in capillary electrophoresis. Journal of Chromatography A 1184 (1–2), 81–105.

Mikkers, F.E.P., Everaets, F.M., Verheggen, T.P.E.M., 1979. High performance zone electrophoresis. Journal of Chromatography 169, 11–20.

Righetti, P.G., 2005. Review. Electrophoresis: the march of pennies, the march of dimes. Journal of Chromatography A 1079, 24–40.

Smithies, O., 1955. Zone electrophoresis in starch gels: group variations in the serum proteins of normal human adults. The Biochemical Journal 61 (4), 629–641.

Svensson, H., 1961. Isoelectric fractionation, analysis, and characterization of ampholytes in natural pH gradients I. The differential equation of solute concen-trations at a steady state and its solution for simple cases. Acta Chemica Scan-danavia 15, 325–341.

Terabe, S., Otsuka, K., Ichikawa, K., Tsuchiya, A., Ando, T., 1984. Electrokinetic separations with micellar solutions and open-tubular capillaries. Analytical Chem-istry 56 (1), 111–113.

Tiselius, A., 1937. A new apparatus for electrophoretic analysis of colloidal mixtures. Transactions of the Faraday Society 33, 524–531.

Zaugg, S., Thormann, W., 2000. Enantioselective determination of drugs in body fluids by capillary electrophoresis. Journal of Chromatography A 875, 27–41.

Relevant Websites

http://www.chromedia.org/—Chomedia.
http://web.natur.cuni.cz/gas/—Peakmaster and Simul: Electrophoresis Simulation Software.

Capillary Electrophoresis in Forensic Chemistry

F Tagliaro and JP Pascali, University of Verona, Verona, Italy
SW Lewis, Curtin University, Perth, WA, Australia

Abbreviations

BGE	Background electrolyte	GC	Gas chromatography
CDT	Carbohydrate-deficient transferrin	GHB	Gamma-hydroxybutyric acid
CE	Capillary electrophoresis	HPLC	High-performance liquid chromatography
CE–ESI–MS	Capillary electrophoresis–electrospray ionization–mass spectrometry		
		MEKC	Micellar electrokinetic chromatography
CZE	Capillary zone electrophoresis		

Introduction

The separation and quantification of chemical substances in a wide variety of complex matrices is a significant analytical challenge for the forensic chemist. While there is no doubt that capillary electrophoresis (CE) has had its largest impact in the area of forensic biology, specifically in the field of DNA analysis, it has also found application in forensic chemical analysis in general. Since the potential of CE for forensic analysis was first demonstrated in the early 1990s, it has been applied to a wide range of analytes of forensic interest including illicit drugs, toxicology samples, explosives residues, and pen ink.

CE is attractive for forensic applications because of its exceptional separating power (up to millions of theoretical plates), rapid analysis times, and high mass sensitivity (from femtomoles—10^{-15} moles—down to yoctomoles—10^{-21} moles). It is an economical technique in terms of reagents and consumables, requiring only minimal amounts of sample. Additionally, owing to the variety of separation modes possible (electrophoretic, electrokinetic, chromatography-like, etc.) and the detection systems available (UV–visible absorbance, luminescence, and mass spectrometry (MS) are all available commercially), it is applicable in the determination of a wide variety of chemical substances including inorganic ions, small organic molecules, chiral compounds, macromolecules, and intact viruses and cells. The Achilles' heel of CE in the past has been its relatively poor detection limits when compared with liquid chromatography (LC) and gas chromatography (GC). However, improved detection optics and electronics for the most commonly encountered detector in CE, namely UV–visible absorbance, and the introduction of new detection techniques such as contactless conductivity detection have led to improved detection limits that are compatible with many forensic applications. Significant improvements in terms of sensitivity and specificity have been achieved in recent years by the hyphenation of CE with MS. CE–MS has become useful in clinical and forensic toxicology, doping control, and workplace drug testing, gaining attractiveness in respect to GC–MS and LC–MS.

The purpose of this article is to provide an overview of the application of CE to forensic analysis, illustrated with recent examples. For more comprehensive treatments of specific areas, the reader is directed to the textbooks, monographs, and review articles listed in Further Reading section.

Applications

Illicit Drug Analysis

CE has been used widely for the analysis of drugs and related compounds in pharmaceutical research and development since its introduction as a commercial analytical technique in the late 1980s. The potential of CE for forensic analytical problems was first demonstrated in the early 1990s with its application to the separation of illicit drugs in synthetic mixtures. Since that time, the determination of illicit drug seizures and clandestine lab materials has become a major application area for this group of techniques. Some examples of the application of CE techniques to such samples are presented on **Table 1**.

In many instances, the choice of CE as an alternative technique to the more traditional GC and high-performance liquid chromatography (HPLC) methods is justified by the minimal amount of sample required and by the shorter and easier sample pretreatment. CE often allows for very short separation

Table 1   Applications of capillary electrophoresis to illicit drugs in seizures and toxicology samples

Analytes	Matrix	Method
Coca alkaloids and sugars	Illicit cocaine	Micellar electrokinetic chromatography (MEKC) with indirect UV detection
D-methamphetamine, L-methamphetamine, D-3,4-methylenedioxymetham-phetamine (MDMA), L-MDMA, D-ketamine, L-ketamine, and heroin	Surfaces of banknotes, plastic bags, and silver paper	Liquid-phase microextraction followed by capillary zone electrophoresis (CZE) using beta-cyclodextrin as a chiral selector, detection by UV absorbance
Heroin, morphine, acetylcodeine, caffeine, paracetamol	Heroin seizures	MEKC with short-end injection, detection by UV absorbance
Glucose, sucrose, lactose, mannitol	Heroin seizures	CZE with borate complexation and short-end injection, detection by UV absorbance
Codeine, ketamine, methamphetamine, morphine, alprazolam, and oxazepam	Urine	MEKC with UV absorbance detection
Methamphetamine, amphetamine, dimethylamphetamine, and *p*-hydroxymethamphetamine	Urine from subjects using methamphetamine and dimethylamphetamine	CZE using cyclodextrins for separation of enantiomers with MS detection
Lysergic acid diethylamide	Blood	CZE with laser-induced fluorescence detection
MDMA	Hair	CZE with UV absorbance detection

times, particularly when using techniques such as short-end injection are being used (see **Figure 1**). These features are beneficial to forensic analysis, particularly to screening for illicit drugs in clandestine preparations. In addition, CE lends itself to the difficult task of separations of enantiomers by the addition of a chiral selector to the background electrolyte (BGE). In addition to determining active illicit drugs, CE is also useful in separating cutting agents and other compounds that might be present, thus making it highly suitable for profiling type analyses.

Toxicology

CE has been successfully applied to a wide range of drugs, both therapeutic and illicit, and their metabolites in a wide range of biological matrices including urine, blood, and serum for forensic toxicological purposes.

CE has been applied to therapeutical drug monitoring, which has both clinical and forensic implications. Lithium salts are one of the most popular therapeutic approaches to the treatment of bipolar disorders, notwithstanding the introduction of modern, less toxic drugs. Because of its narrow therapeutic range, lithium serum concentration must be strictly monitored during the treatment to avoid life-threatening neurotoxicity. Capillary zone electrophoresis (CZE) was successfully applied to the routine determination of lithium in serum samples after a simple sample pretreatment of dilution with water and indirect detection using UV absorbance.

Small organic molecules, such as the central nervous system depressant and hypnotic gamma-hydroxybutyric acid (GHB), feature heavily as analytes in toxicological samples. GHB has

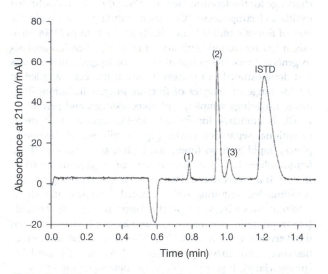

Figure 1   Electropherogram showing the separation of a seized heroin sample by using micellar electrokinetic chromatography with short-end injection (1) morphine, (2) heroin, (3) acetylcodeine, ISTD = internal standard (*N, N*-dimethyl-5-methoxytryptamine). UV absorbance at 210 nm, uncoated fused silica capillary 50 cm × 50 μm I.D. ×360 μm O.D., effective separation length 8 cm, background electrolyte: 15 mM sodium borate, 25 mM sodium dodecylsulfate, 15% (v/v) acetonitrile, pH 9.5, 25°C, −25 kV, hydrodynamic injection: 2 s at −50 mbar. Reprinted from Anastos, N., Lewis, S.W., Barnett, N.W., Pearson, J.R., Kirkbride, K.P., 2005. The rapid analysis of heroin drug seizures using micellar electrokinetic chromatography with short-end injection. Journal of Forensic Sciences 50, 37–42, with permission.

been increasingly used as a recreational drug (owing to its euphoric effects and ability to reduce inhibitions) and as a rape facilitation drug. GHB has also been used as a doping agent for enhancing muscle growth. Analogues of GHB, namely gamma-butyrolactone and 1,4-butanediol, share its biological activity and are rapidly converted in vivo into GHB. CZE, in combination with UV detection, capillary electrophoresis–electrospray ionization–mass spectrometry (CE–ESI–MS), or conductivity detection, has been shown to be a rapid and accurate approach to the determination of GHB and its metabolites in urine and blood serum. Additional examples of illicit drugs determined in toxicological samples by CE are provided in **Table 1** with an example of analysis of hair for 3,4-methylenedioxymetham-phetamine (MDMA) shown in **Figure 2**.

CE can also be used for the determination of large biopolymers. It has been applied in the field of antidoping analysis to identify macromolecules. Recombinant human erythropoietin (rHuEPO) and the novel erythropoiesis-stimulating protein were analyzed by CE–ESI–MS using an ion trap mass spectrometry instrument as the analyzer. Additionally, affinity probe CE/laser-induced fluorescence (LIF) was developed for the detection of rHuEPO-alpha using a specific single-stranded DNA as aptamer probe. After optimization, the method was successfully applied for the quantification of rHuEPO-alpha in buffer, artificial urine, and human serum.

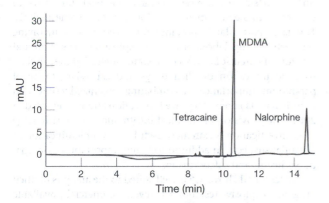

Figure 2 Electropherogram of an extract from a sample of hair from a user of "ecstasy" containing 3,4-methylenedioxymetham-phetamine (MDMA) at a concentration of 4.0 ng mg^{-1}. Tetracaine and nalorphine were added as internal standards. Injection was by electromigration under field-amplified sample stacking conditions. Separation was by capillary zone electrophoresis using 100 mM phosphate pH 2.5 as the running buffer. Detection was by UV absorbance at 200 nm. Reprinted from Tagliaro, F., Manetto, G., Crivellente, F., Scarcerlla, D., Marigo, M., 1998. Hair analysis for abused drugs by capillary zone electrophoresis with field-amplified sample stacking. Forensic Science International 92, 20–211, with permission.

Toxins and venoms are products of living organisms, which in most cases have complex and unstable polypeptide structures. For these reasons, they are, in general, not suitable for GC analysis and are often "difficult" to analyze with HPLC. CE provides an alternative approach for analyses of these challenging analytes. For example, the CE–ESI–MS method, using an ion-trap mass spectrometer, has been used for the identification of the biologically active oligopeptides of Amanita fungi, namely, alpha-, beta-, gamma-amanitin, phalloidin, and phallacidin. These complex analytes were also determined in real samples using a simple CZE separation with UV absorbance detection. Alpha- and beta-amanitin were determined in urine in less than 7 min with a simple sample treatment of dilution in BGE. Urine samples from suspected cases of intoxication with amanitins were analyzed, with beta-amanitin being identified in two samples.

Forensic Medicine

Recently, a number of protein molecules have become attractive as biological markers of chronic alcohol abuse. In particular, carbohydrate-deficient transferrin (CDT) has gained universal acceptance in this context, as reported in recent research papers and reviews. CDT is the collective name of a group of minor glycoforms of transferrin (the main iron transporting protein in human serum) with a low degree of glycosylation. CDT includes asialo-, monosialo-, and disialo-transferrin (Tf). CDT concentrations increase after sustained alcohol intake (≥ 50–80 g day^{-1}), lasting for at least 7–10 days; there is a decrease after cessation of drinking with a half-life of about 14 days.

CE was first applied to CDT analysis in the late 1990s and has since then rapidly gained acceptance. Today, together with HPLC, it is considered one of the most reliable analytical methods in the international literature. After the introduction of multicapillary instrumentation and ready-to-use commercial reagents, CE has become by far the most productive instrumental technique for CDT determination. Most CE methods are based on CZE separations using borate buffers added with organic amines (e.g., with diaminobutane, spermine, or diethylenetriamine) to hinder protein interactions with the capillary wall. Detection is based on absorption of UV radiation at 200–214-nm wavelengths. Examples of its application include CDT determination in blood microsamples collected from newborns using microhematocrit tubes and analysis of cadaveric blood to study the postmortem stability and possible redistribution of CDT. Notwithstanding a relevant hemolysis, CE separation allowed for CDT determination in 41% of the blood samples collected after death, showing an acceptable stability of the protein and the absence of an appreciable postmortem redistribution.

In a similar manner, changes in hemoglobin (HbA) induced by reaction with acetaldehyde, which is the first and most reactive metabolite of ethanol, has been proposed as a possible biomarker of alcohol abuse. A CE–ESI–MS method has been developed to study these adducts and applied to studies *in vitro*. When applied to real samples, this technique led to the identification of stable modifications of hemoglobin even in moderate alcohol drinkers.

Inks

Inks are complex mixtures of colorants, vehicles, and additives that are adjusted in composition to produce the desired writing characteristics. From a forensic point of view, ink analysis is mainly requested for ink-source comparisons, commonly conducted in casework involving such crimes as tax evasion, insurance fraud, and currency counterfeiting. The ability to distinguish different inks can be useful in criminal cases of document alteration, where two or more inks of the same apparent color, but with different dye compositions, were used in a document.

CE in common with other instrumental separation techniques, such as HPLC and GC, has been applied to the forensic analysis of pen ink. There are a number of reports in the literature, for example, of separations of water-soluble inks by CZE, using UV absorbance and LIF detection. CE has also been used to analyze roller ball inks as part of ink aging investigation where the age of various ink samples was determined based on the relative quantities of components separated by CE.

The possibility of comparing inkjet printing inks by using micellar electrokinetic chromatography (MEKC) with diode array detection has also recently been proposed. The analytical procedure discriminated between the electrophoretic profiles of inks (extracted from paper) that were produced by five different manufacturers. The effective differentiation of individual inks was possible in terms of migration time, order, and specific shapes of characteristic peaks. The comparison of the recorded UV–visible spectra also allowed for the identification of the main dyes.

Explosives and Gunshot Residues

Explosives have a long history of criminal use and have become of increasing concern with their widespread use for international terrorism. The provision of information concerning the identity of an explosive at an early stage in an investigation is critical. Explosives and explosive residues can include a wide range of organic and inorganic components, thus necessitating an equally wide range of analytical techniques to identify them in the often complex matrix of postblast debris. Instrumental techniques, such as SEM–EDX, MS coupled with liquid or GC, X-ray spectrometry, infrared spectrometry, and ion chromatography, are used in combination with wet chemical tests (presumptive tests) to provide information on the identity and quantity of explosive residues.

Many organic and inorganic explosives and their residues are amenable to analysis by CE with acceptable limits of detection. CE is particularly well suited to the determination of inorganic ions that might be present in the postblast residue from improvised explosive devices (IEDs). In order to achieve the required level of confidence in identification of an explosive residue, corroboration through analysis by two independent techniques is required. In addition to the advantages of CE referred to earlier, the separation mechanisms in CE are substantially different from those of ion chromatography, thus providing a suitable orthogonal approach.

CE has also been shown to be useful in the separation and identification of components in gunshot residues (GSR). These residues are typically analyzed to identify persons who fired weapons and to investigate the sources and supply chains of ammunition. GSR analysis is traditionally based on the determination of heavy metals (usually lead, barium, and antimony) originating from the primer, but the production of "metal-free" ammunition requires robust analytical methods for the identification of the organic components in the gunshot and explosive residues. Both the inorganic and organic components of GSR can be separated by CE simultaneously through the use of complexation for the metal ions and MEKC for the uncharged organic compounds (see **Figure 3** and **Table 2**). The method was tested on real samples collected from weapons and from hands after firing.

Miniaturization

An area of significant recent research has been the move to develop portable instrumentation for at- or near-scene analysis. This is of particular importance for investigations involving clandestine drug laboratories and explosions. The National Institute of Forensic Sciences in Australia identified the rapid at-scene identification of illicit drugs and explosives to be of paramount importance in combating organized crime and terrorism in its Forensic Science Innovation Strategy reported in 2001. The provision of chemical information at an early stage of an investigation is extremely useful in rapid identification of potential suspects, in addition to being important for occupational health and safety reasons.

As described above, CE is well suited to the analysis of illicit drugs and explosive residues. However, commercially available benchtop instrumentation is too bulky to be used in the field. An area that shows great promise for forensic analysis is microfluidics, the so-called "lab-on-a-chip." Joseph Wang, one of the world leaders in microfluidics, stated in a 2004 review that "microfluidic devices offer great promise for transporting the forensic laboratory to the sample source." Many microfluidic devices rely upon electrophoresis to separate analytes, with the advantage that miniaturization also leads to associated reductions in analysis times. For example, microchip CE has been applied to the analysis of nitrate ester explosives, with

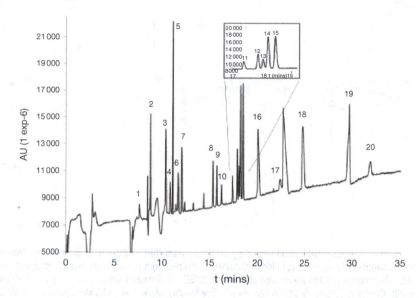

Figure 3 Simultaneous separation of organic and inorganic gunshot residues under optimal conditions. Electrolyte: 40 mM borate buffer, 16 mM SDS, 0.5 mM CDTA, capillary: 79.2 cm (69.2 cm detection length) ×75 μm i.d. Hydrodynamic injection: 0.5 p.s.i. for 5 s at 25 °C, UV detection at 200 nm. (1) Sb (30), (2) resorcinol (11.1), (3) 24-DNT (10.93), (4) 26-DNT (14.57), (5) Fe (10), (6) 23-DNT (18.2), (7) MF (6.0), (8) Ba (30), (9) Ca (20), (10) Mg (20), (11) Al (20), (12) Ni (20), (13) Zn (10), (14) Pb (10), (15) Cu (20), (16) EF (17.8), (17) DPA (16.9), (18) MC (14.4), (19) EC (22.6), (20) BF (10). Standard concentrations in parentheses in milligrams per liter. Reprinted from Morales, E.B., Vázquez, A.L., 2004. Simultaneous determination of inorganic and organic gunshot residues by capillary electrophoresis. Journal of Chromatography A 1061, 225–233, with permission.

Table 2 Characteristic organic and inorganic gunshot residue components listed with abbreviations used in **Figure 3**

Compound	Abbreviation	Usage
Nitroglycerin	NG	Propellant
Resorcinol	Rs	Stabilizer
2,4-Dinitrotoluene	24-DNT	Flash inhibitor
2,6-Dinitrotoluene	26-DNT	Flash inhibitor
2,3-Dinitrotoluene	23-DNT	Flash inhibitor
Dimethyl phthalate	MF	Plasticizer
Diethyl phthalate	EF	Plasticizer
Dibutyl phthalate	BF	Plasticizer
Diphenylamine	DPA	Stabilizer
Methyl centralite	MC	Stabilizer
Ethyl centralite	EC	Stabilizer
Antimony	Sb	Fuel
Iron	Fe	Bullet material
Barium	Ba	Oxidizing agent
Calcium	Ca	Fuel
Magnesium	Mg	Fuel
Aluminum	Al	Fuel
Nickel	Ni	Bullet material
Zinc	Zn	Bullet material
Lead	Pb	Explosive (lead styphnate)
Copper	Cu	Bullet material

Reprinted from Morales, E.B., Vázquez, A.L., 2004. Simultaneous determination of inorganic and organic gunshot residues by capillary electrophoresis. Journal of Chromatography A 1061, 225–233, with permission.

ethylene glycol dinitrate, pentaerythritol tetranitrate, propylene glycol dinitrate, and nitroglycerin being separated in less than 3 min. Amphetamine, methamphetamine, and pseudoephedrine derivatized with a fluorescent label were separated by MEKC and quantified using a commercially available lab on a chip device intended for bioassays. The derivatization was achieved using a dry heating block procedure, which allowed for labeling of the drug analytes in 3 min and could feasibly be used in the field.

In addition to these lab-on-a-chip devices, other workers have focused on using shorter capillaries in combination with higher voltages to achieve rapid separations in portable instrumentation. These have required the development of novel flow-based sample introduction techniques. For example, a simple sequential injection–capillary electrophoresis (SI–CE) instrument with contactless conductivity detection has been developed and applied to the determination of anions relevant to the identification of inorganic IEDs. The portable device was able to separate mixtures of key explosive tracer ions (nitrate, perchlorate, chlorate, and azide) in combination with common background ions (chloride, sulfate, thiocyanate, fluoride, phosphate, and carbonate) within 55 sections (see **Figure 4**).

Software control enabled a high analytical frequency of 60 samples per hour with high repeatability of separation times and detection limits in the 25–50 μg l^{-1} range. National Institute of Justice Guide for the Selection of Commercial

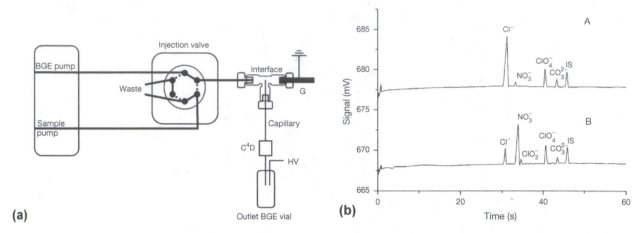

Figure 4   (a) Schematic diagram of the sequential injection–capillary electrophoresis (SI-CE) system: G, ground; HV, high-voltage electrode; C4D, capacitively coupled contactless conductivity detector. (b) Electropherogram obtained from the aqueous extracts of a soil sample after the detonation of a (A) perchlorate/sugar IED; (B) chlorate/perchlorate/nitrate/sulfur/charcoal IED. IS, propanesulfonic acid 5 mg l^{-1}. BGE composition, 50 mM Tris, 50 mM CHES, 0.05% (w/v) PEI. Capillary, 25 μm i.d. 35 cm (25 cm effective length); separation, −25 kV; injection, −1 kV × 1 s. Reprinted from Blanco, G.A., Nai, Y.H., Hilder, E.F. et al., 2011. Identification of inorganic improvised explosive devices using sequential injection capillary electrophoresis and contactless conductivity detection. Analytical Chemistry 83, 9068–9075, with permission.

Explosives Detection Systems for Law Enforcement Applications states that the nominal capability for explosive screening technology is that it "Can detect 100 μg of each target explosive in the swipe collection mode at least 95 percent of the time." For a typical ammonium nitrate–fuel oil explosive, 100 μg translates to approximately 73 μg of nitrate, which if dissolved in 1 ml of water, gives a concentration well above that of the detection limits for the SI–CE instrument.

See also: **Chemistry/Trace/Fire Investigation:** Analysis of Fire Debris; **Chemistry/Trace/Paint and Coating:** Forensic Paint Analysis; **Documents:** Ink Analysis; **Forensic Medicine/Causes of Death:** Gunshot Wounds; **Forensic Medicine/Pathology:** Estimation of the Time Since Death; **Toxicology:** Drug Screening in Sport; Herbal Psychoactive Substances; Volatile Substances and Inhalants; **Toxicology/Alcohol:** Blood; Urine and Other Body Fluids; **Toxicology/Drugs of Abuse:** Drug-Impaired Driving; Drugs in Hair; Urine; Validation of Twelve Chemical Spot Tests for the Detection of Drugs of Abuse.

Further Reading

Anastos, N., Barnett, N.W., Lewis, S.W., 2005. Capillary electrophoresis for forensic drug analysis: a review. Talanta 67, 269–279.

Anastos, N., Barnett, N.W., Lewis, S.W., Pearson, J.R., Kirkbride, K.P., 2005. Rapid determination of carbohydrates in heroin drug seizures using capillary electrophoresis with short-end injection. Journal of Forensic Sciences 50, 1039–1043.

Anastos, N., Lewis, S.W., Barnett, N.W., Pearson, J.R., Kirkbride, K.P., 2005. The rapid analysis of heroin drug seizures using micellar electrokinetic chromatography with short-end injection. Journal of Forensic Sciences 50, 37–42.

Blanco, G.A., Nai, Y.H., Hilder, E.F., et al., 2011. Identification of inorganic improvised explosive devices using sequential injection capillary electrophoresis and contactless conductivity detection. Analytical Chemistry 83, 9068–9075.

Bortolotti, F., Trettene, M., Gottardo, R., Bernini, M., Ricossa, M.C., Tagliaro, F., 2007. Carbohydrate-deficient transferrin (CDT): a reliable indicator of the risk of driving under the influence of alcohol when determined by capillary electrophoresis. Forensic Science International 170, 175–178.

Bortolotti, F., De Paoli, G., Gottardo, R., Trattene, M., Tagliaro, F., 2004. Determination of gamma-hydroxybutyric acid in biological fluids by using capillary electrophoresis with indirect detection. Journal of Chromatography B 800, 239–244.

Brüggemann, O., Meder, M., Freitag, R., 1996. Analysis of amatoxins alpha-amanitin and beta-amanitin in toadstool extracts and body fluids by capillary zone electrophoresis with photodiode array detection. Journal of Chromatography A 744, 167–176.

Caslavska, J., Thormann, W., 2011. Stereoselective determination of drugs and metabolites in body fluids, tissues and microsomal preparations by capillary electrophoresis (2000–2010). Journal of Chromatography A 1218, 588–601.

Chiang, J.F., Hsiao, Y.T., Ko, W.K., Wu, S.M., 2009. Analysis of multiple abused drugs and hypnotics in urine by sweeping CE. Electrophoresis 30, 2583–2589.

De Benedetto, G.E., Fanigliulo, M., 2009. A new CE-ESI-MS method for the detection of stable hemoglobin acetaldehyde adducts, potential biomarkers of alcohol abuse. Electrophoresis 30, 1798–1807.

Gottardo, R., Bortolotti, F., Trettene, M., De Paoli, G., Tagliaro, F., 2008. Rapid and direct analysis of gamma-hydroxybutyric acid in urine by capillary electrophoresis-electrospray ionization ion-trap mass spectrometry. Journal of Chromatography A 1051, 207–211.

Gong, X.Y., Kubán, P., Scholer, A., Hauser, P.C., 2008. Determination of gamma-hydroxybutyric acid in clinical samples using capillary electrophoresis with contactless conductivity detection. Journal of Chromatography A 1213, 100–104.

Guide for the Selection of Commercial Explosives Detection Systems for Law Enforcement Applications (NIJ Guide 100–99). Available at: http://www.nij.gov/pubs-sum/178913.htm (accessed 28 March 2012).

Lloyd, A., Blanes, L., Beavis, A., Roux, C., Doble, P., 2011. A rapid method for the in-field analysis of amphetamines employing the Agilent Bioanalyzer. Analytical Methods 3, 1535–1539.

Meng, L., Wang, B., Luo, F., Shen, G., Wang, Z., Guo, M., 2011. Application of dispersive liquid-liquid microextraction and CE with UV detection for the chiral separation and determination of the multiple illicit drugs on forensic samples. Forensic Science International 209, 42–47.

Morales, E.B., Vázquez, A.L., 2004. Simultaneous determination of inorganic and organic gunshot residues by capillary electrophoresis. Journal of Chromatography A 1061, 225–233.

National Institute of Forensic Sciences (Australia), National Forensic Science Innovation Strategy. Available at: http://www.nifs.com.au/NIFS/NIFS_frame.html?strategy.asp&1 (accessed 28 March 2012).

Pascali, J.P., Liotta, E., Gottardo, R., Bortolotti, F., Tagliaro, F., 2009. Rapid optimized separation of bromide in serum samples with capillary zone electrophoresis by using glycerol as additive to the background electrolyte. Journal of Chromatography A 1216, 3349–3352.

Pascali, J.P., Sorio, D., Bortolotti, F., Tagliaro, F., 2010. Rapid determination of lithium in serum samples by capillary electrophoresis. Analytical and Bioanalytical Chemistry 396, 2543–2546.

Piccin, E., Dossi, N., Cagan, A., Carrilho, E., Wang, J., 2009. Rapid and sensitive measurements of nitrate ester explosives using microchip electrophoresis with electrochemical detection. The Analyst 134, 528–532.

Pumera, M., 2006. Analysis of explosives *via* microchip electrophoresis and conventional capillary electrophoresis: a review. Electrophoresis 27, 244–256.

Rittgen, J., Pütz, M., Pyell, U., 2008. Identification of toxic oligopeptides in Amanita fungi employing capillary electrophoresis-electrospray ionization-mass spectrometry with positive and negative ion detection. Electrophoresis 29, 2094–2100.

Szafarska, M., Wietecha-Posøuszny, R., Woźniakiewicz, M., Kościelniak, P., 2011. Application of capillary electrophoresis to examination of color inkjet printing inks for forensic purposes. Forensic Science International 212, 78–85.

Wang, J., 2004. Microchip devices for detecting terrorist weapons. Analytica Chimica Acta 507, 3–10.

Chromatography: Basic Principles

CE Lenehan, Flinders University, Adelaide, SA, Australia

Abbreviations

GC	Gas chromatography	SEC	Size-exclusion chromatography
HPLC	High-performance liquid chromatography	TLC	Thin-layer chromatography

Glossary

Analytes The analytes are the substances of interest that are being separated from the sample matrix by chromatography.

Chromatogram A chromatogram is a plot showing detector signal versus time; peaks are usually observed on the chromatogram when an analyte is emerging from the column.

Chromatograph A chromatograph is the instrument used to perform a chromatographic separation.

Eluate The eluate is the mobile phase leaving the column; it is usually monitored by some form of detection system.

Eluent The eluent is the solvent carrying the analyte through the stationary phase.

Introduction

In the majority of cases, samples encountered in the forensic science laboratory comprise a complex mixture of substances. Often, the forensic scientist is interested in looking at one or a number of these components (e.g., the level of a drug in a blood sample); however, there are very few analytical methods that are selective for a single chemical species. In reality, most compounds need to be relatively pure in order to identify them. Consequently, the analyte of interest must be separated from other compounds in the sample matrix in order to allow its identification and quantification. Chromatography is a powerful and versatile technique that is routinely used by forensic scientists for this purpose.

All chromatographic separations are based on the distribution of the sample components between two phases; the stationary phase and the mobile phase. The sample is dissolved in the mobile phase (which may be a liquid, solid, or supercritical fluid) and forced through an immiscible stationary phase. The stationary phase is generally solid particles or a viscous liquid fixed to the surface of a column or solid particles. On traveling through the stationary phase, molecules within the sample distribute themselves differently between the two phases. Molecules with a strong affinity for the stationary phase move slowly through the system. Conversely, molecules with a weak affinity for the stationary phase migrate very quickly through the system. This difference in migration rates allows the components to separate into discrete bands that can then be analyzed. A generalized schematic diagram showing a chromatographic separation is shown in **Figure 1**.

Classification of Chromatographic Techniques

There are a multitude of different ways in which chromatographic separations can be performed. Consequently, chromatographic methods are often classified into subcategories. First, the physical setup of the stationary phase can be either planar or column based. In planar chromatography, the stationary phase is fixed onto a flat surface. Thin-layer chromatography is a good example of planar chromatography. Alternatively, column chromatography uses a column to house the stationary phase. Most chromatographic separations used in the forensic laboratory use some form of column

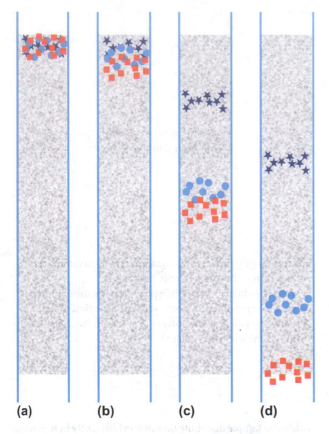

(a)   **(b)**   **(c)**   **(d)**

Figure 1 A diagram showing the principle of chromatographic separations. (a) A small volume of sample is placed at the top of the column, which is filled with stationary phase and solvent. (b–d) Mobile phase is added to the top and allowed to slowly elute through the column, individual molecules interact with the stationary phase to different degrees and thus take differing times to move through the column.

chromatography. Second, the chromatographic technique is often classified according to the physical state of mobile phase (gas, liquid, or supercritical fluid) employed as the eluent. Gas chromatography (GC) and high-performance liquid chromatography (HPLC) are commonly employed in the forensic laboratory, while supercritical fluid chromatography is less commonly found. In recent times, ultrahigh-performance liquid chromatography (UHPLC) has emerged as a more powerful separation technique than HPLC offering reduced run times and increased separation power. UHPLC is increasingly being used in the forensic context.

Chromatographic techniques can be further subclassified on the basis of the separation mechanism involved; these being adsorption, partition, ion exchange, size exclusion, and affinity. Liquid chromatography (LC) often employs separations based on an adsorption mechanism. In this case, molecules or ions adhere (adsorb) to the surface of the stationary phase (the

adsorbent) via weak intermolecular forces. In general, the "like dissolves like" principle can be applied. A nonpolar molecule will adsorb to a nonpolar stationary phase but will have little affinity for a polar stationary phase. Similarly, a polar molecule will adsorb to a polar surface but will be only weakly attracted to a nonpolar surface. Alternatively, most GC separations are based on a partition mechanism, whereby the molecules partition between two immiscible fluid phases. In GC, the stationary phase is most commonly a viscous liquid bonded to the interior of an open tubular column. The molecules being separated move in and out of this liquid in a mechanism analogous to a liquid–liquid extraction. A general schematic diagram showing adsorption and partition mechanisms is shown in **Figure 2**.

Ion-exchange chromatography (often referred to as ion chromatography) allows the separation of ionic molecules on the basis of their charge. The surface of the stationary phase has ionic functional groups that bind to analyte molecules on the basis of Coulombic (ionic) interactions. This type of chromatography is generally further subdivided into two groups: cation-exchange chromatography and anion-exchange chromatography. Cation-exchange chromatography retains cations due to the negatively charged functional groups on the surface of the stationary phase. These can then be eluted from the stationary phase by introducing a competing cation such as H^+ to force the molecules back off the surface and into the mobile phase (thus exchanging places at the surface). Anion-exchange

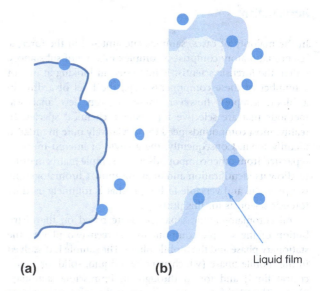

(a)   **(b)**   Liquid film

Figure 2 Schematic diagram showing the interaction of analyte molecules with the stationary phase (shown as a cross section). (a) An adsorption mechanism; analyte molecules are adsorbed directly to the stationary-phase surface and (b) a partition mechanism; analyte molecules are dissolved in a viscous liquid stationary phase bonded to the surface of a particle.

chromatography retains anions as a result of positively charged functional groups on the stationary-phase surface. In this case, the ions are eluted from the column by introducing a competing anion into the mobile phase, for example, hydroxide, which will exchange places with the bound anion. Generalized reaction schemes for the separation of ions by cation and anion exchange are shown below. In general, the higher the charge of the ion the greater the affinity for the charged stationary phase, the more slowly it will move through the system.

$$R^+ - X^- + Y^+ - A^- \underset{\text{Anion–exchange mechanism}}{\rightleftharpoons} R^+ - A^- + Y^+ - X^-$$

$$R^- - Z^- + B^- - C^+ \underset{\text{Cation–exchange mechanism}}{\rightleftharpoons} R - C^+ + B^- - Z^+$$

Size-exclusion chromatography is also known as gel permeation chromatography. As the name indicates, in this form of chromatography, molecules are separated on the basis of their molecular size. Molecules move through a porous stationary phase. Small molecules are able to move into the pores and become trapped, effectively removed from the bulk flow of the mobile phase. Larger molecules are unable to move into the pores and are washed around the stationary phase and elute quickly. The average residence time in the pores depends on the pore size of the stationary phase and the effective size of the analyte molecules (**Figure 3**).

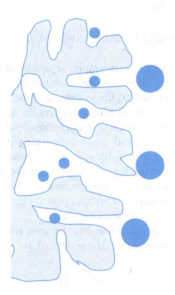

Figure 3 Schematic diagram showing the interaction of analyte molecules with a porous stationary phase. As can be seen, small molecules move into the pores and are retained, while larger molecules are washed through.

LC methods are often subdivided into two further categories, those of normal-phase and reversed-phase chromatography. In normal-phase LC, the stationary phase is generally a polar solid such as silica or alumina, and the mobile phase is nonpolar. Historically, LC separations were generally performed using "normal-phase" strategies. In the 1970s, nonpolar stationary phases were introduced for use with polar mobile phases such as water and methanol. These were termed reversed-phase systems. Reversed-phase systems based on an octadecyl carbon chain (C18) bonded to the surface of the stationary phase are the most commonly employed LC strategy in forensic laboratories.

As stated earlier, chromatographic separations are generally performed in some type of column setup. Column chromatography can be further subdivided into two types based on the type of column used: packed column chromatography and open tubular capillary column chromatography. Packed columns are filled with small particles that either serve as the stationary phase (adsorption chromatography) or serve as the support for a nonvolatile liquid coating that acts as the stationary phase (partition chromatography). A variety of stationary phases is available. Packed columns are commonly used in LC. The use of packed columns in GC is relatively rare; however, they can be employed when increased sample capacity is required. Open tubular capillary chromatography is generally employed in GC and less commonly in LC. There are three types of open tubular columns. In wall-coated open tubular columns, the capillary wall serves as a support for a liquid-film coating that acts as the stationary phase (partition chromatography). Support-coated open tubular columns contain solid microparticles that are coated with stationary phase fixed to the walls of the capillary (partition chromatograph). Finally, adsorption chromatography can be achieved using porous-layer open tubular columns, which have solid microparticles attached to the wall.

Chromatographic Distribution Equilibria

The effectiveness of a chromatographic separation depends in part on the distribution of the sample components between the stationary phase and the mobile phase. This distribution equilibria can generally be described as the transfer of the analyte (S) between the two phases. Therefore we can write

$$S_{(mobile)} \rightleftharpoons S_{(stationary)}$$

As with all equilibrium reactions, this reaction can be described by an equilibrium constant. In this case, it is known as the distribution constant (K_C):

$$K_C = \frac{[S]_{stationary}}{[S]_{mobile}}$$

The magnitude of the distribution constant is governed by the temperature, the type of compound, as well as the chemical composition of the stationary and mobile phases. Should these be kept constant, the separation will be able to be reliably reproduced. Analytes with a large K_C will be more strongly retained by the stationary phase and thus take longer to elute from the column. If, under certain conditions, two analytes had the same K_C they would not be separable, a different set of chromatographic conditions would need to be used. By appropriate choice of the stationary- and mobile-phase compositions, the distribution constants could be adjusted to allow their separation. In an ideal case, the K_C values for each analyte would be considerably different, and all compounds within the mixture would be well separated.

Although the distribution constant is fundamental to chromatographic separations, it is not readily measured. Alternatively, analytes are usually monitored (using some type of detector) as they are eluted from a chromatography column. The result is a plot showing detector signal versus time, known as a chromatogram. **Figure 4** shows a typical chromatogram showing the chromatographic separation of two compounds. In this case, an unretained compound elutes first, followed by a compound that has been retained by the column.

As illustrated in **Figure 4**, the retention time (t_R) for each analyte is the time taken from injection of the sample mixture onto the column until the component reaches the detector. In many cases, a sample may contain species that are not retained by the stationary phase. These unretained compounds travel through the stationary phase in the minimum time possible. The time taken for an unretained peak to reach the detector is known as the void time (t_M). The void time provides a measure of the amount of time an analyte will spend moving in the mobile phase. The adjusted retention time is a measure of the time the analyte spends in/on the stationary phase. This can be

measured by subtracting the void time (t_M) from the observed retention time (t_R) as shown below:

$$t'_R = t_R - t_M$$

The retention factor, k, is the ratio of the adjusted retention time (t'_R) to the void time (t_M) and is often used to compare the migration rates of analytes. That is because, for a fixed set of chromatographic conditions (stationary phase, mobile phase, and analyte) the value for k will be the same, regardless of flow rate:

$$k = \frac{t'_R}{t_M}$$

The retention factor can be related to the distribution coefficient (K_C) as it is effectively a measure of the time the analyte spends in each phase:

$$k = \frac{t'_R}{t_M} = \frac{\text{time spent in stationary phase}}{\text{time spent in mobile phase}} = \frac{[S]_{\text{stationary}}}{[S]_{\text{mobile}}}$$

The separation factor, α, is a measure of the relative retention of two components and can be defined as the ratio of their two adjusted retention times:

$$\alpha = \frac{t'_{R_2}}{t'_{R_1}}$$

where $t'_{R_2} > t'_{R_1}$. Accordingly, the value for α is always >1. In general, the greater the relative retention, the greater the separation between the components. Similarly to k, α is proportional to the ratio of the two analytes distribution coefficients.

Band Broadening in Chromatography

The efficiency of a chromatographic separation depends on two factors: (a) the difference in distribution coefficients as described earlier and (b) the broadness of the band of eluting analyte molecules. Band broadening results as analyte molecules traveling through the stationary phase tend to diffuse into a Gaussian-shaped band. Band broadening occurs to some extent in all chromatographic systems. In general, the wider the bands, the poorer the separation. Additionally, the longer the molecule spends on the stationary phase the broader the band becomes. This results in a broader peak on the chromatogram and thus poorer separation efficiency.

The resolution, R_s, tells us how far apart two analyte peaks are relative to their widths and is defined as

$$R_s = \frac{2(t_{R_2} - t_{R_1})}{W_{b1} + W_{b2}}$$

$$= \frac{0.589(t_{R_2} - t_{R_1})}{W_{1/2 \text{ average}}}$$

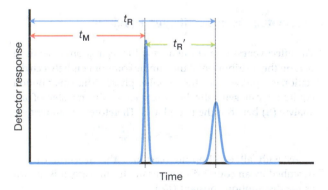

Figure 4 Example chromatogram showing the separation of two compounds. The first compound is unretained by the column and elutes at t_M, the second compound is retained from the column eluting later at t_R.

where W_b is the peak width at baseline and $W_{1/2 \text{ average}}$ is the average peak width at half height as shown on the idealized Gaussian peak in **Figure 5**. As shown below, separations where R_s values are < 1.5 exhibit some overlap between the peaks. For quantitative analysis, a resolution of >1.5 is ideal.

Band broadening within the chromatographic system results from three different broadening processes namely, eddy diffusion (A), longitudinal diffusion (B), and interphase mass transfer (C). These processes are discussed separately, below.

A molecule (or ion) can travel throughout a packed stationary phase via a multitude of different pathways. As shown in **Figure 6(a)**, the length of these pathways can differ significantly. As a result, analyte molecules may reach the detector over a time interval, leading to a broad peak. This broadening effect is termed eddy diffusion and is independent of mobile-phase velocity. Eddy diffusion (A) is related to average particle diameter (d_p) and packing geometry (λ) by

$$A = 2\lambda d_p$$

Eddy diffusion is minimized by using small uniform stationary-phase particles and tighter packing. Typical values are around 1.0 for a well-packed column.

Figure 6(b) illustrates the longitudinal diffusion of analyte molecules. Longitudinal diffusion describes the spread of analyte molecules or ions through random motion from regions of higher concentration to regions of lower concentration. Longitudinal diffusion (B) is related to the diffusion coefficient of the analyte in a given medium (D_M), an obstruction factor resulting from the packing (γ):

$$B = 2\gamma D_M$$

D_M is a function of both the analyte and the mobile phase, and γ is a constant that depends on the quality of the stationary-phase packing. Consequently, the magnitude of B can only be changed by varying the type, pressure, and/or flow rate of the mobile phase. Longitudinal diffusion is particularly important in GC and can be reduced by using high flow rates

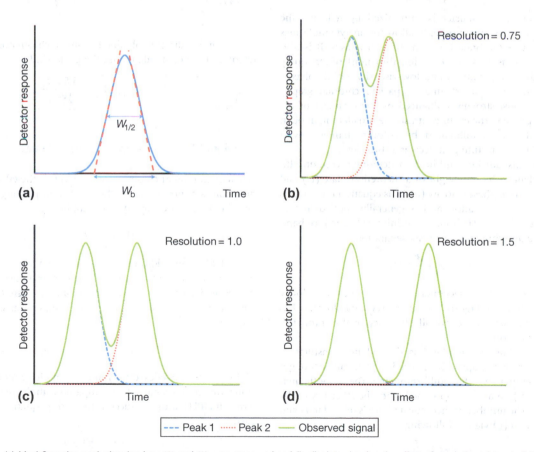

Figure 5   (a) Ideal Gaussian peak showing how W_b and $W_{1/2}$ are measured and (b–d) plots showing the effect of resolution of two individual peaks on the observed chromatogram. The solid line represents the observed signal, with the dashed lines representing the individual peaks.

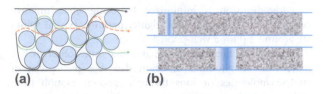

Figure 6 Schematic diagram showing modes of broadening in chromatography. (a) Multiple pathways traveled by the analyte through a packed column (eddy diffusion) and (b) longitudinal diffusion.

and or denser gases. In LC, longitudinal diffusion is generally relatively small.

Broadening, due to interphase mass transfer (C), results from the finite time taken for a molecule to equilibrate as it moves between the two phases. For packed columns interphase mass transfer is dependent on the diffusion coefficient (D_M) and the particle diameter (d_p) and is approximated by

$$C = \frac{1}{6}\frac{d_p^2}{D_M}$$

Interphase mass transfer is minimized by reducing the mobile-phase flow rate in order to allow the analyte molecules more time to equilibrate between the two phases. It is also minimized by using small particles, thin films of stationary phase, higher temperatures, and low-viscosity mobile phases. As a general rule, broadening in packed chromatography columns is most strongly influenced by the diameter of the stationary-phase particles. In contrast, the broadening in open tubular columns is influenced by column diameter, with reduced diameter resulting in decreased broadening.

These terms can be combined to determine column efficiency as defined by the height of a theoretical plate (H) and the linear mobile-phase velocity (u). This equation is known as the van Deemter equation and is generally applied in GC. Ideally, the value for H should be minimized to reduce band broadening and thus improve peak separation.

$$H = A + \frac{B}{u} + Cu$$

A representative van Deemter plot showing linear velocity versus H is shown in **Figure 7**. As can be seen, the flow rate has significant impact on the overall efficiency of the chromatographic separation.

The term "theoretical plate" is derived from distillation theory; in chromatography, the theoretical plate can be thought of a representing a single equilibrium step. The more theoretical plates (N) on a separation, the higher the efficiency of the separation. The number of theoretical plates is related to H and column length (L) via the following:

$$N = \frac{L}{H}$$

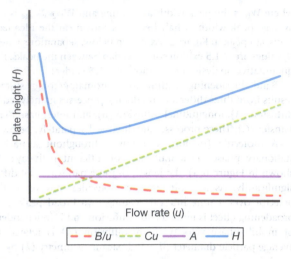

Figure 7 Exemplar van Deemter plot showing effect of flow rate on efficiency as measured by the height equivalent to a theoretical plate (H). Dotted lines show the contribution from the individual diffusion mechanisms.

N can be directly obtained from a chromatogram, the retention time of standard, and the peak width:

$$N = 16\left(\frac{t_R}{W}\right)^2 = \frac{5.545 t_R^2}{W_{1/2}}$$

Additional Comments on Band Broadening

When open tubular columns are used in GC, the effect of eddy diffusion is removed due to the absence of packing materials and the modified Golay equation applies:

$$H = \frac{B}{u} + Cu$$

In HPLC, an additional mass transfer term needs to be incorporated to account for different mass transfer in each phases as described by the Huber equation, where C_s and C_m are the stationary-phase and mobile-mass transfer terms, respectively:

$$H = A + \frac{B}{u} + C_s u + C_m u$$

In general, the eddy diffusion term and longitudinal diffusion term are very small when compared with the mass transfer terms in HPLC, thus a reduced form of this equation is usually used:

$$H = C_s u + C_m u$$

Optimization of Chromatographic Performance

Chromatographic performance is optimized by varying experimental conditions until the components of a mixture are well separated. Consideration is often taken to the time frame of the separation. Optimization experiments are generally aimed at (1) adjusting the distribution equilibria of the analytes (thus changing the migration rates) or (2) reducing band broadening. Adjustments to the distribution equilibria can be achieved by changing the chemical composition of the mobile or stationary phase and adjusting the temperature. As described earlier, band broadening can be reduced by judicious choice of flow rate, minimizing particle or column diameter, and reducing film thickness.

See also: **Methods:** Gas Chromatography; Liquid and Thin-Layer Chromatography; Liquid Chromatography–Mass Spectrometry.

Further Reading

Bayne, S., Carlin, M., 2010. Forensic Applications of High Performance Liquid Chromatography. CRC Press, Boca Raton.

McNair, H.M., Miller, J.M., 2009. Basic Gas Chromatography, second ed. John Wiley & Sons, Inc., Hoboken, NJ.

Miller, J.M., 2005. Chromatography Concepts and Contrasts, second ed. John Wiley & Sons, Inc., Hoboken, NJ.

Pollettini, A., 2011. HPLC in the forensic sciences. In: Corradini, D. (Ed.), Handbook of HPLC. Chromatographic Science Series, , second ed.vol. 101. CRC Press, Boca Raton, FL, pp. 661–682.

Robards, K., Haddad, P.R., Jackson, P.E., 1994. Principles and Practice of Modern Chromatographic Methods, third ed. Academic Press, Elsevier Science Limited, London.

Snyder, L.R., Kirkland, J.J., Dolan, J.W., 2010. Introduction to Modern Liquid Chromatography, third ed. John Wiley & Sons, Inc., Hoboken, NJ.

Relevant Websites

http://www.chromatography-online.org—Chromatography online.
http://www.chromedia.org—Chromedia.

Liquid and Thin-Layer Chromatography

SW Lewis, Curtin University, Perth, WA, Australia
CE Lenehan, Flinders University, Adelaide, SA, Australia

Abbreviations

HPLC	High-performance liquid chromatography	TLC	Thin-layer chromatography

Introduction

Liquid chromatography is a broad classification used to describe a variety of different chromatographic configurations that rely on the use of a liquid mobile phase. Paper, thin-layer, and classical column chromatography techniques, as well as high-performance liquid chromatography (HPLC) and ion chromatography, all belong to the class of liquid chromatography. These techniques are heavily used in forensic science to separate a wide range of analytes including, but not restricted to, illicit drugs, drugs, and drug metabolites in toxicology samples, explosives residues, and textile fiber dyes. A variety of separation mechanisms can be used within liquid chromatography; these include adsorption, ion-exchange, size-exclusion, affinity, and ion-pair formation. A discussion of these separation mechanisms can be found in *Chromatography: Basic Principles*. This chapter gives an overview of classical, high-performance, and thin-layer chromatographic techniques including experimental configurations and forensic applications.

Column (or Liquid–Solid) Chromatography

Column chromatography is commonly used in sample purification and cleanup, particularly in synthetic organic laboratories. One of the simplest chromatographic techniques to set up, column chromatography utilizes commonly available laboratory materials to effect the separation. The column typically comprises either a laboratory pipette or a burette that is filled with a solid stationary phase (typically alumina, silica, or celite). The mixture to be separated is dissolved in an appropriate solvent and added to the top of the column. Mobile phase is continually added to the top of the column and liquid flow is continued through the column. Compounds are separated on the basis of their differential migration through the column. Compounds with a strong affinity for the stationary

phase take a longer time to be eluted. The eluted compounds can be collected, recovered, and examined.

In the 1960s and the 1970s, toxicologists routinely used column chromatography for the isolation and purification of drugs and pesticides from biological fluids. More recently, commercially prepared "solid-phase extraction" (SPE) chromatography columns have become the most commonly used column chromatography system for sample cleanup in the forensic laboratory. Ready to use SPE columns of varying stationary phase composition can be purchased from a variety of chromatographic suppliers. The choice of stationary phase is dependent on the analyte of interest, with SPE columns suitable for proteins, drugs, and pesticides being readily available.

HPLC and Ultrahigh-Performance Liquid Chromatography

In order for a sample to be successfully analyzed by gas chromatography (GC), it must be volatile (vapor pressure at least 1 torr) and stable in the vapor phase at elevated temperatures. Many organic compounds, such as drugs and explosives, do not fit this criterion. For such compounds, HPLC is a viable alternative as it is applicable to a much greater range of compounds than GC. In theory, any compound that can be dissolved is able to be separated by HPLC. There are some limitations; however, appropriate mobile and stationary phases must be available, the compounds must be stable in the solvent system, and suitable detection systems must be at hand. Overall, HPLC is an extremely powerful separation technique that is widely used in all areas of analytical science.

HPLC is an extension of column chromatography and typically uses a stationary phase that has a very small particle size (typically 3–5 μm in diameter) that has been tightly packed into a commercially produced column (generally 3–25 cm in length and 3–5 mm internal diameter). Samples (generally 1–20 µl) are introduced into the column via an injection port. The decreased particle size (compared with classic column chromatography) results in increased contact between stationary phase and the mobile phase and superior resolution to classical column chromatography. A consequence of the decreased particle size and tight packing is that the flow of mobile phase through such a tightly packed column is highly restricted. Therefore, a quality pump capable of sustaining high inlet pressures (up to 400 bar) is employed to propel the mobile phase through the column. Thus, HPLC is often termed "high-pressure" LC. Typical mobile phase flow rates range from 0.3 ml min^{-1} to 1.0 ml min^{-1}. The outlet of the HPLC column is generally coupled to a flow through detection system such that the eluted compounds can be directly detected as they leave the column, without need for further modification. A number of different approaches can be used to detect the eluting analytes, the most common ones being ultraviolet–visible (UV–vis) absorbance spectrophotometry and mass spectrometry (MS). The resulting separation is recorded as a graph of detector response versus time, which is referred to as a chromatogram. Modern HPLC instrumentation is typically fully automated with computer control of the pump, injection, and detector components. The schematic diagram in **Figure 1** shows a typical instrumental setup.

It is well documented in HPLC that decreasing the stationary phase particle size results in improved separation efficiency. However, until recently, the use of smaller particles had been limited as the pressure required for percolating the mobile phase through a column packed with smaller particles was prohibitive using conventional HPLC systems. Over the last decade, ultrahigh-pressure liquid chromatography (UHPLC) instrumentation comprising a combination of innovative reduced particle size solid phase supports capable of withstanding higher pressures and advanced pumping systems able to deliver the mobile phase at these higher pressures (can be up to 1200 bar) has become a commercial reality. Both HPLC and UHPLC operate on the same principles; however, UHPLC offers superior performance with regard to speed and resolution. The use of UHPLC has been reported to decrease run times by a factor of 10 without loss of resolution. Furthermore, the incorporation of longer UHPLC columns can increase resolution of poorly resolved analytes while maintaining an acceptable analytical time frame and achieve greater detection sensitivity.

One of the reasons for the success of HPLC (and UHPLC) as a technique is its flexibility. A wide range of stationary phases is available to the analyst. These are typically of silica or polymeric makeup and are specifically designed to withstand the high pressures within the column. These stationary phases can be used in combination with an almost limitless range of mobile phase compositions to achieve very high degrees of separation efficiencies. HPLC (and UHPLC) can be run in either normal phase (stationary phase more polar than mobile phase) or reversed phase (stationary phase less polar than mobile phase) mode. In reversed phase chromatography, the polar compounds elute first from the column, whereas in normal phase chromatography, nonpolar compounds are the first to elute.

A variety of different separation mechanisms are used in HPLC (and UHPLC), the most common being partition. Further detail regarding the separation mechanisms used in chromatography can be found in *Chromatography: Basic Principles*. A number of variables can be changed in order to improve separations through HPLC (and UHPLC). Most commonly, the mobile phase composition is altered. This can be achieved either by preparing a new mobile phase off-line or by using modern pumps that are able to mix the solvent online. Furthermore, with the use of modern pumps, chromatographers are able to alter the mobile phase composition during a run (gradient elution). Most forensic separations rely on the use of reversed phase chromatography with mobile phases comprising a mixture of an aqueous buffer and an organic solvent. Special care needs to be taken with selecting the mobile phase as small changes in pH and solvent content can result in markedly different separations. In addition to the mobile phase composition, column flow rates and temperature can also be varied in order to effect a separation. If these measures prove unsuccessful, an alternate stationary phase should be considered.

Many molecules exhibit UV–vis absorption, and as a consequence, UV–vis detection is by far the most commonly used detection method coupled with HPLC. (For a detailed

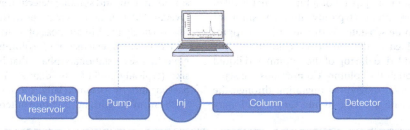

Figure 1   Schematic diagram of the components of a high-performance liquid chromatography system, Inj = sample injector.

discussion of UV–vis spectroscopy, see other chapters in this book). These detectors are generally set at a fixed (programmable) wavelength. Alternatively, diode array detectors are often coupled to the HPLC system, and these allow the collection of the UV–vis spectrum of the eluting compound. Diode array spectra are useful in that they can be used to compare with known compounds using a library search as well as to evaluate the purity of the eluting compounds. For those molecules that do not exhibit a chromophore in the UV–vis region, alternative detection systems are required. A differential refractive index detector compares the refractive index of the eluting compounds with that of the mobile phase. While widely applicable, this detector is generally not suitable for gradient elution as the mobile phase composition (and thus the refractive index) changes throughout the run. Fluorescence detectors can offer a sensitive detection system; however, the use of this detector requires that the compounds of interest are naturally fluorescent or can be made to fluoresce by chemical derivatization. In evaporative light scattering detection, the column eluent is merged with a gas and atomized into small droplets. The mobile phase is allowed to evaporate, leaving fine particles suspended in the gas. These particles scatter light, and the magnitude of the scattering is measured. Theoretically, the detector responds to nonvolatile substances, and the response should be proportional to the mass of solute present. MS is emerging as the HPLC detection system of choice in forensic laboratories as it gives structural as well as quantitative information about the compounds eluting from the HPLC column. There are many ways in which LC can be interfaced with MS, and as such the reader is referred to other chapters in this book.

HPLC has been applied to a wide variety of forensic applications. Examples include the analysis of ballpoint inks from documents, condom lubricants, explosive residues, and hemoglobin in blood. The most common forensic application of HPLC, however, is in the analysis of drugs and toxins. Over the last 10 years, HPLC (especially when combined with MS) has become the method of choice for the analysis of nonvolatile drugs that are difficult to analyze using GC. An example of where HPLC is particularly useful is in the analysis of benzodiazepines. Benzodiazepines are commonly prescribed drugs and can be subject to misuse. As a result, they are commonly tested for as a part of forensic toxicological screening. An example chromatogram given (**Figure** 2) below shows the separation of 35 different benzodiazepine and other drug standards that are achieved using HPLC coupled with MS.

Thin-Layer Chromatography

Thin-layer chromatography (TLC) is a variant of liquid chromatography, with the mobile phases and stationary phases utilized being common to both. However, in TLC, the stationary phase is present as a thin layer on a planar inert rigid support, rather than as a column. This approach was first proposed in the 1930s, but TLC, in the form it is used today, was not established until the 1950s. Today, there is a wide range of premade plates with a variety of different stationary phases available to the scientist. A typical TLC separation involves application of a solution of the sample to be analyzed as a discrete spot or smear on the chromatographic plate. Once the solvent in which the sample was applied has evaporated, the plate is developed by allowing a mobile phase to move by capillary action through the stationary phase, carrying the components contained within the sample with it. These components are retained to different extents by the stationary phase, thus leading to separation.

There are some key differences between TLC and HPLC. In TLC, unlike HPLC, there is no need for the sample solvent to be compatible with the mobile phase as it is evaporated off when applying the sample to the plate. Similarly, there is no

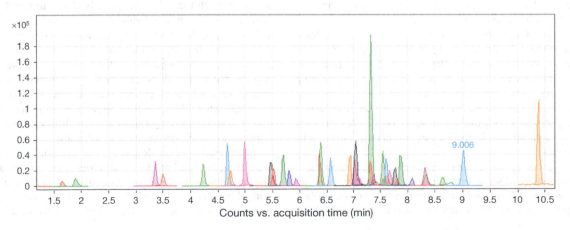

Figure 2 Separation of 35 benzodiazepine and other drug standards by HPLC coupled with mass spectrometric detection.

requirement for the mobile phase to be compatible with detection as is the case with HPLC. TLC is an "open-bed" method, with retention being observable at all stages, unlike in HPLC where if a component is strongly retained, the only indication will be the lack of a peak. In TLC, standards and samples can be run simultaneously on a single plate under identical conditions. A key advantage of TLC is its relative simplicity when compared with other chromatographic techniques. The steps in a TLC analysis have been defined as follows:

1. Selection of a suitable chromatographic stationary phase
2. Application of the sample
3. Selection of a mobile phase
4. Development
5. Visualization and detection

This can also be followed by quantification, by removing the spot of eluted material and extracting into appropriate solvent before subsequent analysis with some other instrumental technique.

There are, however, some disadvantages of TLC. Owing to the reliance on capillary action for development, the flow rate of the mobile phase is difficult to control with any precision. Detection limits are also an issue, with HPLC being far better in this regard. In addition, there is a certain amount of manual dexterity required to load (or "spot") the samples onto the plate, and this can introduce some variability.

A range of stationary phases are available for TLC, which can be classified on the basis of their composition and primary mechanism of retention. The most popular phases in common use are silica gel and alumina, the main retention mechanism for both being due to an adsorption process involving affinity of polar and polarizable compounds to the stationary phase. Nonpolar components are not retained and move further along the TLC plate. Aromatic compounds are readily polarizable; hence, this mode of TLC is well suited, for example, to the separation of fiber dyes that have extensive aromaticity and many other polarizable functional groups.

The stationary phase is laid down as a thin layer (100–2000 μm thick) on an inert rigid support, glass or aluminum. While in earlier times the scientist had to undertake the laborious and time-consuming process of preparing these plates from scratch, there are now many commercial sources of premade plates. Before use, plates need to be stored and prepared in a controlled and reproducible manner, preferably in a humidity-controlled environment to ensure reliable results.

Appropriate application of the sample is highly important for obtaining good separations. In principle, it is very simple; using a glass capillary or micropipette, the dye extract is applied as a spot approximately 2 mm in diameter, typically about 1 cm from the bottom edge of the plate. To ensure good results, there are a number of practical issues that need to be faced. Care needs to be taken not to damage the adsorbent layer or to produce an excessive spot size. The solvent used to load the sample should be able to wet the stationary phase, and it should also be volatile so that it can be driven off before the development of the plate. This process can be accelerated through the application of heat, either applied using a hair dryer or by having the plate rest on a hot surface. To increase the amount of analyte material on the plate, thereby providing a more detectable result, repeated application of sample on the initial spot could be carried out. It is recommended that both questioned samples, and known samples or standard mixtures are run at the same time, with the questioned sample being bracketed by known samples or standards. The applied spots should not be too close to each other, or to the edge of the plate.

There are a number of different approaches to developing TLC plates, with varying levels of complexity. However, the simplest and most widely used approach is the ascending linear method. Once the plate is completely dry, it is placed in a pool of eluent contained within a covered chamber. The eluent used will depend on the stationary phase and the analytes being separated and typically consists of mixtures of various solvents in different proportions, providing different degrees of polarity. Issues that need to be considered when deciding whether a particular eluent system is suitable for a particular analyte mixture include separation and sharpness of bands, the distance the bands have moved from the origin, and the proximity of the solvent front and the concentration of the analytes within the mixture to the separated bands. The development chamber can be as simple as a beaker with a Petri dish cover or, alternatively, a commercially available development chamber. Before use, the eluent needs to stand for a few minutes in the covered chamber to allow the chamber to become saturated with eluent vapor. The depth of eluent should be such that when the plate is placed in the chamber, the eluent level should be below the applied spots; a distance of at least 0.5 cm has been recommended. The eluent will then move up the plate by capillary action; this process takes only a few minutes and separation of the components within the applied dye spots will be observed. Development should be carried out until the eluent has traveled around 2 cm beyond the origin where the spots were applied. Any further than this may lead to the separated spots become diffuse, which makes visualization and interpretation problematic.

Interpretation of the developed TLC plates is carried out by comparing the band position and colors of the questioned and known (standard) components. This can be done under normal laboratory lighting if the analytes are colored (e.g., fiber dyes) or with the use of UV light. Commercially available TLC

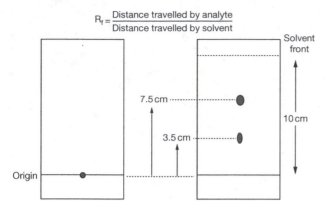

$$R_f = \frac{\text{Distance travelled by analyte}}{\text{Distance travelled by solvent}}$$

Figure 3 Schematic diagram illustrating the measurement of R_f values for a TLC separation.

plates contain a UV fluorescent dye, so separated analyte bands will appear as dark spots against a bright background. A visualizing reagent that reacts with the separated analytes to provide a colored spot may be used; for example, ninhydrin was used to detect amino acids separated by TLC before its application as a latent fingermark detection reagent. The elution characteristics of compounds can be reported as R_f values, which are a measure of the relative distance traveled by each compound from the origin with respect to the solvent front (see **Figure 2**).

However, care must be taken when comparing between plates because of subtle differences in development that lead to different retentions (**Figure 3**).

TLC has found application in forensic testing in areas as diverse as illicit drugs, explosive residues, and particularly, textile dye analysis.

Acknowledgments

The section on TLC in this chapter is substantially based on portions of Lewis S (2009) Analysis of dyes using chromatography. In: Houck M (ed.) *Identification of Textile Fibres*, pp. 203–223. Cambridge: Woodhead Publishing.

> *See also:* **Methods:** Chromatography: Basic Principles; Gas Chromatography; Gas Chromatography–Mass Spectrometry; Liquid Chromatography–Mass Spectrometry.

Further Reading

Bayne, S., Carlin, M., 2010. Forensic Applications of High Performance Liquid Chromatography. CRC Press, Boca Raton, FL.
Bayne, S., Carlin, M., 2010. Forensic Applications of High Performance Liquid Chromatography. CRC Press, Taylor and Francis Group, Boca Raton, FL.
Lewis, S., 2009. Analysis of dyes using chromatography. In: Houck, M. (Ed.), Identification of Textile Fibres. Woodhead Publishing, Cambridge, pp. 203–223.
Miller, J.M., 2005. Chromatography Concepts and Contrasts, second ed. John Wiley & Sons, Inc, Hoboken, NJ.
Pollettini, A., 2011. HPLC in the forensic sciences. In: Corradini, D. (Ed.), Chromatographic Science Series, Handbook of HPLC, second ed., vol. 101. CRC Press, Boca Raton, FL, pp. 661–682.
Robards, K., Haddad, P.R., Jackson, P.E., 1994. Principles and Practice of Modern Chromatographic Methods, third ed. Academic Press Elsevier Science Limited, London.
Snyder, L.R., Kirkland, J.J., Dolan, J.W., 2010. Introduction to Modern Liquid Chromatography, third ed. John Wiley & Sons, Inc, Hoboken, NJ.

Relevant Websites

http://www.chromedia.org/—Chromedia.
http://www.chromatography-online.org/—Chromatography online.

Liquid Chromatography–Mass Spectrometry

F Busetti, Curtin University of Technology, Perth, WA, Australia
L Swann, University of Western Australia, Crawley, WA, Australia

Abbreviations

APCI	Atmospheric Pressure Chemical Ionization		MRM	Multiple Reaction Monitoring
API	Atmospheric Pressure Ionization		MS	Mass Spectrometry
APPI	Atmospheric Pressure Photoionization		MS/MS	Tandem mass spectrometry
ASAP	Atmospheric Solids Analysis Probe		MS^n	Multiple steps of mass spectrometry selection following multiple fragmentations
Da	Daltons			
DART	Direct Analysis in Real Time		m/z	Mass-to-charge ratio
DESI	Desorption Electrospray Ionization		ppm	Parts per million
DI	Direct injection		Q-IT	Quadrupole–Ion Trap
DIOS	Desorption Ionization On porous Silicon		QqQ	Triple quadrupole
ESI	Electrospray Ionization		Q–TOF	Quadrupole–Time of Flight
FT–ICR	Fourier Transform–Ion Cyclotron Resonance		SALDI	Surface-Assisted Laser Desorption/Ionization
FWHM	Full Width at Half Maximum		SELDI	Surface-Enhanced Laser Desorption Ionization
GC	Gas Chromatography			
HPLC	High-Performance Liquid Chromatography		SEND	Surface-Enhanced Neat Desorption
HR	High Resolution		SIM	Single Ion Monitoring
IMS	Ion Mobility Separation		SPE	Solid-Phase Extraction
IRMS	Isotope Ratio Mass Spectrometry		SRM	Single Reaction Monitoring
LC	Liquid Chromatography		TDC	Time-to-Digital Converter
LVI	Large Volume Injection		TOF	Time of Flight
MALDI	Matrix-Assisted Laser Desorption/Ionization		UPLC	Ultraperformance Liquid Chromatography
			UV	Ultraviolet

Introduction

One of the analytical challenges posed by forensic science includes the identification and quantification of complex mixtures containing known, unknown, and suspect compounds within complex matrices. Ultra- and high-performance liquid chromatography (UPLC and HPLC) coupled with soft ionization techniques (e.g., electrospray ionization (ESI) or atmospheric pressure chemical ionization; APCI), along with low-resolution (triple quadrupoles and ion trap) and high-resolution (e.g., quadrupole–time of flight, Orbitrap, and Fourier transform–ion cyclotron resonance)

mass spectrometers, have significantly progressed the molecular-level characterization of complex drugs, metabolites, macrobiomolecules, and synthetic chemicals. In the past, gas chromatography (GC) coupled with mass spectrometry (MS) was recognized as one of the primary analytical techniques used in forensic laboratories. GC–MS was widely used for analysis of illegal substances in body fluids, testing fibers and blood from a crime scene, and detection of explosive residues. However, GC–MS-based techniques often require extensive sample cleanup and, for the analysis of polar compounds, the routine application of derivatization procedures. These limitations have been overcome by the advent of

LC–MS-based techniques. Moreover, the urgency in developing fast and reliable analytical methods with minimal sample preparation has driven solid-phase extraction (SPE) media and column manufacturers to offer a new means of rapidly and effectively cleaning up and injecting samples into mass spectrometers. Ionization sources, sample preparation techniques, emerging injection methods, matrix effects, and state-of-the-art LC–MS instrumentation are critically discussed in the following sections, along with the examples of applications to forensic science taken from the scientific literature. Throughout this article, HPLC is used interchangeably with LC.

Ionization Techniques

In the early 1970s, the introduction of samples into mass spectrometers was "the issue" limiting the development of reliable LC–MS systems. The challenge originated from the difficulty to (1) introduce a sample at atmospheric pressure (760 Torr) into a low-vacuum region ($<10^{-6}$ Torr) without disrupting the vacuum and (2) efficiently convert a liquid mobile phase into a spray of charged ions. The invention of the "thermospray" source along with the introduction of innovative MS designs, including multiple vacuum stages independently pumped, was what made LC and MS finally come together.

Nowadays, at the forefront of available ionization techniques, ESI is by far the most widely used ionization source. This is followed by an APCI source. ESI takes place as a result of impairing a strong electrical charge (kV) to the mobile phase emerging from the nebulizer. The spray of charged droplets undergoes size reduction by solvent evaporation. When the droplets have a sufficient charge density, sample ions are ejected from the surface of the droplets. This phenomenon is known as "ion evaporation" or "Columbian explosion." The main drawback of ESI is that the analytes can ionize in solution with multiple charges (e.g., doubly charged ions will appear in the MS spectra at $m/2z$). Moreover, ESI and other atmospheric pressure ionization (API) techniques suffer from "ion suppression" or "matrix effects," which often limit their direct applicability for quantitative assessment.

APCI produces protonated or deprotonated molecular ions by transferring (in positive mode) or abstracting (in negative mode) a proton from the molecule. The liquid sample coming from the HPLC is vaporized in a heated nebulizer, and it emerges in a plasma made of solvent ions formed within the atmospheric source by corona discharge. The corona discharge produces reactant ions, such as N_2^{o+} and N_4^{o+}, by electron ionization. These ions collide with the vaporized solvent molecules to form other reactant gas ions (e.g., H_3O^+ and $(H_2O)_nH^+$), which undergo repeated collisions with the analyte forming analyte ions. APCI is best suited for analysis of nonpolar and semipolar compounds. Both ESI and APCI provide a "soft" ionization of chemicals, allowing direct mass measurement of thermolabile and polar compounds, while minimizing "in-source" fragmentation.

The atmospheric pressure photoionization (APPI) source was introduced in early 2000. APPI allows ionization of nonpolar and semipolar compounds that usually are poorly ionized under ESI and/or APCI ionization conditions. The APPI source uses a krypton lamp, which emits photons at a specific wavelength, to optimize analyte ionization, while reducing in-source ionization of air and other common HPLC solvents (e.g., methanol and acetonitrile).

New generation ambient ionization methods that have been introduced since 2004 are the DART (direct analysis in real time), DESI (desorption electrospray ionization), and ASAP (atmospheric solids analysis probe) sources. Apart from their smart acronyms, each of these ambient ionization methods utilizes a plasma to ionize sample molecules or use molecules in the atmosphere, which then proceed to ionize the sample. The minimal sample preparation required for ambient ionization is very important to drastically reduce the analysis time. DART, DESI, and ASAP have numerous applications in which real-time "chemical fingerprinting" is required, or where ESI, APCI, and APPI are not effective in ionizing the compounds of interest. Ambient ionization techniques are useful to perform real-time analysis of surfaces, coatings, and materials, analysis of biological samples, in situ histological identification of tissues, food control analysis, drug discovery, pharmaceutical quality assessment, and counterfeit drugs. There are also numerous forensic applications, including the analysis of porous surfaces (e.g., paper) and postmortem analysis of amines from mammalian decomposition fluid or tissues.

Matrix-assisted laser desorption/ionization (MALDI) is a soft ionization technique for the analysis of biomolecules, biopolymers, and in general large organic molecules (e.g., DNA, RNA, proteins, sugars, lipids, oligosaccharides, bacteria, phosphopeptides, and synthetic polymers). Although the real mechanism of MALDI is still under debate, the process includes the following: (1) matrix material desorption triggered by a UV laser beam followed by (2) analyte ionization occurring in the hot plume formed during the ablation process of the upper layer of the highly UV absorbing matrix material. Variations of MALDI includes SELDI (surface-enhanced laser desorption ionization), SALDI (surface-assisted laser desorption/ionization), DIOS (desorption ionization on porous silicon), and SEND (surface-enhanced neat desorption) among others. For example, SELDI is mostly used to analyze proteins in tissue samples, urine, blood, body fluids, or other clinical samples.

Sample Preparation and Injection Techniques

To concentrate and cleanup samples for injection into LC–MS systems, off-line SPE is by far the most used sample preparation technique. SPE typically is performed with sample volumes ranging from milliliters to liters. Samples are loaded onto a preconditioned stationary phase, where analytes are retained based on their polarity or their acidic or basic properties. Cartridges are then washed, and analytes are eluted with excess solvent removed by evaporation. The most common SPE media commercially available include C8–C18 end-capped silica (for hydrophobic interactions), polymeric stationary phases (for hydrophilic/hydrophobic interactions), and mixed mode cationic and anionic resins (for hydrophilic/hydrophobic/ion-exchange interactions). SPE is widely used to extract, concentrate, and cleanup samples, but it is possibly the most "time-consuming" and therefore, expensive means of sample pretreatment. The major costs include the labor required to perform SPE, including method development, purchasing the SPE cartridges, that typically are used once and then disposed solvent usage and disposal, and the large volume of samples to be shipped. If SPE is performed on a stand-alone apparatus (SPE manifold + vacuum pump) or by online SPE instruments (automated SPE extractor), laboratories incur additional costs to purchase such equipment and to optimize, operate, and maintain SPE instrumentation.

Online SPE has been gaining importance in the last decade, as it combines recovery and cleanup typical of "off-line SPE" with minimal sample handling (e.g., centrifugation or filtration), allowing fast and relatively cheap high throughput of samples. However, online SPE requires purchasing of expensive instrumentation such as online SPE cartridges and precolumns, and possibly a second HPLC pump along with multiport valves for high-pressure applications.

Direct injection (DI) and large volume injection (LVI) sample injection techniques are performed simply by introducing crude samples straight into an analytical column followed by spectroscopic and/or spectrometric detection. DI usually employs small volumes (i.e., few microliters) of sample and is recommended when analytes are present at high concentrations in the matrix. LVI instead uses high sample volumes (i.e., 100–5000 μl) for analysis of chemicals present at low concentrations in the matrix. Compared with other techniques requiring extensive sample pretreatment, DI and LVI are easier to set up, only requiring small hardware modifications to existing autosamplers (e.g., LVI may only require a possible increase in loop size and/or upgraded analytical head). As for online SPE, with DI and LVI, tunable gradients can be set up to achieve "on-column" cleanup, while injection valves (usually mounted on most mass spectrometers) can be used to divert unwanted chromatographic slices to waste. Given that sample handling/pretreatment is usually the "rate-determining step" of sample throughput in analytical chemistry, LVI and DI represent valid and cheap alternatives to both off-line and online SPE. Method development and validation, as well as routine analyses are faster and cheaper with DI and LVI, as they reduce sample handling and material involved to a minimum. In the last decade, LVI and DI techniques have been increasingly gaining acceptance among analytical chemists. These sample injection approaches are emerging as analytical tools, which will possibly render SPE redundant for a number of analytical applications.

Matrix Effects

Analytes ionized by API sources are affected by matrix effects, which are responsible for suppressing and, less frequently, for enhancing their absolute response. This often results in variable detection limits and more importantly, in inaccurate quantitative results. The matrix effect was first reported by Tang and Kerbarle back in the early 1990s, where they observed that the detection capability, precision, and resolution in ESI were influenced by coeluting interferences. The matrix effect originates in the early stages of the ionization process and is usually expressed as:

$$\text{Matrix effect } (\%) = 100 \times (A_s - A_m)/A_s$$

where A_s and A_m are the area of the analyte in the standard solution and in the matrix, respectively. It has been reported that matrix components are thought to suppress the analyte response mainly by (1) changing viscosity and surface tension of mobile-phase spray, causing reduced evaporation efficiency, (2) competing with the analyte to gain or lose a charge, therefore limiting the ejection of ions from the charged spray, and (3) neutralization in gas phase via deprotonation reactions with high gas-phase basicity compounds using APCI. Different approaches have been proposed to compensate for matrix effects. These include (1) calibration methods (e.g., inclusion of deuterated homologues and standard addition method), (2) dilution of sample extracts (e.g., with LC mobile phase), (3) injection of reduced volumes (few microliters rather than tens of microliters), (4) specific sample preparation strategies (e.g., off-line and online SPE, protein precipitation), (5) improvement of chromatographic selectivity (e.g., employing different mobile-phase compositions and elution gradients), and (6) "echo-peak" technique.

By far, the most reliable and effective method to account for the matrix effect is the inclusion of deuterated homologues, as the analyte and the coeluting deuterated standard would be subject to almost identical matrix effects. However, deuterated homologues are quite expensive and are not always commercially available, which can limit their possible inclusion in an analytical assay. The second calibration method is the "standard addition method," which consists of analyzing the original sample followed by the same sample containing known amounts of an added standard. This calibration technique has proven to be effective to correct for matrix effects. Autosamplers can be programmed to accurately perform online multiple spiking of the original sample, making the standard addition method more accessible and less time-consuming.

Methods utilizing dilution of sample extracts and/or injection of reduced volumes aim to introduce less matrix into the API interface so that the resulting ionization of analytes is more efficient. The downside of this approach is that the analytes of interest are often at low concentration levels, so dilution of a sample extract or injection of a reduced sample volume also results in a lower absolute amount of analyte entering the mass spectrometer.

Both off-line and online SPE can be used to reduce the matrix effect mainly by selective extraction, inclusion of a "washing step," and selective elution. For example, to extract an acidic drug with a positively charged mixed mode anion-exchange resin, the sample pH should be buffered two pH units above the pKa of the acidic analyte to ensure the analyte is fully deprotonated. After extraction, a washing step with water and methanol is typically applied to selectively elute basic and neutral interferences from the stationary phase. Analyte elution is then performed using mixtures of basic methanol and acetonitrile. Similarly, with online SPE, it is possible to selectively extract and elute analytes, as well as add a washing step by eluting a weak elution strength mobile phase through the online SPE cartridge.

Protein precipitation is used to reduce the matrix effect in biological fluid analyses; however, different problems arise, such as incomplete protein precipitation, low analyte recoveries, and dilution of the final extract, thereby making SPE a better choice.

Changing the mobile-phase composition and elution gradient can improve the selectivity of the separation and is also an effective way to reduce the matrix effect. The two chromatographic areas to avoid are the solvent front, where polar unretained organic and inorganic species elute, and the end of the chromatographic run, where highly retained hydrophobic interfering compounds elute.

The "echo-peak" technique, proposed recently, involves injection of an analytical standard followed by injection of the sample extract, so that analytes in the standard and in the sample are eluting in a "similar chromatographic region" and therefore should be subject to a similar matrix effect.

Although it has been proven that matrix effects are compound and sample dependent, investigations on how the analyte response is affected by matrix components should be taken into consideration during the development and validation of new analytical methods. Understanding how matrix effects qualitatively and quantitatively affect analytical results is recognized as an important step toward "good laboratory practices."

Overview of State-of-the-Art LC–MS Instrumentation

The most commonly used instruments in laboratories around the world are triple quadrupoles (QqQ) and quadrupole–ion traps (Q-ITs). QqQs are known as "transmitting instruments," as the front (Q1) and end (Q3) quadrupoles are set to allow only certain m/z values or ranges to be transmitted for detection. QqQs also feature a collision cell (q), usually full of argon for fragmentation. Beside different acquisition modes, including MS scan, daughter scan, parent scan, neutral loss, and MS survey scan, QqQs feature the multiple reaction monitoring (MRM) data acquisition mode. In the MRM mode, a parent ion is selected in the first quadrupole, fragmented in the collision cell (q) and two (or more) formed daughter ions are selected in the third quadrupole. In MRM, one parent $\rightarrow$ daughter transition is used for quantitative assessment, while the second transition is used to confirm the presence of a certain chemical species in the sample. Monitoring the retention time along with the measured MRM ratio in both the sample and the calibration curve generally confirms detection. Sensitivity and selectivity make QqQ the instrument of choice to quantify low picogram–femtogram levels of known compounds in a variety of complex matrices.

Q-ITs are known as "trapping instruments," as they use constant direct current and radio frequency oscillating electric fields to trap ions. The strength of these systems is that they allow data acquisition in the selected reaction monitoring mode, increasing the specificity of detection of known molecules while offering high sensitivity and selectivity with low risk of false positives. Q-IT can be also operated in MS/MS or MS^n ($n = 2-10$) mode allowing, to some extent, structural elucidation of unknowns. Screening information-dependent acquisition is also used with Q-IT systems, where an automated switching between MS and MS/MS during a scan is triggered on the basis of certain threshold criteria. Both QqQ and Q-IT are generally operated at unit mass resolution, limiting their effectiveness for structural elucidation.

High-end MS systems combine high-resolution and high-resolution capabilities with the diagnostic feature of fragmentation (MS/MS and MS^n). So-called hybrid systems can comprise a combination of a quadrupole and a time of flight (Q-TOF) or a Q-IT coupled to a high-precision electrostatic ion trap (Q-IT-Orbitrap). Q-TOFs usually present a front quadrupole (Q) for parent ion selection, followed by a collision cell, in which ions are fragmented before being subjected to accurate mass analysis in a TOF mass spectrometer. TOF works by accelerating ions to the same kinetic energy. The time the ions take to travel through a defined path length is measured, and this information is used to calculate the mass-to-charge ratio for each ion. Q-TOFs are usually operated at 15 000 resolving power in "sensitivity mode," or at 30 000 resolving power in "mass resolution" mode. The latest generation Q-TOFs, introduced in the late 2010 by AB Sciex, feature 40 GHz, four-channel time-to-digital converter (TDC) and detector, enabling unprecedented speed acquisition rates (e.g., 100 scans per second with "MRM-like" sensitivity in MS mode and up to 50 scans per second in MS/MS mode) with high resolving power even in the low mass range. This allows for fast screening, identification, and quantitation on known, suspect, and unknown compounds in a few seconds. Given the fast scan rate of Q–TOF technologies, the inclusion of an UPLC for faster and more efficient chromatography is certainly an option to be considered to increase sample throughput. Recent developments in ion mobility separation (IMS) technology have enabled coupling to Q–TOF MS by Waters. The inclusion of a high-resolution traveling wave IMS cell allows ions to be separated on the basis of size and shape, as well as mass-to-charge ratio before being introduced in the mass analyzer.

The other class of hybrid instruments is based on the patented "Orbitrap" technology. These instruments, built by Thermo-Fisher Scientific, combine a Q-IT with a high-precision ion trap (Orbitrap). Orbitrap measures the oscillation of ions back and forth within an electrostatic field. A Fourier transform mathematical operation is then used to convert those frequencies to a mass spectrum. Q-IT can be operated as a mass analyzer independent from the Orbitrap, or as an ion storage and injection system for the Orbitrap mass analyzer. The Q-IT can be operated in full scan, single ion monitoring (SIM), MS/MS product ions, MS^n ($n = 2-10$), and SRM. The Orbitrap allows resolving power up to 100 000 at $m/z = 400$, with mass resolution less than 3 ppm with external calibration. The main strength of this hybrid system is that it allows multiple scan modes, multiple collision cells, multiple dissociation methods, multiple mass analyzers, and multiple detectors for MS^M experiments. For example, in the "dual detection" mode, low-resolution MS/MS or MS^n data can be acquired in the Q-IT, while at the same time high resolution (e.g., 100 000) and high mass resolution (<2 ppm, with internal calibration) MS data are acquired in the Orbitrap over the same analytical run. The main downside of the Q-IT Orbitrap is that MS resolution depends on the scan rate. The relatively slow scan rate of the Orbitrap at high resolving power somehow limits the applicability of this technology to fast UPLC separation. Nevertheless, Q-IT Orbitrap along with Q-TOF technologies offers unparalleled levels of structural elucidation though high resolution and high mass resolution fragmentation experiments.

Fourier transform–ion cyclotron resonance–mass spectrometers (FT–ICR–MSs) are the current pinnacle of MS performance. This type of mass analyzer is used to determine the mass-to-charge ratio (m/z) of ions based on the cyclotron frequency of the ions in a fixed magnetic field. FT–ICR–MS combines ultrahigh resolving power (~1 000 000) and very high mass accuracy (<1 ppm) along with various fragmentation techniques, achieving unprecedented characterization of unknown polar compounds in complex mixtures. FT–ICR generally offers 10–100 times higher mass resolution and mass accuracy than other mass analysis techniques, allowing direct determination of elemental composition ($C_XH_yO_zN_j...$) and molecular structure even without prior chromatographic separation (i.e., through direct infusion in ESI). Owing to the mass defect of the elements, FT–ICR is especially useful to study the molecular composition of large multiple charged biomolecules in complex mixtures. Forensic applications of FT–ICR are various and include the direct determination of ignitable liquids in criminal investigations of suspected arson fires. The drawback of both FT techniques (i.e., ICR and Orbitrap) is that the resolving power comes at the expense of scan speed. FT–ICR systems are also very expensive to purchase and operate, and this limits their widespread application in analytical laboratories. The main characteristics of the MS technologies described in this section are summarized in **Table 1**.

The values reported for resolving power, mass accuracy, sensitivity, dynamic range, and scan speed can vary from one MS manufacturer to another, and they should be considered as a broad guide only.

Application of LC–MS to Forensic Sciences

HPLC coupled with tandem MS has become the technique of choice for the analysis of pharmaceutical samples and biological specimens, particularly with reference to small molecule drugs and metabolites in biological matrices such as blood, plasma, serum, and other biological matrices. The advantage of LC over widely established techniques such as GC is the ability for the separation of compounds that are characterized by low to high molecular weight, having low volatility, are thermolabile, and that have a wide range of polarity (from highly polar to hydrophobic).

In the current available literature, the vast majority of forensic papers detailing LC coupled with tandem MS separations involve illicit drugs, therapeutic drugs, metabolites, and poisons. Several reviews have also been written on the subject. There are reports of LC–MS being used to separate amino acids and hypoxanthine in vitreous humor and cerebrospinal fluid with the potential to aid in postmortem interval estimation. Biogenic amines and amino acids in mammalian decomposition fluid have also been analyzed by DI LC–ESI–MS/MS. These compounds showed potential in relating semiquantitative concentrations and cyclic behavior in target compounds back to the estimation of postmortem interval. To a somewhat lesser extent, LC–MS/MS has also been used for the analysis of gunshot residues, explosives, fiber dye analysis, amino acid analysis from eccrine fingerprint deposits, and chemical and biological warfare agents.

Owing to their chemical instability and polarity, LC is often the technique of choice to separate explosives from other interferences. The analysis of explosives has been typically performed using LC with APCI in the negative ion mode. The identification of compounds such as nitrate esters and 2,4,6-trinitrotoluene is of high importance for forensic identification of postblast debris at bombing scenes and also for the detection and monitoring of trace amounts that may be

Table 1 Resolving power, mass accuracy, sensitivity, linear dynamic range, scan speed, strength, and weakness of various commercially available mass spectrometry (MS) spectrometers

Mass spectrometer	Resolving power (mass/FWHM)[a]	Mass accuracy (ppm)[b]	Sensitivity	Linear dynamic range	Scan speed[c]	Strength	Weakness
QqQ	Up to 5000[d]	~5–50	fg–pg (SRM, multiple reaction monitoring (MRM))	10^4–10^6	Up to 15 000 Da/s	• Reliable for quantitation • MRM data acquisition • Low risk of false positives • High-performance liquid chromatography (HPLC)/Ultraperformance liquid chromatography (UPLC) ready • Relatively cheap	• Limited diagnostic power because of low sensitivity in MS scan • Limited resolution and MS accuracy
Q-IT	Up to 10 000	~5–50	fg–pg (SRM, MS scan)	10^3–10^4	Up to 66 700 Da/s	• Reliable for quantitation in SRM • Good diagnostic power in MS^n • Information-dependent acquisition data • HPLC/UPLC ready • Relatively cheap	• Resolution depends on scan rate • Limited MS accuracy/resolution
Q-TOF	Up to 40 000 at $m/z \sim 300$	< 3[e] < 2[f]	fg–pg (MS scan)	10^2–10^4	100 Hz in MS scan and 50–100 Hz in MS/MS at 30 000 resolving power	• Fast scan rate • Good diagnostic power because of HR MS/MS capability • Good MS accuracy • Unlimited m/z range • HPLC/UPLC ready	• Resolution depends on m/z range and decreases at low m/z • High sensitivity or high-resolution modes are possible but not simultaneously • Loss of sensitivity moving to HR • Expensive • Daily MS calibration required
Q-IT Orbitrap	Up to 100 000 at $m/z \sim 400$	< 3[e] < 2[f]	fg–pg (MS scan)	10^4	1 Hz at m/z 400 and 100 000 resolving power[g]	• High diagnostic power because of HR MS/MS and MS^n capability • Information-dependent acquisition data • Very good MS resolution and accuracy • Dual detections on IT/FTIR • MS^M capable • MS calibration done weekly	• Resolution depends on scan rate • Limited m/z range (50–4000) • HPLC only is recommended for most applications • Expensive
FT-ICR	Up to 1 000 000 at $m/z \sim 400$	< 1	Low fg–pg (MS scan)	10^4		• Ultimate diagnostic power because of ultra HR MS/MS capability • Very high MS resolution and accuracy	• Very expensive to purchase, operate, and maintain

FT-ICR, Fourier transform–ion cyclotron resonance MS; HR, high resolution; Q–IT, 2D linear ion trap MS; Q–IT Orbitrap, 2D linear ion trap Orbitrap MS; QqQ, triple quadrupole MS; Q-TOF, quadrupole–time of flight (FWHM).

[a]Mass resolution indicates the ability to discriminate two ions with an m/z difference of Δm; resolving power is measured as the observed m/z value divided by the full width at half maximum height (FWHM).

[b]Mass accuracy indicates the difference between the measured m/z and the calculated m/z; mass accuracy is expressed as the relative error $= (Mass_{measured} - Mass_{calculated})/Mass_{calculated} \times 10^6$ and is given in ppm.

[c]MS scan speed: is given as Dalton per second for QqQ and Q–IT or number of scans per second at a given m/z and a fixed resolving power for Q–TOF, Q-IT Orbitrap, and FT-ICR. Resolution and resolving power change as a function of m/z, and the extent of the change depends on the mass analyzer.

[d]Usually QqQ are operated at unit mass resolution.

[e]Mass accuracy with external calibration.

[f]Mass accuracy with internal calibration.

[g]MS/MS is done in the Q–IT for speed.

released into the environment. The use of APCI coupled to tandem MS provides a highly specific and sensitive analytical method for the identification of explosive compounds through the formation of an adduct ion in the APCI source. Work by Sanchez et al. developed an LC–APCI–MS method with high levels of reproducibility following a relatively fast analysis time (<30 min) with detection limits in the femtogram-per-liter (fg/L) range. When coupled with tandem MS in forensic cases, the potential for false positives is minimized, making this an attractive analytical method in the forensic field.

Forensic cases involving illicit drugs can present a multitude of issues with regard to analysis, typically as drug seizures often involve large sample numbers with unknown origin and composition. As samples are usually a mixture containing unknown analytes and interferences, analyte extraction and sample cleanup procedures available to the analyst can be varied. Typically, SPE is the most commonly used viable technique. Initially, LC–MS was used where samples were not amenable to analysis by GC–MS because of low volatility (or those that cannot be made volatile by derivatization) or lack of thermal stability. Examples include analysis of LSD (lysergic acid diethylamide), benzodiazepines, tricyclic antidepressants (amitriptyline), and acetaminophen.

High-resolution TOF MS has led some laboratories to implement TOF methods for screening and identification purposes. The ability of TOF to give elemental compositions of compounds allows for the development of exact mass databases. This is particularly useful when new so-called "designer drugs" are developed, as it allows the drug itself as well as the potential metabolites to be monitored. An example of the application of LC–TOF–MS can be seen in the work by a research group based in Finland, where hair samples were analyzed for 35 different drugs from different classes. The results obtained were in good agreement with the established procedures that utilized analysis of blood and urine by GC–MS.

Currently, LC coupled with isotope ratio mass spectrometry (IRMS) has limited applications in forensic science. Only as recently as 2004, some of the first results were published, detailing the separation of drug molecules using this technique. For example, paracetamol and aspirin, two mass produced and readily available drugs, were separated and identified by monitoring the δ^{13}C values with direct loop injection. Although IRMS has the potential to be applied to several forensic samples and cases, the relatively new nature of the technique means that each laboratory has its own experimental design, acceptable standards, calibration methods, and data analysis. IRMS has

also been used in a forensic context to analyze explosives, to analyze cotton fibers, and for bullet characterization.

> *See also:* **Methods:** Gas Chromatography–Mass Spectrometry; Mass Spectrometry; **Toxicology:** Methods of Analysis—Confirmatory Testing; Toxicology: Overview and Applications.

Further Reading

Bell, S., 2009. Forensic chemistry. Annual Review of Analytical Chemistry 2, 297–319.

Benson, S., Lennard, C., Maynard, P., Roux, C., 2006. Forensic applications of isotope ratio mass spectrometry – a review. Forensic Science International 157, 1–22.

Busetti, F., Backe, W.J., Bendixen, N., Maier, U., Place, B., Giger, W., Field, J.A., 2012. Trace analysis by large-volume injection into liquid chromatography-mass spectrometry. Analytical and Bioanalytical Chemistry 402 (1), 175–186.

Ferrer, I., Thurman, E.M., 2009. Liquid Chromatography Time-of-flight Mass Spectrometry: Principles, Tools and Applications for Accurate Mass Analysis. John Wiley and Sons, New York.

Gentile, N., Besson, L., Pazos, D., Delemont, O., Esseiva, P., 2011. On the use of IRMS in forensic science: proposals for a methodological approach. Forensic Science International 212, 260–271.

Jessome, L.L., Volmer, D.A., 2006. Ion suppression: a major concern in mass spectrometry. LCGC North America 24 (5), 83–89.

Krauss, M., Singer, H., Hollender, J., 2010. LC–high resolution MS in environmental analysis: from target screening to the identification of unknowns. Analytical and Bioanalytical Chemistry 397, 943–951.

Krummen, M., Hilkert, A.W., Juchelka, D., 2004. A new concept for isotope ratio monitoring liquid chromatography/mass spectrometry. Rapid Communications in Mass Spectrometry 18, 2260–2266.

Pullen, F., 2010. The fascinating history of the development of LC-MS; a personal perspective. Chromatography Today 3 (1).

Swann, L.M., Busetti, F., Lewis, S.W., 2012. Determination of amino acids and amines in mammalian decomposition fluid by direct injection liquid chromatographyelectrospray ionisation-tandem mass spectrometry. Analytical Methods 4 (2), 363–370.

Tang, L., Kebarle, P., 1991. Effect of the conductivity of the electrosprayed solution on the electrospray current – Factors determining analyte sensitivity in electrospray mass-spectrometry. Analytical Chemistry 63 (24), 2709–2715.

Relevant Websites

Gas Chromatography–Mass Spectrometry

E Stauffer, Commissariat d'identification judiciaire, Police cantonale Fribourg, Fribourg, Switzerland

Abbreviations

EIC	Extracted ion chromatogram		MS	Mass spectrometry or mass spectrometer
EIP	Extraction ion profile		*m/z*	Mass-to-charge ratio
FID	Flame ionization detector		SIM	Selected ion monitoring
GC	Gas chromatography or gas chromatograph		TIC	Total ion chromatogram
GC × GC	Two-dimensional comprehensive gas chromatography		TOF	Time-of-flight

Glossary

Chromatogram A graphical representation of chromatographic data. It is the record of detector response as a function of time.

Extracted ion chromatogram Graphical representation of the abundance of a single ion versus retention time (RT). Abbreviated EIC.

Extracted ion profile Graphical representation of the abundance of the sum of several ions versus RT. Abbreviated EIP.

Gas chromatography A separation technique in which the mobile phase is a gas. Gas chromatography is always carried out in a column. Abbreviated GC.

Gas chromatography–mass spectrometry A separation technique (gas chromatography) coupled with a detection technique (mass spectrometry). Abbreviated GC–MS.

m/z **ratio** Mass-to-charge ratio: the mass of an ion divided by its charge.

Mass spectrometry An analytical technique that is used to identify unknown compounds, to quantify known compounds, and to elucidate the structure and chemical properties of molecules. This is done by converting components of a sample into rapidly moving gaseous ions and separating them on the basis of their mass/charge ratio. Abbreviated MS.

Resolution In chromatography, it is the measure of the separation of two components. It is a function of the peak width and RT. In mass spectrometry, it is the measure of the ability of the instrument to distinguish ions of different masses.

Retention time The length of time required for a compound to pass through a chromatographic column and be detected.

Total ion chromatogram Graphical representation of the abundance of a full scan range versus RT. Abbreviated TIC.

Two-dimensional comprehensive gas chromatography A procedure in which all of the separated sample components are subjected to an additional separation step. This is achieved by coupling (using a thermal modulator) two different chromatographic columns. Abbreviated GC × GC.

Introduction

Chromatographic techniques have the power to separate analytes from complex mixtures. However, separating these analytes would not be useful if it was not possible to either detect them or, better yet, to identify them. For this reason, different detectors have been used throughout the years. With simple thin-layer chromatography, or paper chromatography, the naked eye, or an alternate light source, would suffice to detect some analytes. Eventually, a chemical reaction would be triggered. On the more modern gas chromatograph (GC), flame ionization detector (FID) or photoionization detector is used, depending on the type of analytes to be detected.

However, the common ground of all these detectors is that they only provide two types of information: the number of analytes and their concentration. Nowadays, particularly in the forensic field, this information does not suffice. One needs to know the identity of a compound or of a series of compounds from a complex mixture.

Mass spectrometry (MS) does not simply detect the presence or absence of analytes; it provides structural information about the molecule, often leading to its identification. As such, it is an extremely powerful instrument, but one which quickly becomes impractical when analyzing complex mixtures of analytes. As a matter of fact, its optimal use consists in analyzing pure compounds. This is when the chances of identifying the unknown compounds are greatest.

Thus, the separation power of GC and the analytical power of MS needed to be combined in one full analytical instrument in order to exploit the capabilities of both techniques to their maximum. Chromatography was invented in 1906 by Russian chemist Mikhail Semenovich Tswett and MS in 1913 by British physicist Joseph John Thomson. GC was invented in 1952 by James and Martin, which allowed the first combined use of GC and MS as a hyphenated technique in 1956 by Roland Gohlke and Fred McLafferty.

The typical setup of a gas chromatograph–mass spectrometer (GC–MS) is shown in **Figure 1**. The sample is injected into the GC, separated through the column, then goes through the transfer line and is analyzed in the MS. A computer controls the overall instrument.

GC–MS does not simply add the capability of one to another; it literally multiplies both capabilities and leads to a full analytical instrument. While the specificities of GC alone (with a simple detector such as FID) and MS alone are not great, the combination of both results in an enormous increase in specificity. If two compounds were not to be separated by the chromatographic process, there is a good chance that they would exhibit different structural data and, thus, be distinguished through the MS. Similarly, two

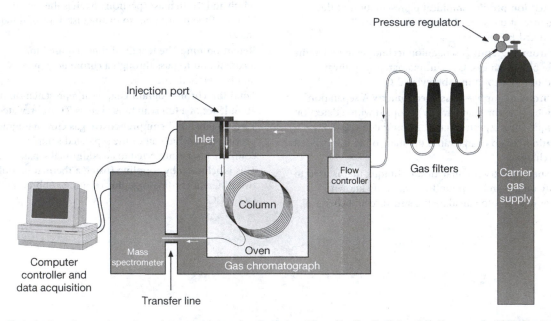

Figure 1 Typical setup of a gas chromatograph–mass spectrometer. Reproduced from Stauffer, E., Dolan, J.A., Newman, R., 2008. Fire Debris Analysis. Elsevier Academic Press, Burlington, MA, p. 246. Copyright © 2008, Elsevier.

compounds exhibiting a very close mass spectrum may have a good chance of being separated by the chromatographic process, thus allowing for their distinction. However, one will always find compounds that have very close chromatographic and structural characteristics, for which GC–MS will not be able to make a distinction. This is the case with some structural isomers.

Multiplied Powers

When considering a regular chromatogram, obtained with a simple detector such as FID, the sole information available is the curve constituting the chromatogram. One can extract the retention time (RT) and the peak area, thus the concentration of the analyte if a calibration curve is available. However, it is very possible that another analyte elutes exactly at the same time as the analyte of interest. As such, it is not possible to be sure that the peak in question is the sought-after analyte.

When considering a chromatogram obtained from a GC–MS, the resulting data actually hides another whole layer of information. For each point on the curve, it is possible to extract a mass spectrum, providing the structural information of the analyte(s) eluting at that time. **Figure 2** illustrates this.

This information consists of a series of mass-to-charge ratio (m/z) peaks with their relative abundance. The most important of these peaks is the molecular ion peak, which corresponds to the unfragmented compound, and the base peak, the most intense peak of the spectrum, normalized to 100%. The other peaks represent the fragments of the molecule, fragments with distribution and relative abundances that are characteristic of the structure of the molecule.

As such, in addition to RT data, one benefits from structural data to identify an analyte. If each analyte in the complex mixture is completely separated from the others, it is then possible to identify with certainty the nature of each analyte. This is where the power of GC–MS comes into play: the capability of identifying almost every component from a complex mixture.

Different Ways of Looking at Data

One great advantage of GC–MS lies in the different ways it is possible to acquire and look at data. Typically, one acquires data using a full scan range, which means that the MS is configured to acquire all the m/z within a given range (e.g., 33–400 m/z). The resulting data is called a total ion chromatogram (TIC). It can be seen as a chromatogram identical to one that would be obtained with another simple detector, except that each data entry making the chromatographic pattern contains a full mass spectrum.

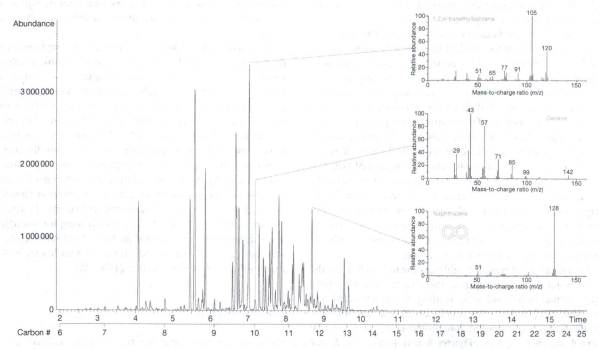

Figure 2   Total ion chromatogram of a 75% evaporated gasoline sample. Each point on the chromatogram contains a full mass spectrum, as shown with the peaks of 1,2,4-trimethylbenzene, decane, and naphthalene.

The great advantage of the TIC is that all the analytes present in a given sample are detected and recorded. Thus, the chromatogram truly and fully represents the overall content and the analyst has a good panoramic view of what is in the sample. A few disadvantages also exist. The first one is that carrying out a full scan takes time and the resolution of the chromatogram may not be optimal, thus not allowing for a full separation of some analytes. Second, if one is only interested in the presence of a given or a set of given analytes, these may not stand out within the overall pattern of the mixture. Third, the sensitivity of the full scan range is not as good as the one that would result from the scan of just a few ions. The more m/z are scanned, the worse the sensitivity. Thus, some trace analytes may simply not be detected or distinguished from the background signal.

As an alternative, it is possible to use a selected ion monitoring (SIM) rather than a full scan. In this situation, the user decides which ions must be monitored. The MS will then scan only for these m/z and ignore all of the others. This allows for a quasi-complete suppression of the matrix interferences: only the analytes sought after are detected. It also significantly improves the sensitivity since each scan covers only a couple of dozens m/z rather than a full range of 300 or more m/z, for example. One major disadvantage in this configuration is that the analyst completely loses the overall view of the sample. Because only a partial image of what is in the sample is obtained, it is not possible to take into account the overall composition of the sample during the interpretation of the results. If the full scan corresponds to a wide-angle view, SIM would correspond to a super telephoto view.

Some analyses are better carried out using SIM and some others using a full scan. Analyzing a sample of unknowns would naturally require a full scan, since one does not know in advance which analytes are sought after. Conversely, performing routine analysis for some specific known metabolites in trace amounts, for which their presence and quantity are not influenced by the content of the matrix, is best performed using a SIM configuration. In fire debris analysis, for example, even though the analytes sought after are quite known, it is not recommended to carry out only SIM. As a matter of fact, it is important to have a good view of the content given off by the sample's matrix, since it is taken into consideration in the interpretation of the results. However, it is recommended in some instances, after performing a full scan range, to carry out a second analysis, under a SIM mode, to improve the sensitivity of the GC–MS and to provide further data.

When using a full scan, it is still possible to benefit from the mass spectral data. Starting from the TIC, one can selectively display some individual m/z, leading to an extracted ion chromatogram (EIC), as shown in **Figure 3**, or a sum of several m/z, leading to an extracted ion profile (EIP), as shown in **Figure 4**. When comparing **Figures 3 and 4** to **Figure 2**, one quickly realizes the advantage of extracted ions in interpreting chromatograms and identifying classes of compounds.

This provides the advantage of first having a complete view of the sample through the full scan and second, looking at specific compound-related patterns through the EIC or EIP. This allows the data to be filtered through the partial removal of matrix interferences or other analytes and for the pertinent data to be revealed. The great advantage of EIC and EIP is that it does not filter at the data acquisition, thus the full data always remain available.

Requirements

In order to combine a GC to a MS, a few conditions must be met.

First of all, the sample must be suitable for injection into the MS. This is naturally achieved because the mobile gas phase exiting the GC with the analytes is perfectly suitable for entry into the MS, where it will first be ionized and then filtered, to be finally detected.

Second, it is important to realize that in order to obtain a mass spectrum, a certain amount of time is required. This time depends on the type of detector and the scan range (typically something like 30–400 m/z). The larger the scan range, the longer the scan takes. In order to obtain full separation of coeluting compounds, the resolution of the chromatogram must be high enough to allow for the separation of the peaks. Thus, if two compounds elute within 4 s and the MS makes one full scan every 4 s, the compounds will not be separated and the specificity of the instrument will strongly suffer.

In practice, all modern MS exhibit a scan rate high enough (2–10 Hz) to allow for a good chromatographic resolution. However, the chromatographic resolution obtained with a regular GC–MS is definitely lower than that obtained from a GC–FID, for example. The reason is that the FID has a scan rate of approximately 200 Hz. Actual MS scan rates are not considered an issue for regular GC–MS; however, they become a concern with new methods such as two-dimensional comprehensive gas chromatography–mass spectrometry (GC × GC–MS). In this case, all the components coming out of the first GC are subjected to a second separation (based on different characteristics) in another chromatograph. The scan rate must be of at least 50 Hz, thus allowing for enough MS scans during the time required for the second separation. This scan rate can only be achieved with a different MS technology: time-of-flight mass spectrometry (TOF-MS).

Instrumentation

There are very few variations regarding the GC. All modern chromatographs use a capillary column with a coated stationary phase, which offers a very high resolution. The

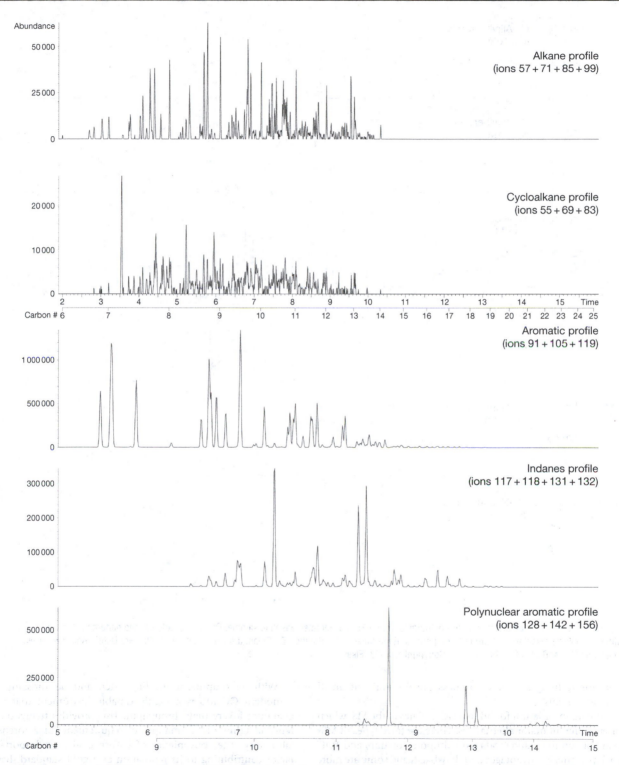

Figure 3 Example of extracted ion profiles from a 75% evaporated gasoline sample. One can clearly see the patterns exhibited by the different classes of compounds. Reproduced from Stauffer, E., Dolan, J.A., Newman, R., 2008. Fire Debris Analysis. Elsevier Academic Press, Burlington, MA, p. 246. Copyright © 2008, Elsevier.

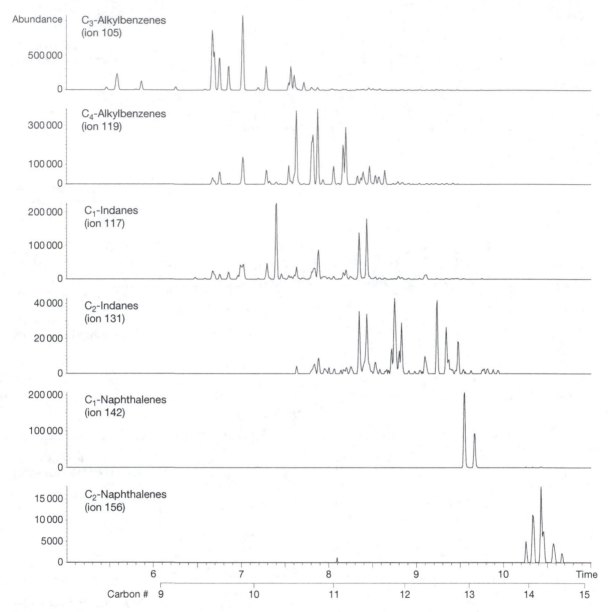

Figure 4 Example of extracted ion chromatograms from a 75% evaporated gasoline sample. One can clearly see the patterns exhibited by the different ions representative of organic compounds. Reproduced from Stauffer, E., Dolan, J.A., Newman, R., 2008. Fire Debris Analysis. Elsevier Academic Press, Burlington, MA, p. 246. Copyright © 2008, Elsevier.

injection techniques, split or splitless, are also available on all gas instruments.

The main variation found in a GC–MS lies in the MS, which offers different major alternatives. There are three types of MSs available on the market today: quadrupole, ion trap, and TOF. Each presents its advantages and drawbacks and some are more suitable for some types of analysis than others. **Figure 5** shows a typical GC–MS setup in a forensic laboratory.

With the computer controlling system and the autosampler, a modern GC–MS is a highly capable instrument that can guarantee a very high throughput. This provides tremendous relief in terms of the manpower requirement for a forensic laboratory. The convenience of its use is also an important factor contributing to its reputation as a gold standard. Basically, it is possible to fully automate the separation of 150 complex mixtures, including the identification of their analytes.

Figure 5 An Agilent 6890N-5975 gas chromatograph–mass spectrometer. An Agilent 7683B autosampler is present above the GC on the left. Reproduced from Stauffer, E., Dolan, J.A., Newman, R., 2008. Fire Debris Analysis. Elsevier Academic Press, Burlington, MA, p. 246. Copyright © 2008, Elsevier.

In other words, one can let the instrument run by itself for several days without worrying about it and just concentrate on the interpretation of the results.

Forensic Applications

The applications of GC–MS to the forensic field are extremely diverse. Basically, all analytes that can go through a GC can be analyzed by GC–MS. So, everything that is volatile under 300–500 °C, does not decompose at these temperatures, and exhibits a molecular weight below 600 amu (up to 1000 with new MS) can be analyzed by GC–MS. This leaves room for many different applications, which is the reason why GC–MS is one of the most versatile analytical instruments that one can find in a forensic laboratory.

The most common applications in forensic science are the analysis of fire debris, drugs, explosives, and toxins. Other applications, less often encountered, include the analysis of hydrocarbons in environmental crime investigations, vegetable oil residues, and, when using pyrolysis-GC–MS, paints, fibers, and plastics.

In fire debris analysis, ignitable liquid residues extracted from fire debris samples are analyzed in order to detect for the presence of an ignitable liquid, possibly used as an accelerant at a fire scene. These samples consist of complex mixtures of hydrocarbons, often unresolved. The power of MS is fully exploited by using EIC and EIP to interpret the complex chromatograms. Because of the type of organic molecules, it is possible to extract different profiles using several specific ions and, thus, to facilitate the interpretation of the chromatograms.

Fire debris analysis is mostly concerned with qualitative, maybe semiquantitative, analysis.

In drug analysis, the forensic scientist is presented with unknown samples of powder or liquid and must determine the nature and quantity of its components. Not all drugs can be analyzed through GC–MS, given that some are sensitive to the heat of the injector, for example. However, the analysis can be carried out on most drugs. With many drugs, such as cocaine and heroin seized from the street, GC–MS provides a very thorough analysis. Determining that an active substance is present and at what quantity is an important element for the prosecution. However, identifying the adulterants and the contaminations/impurities also present brings a whole new edge to the investigation. As a matter of fact, adulterants and contaminations/impurities are used to perform drug profiling, a method capable of establishing links between individual seizures and identifying the drug network. GC–MS is a primordial tool in this regard, since it allows for a complete separation and identification of unknowns in a substance. Because MS is not always optimal in quantitative analysis, it is often used in conjunction with other detectors, such as FID, to obtain both qualitative and quantitative accurate results.

In explosive analysis, the goal is to analyze seized substances or residues of possible explosives. Again, the scientist not necessarily being aware of the type of substance involved, GC–MS's versatility brings a great advantage to the identification of explosives and residues. It is considered as a sufficient technique to allow for the identification of many explosives without any other testing.

Forensic toxicology is a wide field concerned with the detection of drugs, metabolites, or toxins in the human body. This ranges from simple medication to alcohol consumption and other drug-related substances. The samples are body fluids such as blood and urine and other body samples, such as hair, tissues, or fingernails. The separation and identification power of GC–MS presents an interesting advantage, even though not all substances can be run through GC–MS. A forensic toxicology lab includes many other analytical instruments such as liquid chromatography, capillary electrophoresis, and immunoassay. As such, GC–MS is one important tool among others, such as liquid chromatography–mass spectrometry (LC–MS), in a forensic toxicology laboratory.

In environmental crime investigation, one is often confronted with hydrocarbon spills or contaminations. Because hydrocarbons are extremely complex mixtures of hundreds of components, the separation power exhibited by GC and the characterization power of MS are fully necessary. As a matter of fact, environmental laboratories often use specific parameters, in terms of separation, that are quite different from parameters used in traditional forensic settings, because of the complexity of the substances they are dealing with. The ultimate goal of an environmental investigation is not to simply demonstrate that the pollution exists, as one rarely needs a GC–MS for that;

however, it is to identify the source of the pollution. In this scope, different techniques of oil spill fingerprinting, for example, have been developed over the years.

The analysis of vegetable oils (or rather their derivates) by GC–MS has been well known for many years in the food industry. In fire investigation, a method has been developed to recover vegetable oil residues from a fire that could have been triggered by the autoignition of oil residues. This method uses GC–MS to analyze the extract and to identify the type of oil involved. GC–MS is clearly the best instrument to carry out this type of analysis, because of its combined separation and analytical power.

Finally, many other samples can be analyzed by GC–MS. This is the case with plastics, polymers, paints, and fibers whose composition can be analyzed after being pyrolyzed. This provides important information regarding a common source between a questioned and a comparison samples. In this regard, pyrolysis-GC–MS was developed, allowing for the direct injection of pyrolysis products into the GC. This technique, less often encountered, has also been used for many years in different crime laboratories around the world.

See also: **Chemistry/Trace/Drugs of Abuse:** Analysis of Controlled Substances; **Chemistry/Trace/Explosives:** Explosives: Analysis; **Chemistry/Trace/Fire Investigation:** Analysis of Fire Debris; Interpretation of Fire Debris Analysis; **Methods:** Gas Chromatography; Liquid Chromatography–Mass Spectrometry; Mass Spectrometry; **Toxicology/Drugs of Abuse:** Drugs in Hair; Validation of Twelve Chemical Spot Tests for the Detection of Drugs of Abuse.

Further Reading

Gohlke, R.S., McLafferty, F.W., 1993. Early gas chromatography/mass spectrometry. Journal of the American Society for Mass Spectrometry 4, 367–371.

Levine, B. (Ed.), 2010. Principles of Forensic Toxicology, third ed. American Association for Clinical Chemistry, Washington, DC.

Silverstein, R.M., Webster, F.X., Kiemle, D., 2005. Spectrometric Identification of Organic Compounds, seventh ed. John Wiley and Sons, Hoboken, NJ.

Smith, F.P. (Ed.), 2005. Handbook of Drug Analysis. Elsevier Academic Press, Burlington, MA.

Sparkman, O.D., Penton, Z., Kitson, F.G., 2011. Gas Chromatography and Mass Spectrometry: A Practical Guide, second ed. Elsevier Academic Press, Burlington, MA.

Stauffer, E., Dolan, J.A., Newman, R., 2008. Fire Debris Analysis. Elsevier Academic Press, Burlington, MA.

Terrettaz-Zufferey, A.L., Ratle, F., Ribaux, O., Esseiva, P., Kanevski, M., 2007. Pattern detection in forensic case data using graph theory: Application to heroin cutting agents. Forensic Science International 167, 242–246.

Wang, Z., Stout, S., 2006. Oil Spill Environmental Forensics: Fingerprinting and Source Identification. Elsevier Academic Press, Burlington, MA.

Wong, R.C., Tse, H.Y. (Eds.), 2005. Drugs of Abuse: Body Fluid Testing. Humana Press, Totowa, NJ.

Yinon, J., Zitrin, S., 1996. Modern Methods and Applications in Analysis of Explosives. John Wiley and Sons, Hoboken, NJ.

Zoro, J.A., Hadley, K., 1976. Organic mass spectrometry in forensic science. Journal of the Forensic Science Society 16 (2), 103–114.

Relevant Websites

http://www.agilent.com—Agilent.
http://www.perkinelmer.com—PerkinElmer Inc.
http://www.restek.com—Restek Corporation.

Nonchromatographic Separation Techniques

SW Lewis, Curtin University, Perth, WA, Australia

This article is a revision of the previous edition article by C. Bommarito, volume 1, pp. 172–179, © 2000, Elsevier Ltd.

Glossary

Derivatization Use of a chemical reaction to convert analyte into a form that may be more detectable or amenable to separation.

Enantiomers A pair of chemical compounds whose molecular structures are nonsuperimposable mirror images of each other.

Ion mobility spectrometry Instrumental analytical technique based upon separation via differential migration of gas phase ions through an electric field.

Liquid–liquid extraction Transfer of a dissolved substance from one liquid phase to another immiscible (or partially immiscible) liquid in contact with it.

Solid-phase extraction The separation method by which compounds adsorbed on a solid phase are preferentially removed by use of a suitable solvent. Processes involved are essentially chromatographic in nature.

Introduction

Many types of evidence that are encountered in the forensic science laboratory consist of complex mixtures of substances. The complexity of these materials is a double-edged sword to the forensic scientist. The more complex and variable a mixture, the greater is its probative value when comparing known and questioned samples. However, complex mixtures also create analytical problems, as most compounds need to be relatively pure in order to be identified by analytical techniques, such as spectroscopy. While chromatographic and electrophoretic separations are used widely in forensic science, other separation techniques are also important. These can be used both to clean up samples before analysis and for determining useful information about the sample of interest. This chapter provides an overview of nonchromatographic/electrophoretic separation techniques that are often encountered in forensic analysis.

Physical Separations

Physical separations are commonly used in forensic chemistry. Examination of a mixture under a stereoscope may yield variation of its component particles. These particles may vary in their shape, size, color, opacity, texture, or other physical properties, which can be observed microscopically. The particles may then be physically separated from the mixture. Particle selection or "picking" is the major separation technique used in most areas of trace evidence. A skilled examiner can recognize and pick out critical particles in explosive residue. Paint examiners can select uncontaminated particles out of a mixed smear of paint for examination and comparison. This type of separation can also be utilized in mixtures containing cocaine hydrochloride. This salt form of cocaine has a translucent, shale-like appearance, which can be easily distinguished from the coarse grains of most diluents and excipients used as cutting agents in cocaine mixtures.

Forensic geologists have long used particle size to separate soil components for analysis. A novel example of this is the use of a mesh screen for separation of sand grains onto an SEM stub for automated elemental analysis and mineral identification (**Figure 1**). Manual separation of particles should always be explored before attempting a chemical separation.

Volatile Materials

Volatile materials are often present in drug and fire debris cases submitted to forensic laboratories. These materials (primarily solvents and flammables) can be easily separated from relatively nonvolatile substances by techniques such as distillation, sublimation, absorption–elution, and solid-phase microextraction (SPME).

Figure 1 Photograph of sand particles separated using a mesh screen and mounted on an SEM stub. Courtesy McVicar, M.J., Graves, W.J., 1997. The forensic comparison of soils by automated scanning electron microscopy. Journal of the Canadian Society of Forensic Science 30, 241–261.

Distillation and sublimation are the techniques occasionally used in analysis of drugs. Amines, such as amphetamine and methamphetamine, are relatively volatile and can be flash distilled to separate the drug from a complex mixture. Dimethylsulfone is currently one of the most common cutting agents used with methamphetamine in the United States. It is far more volatile than methamphetamine, sublimating at 35–38 °C (90–100 °F). It can be easily removed from methamphetamine by placing the mixture on a watch glass and sublimating the dimethylsulfone over a steam bath. The purified methamphetamine can then be analyzed via infrared spectrometry.

Examination of fire debris for the presence of ignitable liquids (e.g., petrol, kerosene, and diesel) requires that the residual amounts of these liquids be separated from the debris. Samples of debris are sealed into airtight nylon bags or paint cans and heated to volatilize the ignitable liquid into the headspace of the container. The vapor in the headspace can then be analyzed directly by removing a portion with a syringe. Often the concentration of the volatile material in the headspace is insufficient for direct analysis. In these cases, a process known as absorption–elution can be used to concentrate the volatile species. In this process, the volatiles are absorbed by a material (usually activated charcoal) and then extracted from the absorbent in a concentrated form by a solvent. The process of absorption can be active or passive. In active or dynamic absorption, the material containing the volatile species is

heated and the vapor forced through a vessel containing absorbent. A typical setup may consist of charcoal housed inside a disposable pipette or hypodermic needle connected to a vacuum pump. The open end of the vessel is placed in the headspace of the sample and the air containing the ignitable liquid is drawn through the vessel. The charcoal would then be removed for solvent extraction of the captured volatile substances (elution). Passive absorption entails placing the absorbent material directly inside the airtight container while heating to volatilize the ignitable liquids. Vaporized molecules of the volatile species contact the absorbent in a random fashion. Because the volatile compounds are not forced to contact the absorbent, the time of exposure of the absorbent to the vapor must be dramatically increased in order to ensure proper absorption.

SPME is a relatively recently introduced technique that is being used increasingly in forensic chemical analysis. This technique is based around a special syringe containing a spring-loaded fiber coated with a bonded phase. The fiber in the syringe can be extended and retracted. The sample containing the volatile compounds is sealed in an airtight container. The syringe is then inserted into the headspace of the container and the fiber extended and exposed. The container is heated for a period of time to release the volatile species into the headspace. The volatile substances are adsorbed onto the fiber, which are then retracted into the syringe. The syringe is then used for injection into a gas chromatograph. The fiber is extended from the syringe into the injector port and the heat of the injector port desorbs the volatile species from the fiber (**Figure 2**). SPME may also be used to concentrate analytes from a liquid solution onto the SPME fiber. A variety of bonded phase chemistries are commercially available allowing manipulation of selectivity. This technique is increasingly being used in the areas of solvent, drug, fire debris, and high-explosives analysis.

Chemical Separations

Solvent Extraction

Although chemical separations have increasingly become chromatographic in nature, solvent extraction is still frequently used in the forensic laboratory, especially in drug analysis, where chemical separations are generally followed by confirmatory qualitative techniques such as infrared spectrometry. Solvent extractions can be either single phase or multiphase in nature. The theory and process of both types of solvent extractions are based on many criteria, the most important of which is solubility.

In a single-phase extraction, components of a mixture are separated based on the solubility of the components in a solvent. In this type of extraction, solvent selection is critical. The target component of the mixture must either be soluble in

Figure 2 Photograph of an SPME fiber inserted into headspace of a sampling vial. Courtesy R Mindrup, Supelco Inc.

the solvent, while all remaining components are insoluble, or vice versa. The solvent is added to the mixture and then filtered to separate undissolved solute and solvent. If the target compound is soluble in the solvent, it is then recovered by evaporation of the solvent. If the target compound is insoluble in the solvent and the other components are soluble, the filter paper is then dried and the material is recovered. This process is also known as "solvent washing." In complex mixtures, it is usually not possible to find a suitable single solvent to separate all components of the mixture. If this is the case, several solvents are selected and applied in a serial manner to effect the separation. The selection of solvent generally proceeds from the solvents in which few compounds are soluble (hexane and ether) to those in which a moderate number are soluble (acetone, dichloromethane, and chloroform) to those in which most substances are soluble (alcohols and water). Use of acidified or basified solvents may increase the specificity of the extraction.

In multiphase or liquid–liquid extractions, components of a mixture are separated based primarily on their solubility in two immiscible solvents. The mixture to be separated is added to a solvent (generally aqueous) and second solvent (usually organic) is then added. The components of the mixture then partition into the solvent or solvents in which they are most

soluble. This type of extraction is extremely flexible as solvent components can be selected, mixed, their pH changed, heated or cooled, used in vastly different proportions, and so on, to effect the desired separation. The most commonly modified variable in multiphase extractions is the pH of the aqueous solvent phase, which is varied by addition of strong acids or bases. The solubility of components dissolved in this phase is directly affected by these pH changes. By adjusting the pH of the aqueous phase to make a particular analyte relatively insoluble in the aqueous phase, the stage is set for the analyte to be extracted into the second solvent, which is then added.

Drugs, in particular, are amenable to separations based on changes of pH in multiphase extractions, lending to a terminology based on their behavior on extraction. "Acidic drugs" are relatively insoluble in acidic solutions and may generally be extracted from acidic aqueous solutions into an organic solvent. "Basic drugs" are relatively insoluble in basic solutions and may generally be extracted from basic aqueous solutions into an organic solvent. "Neutral drugs" are generally unaffected by changes in pH and they will usually stay in whichever phase they are more soluble.

An example of such an extraction is the separation of a mixture of codeine, butalbital, and acetaminophen. **Figure 3** is a flow diagram illustrating this extraction. Butalbital is an acidic drug, whereas codeine and acetaminophen are basic drugs. The drug mixture is added to some acidic water, mixed, and dichloromethane is added. The butalbital will partition into the organic phase, which can then be drawn off and evaporated to recover the drug. The codeine and acetaminophen remain in the aqueous phase, which are then made basic with the addition of a strong base, such as NaOH. Additional dichloromethane is then added. Although acetaminophen is a basic drug, it is mostly insoluble in dichloromethane; therefore, most will remain in the aqueous phase. The organic phase containing the codeine and a small amount of acetaminophen are drawn off and additional basic water is added. The remaining acetaminophen is partitioned into the aqueous phase in which it is more soluble, and the organic phase can then be drawn off and evaporated to recover the codeine.

Solvent extraction is used in the analysis of fiber dyes not only to extract a dye from an evidential fiber, but also to classify the dye. A comprehensive approach to fiber dye extraction has been developed by the Forensic Science Service in the United Kingdom; an example of this approach is shown in **Figure 4**. The reader is directed to the Further Reading for details.

Solid-Phase Extraction

In some situations, liquid-phase extraction may not be suitable. For example, a separation may not be possible if the compounds to be separated are very similar in polarity, or exhibit similar acid/base properties. There also may be issues when sample amount is limited or there are significant matrix

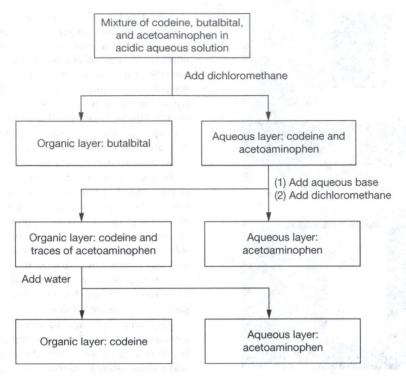

Figure 3 Flow diagram for separation of acid and basic drugs by solvent extraction.

issues, for example, biological samples such as blood and urine. In these situations, solid-phase extraction, which relies upon adsorption of components on a solid phase, can be used. The adsorbed analytes can be preferentially removed by use of a suitable solvent (**Figure 5**). This approach, which strictly is a miniaturized form of liquid–solid chromatography, is widely used in analytical chemistry to "clean up" dirty samples and preconcentrate target analytes for subsequent measurement. A wide range of different adsorbent chemistries are available in prepackaged polymer or glass cartridges. SPME (described above) is a recent variation on this theme.

Purification via Chemical Reaction

Purification can also be achieved by salt formation or chemical derivatization. Both techniques involve addition of a chemical to react with the target component to form a complex, which has properties allowing it to be separated from the rest of the mixture. An example of this is the separation of inorganic acids from a solution. These types of liquids are often encountered in poisoning cases (e.g., a suspect puts an acidic solution in a victim's drink) or in clandestine laboratories where acids are utilized in the production of illicit drugs. Knowing that an acid plus a base yields a salt plus water, concentrated ammonium hydroxide is added to the acidic solution, which forms an

ammonium salt with the acid. As these salts are insoluble in acetone, addition of this solvent precipitates the ammonium salt from solution. Infrared analysis of the ammonium salt allows the analyst to determine the composition of the acid originally in solution. Production of ammonium chloride indicates that hydrochloric acid was present, and ammonium sulfate indicates that sulfuric acid was present.

There are hundreds of chemicals used to derivatize compounds with the added benefit that the complex formed by derivatization is generally more stable than the underivatized compound. An example of this additional stability is the silylation of psilocybin with BSTFA (N, O-bis-(trimethylcilyl)-trifluoroacetamide). Psilocybin (the active drug present in psilocybin mushrooms) undergoes thermal decomposition on heating due to the loss of the dihydrogen phosphate ester group; therefore, due to the heat of the injector, gas chromatography–mass spectrometric (GC-MS) analysis produces chromatograms and spectra that are identical with psilocin. Silylation of the psilocybin before GC-MS analysis "locks in" the phosphate group, eliminating its thermal instability on injection.

Separation of Enantiomers

Enantiomers (isomers that are mirror images of each other) are traditionally difficult to separate. Enantiomers have

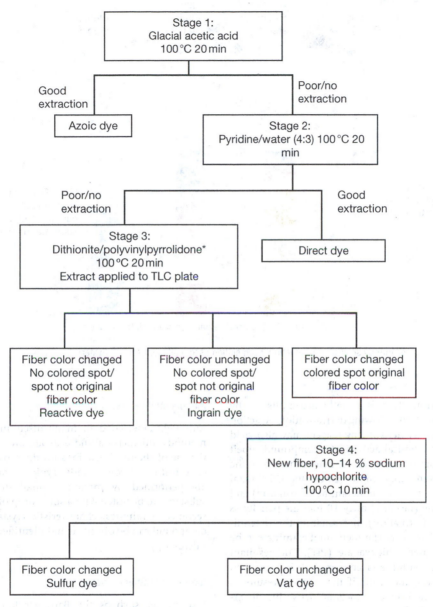

*sodium dithionite (80 mg), polyvinylpyrrolidone (30 mg), sodium hydroxide (10%, 450 μl), and water (9 ml); use immediately and discard excess

Figure 4 Extraction and classification of dyes from cotton and viscose. Reproduced from Lewis, S.W., 2009. Analysis of dyes using chromatography. In: Houck, M.M., (Ed.), Identification of Textile Fibres. Woodhead Publishing, Cambridge, pp. 203–223 after Wiggins, K.G., 1999. Thin layer chromatographic analysis of fibre dyes. In: Robertson, J., Grieve, M., (Eds.), Forensic Examination of Fibres, second ed. Taylor & Francis, London.

identical melting points, boiling points, density, dissociation strengths, reaction rates, and solubilities. The only variable in which they can be distinguished is the direction of their refraction of plane-polarized light (optical activity). Products formed by the reaction of enantiomers with optically inactive reagents are identical, as are the rates of reaction. The reaction rate of enantiomers with reagents that are themselves optically active is not identical and may be so different that one isomer does not react at all. Derivatization of enantiomers with optically active reagents may lead to their separation and their

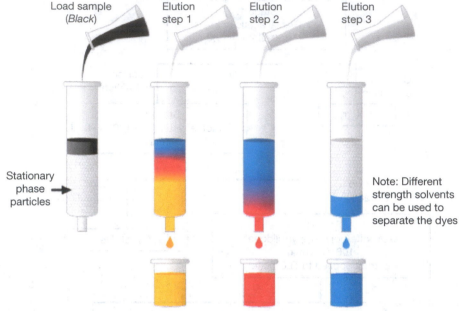

Load sample
(*Black*)

Elution
step 1

Elution
step 2

Elution
step 3

Stationary
phase
particles

Note: Different
strength solvents
can be used to
separate the dyes

One SPE cartridge can separate all three dyes

Figure 5   Separation of dye mixture by solid-phase extraction. Each elution used a different solvent (water).

isomeric determination. This is usually accomplished by a chromatographic method following derivatization. Reaction with an optically inactive derivatizing reagent may also yield information about the optical activity of a compound, albeit indirectly. An example of this is in the determination of the optical isomer of methamphetamine. Under the US Federal sentencing guidelines, D-methamphetamine (+ rotation) and D,L-methamphetamine (racemic) carry 10-fold the penalty as L-methamphetamine (- rotation), necessitating the determination of the optical isomer. The methamphetamine can be derivatized with phenylisothiocyanate (PIT). The resultant derivative precipitates with the racemic mixture but not with the single enantiomers; therefore, if the reaction results in precipitation of the derivative, a racemic derivative of D,L-methamphetamine–PIT forms and its chemical structure is confirmed via infrared spectrometry. If no precipitation occurs, standard L-methamphetamine can be added to the PIT-sample complex and if precipitation occurs after the addition, it can be concluded that D-methamphetamine was initially present. If no precipitation occurs, the entire process must be repeated with the addition of standard D-methamphetamine instead of L-methamphetamine. If precipitation occurs upon the addition of D-methamphetamine to the PIT-sample complex, it can be concluded that L-methamphetamine was initially present.

Microcrystalline Tests

Although superseded in many disciplines by instrumental methods, microcrystalline tests are an excellent example of the use of chemical reactions for the separation and identification of some compounds. Typically microcrystalline tests are performed by mixing a small drop containing the substance to be tested with a small drop of reagent. After a few seconds to minutes, characteristic crystals of the resulting compound can be observed and identified via polarized light microscopy.

Ion Mobility Spectrometry

Instruments, such as the Barringer Ionscan, have become increasingly popular due to their portability, sensitivity, and speed of analysis. Ion mobility spectrometry (IMS) has been used as a forensic screening technique in the areas of drug and explosive residue. In this technique, samples are swabbed with a filter paper and inserted into a heated sampling device, which serves to ionize the sample. The ions are released into a separation region that is under the influence of an electric field. The ions move through this region at a rate proportional to their mass and against the flow of a gas. Negatively charged ions move quickly through the field toward the cathode and their time of flight recorded. This time of flight can be compared to the time of flight of a variety of substances across the field allowing tentative identification of the substance. These instruments are commonly used in airports to rapidly screen luggage for explosives and drugs. In the last few years, they have been increasingly used at the scenes of clandestine laboratory and bombing investigations and prison inspections.

Acknowledgment

The author would like to acknowledge the contribution of Christopher Bommarito, who wrote this chapter for the first edition, as a significant amount of the original material has been used in the revised chapter.

See also: **Chemistry/Trace/Fibers:** Color Analysis; **Chemistry/Trace/Fire Investigation:** Analysis of Fire Debris; **Chemistry/Trace/Forensic Geosciences:** Soils; **Methods:** Capillary Electrophoresis: Basic Principles; Capillary Electrophoresis in Forensic Biology; Capillary Electrophoresis in Forensic Chemistry; Chromatography: Basic Principles; Gas Chromatography; Gas Chromatography–Mass Spectrometry; Liquid and Thin-Layer Chromatography; Liquid Chromatography–Mass Spectrometry; Presumptive Chemical Tests.

Further Reading

Bell, S., 2006. Forensic Chemistry. Pearson Education, Upper Saddle River, NJ.

Frenkel, M., Tsaroom, S., Aizenshtat, Z., Kraus, S., Daphna, D., 1984. Enhanced sensitivity in analysis of arson residues: an adsorption-tube gas chromatograph method. Journal of Forensic Sciences 29, 723–731.

Harris, D.C., 2010. Quantitative Chemical Analysis, eighth ed. W. H. Freeman and Company, New York.

Hopen, T.J., Kilbourn, J.H., 1985. Characterization and identification of water soluble explosives. Microscope 33, 1–22.

Houck, M.M., Siegel, J.A., 2010. Fundamentals of Forensic Science, second ed. Elsevier, Burlington, MA.

Karpas, Z., 1989. Forensic science applications of ion mobility spectrometry. Forensic Science Review 1, 103–119.

Kirkbride, K.P., Klass, G., Pigou, P.E., 1998. Application of solid-phase microextraction to the recovery of organic explosives. Journal of Forensic Sciences 43, 76–81.

Lewis, S.W., 2009. Analysis of dyes using chromatography. In: Houck, M.M. (Ed.), Identification of Textile Fibres. Woodhead Publishing, Cambridge.

McVicar, M.J., Graves, W.J., 1997. The forensic comparison of soils by automated scanning electron microscopy. Journal of the Canadian Society of Forensic Science 30, 241–261.

Moffat, A.C., Jackson, J.V., Moss, M.S., Widdop, B. (Eds.), 1986. Clarke's Isolation and Identification of Drugs in Pharmaceuticals, Body Fluids, and Post-mortem Material, second ed. The Pharmaceutical Press, London.

Ren, Q., Bertsch, W., 1999. A comprehensive sample preparation scheme for accelerants in suspect arson cases. Journal of Forensic Sciences 44, 504–515.

Skoog, D.A., West, D.M., Holler, F.J., Crouch, S.R., 2004. Fundamentals of Analytical Chemistry, eighth ed. Brooks/Cole, Belmont, CA.

Souter, R.W., 1985. Chromatographic Separations of Stereoisomers. CRC Press, Boca Raton, FL.

Wiggins, K.G., 1999. Thin Layer Chromatographic Analysis of Fibre Dyes. In: Robertson, J., Grieve, M. (Eds.), Forensic Examination of Fibres, second ed. Taylor & Francis, London.

Spectroscopic Techniques

KF Lim, Deakin University, Burwood, VIC, Australia
SW Lewis, Curtin University, Perth, WA, Australia

This article is a revision of the previous edition article by K.P. Kirkbride, volume 1, pp. 179–191, © 2000, Elsevier Ltd.

Nomenclature

AAS Atomic absorption spectroscopy
AES Atomic emission spectroscopy
cm^{-1} Unit used to measure the number of wavelengths per centimeter
DRIFTS Diffuse reflectance infrared Fourier transform spectroscopy
IR Infrared
IRS Internal reflectance spectroscopy

NMR Nuclear magnetic resonance
SEM–EDX Scanning electron microscopy–energy-dispersive X-ray
SEM–WDS Scanning electron microscopy–wavelength-dispersive spectroscopy
UV–vis Ultraviolet–visible
XRF X-ray fluorescence

Glossary

Chemiluminescence The emission of radiation (light) by a sample, after the sample undergoes a chemical reaction.
Fluorescence The emission of radiation (light) by a sample, after the sample absorbs radiation (light), usually of a different wavelength.
Spectrometer An instrument designed to measure the amount and wavelength distribution of light either absorbed or emitted by a sample.

Spectroscopy A set of techniques which measure the amount and wavelength distribution of light either absorbed or emitted by a sample.
Synchrotron A large device (usually 100–200 m in diameter) that produces extremely intense light by accelerating electrons close to the speed of light, around an almost circular track.

Introduction

Spectroscopic techniques are widely used in forensic laboratories for quantitative and qualitative analysis. The techniques described in this chapter are those that are most commonly encountered in forensic laboratories. Generally, these can be classified as being used for either identification or measurement of substances or elements, although some techniques can be used for both.

Identification of Substances

Infrared Spectroscopy

Infrared (IR) spectroscopy is unsurpassed as a universal technique for the identification of the class of compounds present within a specimen. For example, it is very easy to identify fibers on a generic basis such as acrylics, nylons, and polyesters, or paints on a generic basis such as alkyds, acrylics, urethanes, and nitrocellulose. With the advent of computerized spectral databases and chemometrics, it is now possible to extend the technique to allow subgeneric discrimination. Unique identification of a particular substance is possible if the sample is not a mixture. However, as similar substances within a particular class have similar functional groups, it is often difficult to discriminate between substances within a class, particularly if mixtures of members of the class are present. **Figure 1** gives the spectral data for three common phthalate ester plasticizers. Another example of the limitation of the technique is differentiation of paints within the alkyd class.

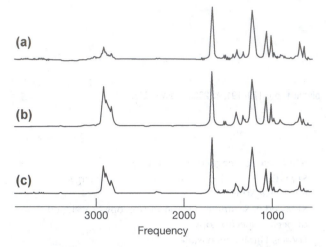

Figure 1 Infrared spectral data from three phthalate ester plasticizers: (A) dimethyl phthalate; (B) diisooctyl phthalate; and (C) dihexyl phthalate.

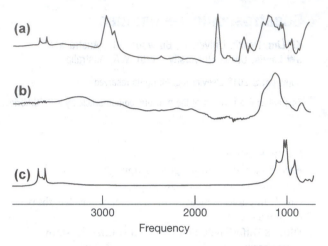

Figure 2 Infrared spectroscopy of paint films allows identification of inorganic compounds as well as the polymeric binder. In this example, neither the binder nor the inorganic substances dominate the spectrum. (A) Paint film; (B) infrared spectrum for silica; and (C) infrared spectrum for kaolin.

IR spectroscopy can be used to elicit structural information that might be difficult or impossible to arrive at using other techniques. One area of great utility is the characterization of chemical isomers. For example, the diastereoisomers ephedrine and pseudoephedrine are difficult to distinguish by mass spectrometry, and depending on the stationary phase used, might exhibit identical retentions in a gas chromatograph. As absorption wave numbers depend on molecular geometry, IR spectroscopy can distinguish between diastereoisomers (e.g., ephedrine and pseudoephedrine), positional isomers of aromatic substances (e.g., the various isomers of dimethoxyamphetamine, or trimethyl benzene), other stereoisomers (e.g., cocaine, allococaine, pseudococaine, and pseudoallococaine), and isomeric functional groups (e.g., butyl nitrite, isobutyl nitrite, and sec-butyl nitrite). Subtle chemical changes can result in significant changes in the IR absorption. For example, the N–H stretch in amine salts of drugs is found between 2500 and 3000 cm^{-1}, while the N–H stretch in their free bases is found well above 3000 cm^{-1}.

IR spectroscopy can provide information relating to the total composition of the specimen, unlike chromatographic techniques that usually require an extraction step and have restrictions due to volatility and solubility. Such techniques therefore can only provide partial information as to the specimen. In the examination of paint, for example, IR spectroscopy can provide information as to the polymeric binder as well as the inorganic extenders and pigments. **Figure 2** shows the spectrum of a paint specimen and spectra for kaolin and silica. Spectral features due to those minerals as well as the polymer are evident in the spectrum of the paint. Inorganic halides are virtually transparent to IR radiation; therefore, the presence of, for example, common salt or potassium bromide in a specimen cannot be deduced. Metals and some of their oxides also do not give useful data.

However, while quantitative measurements are possible using IR spectroscopy, they are difficult. First, the limit of detection of a substance in the presence of another is about 5%. IR spectroscopy is therefore not a good technique for the detection or identification of trace copolymers, residual solvents, low-level pigments, some additives in polymer samples (e.g., fibers or paints), manufacturing impurities, or trace contaminants in illicit drugs. Second, the matrix contribution must be accounted for in quantitative IR spectroscopy. Hence, the matrix must be well characterized. For example, relatively accurate quantitative analysis of unknown mixtures of heroin in sucrose can be performed by using a set of calibration data comprising various known mixtures of heroin in sucrose, and if no other substances are present in the mixture, but the level of heroin in glucose cannot be determined using heroin–sucrose calibration data.

The presence of different substances in a mixture can mask or disguise the absorption of other components. **Figure 3** shows the spectrum obtained from a sample of colored matter (apparently electrical wire insulation) taken from a pair of wire cutters suspected of being used to disable a burglar alarm. Spectral features due to the polymer (polyvinyl chloride) are almost nonexistent; the majority of peaks are due to plasticizer (a phthalate ester, or a mixture of them) and calcite. As a means of comparison between the recovered chips of plastic and insulation taken from wire in the burglar alarm, IR spectroscopy is particularly poor. Spectral features, due to the important polymer component, are masked by peaks due to additives.

IR spectroscopy can be carried out on microscopic specimens (down to about 10 μm^2) using an IR microscope. This instrument is simply a device that condenses the IR beam from

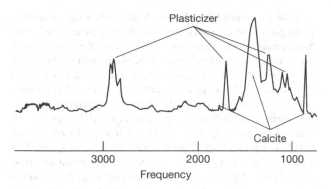

Figure 3 Infrared spectrum recorded from a small piece of plastic electrical insulation. Peaks indicated are due to plasticizer or calcite. In this spectrum, the inorganic fillers dominate; therefore, the polymeric substance (polyvinylchloride) is very difficult to identify.

its standard size (usually about 10 mm) to much smaller dimensions (about 0.18 mm). This task is accomplished with a microscope that is also used to allow high-magnification viewing of the specimen and accurate positioning of it in the beam. The technique is referred to as IR microscopy or, more accurately, IR microspectroscopy.

IR microspectroscopy is the usual technique employed in the analysis of small samples of paint (e.g., motor vehicle accidents, breaking, and entering), single textile fibers (evidence of contact), particulate material (explosive residues such as ammonium nitrate, smokeless powder, etc.), and concentrated extracts of low-dosage drugs (e.g., an extract from a lysergic acid diethylamide (LSD) dose evaporated to a microscopic spot). It is possible to record spectra from a few nanograms of material using an IR microscope.

In practice, IR microspectroscopy differs a little from IR spectroscopy. Sample preparation is a little more tedious, as manipulations must be carried out with the aid of a microscope. In most instances, steps must be taken to reduce the thickness of the specimen to about 10–30 μm, otherwise bad artifacts will be evident in the spectrum. As with any other spectroscopic technique, the homogeneity of the specimen is an important issue. For example, in some paint samples, the granule size of some inorganic fillers can be relatively large: on the microscopic scale, some samples are quite heterogeneous. Even though it is possible to see very small objects (<10 μm) with the IR microscope, diffraction of the IR beam inhibits the acquisition of high-quality spectra. A description of diffraction and its effects on microspectroscopy is beyond the scope of this chapter; the reader is referred to the bibliography for useful references.

Much of the above has described the measurement of absorbed IR radiation being transmitted or passing through a specimen. There are two other techniques in widespread use in forensic laboratories; in both internal reflectance spectroscopy (IRS, sometimes referred to as attenuated total reflectance spectroscopy) and diffuse reflectance spectroscopy, the IR

radiation interacts with the surface of a sample instead of passing through the sample.

In IRS, the IR beam is caused to reflect inside a special crystal that is in contact with the sample. Some components of the IR electromagnetic radiation extend beyond the crystal and interact with the surface of the sample to a depth of about 1 μm. The absorption of the IR radiation by the specimen is recorded as the IRS spectrum. The physics of IRS means that absorption of longer wavelengths (smaller wave numbers) is enhanced compared to the absorption of shorter wavelengths.

In diffuse reflectance spectroscopy, the IR beam is directed onto a finely powdered sample. The IR beam is reflected from both the surface layer and from particles below the immediate surface. In a manner similar to other IR techniques, the absorption of IR radiation by the sample is recorded as the diffuse reflectance spectrum. Note that the acronym DRIFTS (diffuse reflectance IR Fourier transform spectroscopy) is sometimes used, where the Fourier transform refers to the type of spectrometer used to collect the IR spectrum.

Raman Spectroscopy

Raman spectra look like, and give similar information to, IR spectra. As Raman signals arise from a simultaneous absorption/emission event, while IR signals arise from absorption only, some peaks will present in only either IR or Raman spectra, while most peaks will present in both.

Raman spectroscopy can be done with any single-wavelength incident beam, which is higher in energy than the IR absorption, but in practice, visible laser sources are often used. Fluorescence from the specimen (e.g., ink) or from the background matrix (e.g., paper) can make it difficult to detect the Raman signals, but this is usually overcome by use of a different light of slightly longer wavelength.

There are several advantages of Raman spectroscopy. First, the single-wavelength incident beam permits the use of laser light sources, whereas the sources in IR spectroscopy must cover all IR wavelengths, requiring the use of less intense light sources. Second, the minimum beam diameter and spatial resolution is related to the wavelength, which means that a Raman source can be focused to about 1 μm, significantly smaller than for IR. This has special advantages for Raman microspectroscopy. This means that if two different substances are present side by side, such as adjacent layers of paint or the two components of a bicomponent fiber, it is much easier to achieve a spectrum of one of the substances free of spectral interference from the other. Third, as Raman spectroscopy is not a transmission technique, there is no requirement to make the specimen thin enough to transmit radiation, as is the case in IR microspectroscopy; therefore, specimen preparation is very simple. Fourth, specimens can easily be analyzed as solutions in water or as films on a glass microscope slide, as these media do not absorb the visible Raman beam; this is not possible for

IR spectroscopy. Finally, developments in confocal Raman microspectroscopy will allow accurate control over the probe beam so it can be brought into focus in a very small volume within the specimen, not just on its surface. This will allow evaluation of the entire specimen, and might be a useful way of avoiding excess fluorescence arising from surface contamination, textile brighteners, etc.

X-ray Fluorescence and Scanning Electron Microscopy–Energy-Dispersive X-ray

X-ray fluorescence (XRF) is primarily a method for identifying the elemental composition of a sample. The way in which the atoms are combined or bonded to other atoms in the sample does affect the energies of the XRF, but this subtle change in energy is difficult to use for identification, unless there is additional information from other analyses. Therefore, XRF is used to determine the chemical elements present in the specimen, but not the chemical speciation or functional group of those elements. For example, XRF can be used to identify particles containing chlorine arising from chlorate-, perchlorate-, or hypochlorite-containing improvised explosive devices, but XRF is not used to distinguish these oxyanions from each other, or from chloride, which is not characteristic of explosive residues. Similarly, in cases of black powder explosions, XRF can be used to identify the presence of potassium and sulfur, but not to prove whether the sulfur is present as one of its oxyanions, or as elemental sulfur, or sulfide.

MicroXRF is a version of XRF that is used for the analysis of microscopic specimens. A light guide is used to "focus" X-rays in a spot about 10 μm in diameter. The specimen is viewed under low magnification with the aid of a video camera, which allows control over the area illuminated by the X-ray beam and therefore the region in the specimen that is analyzed.

X-rays will penetrate a long way into the specimen and interact with a relatively large volume of the specimen. Therefore, with thin, microscopic specimens, such as small flakes of glass or thin pieces of paint, most of the X-ray beam will pass right through and fluorescence will be minimal. Hence, XRF is most useful for the elemental analysis of relatively large, easy-to-find specimens such as thickly layered paints, big chips of glass, fibers, and pieces of automotive accessories.

Emission of X-rays can also be achieved by irradiating the specimen with an electron beam, which causes similar electronic excitation and subsequent X-ray emission. The spectral information is the same as from XRF, but this process is not called fluorescence because the initial excitation is not from the absorption of electromagnetic radiation. In scanning electron microscopy (SEM), as an electron beam is moved over the specimen, back-scattered electrons and secondary electrons, which are emitted from the specimen, are detected. The correlation between the number of detected electrons and the position of the electron beam builds up a point-by-point picture of the specimen. The electron beam also causes X-ray emission. The correlation between the X-ray wavelength and intensity and the position of the electron beam builds up an elemental map of the specimen. As the electron beam does not penetrate the sample to any great extent, this spectroscopic technique examines the chemical elements present in the surface of the specimen. The emitted X-rays can be analyzed by passing the X-rays through a special crystal that acts like a prism and disperses the radiation in space. This technique is referred to as wavelength-dispersive spectroscopy (WDS). Alternatively, the X-rays can be analyzed on the basis of their energy: this approach is called energy-dispersive X-ray (EDX) microanalysis, or energy-dispersive spectroscopy (EDS). While wavelength-dispersive spectrometers have superior performance, EDX spectrometers are more commonly used in forensic laboratories because of their lower cost.

In SEM–WDS and SEM–EDX, the electron microscope can achieve a wide range of magnifications simply by causing the electron beam to impinge on either a very small area (high magnification, with less than 1 μm diameter) or relatively large area (low magnification) of the specimen. SEM–WDS and SEM–EDX give higher spatial resolution than XRF and without the problems of X-ray emission from underlying layers or the mounting substrate. For large homogeneous samples, inductively coupled plasma or atomic absorption techniques, or even XRF, have significantly lower limits of detection than SEM–WDS and SEM–EDX. However, for specimens that are heterogeneous on microscopic scales, SEM–WDS and SEM–EDX are far superior to the other techniques.

For example, one common application of SEM–EDX is in the detection and analysis of gunshot residue (GSR) particles. Most GSR particles are characterized by their spherical shape and the presence of lead, barium, and antimony. If atomic absorption spectroscopy (AAS) or XRF was used to find lead, barium, and antimony in a sample, interpretation would be difficult, because these other techniques would be unable to distinguish between true GSR and microscopic heterogeneous mixtures of pure lead particles, pure antimony particles, and pure barium particles, a situation that does not point to the presence of GSR particles.

Both XRF and the hyphenated SEM X-ray techniques work best for heavy elements, which have large numbers of electrons in each atom. With appropriate signal processing, the SEM image can be tuned to show only elements of high atomic mass such as lead, while light elements remain invisible. Under these circumstances, searching a large matrix for minute amounts of heavy elements, such as those in GSR particles, can be automated, as long as there is enough contrast between the heavy elements and the matrix.

Although SEM–EDX has a few shortcomings, it is a very versatile and efficient technique for elemental analysis.

Although it suffers from an apparently high limit of detection, the ability to analyze submicrometer particles or specimen areas compensates to a great extent. If a particle or unusual region in the specimen can be found using the imaging options, then it can be analyzed, giving the technique an extremely low working limit of detection. Furthermore, the instrument allows imaging of specimens at high or low magnification with very high depth of focus. This facility can provide useful morphological information relating to trace evidence, such as fiber cross section and surface morphology. Finally, an important consideration is that often the specimen needs little or no treatment before analysis.

Nuclear Magnetic Resonance Spectroscopy

In a forensic context, nuclear magnetic resonance (NMR) spectroscopy finds its greatest application in the analysis of organic compounds. However, the impact and use of NMR in the forensic context has been limited by the high purchase cost of NMR spectrometers, the operating cost of liquid helium and liquid nitrogen to maintain the cold temperature of the superconducting magnets, the limitation that analytical mixtures must be relatively simple as commercial instruments with interfaces to chromatographic techniques are not available and the relatively high limits of detection.

The main use of NMR in the forensic context is to analyze and characterize illicit drugs (especially new designer drugs) and unusual precursors or intermediates in clandestine laboratories. NMR is normally operated in one of two modes, proton mode, which detects signals from the nuclei of hydrogen atoms, and carbon-13 mode, which detects signals from ^{13}C nuclei. In carbon-13 mode, it is usual to see a signal for every nonequivalent carbon atom within the specimen. Therefore, if the specimen is a pure sample heroin, for example, 21 distinct signals at characteristic frequencies are observed. This is an extremely high level of discrimination. In proton mode, the situation is analogous.

The ability of NMR to provide enormous structural detail becomes a limitation in the case of complex mixtures, because it is difficult to determine which signals are associated with which component in the mixture. Furthermore, NMR is often not able to resolve large numbers of overlapping signals, especially those that arise from very similar environments, such as the spectra of polymers and oligomers. Therefore, NMR is not useful in the forensic discrimination of paints or fibers, or in trace analysis, for example, detection of explosives in bombing debris, or drugs in body fluid.

One of the greatest benefits of NMR spectroscopy is the predictive structural information that can, with skill, be elucidated from the spectrum of an unknown substance. The number of distinct carbon and hydrogen atoms within the unknown molecule can be deduced from the carbon-13 and proton spectra. Furthermore, the proton NMR spectrum gives information about which protons are neighbors to other protons. The presence of heteroatoms and carbon–carbon multiple bonds can be inferred by careful examination of the position of each peak in the carbon-13 and proton spectra. Finally, more sophisticated NMR spectra, using complicated sequences of radio pulses, can be used to determine not only the connectivity of the moieties, but also the three-dimensional arrangement of parts of the unknown substance.

Specimen preparation is very simple; the substance can be dissolved in a suitable solvent (heavy water, deuterochloroform, and deuterated methanol) or basic drugs can be extracted from alkaline aqueous solution using a suitable solvent (deuterochloroform and carbon tetrachloride). If the instrument is calibrated and an internal standard is included in the protocol, then the test can be quantitative as well as qualitative. The extremely high level of discrimination gives the test a very high probative value. If required, NMR can be used to probe other nuclei, such as ^{31}P or ^{33}S, though the low natural abundance of some isotopes makes the collection of those spectra very difficult and time-consuming. Finally, as the sample can be recovered from the solvent, NMR is also a nondestructive technique.

Quantification of Substances

Spectroscopic methods can be used to measure the quantities of a substance present in a sample. The Beer–Lambert law (or the Beer–Lambert–Bouguer law) states that the absorbance of radiation at a particular wavelength is proportional to both the distance the radiation travels through a specimen and the concentration of the species that absorbs the radiation:

$$A = \varepsilon c l$$

where A is the absorbance; ε is the extinction coefficient; c is the concentration of the absorbing species, and l is the path length of radiation through the specimen. The constant of proportionality, ε, in Beer's law is called the extinction coefficient. It is a measure of how well a compound absorbs radiation at a given wavelength; it is as characteristic of that compound as other physical constants such as melting point, boiling point, or molecular weight. The chemical literature abounds with extinction coefficients for many substances, including pure drugs and their salts in a variety of solvents at a variety of wavelengths, mostly in the ultraviolet (UV) and visible regions of the electromagnetic spectrum.

UV and Visible Spectroscopy

Visible (vis) spectroscopy and UV spectroscopy are usually referred to as a single technique (UV–vis) because the absorption or emission of UV and/or visible light are associated with the same physical and chemical processes in both of these adjacent regions of the electromagnetic spectrum. As many compounds absorb UV and/or visible light, UV–vis is widely applicable to the determination of a wide range of substances. Most of these, especially liquid- and solid-phase samples, have broad peaks and features in their UV and visible spectra that are difficult to use for qualitative identification. However, UV–vis is very widely used in analytical chemistry for quantitative analysis, either as a stand-alone technique or as the most common mode of detection in liquid chromatography and capillary electrophoresis (**Figure 4**).

A common use for UV–vis spectroscopy in the forensic laboratory as a stand-alone technique is screening powders for the presence of illicit drugs. In this application, UV–vis is quite successful because the technique has a very low limit of detection, powders are usually simple mixtures, and illicit drugs give good signals. Many useful solvents such as water, methanol, ethanol, and acetonitrile are virtually transparent throughout the visible and UV spectrum. It is therefore very easy to prepare a solution of the illicit preparation to an accurate concentration in a solvent that does not interfere with the absorption spectrum. Using the Beer–Lambert law, the absorbance of the specimen, the optical path length (usually 1 cm in standard sample cells), and the extinction coefficient of the drug, the concentration of drug present in the solution of the illicit preparation can be determined. In practice, it is more common to compare the absorbance of the specimen against standard solutions of known concentration, rather than relying on the literature extinction coefficients, because the standards can be prepared to include impurities that are present in the specimen and that may change the effective extinction coefficient. The attraction of such an analytical strategy is that it is very inexpensive, rapid, and simple. Furthermore, if the UV–vis spectrometer has been properly calibrated using absorbance and wavelength references, a pure reference drug standard may be not absolutely necessary in order to quantify the drug because extinction coefficients are universal constants.

This facility for accurate, standardless quantification is unique to UV–vis spectroscopy; separation techniques (e.g., gas chromatography, liquid chromatography, capillary electrophoresis) require a reference substance in order to calibrate the response with respect to amount, and for other spectroscopic techniques (e.g., IR spectroscopy), extinction coefficients are not available. UV–vis spectroscopy is not generally applied to the quantitative assay of illicit drug preparations, however, because the technique in general has severe limitations for the analysis of uncharacterized mixtures. However, when a mixture is well characterized and there is some degree of separation between the spectral peaks arising from the compounds in the mixture, UV–vis spectroscopy can be useful.

Another example is the estimation of carboxyhemoglobin in human blood. The spectral characteristics (i.e., absorption maxima and extinction coefficients) for carboxyhemoglobin and interfering blood pigments (e.g., oxyhemoglobin and methemoglobin) are well known. For a blood specimen of unknown carboxyhemoglobin saturation, it is a simple matter to deconvolute mathematically the spectral contributions of interfering blood pigments from the bands due to carboxyhemoglobin.

A major application of visible spectroscopy is the objective color comparison of evidential material such as fibers or paint. The human eye and brain interpret the visible spectrum of light reflected from an object as its color. However, the human eye is a low-resolution transducer, and it can be fooled into interpreting two closely related colors as identical. **Figure 5** shows visible spectra acquired from two different turquoise wool fibers. Even though the spectra from the two fibers are noticeably different, the eye perceives the two fibers to be identical in color. In the modern forensic laboratory, therefore, visible spectroscopy is invaluable as a means of confirming whether two objects are of the same color, or refuting the observation.

Conventional UV–vis spectrometers cannot acquire spectral data from microscopic samples of paint, or from short pieces of single textile fibers. The instrument used is referred to as a visible microspectrometer, and it functions in the same way as the IR microscope described earlier. Unlike the IR microscope, visible microspectrometers allow analysis and visualization of objects less that 10 μm in size. This is possible because visible light suffers less diffraction than IR radiation. Visible spectroscopy should be considered a color analysis technique, not a pigment analysis technique. This is because visible spectroscopy is not always capable of resolving different compounds (or different blends of compounds) that have the same color. Reliable pigment analysis is achieved only when visible spectroscopy is used in conjunction with other techniques. For

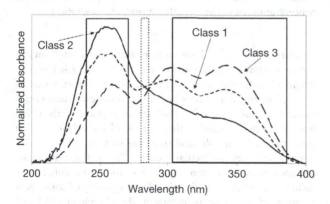

Figure 4 Ultraviolet absorbance spectra obtained from exemplars of three different classes of automotive clear coat. The differences between Class 1 (2000 Toyota MR-2), Class 2 (2002 Honda Civic), and Class 3 (1995 Chevy Sebring 434) were characterized using principal component analysis. Reproduced from Liszewski, E.A., Lewis, S.W., Siegel, J.A., Goodpaster, J.V., 2010. Characterization of automotive paint clear coats by ultraviolet absorption microspectrophotometry with subsequent chemometric analysis. Applied Spectroscopy 64, 1122–1125, with permission from Society for Applied Spectroscopy.

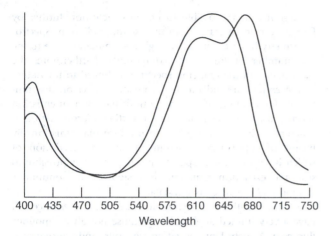

400 435 470 505 540 575 610 645 680 715 750
Wavelength

Figure 5   Visible microspectra of two different, metameric turquoise wool fibers. Although these fibers are of an identical color to the human eye, they are easily distinguished using visible microspectroscopy.

example, thin-layer chromatography (TLC) could be attempted on pigments extracted from fibers, or SEM–EDX microanalysis could be used to characterize pigments in paint.

Pigments absorb radiation in the UV region as well as in the visible region, and paints designed for outdoor application can contain compounds that are active in the UV. Therefore, compared to visible spectroscopy, UV–vis spectroscopy can be expected to offer enhanced discrimination. However, the standard optics present in visible microspectrometers are usually made of glass, and these strongly attenuate UV radiation. It is possible to purchase microspectrometers equipped with quartz optics, which allow the spectrometer to cover the UV and visible range. When faced with the high cost of quartz optics, however, forensic laboratories tend to rely on visible microspectroscopy and enhance pigment discrimination with a simple, inexpensive technique such as TLC.

AAS and Atomic Emission Spectroscopy

AAS and atomic emission spectroscopy (AES) are normally used to quantify metallic elements present in a specimen. A specimen is dissolved in a suitable solvent. Chemical treatment may also be required if the sample is not soluble. Depending on the exact instrumentation, the solution is aspirated into a flame or plasma torch, which converts the analytes into gaseous atoms. Atomic absorption spectrometers use lamps that are specific to the measurement of a single metallic element, or multielement lamps that are specific to a small number of metallic elements.

Using the Beer–Lambert law, the absorbance of light by the sample at a wavelength that is specific to that metal gives

a measure of the amount of that metal present in the sample. Note that this method gives a measure of the total amount of a specific metal that is present, and that there is no information about the original speciation of that metallic element. AES is similar to AAS in many regards, except that the emission of the heated gaseous metallic atoms is measured.

The primary advantages of AAS and AES for the forensic scientist are unsurpassed limits of detection, accuracy, and precision for elemental analysis. However, AAS and AES are not necessarily the most effective means by which a forensic scientist can conduct elemental analysis. First, atomic spectroscopy is destructive; the sample presented for analysis is usually treated with a very strong acid to form a solution, and then irreversibly aspirated into the instrument. Second, because the sample is homogenized by dissolution, atomic spectroscopy cannot yield any information as to spatial distribution, or compounds present in the specimen. For example, a sample might be found to contain Fe and Cr. Although this suggests that the sample contains a chromium–steel alloy, one cannot rule out the possibility that iron chromate and iron dichromate are present, or that the sample might contain granules of iron, chromium, iron oxides, etc. Third, any contaminant associated with the specimen will be digested along with it, and will contribute to the results. Fourth, although atomic spectroscopic techniques do have very low limits of detection, they are often not low enough to detect trace elements in trace evidence. This is because the specimen must be made into a solution of relatively large volume (usually 0.5–5 ml). As a consequence, trace elements in, for example, small chips of glass or paint yield very dilute solutions. Finally, some techniques, such as flame AAS, only allow sequential analysis of target elements; one analytical test provides data with respect to only one element. As it is not possible to screen a specimen for many elements in one test, the analysis is not particularly efficient, especially with regard to specimen consumption.

Paradoxically, given the very low limits of detection for these techniques, they are of greatest use in the analysis of relatively large specimens, and given that the technique is destructive, specimens must be big enough to allow subsampling. Such specimens could be human tissue for toxicological analysis and milligram-size pieces of glass, paint, and metals.

Another strong application of atomic spectroscopy is the analysis of illicit drug powder samples. The low limits of detection that can be achieved allow many trace elements to be detected in heroin, for example. It is possible to identify the source country of the drug on the basis of the suite of elements it contains.

Some of the major shortcomings of atomic spectroscopy can be rectified by the use of a laser ablation source. In this technique, a laser beam is used to vaporize very small quantities of the specimen, which are then swept into the instrument, without the need for digestion of the specimen. It is possible to allow the laser beam to dwell on the specimen for some time before analysis, thereby effectively removing any surface contamination. As the laser beam can be focused to a small spot size, it is possible to sample and analyze discrete regions within the specimen. This allows some identification of the spatial distribution of compounds within the specimen. Finally, the laser ablates only a tiny amount of material, leaving the remainder of the specimen intact for further analysis.

Related Techniques

Molecular Fluorescence and Chemiluminescence

Fluorescence has three important applications in forensic science. Perhaps the most widespread use is not in relation to spectroscopy at all, but image or specimen enhancement in the fields of ink comparison, latent fingerprint enhancement, and classification of textile fibers. Another use is in relation to chromatographic detection associated with separation techniques, such as high-performance liquid chromatography and capillary electrophoresis, where extremely low limits of detection can be realized. Finally, molecular fluorescence can be used as a spectroscopic technique (spectrofluorimetry).

Chemiluminescence is a related emission technique, where molecules are elevated to an excited state by a chemical reaction, rather than absorption of light. Chemiluminescence is most commonly used for image or specimen enhancement in the detection of blood at crime scenes, as a quantification method either by itself or in relation to chromatographic detection and is finding increasing use for the rapid screening of illicit drugs. While chemiluminescence is a spectroscopic process, in these forensic applications, it is not used as a spectroscopic technique and will not be discussed further here.

Although spectrofluorimetry is related to UV–vis spectroscopy, there are some significant differences. One distinguishing property of fluorescence, a feature that is both its biggest asset and its biggest drawback, is that not all molecules exhibit this behavior. In general terms, only some inorganic compounds, aromatic compounds, or highly conjugated organic systems are fluorescent, particularly if oxygen or nitrogen atoms are attached. The presence of electron-withdrawing groups (e.g., halogen atoms, nitro groups) diminishes or even completely quenches fluorescence in these substances. On the positive side, therefore, techniques based on fluorescence can have very low limits of detection because spurious background signals are not likely to arise. As the excitation radiation is of a shorter wavelength than the

fluorescence, it is possible to enhance detection further by filtering out interference from the exciting radiation. Spectrofluorimetry has a potential for high discrimination due to the low number of fluorescent compounds. Furthermore, the exact nature of the emission spectrum is linked to the nature of the excitation, and this has a positive effect on discrimination. For example, if two compounds have similar emission spectra, there is the potential for further discrimination if different excitation is required to produce that emission. By means of sophisticated instrumentation (a description of which is beyond the scope of this chapter), it is possible to scan the excitation radiation in a stepwise or continuous fashion and record emission data.

On the negative side, techniques based on fluorescence will have a very limited applicability because not all compounds fluoresce. As petroleum-based greases, oils, and concentrated fuel residues contain aromatic compounds (in particular, polyheteronuclear aromatic compounds), spectrofluorimetry can be used as a means to characterize them. Some drugs (e.g., LSD, phenothiazine, quinine, and quinidine) are fluorescent, and therefore amenable to qualitative and quantitative analysis using spectrofluorimetry. Some metal atoms can also fluoresce; this finds some application in glass analysis. A major application of fluorescence is through the use of fluorescent labels in DNA sequencing.

Synchrotron Techniques

Synchrotrons are facilities that produce extremely intense light. The actual spectroscopic techniques include IR absorption, XRF, and molecular fluorescence. The much more powerful light sources give significantly better limits of detection, spatial resolution, etc.

In a synchrotron, electrons are accelerated to almost the speed of light and circulate around an almost circular track. As the electrons change direction of travel from one straight section to another, intense electromagnetic radiation is emitted. Depending on the spatial arrangement of the magnetic fields used to contain and bend the electrons, emission in particular regions of the electromagnetic spectrum can be optimized. Each emission station or beamline is dedicated to a particular spectroscopic technique.

Limited access to synchrotron facilities means that synchrotron techniques may never become routine in forensic science, but there are many interesting possibilities. Synchrotron XRF has been used for the forensic discrimination of glass samples by analyzing the quantities of Ba, Ce, and Sm at picogram levels and Sr, Zr, Sn, and Hf at 10 pg levels. In another case, synchrotron XRF and X-ray absorption near-edge spectroscopy was used to map the distribution and characterize the form of the arsenic within hair samples; it was possible to

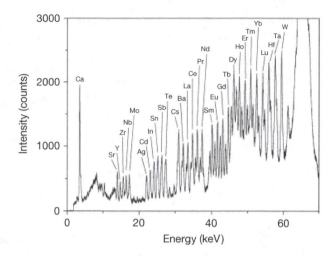

Figure 6 Synchrotron radiation X-ray fluorescence spectrum of NIST SRM 612 glass sample. Reproduced from Nakanishi, T., Nishiwaki, Y., Miyamoto, N. et al., 2008. Lower limits of detection of synchrotron radiation high-energy X-ray fluorescence spectrometry and its possibility for the forensic application for discrimination of glass fragments. Forensic Science International 175, 227–234, with permission from Elsevier.

distinguish between arsenic that has been ingested and arsenic applied postmortem (**Figure 6**).

See also: **Chemistry/Trace/Drugs of Abuse:** Analysis of Controlled Substances; **Chemistry/Trace/Explosives:** Explosives: Analysis; **Chemistry/Trace/Fibers:** Color Analysis; **Chemistry/Trace/Glass:** Glass Analysis; **Chemistry/Trace/Paint and Coating:** Forensic Paint Analysis; **Documents:** Analytical Methods; Ink Analysis; **Investigations:** Fingerprints; **Methods:** Liquid and Thin-Layer Chromatography; Microscopy (Electron).

Further Reading

Ahuja, S., Jespersen, N. (Eds.), 2006. Modern Instrumental Analysis. Elsevier, London.

Brettell, T.A., Butler, J.M., Almirall, J.R., 2009. Forensic science. Analytical Chemistry 81, 4695–4711.

Cervelli, F., Carrato, S., Mattei, A., et al., 2011. Imaging using synchrotron radiation for forensic science. In: Astola, J.T., Egiazarian, K.O. (Eds.), Image Processing: Algorithms and Systems IX, Proceedings of the SPIE, vol. 7870. Society of Photo-Optical Instrumentation Engineers (SPIE), San Francisco, pp. 78700B–78709B-9.

Chalmers, J.M., Edwards, H.G.M., Hargreaves, M.D. (Eds.), 2012. Infrared and Raman Spectroscopy in Forensic Science. Wiley, New York.

Cullen, M. (Ed.), 2003. Atomic Spectroscopy in Elemental Analysis. Blackwell, Oxford.

Friebolin, H., 2005. Basic One- and Two-Dimensional NMR Spectroscopy. Wiley-VCH, New York.

Goldstein, J.I., Newbury, D.E., Echlin, P., et al., 2003. Scanning Electron Microscopy and X-ray Microanalysis, third ed. Plenum, New York.

Goodhew, P.J., Humphreys, J., Beanland, R., 2000. Electron Microscopy and Analysis, third ed. Taylor and Francis, London.

Harris, D.C., 2010. Quantitative Chemical Analysis, eighth ed. W. H. Freeman and Company, New York.

Hesse, M., Meier, H., Zeeh, B., 1997. Foundations of Organic Chemistry: Spectroscopic Methods in Organic Chemistry. Thieme, New York.

Humecki, H.J., 1995. Practical Spectroscopy. In: Practical Guide to Infrared Microspectroscopy, vol. 19. Marcel Dekker, New York.

Keeler, J., 2010. Understanding NMR Spectroscopy, second ed. John Wiley and Sons, New York.

Kirkbride, K.P., Skinner, W.M., Coumbaros, J., 2005. Applications of synchrotron radiation in forensic trace evidence analysis. Talanta 67, 286–303.

Lajunen, L.H.J., Perämäki, P., 2004. Spectrochemical Analysis by Atomic Absorption and Emission, second ed. Royal Society of Chemistry, Cambridge.

Lambert, J.B., Shurvell, H.F., Lightner, D.A., Cooks, R.G., 1998. Organic Structural Spectroscopy. Prentice Hall, Upper Saddle River.

Larkin, P., 2011. Infrared and Raman Spectroscopy; Principles and Spectral Interpretation. Elsevier, San Diego.

Messerschmidt, R.G., Harthcock, M.A. (Eds.), 1988. Infrared Microspectroscopy. Theory and Applications. Marcel Dekker, New York.

Moffat, A.C. (Ed.), 1986. Clarke's Isolation and Identification of Drugs in Pharmaceuticals, Body Fluids, and Post-mortem Material. Pharmaceutical Press, London.

Nelson, J.H., 2003. Nuclear Magnetic Resonance Spectroscopy. Prentice Hall, Upper Saddle River.

Robertson, J.R. (Ed.), 1992. Forensic Examination of Fibres. Ellis Horwood, London.

Roush, P.B. (Ed.), 1987. The Design, Sample Handling, and Applications of Infrared Microscopes. American Society for Testing and Materials, Philadelphia.

Silverstein, R.M., Webster, F.X., Kiemle, D., 2005. Spectroscopic Identification of Organic Compounds, seventh ed. Wiley, New York.

Skoog, D.A., Holler, F.J., Crouch, S.R., 2007. Principles of Instrumental Analysis, sixth ed. Cengage, Belmont.

Skoog, D.A., West, D.M., Holler, F.J., Crouch, S.R., 2004. Fundamentals of Analytical Chemistry, eighth ed. Brooks/Cole, Belmont.

Van Grieken, R., Markowicz, A., 2001. Handbook of X-ray Spectrometry, second ed. CRC Press, Boca Raton.

Welz, B., Sperling, M., 1998. Atomic Absorption Spectrometry, third ed. Wiley-VCH, Weinheim.

Williams, K.L., 1987. An Introduction to X-ray Spectrometry. Allen and Unwin, London.

Williams, D.H., Fleming, I., 2007. Spectroscopic Methods in Organic Chemistry, sixth ed. McGraw Hill, London.

Spectroscopy: Basic Principles

SW Lewis, Curtin University, Perth, WA, Australia
KF Lim, Deakin University, Burwood, VIC, Australia

This chapter is a revision of the previous edition article by K.P. Kirkbride, volume 3, pp. 191–194, © 2000, Elsevier Ltd.

Glossary

Spectrometer An instrument designed to measure the amount and wavelength distribution of light either absorbed or emitted by a sample.

Spectroscopy A set of techniques which measure the amount and wavelength distribution of light either absorbed or emitted by a sample.

Introduction

Spectroscopy is the study of electromagnetic radiation and its production from, or its interaction with, matter. Historically, spectroscopy has played an essential role in the development of atomic theory, and it is still extensively used for fundamental studies. Spectroscopic techniques are widely used in forensic laboratories for quantitative and qualitative analysis. This chapter provides an overview of the basic principles of spectroscopy as applied to analytical measurements; for more in-depth details concerning specific matter–radiation interactions, instrumentation, and techniques, readers are directed to the reference works listed under Further Reading.

Electromagnetic Radiation and Light

Electromagnetic radiation is a traveling disturbance in space that comprises electric and magnetic components. Unlike the field associated with a common magnet or the earth, the magnetic field associated with electromagnetic radiation is constantly changing its direction and strength. The electric field component undergoes exactly the same behavior. **Figure 1** illustrates what would be observed if it was possible to see the electric and magnetic components of a ray of radiation as it passes. It is the interaction of the electric and magnetic components of radiation with matter that are responsible for all the phenomena that are associated with radiation, such as human vision, sunburn, microwave cookery, radio and television, and of course spectroscopy.

There are some important fundamental features of electromagnetic radiation. The periodicity of the disturbance, or the distance between adjacent troughs or adjacent peaks, is referred to as the wavelength of the radiation. The number of times the electromagnetic field undergoes a complete cycle per unit time is called the frequency. The speed with which radiation can travel is limited, and moreover, radiation of all wavelengths travels at a single speed. This is referred to as the speed of light, universally denoted by the symbol c. The speed of light (and every other radiation) is dependent on the substance through which it travels, and reaches a maximum in a vacuum. The speed of light is a constant of proportionality between frequency and wavelength as described by the following equation:

$$c = v\lambda$$

where v is the radiation frequency, λ is the radiation wavelength, and c is the speed of light.

The interpretation of this equation is that wavelength and frequency are related. Electromagnetic radiation of long wavelength must have a low frequency, whereas radiation of short wavelength must have a high frequency. At the long-wavelength (low-frequency) end of the electromagnetic radiation spectrum are radio waves, while at the other end is high-frequency (short-wavelength) radiation such as gamma rays. Between these extremes lie other forms of radiation, including microwaves, infrared (IR), ultraviolet (UV), and the narrow band of radiation that can be directly observed by humans, visible light.

Radiation carries energy with it, a phenomenon that is made use of in the domestic microwave oven, for example. The radiation is carried in small discrete quantities or "quanta" (singular: "quantum"). The amount of energy carried in each quantum is proportional to the frequency of the radiation. As frequency and wavelength have an inversely proportional relationship, the energy quantum carried is inversely proportional to

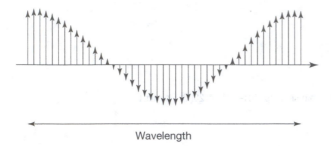

Figure 1 Representation of a ray of electromagnetic radiation traveling through space, left to right. The small vertical arrows represent the strength and direction of the electric field component of the radiation at discrete locations (the magnetic field behaves in an analogous manner). The disturbance is periodic, with the distance between field components of identical strength and direction being the wavelength of the radiation.

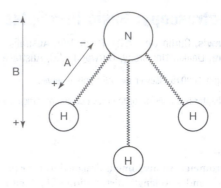

Figure 2 Electrical moments in the ammonia molecule. "A" represents the electrical field resulting from unequal sharing of electrons between nitrogen and hydrogen nuclei. "B" represents the overall field resulting from combination of three "A" moments.

wavelength. Radiation of high frequency and short wavelength (e.g., X-rays, gamma rays), therefore, is of high energy, whereas low-frequency radiation that must have long wavelength (e.g., radio waves) carries little energy.

Matter

Given that radiation is an electromagnetic phenomenon, the main feature of matter as far as its interaction with radiation is concerned is the distribution of its electric and magnetic components.

From the subatomic scale to the molecular, matter exhibits a variety of electric and magnetic features with which radiation can interact. **Figure 2** depicts some of these features for a molecule of ammonia. The forces that hold the molecule together arise from attraction between negatively charged electrons shared between the positively charged nuclei of the nitrogen and hydrogen atoms. The nuclei of each of the hydrogen atoms contain a single-charged particle, a proton. The share of electrons between the hydrogen nuclei and the nitrogen nucleus is not equal; nitrogen commands a larger share. Each nitrogen–hydrogen bond, therefore, has a heterogeneous distribution of charges resulting overall in a positively charged end (toward the hydrogen atom) and a negatively charged end. Such a bond is described as having a dipole moment or being polarized. As each nitrogen–hydrogen bond has a similar polarization, there is an additive effect with the result that the entire molecule is polarized or has a dipole moment.

Each nucleus of the hydrogen atoms comprises a single positively charged proton; each acts like a small rotating bar magnet, or is said to possess magnetic spin. Potentially, the entire ammonia molecule, its bonds, its protons, and its electrons, all have the necessary prerequisites to interact with radiation.

Interaction Between Radiation and Matter

In the previous section, it was shown that matter can be thought of as possessing many minute electric and magnetic moments on the subatomic and molecular scale. Radiation, which is also electromagnetic in nature, therefore, potentially can interact with matter on this scale. If interaction is to be significant, however, there has to be a match between the frequency of the electromagnetic oscillations executed by the radiation and oscillations of the electromagnetic moments within the matter. The situation is analogous to that of pushing a person on a swing. Say the person on the swing completes a cycle once every second. If the pushes are at some other frequency, then the energy transfer from the pushes is not efficient. The most effective transfer of energy takes place when pushes are in unison with the motion of the swing (i.e., with a frequency of one per second). The interaction between radiation and matter can lead to the occurrence of a variety of phenomena; important ones as far as spectroscopy is concerned are absorption, emission, and scattering.

Absorption

Absorption occurs when electromagnetic radiation is absorbed by atoms, ions, or molecules within a sample. The basis of absorption spectroscopy is the measurement of the manner in which matter absorbs radiation. An appreciation of absorption can be gained by considering the properties of the lens in a pair of sunglasses. Through the lens, the image of the outside world is duller; some of the radiation (light) encountering the lens does not pass through, the lens absorbs it. It leads to an increase in internal energy of the chemical species producing an excited state. This rise in internal energy is related to various transitions in the atom or molecule under investigation, the specific

Table 1   Spectroscopic techniques

Type	Wavelength (m)	Quantum transition
Gamma ray emission	$0.005–1.4 \times 10^{-10}$	Nuclear
X-ray absorption, emission fluorescence, or diffraction	$0.1–100 \times 10^{-10}$	Core electron transitions
Ultraviolet/visible absorption, emission, and fluorescence	$10–780 \times 10^{-9}$	Valence electron transitions
Infrared absorption and Raman shifts	$0.78–300 \times 10^{-6}$	Rotation/vibration of molecules
Microwave absorption	$0.75–3.75 \times 10^{-3}$	Rotation of molecules
Electron spin resonance	3×10^{-2}	Spin of electrons in a magnetic field
Nuclear magnetic resonance	$0.6–10$	Spin of nuclei in a magnetic field

transition being related to the wavelength of electromagnetic radiation being used (see **Table 1**). These transitions occur at particular wavelengths depending upon the chemical species being studied; this forms the basis of the use of spectroscopy for qualitative purposes. In addition, under particular conditions, the energy absorbed by the chemical species is proportional to the concentration of the absorbing species, allowing quantitative measurements.

Emission

Emission describes the production of electromagnetic radiation by matter as an excited state returns to the ground state. The chemical species may have been raised to the excited state by absorption of electromagnetic radiation or by a chemical reaction. Since emission is the reverse of absorption, the specific wavelength of electromagnetic radiation observed will depend upon the transition occurring. The basis of emission spectroscopy is the measurement of the manner in which matter emits radiation.

Scatter

Scatter occurs when a small fraction of electromagnetic radiation is scattered at all angles from the original path. Scatter is essentially radiation bouncing off atoms, ions, or molecules.

Instrumentation and Techniques

Spectrometers

Figure 3 depicts the important features of simple instrumentation that can be used for absorption spectroscopy, and a typical spectrum. Although all absorption spectrometers might not be exactly described by **Figure 3**, as far as this chapter is concerned, the important issue is the process leading to the spectroscopic output, and the features of the output itself, rather than the exact mechanism by which it was generated.

Three basic elements are present: a radiation source, a monochromator, and a transducer. It is usual for the source to emit radiation of many frequencies within a region of the entire electromagnetic spectrum, for example, the IR region, the visible light region, X-rays, and so on. The region over which the source operates in a given spectroscopic technique is often used as a means to name that technique. For example, if an IR source is used, the technique is referred to as IR spectroscopy.

The monochromator isolates the wavelength of interest from the source. Ideally it should allow radiation of only one frequency at a time to pass through although, in practice, a band of wavelengths centered around this wavelength is passed through. The radiation is then allowed to impinge on the specimen to be analyzed. The transducer then collects the radiation that is transmitted by the specimen and converts it into an electrical signal, thus allowing measurement of its intensity. Spectroscopic measurement of the specimen is performed by "sweeping" the filter through its entire wavelength range allowing (ideally) the detector to measure the radiation transmitted by the specimen one wavelength at a time. A graphical representation of measurements made by the detector is the spectrum of the specimen; typical output is shown in **Figure 3**.

The horizontal axis in the spectrum defines the range of wavelengths (frequencies) of the radiation that strikes the specimen. The vertical axis indicates how much of each wavelength is absorbed by the specimen (i.e., a peak at a certain wavelength indicates that the specimen absorbs at that wavelength).

Spectrometers can come as single-beam instruments, which have the advantage of simplicity, or as double-beam instruments (see **Figure 3**). Double-beam instruments have the advantage of being able to compensate for fluctuations in the radiant output of the source and for variation in source intensity with wavelength. Array spectrometers (**Figure 4**) have begun to be widely used for UV–visible (UV–vis) absorption measurements. They have the advantage of obtaining a complete spectrum at once, which can aid in multianalyte determinations and allow the use of measurement statistics to improve quantitative data.

The ideal of spectroscopy is that because different substances undergo different motions on the subatomic or molecular scale, the spectrum of each must have a unique pattern of peaks. The reality is that substances with very similar structures could behave in a very similar manner, with the result that instrumentation is not capable of discriminating them.

Throughout this chapter, the term spectrometer has been used to describe the device that acquires a spectrum, whereas spectroscopy has been used to describe the technique. This usage is common in modern publications, but it is by no means

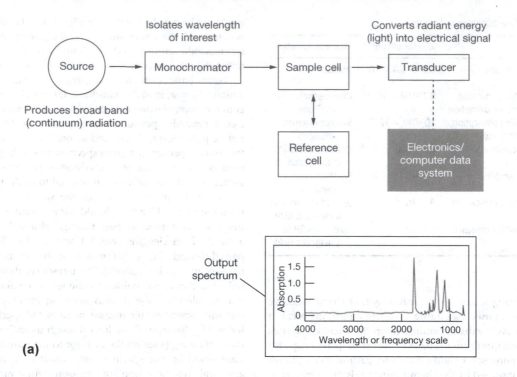

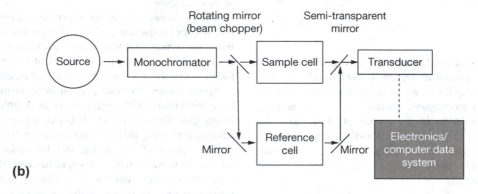

Figure 3 Schematic diagram of (A) single-beam spectrometer. The spectral output is a plot showing the extent of absorption as a function of the range of frequencies (or wavelength) that strike the specimen (B) dual-beam spectrometer.

the only terminology that might be encountered. The words spectrograph, spectrophotometer, and spectroscope are used to describe apparatus, whereas spectrometry and spectrophotometry are used interchangeably with spectroscopy.

Techniques

As mentioned above, the range of the electromagnetic spectrum that is utilized for particular measurements defines the technique used (see **Table 1**). From a forensic point of view, the following techniques find the widest application for analysis.

Molecular UV and visible absorbance spectroscopy

UV and visible absorbance spectroscopy are usually referred to as a single technique (UV–vis), as the absorption of UV and/or visible light is associated with the same physical and chemical processes. UV–vis absorbance involves electronic transitions, and as many compounds absorb UV or visible light, it is widely applicable in chemical analysis. Liquid- and solid-phase samples exhibit broad, featureless, absorbance peaks, and thus, UV–vis absorbance is not generally very useful for identification purposes. However, it is very widely used for quantitative measurements.

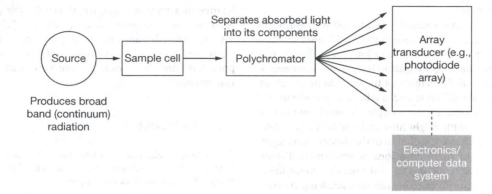

Figure 4 Schematic diagram of an array spectrometer.

Molecular luminescence spectroscopy

As described above, when molecules absorb visible or UV radiation, they are elevated to an excited state of high potential energy. From that state, the molecule can undergo a variety of actions in order to relax. One activity is to emit radiation of lower frequency than that which caused the excitation in the first place. The emitted radiation (fluorescence or phosphorescence) consists of many frequencies of characteristic intensity. Similar to the UV–vis spectrum, the emission spectrum (i.e., the plot of emitted radiation intensity versus wavelength) of a substance can be a means of characterizing that substance. Luminescence has the advantage of improved selectivity, as relatively few compounds exhibit fluorescence or phosphorescence, and sensitivity. It can also be used in imaging, as is commonly done with the detection of latent fingermarks (**Figure 5**). Chemical species can also be elevated to an excited state through a chemical reaction leading to the phenomenon of chemiluminescence, best known forensically through the luminol test for bloodstains.

Atomic absorption spectroscopy and atomic emission spectroscopy

Atomic absorption spectroscopy involves absorbance of light by metallic atoms in the gas phase, the light typically being sourced from a lamp specific to the measurement of a single element. Atomic emission is similar but instead measures the emission from heated gaseous metallic atoms. Both of these techniques are widely used for the quantification of metallic elements.

IR spectroscopy

The atoms of substances are constantly in motion with characteristic vibrational frequencies of 10^{12}–10^{13} Hz. Most of these vibrations can interact with electromagnetic radiation to absorb in the IR region of the spectrum. Wave number or

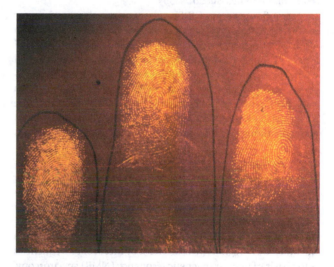

Figure 5 Luminescence from latent fingermarks on a paper surface developed with 1,2-indanedione. Excitation using a Polilight PL500 at 505 nm and viewed through a KV550 filter.

reciprocal wavelength measured in cm^{-1} units is normally used. The absorptions in the mid-IR range, 4000–500 cm^{-1}, are commonly used in forensic science.

The exact absorption wave number will depend on the bond strength, the relative atomic masses, and the molecular geometry, giving rise to complicated spectra. Particular combinations of atoms, which are bonded together, called chemical functional groups, have distinctive wave number patterns. For example, intense narrow peaks near 1700 cm^{-1} are characteristic of a carbonyl group, found in aldehydes, ketones, organic acids, and organic acid derivatives, including proteins and esters. Both IR and Raman spectroscopy are used mainly for the qualitative determination of functional groups.

Raman spectroscopy

In Raman spectroscopy, a sample absorbs the incident beam (usually visible light of a single wavelength) and simultaneously emits radiation of the same or longer wavelength. It is a scattering phenomenon that also changes the wavelength. The Raman shift is the difference in the wave numbers of the incident and Raman radiation and is related to the vibrational motions of the atoms in the sample. A small number of molecules in the sample might initially be in an excited state, resulting in the emission of radiation of the shorter wavelength, but the intensity of these emissions is very small. Raman spectra look similar to IR spectra and provide similar information, thus Raman spectroscopy can be considered complementary to IR spectroscopy.

X-ray fluorescence spectroscopy

In X-ray fluorescence (XRF) spectroscopy, the specimen is irradiated with X-rays, which causes electrons associated with atoms in the specimen to attain an excited state of potential energy. These excited-state electrons can release that potential energy by emitting energy (fluorescence) in the form of new X-rays. The X-rays are emitted at energies, measured in electron volts (eV), which are characteristic of the atoms present in the specimen. XRF is used mainly for qualitative determination of elements though some quantification is possible.

Nuclear magnetic resonance spectroscopy

In a magnetic field, the nuclei of certain isotopes can absorb or emit radio waves to change their nuclear spin. The exact energies of the spin states depend very markedly on the molecular environment the atoms are in. Nuclei in different environments, therefore, absorb or emit different frequencies within the radio wave region. Measurement of these radio frequencies is the basis of nuclear magnetic resonance (NMR) spectroscopy, with almost all NMR instruments measuring the emission (fluorescence) of radio waves from excited nuclei. There is such a sensitive correlation between the environment and the signal associated with the nuclei that NMR is capable of yielding an enormous amount of information regarding molecular structure, and therefore, unsurpassed specimen discrimination. Furthermore, NMR can be used to analyze a wide range of substances, not limited by molecular mass, volatility, or polarity.

Instruments are categorized by the NMR frequency of protons in the sample. In turn, this frequency depends on the strength of the magnetic field in the instrument, where a stronger magnetic field correlates to great resolving power. Differences in bonding and the molecule near each proton or ^{13}C nucleus cause subtle changes in the NMR frequencies. The changes in frequencies are called chemical shifts and are measured as part per million (ppm) shifts in frequencies relative to a reference frequency, usually the proton or ^{13}C resonance of tetramethylsilane (TMS, $(CH)_3Si$). The necessity to maintain an unchanging magnetic field and the electronics required to measure shifts in frequency at the ppm level are the reason for the very high cost of NMR instruments.

Acknowledgment

The authors would like to acknowledge the contribution of Paul Kirkbride, who wrote this chapter for the first edition, as some of his material has been used for this chapter.

See also: **Chemistry/Trace/Drugs of Abuse:** Analysis of Controlled Substances; **Chemistry/Trace/Explosives:** Explosives: Analysis; **Chemistry/Trace/Fibers:** Color Analysis; **Chemistry/Trace/Glass:** Glass Analysis; **Chemistry/Trace/Paint and Coating:** Forensic Paint Analysis; **Documents:** Analytical Methods; Ink Analysis; **Investigations:** Fingerprints; **Methods**: Liquid and Thin-Layer Chromatography; Microscopy (Electron); Spectroscopic Techniques; **Pattern Evidence/ Fingerprints (Dactyloscopy):** Sequential Treatment and Enhancement; Visualization or Development of Crime Scene Fingerprints.

Further Reading

Ahuja, S., Jespersen, N. (Eds.), 2006. Modern Instrumental Analysis. Elsevier, London.

Chalmers, J.M., Edwards, H.G.M., Hargreaves, M.D. (Eds.), 2012. Infrared and Raman Spectroscopy in Forensic Science. Wiley, New York.

Cullen, M. (Ed.), 2003. Atomic Spectroscopy in Elemental Analysis. Blackwell, Oxford.

Friebolin, H., 2005. Basic One- and Two-dimensional NMR Spectroscopy. Wiley-VCH, New York.

Goldstein, J.I., Newbury, D.E., Echlin, P., et al., 2003. Scanning Electron Microscopy and X-Ray Microanalysis, third ed. Plenum, New York.

Harris, D.C., 2010. Quantitative Chemical Analysis, eighth ed. W. H. Freeman and Company, New York.

Hesse, M., Meier, H., Zeeh, B., 1997. Foundations of Organic Chemistry: Spectroscopic Methods in Organic Chemistry. Thieme, New York.

Keeler, J., 2003. Understanding NMR Spectroscopy. University of Cambridge, Cambridge, UK.

Lajunen, L.H.J., Perämäki, P., 2004. Spectrochemical Analysis by Atomic Absorption and Emission, second ed. Royal Society of Chemistry, Cambridge.

Lambert, J.B., Shurvell, H.F., Lightner, D.A., Cooks, R.G., 1998. Organic Structural Spectroscopy. Prentice Hall, Upper Saddle River, NJ.

Larkin, P., 2011. Infrared and Raman Spectroscopy; Principles and Spectral Interpretation. Elsevier, San Diego.

Nelson, J.H., 2003. Nuclear Magnetic Resonance Spectroscopy. Prentice Hall, Upper Saddle River, NJ.

Silverstein, R.M., Webster, F.X., Kiemle, D., 2005. Spectroscopic Identification of Organic Compounds, seventh ed. Wiley, New York.

Skoog, D.A., Holler, F.J., Crouch, S.R., 2007. Principles of Instrumental Analysis, sixth ed. Cengage, Belmont, CA.

Skoog, D.A., West, D.M., Holler, F.J., Crouch, S.R., 2004. Fundamentals of Analytical Chemistry, eighth ed. Brooks/Cole, Belmont, CA.

Van Grieken, R., Markowicz, A., 2001. Handbook of X-Ray Spectrometry, second ed. CRC Press, Boca Raton.

Welz, B., Sperling, M., 1998. Atomic Absorption Spectrometry, third ed. Wiley-VCH, Weinheim.

Williams, D.H., Fleming, I., 2007. Spectroscopic Methods in Organic Chemistry, sixth ed. McGraw Hill, London.

Williams, K.L., 1987. An Introduction to X-ray Spectrometry. Allen and Unwin, London.

Key Terms

Absorption, Analyzer, Atomic absorption, Atomic emission, Basic principles, Capillary electrophoresis, Chemiluminescence, Chromatogram, Chromatography, Direct injection, Distillation, DNA sequencing, Electrokinetic chromatography, Emission, Enantiomers, Explosives, Forensic medicine, Forensic science, Gel electrophoresis, Gold standard, Gunshot residue, High-performance liquid chromatography (HPLC), Identification of substances, Illicit drugs, Infrared, Inks, Instrumental analysis, Ion mobility spectrometry, Ionization techniques, Isotachophoresis, Large-volume injection, Liquid chromatography, Mass spectrometry, Mass spectrum, Matrix effects, Miniaturization, Molecular fluorescence, Molecular luminescence, Molecular ultraviolet and visible absorbance, Nuclear magnetic resonance, Purification, Quantification of substances, Raman, Raman spectroscopy, Sample cleanup, Sample preparation, Scatter, Separations, Sieving electrophoresis, Solid-phase extraction, Solid-phase microextraction, Solvent extraction, Spectrometer, Spectroscopy, STR separation, Sublimation, Synchrotron techniques, Thin-layer chromatography (TLC), Toxicology, UV–visible, X-ray fluorescence, Zone electrophoresis.

Review Questions

1. What role does electroosmotic flow play in chromatographic separation, that is, resolution? What factors affect electroosmotic flow and how does this relate to separation?
2. How does CE used in chemistry differ from its application in biology? What aspects are the same?
3. What factors determine the distribution constant, K_c? Describe the relationship between K_c, retention time (t_R), and void time (t_M).
4. What is a theoretical plate? Why is the number of theoretical plates important in chromatography? Write the equation for the relationship between the number of theoretical plates and column length (L). Why is this important to band broadening?
5. List the various methods of chromatography, the sample forms they can accept, the types of applications they are used for, and the strengths and weaknesses of each.
6. When would a split injection port be used? When would a splitless port be used? Why?
7. What are the main types of detectors used in GC? How do they differ? When would they be used and for what applications?
8. What is the main benefit of coupling a GC with an MS? Why does this matter in forensic science?
9. Describe how a mass spectrometer works. What is "time of flight" and how does it differ from standard mass spectrometry? What is an "MS/MS" and how does it work?
10. What is mass-to-charge ratio? What is its relevance to mass spectrometry?
11. Describe how absorption, emission, and scatter originate in spectroscopy and what they indicate about a material.
12. What are main spectroscopic methods? How are they organized? Do any overlap; why or why not? Which ones allow for quantitation?
13. What is more important in microscopy, magnification or resolution? Why?
14. How do light microscopes and electron microscopes differ? What are their strengths and weaknesses?
15. Why do chemical tests need to be confirmed by instrumental methods?
16. List three color tests, their main reagents, and what they test for.
17. List five crystal types resulting from microcrystalline tests and describe them.
18. List five nonchromatographic separation methods, the types of samples they can be used for, and how they work.
19. What is SPME?
20. What is the analytical benefit of purification via chemical reaction? When would it be beneficial?

Discussion Questions

1. Discuss isomers in relation to chromatography and spectrometry, especially GC–MS. How are isomers best identified and analyzed? How would an analytical scheme (or standard operating procedure) change if isomers are to be considered?

2. What does the current range of analytical capabilities mean for the modern forensic toxicology laboratory's limited budget? If a laboratory is required to analyze drugs, trace materials (paints, fibers, and tape, for example), *and* toxicology samples, what would be the highest quality, lowest cost array of instrumentation? How does maintenance of instrumentation affect the decision?

3. An important part of forensic science is explaining methods, results, and interpretations to a jury of nonscientists. Pick an instrumental method and work out how you would describe it to someone who knows nothing about it or chemistry. What technical words to you have to use (do not forget to define them) and which ones can you ignore?

4. Why are most toxicology laboratories part of medical examiner offices and not forensic laboratories? Why would not they be a part of a forensic laboratory under a police department (like 95% of forensic laboratories are now)?

5. The average budget for a forensic laboratory is about $3.5 million[1] and personnel consume about 70% of that money; that leaves about $1.05 million. Assume a budget *one-tenth of that*, $105,000. How would you conduct toxicological tests? What evidence types could you analyze? What methods would you use?

Additional Readings

Barron, L., Gilchrist, E., 2014. Ion chromatography-mass spectrometry: a review of recent technologies and applications in forensic and environmental explosives analysis. Analytica Chimica Acta 806 (2), 27–54.

Fritz, P., van Bronswijk, W., Lepkova, K., Lewis, S., Lim, K., Martin, D., Puskar, L., 2013. Infrared microscopy studies of the chemical composition of latent fingermark residues. Microchemical Journal 111, 40–46.

Palermo, A., Botrè, F., de la Torre, X., Fiacco, I., Iannone, M., Mazzarino, M., 2016. Drug-drug interactions and masking effects in sport doping: influence of miconazole administration on the urinary concentrations of endogenous anabolic steroids. Forensic Toxicology 34 (2), 386–397.

Remane, D., Wissenbach, D.K., Peters, F.T., 2016. Recent advances of liquid chromatography–(tandem) mass spectrometry in clinical and forensic toxicology—an update. Clinical Biochemistry 49 (13), 1051–1071.

---

[1] Durose, M., Walsh, K., and Burch, A. 2012. *Census of Publicly Funded Forensic Crime Laboratories (2009)*. US Department of Justice, Office of Justice Programs, Bureau of Justice Statistics: Washington, D.C.

Section 3. Pharmacology and Drugs

Drug chemists need to know a lot to do their jobs. Toxicologists need to know all of that, plus other chemicals (like poisons and toxins) and how the body works. This additional burden is what makes toxicology such a complicated discipline. For example, terminology. In medicine and zoology, toxins are poisons produced by organisms (plant and animal) but venoms are toxins injected by a sting or a bite from an animal.

Pesticides are poisons used to kill pests, like rats and insects, but are only used by humans. Unintentional poisonings occur quite frequently; for example, 3.3 million cases of unintentional poisonings were reported in 2013, resulting in 98,000 deaths worldwide[1]. The point here is that a toxicologist must be familiar with all these issues and chemicals, not only drugs of abuse.

Analysis of Controlled Substances

N NicDaéid and H Buchannan, University of Strathclyde, Glasgow, UK

Abbreviations

BSIA	Bulk stable isotope analysis	HPLC	High-performance liquid chromatography
CF-IRMS	Continuous flow isotope ratio mass spectrometry	IRMS	Isotope ratio mass spectrometry
CSIA	Compound-specific isotope analysis	NMR	Nuclear magnetic resonance spectroscopy
EA-IRMS	Elemental analyzer isotope ratio mass spectrometry	TC/EA-IRMS	Temperature conversion/elemental analyzer isotope ratio mass spectrometry
GC-IRMS	Gas chromatography isotope ratio mass spectrometry	TLC	Thin-layer chromatography
GCMS	Gas chromatography mass spectroscopy		

Introduction

One of the main activities in a forensic chemical laboratory is the examination of powders, pills, and plant materials thought to be illicit or controlled substances. The analysis of suspected drugs of abuse occurs over a number of stages. These involve

a physical examination of the item, including its packaging, followed by sampling, and subsequent presumptive and confirmatory testing. A variety of analytical tests are used in drug analysis, and the analytical test is selected according to the nature of the suspect material and the ultimate question being asked about it: that is, identification, quantification, or chemical profiling. This chapter explores, in brief, the analytical techniques used in conventional drug analysis. The data derived from the analysis of such substances are used in the production of forensic science reports for use within the criminal justice system and/or used by the police in the development of intelligence information for disrupting dealer-user networks and clandestine manufacture at national and international levels.

---

[1] Vos, T., Barber, R.M., Bell, B., Bertozzi-Villa, A., Biryukov, S., Bolliger, I., Charlson, F., Davis, A., Degenhardt, L., Dicker, D., Duan, L., 2015. Global, regional, and national incidence, prevalence, and years lived with disability for 301 acute and chronic diseases and injuries in 188 countries, 1990–2013: a systematic analysis for the Global Burden of Disease Study (2013). The Lancet, 386 (9995), 743.

Analytical Strategy

The strategy chosen by the drug analyst in the investigation of drug samples will depend upon the ultimate question at issue balanced by the resource and time implications. Within the laboratory, this may involve decisions in relation to the necessity to identify, quantify, or profile the drug sample in question. In general circumstances, samples will be physically examined (including examination of the packaging materials), will undergo presumptive and/or thin-layer chromatographic analysis, and be analyzed using a variety of confirmatory tests.

Physical Examination

Once a drug sample is presented for examination, its packaging should be checked to ensure that it is intact. Any breech of the packaging should be recorded and a decision taken as to whether the analysis of that item should continue.

The physical description of an item, as well as the analyses undertaken, depends upon whether that item is considered a bulk or trace sample. Each item should be described fully (with diagrams if appropriate), including a description of color, smell, and packaging materials. Any logos (e.g., on tablets) or marks (such as stamp marks on blocks of resin or packages of drugs) must also be fully described and recorded. Microscopic examination may also be required to examine the morphological characteristics of the material, particularly for plant-based substances.

Specific analysis of packaging material also is beneficial. In particular, such examinations can provide intelligence information for case-to-case linkages. Examination of packaging material not only can include a general physical characterization of the materials used but may also include DNA, fingerprint, and specific chemical analysis of materials such as plastic and duct tape using, for example, isotope ratio mass spectrometry (IRMS).

Presumptive Tests

A sample is initially subjected to presumptive colorimetric tests to give an indication of the class of drug, which may be present in the sample. These tests are widely accepted. Presumptive tests are also used extensively as field tests where various commercial kits are available. In the laboratory, presumptive tests are generally performed on clean porcelain tiles, in solution, or on adsorbent substrates. The most common type of presumptive test involves the addition of reagents to the sample to produce a color. Other tests utilize microscopy to identify plant components (e.g., trichomes in suspected cannabis samples) or microcrystalline tests in which the formation of specific crystals is indicative of the class of drug

present. In all cases, appropriate positive and negative control samples must be used. Although presumptive tests are cheap, quick, and easy to use, they may be subjective in nature and prone to spurious positive results when drug mixtures are encountered. Furthermore, "false positive" results may be obtained when a color change occurs due to the presence of certain noncontrolled substances within the drug sample.

Fourier Transform Infrared Spectroscopy

Infrared (IR) spectroscopy is a technique available for the identification of functional groups within molecules. When IR light is passed through an organic compound, some wavelengths of light are absorbed. This absorption of light causes an energy transition in the form of vibrational excitation of bonds within the molecule. One example of this vibrational excitation is the stretching and bending of bonds. Light of wavelength λ will only be absorbed if there is an energy transition (ΔE) according to the following equation:

$$\Delta E = \frac{hc}{\lambda}$$

where h is Planck's constant (6.626×10^{-34} J s), c is the speed of light (3.0×10^8 m s^{-1}), and λ is the wavelength of light in meters.

After the light has passed through the sample, the frequencies that have been absorbed are detected due to their absence, and the intensities are recorded as troughs in the resultant spectrum.

Different types of bonds have different vibrational frequencies, so the presence or absence of characteristic frequencies in the spectrum can provide information about the functional groups present in an organic molecule; most useful for functional group identification are the absorptions above 1400 cm^{-1} and below 900 cm^{-1}. [The per cm unit, or "wavenumber," is the reciprocal of wavelength (λ).] For example, carbonyl compounds generally absorb IR at 1670–1780 cm^{-1}, alkenes (nonterminal) at 1640–1680 cm^{-1}, and amines at 3300–3500 cm^{-1} (for N–H) and 1030–1230 cm^{-1} (for C–N). The range from 1400 to 900 cm^{-1} is termed the "fingerprint region" and contains a complex pattern of absorptions, which can be characteristic of the analyzed molecule. This region is valuable for direct comparison between two spectra, but it is generally of little use for determining the presence or absence of functional groups. Fourier transform IR is often used in the confirmation of the identity of a pure drug substance or the determination of functional groups in an unknown drug compound.

Nuclear Magnetic Resonance Spectroscopy

"Nuclear magnetic resonance" (NMR) occurs because nuclei of certain atoms spin, thus creating a weak magnetic field around the nucleus. The instrument applies an external magnetic field to the sample, which causes the spinning nuclei to reorient themselves. In the case of proton (^{1}H) and carbon (^{13}C) NMR spectroscopy, the nuclei become aligned with or against the external magnetic field. The former is the lower energy state, and the latter is the higher energy state. When radio frequency radiation of the appropriate frequency is applied, nuclei in the lower energy state can jump to the higher energy state; that is, nuclei that are parallel to the applied magnetic field can invert so that they are antiparallel. When this occurs, NMR has been induced. The nuclei in the higher energy state then relax to the lower energy state, and a very small amount of energy is released. This small pulse of radio frequency electromagnetic radiation is detected and converted to intensity against frequency signal.

A nucleus is surrounded by circulating electrons, each of which creates a magnetic field that acts in opposition to the external magnetic field; thus, the nucleus is shielded from the applied magnetic field by the electron cloud. Different degrees of shielding require different frequencies in order to attain resonance, and, in this way, the different chemical environments can be discriminated. Nuclei that are deshielded resonate at higher frequencies and that are shielded resonate at lower frequencies.

The frequency differences between nuclei in different chemical environments are plotted in an NMR spectrum as chemical shift. Chemical shift (δ) is a relative measure of frequency (v) in parts per million:

$$\delta = \frac{v - v_{ref}}{v_{ref}}$$

where the reference compound for proton and carbon NMR is tetramethylsilane, and the chemical shift for this compound is defined arbitrarily as 0.0 ppm.

Both ^{1}H and ^{13}C NMR are routinely used for the identification of organic compounds. ^{1}H is more powerful than ^{13}C NMR for two reasons: first, ^{1}H NMR is more sensitive than ^{13}C NMR because ^{13}C is not the dominant isotope of carbon and only exists in 1.1% abundance. ^{1}H is, however, the dominant isotope and naturally occurs in >99% abundance. Second, the signal intensity in ^{1}H NMR relates to the number of nuclei in a particular chemical environment, but this does not hold true for ^{13}C NMR.

NMR is increasingly used in the forensic analysis of unknown drug samples, particularly to elucidate the structure of the compound.

Chromatography

The International Union of Pure and Applied Chemistry (IUPAC) defines chromatography as "a physical method of separation in which the components to be separated are distributed between two phases, one of which is stationary while the other moves in a definite direction." Three different types of chromatography techniques are most commonly used in the analysis of drugs of abuse: thin-layer chromatography (TLC), in which the stationary phase is coated onto an inert support and the mobile phase is a solvent or mixture of solvents, gas chromatography (GC), in which the mobile phase is a carrier gas and the stationary phase is a thin coating on the inside of a capillary column, and high-performance liquid chromatography (HPLC), in which the mobile phase is a liquid and the stationary phase is a packed column containing silica. The choice of method normally depends on the laboratory procedure, analytical efficiency, and cost. Some drug compounds are susceptible to thermal degradation and are derivatized (i.e., their chemical structure is modified to impart greater stability) prior to analysis by GC. Derivatization is not required for analysis by HPLC.

Thin-Layer Chromatography

TLC is a technique that has the advantages of being both rapid and cheap. With TLC, the sample is separated according to the relative strength of interaction of the sample analytes with a stationary phase (often a silica plate) and a mobile phase (composed generally of a solvent mixture). The sample is prepared by dissolution in a small volume of a suitable solvent (often methanol). An ideal solvent for drug analysis is one in which the drug of interest is freely soluble, does not react with the drug or catalyze breakdown, and is volatile for easy concentration of the sample. The sample to be analyzed, together with positive and negative controls, should all be spotted onto the same TLC plate and developed in the usual manner.

After development, the plate is viewed under ultraviolet (UV) light and any visible spots recorded. Depending on the suspected class of drug present in the sample, other visualization techniques are commonly used, usually involving spraying the plates with reagents. The R_f values of the sample are compared with the controls run on the same plate, and they may also be compared with literature values using the same solvent system (though these should be interpreted with care).

High-Performance Liquid Chromatography

HPLC systems are generally comprised of a pump, an injector to introduce the sample, a column containing the stationary phase, a detector, and a recorder or other data handling system. The pump delivers the mobile phase through the system at high pressure. The sample is introduced into an injection port equipped with a fixed volume sample loop, which ensures that the injection volume remains constant and reproducible for every injection. The column, usually 5–25 cm long with an internal diameter of 2–5 mm, is packed with adsorbent. In normal-phase chromatography, the stationary phase is polar and the mobile phase is less polar; in reversed-phase chromatography, the stationary phase is nonpolar and the mobile phase is polar.

UV detectors are the most commonly used type of HPLC detector. UV spectrophotometers monitor the light absorbed by the solute molecules from the incident beam. Absorbance in solution is proportional to concentration according to the Beer–Lambert law:

$$A = \log\left(\frac{I_0}{I_t}\right) = \varepsilon c l$$

where A is the absorbance (dimensionless), I_0 and I_t are the intensities of the incident and transmitted radiation, respectively, ε is the absorptivity (L cm^{-1} mol^{-1}), c is the concentration (mol L^{-1}), and l is the path length through the absorbing volume (cm).

Flow cells, which are of small volume and avoid excessive band broadening, are required. Typically, flow cells have a path length of 10 mm and a bore of 1 mm, resulting in a volume of 8 μl. There are two general types of UV detector in use for drug analysis: fixed wavelength and variable wavelength. Fixed-wavelength detectors use mercury vapor lamps to produce radiant energy that is passed through the sample. Variable-wavelength detectors utilize deuterium and tungsten lamps combined with manually adjustable diffraction grating monochromators to allow the user to choose the optimum wavelength. Photodiode array detectors (DADs) allow continuous scanning of the absorbance spectrum of the eluant. With this setup, all of the light (rather than single wavelengths) is passed through the sample. The transmitted light is then dispersed into single wavelengths that are simultaneously focused onto an array of up to 1056 photodiode detectors.

Gas Chromatography

In GC, the vaporized sample is transported by a carrier gas (the mobile phase) through a column containing the stationary phase. The column, which is heated in an oven, is where separation of the components of the injected sample occurs, and each component is detected when it elutes from the column. A variety of detectors can be used, but increasingly a mass spectrometer (MS) is favored.

In the injection port, the sample (usually 1–2 μl) is injected onto the column through a self-sealing rubber septum. The temperature of the injection port is such that the sample is immediately vaporized, ideally without thermal decomposition of the sample. Injections can be split or splitless. In both cases, a glass liner is positioned between the injection port and top of the column with a needle valve positioned between the

liner and top of the column. The liner may also contain a plug of glass wool to trap nonvolatile components. In a split injection, the valve is opened to allow the majority of the sample to be vented to waste. Typically, only 1–2% of the sample enters the column with split ratios ranging from 1:10 to 1:100. Splitless injections require the split needle valve to be fully closed initially.

Normally, capillary columns are used for drug analysis consisting of a long length of tubing, typically 10–100 m, with a small internal diameter, 0.1–0.7 mm, which is coated with a thin layer of the stationary phase. Introduction of the GC effluent into the high vacuum of the MS can be achieved relatively easily when capillary columns are in use. Due to the narrow bore of the column, mobile phase flow rates are low (generally <2 ml min^{-1}) and the end of the column can be directly connected to the ion source of the MS. The interface between the GC and MS consists of a transfer line of glass or glass-lined metal that is also heated to prevent condensation of the analytes. The carrier gas is then pumped away by the vacuum system of the MS.

Quantitative Chromatographic Analysis

The area under a component peak is proportional to the concentration of the component in the sample. A simple method of quantification requires the peak area of a component to be expressed as a percentage of total peak area of all the components in the sample. The accuracy of this method, however, depends on all the components being detected with the same sensitivity.

The use of external standards allows precise and rapid quantification of an unknown component, so long as the detector has a linear response for the encountered concentration(s) of the unknown component. An internal standard can be added to the sample matrix itself to achieve quantification as well as compensate for slight variations in injection volumes. Component peak areas are then divided by the internal standard's peak area and the resulting "normalized" peak area used for quantification or comparison of components between samples.

HPLC and gas chromatography mass spectroscopy (GCMS) are both commonly used for quantitative analysis of drugs of abuse, and GCMS is generally used for impurity identification in drug profiling.

Mass Spectrometry

MS is a technique used for the identification of compounds by determination of molecular weight as well as detection of positions within the molecule at which fragmentation can occur during ionization. MSs have three main components: an ion source for ionizing the sample, a magnetic sector for separating the ionized particles according to mass-to-charge ratio (m/z), and a detector. Two methods are used for the ionization of molecules: electron impact (EI) and chemical ionization. EI is most commonly used, so only this method will be addressed here. In EI MS, an organic molecule is bombarded with electrons and converted to a positively charged ion; loss of an electron from this starting molecule leads to a radical cation, which is called the molecular ion or parent ion and is denoted by $M^{+\bullet}$. The molecular ion is then broken apart into fragment or daughter ions. The molecular ion usually breaks up into a pair of fragments:

$$M^{+\bullet} \rightarrow m_1^+ + m_2^\bullet \quad \text{or} \quad m_1^{+\bullet} + m_2.$$

All of these ions are subjected to a variable magnetic field where they are separated according to their mass and charge (which is usually one) in a high vacuum. At the collector, each ion generates a current in proportion to its relative abundance. This current is then converted and plotted as relative abundance against the mass-to-charge ratio (m/z) of the ion. Neutral particles, such as $m^\bullet$ or m, cannot be detected.

The electrons used to fragment the sample molecule are produced by a heated tungsten filament. The number and energy of electrons emitted are dependent on the temperature and potential of the filament, respectively. At low potential (10 V), fragmentation does not occur so readily, which is useful for determination of molecular weight since the molecular ion tends to dominate the spectrum. At higher potential (70 V), structural determination is better achieved due to extensive fragmentation.

The ion source, which is heated at 200–250 °C, is kept at low pressure. This helps prevent collisions between sample molecules and ions, reduces background spectra, and maintains the mean free path of the ions within the source.

The mass analyzer, which separates ions according to their m/z ratio, is commonly a quadrupole consisting of four conducting rods positioned parallel to the direction of travel of the ions. Adjacent rods are of opposite charge. By application of a fixed direct current (DC) potential and an oscillating radio frequency (rf) field, an electric field is generated within the region bound by the four rods. This causes the ions to travel in spiral paths, and the DC:rf ratio is set so that the ions within a narrow m/z range, typically 0.8 m/z, reach the detector without colliding with the rods. Ions outside this narrow range collide with the rods and are not detected. In scanning mode, the DC:rf ratio is varied so that ions with increasing m/z reach the detector. In a technique such as GCMS, the quadrupole mass analyzer has a fast scan rate of up to 780 mass units per second, which achieves the full mass spectrum for each eluted component.

After separation of ions according to m/z, they are detected and their relative abundance recorded. The detector consists of a glass tube drawn out into multiplication tubes with ring-shaped electrodes, called dynodes, along the length of the tube. These dynodes are coated with a substrate, typically PbO, which readily emits secondary electrons. The ion beam from the mass analyzer is attracted to the multiplication tube by application of a high voltage (-2600 to -3500 V). Ions collide with the dynodes, thus causing emission of one or more secondary electrons. These electrons are accelerated along the tube and further collisions occur, resulting in the emission of more secondary electrons. In this way, the original low-intensity ion beam is amplified, usually in the order of 10^5–10^7.

Isotope Ratio Mass Spectrometry

In recent years, considerable attention has been paid to the applications of IRMS in forensic science, including the analysis of drugs of abuse.

Isotopes of an element have different mass numbers (i.e., the same number of protons but a different number of neutrons in their nuclei). The lighter isotope (lower mass number) usually dominates in natural abundance, with one or more heavier isotopes existing in less than a few percent. The dominant isotope is often referred to as the major isotope, with the heavier isotope(s) called the minor isotope(s). Normally, IRMS analysis of drugs of abuse involves the determination of the relative isotope abundances of hydrogen (^1H and ^2H), carbon (^{12}C and ^{13}C), nitrogen (^{14}N and N^{15}), and oxygen (^{16}O, ^{17}O, and ^{18}O). The terrestrial isotope ratios were determined when the earth was formed and are, for the most part, fixed. Compartmentally (e.g., between species or climatic regions), isotope ratios vary constantly as a result of biological, biochemical, chemical, and physical processes. Any such process, which changes the relative abundances of an element's isotopes, is called isotopic fractionation. Two different types of effects result in isotopic fractionation: kinetic isotope effects (KIEs) and thermodynamic isotope effects (TIEs).

KIEs, or mass discriminating effects, are due to differences in reaction rates as a result of different bond strengths between heavier and lighter elements. Statistical models predict that lighter isotopes form weaker bonds; therefore, lighter isotopes are more reactive and will be concentrated in the products, while the heavier isotopes will be concentrated in the reactants. When this occurs, the effect is said to be *normal*. If, on the other hand, the products are enriched with the heavier isotopes and the reactants with the lighter ones, the effect is termed *inverse*.

Isotope fractionation is associated with differences in melting point, boiling point, vapor pressure, IR absorption, and other physicochemical properties. In contrast with KIEs, TIEs are evident in processes in which chemical bonds are neither broken nor formed.

IRMS measures natural-abundance isotope ratios *relative* to a standard; it does not measure absolute natural abundance. Data are generally quoted as delta values, δ, which can be calculated by the following equation:

$$\delta^{13}C = 1000\left(\frac{R_{samp}}{R_{std}} - 1\right),$$

where R_{samp} is the ratio of the number of atoms of the heavy isotope to the number of atoms of the light isotope of an element and R_{std} is the equivalent ratio corresponding to the standard. Because differences in isotope abundance ratios between the sample and the standard are typically only 0.001–0.05%, δ values include multiplication by 1000 for ease of discussion and are therefore quoted "per mill" (‰). A negative δ value indicates that the sample is enriched in the light isotope relative to the standard, and a positive δ value indicates the sample is enriched in the heavy isotope relative to the standard.

Natural abundances of isotopes vary constantly despite fixed whole earth isotope abundances. Given that the synthesis of most illicit substances starts with a natural product (e.g., safrole from the sassafras tree in the case of 3,4-methylenedioxymethylamphetamine (MDMA), coca leaf in the case of cocaine, and opium from poppies in the case of heroin), the isotopic fractionation occurring in these plants may play an important role in determining the final isotopic composition of a specific product.

Analysis of a plant's natural carbon isotope abundance can allow determination of the pathway by which the plant fixes (or assimilates) atmospheric CO_2 into carbohydrate. For example, plants that assimilate CO_2 by the Calvin cycle, that is, they convert CO_2 into carbohydrates via the three-carbon-chain molecule phosphoglyceric acid, are called C_3 plants. These plants generally have $\delta^{13}C$ values of -34 to -24‰. Plants that assimilate CO_2 by the Hatch–Slack cycle, that is, they convert CO_2 into carbohydrates via the four-chain molecule oxaloacetic acid, are called C_4 plants. Plants with this type generally have $\delta^{13}C$ values of -16 to -9‰. Humidity, temperature, isotopic composition of the soil, and isotopic composition of CO_2 also affect these $\delta^{13}C$ values.

Hydrogen and oxygen isotope abundances of terrestrial waters are affected by evaporation. For example, citrus trees growing in subtropical climates may be subjected to extensive evaporation that causes ^2H enrichment in the cellular water of the fruit. Variation in nitrogen isotope abundance is caused by many chemical and physical processes, resulting in variable isotope ratios of common materials.

The IRMS system can be interfaced with different sample preparation techniques, which allow either bulk stable isotope analysis (BSIA) or compound-specific isotope analysis (CSIA) to be undertaken. BSIA measures the isotope ratios for the sample as a whole. If carbon is the target element for analysis, then the $^{13}C/^{12}C$ ratio returned by the instrument will represent *all* of the carbon atoms in *every* compound present in the sample. CSIA measures the isotope ratio for one compound in the sample. The separation of the sample can be achieved by the coupling of the IRMS to a GC instrument. In this case, the sample is dissolved in an organic solvent and injected onto the first GC column. Baseline separation of the peaks is essential, as accurate determination of isotope ratios cannot be achieved from a partial GC peak.

Conclusions

Most analysis of drugs of abuse is undertaken using conventional analytical techniques. The implementation of techniques such as IRMS has specific values in drug profiling but is not used for routine analysis. In selecting the appropriate analytical regime, a balance must be struck between required laboratory efficiencies and desired scientific result to the specific task at hand (e.g., identification, quantification, and intelligence).

> *See also:* **Chemistry/Trace/Drugs of Abuse:** Clandestine Laboratories; Classification; Designer Drugs.

Further Reading

Besacier, F., Chaudron-Thozet, H., Rousseau-Tsangaris, M., Girard, J., Lamotte, A., 1997. Comparative chemical analyses of drug samples: general approach and application to heroin. Forensic Science International 85 (2), 113–125.

Braithwaite, A., Smith, F.J., 1996. Chromatographic Methods, fifth ed. Blackie Academic & Professional, Glasgow.

Carter, J.F., Titterton, E.L., Grant, H., Sleeman, R., 2002. Isotopic changes during the synthesis of amphetamines. Chemical Communications 21, 2590–2591.

Carter, J.F., Titterton, E.L., Murray, M., Sleeman, R., 2002. Isotopic characterisation of 3,4-methylenedioxymethylamphetamine and 3,4-methylenedioxymethylamphetamine (ecstasy). Analyst 127, 830–833.

Casale, J., Casale, E., Collins, M., Morello, D., Cathapermal, S., Panicker, S., 2006. Stable isotope analyses of heroin seized from the merchant vessel Pong Su. Journal of Forensic Sciences 51 (3), 603–606.

Desage, M., Guilluy, R., Brazier, J.L., et al., 1991. Gas-chromatography with mass-spectrometry or isotope-ratio mass-spectrometry in studying the geographical origin of heroin. Analytica Chimica Acta 247 (2), 249–254.

Kurashima, N., Makino, Y., Sekita, S., Urano, Y., Nagano, T., 2004. Determination of origin of ephedrine used as precursor for illicit methamphetamine by carbon and nitrogen stable isotope ratio analysis. Analytical Chemistry 76 (14), 4233–4236.

Lurie, I.S., Wittwer Jr., J.D., 1983. High-Performance Liquid Chromatography in Forensic Chemistry, vol. 24. Marcel Dekker, New York.

Mas, F., Beemsterboer, B., Veltkamp, A.C., Verweij, A.M.A., 1995. Determination of common-batch members in a set of confiscated 3,4-(methylenedioxy)methyl-amphetamine samples by measuring the natural isotope abundances – a preliminary study. Forensic Science International 71 (3), 225–231.

Meier-Augenstein, W., Liu, R.H., 2004. Forensic applications of isotope ratio mass spectrometry. In: Yinon, J. (Ed.), Advances in Forensic Applications of Mass Spectrometry. CRC Press, Boca Raton, FL, pp. 149–180.

Palhol, F., Lamoureux, C., Chabrillat, M., Naulet, N., 2004. $^{15}N/^{14}N$ isotopic ratio and statistical analysis: an efficient way of linking seized ecstasy tablets. Analytica Chimica Acta 510 (1), 1–8.

Willard, H.H., Merritt Jr., L.L., Dean, J.A., Settle Jr., F.A., 1988. Instrumental Methods of Analysis, seventh ed. Wadsworth Publishers, Belmont, CA.

Classification

N NicDaéid and KA Savage, University of Strathclyde, Glasgow, UK

Introduction

Drugs can be classified depending upon how they are derived. This classification is as natural products, semisynthetic drugs, synthetic drugs, and designer drugs. Natural drugs are active ingredients and/or secondary metabolic products of plants and other living systems that may be isolated by extraction (e.g., morphine). Semisynthetic drugs are products from natural sources, which are subject to some chemical process to modify their structure (e.g., diamorphine or cocaine). Synthetic drugs are artificially produced substances for the licit or illicit market, which are almost wholly manufactured from chemical compounds in a laboratory (e.g., amphetamine and benzodiazepines). Designer drugs are substances, either natural or synthetic, whose molecular structure has been modified in order to optimize their effect, on the one hand, and in order to bypass laws and regulations governing the control of substances, on the other hand.

Natural Drugs

Cannabis

Cannabis is the most consumed illicit drug in the world, and therefore the subject of the most illegal trafficking in one form or another. The botanical name of cannabis is *Cannabis sativa* and it is referred to as marijuana (herbal cannabis) and hashish (cannabis resin), terms associated with cannabis grown for its illicit use, or as hemp, a term usually associated with *Cannabis* plants grown for their fiber content.

Cannabis is native to the mountainous areas of central and south Asia and the plant has been used by man for over 6000 years. *Cannabis* grows over a wide variety of geographic terrains, altitudes, and latitudes. It is grown in many countries and on all continents. Although it prefers the higher temperatures and longer growing seasons of the equatorial areas of the world, it has been cultivated as far north as 60° latitude. With the more recent prevalence for hydroponic growth, *Cannabis* is known to be grown in 172 countries around the globe.

Cannabis and its related products comprise over three quarters of the drug materials submitted to Forensic Science Laboratories in the United Kingdom for analysis. A number of forms of the drug may be encountered, including plant material, resin, and "hash oil." The active ingredient in all of these is Δ^9-tetrahydrocannabinol (THC). Also found is Δ^9-tetrahydrocannabinolic acid (THCOOH), which is converted to THC through smoking. Also present are the compounds Δ^8-THC (an isomer of the active ingredient), cannabidiol (CBD—the precursor), and cannabinol (CBN—the metabolite), as well as upward of 50 minor CBNs. The chemical structures of these compounds are presented in **Figure 1**.

Fresh plant material

Cannabis plant material can occur as live plants, or as dried plant material. It is important when examining plant material that it should be in the dried state as water content will affect any weight measurements, a crucial factor in determining the seriousness of any charges. Male and female *Cannabis* plants are separate, with the male plant flowering before the female to ensure cross-pollination. The plant grows between 30 cm and 6 m in height and grows from seed to maturity in about 3 months, though harvesting can occur after 2 months. The leaves are palmate with serrated edges and are opposite and alternate around a hollow four-cornered stem. The leaves are coated with upward-pointing unicellular hairs called trichomes. Nonglandular trichomes are found on the stems and leaves together with a few glandular trichomes, which contain the THC. The greatest concentration of glandular trichomes is in the flowering tops of the plants and those of the female plant have a greater concentration of THC. Material prepared from the flowering tops or leaves is commonly called marijuana and usually contains 0.5–5% THC. *Cannabis* plants grown under controlled hydroponic conditions, which are predominantly female plants (skunk), generally have a higher quantity of THC (9–25%) and can reach full maturity in about 13 weeks.

Dried plant material

This may occur in various ways. Low-quality products contain stalks, seeds, leaves, and flowering tops. This may be compressed into blocks (west African and Caribbean material) as loose material or rolled up and wrapped in vegetable leaves (central and southern Africa). High-quality material contains mostly flowering tops and can be found rolled up or wrapped around bamboo sticks ("Buddha" or "Thai" sticks) or sieved ("Kif") and generally originates from southeast Asia or parts of Africa.

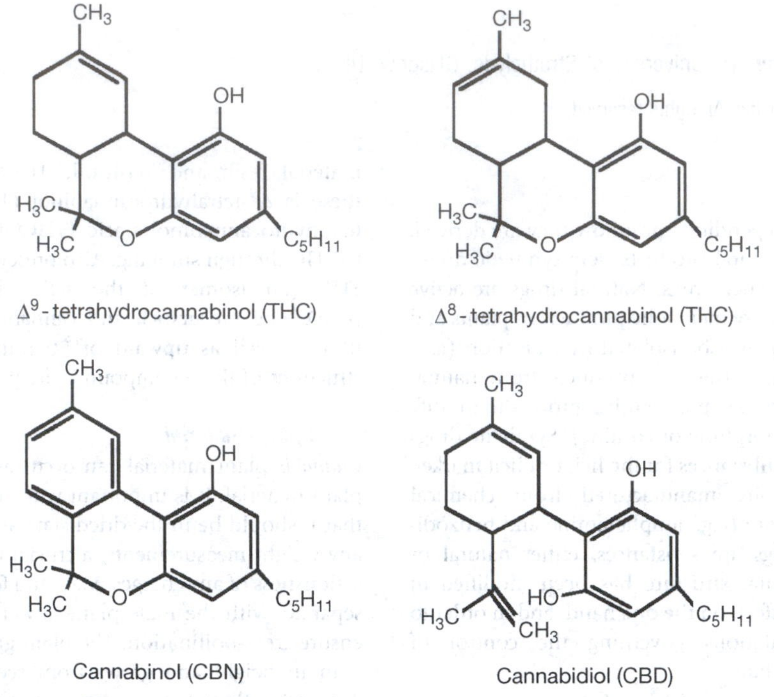

Figure 1   Chemical structures of the main cannabinoids.

Resin

This is also produced directly from the plant material. The glandular trichomes produce a resin that is scraped from the surface of the plant and pressed into blocks. Hashish contains about 2–10% by weight of the active constituent, Δ^9-THC. Most resin is produced either in the Indian subcontinent or parts of the Mediterranean. Usually between 100 and 400 mg of resin are used in a joint, though this varies from user to user. Mediterranean resin is made by threshing the herbal material, sieving to remove seeds and stems, and the remainder compressed into slabs. The final material is light in color and quite brittle. Indian subcontinent resin is quite sticky and is removed from the plant by rubbing the plant and then molded into slabs. The final material is dark brown and sticky. When examining resin, several facts are recorded, including whether or not the blocks seized fit together, any striation marks (cutting marks) which may be present, and whether these can then be linked to a cutting instrument. The color and different layers within the resin block should also be examined and recorded. Packaging material (commonly cling film) can also be examined for physical fits linking blocks together.

Hash oil

This is a manufactured product of cannabis and is produced by extracting the whole plant material using an organic solvent (usually alcohol, ether, or benzene). On extraction the resulting

oil can contain between 10 and 30% by weight of Δ^9-THC. The oil is used in various ways including smoking in special pipes with tobacco.

The effect caused by cannabis depends largely on the expectations, moods, and motivations of the user. The most sought after effects are pleasurable sensations and greater sensory awareness, though inexperienced users on high doses can experience psychological distress. In general, *Cannabis* is recognized by the characteristics of the plant including odor, shape, and presence of trichomes.

Mushrooms and Cacti

Psilocybin and *psilocin* are found in at least 15 species of mushrooms—so-called "magic mushrooms"—belonging to the genera *Psilocybe*, *Panaeolus*, and *Conocybe*. If a seizure contains whole or parts of mushrooms, the examination should include a description of the shape, size, and color of the fungus, as well as information regarding the gills, spores, cap, and stalk. Identification of fungi is difficult and should be performed by experts in that field. Illicit trafficking of cacti, which contain the psychoactive agent, mescaline, is also known. This drug occurs in at least three species of cacti. The most common illicit form of mescaline is produced as dried disk-shaped cuttings taken from the tops of the cacti and are called "mescal buttons." The main compounds are presented in **Figure 2**.

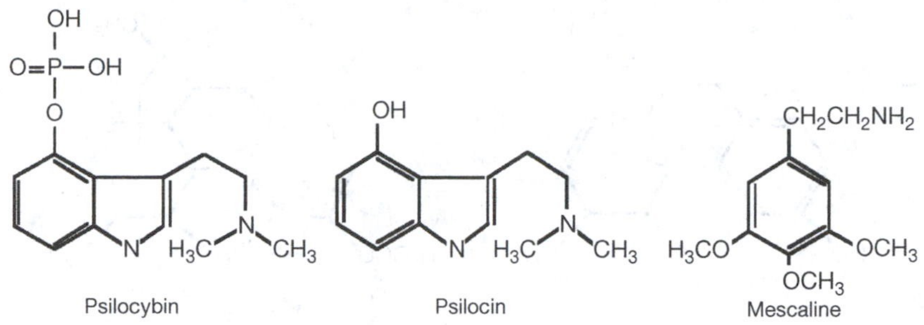

Figure 2   Chemical structure of psilocybin, psilocin, and mescaline.

Semisynthetic Drugs

Opiates

Opium is a natural product obtained from unripe poppy capsules. There are over 100 species of the genus *Papaver* (or poppy) known; however, only two, *Papaver somniferum* and *Papaver setigerum* DC., are known to produce opium.

An incision is made in the poppy capsule, and the latex that oozes from the incision is scraped-off and collected to produce a raw opium gum. When fresh, the material is a sticky tar-like brown substance with a licorice-like odor, which becomes brittle as it dries. Raw opium is a complex mixture containing sugars, proteins, lipids, and water, as well as the active alkaloid compounds (10–20%). About 40 alkaloids are known and fall broadly into two categories:

- Phenanthrene alkaloids such as morphine, codeine, and thebaine
- Isoquinoline alkaloids such as papaverine and noscapine

The relative amounts of these alkaloids vary and are dependent on factors such as climate, soil fertility, altitude, available moisture, and age of the plant.

Raw opium can be used for smoking but must first be extracted most commonly with water. Morphine can still be detected in the leftover dross that remains in the opium pipe. Several purification processes can be used in the preparation of crude morphine from raw opium. Morphine-free base is further refined to produce diamorphine. Because of the nature of the raw opium starting material, the production process, and the addition of excipients to produce "street" heroin samples, there can be a considerable intersample variation. The main alkaloids encountered in heroin street samples are presented in **Figure 3**.

Cocaine

Cocaine is derived from ecgonine alkaloids in the leaf of the coca (*Erythroxylon*) plant. There are various varieties of plant, which produce leaves of different size and appearance. In all species, the upper side of the leaf is darker in color. The underside of the leaf has two lines running parallel to the midrib of the leaf and is considered characteristic of the coca leaf. The production of cocaine from the plant is via an intermediate stage producing coca paste.

Coca leaves are mixed with calcium hydroxide (lime) and water. The mixture is crushed and stirred in a hydrocarbon solvent, usually kerosene. The extracted coca leaf residue is removed and the kerosene extracted with acidified water. The cocaine alkaloids (presented in **Figure 4**) are extracted into the aqueous layer and coca paste is precipitated by the addition of base. This paste contains crude cocaine as well as a mixture of inorganic salts and is further refined to extract cocaine.

Tryptamines

Tryptamines (**Figure 5**) are naturally occurring alkaloids found in a variety of plants and life forms around the world and exist in more than 1500 natural varieties. The basic element of tryptamine is the indol-structure and tryptamine itself is an endogenous amine found in the human brain; for example, serotonin and melatonin are two essential tryptamines present as neurotransmitters in the brain. Tryptamines can also be produced either completely synthetically or semisynthetically.

The main tryptamines found on the illicit market are dimethyltryptamine (DMT) and bufotenin. DMT is an active component of various South American snuff products, such as "COHOBA" and "YOPO" and has been produced synthetically for a number of years. Its abuse has been restricted to a small number of dedicated users. Bufotin is chemically very similar to DMT and can be found either in the skin secretions of toads or in combinations with DMT in different trees in South America (e.g., the YOPO tree).

Lysergic acid diethylamide (LSD) (**Figure 6**) is a semisynthetic drug incorporating the tryptamine structure and first synthesized by Albert Hofmann in 1938. The starting materials are lysergic acid compounds derived from ergot spores of some mushrooms. On the illicit drug market, LSD has been sold impregnated as an alcohol solution onto paper (blotters acids "trade marked" with various designs), microdots, thin squares of gelatine (window panes), or impregnated on sugar cubes.

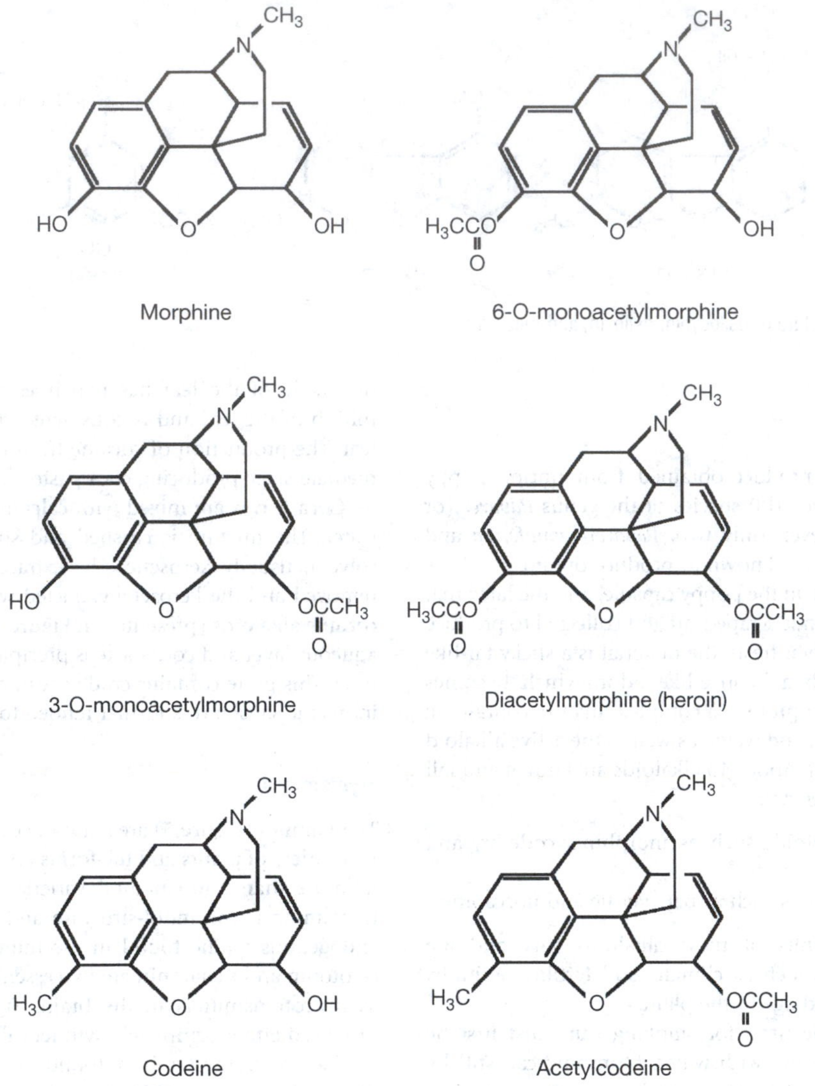

Morphine

6-O-monoacetylmorphine

3-O-monoacetylmorphine

Diacetylmorphine (heroin)

Codeine

Acetylcodeine

Figure 3   Chemical structures of common opiates.

Synthetic Drugs

Amphetamine and Amphetamine-Type Stimulants

Amphetamine-type stimulants (ATS) drugs are generally divided into two groups, the amphetamines group (amphetamine sulfate and methylamphetamine) and the ecstasy group (methylenedioxy methylamphetamine (MDMA), methylenedioxy amphetamine (MDA), methylenedioxy ethylamphetamine (MDEA), MDE). ATS precursor and pre-precursor chemicals are also controlled. From a chemical point of view, all ATS are related to β-phenethylamine that is the basic element of neurotransmitters in the body (such as dopamine and adrenaline).

The most common amphetamine derivatives (**Figure 7**) available on the illicit drug market include amphetamine sulfate, methylamphetamine, MDA, MDMA, and MDEA. Dosages in powders and tablets vary considerably but are generally in the range of 10–110 mg of drug in a single dose. Street samples of amphetamine sulfate typically contain as little as 5% drug, whereas ecstasy tablets can be up to 56–60% pure. Most, if not all, amphetamine and related compounds are synthesized in clandestine laboratories by various synthetic routes.

Ecstasy group

When the term Ecstasy was first used in the early 1970s, it was an American street name for preparations containing the active agent

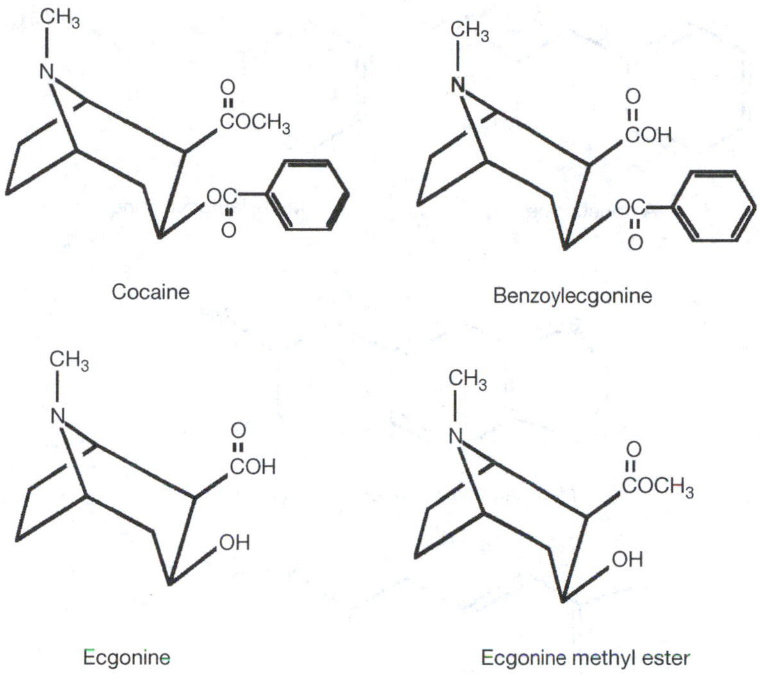

Cocaine

Benzoylecgonine

Ecgonine

Ecgonine methyl ester

Figure 4 Chemical structures of cocaine and analogues.

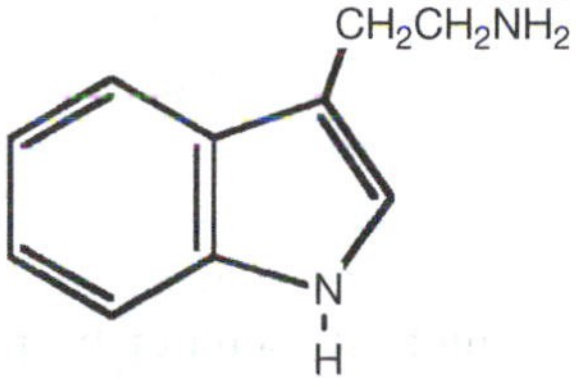

Figure 5 Tryptamine structure.

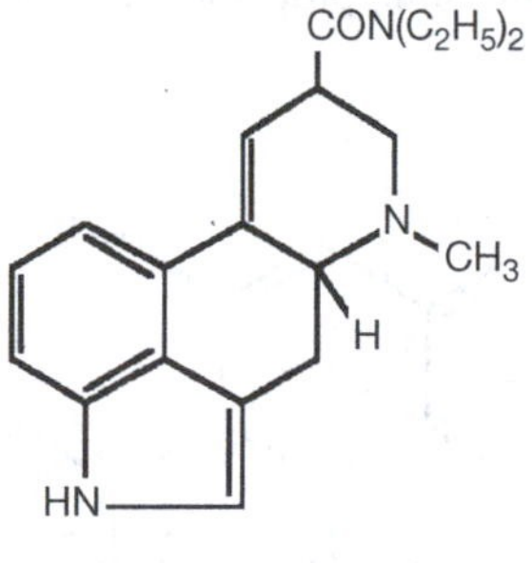

Figure 6 Chemical structure of LSD.

MDMA. Now the term describes tablets or capsules predominantly containing one or more (or combinations) of psychotropic active agents derived from the β-phenethylamine group. It is becoming more and more common to compress amphetamine/

methamphetamine into tablets that are then also marketed as ecstasy. In more recent years, other relatively new ATS are appearing in tablets. These include para-methoxymethamphatamine (PMA; 3,4-methylenedioxyphenylpropan-2-ol), ketamine (an anesthetic used in veterinary medicine), and even gamma-hydroxybutyric acid (GHB).

Amphetamine group

Amphetamine was first synthesized in 1887 but was not used for medical purposes until the early 1930s, when it was found that it increased blood pressure, stimulated the central nervous system, was effective against asthma, and useful in treating epileptic seizure disorders. On the illicit drug market, amphetamines have been sold in the form of powders, liquids, crystals, tablets, and capsules.

Barbiturates

Barbiturates (**Figure 8**) are therapeutically used as sedatives, hypnotics, anesthetics, and anticonvulsants. Virtually all barbiturates on the illicit drug market come from licit sources. There are 12 barbiturates recognized and scheduled by the United Nations and occur mainly as capsules and tablets and in some cases as injectable solutions. Illicit compounds occur as mixtures of barbiturates, or mixed with other drugs such as caffeine, aspirin, codeine, or, in some cases, heroin.

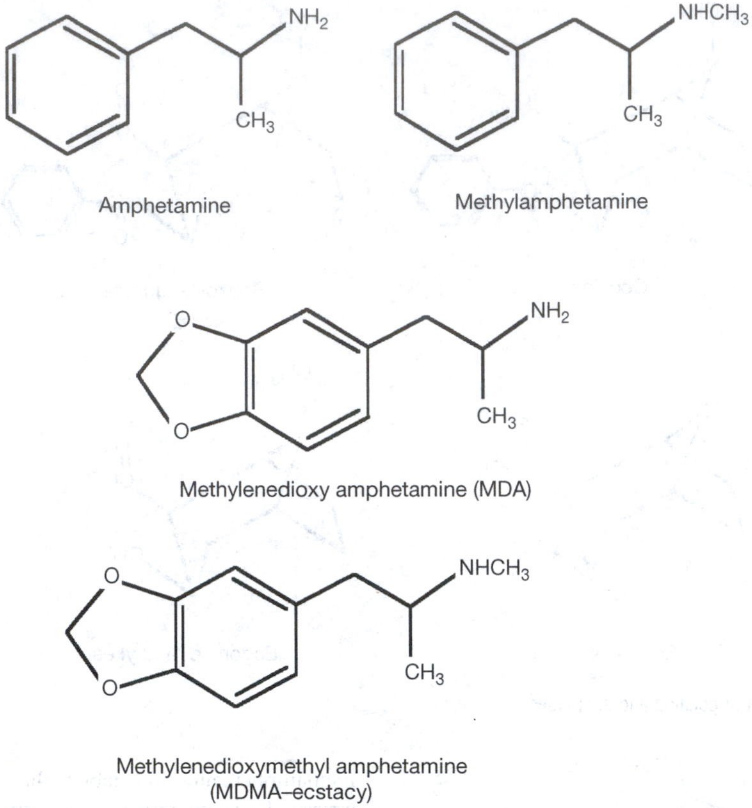

Amphetamine

Methylamphetamine

Methylenedioxy amphetamine (MDA)

Methylenedioxymethyl amphetamine
(MDMA–ecstacy)

Figure 7   Amphetamine and related compounds.

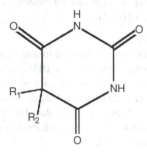

Figure 8   Barbiturate structure.

Methaqualone and Meclaqualone

Methaqualone was first synthesized in 1951 and introduced as a new drug that produced sedation and sleep in 1956. Methaqualone has been initially designed to counter the nervous damage caused by long-term consumption of barbiturates and to reduce the risk of dependency on barbiturates. Methaqualone and meclaqualone were also prepared as nonbarbiturate sleeping tablets, though they have also legally been used as hypnotics in some European countries. Interest in methaqualone has risen dramatically in recent years. Its popularity was due to its undeserved reputation as an "aphrodisiac" often in combination with diphenhydramine. Methaqualone was effectively removed from the market in 1984 because of its strong addiction-forming properties. Their structures are presented in **Figure 9**.

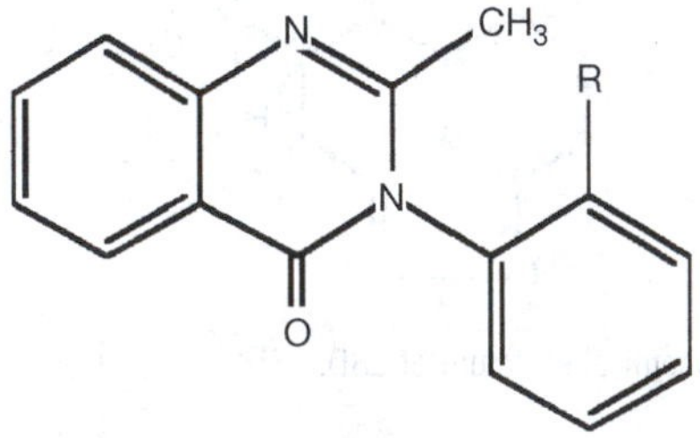

R = CH$_3$ Methaqualone
R = Cl Meclaqualone

Figure 9   Methaqualone and meclaqualone.

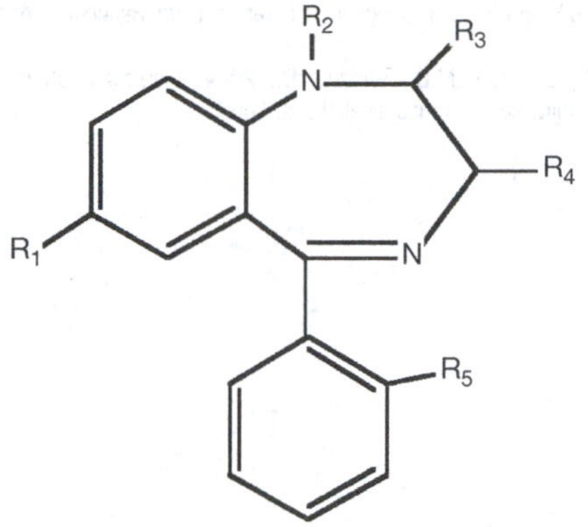

Figure 10 Benzodiazapine structure.

They appear on the illicit drug market either through diversion from the legitimate pharmaceutical trade or through illicit synthesis. The illicit samples are usually brown or gray powders with varying degrees of purity. Methaqualone is also used sometimes as a cutting agent for heroin.

Benzodiazepines

Benzodiazepines (**Figure 10**), therapeutically used as tranquillizers, hypnotics, anticonvulsants, and centrally acting muscle relaxants, rank among the most frequently prescribed drugs. In 1960, the first benzodiazepine, chlordiazepoxide, was introduced. To date, more than 50 benzodiazepines have been marketed in over 100 different preparations. They appear mainly as capsules and tablets; however, some are marketed in other forms such as injectable solutions or powders. Benzodiazepines were introduced to replace barbiturates and methaqualone as tranquillizers, hypnotics, anticonvulsants, and muscle relaxants. Currently, there are 33 benzodiazepines on the control list all of which appear as tablets or capsules, though some also appear as vials or powders for preparation for injection.

On the illicit drug market, diazepam ("Valium"), temazepam (often referred to as "jellies"), and flunitrazepam ("Rohypnol") are used as drug substitutes, as additives in drug preparations, or in combination with alcohol, as methods of incapacitating individuals ("Rohypnol" is sometimes known as a "date rape drug"). Virtually all benzodiazepines on the illicit market result from diversion from legitimate sources and there is no evidence of clandestine manufacture.

Phencyclidine and Analogues

Phencyclidine (PCP) was synthesized and tested in the early 1950s and recommended for clinical trials as an anesthetic in humans in 1957. In 1965, further human clinical investigation of PCP was discontinued and the compound was marketed

commercially as a veterinary anesthetic. PCP became available through the drug culture in the late 1960s, referred to as "PeaCe-Pill," commonly sold as "angel dust," "crystal," or "hog" in powder, tablet, leaf mixture, and 1 g "rock" crystal forms, usually taken orally, by smoking, snorting, or intravenous injection. The laboratory synthesis of PCP and approximately 120 related substances, such as Eticyclidin (PCE) or Tenocyclidin (TCP), is cheap but also work intensive and time consuming.

A structurally related anesthetic, ketamine ("special K"), has been developed and has gained popularity in recent years.

Gamma-Hydroxybutyric Acid

GHB is a drug, which is very similar to a natural chemical in the human brain called gamma-aminobutyric acid. GHB is a simple sodium (or potassium) salt of 4-gamma-hydroxybutyric acid. The street names are "liquid E," "liquid ecstasy," or "fantasy," and they are currently not listed as a controlled substance. The forms of use are tablets, white powder, or dissolved in water or other liquids. GHB (like Rohypnol) is sometimes added to alcoholic drinks as methods of incapacitating individuals and is also known as a "date rape drug."

Originally GHB was marketed as a supplement replacement for L-tryptophan (an amino acid). Since the early 1990s, it has been illicitly used by athletes and bodybuilders believing that its growth hormone releasing effects contribute to anabolism and lipolysis, or misused as a sleep aid and for weight control.

GHB can be very easily prepared from gamma butyrolactone—a common industrial chemical for paint removers—by alkaline hydrolysis. The clandestine manufacture of GHB requires no prior chemical expertise as evidenced by the simplistic instructions given in the underground publications or on the Internet.

"Legal Highs"

"Legal highs" have the same or similar effects as illegal drugs, but are structurally different enough from the drugs that they mimic to avoid control under the Misuse of Drugs Act. In order to circumvent the Medicines Act, they are sold as, for example, plant food or bath salts. Legal highs are widely available over the Internet and may be known as, for example, "legal marijuana," Spice, NRG, Ivory Wave.

Mephedrone is a synthetic compound similar to methcathinone, the active ingredient in Khat, and has been found in some legal high substances. Mephedrone may be known as M-Cat, Miew-miew, among other names. Mephedrone has recently been classified as an illegal Class B drug.

See also: **Chemistry/Trace/Drugs of Abuse:** Analysis of Controlled Substances; **Chemistry/Trace/Fire Investigation:** Interpretation of Fire Debris Analysis.

Further Reading

Karch, S.B., 2007. A Drug Abuse Handbook. CRC Press, Boca Raton, FL.

King, L.A., 2009. Forensic Chemistry of Substance Misuse. Royal Society of Chemistry, Cambridge.

Laing, R. (Ed.), 2003. Hallucinogens a Forensic Drug Handbook. Academic Press, London.

Moffat, A.C., Osselton, M.D., Widdop, B., 2004. Clarke's Analysis of Drugs and Poisons, third ed. Pharmacutical Press, London.

Designer Drugs

S Fu and N Stojanovska, University of Technology Sydney, Broadway, NSW, Australia

Glossary

Adulterant Any material that lessens the purity or effectiveness of a substance, especially a pharmacologically active drug.

Date-rape An act of sexual intercourse regarded as tantamount to rape, especially if the victim was under the influence of alcohol or other drugs.

Designer drug A drug with properties and effects similar to a known illicit or prohibited drug but having a slightly altered chemical structure, especially such a drug created in order to evade legislative controls.

Herbal High A recreational drug mixture consisting mainly of natural and/or synthetically derived compounds producing drug-like effects.

Smart Shops/Head Shops Retail outlets specializing in drug paraphernalia (e.g., pipes to smoke cannabis) used for the consumption/ingestion of recreational drugs.

Spice A mixture of plant materials fortified with synthetic chemicals that mimic the effect of cannabis when smoked by users.

Introduction

The term designer drug is used to describe drugs that are modified in an attempt to circumvent legislative controls. This is usually done by modifying the chemical structure of current illegal drugs or by finding drugs with entirely different chemical structures that have similar subjective effects to current recreational/illicit drugs. Besides the classic examples of amphetamine (AP)-type designer drugs such as 3,4-methylenedioxyamphetamine (MDA) and 3,4-methylenedioxymethamphetamine (MDMA), which have been widely abused for decades, a number of new drug classes have appeared on the illicit drug market in recent years. These new drug classes include 2,5-dimethoxyamphetamines, 2,5-phenylamines (2C drugs), β-keto amphetamines (cathinones), phencyclidines, piperazines, pyrrolidinophenones, fentanyls, piperidines, and tryptamine derivatives. A number of "Herbal Highs" such as "Kratom," a *Mitragyna* plant native to Thailand and other southeast Asian countries, and more recently "Spice," which contains added synthetic cannabinoids, have also been encountered in many illicit drug markets. Some designer steroids have emerged and are particularly popular among athletes seeking to avoid detection of steroidal abuse in order to gain unfair performance enhancement advantages. The chemical structures of some of these designer drugs are presented in **Figure 1** and **Table 1**.

The continual emergence and rapid spread of novel designer drugs not only pose a serious health risk to consumers due to the limited pharmacokinetics and toxicological data available but also present an ongoing challenge to forensic chemists, forensic toxicologists, and law enforcement agencies. To effectively combat the problems associated with designer drugs, a collective effort needs to be in place from forensic scientists, health professionals, and law enforcement authorities. It is important to stay at the forefront of drug detection techniques and strategies to allow speedy identification of new substances as they emerge. Metabolism and toxicity data need to be collected to facilitate diagnosis and treatment of designer drug-induced intoxication. At the same time, drug scheduling authorities need to schedule these drugs promptly to enable laws to be applied to the production, distribution, and consumption of these illicit substances to safeguard society.

Designer Drugs of Various Structural Types

AP-Type Designer Drugs

There are many designer drugs that are structural analogues of AP and methamphetamine (MA). The most common way for the construction of an AP-type designer drug is the introduction of N-alkyl substituents of a different size into the molecule of a parent drug of known activity. Consequently, a number of MDA homologues, such as MDMA, 3,4-methylenedioxyethylamphetamine (MDEA), N,N-dimethyl-3,4-methylenedioxyamphetamine (DMMDA), N-propyl-3,4-methylenedioxyamphetamine (N-propyl-MDA), and N-isopropyl-3,4-methylenedioxyamphetamine (N-isopropyl-MDA), were synthesized and introduced into the illicit drug market. In addition, benzodioxolylbutanamine (BDB) and N-methylbenzodioxolylbutanamine (MBDB) have also been encountered in recent years. N-Hydroxy analogues, such as N-hydroxy-MDA and N-hydroxy-MDMA,

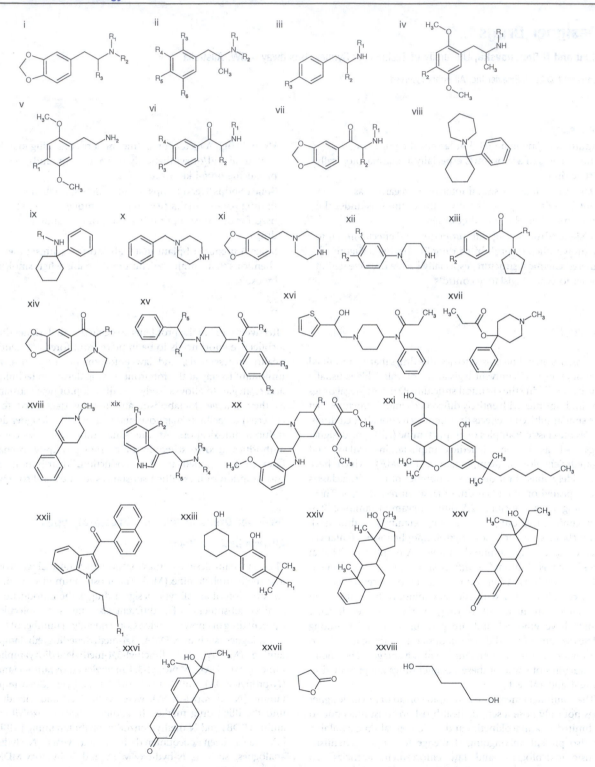

Figure 1 Structures of some common designer drugs. Amphetamine types (i–iii); 2,5-dimethoxyamphetamines (iv); 2,5-phenethylamines (v); β-keto amphetamines (vi, vii); phencyclidines (viii, ix); piperazines (x–xii); pyrrolidinophenones (xiii, xiv); fentanyls (xv, xvi); piperidines (xvii, xviii); tryptamines (xix); "Kratom" alkaloids (xx); synthetic cannabinoids (xxi–xxiii); synthetic steroids (xxiv–xxvi); GHB-related substances (xxvii, xxviii).

Table 1   Names and chemical structures of common designer drugs with parent molecular features illustrated in **Figure 1**

Drug name	Parent structure	Substituents					
		R_1	R_2	R_3	R_4	R_5	R_6
3,4-Methylenedioxyamphetamine (MDA)	i	H	H	CH_3	–	–	–
3,4-Methylenedioxymethamphetamine (MDMA)		CH_3	H	CH_3	–	–	–
3,4-Methylenedioxyethylamphetamine (MDEA)		CH_2CH_3	H	CH_3	–	–	–
N,N-Dimethyl-MDA (DMMDA)		CH_3	CH_3	CH_3	–	–	–
N-Propyl-MDA		$CH_2CH_2CH_3$	H	CH_3	–	–	–
N-Isopropyl-MDA		$CH(CH_3)_2$	H	CH_3	–	–	–
Benzodioxolylbutanamine (BDB)		H	H	CH_2CH_3	–	–	–
N-Methylbenzodioxolylbutanamine (MBDB)		CH_3	H	CH_2CH_3	–	–	–
N-Hydroxy-MDA		OH	H	CH_3	–	–	–
N-Hydroxy-MDMA		OH	CH_3	CH_3	–	–	–
4-Methylthioamphetamine (4-MTA)	ii	H	H	H	H	SCH_3	H
4-Methylthiomethamphetamine (4-MTMA)		CH_3	H	H	H	SCH_3	H
4-Methylthioethylamphetamine (4-MTEA)		CH_2CH_3	H	H	H	SCH_3	H
4-Methylthiodimethamphetamine (4-MTDMA)		CH_3	CH_3	H	H	SCH_3	H
4-Methylthiopropylamphetamine (4-MTPA)		$CH_2CH_2CH_3$	H	H	H	SCH_3	H
4-Methylthiobutylamphetamine (4-MTBA)		$CH_2CH_2CH_2CH_3$	H	H	H	SCH_3	H
p-Methoxyamphetamine (PMA)		H	H	H	H	OCH_3	H
p-Methoxymethylamphetamine (PMMA)		CH_3	H	H	H	OCH_3	H
2-Fluoroamphetamine		H	H	F	H	H	H
3-Fluoroamphetamine		H	H	H	F	H	H
4-Fluoroamphetamine		H	H	H	H	F	H
5-Fluoro-2-methoxyamphetamine		H	H	OCH_3	H	H	F
3-Fluoro-4-methoxyamphetamine		H	H	H	F	OCH_3	H
N-Methyl-4-fluoroamphetamine		CH_3	H	H	H	F	H
N-Ethyl-4-fluoroamphetamine		CH_2CH_3	H	H	H	F	H
N-Ethyl-4-methoxyamphetamine	iii	CH_2CH_3	CH_3	OCH_3	–	–	–
1-(4-Fluorophenyl)-butan-2-amine		H	CH_2CH_3	F	–	–	–
4-Bromo-2,5-dimethoxyamphetamine (DOB)	iv	H	Br	–	–	–	–
4-Iodo-2,5-dimethoxyamphetamine (DOI)		H	I	–	–	–	–
4-Chloro-2,5-dimethoxyamphetamine (DOC)		H	Cl	–	–	–	–
2,5-Dimethoxy-4-methyl-amphetamine (DOM)		H	CH_3	–	–	–	–
4-Bromo-2,5-dimethoxymethamphetamine (MDOB)		CH_3	Br	–	–	–	–
2,4,5-Trimethoxyamphetamine (TMA)		H	OCH_3	–	–	–	–
4-Bromo-2,5-dimethoxyphenethylamine (2C–B)	v	Br	–	–	–	–	–
4-Iodo-2,5-dimethoxyphenethylamine (2C–I)		I	–	–	–	–	–
4-Methyl-2,5-dimethoxyphenethylamine (2C–D)		CH_3	–	–	–	–	–
4-Ethyl-2,5-dimethoxyphenethylamine (2C–E)		CH_2CH_3	–	–	–	–	–
4-Chloro-2,5-dimethoxyphenethylamine (2C–C)		Cl	–	–	–	–	–
4-Ethylthio-2,5-dimethoxyphenethylamine (2C-T-2)		SCH_2CH_3	–	–	–	–	–
4-(n)-Propylthio-2,5-dimethoxyphenethylamine (2C-T-7)		$SCH_2CH_2CH_3$	–	–	–	–	–
4-(2-Fluoroethylthio)-2,5-dimethoxyphenethylamine (2C-T-21)		SCH_2CH_2F	–	–	–	–	–
Cathinone	vi	H	CH_3	H	H	–	–
Ephedrone (methcathinone)		CH_3	CH_3	H	H	–	–
Mephedrone (bk-MMA)		CH_3	CH_3	CH_3	H	–	–
3-Fluoromethcathinone		CH_3	CH_3	H	F	–	–
Butylone (bk-MBDB)	vii	CH_3	CH_2CH_3	–	–	–	–
Ethylone (bk-MDEA)		CH_2CH_3	CH_3	–	–	–	–
Methylone (bk-MDMA)		CH_3	CH_3	–	–	–	–

(Continued)

Table 1   Names and chemical structures of common designer drugs with parent molecular features illustrated in Figure 1—cont'd

Drug name	Parent structure	Substituents					
		R_1	R_2	R_3	R_4	R_5	R_6
Phencyclidine (PCP)	viii	–	–	–	–	–	–
N-(1-Phenylcyclohexyl)propanamine (PCPPA)	ix	$CH_2CH_2CH_3$	–	–	–	–	–
N-(1-Phenylcyclohexyl)-3-methoxypropanamine (PCMPA)		$CH_2CH_2CH_2OCH_3$	–	–	–	–	–
N-(1-Phenylcyclohexyl)-2-methoxyethanamine (PCMEA)		$CH_2CH_2OCH_3$	–	–	–	–	–
N-(1-Phenylcyclohexyl)-2-ethoxyethanamine (PCEEA)		$CH_2CH_2OCH_2CH_3$	–	–	–	–	–
N-Benzylpiperazine (BZP)	x	–	–	–	–	–	–
1-(3,4-Methylenedioxybenzyl)piperazine (MDBP)	xi	–	–	–	–	–	–
Trifluoromethylphenylpiperazine (TFMPP)	xii	CF_3	H	–	–	–	–
m-Chlorophenylpiperazine (mCPP)		Cl	H	–	–	–	–
Methoxyphenylpiperazine (MeOPP)		H	OCH_3	–	–	–	–
Fluorophenylpiperazine (FPP)		H	F	–	–	–	–
α-Pyrrolidinopropiophenone (PPP)	xiii	CH_3	H	–	–	–	–
4-Methoxy-α-pyrrolidinopropiophenone (MOPPP)		CH_3	OCH_3	–	–	–	–
4-Methyl-α-pyrrolidinopropiophenone (MPPP)		CH_3	CH_3	–	–	–	–
4-Methyl-α-pyrrolidinohexanophenone (MPHP)		$CH_2CH_2CH_2CH_3$	CH_3	–	–	–	–
3,4-Methylenedioxy-α-pyrrolidinopropiophenone (MDPPP)	xiv	CH_3	–	–	–	–	–
3,4-Methylenedioxypyrovalerone (MDPV)		$CH_2CH_2CH_3$	–	–	–	–	–
α-Methylfentanyl	xv	CH_3	H	H	CH_2CH_3	H	–
p-Fluorofentanyl		H	F	H	CH_2CH_3	H	–
α-Methylacetylfentanyl		CH_3	H	H	CH_3	H	–
3-Methylfentanyl		H	H	CH_3	CH_2CH_3	H	–
β-Hydroxyfentanyl		H	H	H	CH_2CH_3	OH	–
β-Hydroxy-4-methylfentanyl		H	CH_3	H	CH_2CH_3	OH	–
β-Hydroxythiofentanyl	xvi	–	–	–	–	–	–
1-Methyl-4-phenyl-4-piperdyl propionate (MPP)	xvii	–	–	–	–	–	–
1-Methyl-4-phenyl-1,2,5,6-tetrahydropyridine (MPTP)	xviii	–	–	–	–	–	–
N,N-Diisopropyl-5-methoxy-tryptamine (5-MeO-DIPT)	xix	OCH_3	H	$CH(CH_3)_2$	$CH(CH_3)_2$	H	–
5-Methoxy-N,N-dimethyltryptamine (5-MeO-DMT)		OCH_3	H	CH_3	CH_3	H	–
α-Methyltryptamine (AMT)		H	H	H	H	H	CH_3
N-Isopropyl-5-methoxy-N-methyltryptamine (5-MeO-MIPT)		OCH_3	H	$CH(CH_3)_2$	CH_3	H	–
5-Methoxy-α-methyltryptamine (5-MeO-AMT)		OCH_3	H	H	H	H	CH_3
N,N-Diisopropyl-4-acetoxytryptamine (4-Acetoxy-DIPT)		H	$OCOCH_3$	$CH(CH_3)_2$	$CH(CH_3)_2$	H	–
α-Ethyltryptamine (AET)		H	H	H	H	H	CH_2CH_3
N,N-Diisopropyltryptamine (DIPT)		H	H	$CH(CH_3)_2$	$CH(CH_3)_2$	H	–
N,N-Dipropyltryptamine (DPT)		H	H	$CH_2CH_2CH_3$	$CH_2CH_2CH_3$	H	–
Mitragynine (MG)	xx	CH_2CH_3	–	–	–	–	–
Paynantheine (PAY)		$CHCH_2$	–	–	–	–	–
HU-210	xxi	–	–	–	–	–	–
JWH-018	xxii	CH_3	–	–	–	–	–
JWH-073		H	–	–	–	–	–
CP 47,497	xxiii	C_6H_{14}	–	–	–	–	–
CP 47, 497–C_8 homologue		C_7H_{16}	–	–	–	–	–
Desoxymethyltestosterone	xxiv	–	–	–	–	–	–
Norbolethone	xxv	–	–	–	–	–	–
Tetrahydrogestrinone (THG)	xxvi	–	–	–	–	–	–
γ-Butyrolactone (GBL)	xxvii	–	–	–	–	–	–
1,4-Butanediol	xxviii	–	–	–	–	–	–

have recently been distributed as new designer drugs in some drug markets. These psychoactive drugs produce emotional and social effects similar to those of MDMA. Despite mostly producing stimulant effects, these drugs can commonly result in feelings of empathy, love, and emotional closeness to others.

A number of N-alkyl homologues of 4-methylthio-amphetamine (4-MTA), including 4-methylthiomethamphetamine (4-MTMA), 4-methylthioethylamphetamine (4-MTEA), 4-methylthiodimethamphetamine (4-MTDMA), 4-methylthio-propylamphetamine (4-MTPA), and 4-methylthiobutylamphetamine (4-MTBA), some of which have been encountered as early as in the 1990s as research chemicals, are becoming more prevalent as designer drugs of abuse. In addition, the modification of p-methoxyamphetamine (PMA) to its N-methyl homologue, p-methoxymethylamphetamine (PMMA), has been performed several years ago. The presence of N-ethyl-4-methoxyamphetamine has also been identified in illicit samples in the United States. The effects resulting from the homologues of 4-MTA appear to mimic the sympathomimetic effects of PMA. However, their potency appears to decrease with the increasing size of the N-alkyl substituent, for example, N-propyl 4-MTA was found to be less potent than N-methyl 4-MTA.

In January 2003, a series of clandestinely prepared fluoro-α-methoxy-substituted phenylalkylamines were seized in Germany, which were unknown on the illicit market at the time of their appearance. They include 2-fluoroamphetamine sulfate and hydrochloride salts of 3-fluoroamphetamine, 4-fluoroamphetamine, 5-fluoro-2-methoxyamphetamine, 3-fluoro-4-methoxyamphetamine, N-methyl-4-fluoroamphetamine, N-ethyl-4-fluoroamphetamine, and 1-(4-fluorophenyl)butan-2-amine. These materials were marketed as white powders with very high purities.

2,5-Dimethoxyamphetamine Designer Drugs

The most common drugs of this class include 4-bromo-2,5-dimethoxyamphetamine (DOB), 4-iodo-2,5-dimethoxyamphetamine (DOI), 4-chloro-2,5-dimethoxyamphetamine (DOC), 2,5-dimethoxy-4-methyl-amphetamine (DOM), 4-bromo-2,5-dimethoxymethamphetamine (MDOB), and 2,4,5-trimethoxyamphetamine (TMA).

Most of these drugs are sold in "Smart Shops" either alone or as mixtures with other designer drugs in tablets, powder, liquids, and blotters. The 2,5-dimethoxyamphetamines exhibit hallucinogenic-like activity. It is thought that the methyl group in the α position is responsible for increased *in vivo* potency and duration of action.

2,5-Phenethylamine Designer Drugs (2C Drugs)

The 2,5-dimethoxyphenethylamines are analogues of the just-mentioned 2,5-dimethoxyamphetamines. Some common 2C drugs include 4-bromo-2,5-dimethoxyphenethylamine (2C–B),

4-iodo-2,5-dimethoxyphenethylamine (2C–I), 4-methyl-2,5-dimethoxyphenethylamine (2C–D), 4-ethyl-2,5-dimethoxy phenethylamine (2C–E), 4-chloro-2,5-dimethoxyphenethylamine (2C–C), 4-ethylthio-2,5-dimethoxyphenethylamine (2C-T-2), 4-(n)-propylthio-2,5-dimethoxyphenethylamine (2C-T-7), and 4-(2-fluoroethylthio)-2,5-dimethoxyphenethylamine (2C-T-21). The synthesis of 2C–I was published first in 1991 and the drug became popular in tablet form as a club drug in the United Kingdom around 2003.

The name 2C comes from the two carbon atoms that separate the amine from the phenyl ring. These drugs have hallucinogenic properties and are sometimes sold as MDMA. Little is known about the pharmacological and toxicological properties of the 2C drugs, but their affinity to type-2 serotonin receptors has been demonstrated.

β-Keto Amphetamine Designer Drugs

Some common β-keto designer drugs include cathinone, ephedrone (methcathinone), mephedrone (2-methylamino-1-p-tolylpropane-1-one, 4-methylmethcathinone, bk-methylmethamphetamine, bk-MMA), butylone (2-methyl-amino-1-(3,4-methylenedioxyphenyl)butan-1-one, bk-MBDB), ethylone (3,4-methylenedioxyethylcathinone, bk-methylenedioxyethylamphetamine, bk-MDEA), and methylone (3,4-methylenedioxymethcathinone, bk-MDMA).

Cathinone can be extracted from *Catha edulis* or synthesized from α-bromopropiophenone, a compound that can be made from propiophenone. Methcathinone can be prepared from oxidation of ephedrine. Even the chiral synthesis of these materials has been reported, using amino acids as precursors, with ease. The ease of preparation of these materials has contributed to the emergence of an increasing number of cathinone analogues in the illicit market.

Despite being relatively new as drugs of abuse, these β-keto designer drugs have been around since the 1930s. Ephedrone, originally used as an antidepressant in the 1930s, went on to be used recreationally in the Netherlands and in the United States during the 1970s–1990s. Similarly, mephedrone was first synthesized in the late 1920s but did not become widely known until early 2000s. Intelligence from Australia Customs and Border Protection Service has identified China and the United Kingdom as being the principal sources of mephedrone. The compound 3-fluoromethcathinone has been identified in capsules marketed as plant feeders available from Internet suppliers in the United Kingdom. Other materials were also identified in the tablet and include caffeine and methylamine salt. Methylone was found in street drugs in the Netherlands in 2004 and is the main ingredient of a new liquid designer drug that appeared on the Dutch drug market called "Explosion."

When administered to experimental animals, methcathinone and cathinone were found to cause hyperactivity, with methcathinone being ~10 times more potent than cathinone.

The subjective effects of methylone exhibit subtle differences with those of MDMA. A vast majority of the drugs in this class, particularly those recently introduced, do not have any pharmacological and toxicological data recorded thus far.

Phencyclidine-Derived Designer Drugs

Developed in the 1950s as an intravenous anesthetic, phencyclidine (1-(1-phenylcyclohexyl)piperidine, or PCP) was never approved for human use because of its side effects, including intensely negative psychological effects observed during clinical studies. Illicit use of this classical designer drug is in the form of tablets, capsules, or powder. It can be snorted, smoked, or ingested.

Several PCP-derived designer drugs have been encountered in Germany in recent years. These designer drugs include N-(1-phenylcyclohexyl)propanamine (PCPPA), N-(1-phenylcyclohexyl)-3-methoxypropanamine (PCMPA), N-(1-phenylcyclohexyl)-2-methoxyethanamine (PCMEA), and N-(1-phenylcyclohexyl)-2-ethoxyethanamine (PCEEA). Due to the lack of information on the pharmacological properties of these substances, their psychotomimetic and anesthetic properties are only assumed based on their structural similarities with PCP and ketamine.

Piperazine-Derived Designer Drugs

N-Benzylpiperazine (BZP) and its analogues such as 1-(3, 4-methylenedioxybenzyl)piperazine (MDBP), trifluoromethyl-phenylpiperazine (TFMPP), m-chlorophenylpiperazine (mCPP), methoxyphenylpiperazine (MeOPP), and fluorophenylpiper-azine (FPP) have been found to be the active ingredients of some recently encountered "party pills." They are used extensively as recreational drugs globally despite their prohibition in several countries.

These piperazines became known as drugs of abuse in the United Kingdom in early 2008. A few nonfatal and fatal cases have been published and typically involve other drugs. In the United Kingdom, in recent years, the presence of BZP and TFMPP have been confirmed in three fatalities (road traffic deaths and a fatal fall off a building), with two of these involving both drugs. Research has shown that drug users are ingesting piperazine analogues, like BZP and TFMPP, in order to mimic the psychoactive effects of MDMA. It has been demonstrated that BZP/TFMPP and MDMA share the ability to evoke monoamine release, but dangerous drug synergism may occur when piperazines are coadministered in high doses.

Pyrrolidinophenone-Derived Designer Drugs

Pyrrolidinophenone-type drugs such as α-pyrrolidinopro-piophenone (PPP), 4-methoxy-α-pyrrolidinopropiophenone (MOPPP), 3,4-methylenedioxy-α-pyrrolidinopropiophenone (MDPPP), 4-methyl-α-pyrrolidinopropiophenone (MPPP),

and 4-methyl-α-pyrrolidinohexanophenone (MPHP) have gained popularity and notoriety as "rave" drugs. Very little experimental data on pharmacology and toxicology of this drug class has been published. Pyrrolidinophenones are thought to possess AP-like effects. 3,4-Methylenedi-oxypyrovalerone (MDPV) is the methylenedioxy derivative of pyrovalerone. In 2008, MDPV was seized in the United States and is thought to be a drug of abuse. MDPV is a white or light tan powder and is commonly described as boosting a user's libido; however, it is also associated with extreme anxiety at higher dosages.

Fentanyl-Derived Designer Drugs

"China White," as it has become known on the heroin market, is an opioid analgesic designer drug called α-methylfentanyl. "China White" was encountered as early as 1979 and it was significant as the first example of a designer drug that had been developed entirely by clandestine chemists for sale as an illicit recreational drug rather than as a product of legitimate scientific research. Following the appearance of α-methylfentanyl on the market, several new analogues of fentanyl have been reported, including para-fluorofentanyl, α-methylacetylfentanyl, and the highly potent 3-methylfentanyl. 3-Methylfentanyl was allegedly used as a chemical warfare agent by the Russian army. Subsequently, many other fentanyl derivatives have been encountered, including β-hydroxyfentanyl, β-hydroxythiofentanyl, and β-hydroxy-4-methylfentanyl. There have been a significant number of reported fatalities associated with the use of fentanyl derivatives in the past.

Piperidine Analogues

One of the representative compounds for this class of designer drugs is 1-methyl-4-phenyl-4-piperdyl propionate (MPP). Despite being a powerful analgesic, MPP has never been used in clinical medicine. Its synthesis was solely for the purpose of recreational drug use. One MPP product that was sold as "synthetic heroin" on the black market caused what was termed by clinicians as a "designer drug disaster" in the 1980s. Many of the individuals who used the product developed irreversible Parkinsonism. It was later found that the toxic properties of the product were attributable to 1-methyl-4-phenyl-1,2,5,6-tetrahydropyridine (MPTP), a by-product formed during the synthesis of MPP. MPTP is known to cause permanent Parkinsonism by destroying neurons in the brain of the subject.

Tryptamine-Derived Designer Drugs

Hallucinogenic tryptamines are derivatives of indoleethyl-amine with substitutions on the indole ring and ethylamine side chains that are responsible for its hallucinogenic properties. N,N-Diisopropyl-5-methoxy-tryptamine (5-MeO-DIPT), also known as "Foxy," emerged as a drug of abuse in 1999 and has been used increasingly since its appearance. Some effects that have been encountered by users of "Foxy" include euphoria, visual and auditory hallucinations, loss of inhibition, and feelings of empathy for others. In general, the effects of "Foxy" mimic the effects of MDMA. 5-MeO-DIPT is several times more potent than N,N-dimethyltryptamine and is widely available over the Internet.

Some other designer tryptamines that have been encountered include 5-methoxy-N,N-dimethyltryptamine (5-MeO-DMT), α-methyltryptamine (AMT), N-isopropyl-5-methoxy-N-methyltryptamine (5-MeO-MIPT), 5-methyoxy-α-methyltryptamine (5-MeO-AMT), N,N-diisopropyl-4-acetoxytryptamine (4-Acetoxy-DIPT), α-ethyltryptamine (AET), N,N-diisopropyltryptamine (DIPT), and N,N-dipropyltryptamine (DPT).

Herbal Drug "Kratom"

"Kratom" is the Thai name for the plant *Mitragyna speciosa* Korth., which is native in Thailand and other southeast Asian countries and contains several alkaloids including mitragynine (MG) and paynantheine (PAY). "Kratom" has been used as a traditional medicine to treat illnesses, including coughing, diarrhea, muscle pain, and hypertension. It is also effective in relieving opiate withdrawal symptoms for heroin or morphine addicts. "Kratom" is misused as an herbal drug of abuse mainly because of its stimulant and euphoric effects. The herbal drug has been controlled in Thailand since 1946 and in Australia since 2005.

Synthetic Cannabinoids in "Spice"

Since 2004, herbal mixtures such as "Spice" (also known as "K2" or "Spice Gold") have been sold in Switzerland, Austria, Germany, and other European countries in "Head Shops" or "Smart Shops" and over the Internet. These products are marketed as "Incense" as a result of their rich aromas, although users utilize them in the same way as cannabis, by inhaling the smoke. "Spice" is said to contain ingredients of natural origin (inactive herbs) mixed with other synthetically derived cannabinoids (active component of mixture). Some inactive herbs that have been encountered in mixtures of "Spice" include *Canavalia maritime, Nymphae caerulea, Scutellaria nana, Pedicularis densiflora, Leonotis leonurus, Zornia latifolia, Nelumbo nucifera, and Leonurus sibiricus.* Synthetic cannabinoids have received a lot of attention recently due to their ability to mimic the effects of cannabis. Synthetic cannabinoids bind to cannabinoid-like receptors, producing effects that are stronger than natural cannabis with users typically ingesting less than 1 mg. The main synthetic cannabinoids found in "Spice" include HU-210, JWH-018, JWH-073, CP-47,497 and the C_8 homologue of CP-47,497, among hundreds of their analogues. Some "Spice" products contain only a single cannabinoid, while others may contain multiple cannabinoid compounds.

Users have reported addiction syndrome and withdrawal effects that parallel those resulting from natural cannabis use. Accidental overdosing may lead to severe psychiatrical complications and life-threatening conditions in the case of cannabinoid receptor agonist. However, pharmacological and toxicological studies of these "Spice" mixtures in human are rare; therefore, potential health risks or possible psychoactive effects of these products cannot be clearly defined. It remains unclear where and how actual production of the herbal mixtures takes place; however, it is clear that producers are purposely risking the health of consumers for high profits.

Designer Steroids

Several designer steroids such as desoxymethyltestosterone, norbolethone, and tetrahydrogestrinone (THG) have appeared either in confiscated powders or in urine samples of elite athletes in recent years. While many anabolic steroids abused by athletes are pharmaceuticals intended for veterinary or human use, or discontinued, designer steroids are typically those that were given to athletes without toxicity or teratogenicity assessment and thus pose greater health risks to users.

Norbolethone was first detected in urine of athletes in competition in the early 2000s. It is an anabolic steroid agent that was synthesized and trialed clinically in the 1960s to encourage weight gain and for the treatment of short stature. Norbolethone was never marketed commercially, possibly due to its toxicity concerns. Detection of norbolethone in athletes' urine after three decades of its abandonment by the pharmaceutical industry suggests strongly that a clandestine source may exist.

THG was identified in the residue of a spent syringe provided anonymously to the United States Anti-Doping Agency (USADA) in 2004. THG is considered the first true "designer steroid," as the substance was designed, synthesized, and distributed only to beat the test. THG as a sports doping agent reflects both an alarmingly sophisticated illicit manufacturing facility and an underground network of androgen abusers in sports. Since the implementation of testing methods for THG by anti-doping laboratories, THG has never been detected again in sport drug testing programs up until this date.

Desoxymethyltestosterone (or madol) was first discovered in 2005 and is another steroid (never commercially marketed) to be found in the context of performance-enhancing drugs in sports. Desoxymethyltestosterone was synthesized in the early 1960s. There is very limited data on the safety and efficacy of the substance and the drug has never been approved for human use.

Other Designer Drugs

Other designer drugs, which are rarely mentioned in literature and fall outside the groups discussed above, include 1,4-butanediol and γ-butyrolactone (GBL). Both drugs are metabolized to γ-hydroxybutyric acid (GHB) in the human body, thus producing symptoms that parallel those of GHB ingestion alone. Some common effects of these drugs include euphoria, enhanced sensuality, and empathy toward others. GHB, GBL, and 1,4-butanediol are commonly used as "date-rape" drugs due to their profound sedative effects. Determination of these drugs or their metabolites in a victim's urine is challenging due to firstly their short detection windows and secondly the presence of a low level of endogenous GHB in the testing samples.

Forensic Relevance

Forensic Chemistry

Driven by burgeoning appetite for profit, clandestine industries are constantly developing new illicit products for street sale. They are well aware of the legal framework of drug control legislations and are more aware of the drug market and thus may have sophisticated drug synthesis and release strategies in place. They market new drugs in the form of tablets, powder, liquids, or blotters, as research chemicals, fertilizers, and more recently as "Spice" or "Incense" products and sell via the Internet and other distribution channels.

Since the black market changes more quickly than testing reference standards can be developed legitimately, effective identification of these new designer drugs becomes an ongoing challenge for forensic chemists. First, many new designer drugs may be present at a low concentration and coexist with many masking interfering substances such as in the case of "Herbal Highs," and correct identification of these minor illicit drug components will not be easy. Secondly, some designer drug preparations contain many structural isomers, which make structural identification difficult. For instance, TFMPP, mCPP, and MeOPP have structural isomers relating to substitution at the 2-, 3-, and 4- positions relating to ortho-, meta-, and para- positions, respectively. The existence of these structural isomers complicates identification of these piperazines. And thirdly, due to lack of reference materials, reference spectra of mass spectrometry, ultraviolet, and infrared will not be available in the respective reference libraries, therefore rendering these spectroscopy-based drug screening techniques inadequate.

To keep up with the dynamic and changing market of the designer drugs, it is important not only to utilize and adapt existing analytical methods but also to develop new ones that allow determination of these new drugs. Gas chromatography–mass spectrometry (GC–MS) and liquid chromatography–mass spectrometry (LC–MS) have been very useful in analyzing illicit drugs in the past and will continue to be so in the future. Direct coupling of LC with high-resolution nuclear magnetic resonance (NMR) or coupling novel techniques such as desorption electrospray ionization with mass spectrometry may become the methods of choice in speedy screening and identification of novel drugs and drug analogues.

Forensic Toxicology

Although many toxicokinetic studies have been recorded in the literature on some classic designer drug classes such as the AP-type drugs, they are scarce or not existent for newer designer drugs. For instance, only little information is available on toxicological properties of the 2C series. Even less is known about the toxicokinetics of synthetic cannabinnoids recently encountered in "Spice" preparations. Due to the growing global interest in "Spice" and related "Herbal High" products, a number of certified reference materials including JWH-018, JWH-073, and their deuterated counterparts have been made available commercially. Availability of these standards allows accurate determination of these species in biological fluids such as blood. However, for many designer drugs, toxicological analyses, especially urine analyses, are difficult, as urinary metabolites are unknown and reference standards do not exist. Therefore, it is important that forensic toxicologists conduct metabolic studies in order to better understand the metabolic pathways and search for appropriate metabolites as markers for urine analysis. The importance of these studies also lies in the belief that many metabolites may contribute to some of the toxic effects of the parent drugs, including life-threatening serotonin syndrome, hepatotoxicity, neurotoxicity, and psychopathology. For example, demethylenation of MDMA gives rise to a toxic catechol, which can be further metabolized into a neurotoxin following aromatic hydroxylation. Thus, knowledge of their metabolism is a prerequisite for toxicological risk assessment of these designer drugs of abuse.

Drug monitoring in nonconventional biological matrices (e.g., oral fluid, hair, nails, and sweat) has recently gained much attention because of its possible applications in clinical and forensic toxicology. An individual's past history of medication, compliance, or drug abuse can be obtained from testing of hair and nails, whereas data on current status of drug use can be provided by analysis of sweat and oral fluid. Countries such as Australia have been testing oral fluid at the roadside by police for the presence of MDMA along with other drugs such as MA and tetrahydrocannabinol (THC). Oral fluid testing for the presence of synthetic cannabinoids, for example, JWH-018 and JWH-073, is anticipated to take place in the near future should the problem of "Spice" drug abuse continue to grow.

Clinical Intoxication

Unlike therapeutical substances, new designer drugs enter the black market without any safety testing and thus pose a serious health risk. Emergency physicians have had to deal with overdoses and symptoms, the characteristics of which they may not have seen before. Since studies for risk assessment of these drugs are limited for ethical reasons, corresponding metabolic and especially toxicokinetic data for humans can only be obtained from authentic clinical or forensic cases. Undesired side effects of using these drugs may also be gathered from Internet sites such as drug user forums.

History has seen many severe or fatal poisoning cases as a result of designer drug abuse. 4-MTA has led to several fatal poisonings in the past. No deaths have been reported following the sole ingestion of BZP; however, there have been at least two reported deaths from the combination of BZP and MDMA. Coingestion of ethanol and BZP increases the likelihood of common and distressing symptoms related to BZP ingestion; however, it reduces the incidence of BZP seizures. Some fatal intoxications involving 2C-T-7 and PMA have also been reported. There have been dozens of reported fatalities during the period of 2008–10 in the United Kingdom and other European countries in which mephedrone has been implicated. Over 150 deaths resulted from the use of α-methylfentanyl ("China White") and other fentanyl derivatives in late 1970s and early 1980s. There have been only a limited number of clinical emergency cases in the literature so far related to the use of the synthetic cannabinoids of "Spice." The health risks, especially the risks at developing "Spice" drug-associated dependence and psychosis, are yet to be further assessed.

5-MeO-DIPT as well as other tryptamine-derived designer drugs are increasingly common drugs of abuse and are not detectable by routine toxicology screening. The possibility of intoxication with these agents should be noted, and clinicians should be aware of the potentially serious morbidity and mortality associated with their use. In addition, it should be realized that possible health risks may depend on individual users and their behavior; therefore, each case of intoxication should be treated individually, keeping in mind any known health risks associated with the drug taken.

Legislation

Different countries have different drug control legislations. A drug controlled in one country may not necessarily be controlled in others. For example, BZP is illegal in many countries, including the United States, Australia, and New Zealand; however, it remains legal in other countries such as Canada and the United Kingdom.

Synthetic cannabinoids are controlled substances in Australia, Europe, the United States, and Canada. In the United States, MDPV is currently unscheduled, while 5-MeO-DIPT, also known as "Foxy," is classified as a Schedule 1 Drug of the Controlled Substances Act.

Some countries such as Germany, Canada, the United States, and the United Kingdom ban new drugs as they become a concern. Other countries such as Australia and New Zealand ban drugs together with their structural analogues, including those that may have never been made. Regardless of the difference in drug scheduling acts, fast and accurate detection and identification of designer drugs are the key to effective drug control and law enforcement. Nonscheduling of a drug in a country does not necessarily mean that the drug poses less health concerns to the community, but might be attributable to the inability of toxicologists to detect the drug substance. It is therefore necessary for scientists and authorities to promote the availability of relevant standards, validated assays, and scientific knowledge regarding these designer drugs of abuse.

Conclusions

Designer drugs of abuse exist in a dynamic market with new drugs appearing all the time. They pose a serious health risk to society and present an ongoing challenge to forensic chemists, forensic toxicologists, health professionals, and law enforcement agencies. Scientists and authorities must keep a close eye on the drug trends as in-depth investigations on chemical, analytical, toxicological, and metabolic properties of these emerging drugs are critical in combating the problem of drug abuse.

> See also: **Chemistry/Trace/Drugs of Abuse:** Clandestine Laboratories; **Toxicology/Drugs of Abuse**: Validation of Twelve Chemical Spot Tests for the Detection of Drugs of Abuse.

Further Reading

Antia, U., Lee, H.S., Hydd, R.R., Tingle, M.D., Russell, B.R., 2009. Pharmacokinetics of 'party pill' drug N-benzylpiperazine (BZP) in healthy human participants. Forensic Science International 186, 63–67.

Archer, R.P., 2009. Fluoromethcathinone, a new substance of abuse. Forensic Science International 185, 10–20.

Baumann, M.H., Clark, R.D., Budzynxki, A.G., et al., 2005. N-Substituted piperazines abused by humans mimic the molecular mechanism of 3,4- methylenedioxymethamphetamine (MDMA, or 'Ecstasy'). Neuropychopharmacology 30, 550–560.

Blachut, D., Wojtasiewicz, K., Czarnocki, Z., Szukalski, B., 2009. The analytical profile of some 4-methylthioamphetamine (4-MTA) homologues. Forensic Science International 192, 98–114.

Bossong, M.G., Van Dijk, J.P., Niesink, R.J.M., 2005. Methylone and mCPP, two new drugs of abuse? Addiction Biology 10, 321–323.

Drees, J.C., Stone, J.A., Wu, A.H.B., 2009. Morbidity involving the hallucinogenic designer amines MDA and 2C-I. Journal of Forensic Sciences 54, 1485–1487.

Elliott, S., Smith, C., 2008. Investigation of the first deaths in the United Kingdom involving the detection and quantitation of the piperazines BZP and 3-TFMPP. Journal of Analytical Toxicology 32, 172–177.

Glennon, R.A., 1990. Phenylalkylamine stimulants, hallucinogens, and designer drugs. NIDA Research Monograph 105, 154–160.

Maurer, H.H., 2010. Chemistry, pharmacology, and metabolism of emerging drugs of abuse. Therapeutic Drug Monitoring 32, 544–549.

Peters, F.T., Schaefer, S., Staack, R.F., Kraemer, T., Maurer, H.H., 2003. Screening for and validated quantification of amphetamines and of amphetamine- and piperazine-derived designer drugs in human blood plasma by gas chromatography/mass spectrometry. Journal of Mass Spectrometry 38, 659–676.

Rosner, P., Quednow, B., Girreser, U., Junge, T., 2005. Isomeric fluoro-methoxy-phenylalkylamine: a new series of controlled-substance analogues (designer drugs). Forensic Science International 148, 143–156.

Shulgin, A., Shulgin, A., 1991. Pihkal: A Chemical Love Story. Transform Press, Berkley, CA.

Takahashi, M., Nagashima, M., Suzuki, J., et al., 2008. Analysis of phenethylamines and tryptamines in designer drugs using gas chromatography– mass spectrometry. Journal of Health Science 54, 89–96.

Relevant Websites

http://www.crimecommission.gov.au/publications—Australian Crime Commission Publications.

http://www.justice.gov/dea—DEA United States Drug Enforcement Administration.

http://www.drugs-forum.com—Drugs Forum.

http://www.emcdda.europa.eu—European Monitoring Centre for Drugs and Drug Addiction.

http://www.mixmag.net/drugsurvey—Mixmag | Mixmag's Drug Survey: The Results.

http://www.rednetproject.eu—ReDNet Research Project.

http://www.unodc.org/unodc/en/scientists/smart.html—United Nations Office on Drugs and Crime Global SMART Programme.

Pharmacology and Mechanism of Action of Drugs

LP Raymon, NOVA Southeastern College of Osteopathic Medicine, Fort Lauderdale, FL, USA

Glossary

Affinity Attraction between molecules based on chemical interactions between atoms, resulting in binding of a ligand to its receptor.

Agonist A drug eliciting a response subsequent to its binding to a receptor.

Antagonism The property of blocking the effect of an agonist.

Antagonist A drug blocking responses from an agonist subsequent to its binding to a receptor.

Craving The compelling need to seek a drug for a desired effect to return.

Dependence A behavior accompanied by craving and possible physical symptoms when a drug use is terminated.

Efficacy The ability to produce a response after binding to a receptor.

G-protein A trimeric protein using GTP as a source of energy to transmit signals from outside the cell into that cell bridging receptors to an intracellular enzyme.

Induction The process of enhancing gene expression through DNA interaction with transcription factors.

Kinase Enzyme acting through phosphorylation to activate or inactivate substrates.

Phosphatase Enzyme acting through dephosphorylation to activate or inactivate substrates.

Potency A comparative measure of doses required to elicit a response. The smaller the dose, the more potent the drug.

Potentiation The property of enhancing the effect of an agonist.

Receptor The molecular target of a drug.

Repression The process of silencing gene expression through DNA interaction with transcription factors.

Sensitization An increased sensitivity of receptors, resulting in greater than expected responses for a given dose of agonist. Desensitization is the opposite.

Tolerance The loss of response to a drug in spite of its presence.

Upregulation An increased availability of receptors, resulting in greater than expected responses for a given dose of agonist. Downregulation is the opposite.

Withdrawal A syndrome of physical and psychiatric symptoms triggered by sudden cessation of drug use.

Introduction

The pharmacology of drugs results from the interaction of a chemical with endogenous receptors, and pharmacodynamics is the science concerned with the mechanisms of drug action. Although proteins are best characterized as targets for drugs to bind to, nucleic acids and complex lipids can also behave as binding sites. Pharmacologic and toxic effects can be understood through the interaction between a drug or poison and these endogenous macromolecules are called receptors. More importantly in toxicology, it is the number of actual receptors that the xenobiotic binds to that best correlates with the magnitude of the effects observed. It is the complex interaction of the drug and the receptor that results in mediation of the actions of agonists and antagonists.

Affinity, Efficacy, and Potency

Drugs can be classified as agonists or antagonists of receptors. The recognition of a specific binding site is called the affinity of the drug for its target. This affinity is responsible for the selectivity of drug action. Parameters such as size, shape, charge, and solubility determine the affinity with which a particular drug will recognize a particular site to bind to. Both agonists and antagonists have affinity. When a binding elicits a response, it is called efficacy. Only agonists have efficacy (i.e., constrict blood vessels known as vasoconstriction), antagonists have zero efficacy (i.e., prevent vasoconstriction), and inverse agonists have the opposite effect (i.e., vasodilate). Once receptors are occupied, they transmit a signal that results in a multistep biochemical and biophysical cascade, which culminates in a change in cellular activity. Pharmacologists have studied these effects using log dose–response

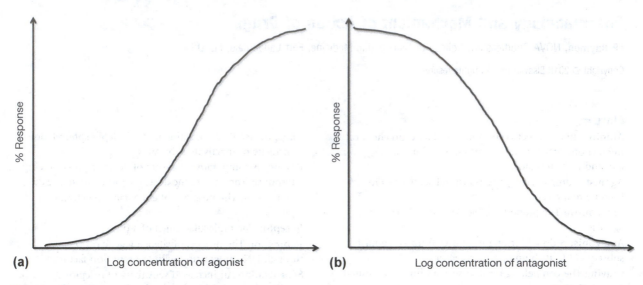

(a) Log concentration of agonist

(b) Log concentration of antagonist

Figure 1 Log dose–response curves. (a) Increasing concentrations of a full agonist along the X-axis increase responses to a maximum, read on the Y-axis. (b) Increasing concentrations of an antagonist block responses.

curves to illustrate these mechanisms. Whereas the X-axis represents increasing concentrations or amounts of an endogenous hormone, neurotransmitter, or chemical, the Y-axis measures the percentage of response elicited by the endogenous substance (**Figure 1**).

Partial agonists are drugs that bind and elicit partial (ceiling) responses, always less than the maximal efficacy of a full agonist. Partial agonists have duality of action: when alone, increasing doses cause more and more response with eventually the ceiling effect being reached; but when acting together with a full agonist, they can behave as an antagonist (blocker), never fully antagonizing, but displacing the full responses of the agonist and replacing them with the lesser efficacies of their ceiling effect (**Figure 2**).

Potency finally is a comparative measure. It is used to compare the doses required to reach a particular size effect: the most potent agonist is the one for which the smallest dose was given for the required response. Potency is often related to affinity, with the drug having the greatest affinity and also having the highest potency.

Antagonism and Potentiation

Drugs interact with cellular responses in two distinct ways: inhibiting by antagonizing the process or augmenting by potentiating the responses. On a log dose–response curve, the curve labeled "control" is obtained by increasing the concentration of the endogenous substrate alone and measuring the increasing responses. Potentiation is illustrated as a left shift of the curve: essentially, one needs less endogenous chemical to elicit the responses, as if now the endogenous compound is

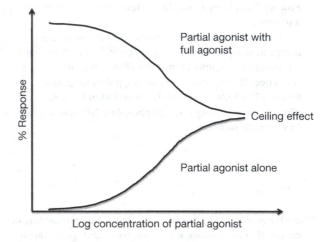

Log concentration of partial agonist

Figure 2 Duality of partial agonists. Partial agonists alone behave as agonists but have a ceiling effect (less than maximal response; bottom curve). In the presence of a full agonist response, increasing concentrations of partial agonists will antagonize the full response until the lesser ceiling effect is reached (top curve).

more potent (benzodiazepines, which are sedatives/hypnotics potentiate gamma-aminobutyric acid (GABA), the major inhibitory transmitter in the human brain, e.g., while cocaine, a stimulant, potentiates norepinephrine, the major mediator of cardiovascular and stimulant responses). Antagonism is represented by a right shift of the curve. There are two types of pharmacological antagonism. When the antagonist competes with the endogenous agonist substance for binding (i.e., both recognize the same site on the receptor), increasing the concentration of the endogenous chemical will eventually displace the blocking drug and reinstate the full efficacy, albeit with higher concentrations needed (hence the shift to the right). Most blockers act in this manner and are called competitive antagonists. In some cases, the antagonist may bind to a different site (allosteric binding) or may create a covalent or other strong bond at the binding site. In this case, increasing the concentrations or amount of the endogenous substance fails to fully recover the responses, and the curve is still shifted to the right but never reaches the maximum efficacy. Few drugs act irreversibly, since this property would result in unsafe effects that cannot be overturned easily. Finally, although pharmacological antagonism is classic, one cannot rule out physiological antagonism (**Figure 3**).

Physiological antagonism occurs when two agonists are administered, each having an opposing action: a bronchodilator and a bronchoconstrictor, for example, effectively resulting in canceling each other's effect. In rare instances, chemicals may also antagonize themselves simply by binding to each other, as in heparin's anticoagulant effect being antagonized by the antidote protamine sulfate.

Signal Transduction

Receptors are found in two broad locations: on the cell membrane or inside the cell.

Intracellular Receptors

Intracellular receptors are generally reserved for highly lipid-soluble drugs such as antiinflammatory steroids, thyroid hormones, and vitamin A or D. These receptors belong to a superfamily of DNA-binding proteins. When activated by the binding of an agonist, they translocate to the nucleus of the cell and recognize specific binding sites along the chromosomal DNA called response elements. These DNA-binding sites are not part of genes in that they are not expressed. Rather, these DNA-binding sites are scattered along spacer DNA (the DNA between genes), and when activated, they can alter the patterns of gene expression. Drugs that control gene expression not only have a slow onset of action (it can take hours or days to see the protein products) but also have a much longer duration of action, likely lasting beyond the drug's presence in the body. These receptors have specific structural elements to recognize on the one hand, the drug, and the DNA spacer elements on the other. Classic structures allowing DNA binding include zinc finger motifs, leucine zippers, helix-turn-helix, Rev domains, and many others. One can understand these intracellular receptors as specialized transcription factors that control as to when, where, and how much a specific gene or set of related genes will be expressed. Examples include the binding to peroxisome proliferator-activated receptors by thiazolidinediones (e.g., rosiglitazone) and fibrates (e.g., gemfibrozil) in the management of diabetes and hyperlipidemia, respectively.

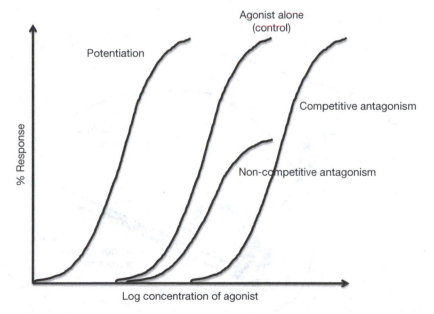

Figure 3 Antagonism and potentiation. The control curve is obtained from a full agonist alone. All other curves are the full agonist in presence of another drug. When the curve is to the right of the control, more agonist is needed for the responses to occur: that is, an antagonist was added. When the curve is to the left of the control, less agonist is needed for the responses to occur: that is, a potentiator was added. Note that there are two forms of antagonism, competitive and noncompetitive.

In the case of fibrates, the induction of lipoprotein lipase (LPL) activity (induction meaning more LPL enzyme is expressed by the cell in contrast to activation meaning greater affinity of existing LPL enzymes) is responsible for the digestion of endogenous and exogenous lipoproteins and the removal of triglycerides from the patient's blood (**Figure 4**).

Membrane-Bound Receptors

Ion channels

Membrane-bound receptors include the family of ion channels. Ion channels can be classified as gated and ungated. And gated ion channels fall in two major families: voltage and ligand gated. Conductance is the term reflecting the number of channels opened. Whereas ungated channels always have maximal conductance, gated channels require a change in membrane potential (mV) or a ligand binding to be opened. When a channel is open, ions may flow through the channel pore, called an ionophore, provided a net force is exerted on that ion (i.e., the ion is not at equilibrium). The net force is a combination of concentration force (ions flow down a concentration gradient) and electrical force (opposite charges attract each other and same charges repel each other). Changes in mV result from the movement of charged ions across the membrane. In general, cells have a resting potential more negative than that of the extracellular medium. Excitation follows depolarization, that is, the cells become more positive

(positive ions like sodium going in or positive charges like potassium not leaving the cell); inhibition follows hyperpolarization, that is, the cells become more negative (negative ions like chloride going in or negative charges like potassium leaving the cell). mV changes are extremely rapid and can result in responses elicited within milliseconds. Ungated channels are the targets of certain diuretics (amiloride, triamterene). Voltage-dependent channels are blocked by a variety of anti-seizure and antiarrhythmic medications (phenytoin, carbamazepine and quinidine, lidocaine, amiodarone, verapamil for a few examples). Ligand-gated channels include nicotinic acetylcholine receptors of the neuromuscular junction (blocked by curare-like drugs), those of neuronal tissues (stimulated by nicotine), GABA receptors (potentiated by benzodiazepines, prolonged in their opening by barbiturates or alcohol), several glutamate receptors (N-Methyl-D-aspartate and felbamate or ketamine, phencyclidine blocking it; 2-amino-3-(5-methyl-3-oxo-1,2-oxazol-4-yl)propanoic acid and topiramate), serotonin $5HT_3$ receptors (blocked by the antiemetic ondansetron), and more (**Figure 5**).

G-protein-coupled receptors

The classic G-protein-coupled receptor (GPCR) remains the best characterized and most common signal transduction system. The human genome has close to a 1000 genes coding for GPCRs. Ultrastructurally, the presence of seven-transmembrane domains defines GPCR. While a drug binds

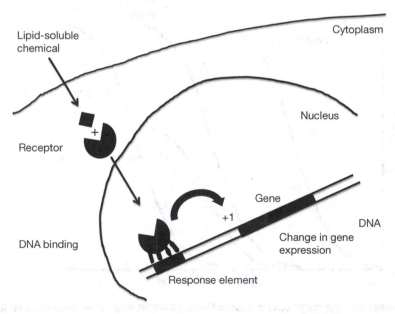

Figure 4 Intracellular receptors. Once stimulated by lipid-soluble ligands, intracellular receptors translocate to the nucleus and bind to response elements of the spacer DNA, altering the rate of gene expression. +1 represents the transcription start. An example would be steroid receptors binding to hormone response elements (HRE), through zinc finger motifs, allowing a steroid response to occur.

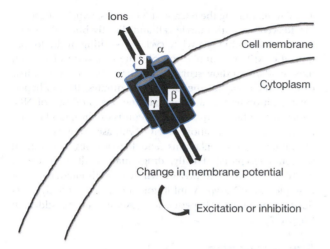

Figure 5 Ion channels. Ion channels allow charged particles to change the membrane potential. If the ion flow results in more positive potentials, the cell is depolarized and excited (cations entering or anions leaving a cell). Conversely, if the ion flow results in more negative potentials, the cell is hyperpolarized and less excitable (anions entering or cations leaving the cell).

to the outside segments of the receptor, the resulting change in shape activates a guanosine-5'-triphosphate (GTP)-binding protein coupled to the receptor on the inside face of the cell. G-proteins are trimeric, comprising alpha, beta, and gamma subunits. It is the alpha subunit that has a GTPase activity, and when GTP is "burnt" to guanosine-5'-diphosphate (GDP), the

G-protein transmits downstream the signal of a drug binding to the receptor outside of the cell. They function as switches to turn on or off enzymes, open or close ion channels, controlling transporters, transcription factors, and other targets of the cell's machinery. Although the alpha subunit seems the most important in transmitting signals, the beta–gamma subunits are increasingly recognized as having their own roles (such as controlling potassium channels). Two major pathways are used by many of the drugs prescribed in medicine: the cyclic adenosine-5'-monophosphate (cAMP) pathway and the PIP_2 pathway (**Figure 6**).

The pattern followed includes a five-step transduction, starting with the binding of a drug to a GPCR. A G-protein is activated. It stimulates (Gs, Gq) or inhibits (Gi) an enzyme. The enzyme makes more or less of a "second messenger," such as cAMP or from a membrane phospholipid like PIP_2, inositol trisphosphate (IP_3), and diacylglycerol (DAG). The second messenger is a metabolite that in turn controls the activity of a family of phosphorylating enzymes called serine/threonine kinases (protein kinase A in the cAMP cascade and protein kinase C in the PIP_2 cascade). When kinases phosphorylate substrates, they alter their activity. For example, an enzyme may be activated or inhibited by phosphorylation and an ion channel may be closed or opened. Interestingly, receptors localized on the same cell may well modulate the cellular activity through coupling to opposite G-proteins. Whereas Gs coupling would increase cAMP and result in phosphorylation by protein kinase A of effector proteins, a Gi-coupled receptor would undo this effect by decreasing cAMP in the same cell. An example would be norepinephrine stimulating the Gs coupling

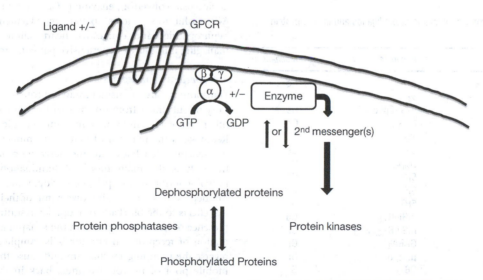

Figure 6 G-protein-coupled receptors. These receptors interact with G-proteins (Gs, Gi, and Gq) to alter second messenger levels and protein kinase activity in the cell. Phosphorylation alters the activity of select enzymes, receptors, channels, transcription factors, structural proteins, and so on. Phosphatases return the target proteins to their initial state.

of its β_1 receptor, causing an increased firing rate and conduction of electrical potential in selective heart tissue, whereas acetylcholine through its Gi-coupled muscarinic M_2 receptors does the opposite. The resulting effects are an increased heart rate in the presence of sympathetic stimulation of the heart (mediated by norepinephrine) and a decreased heart rate from parasympathetic stimulation of the heart (mediated by acetylcholine). Major pharmacological systems follow this pattern. In particular, catecholamine (dopamine, norepinephrine, and epinephrine) receptors, muscarinic receptors to acetylcholine, six out of seven subtypes of serotonin receptors, many hormonal receptors (thyroid stimulating hormone, antidiuretic hormone, V_2 receptors, parathyroid hormone), metabotropic glutamate receptors, and $GABA_B$ receptors, all have in common this signal transduction pattern involving a seven-transmembrane receptor, a G-protein, an enzyme, a second messenger, and a kinase (**Table 1**).

Other transduction systems may in part mimic that of the classic GPCRs. An example is the pathways involving cGMP. In one instance, the receptor to atrial natriuretic factor (ANF) (stimulated by the drug nesiritide used in congestive heart failure) has the activity of the enzyme guanylate cyclase. Its stimulation by the endogenous atrial natriuretic peptide or the recombinant drug nesiritide immediately results in the formation of the second messenger cGMP and the subsequent activation of protein kinase G, resulting in a phosphatase activation and the dephosphorylation of the contractile protein myosin light chain with resulting vasodilation. But more relevantly, in another variation on the pathway, arginine is metabolized by nitric oxide synthase in the endothelium of the vasculature, causing the release of NO, a gas, which diffuses to the adjacent smooth muscle cell and directly binds the heme groups of a soluble guanylate cyclase, resulting in the formation of cGMP and, similar to ANF, the relaxation of smooth muscle. Many cardiovascular drugs share that pathway: nitric oxide donors, such as the antianginal nitrates, the antihypertensive nitroprusside, and hydralazine, are prodrugs of NO. Others may bind to Gq-coupled receptors on the endothelium, resulting in the activation of NO synthase (muscarinic M_3, histamine H_1, prostaglandins, and leukotrienes, and certain serotonin receptors). Finally, drugs may result in increased cGMP by preventing its breakdown by phosphodiesterases; for example, the PDE-type V inhibitors, used in erectile dysfunctions or pulmonary hypertension, exemplified by sildenafil (**Figure 7**).

Enzymes as receptors

Several classes of drugs bind to enzymes and directly control their activity. Acetylcholinesterase is the main mode of degradation of the neurotransmitter acetylcholine once released in the synapse. Its inhibition by organophosphate or carbamate insecticides will result in dramatic increase in synaptic acetylcholine and overstimulation of muscarinic and nicotinic receptors with ensuing life-threatening toxicity. It is also the target of drugs like neostigmine, used to reverse neuromuscular blockade from curare-like drugs, diagnose or treat myasthenia gravis, or reverse the toxic overdose of antimuscarinic drugs like atropine. Another example would be the nonsteroidal antiinflammatory drugs like aspirin inhibiting the enzyme cyclooxygenase and the production of inflammatory prostaglandins and the platelet aggregant thromboxane A_2. The blockade of angiotensin-converting enzyme (ACE) by captopril and other ACE inhibitors allows better management of diabetic nephropathies and congestive heart failure patients while managing millions of hypertensive patients around the world.

Transporters as receptors

Transporters are transmembrane proteins specialized in carrying substrates from one side of the cell membrane to the other. Reuptake pumps are a relevant example of transporters. Reuptake is the removal of neurotransmitter molecules from the synaptic cleft back into the nerve terminal that released them. It is the main mode of termination of action for norepinephrine in the periphery, dopamine, and serotonin. Antidepressants and cocaine owe some of their pharmacological effects to the blockade of reuptake, resulting in prolonged presence of neurotransmitters in the synapse and longer stimulation of receptors on effector cells. Amphetamines in part reverse the pumping mechanism and cause the release of the mobile pool of neurotransmitters back in the synapse (the mobile pool represents the nonvesicular neurotransmitter that was freshly reuptaken but not yet repackaged into synaptic vesicles).

Table 1   Receptor subtypes to select ligands and their G-protein coupling.

Ligand	Receptor	Mechanism
Epi, norepinephrine	α_1	Gq
	α_2	Gi
	$\beta_{1,2}$ (Epi only)	Gs
Acetylcholine	$M_{1,3,5}$	Gq
	$M_{2,4}$	Gi
Dopamine	$D_{1a,b}$	Gs
	$D_{2a,b,c}$	Gi
Serotonin	$5HT_{1,5}$	Gi
	$5HT_2$	Gq
	$5HT_{4,6,7}$	Gs
Glutamate	$mGluR_{1,5}$	Gq
	$mGluR_{2,3,4,6,7,8}$	Gi
GABA	$GABA_B$	Gi
Opioid peptides	μ, κ, δ	Gi
Cannabinoids	$CB_{1,2}$	Gi

Gs stimulates adenyl cyclase and raises intracellular levels of cAMP, whereas Gi inhibits adenyl cyclase and decreases cAMP concentrations. Gq stimulates phospholipase C and increases intracellular IP_3, DAG, and calcium.

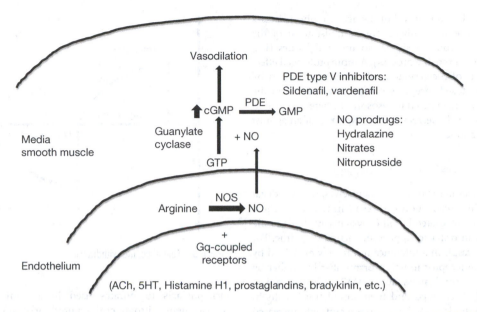

Figure 7 Nitric oxide (NO) signaling cascade. The activity of nitric oxide synthase (NOS) is controlled by Gq-coupled receptors on the endothelium of vessels (e.g., acetylcholine (ACh) M_3 receptors, serotonin (5HT) and $5HT_2$ receptors). The NO produced diffuses to the adjacent smooth muscle cells and causes relaxation and vasodilation through increased levels of cGMP. Many drugs interfere with this pathway. PDE, phosphodiesterase.

Receptors with intrinsic enzymatic activity

As discussed previously, this class of receptors includes the ANF receptor, which has guanylate cyclase activity. But it also encompasses the large family of receptors that have tyrosine kinase activity. Tyrosine kinase distinguishes itself from the other classes of serine/threonine kinases such as protein kinases A, C, and G. It is intrinsic to the receptor, and as its name indicates, the activation of the receptor results in the phosphorylation of tyrosine residues, first on the receptor itself, and then on a number of effector proteins. Insulin receptors belong to this group. The activation of the receptor by insulin triggers a signal transduction system that is drastically different from the one shared by GPCRs. In particular, the final element often involves phosphatases that can dephosphorylate proteins previously phosphorylated by kinases, thereby offering a modulation in cellular activity. For example, glucagon and epinephrine oppose insulin on most metabolic responses. Whereas glucagon and epinephrine share a Gs-coupled mechanism through their respective receptors, which causes effector enzymes to be phosphorylated, insulin results in the dephosphorylation of the same enzymes, causing the opposite activity. Most growth factors and cytokines bind to receptors with intrinsic tyrosine kinase activity. For cytokine receptors, the tyrosine kinase is referred to as a Janus kinase (JAK), and its substrate is transcription factors called signal transducer and activator of transcription (STAT). A number of cancers share abnormal signaling involving these tyrosine kinases. A class of anticancer drugs, such as imatinib for chronic myelogenous leukemia and erlotinib for certain types of lung cancers, actually aims at blocking tyrosine kinases.

Tolerance and Dependence

Receptor Adaptation and Tolerance

Continuous presence of a drug can result in a blunting of the responses over time in spite of the presence of the drug. In the case of GPCRs discussed previously, receptor regulation can result in rapid fluctuation in responsiveness. Two key words are used to describe changes in the receptor function: sensitization/ desensitization and upregulation/downregulation. Whereas sensitization/desensitization is a rapid change in affinity of existing receptors in the membranes of cells, up- and down-regulation reflect changes in the number of receptors in the cell membrane. Intuitively, agonists could result in desensitization or downregulation, whereas antagonists would result in sensitization or upregulation. The process remarkably results in a loss of efficacy of the drugs administered. If the process is very rapid, acute tolerance is sometimes referred to as tachyphylaxis. The mechanism of rapid desensitization of β receptors (and many other GPCRs) involves phosphorylation of the receptor itself by a GPCR kinase called GRK. When agonists bind to the receptors, they activate GRKs, which in turn phosphorylate the receptors themselves. The phosphorylated serine residues then bind to beta-arrestin, which prevents the interaction of the receptors with their respective G-protein, thereby stopping the signaling cascade. Upon removal of the agonist, phosphatases "reactivate" the receptors: subsequent administration of the agonist results in responses similar to the initial ones (i.e., desensitization is a reversible process). A more prolonged effect is the endocytosis of the receptors, also mediated in part by β-arrestin. Endocytosed receptors can be reversed unless the engulfed receptors are targeted to lysosomes where they would be degraded, effectively decreasing the responses of an agonist for a prolonged period of time.

Compensatory Responses and Drug Tolerance

Rather than changes in the receptors themselves, changes distal to the receptor in transduction can result in tolerance. These changes tend to be mediated by other systems available to the cell or organism in order to oppose the action of a drug. For instance, opiates result in a tolerance not readily explained by changes in opiate receptor function or number but rather by changes in the second messenger cAMP. Whereas opiate receptors are all Gi coupled and their stimulation results in a decreased intracellular cAMP level, in tolerant cells, increased cAMP levels are seen, likely mediated by other receptor system compensating for the continuous inhibitory influence of the opiate drug. Tolerance to central nervous system (CNS) depressants in general is well established, often with cross-tolerance between drugs acting in similar ways (such as benzodiazepines, barbiturates, and ethanol). But tolerance is not seen with CNS drugs alone. Drugs acting peripherally can also exhibit tolerance. An example is the homeostatic responses elicited by drugs that alter blood pressure: antihypertensives trigger autonomic and endocrine responses aimed at antagonizing the antihypertensive effect of the drug administered. As blood pressure drops, sympathetic responses alter hemodynamic parameters such as heart rate and contractility of the heart muscle and blood vessel tones through baroreceptor reflexes, while the renin–angiotensin–aldosterone system regulates not only the blood vessel tone but also the blood volume. Increased sympathetic and renin activity act in concert to increase the blood pressure back to initial baseline in spite of the antihypertensive drug's presence. This explains the need for several drugs, including beta blockers and diuretics in most cases, in the management of hypertension to maintain the antihypertensive effect of the primary drug (**Figure 8**).

Reduced Availability of Response Mediators

In a similar way, reduced availability of response mediators can result in tolerance. A classic example involves the amphetamines or the food amine tyramine that owes its action to the release of neurotransmitters from its mobile pool in the nerve terminal. Once the pool is exhausted (i.e., completely released), administration of more amphetamine cannot elicit further responses. Another example is represented by the

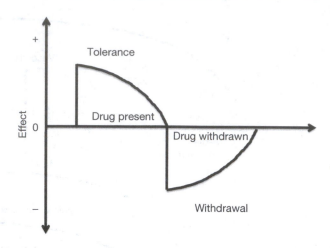

Figure 8 Tolerance and withdrawal.

tachyphylaxis to nitrates used in ischemic heart disease management. Nitroglycerin is a prodrug of NO, which requires the presence of glutathione in its activation. The finite stores of glutathione can result in depletion if the drug is used too often. Once depleted, the nitrates can no longer be activated.

Metabolic Tolerance

Another mode of tolerance is metabolic rather than pharmacodynamic: induction of the microsomal oxidizing system of cytochrome P450 enzymes can result in a more rapid metabolic clearance of a drug, requiring larger doses to get the same effect. For instance, barbiturates and carbamazepine can induce their own metabolism, resulting in decreased duration of action and requiring greater doses to achieve a similar depressant effect. Chronic ethanol also induces metabolic tolerance.

Behavioral Factors

Behavioral factors also contribute to tolerance and dependence. Animal studies have shown that tolerance can be altered by varying the experimental conditions, such as time of administration and prior experiences of the test animal. Similarly, environmental cues are known to trigger withdrawal in human addicts if withdrawal was previously experienced under such conditions.

Dependence

Dependence is characterized by overt symptoms on withdrawal of the drug, resulting in physical symptoms or psychological changes (craving). The assumption has been that the same mechanisms responsible for tolerance are also fundamentally responsible for dependence on the drug. Altered sensitivity or numbers of receptors, changes in other receptors, increased activity of enzymes, and compensatory mechanisms predict that tolerance and dependence are associated processes. Dependence would require the presence of adaptive changes induced by the drug causing tolerance. Yet, it is also evident that some of the mechanisms causing tolerance are not necessarily associated with dependence: the rapid phosphorylation of beta receptors caused tolerance to an agonist, but its rapid dephosphorylation upon agonist withdrawal reset the receptor to normal, for example. The duration of changes elicited by the drug presence is important: if they exceed the drug's presence, then dependence will likely result from withdrawal of the drug.

Conclusions

Several hundreds if not thousands of discrete intracellular and extracellular receptors recognize endogenous and exogenous molecules. In spite of this evergrowing variety, general patterns of signal transduction underlying the mechanisms of action of drugs have emerged. These pathways are responsible for amplifying the biochemical and physical responses of the various subtypes of cells and tissues making the human body in a cell-dependent manner. An important aspect of having a far greater number of receptor types than pathways is the potential for pharmacodynamic interactions between drugs of different structure and different pharmacological profile. An interesting concluding note would relate this possibility well. In the case of beta-blocker overdose, rather than a beta agonist, glucagon is administered. Both beta receptors and glucagon receptors share Gs coupling and have similar tissue distribution allowing a hormone to undo the detrimental effects of a cardiac drug through its action on a different type of receptor. Whereas more immediate responses from cellular events are well established, recent advances and emphasis on DNA machinery, its plasticity, and gene expression control will undoubtedly contribute to even greater, potential understanding of drug action, in particular when it relates to chronic effects, and mechanisms of tolerance and dependence.

See also: **Toxicology:** Behavioral Toxicology; Herbal Medicines and Phytopharmaceuticals—Contaminations; Herbal Psychoactive Substances.

Further Reading

Brunton, L.L., Lazo, J.S., Parker, K.L., 2006. Goodman & Gilman's: The Pharmacological Basis of Therapeutics. Section I, ch. 1 and 2, eleventh ed. McGraw-Hill, New York.
Katzung, B.G., Masters, S.B., Trevor, A.J., 2009. Basic and Clinical Pharmacology, eleventh ed. McGraw-Hill, New York (Section I: Basic Principles).
Pratt, W.B., Taylor, P., 1990. Principles of Drug Action: The Basis of Pharmacology. Ch. 2 and 10, third ed. Churchill Livingstone, New York.

Relevant Websites

http://www.icp.org.nz—Interactive Clinical Pharmacology.
http://www.rxlist.com—The Internet Index for Prescription Drugs and Medications.
http://www.pharmacology2000.com—Medical Pharmacology and Disease-Based Integrated Instruction.
http://www.drugs.com—Prescription Drug Information and News for Professionals and Consumers.

Volatile Substances and Inhalants

RJ Flanagan and DS Fisher, King's College Hospital NHS Foundation Trust, London, UK

Glossary

Abuse Excessive or improper use of drugs or other substances.

Acute Sudden or short term.

Anesthetic A substance producing either local or general loss of sensation.

Arrhythmia Any variation from the normal rhythm of the heartbeat.

Biological specimens Samples of tissues (including blood, hair), secretions (breast milk, saliva, sweat), excretion products (bile, exhaled air, urine), and other material such as stomach contents or vomit derived from a patient.

First-pass metabolism The portion of an oral dose metabolized in the intestine, gut wall, or liver before reaching the systemic circulation.

Headspace The space above a solid or liquid in a container.

Ingestion Taking of substances into the body by mouth.

Intoxication Excitement or elation induced by alcohol or other drugs (also referred to as inebriation).

Limit of detection The smallest amount of a substance that can be revealed by a test carried out in a prescribed manner.

Methemoglobinemia The presence of abnormal amounts of oxidized hemoglobin in blood.

Pharmacokinetics The study of the rates of the processes involved in the absorption, distribution, metabolism, and elimination of drugs and other agents.

Plasma half-life The time taken for the plasma concentration of a substance to decrease by half.

Scene residue Material found at the scene of a crime, suicide, or other event.

Acute poisoning with volatile substances is encountered most commonly following the deliberate inhalation of vapor in order to become intoxicated ("glue sniffing," "huffing," "dusting," "bagging," inhalant abuse, solvent abuse, volatile substance abuse (VSA), volatile substance misuse). Solvents from adhesives and in paint thinners such as toluene, hydrocarbons such as those found in cigarette lighter refills and aerosol propellants (often purified liquefied petroleum gas (LPG)), polyhalogenated hydrocarbons such as those used as refrigerants and in "chemical dusters," and anesthetic gases such as nitrous oxide are among the compounds/products that may be abused in this way (**Tables 1 and 2**).

Since the mid-1970s, in many countries, there has been phased withdrawal of volatile organochlorine and organobromine compounds, such as hydrochlorofluorocarbon (HCFC) refrigerants and aerosol propellants, thought to be potent ozone depleters. This has led to increased use of polyfluorinated compounds such as difluoromethane (HFC 32), pentafluoroethane (HFC 125), 1,1,1,2-tetrafluoroethane (HFC 134a), and 1,1,1-trifluoroethane (HFC 143a), and to a lesser extent perfluoropropane (PFC 218). In addition, 1, 1-dichloro-1-fluoroethane (HCFC 141b) has been introduced as a degreasing and foam-blowing agent (**Table 1**). However, the misuse potential of the newer compounds/products is just as high as those they have replaced.

LPG arises from the cracking of oil to make petrol (petroleum spirit, gasoline, benzine) and also in the gases trapped above oil fields. There are at least two grades of LPG available to volatile substance abusers, namely (1) unpurified gas intended for direct use as a fuel and (2) purified gas intended primarily for cigarette lighter refills and as a propellant in aerosols and related products. The composition of LPG can vary depending on the source although its major components are usually butane, isobutane, and propane. Some unpurified LPGs can contain up to 40% (v/v) unsaturates (butenes and propene). Petrol itself is often abused, especially in less-developed communities where access to other abusable volatiles is limited.

Isobutyl, isopentyl ("amyl"), and isopropyl nitrites and related compounds ("poppers") may also be inhaled in order to experience their vasodilator properties, sometimes by men who have sex with men. Inhalation of the vapor of a range of other substances ranging from mothballs (naphthalene or 1,4-dichlorobenzene) to chlorine has also been reported, but such pastimes are uncommon. On the other hand, diesel fuel, aviation fuel (kerosene, Avgas), white spirit, turpentine (or

Table 1   Some volatile substances that may be abused by inhalation

Hydrocarbons

Aliphatic	Acetylene
	Butane[a]
	Isobutane (2-methylpropane)[a]
	Hexane[b]
	Propane[a]
Alicyclic/ aromatic	Cyclopropane (trimethylene)
	Toluene (toluol, methylbenzene, phenylmethane)
	Xylene (xylol, dimethylbenzene)[c]
Mixed	LPG[d]
	Petrol (gasoline)[e]
	Petroleum ethers[f]
Halogenated	Bromochlorodifluoromethane (BCF, CFC 12B1)
	Carbon tetrachloride (tetrachloromethane)
	Chlorodifluoromethane (HCFC 22)
	Chloroform (trichloromethane)
	Chloropentafluoroethane (CFC 115)
	1-Chloro-1,2,2,2-tetrafluoroethane (HCFC 124)
	Dichlorodifluoromethane (CFC 12)
	1,1-Dichloro-1-fluoroethane (HCFC 141b, Genetron 141b)
	Dichloromethane (methylene chloride)
	1,2-Dichloropropane (propylene dichloride)
	2,2-Dichloro-1,1,1-trifluoroethane (HCFC 123)
	1,1-Difluoroethane (HFC 152a)
	Difluoromethane (HFC 32)
	Ethyl chloride (monochloroethane)
	Fluothane (halothane, (R,S)-2-bromo-2-chloro-1,1,1-trifluoroethane)
	1,1,1,2,3,3,3-Heptafluoropropane (HFC 227ea, HFC 227)
	1,1,1,3,3,3-Hexafluoropropane (HFC 236fa)
	Pentafluoroethane (HFC 125)
	1,1,1,3,3-Pentafluoropropane (HFC 245fa)
	Perfluoropropane (octafluoropropane, PFC 218)
	Tetrachloroethylene (perchloroethylene)
	1,1,1,2-Tetrafluoroethane (HFC 134[a])
	1,1,1-Trichloroethane (methylchloroform, Genklene)
	1,1,1-Trifluoroethane (HFC 143[a])
	Trifluoromethane (HFC 23)
	1,1,2-Trichlorotrifluoroethane (HCFC 113)
	Trichloroethylene ("trike," Trilene)
	Trichlorofluoromethane (CFC 11)

Oxygenated compounds and others

	Butanone (2-butanone, methyl ethyl ketone, MEK)
	Desflurane ((R,S)-difluoromethyl 1,2,2,2-tetrafluoroethyl ether)
	Diethyl ether (ethoxyethane)
	Dimethyl ether (DME, methoxymethane)
	Enflurane ((R,S)-2-chloro-1,1,2-trifluoroethyl difluoromethyl ether)
	Ethyl acetate
	Ethyl tert-butyl ether (ETBE)
	Helium[g]
	Isoflurane ((R,S)-1-chloro-2,2,2-trifluoroethyl difluoromethyl ether)

(Continued)

Table 1   Some volatile substances that may be abused by inhalation—(Continued)

Isopentyl nitrite (3-methylbutan-1-ol, isoamyl nitrite, "amyl nitrite")[h,i]
Methoxyflurane (2,2-dichloro-1,1-difluoroethyl methyl ether)methyl acetate
Methyl tert-butyl ether (MTBE)
Methyl butyl ketone (MBK, 2-hexanone)
Methyl ethyl ether
Methyl isobutyl ketone (MIBK, isopropyl acetone, 4-methyl-2-pentanone)
Nitrites[h] (amyl[i], butyl, cyclohexyl, isobutyl, isopropyl, isopentyl)
Nitrogen[g]
Nitrous oxide (dinitrogen monoxide, "laughing gas")
Sevoflurane (fluoromethyl 2,2,2-trifluoro-1-(trifluoromethyl)ethyl ether)
Xenon[g]

[a]Principal components of purified liquefied petroleum gas (LPG).
[b]Commercial "hexane" mixture of hexane and heptane with small amounts of higher aliphatic hydrocarbons.
[c]Mainly m-xylene (1,3-dimethylbenzene).
[d]LPG composition may vary depending on its intended use: unpurified for fuel (may contain unsaturates) and purified in aerosols and cigarette lighter refills, although its major components are usually butane, isobutane, and propane.
[e]Mixture of aliphatic and aromatic hydrocarbons with boiling range of 40–200 °C.
[f]Mixtures of pentanes, hexanes, and so forth with specified boiling ranges (e.g., 40–60 °C).
[g]Asphyxiant gas.
[h]Abused primarily for their vasodilator properties.
[i]Commercial "amyl nitrite," mainly isopentyl nitrite but other nitrites also present.

substitute), and paraffin are not sufficiently volatile to be abused by inhalation. Similarly, nail varnish or varnish remover (acetone and esters) and nitroethane (used as an artificial fingernail remover) do not have properly documented examples of abuse, probably because they are either too water-soluble or too involatile to be intoxicants. By the same token, acetone has never been used as an anesthetic.

In addition to those who deliberately inhale volatiles, people who ingest, or even more rarely inject, solvents or solvent-containing products, either accidentally or deliberately, and the victims of clinical, industrial, and domestic accidents may be poisoned by the compounds under consideration. Finally, chloroform (trichloromethane), diethyl ether, and other volatiles are still used occasionally in the course of crimes such as rape and murder, while a further volatile compound, chlorobutanol (1,1,1-trichloro-2-methyl-2-propanol), sometimes employed as a sedative and a preservative, has been used in doping racing greyhounds.

VSA can produce dose-related central nervous system effects similar to those of ethanol. Small doses can lead rapidly to euphoria and other behavioral disturbances, and may also induce more profound effects such as delusions and hallucinations. Heightened sexual (self-) gratification may also be

Table 2 Some products that may be abused by inhalation

Product	Major volatile components
Adhesives	
Balsa wood cement	Ethyl acetate
Contact adhesives	Butanone, hexane, toluene, and esters
Cycle tire repair cement	Toluene and xylenes
Polyvinylchloride (PVC) cement	Acetone, butanone, cyclohexanone, and trichloroethylene
Woodworking adhesives	Xylenes
Aerosols	
Air freshener	LPG, DME, and/or fluorocarbons[a]
Deodorants, antiperspirants	LPG, DME, and/or fluorocarbons[a]
Fly spray	LPG, DME, and/or fluorocarbons[a]
Hair lacquer	LPG, DME, and/or fluorocarbons[a]
Paint	LPG, DME, and/or fluorocarbons[a] and esters
Anesthetics/analgesics	
Inhalational	Nitrous oxide, cyclopropane, diethyl ether, halothane, enflurane, desflurane, isoflurane, methoxyflurane, sevoflurane, and xenon
Topical	Ethyl chloride and fluorocarbons[a]
Balloon gas	Helium, nitrous oxide
Carburettor cleaner, commercial dry cleaning and degreasing agents, surgical plaster/chewing gum remover	DME, dichloromethane, HCFC 113, HCFC 141b, methanol, 1,1,1-trichloroethane, tetrachloroethylene, toluene, and trichloroethylene (now very rarely carbon tetrachloride, 1,2-dichloropropane)
Cooking oil sprays	Diethyl ether
Domestic spot removers and dry cleaners	Dichloromethane, 1,1,1-trichloroethane, tetrachloroethylene, and trichloroethylene
Dust removers ("air brushes")	DME and fluorocarbons[a]
Firefighting agent (older products)	(BCF, HCFC 11, HCFC 12), HFC 125, HFC 227ea, HFC 236fa, HFC 23, HCFC 123
Fuel gases	
Cigarette lighter refills	LPG
"Butane"	LPG
"Propane"	Propane and butanes
Starting fluid	Diethyl ether, DME, heptane, and LPG
Injected oxidant (racing fuel supercharge, blowtorches)	Nitrous oxide
Paints (including spray paints)/paint thinners	Acetone, butanone, esters, hexane, methanol, toluene, trichloroethylene, and xylenes
Paint stripper	Dichloromethane, methanol, and toluene
Refrigerant (or coolant) gas	DME, HFC 125, HFC 134a, HFC 143a, HFC 32, HCFC 124
Room odorizer	Isobutyl nitrite
Typewriter correction fluids/thinners (older products)	1,1,1-Trichloroethane
Varnishes/lacquers	Xylenes
Whipped cream dispensers	Nitrous oxide

See **Table 1** for full chemical names of some compounds.
[a]Mainly HFC 134a and/or HFC 152a, HFC 227ea.

a feature, sometimes in association with partial asphyxia. Once exposure ceases, rapid recovery normally ensues—rapid recovery after exposure may be a factor in the continuing popularity of VSA among children of high school age (13–18 year olds) in some countries. On the other hand, psychological dependence is common in chronic users. VSA has now been reported from most parts of the world, mainly among adolescents, individuals living in remote communities, and those with occupational access to abusable volatiles.

Indirect toxicity from VSA may also occur. For example, lead poisoning was common when lead-containing petrol was abused, methanol toxicity has been reported in Native American Indian communities secondary to abuse of carburettor cleaning solution, and there has been a report of deposition of titanium-containing granules in lung after presumed inhalation of toluene-based spray paint. There is also the risk of explosion and fire when flammable volatiles such as LPG are abused in confined spaces and a source of ignition is at hand. Hydrofluoric acid burns have been observed following ignition of 1,2-difluoroethane from compressed air cleaners.

The major risk from VSA is that of sudden death. There were at least 2 343 (2000 male) VSA-related deaths in the United Kingdom during 1971–2008 (**Figure 1**), some 5% of which are thought to have been suicides. There have been

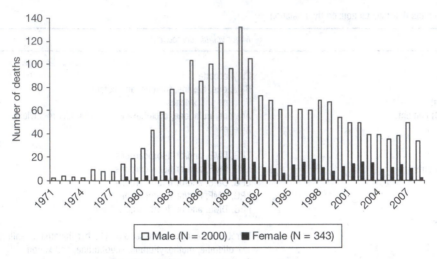

Figure 1   UK VSA-related sudden deaths, 1971–2008 (*N* = 2 343). Data from Ghodse, H., Ahmed, K., Corkery, J., Naidoo, V., Schifano, F., 2010. *Trends in UK Deaths Associated with Abuse of Volatile Substances, 1971–2008*. International Centre for Drug Policy, St George's, University of London, London. http://www.solveitonline.co.uk/images/vsa-annual-report-23-2010-final-version.pdf (accessed 24 August 2011).

many reports of VSA-related sudden deaths worldwide, again predominantly in adolescent males, although epidemiological studies indicate that equal numbers of males and females experiment with VSA. Overall, some 49% of UK VSA-related sudden deaths occurred in adolescents aged 14–18 years, with a further 5% in children aged 7–14 years, although there has been a trend toward an increase in the age at death in recent years. Some deaths were attributed to "indirect" causes such as inhalation of vomit (8.9% of UK VSA-related deaths, 1999–2008), asphyxia associated with the use of a plastic bag

to contain the vapor being inhaled (11.9%), and trauma (5.2%). However, most UK deaths in this period (70.9%) were attributed to direct. toxicity ("sudden sniffing death"), predominantly in relation to the abuse of fuel gases, aerosol propellants, and halogenated solvents as compared to deaths due to abuse of solvents from adhesives. In 2008, some 83% of UK VSA-related deaths were attributed to the abuse of LPG or other fuel gases (**Figure 2**).

The implementation of a European Union Directive (2005/95/EC) that restricts the use of toluene in household and other

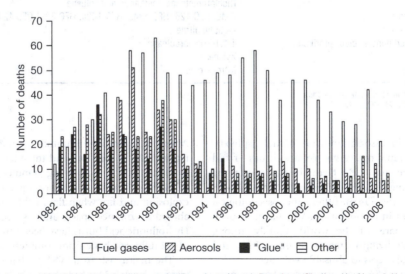

Figure 2   UK VSA-related deaths, 1982–2008 (*N* = 2 244) by type of product abused. Data from Ghodse, H., Ahmed, K., Corkery, J., Naidoo, V., Schifano, F., 2010. *Trends in UK Deaths Associated with Abuse of Volatile Substances, 1971–2008*. International Centre for Drug Policy, St George's, University of London, London. http://www.solveitonline.co.uk/images/vsa-annual-report-23-2010-final-version.pdf (accessed 24 August 2011).

products (December 2006), together with the introduction (January 2007) of the first phase of the provisions of the volatile organic compounds (VOCs) in Paints, Varnishes and Vehicle Refinishing Products Regulations 2005 has served to restrict the availability of some easily abusable products. Legislation in England and Wales to restrict the sale of cigarette lighter refills to those under the age of 16 has also been enacted, and these measures may have contributed to the decline in UK VSA-related deaths in recent years. The use of "poppers" (alkyl nitrites) is also restricted in the United Kingdom and in many countries on product safety grounds as some of these compounds are classed as carcinogens.

These factors may also have helped reduce crime associated with VSA in the United Kingdom. An audit of press reports of VSA-related crime/antisocial behavior in 1997–2007 (589 individuals) showed that, in line with the trend seen in UK VSA-related deaths, not only were 89% of offenders male, but also that there was a decrease in reports of VSA-related offenses with time (84 in 1997, 20 in 2007). The agents reported (17 individuals, 2 agents) were "glue" 225, LPG/"butane"/aerosol propellants 176, "solvents" 158, and petrol (gasoline) 27. The offenses cited (most serious crime) included homicide (35), rape or other sexual assault (34), and arson (25). Many of the offenders were recidivists, and 66% were aged 20 years or more at the time of the first offense.

VSA is often a solitary pastime and the intent to achieve intoxication may be clear, although when someone has died, the circumstances under which death occurred may be disguised. However, VSA is sometimes a shared habit, on occasions accompanied by sexual or attempted sexual activity. If one or indeed both partners die during or immediately after the episode of VSA, then it can be very difficult to ascertain intent, the options being accident, suicide, manslaughter (culpable homicide), and even murder. There have long been suicides facilitated by use of volatile compounds, especially among anesthetists and others with access to not only the agent, but also the necessary equipment with which to self-administer the agent. Often the circumstances of the death help guide the diagnosis, although even here it is sometimes difficult to ascertain intent. A more recent trend reported from several countries has been the use of asphyxiant gases such as helium or nitrogen to facilitate suicide, a trend made possible by the widespread availability of compressed gas in cylinders. Deaths attributed to deliberate helium inhalation in the United Kingdom increased from 2 in 2001 to 25 in 2008, for example. Clearly, such cases present especial problems to the analyst charged with helping investigate the death.

Diagnosis of VSA

Clinically, VSA should be considered in children and adolescents with "drunken" behavior, unexplained listlessness, anorexia, and moodiness. The hair, breath, and clothing may smell of solvent, and empty adhesive tubes or other containers, potato crisp bags, cigarette lighter refills, or aerosol spray cans are often found in unusual places such as secreted in bed clothes. The smell of solvent in the breath is related to the dose and duration of exposure and may last for many hours. The so-called glue-sniffer's rash (perioral eczema) is probably caused by repeated contact with glue in a plastic or other bag held to the face. Adolescents who indulge in VSA often have a personal history of trauma, suicidality, psychiatric distress, and antisocial behavior. Although primarily a phenomenon of adolescence, it must be remembered that adults, especially those with occupational access to abusable volatiles, also indulge in VSA. In the late 1970s, for example, it was estimated that some 1–1.6% of US dentists were abusing nitrous oxide.

Although chronic abuse of some volatiles may give rise to long-term sequelae, for example, abuse of nitrous oxide may cause myeloneuropathy secondary to vitamin B_{12} deficiency, the underlying mechanism of toxicity is not always clearly defined. If substances such as LPG are sprayed directly into the throat, this may cause rapid cooling of the vagus nerve, and may also cause laryngeal edema, laryngospasm, and even frostbite. Stimulation of the vagus nerve can lead to bradycardia, myocardial ischemia, coronary vasospasm, and cardiac arrest. The contents of lighter refills may be inhaled more easily by simply grasping the nozzle between the teeth and pressing while keeping the cylinder upright. Aerosols are either sprayed into a plastic bag to allow the aerosol to settle before inhaling the gas, or simply bubbled through water to remove the product before inhaling the propellant. In either case, displacement of oxygen in the inspired air may lead to asphyxia, but if exposure is continued, butane, especially, may accumulate in the body.

It is thought that butane and most halogenated hydrocarbons sensitize the heart to adrenaline, that is, there is an excessive response to release of adrenaline particularly in the context of a "fight or flight" situation (sudden shock), or pronounced sexual stimulation, especially if accompanied by physical restriction on the ability to inspire oxygen (sexual asphyxia). In turn, this may give rise to cardiac arrhythmia, ventricular fibrillation, and eventually cardiac arrest. Although it is rare for someone who has suffered a cardiac arrest after inhaling volatiles to be resuscitated, it has been suggested that emergency staff should administer amiodarone and use physical measures to normalize heart function rather than giving adrenaline in such a situation.

Laboratory Analysis

The analytical toxicology laboratory may be asked to perform analyses for solvents and other volatile compounds in biological samples and related specimens to (1) confirm a suspicion of chronic VSA in the face of denial from the patient and/or a caretaker; (2) aid the investigation of deaths where poisoning by volatile compounds is a possibility, including deaths associated with anesthesia; (3) aid investigation of rape or other assault, or other offense such as driving a motor vehicle or operating machinery, which may have been committed while the victim and/or the accused may have been under the influence of volatile substances; (4) aid investigation of incidents such as rape or other assault in which volatile substances may have been forcibly administered to the victim; (5) help investigate fire or explosion where VSA might have been a contributory factor; and (6) assess occupational or environmental exposure to anesthetic or solvent vapor. However, other techniques such as ambient air monitoring or, in a few instances, the measurement of urinary metabolite excretion may be more appropriate in this latter context.

The laboratory analysis of volatile substances presents particular problems. First, many of the compounds of interest occur commonly either in the environment or in laboratories, and this necessitates special precautions against contamination and interference. Second, collection, storage, and transport of biological samples must be controlled as far as practicable in order to minimize loss of analyte—quantitative work is futile if very volatile compounds such as propane are encountered unless special precautions are taken to prevent the loss of analyte from the sample prior to the analysis. Third, many compounds of interest are excreted unchanged via the lungs (**Table 3**) and thus whole blood (and/or other tissues in fatalities), and not urine, is usually the sample of choice. Finally, the interpretation of results can be difficult, especially if legitimate exposure to solvent vapor is a possibility.

Analytical Methods

The analysis of biological samples for solvents and other volatiles has similarities to the analysis of ethanol, methanol, and 2-propanol. Headspace gas chromatography (HS-GC) with flame ionization detection (FID) and/or electron capture detection (ECD) or mass spectrometric (MS) detection is widely used in the analysis of volatiles in blood and other biological specimens. Headspace solid-phase microextraction has also been employed. Nitrous oxide and most halogenated compounds respond to the ECD. Use of nitrogen as a carrier gas has facilitated detection of helium in postmortem specimens.

Direct MS of expired air can detect many compounds several days postexposure. However, the use of this technique is somewhat limited by the need to take breath directly from the patient. Inertial spray MS allows introduction of biological fluids directly into the MS without prior chromatographic analysis and has been used in the analysis of halothane in blood during anesthesia. Vapor-phase infrared (IR) spectrophotometry may be useful in the analysis of abused products or ambient atmospheres. High-performance liquid chromatography may be useful in the analysis of certain solvent metabolites such as hippuric acid (**Table 4**).

If the analyte is very volatile (e.g., propane, butane) and a quantitative analysis is required, a blood sample should be collected directly into the headspace vial in which the analysis will be carried out. Other less volatile compounds are relatively stable in blood and other tissues if simple precautions are taken. In the case of blood, the container used for the sample should be glass, preferably with a cap lined with metal foil; greater losses may occur if plastic containers are used. The tube should be as full as possible and should only be opened when required for analysis, and then only when cold (4 °C). If the sample volume is limited, it is advisable to select the container to match the volume of blood so that there is minimal headspace. An anticoagulant (sodium ethylenediamine tetraacetate (EDTA) or lithium heparin) should be used. Specimen storage between -5 and 4 °C is recommended and 1% (w/v) sodium fluoride should be added to minimize esterase and other enzymic activity.

Tissues (~10 g each of brain, lung, liver, kidney, and subcutaneous fat) should also be obtained if a necropsy is performed in addition to standard toxicological specimens (femoral blood, urine, stomach contents, vitreous humor). Tissues should be stored before analysis in the same way as blood. No preservative should be added. Any products thought to have been abused or otherwise implicated in the incident (and stomach contents if ingestion is suspected) should be packed, transported, and stored entirely separately from (other) biological specimens to avoid cross-contamination. Investigation of deaths occurring during or shortly after anesthesia should include the analysis of any residue of the anesthetic used in order to exclude an administration error.

The likelihood of detecting exposure to volatile substances in blood is influenced by the dose and duration of exposure, the time of sampling in relation to the time elapsed since exposure, and the precautions taken in the collection and storage of the specimen. In postmortem work, other factors may be important such as the time elapsed between death and sampling. In a suspected VSA- or anesthetic-related fatality, analysis of tissues (especially brain) may prove useful as high concentrations of volatile compounds may be present even if very little is detectable in blood. Detection of the volatile compounds in adipose tissue may, however, suggest chronic rather than acute exposure.

Gas Chromatography

Bonded-phase wide-bore capillary columns permit relatively large-volume septum injections and offer good efficiency, reproducibility, and reliability. A 60 m × 0.53 mm i.d. fused silica capillary coated with the dimethylpolysiloxane SPB-1 (5 μm film thickness) programmed from 40 to 200 °C offers many advantages over packed column systems. Improved resolution of very volatile compounds is obtained and, even with an initial temperature of 40 °C, the total analysis time can

Table 3   Physical properties and pharmacokinetic data of some volatile compounds

Compound	CAS registry number	WEL[a] (mg m^{-3})	Vapor pressure (20 °C, 760 mmHg)[b]	Inhaled dose absorbed (%)	Proportion absorbed dose (%) Eliminated unchanged	Proportion absorbed dose (%) Metabolized	Plasma half-life[c] (h)	Brain/blood distribution ratio (deaths)	Partition coefficient (blood/gas) (37 °C)
Acetone	67-64-1	1 210	183	–	–	–	3–6[d]	–	330
Benzene	71-43-2	3.25	75	46	12	87	9–24	3–6	6–9
Butane	106-97-8	1450[e]	(1 554)	30–45	–	–	–	–	–
Isobutane CAS 75-28-5		1450[e]	(2 282)	–	–	–	–	–	–
Butanone	78-93-3	600	75	70	99+	0.1	0.5	–	116
Carbon disulfide	75-15-0	15	294	40	<30	50–90	<1	–	2.4
Carbon tetrachloride	56-23-5	13	90	–	50?	50?	48	–	1.6
Chlorobenzene	108-90-7	4.7	–	–	–	>90	1.5–3	–	–
Chloroform	67-66-3	9.9	157	–	>40	>30	1.5	4	8
Cyclopropane	75-19-4	–	(4 701)	–	99	0.5	–	1.5–3.6	0.55
Desflurane	57 041-67-5	–	669	–	–	0.02	23[f]	1.3[g]	0.4
Dichloromethane	76-09-2	350	350	–	50?	<40	0.7	0.5–1	5–10
Diethyl ether	60-29-7	310	438	–	>90	–	–	1.1	12
Dimethylformamide	68-12-2	15	–	–	–	–	2–6	–	–
Enflurane	13838-16-9	383	172	90+	>80 (5 d)	2.4	36	1.4[e]	1.9
Ethanol	64-17-5	1920	–	–	–	95	2–14	–	–
Ethyl acetate	141-78-6	720	72	–	<0.1	–	0.2–0.5	–	–
Ethyl *tert*-butyl ether	637-92-3	–	–	33	50	–	–	–	–
Fluoride	16 984-48-8	2.5	–	–	–	–	2–9	–	–
Formaldehyde	50-00-0	2.5	–	–	–	–	2.5[h]	–	–
Halothane	151-67-7	82	244	90+	64	–	43[f]	2–3	2.1
HCFC 11	75-69-4	–	667	92	80	<0.2	1.5	2.5	0.87
HCFC 12	75-71-8	–	(3 639)	35	99	<0.2	–	1.4	0.15
HCFC 22	75-45-6	3 590	(6 701)	–	–	–	2.6	1.9	–
Hexane	110-54-3	72	122	–	>20	–	1.5–2.0	–	–
Hydrogen cyanide	74-90-8	–	–	–	–	>90	0.7–2.1	–	–
Isoflurane	26675-46-7	383	240	–	>99	0.2	58[f]	1.57[g]	1.38
Methoxyflurane	76-38-0	–	23	–	19 (10 d)	>44	–	2–3	13
Methyl butyl ketone	591-78-6	21	–	–	–	–	–	–	–
Methyl isobutyl ketone	108-10-1	208	15	–	<1	–	1.2	–	–
Methyl *tert*-butyl ether	1634-04-4	183.5	–	45	30	–	1.7–3.5	–	–
Nitrous oxide	10 024-97-2	183	(39 800)	–	>99	–	0.1	1.1	0.47
Petroleum fumes (asphalt)	8 052-42-4	5	–	–	–	–	–	–	–
Propane	74-98-6	1450[e]	(6269)	–	>60	–	–	–	0.6
Sevoflurane	28 523-86-6	–	157	–	40	3	20[f]	1.7[g]	0.6
Styrene	100-42-5	430	4	–	1–2	>95	13	–	32
Tetrachloroethylene	127-18-4	345	14	60+	>90	1–2	33–72	9–15	9–19
Toluene	108-88-3	191	22	53	<20	80	3–6	1–2	8–16
1,1,1-Trichloroethane	71-55-6	555	98	–	60–80 (1 w)	2	20–26	2	1–3
Trichloroethylene	79-01-6	550	58	50–65	16	>80	30–38	2	9.0
"Xylene"	1 330-20-7	220	6	64	5	>90	20–30	–	42.1

CAS, Chemical Abstracts Service.
[a]The UK Workplace Exposure Limit (8 h time-weighted average).
[b]Figures in parentheses indicate compound gas at 20 °C.
[c]Terminal phase elimination half-life.
[d]Longer after high doses.
[e]As components of liquefied petroleum gas (LPG).
[f]From fat.
[g]Experimental: 37 °C.
[h]Formic acid.

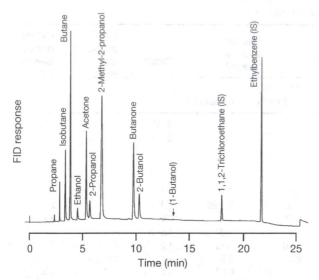

Figure 3 Analysis of a whole blood sample obtained postmortem from a patient who had inhaled the contents of a cigarette lighter refill. Sample preparation: internal standard (IS) solution (ethylbenzene and 1,1,2-trichloroethane (~25 and 10 mg l⁻¹, respectively) in outdated blood-bank whole blood) (200 µl) incubated (65 °C, 15 min) with specimen (200 µl) in a sealed 10 ml glass septum vial. Chromatographic conditions: column: 60 m × 0.53 mm i.d. SPB-1 (5 µm film). Oven temperature: 40 °C (6 min), then to 80 °C at 5 °C min⁻¹, then to 200 °C at 10 °C min⁻¹. Injection: 300 µl headspace.

be reduced to 26 min, and good peak shapes can be obtained even for alcohols (**Figure 3**). Moreover, splitless septum injections of up to 300 µl headspace can be performed with no noticeable effect on column efficiency; hence, sensitivity is as least as good as that attainable with a packed column.

The use of a capillary column together with two different detectors confers a high degree of selectivity, particularly for low formula mass compounds where there are few alternative structures. However, GC–MS can be difficult when the fragments produced are less than m/z 40, particularly if the instrument is used for other purposes as well as solvent analyses. In particular, the available sensitivity and spectra of the low-molecular-weight alkanes renders them very difficult to confirm by GC–MS. GC combined with Fourier transform infrared (FTIR) spectrometry may have some advantages over GC–MS in the analysis of volatiles, but sensitivity is poor, particularly when compared with the ECD. In addition, interference, particularly from water and carbon dioxide in the case of biological specimens, can be troublesome.

"Purge and trap" and multiple headspace extraction offer ways of increasing sensitivity and, although not needed for most clinical and forensic applications, have been used either in conjunction with GC-FTIR or in occupational/environmental monitoring. Pulse heating has also been employed in

the analysis of volatiles in biological specimens. Advantages of this latter technique include use of a small sample volume (0.5–5 µl), short extraction time, and lack of matrix effects.

Interpretation of Analytical Results

A diagnosis of VSA should be based on a combination of circumstantial, clinical, and analytical evidence rather than on any one factor alone. It is especially important to consider all circumstantial evidence in cases of possible VSA-related sudden death as suicide or even homicide cannot be excluded simply on the basis of the toxicological examination. There has been one example in the United Kingdom of a serial murderer whose victims were thought initially to have died accidentally as a result of VSA.

Knowledge of the pharmacokinetics of volatile compounds is important in understanding the rate of onset, the intensity, and the duration of intoxication with these substances. The UK Workplace Exposure Limits (**Table 3**) provide information on the relative toxicities of different compounds after chronic exposure to relatively low concentrations of vapor. The solubility of a volatile compound in blood is an important influence on the rate of absorption, tissue distribution, and elimination of the compound. Due to the large surface area of the lungs, blood concentrations peak minutes after inhalational exposure, distributing rapidly into well-perfused tissues (i.e., brain, heart). If exposure continues, the inhalant will distribute into the poorly diffused tissues such as fat. After ingestion, hepatic metabolism may reduce systemic availability ("first-pass" metabolism), and diffusion into tissues often limits the amount of substance available to get to the brain. Moreover, there may be less displacement of oxygen from the lungs than if solvent vapor had been inhaled directly.

The partition coefficients of a number of compounds between air, blood, and various tissues have been measured *in vitro* using animal tissues, and some *in vivo* distribution data have been obtained from postmortem tissue measurements in man (**Table 3**). However, these latter data must be used with caution as there are many difficulties inherent in such measurements (sampling variations, analyte stability, external calibration, etc.). Similarly, published data on the elimination half-lives of volatile substances (**Table 3**) are not easily comparable, either because too few samples were taken, or the analytical methods used did not have sufficient sensitivity to measure the final half-life accurately. Plasma concentrations of some compounds may fall monoexponentially, while others may exhibit two (or more) separate rates of decline (half-lives) due to distribution to, and elimination from, poorly perfused tissues.

Exogenous compounds may be metabolized in a number of ways, a frequent result being the production of metabolites of greater polarity (water solubility) and thus lower volatility than the parent compound. The pharmacological activity and pharmacokinetics of any metabolite(s) often differ from those of the parent compound(s). However, many volatile substances, including not only inert gases such as helium and nitrogen, but also butane, dimethyl ether (DME), most fluorocarbon refrigerants/aerosol propellants/anesthetics, isobutane, nitrous oxide, propane, tetrachloroethylene, and 1,1,1-trichloroethane are largely eliminated unchanged in exhaled air. Others are partly eliminated in exhaled air and also metabolized in the liver and elsewhere (**Table 4**), the metabolites being eliminated in exhaled air or in urine, or incorporated into intermediary metabolism.

When interpreting the results of qualitative analyses, it is important to remember that some compounds often occur in association with one another on HS-GC (**Table 5**). Analysis of metabolites in urine may extend the time in which exposure may be detected but, of the compounds commonly abused, only toluene, the xylenes, and some chlorinated solvents, notably trichloroethylene, have suitable metabolites (**Table 4**). Chronic petrol "sniffing" has been diagnosed by the measurement of blood lead concentrations, or by detection of aromatic components such as toluene and ethylbenzene. Abuse of the fluorinated anesthetic methoxyflurane has been detected by measuring serum and urine fluoride ion. With some petrol and other complex mixtures such as petroleum ethers (**Table 1**), however, the blood concentrations of the individual components are often below the limit of detection of HS-GC methods even after significant inhalational exposure.

Table 4 Summary of the metabolism of some solvents and other volatile substances

Compound	Principal metabolites (% absorbed dose)	Notes
Acetone	2-Propanol (minor) and intermediary metabolites (largely excreted unchanged at higher concentrations)	Endogenous compound produced in large amounts in diabetic or fasting ketoacidosis; also the major metabolite of 2-propanol in man
Acetonitrile	Inorganic cyanide (at least 12%) thence to thiocyanate	Cyanide/thiocyanate may accumulate during chronic exposure
Benzene	Phenol (51–87%), catechol (6%), hydroquinone (2%), trans, trans-muconic acid	Excreted in urine as sulfate and glucuronide conjugates; urinary phenol excretion has been used to indicate exposure but is variable and subject to interference
Bromomethane	Inorganic bromide	Serum bromide has been used to monitor exposure, although the concentrations associated with toxicity are much lower than when bromide itself is given orally
Butanone	3-Hydroxybutanone (0.1%)	3-Hydroxybutanone excreted in urine; most of an absorbed dose of butanone excreted unchanged in exhaled air
Carbon disulfide	2-Mercapto-2-thiazolin-5-one, 2-thiothiazolidine-4-carboxylic acid (TCCA), thiourea, inorganic sulfate, and others	2-Mercapto-2-thiazolin-5-one glycine conjugate and TCCA glutathione conjugate of carbon disulfide; urinary TCCA excretion is a reliable indicator of exposure
Carbon tetrachloride	Chloroform, carbon dioxide, hexachloroethane, and others	Trichloromethyl free radical (reactive intermediate) is probably responsible for hepatorenal toxicity
Chloroform	Carbon dioxide (up to 50%), diglutathionyl dithiocarbonate	Phosgene (reactive intermediate) depletes glutathione and is probably responsible for hepatorenal toxicity
Cyclohexanone	Cyclohexanol, trans-1,2-cyclohexanediol, trans-1,4-cyclohexanediol	Metabolites excreted mainly as glucuronides in adults
Desflurane	Trifluoroacetic acid (<0.02%), inorganic fluoride	–
Dichloromethane	Carbon monoxide (approximately 35%)	Carboxyhemoglobin half-life 13 h (carboxyhemoglobin half-life 5 h after inhalation of CO); blood carboxyhemoglobin measurement is a useful indicator of chronic exposure
Dimethylsulfoxide	Dimethylsulfide (3%), dimethysulfone (18–22%)	After oral/dermal administration, dimethyl sulfide excreted in exhaled air and dimethylsulfone in urine
Dioxane	β-Hydroxyethoxyacetic acid (HEAA)	HEAA excreted in urine
Enflurane	Difluoromethoxydifluoroacetic acid (>2.5%), inorganic fluoride	–
Ethyl acetate	Ethanol, acetic acid	Rapid reaction catalyzed by plasma esterases
Ethylbenzene	Methylphenylcarbinol (5%), mandelic acid (64%), phenylglyoxylic acid (25%)	Methylphenylcarbinol excreted in urine as conjugate, others as free acids; mandelic acid excretion has been used to monitor ethylbenzene exposure
Halothane	2-Chloro-1,1,1-trifluoroethane, 2-chloro-1,1-difluoroethylene, trifluoroacetic acid, inorganic bromide, and others	The formation of reactive metabolites may be important in the etiology of the hepatotoxicity ("halothane hepatitis") that may occur in patients reexposed to halothane or similar compounds

(Continued)

Table 4   Summary of the metabolism of some solvents and other volatile substances—(Continued)

Compound	Principal metabolites (% absorbed dose)	Notes
Hexane	2-Hexanol, 2-hexanone, 2,5-hexanedione	2-Hexanol excreted in urine as glucuronide; 2,5-hexanedione thought to cause neurotoxicity; methyl butyl ketone also neurotoxic and also metabolized to 2,5-hexanedione
Isobutyl nitrite	2-Methyl-1-propanol (99%+), inorganic nitrite	Parent compound not normally detectable in blood; blood methemoglobin can be used to monitor exposure
Isoflurane	Trifluoroacetic acid (<0.2%), inorganic chloride, inorganic fluoride	–
Isopentyl nitrite	3-Methyl-1-butanol (99%+), inorganic nitrite	Parent compound not normally detectable in blood; blood methemoglobin can be used to monitor exposure
Isopropyl nitrite	2-Propanol, inorganic nitrite	Parent compound not normally detectable in blood; blood methemoglobin can be used to monitor exposure
Methanol	Formaldehyde (up to 60%), formic acid	Urinary formic acid excretion has been advocated for monitoring methanol exposure
Methoxyflurane	Methoxydifluoroacetic acid, dichloroacetic acid, oxalic acid, inorganic fluoride	Abuse has been manifested as chronic fluoride poisoning (fluorosis)
2-Propanol	Acetone (80–90%) thence others	2-Propanol half-life approximately 2 h, acetone half-life approximately 22 h
Sevoflurane	1,1,1,3,3,3-Hexafluoropropanol (<3%), inorganic fluoride	1,1,1,3,3,3-Hexafluoropropanol excreted as glucuronide in urine
Styrene	Mandelic acid (85%) and phenylglyoxylic acid (10%); hippuric acid may be minor metabolite	Urinary mandelic acid excretion indicates exposure; ethanol inhibits mandelic acid excretion
Tetrachloroethylene	Trichloroacetic acid (<3%)	Urinary trichloroacetic acid excretion serves only as qualitative index of exposure
Toluene	Benzoic acid (80%) and o-, m-, and p-cresol (1%)	Benzoic acid largely conjugated with glycine giving hippuric acid that is excreted in urine (half-life 2–3 h); not ideal index of exposure since there are other (dietary) sources of benzoic acid
1,1,1-Trichloroethane	2,2,2-Trichloroethanol (2%) and trichloroacetic acid (0.5%)	Urinary metabolites serve as qualitative index of exposure only (compare tetrachloroethylene)
Trichloroethylene	2,2,2-Trichloroethanol (45%) and trichloroacetic acid (32%)	Trichloroethanol (glucuronide) and trichloroacetic acid excreted in urine (half-lives about 12 and 100 h, respectively); trichloroacetic acid excretion can indicate exposure
Xylenes	Methylbenzoic acids (95%) and xylenols (2%)	Methylbenzoic acids conjugated with glycine and urinary methylhippuric acid excretion used as index of exposure—no dietary sources of methylbenzoates

Detection of a volatile compound in blood does not always indicate VSA or occupational/environmental exposure to solvent vapor. Acetone and some of its homologs may occur in high concentrations in ketotic patients. Large amounts of acetone and butanone may also occur in blood and urine from children with β-ketothiolase deficiency. In addition, acetone is the major metabolite of 2-propanol in man (**Table 4**). Conversely, 2-propanol has been found in blood from ketotic patients. Other ketones may also give rise to alcohols *in vivo*. Cyclohexanol, for example, is the principal metabolite of cyclohexanone in man. Other compounds such as halothane or chlorobutanol may be used in therapy, or inadvertently added to the sample as a preservative. Ethyl chloride may give a peak resembling ethanol on GC-FID.

Use of aerosol disinfectant preparations when collecting specimens may contaminate the sample if an aerosol propellant is used. Contamination of blood samples with ethanol or 2-propanol may also occur if an alcohol-soaked swab is used to cleanse skin prior to venepuncture. Contamination with technical xylene (a mixture of o-, m-, and p-xylene together with ethylbenzene) has been found in blood collected into Sarstedt Monovette Serum Gel blood collection tubes; contamination with toluene (up to 22 mg l^{-1}), 1-butanol, ethylbenzene, and xylene was found in batches of these same tubes. Contamination with 1-butanol or 2-methyl-2-propanol occurs commonly in blood collected into tubes coated with EDTA. Care should be taken when handling frozen tissue prior to analysis as any compounds present in ambient air may condense on the cold surface and give rise to false positives. Processing blank frozen tissue can help control for this possibility.

Table 5 Associated volatile compounds: headspace gas chromatography

Compound	Associated compound(s)
Acetone	Butanone and higher ketones in ketoacidosis, 2-propanol (metabolite, rare)
BCF	HCFC 11
Butane	Butanone (metabolite[a]), isobutane, 2-butanol (metabolite[a]), propane
Cyclohexanone	Cyclohexanol (metabolite)
Dimethyl ether	HCFC 22 or other fluorocarbons
Ethanol	Propanols and higher order alcohols if bacterial fermentation has occurred; methanol or other volatile poisons if denatured alcohol has been consumed
Ethyl acetate[b]	Ethanol (metabolite)
Ethylbenzene	See xylenes below
HCFC 11	BCF, HCFC 12
HCFC 12	HCFC 11
HCFC 22	Dimethyl ether
Halothane	2-Chloro-1,1-difluoroethylene, 2-chloro-1, 1,1-trifluoroethane (metabolites[a])
Isobutane	Butane, 2-methyl-2-propanol (metabolite[a]), propane
Isobutyl nitrite[b]	2-Methyl-1-propanol (degradation product)
Isopentyl nitrite[b]	3-Methyl-1-butanol (degradation product)
Isopropyl nitrite[b]	2-Propanol (degradation product)
Methyl acetate[b]	Methanol (metabolite)
Propane	Butane, isobutane, 2-propanol (metabolite[a])
2-Propanol	Acetone (metabolite)
1,1,1-Trichloroethane	Isopropyl nitrate (stabilizer[a])
2,2,2-Trichloroethanol	Trichloroethylene
Trichloroethylene	2,2,2-Trichloroethanol (metabolite), chloroform (possibly from thermal degradation of trichloroacetic acid (metabolite) *in vitro* at temperatures above approximately 45 °C)
Xylenes	*o*-, *m*-, and *p*-xylene occur together in technical xylene, *m*-xylene predominating; ethylbenzene also contaminant in technical xylene

See **Table 1** for full chemical names of certain compounds.
[a]Rarely found.
[b]Parent compound not normally detected in blood.

Data to aid the interpretation of quantitative analytical results for primarily whole blood for a range of solvents, metabolites, and so on are given in **Table 6**. As a general rule, whole blood concentrations in the range of 10–100 mg l^{-1}, perhaps more, are attained during VSA and may be expected in postmortem specimens. However, there is usually a big overlap in the blood concentrations of volatile compounds attained after workplace exposure and as a result of deliberate inhalation of vapor. Similarly, the blood concentrations of volatile anesthetics attained during anesthesia may far exceed those found in VSA-related deaths. This reflects the fact that VSA-related deaths are often sudden and perhaps multifactorial

(indirect toxicity such as inhalation of stomach contents, possible hypoxia, catecholamine release, etc., as discussed earlier), and that toxicity varies greatly depending on the route and intensity of exposure (blood concentrations may not necessarily reflect concentrations in vital areas of the brain or heart). Moreover, there is always the possibility of loss of volatile analytes from blood or other biological samples prior to the analysis.

The interpretation of case data involving chloroform may be particularly difficult. In addition to sometimes being present in drinking water at low concentrations (following chlorination of drinking water), chloroform is found in a variety of medicinal preparations, in cigarette smoke, soft drinks, margarines, and in swimming pools. A further possible source of chloroform on HS-GC is from thermal decomposition of trichloroacetic acid at temperatures above 40 °C or so. Trichloroacetic acid is a metabolite of several compounds including the solvent trichloroethylene (**Table 4**) and the drugs chloral hydrate, dichloralphenazone, and triclofos (2,2,2-trichloroethanol dihydrogen phosphate). Trichloroacetic acid has a half-life in blood of 3–5 days and thus may be detected for a relatively long time after exposure to, or ingestion of, a precursor. Trichloroacetic acid plasma concentrations of up to 40 mg l^{-1} have been reported after occupational exposure to trichloroethylene vapor.

In 25 Caucasian adult women in Florida, USA, over a period of 6 months average plasma chloroform concentrations were generally less than 25 µg l^{-1}, but in two subjects, plasma chloroform concentrations of 2.9 and 4.0 mg l^{-1}, respectively, were found during routine sampling. All subjects were carefully screened to exclude occupational and recreational exposure to chloroform and other compounds that could give rise to chloroform on HS-GC. At the other extreme, postmortem blood chloroform concentrations in fatalities involving this agent have been reported as 10–50 mg l^{-1}. During anesthesia, blood chloroform concentrations of 50 mg l^{-1} or more were expected (**Table 6**).

It is well known that ethanol may be both produced and metabolized by microbial action in biological specimens. Higher-order alcohols (fusel oils) may also be produced as a result of fermentation. Dimethylsulfide is a common product of putrefaction. Small amounts of hexanal may arise from degradation of fatty acids in blood on long-term storage even at -5 to -20 °C. Hexanal is resolved from toluene on the SPB-1 capillary GC system discussed earlier, but resolution may be lost if an isothermal quantitative analysis is performed. Interference from hexanal is only likely to be important, however, if very low concentrations of toluene (0.1 mg l^{-1} or less) are to be measured.

For very volatile compounds such as propane and butane, detection followed by an estimate of the quantity present in the sample at the time of the analysis (low, high, similar to that seen in other VSA-related deaths, etc.) is often all that can be

Table 6   Solvents and other volatile compounds: simple guide to the interpretation of analytical toxicology results

Analyte	"Therapeutic" or "normal" whole blood concentration (less than)	Whole blood concentration associated with serious toxicity[a]	Relative molecular mass
Acetaldehyde	0.2 mg l^{-1}	(Not known)	44.1
Acetone (see also 2-propanol[b]) (urine)	10 mg l^{-1} (1 g l^{-1} in ketosis) 10 mg l^{-1} (2 g l^{-1} in ketosis) 80 mg l^{-1c}	(Not known)	58.1
Acetonitrile (see also cyanide[b])	–	50 mg l^{-1}	41.1
Amyl nitrite: see nitrite[b]			
Benzene	0.2 μg l^{-1} (nonsmokers) 0.6 μg l^{-1} (smokers)	1 mg l^{-1}	78.1
Benzoate (plasma)	0.01 g l^{-1} (dietary)	0.5 g l^{-1} (neonates)	122.1
Benzyl alcohol (plasma) (see also benzoate[d])	–	50 mg l^{-1} (neonates)	108.1
Bromide (plasma)	3–5 mg l^{-1} (dietary)	500 mg l^{-1} (inorganic bromide exposure) 40 mg l^{-1} (organobromine alkylating agents)	79.9
Bromomethane: see bromide[b]			
Bromopropane: see bromide[b]			
Butanone	10 mg l^{-1} (occupational exposure) 5 mg l^{-1} (urine)[c]	500 mg l^{-1}	72.1
Butyl nitrite: see Nitrite[b]			
Carbon disulphide: see 2-thiothiazolidine-4-carboxylate[d]			
Carbon monoxide (as carboxyhemoglobin saturation)	1% HbCO (nonsmokers) 15% HbCO (heavy smokers) 5% HbCO[c]	20% HbCO	–
Carbon tetrachloride	3.5 μg l^{-1c}	0.5 mg l^{-1} (2 h postexposure)	153.8
Chloral hydrate: see 2,2,2-trichloroethanol[b]			
Chlorobenzene	0.2 mg l^{-1} 25 mg g^{-1} creatinine (urine)[c]	– –	112.6
Chlorodifluoromethane (HCFC 22)	2 mg l^{-1} (occupational)	–	86.5
Chloroform	50 mg l^{-1} (anesthesia) 0.03 mg l^{-1} (dietary)	–	119.4
Cresol (see also toluene) (urine)[d]	1.5 mg l^{-1c}		
Cyanide (see also thiocyanate[d])	0.1 mg l^{-1} (nonsmokers) 0.2 mg l^{-1} (heavy smokers)	0.1 mg l^{-1} (chronic) 1 mg l^{-1} acute	26.0
Cyclohexane	0.4 mg l^{-1} (occupational exposure) 150 μg g^{-1} creatinine (urine)[c]	Not known	84.2
Cyclopropane	100 mg l^{-1} (anesthesia)	–	42.1
Desflurane	300 mg l^{-1} (anesthesia)	–	168.0
1,1-Dichloro-1-fluoroethane (HCFC 141b)	–	10 mg l^{-1}	117.0
Dichlorordifluoromethane (CFC 12)	1.2 mg l^{-1} (occupational)	–	120.9
Dichloromethane (see also carbon monoxide[d])	1 mg l^{-1}	50 mg l^{-1}	84.9
Diethyl ether	500 mg l^{-1} (anesthesia)	–	74.1
N,N-Dimethylformamide	5 mg l^{-1} 35 mg l^{-1} (urine)[c]	Not known Not known	59.1
1,4-Dioxane	12 mg l^{-1} (occupational exposure)	Not known	88.1
β-Hydroxyethoxyacetate[d]	0.5 g l^{-1} (occupational exposure, urine)		120.1
Enflurane	100 mg l^{-1} (anesthesia)	–	184.5
Ethanol	<0.1 g l^{-1}	0.5 g l^{-1} (children) 2 g l^{-1} (adolescents/adults)	46.1
Ether: see diethyl ether			
Ethyl acetate: see ethanol[b]			

(Continued)

Table 6 Solvents and other volatile compounds: simple guide to the interpretation of analytical toxicology results—(Continued)

Analyte	"Therapeutic" or "normal" whole blood concentration (less than)	Whole blood concentration associated with serious toxicity[a]	Relative molecular mass
Ethylbenzene: see mandelate	0.001 mg l^{-1} (environmental) 300 mg l^{-1} (urine)[c]	Not known	106.2
Ethyl *tert*-butyl ether	1 mg l^{-1}	–	102.2
Fluoride (serum) (urine)	0.05 mg l^{-1} (dietary) 3 mg l^{-1}	2 mg l^{-1}	19.0
Formaldehyde (see also formate[b])	4 mg l^{-1} (occupational exposure)	–	30.0
Formate (plasma)	10 mg l^{-1}	Not known	46.0
GHB: see 4-hydroxybutyrate			
Glycol ethers: see 2-butoxyethanol, 2-ethoxyethanol			
Halothane (see also trifluoroacetate[d])	50 mg l^{-1} (anesthesia)	–	197.4
Hexachlorobenzene (plasma)	150 µg l^{-1c}	Not known	284.8
Hexane (*n*-Hexane) (see also 2,5-hexanedione)	5 µg l^{-1} (environmental) 400 µg l^{-1} (occupational)	Not known	86.2
2,5-Hexanedione (+ 4,5-dihydroxy-2-hexanone) (urine)[d]	5 mg l^{-1c}		_[e]
2-Hexanone: see 2,5-hexanedione[d]			
Hippurate (urine)	0.2 g l^{-1} 2 g l^{-1e}		179.2
4-Hydroxybutyrate (plasma)	–	100 mg l^{-1}	104.1
Isoamyl nitrite: see nitrite[b]			
Isobutyl nitrite: see nitrite[b]			
Isoflurane	100 mg l^{-1} (anesthesia)	–	184.5
Isopropanol: see 2-propanol			
Mandelate (urine)	0.005 g l^{-1}		152.1
MBK: see 2-hexanone			
MEK: see butanone			
Methanol (see also formate[d])	0.002 g l^{-1} (dietary) 0.03 g l^{-1} (urine)[c]	0.5 g l^{-1} (2 h postingestion) 0.2 g l^{-1} (6 h postingestion)	32.0
Methoxyflurane	200 mg l^{-1} (anesthesia)	–	165.0
Methyl bromide: see bromide[b]			
Methyl butyl ketone: see 2-hexanone			
Methyl ethyl ketone: see butanone			
Methyl *tert*-butyl ether	<0.1 µg l^{-1} (environmental) 1 mg l^{-1} (occupational)	Not known	88.2
Methylhippurates (total, urine)[d]	2 g l^{-1c}		193.2
Methyl isobutyl ketone: see 4-methyl-2-pentanone			
4-Methyl-2-pentanone (urine)	3.5 mg l^{-1c}		100.2
MIBK: see 4-methyl-2-pentanone			
Nitrite (plasma) (urine)	1 mg l^{-1} (environmental) –	Not known 10 mg l^{-1}	46.0
Nitrous oxide	100 mg l^{-1} (anesthesia)	–	44.0
2-Propanol (see also acetone[d])	–	2.5 g l^{-1}	60.1
Sevoflurane	100 mg l^{-1}	–	200.1
Styrene	0.001 mg l^{-1} (environmental) 2 mg l^{-1} (occupational)	Not known	104.2
Tetrachloroethylene	1 mg l^{-1}	10 mg l^{-1}	165.8
Tetrahydrofuran (urine)	2 mg l^{-1c}		72.1
Thiocyanate (plasma)	4 mg l^{-1} (nonsmokers) 20 mg l^{-1} (heavy smokers) 100 mg l^{-1} (nitroprusside therapy)	120 mg l^{-1}	58.1
2-Thiothiazolidine-4-carboxylate (TTCA) (urine)	2 mg g^{-1} creatinine (urine)[c]	–	163.2

(Continued)

Table 6   Solvents and other volatile compounds: simple guide to the interpretation of analytical toxicology results—(Continued)

Analyte	"Therapeutic" or "normal" whole blood concentration (less than)	Whole blood concentration associated with serious toxicity[a]	Relative molecular mass
Toluene (whole blood) (see also cresol[d])	0.60 mg l^{-1c}	10 mg l^{-1}	92.1
2,2,2-Tribromoethanol	–	50 mg l^{-1}	282.8
Trichloroacetate (urine)	100 mg l^{-1c}		163.4
1,1,1-Trichloroethane	0.55 mg l^{-1c}	10 mg l^{-1}	133.4
2,2,2-Trichloroethanol	10 mg l^{-1}	50 mg l^{-1}	149.4
Trichloroethylene (see also trichloroacetate[d], 2,2,2-Trichloroethanol[b])	–	10 mg l^{-1}	131.4
Trichlorofluoromethane (CFC 11)	5 mg l^{-1}	–	137.4
Trifluoroacetate (from halothane)	2.5 mg l^{-1c}		114.0
TTCA: see 2-thiothiazolidine-4-carboxylate Xylene (total) (see also methylhippurates[d])	0.01 mg l^{-1} (environmental) 1.5 mg l^{-1c}	Not known	106.2

[a]An en-dash indicates that concentration which could be associated with serious toxicity may be no greater than "therapeutic" concentration in other patients.
[b]Active metabolite/decomposition product.
[c]Biologische Arbeitsstoff-Toleranzwerte (BAT) value 2011—biological tolerance value.
[d]Metabolite/decomposition product.
[e]Suggestive of recent toluene exposure, but dietary benzoate may give elevated hippurate excretion.

attempted. In some deaths attributed to the abuse of LPG, only butane, isobutane, and propane are detected on HS-GC of postmortem blood. In other cases, these three compounds may occur together with 2-propanol, acetone, 2-methyl-2-propanol, 2-butanol, and butanone (**Figure 3**). By analogy with the metabolism of hexane (**Table 4**), these additional compounds probably arise from the metabolism of the butanes and propane (**Figure 4**).

The alkyl nitrites (e.g., isobutyl nitrite, isopropyl nitrite) are a special case in that (a) they are extremely unstable and break down rapidly *in vivo* to the corresponding alcohols, and (b) they usually also contain other isomers such as butyl nitrite or propyl nitrite. Any products submitted for analysis will usually contain the corresponding alcohols as well as the nitrites. Methemoglobinemia usually only occurs when exposure has been substantial, for example, after ingestion.

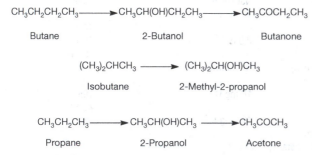

Figure 4 Summary of the metabolism of butane, isobutane, and propane in man.

In the occupational setting, blood toluene concentrations after exposure up to 127 ppm toluene (UK Occupational Exposure Limit at the time 100 ppm) for 8 h ranged between 0.4 and 6.7 mg l^{-1}. After brief exposure, only signs of moderate intoxication such as slurred speech and unsteady movements have been associated with blood toluene concentrations as high as 30 mg l^{-1}. Blood toluene concentrations in samples from 132 patients who were thought to have engaged in VSA ranged from 0.2 to 70 mg l^{-1}, and were above 5 mg l^{-1} in 22 of 25 deaths. On the other hand, 13 patients with blood toluene concentrations greater than 10 mg l^{-1} were either asymptomatic or only mildly intoxicated (headache, nausea, vomiting, and/or drowsiness), although these manifestations of toxicity can lead to "indirect" acute VSA-related death. Similarly, after exposure to 350 ppm 1,1,1-trichloroethane (UK maximum exposure limit at the time) for 1 h, the mean blood 1,1,1-trichloroethane concentration was 2.6 mg l^{-1}. Blood 1,1,1-trichloroethane concentrations ranged from 0.1 to 60 mg l^{-1} in samples from 66 patients suspected of VSA, 29 of whom died. There was a broad relationship between blood 1,1, 1-trichloroethane concentration and the severity of poisoning, but as in the case of toluene, there was a big overlap between the blood concentrations encountered in fatalities and those attained after occupational exposure.

Some 80% of a dose of toluene is converted to hippuric acid (**Table 4**), which is excreted in urine. Similarly, more than 90% of a dose of xylene is metabolized to methylhippuric (toluric) acids. The principal isomer found in urine is 3-methylhippurate, from *m*-xylene (**Table 1**). Methylhippurates are not normal urinary constituents, but hippuric acid may arise from the metabolism of benzoates in medicines and also from foods containing primary phenols and simple aromatic acids such as bilberries and cherries. Hippurate and methylhippurate excretion is often expressed as a ratio to creatinine. Occupational exposure to toluene can give rise to ratios of up to 1 g hippurate per gram creatinine or more; in patients suspected of VSA, a ratio of more than 1 g hippurate per gram creatinine strongly suggests, but does not prove, toluene exposure. Measurement of urinary *o*-cresol has been proposed as an alternative means of monitoring toluene exposure selectively, particularly in occupational circumstances, but the assay procedure is relatively complex and is not widely used.

See also: **Chemistry/Trace/Drugs of Abuse:** Classification; **Methods:** Gas Chromatography; Mass Spectrometry; Spectroscopic Techniques; **Toxicology/Drugs of Abuse:** Postmortem Blood.

Further Reading

Austin, A., Winskog, C., van den Heuvel, C., Byard, R.W., 2011. Recent trends in suicides utilizing helium. Journal of Forensic Sciences 56, 649–651.

Auwaerter, V., Perdekamp, M.G., Kempf, J., Schmidt, U., Weinmann, W., Pollak, S., 2007. Toxicological analysis after asphyxial suicide with helium and a plastic bag. Forensic Science International 170, 139–141.

Baselt, R.C., 2011. Disposition of Toxic Drugs and Chemicals in Man, ninth ed. Biomedical Publications, Seal Beach, CA.

Bowen, S.E., 2011. Two serious and challenging medical complications associated with volatile substance misuse: Sudden sniffing death and fetal solvent syndrome. Substance Use and Misuse 46 (Suppl. 1), 68–72.

Byard, R.W., Gilbert, J.D., Terlet, J., 2007. Death associated with volatile substance inhalation–histologic, scanning electron microscopic and energy dispersive X-ray spectral analyses of lung tissue. Forensic Science International 171, 118–121.

Deutsche Forschungsgemeinschaft, 2011. List of MAK and BAT Values Maximum Concentrations and Biological Tolerance Values at the Workplace. Commission for the investigation of health hazards of chemical compounds in the work area. Report 47. WILEY-VCH, Weinheim.

Flanagan, R.J., Fisher, D.S., 2008. Volatile substance abuse and crime: Data from UK press cuttings 1996–2007. Medicine Science and the Law 48, 295–306.

Flanagan, R.J., Pounder, D.J., 2010. A chloroform-related death. Analytical and forensic aspects. Forensic Science International 197, 89–96.

Flanagan, R.J., Streete, P.J., Ramsey, J.D., 1997. Volatile Substance Abuse. United Nations International Drug Control Programme Technical Series, vol. 5. UNODC, Vienna. http://www.unodc.org/pdf/technical_series_1997-01-01_1.pdf (accessed 13 January 2012).

Foster, K.N., Jones, L., Caruso, D.M., 2003. Hydrofluoric acid burn resulting from ignition of gas from a compressed air duster. Journal of Burn Care and Rehabilitation 24, 234–237.

Hathout, L., El-Saden, S., 2011. Nitrous oxide-induced B_{12} deficiency myelopathy: Perspectives on the clinical biochemistry of vitamin B_{12}. Journal of the Neurological Sciences 301, 1–8.

Himmel, H.M., 2008. Mechanisms involved in cardiac sensitization by volatile anesthetics: General applicability to halogenated hydrocarbons? Critical Reviews in Toxicology 38, 773–803.

Howard, M.O., Bowen, S.E., Garland, E.L., Perron, B.E., Vaughn, M.G., 2011. Inhalant use and inhalant use disorders in the United States. Addiction Science and Clinical Practice 6, 18–31.

Pihlainen, K., Ojanperä, I., 1998. Analytical toxicology of fluorinated inhalation anaesthetics. Forensic Science International 97, 117–133.

Walker, R., Flanagan, R.J., Lennard, M.S., Mills, G.A., Walker, V., 2006. Solid phase micro-extraction: Investigation of the metabolism of substances that may be abused by inhalation. Journal of Chromatographic Science 44, 387–393.

Wille, S.M., Lambert, W.E., 2004. Volatile substance abuse – Post-mortem diagnosis. Forensic Science International 142, 135–156.

Relevant Websites

http://www.emcdda.europa.eu—European Monitoring Centre for Drugs and Drug Addiction (EMCDDA).

http://www.inhalants.org/—National Inhalant Prevention Coalition.

http://www.re-solv.org/—Re-Solv.

http://www.drugabuse.gov—The National Institute on Drug Abuse (NIDA).

Alcohol Congeners and the Source of Ethanol

OH Drummer, Monash University, Southbank, VIC, Australia

Abbreviations

ADH	Alcohol dehydrogenase	GC	Gas chromatography
BAC	Blood alcohol concentration (referring to ethanol)	MS	Mass spectrometry
		SPME	Solid-phase microextraction
FID	Flame ionization detector	TOF	Time of flight

Introduction

The consumption of alcohol by the community in many parts of the world continues at a significant rate. For example, per capita consumption in most of Europe as well as the United States, Australia, and New Zealand ranges from 8 to 12 l. The main types of alcoholic beverages are beer, wine, and spirits, although each category comprises many different products, made from different ingredients and by different processes. Moreover, the concentration of alcohol varies between these products, from about 2–6% for beer, about 10–12% for wine, and over 20% for spirits and liqueurs.

While alcohol (chemically, ethanol) is the main active substance, several other constituents are also present that contribute to the taste of these beverages. Many of these constituents are volatile and can be analyzed to determine the source and type of alcoholic beverage.

The lower-molecular-weight alcohols have been used to characterize the source of particular types of alcoholic beverages, that is, beer, wines, and spirits. These substances are often termed congeners. While these are not individually characteristic of a particular alcoholic beverage, their combination can sometimes be used to help to determine the source and type of alcoholic beverage.

Congener Content of Beverages

In beer, a number of volatile compounds contribute to the odor and flavor. These include acetaldehyde, ethyl acetate, 1-propanol, 2-methyl-1-propanol, 2-methyl-1-butanol, 3-methyl-1-butanol, isoamyl acetate, 2-phenyl-ethanol, 2-phenyl-ethyl acetate, and many others. In wines, there are hundreds of substances that contribute to the color and taste including lower and high alcohols, phenols, esters, and terpenes.

Congeners of the type listed above and in **Table 1** are present in quite low concentrations, but most of them are detectable using modern analytical techniques. Their source depends on the type of fermentation process, the type of material being fermented, and the remaining processes used to prepare the final product.

Methanol derives from bacterial action on pectin, a heteropolysaccharide commonly found in fruits and, as such, it is found in the highest quantities in brandies made from apples, plums, and cherries.

The higher alcohols are by-products of fermentation and depend on the source of the sugars used in the fermentation and the presence of amino acids.

The quality and type of the distillation process will also affect the content of the congeners. Vodka contains some methanol but effectively no other congeners, while other alcoholic products contain variable types and content of congeners.

Congener analysis has been extensively used to determine the type of whiskey (i.e., Scotch, Irish, and Bourbon), including distinguishing counterfeit whiskeys. The relative amounts of the fusel oils 1-propanol, 2-methyl-1-propanol, 2-methyl-1-butanol, and 3-methyl-1-butanol have been used to distinguish these whiskeys. When the 3-methyl-1-butanol/2-methyl-1-butanol ratio is relatively high (>5.0), a spirit of noncereal origin is suspected.

In some alcohol products, particular characteristic chemicals can be targeted. For example, (*E*)-1-methoxy-4-(1-propenyl)benzene or *trans*-anethole is a volatile compound that is found naturally in aniseed (*Pimpinella anisum*), star anise

Table 1   Congener content (mg l^{-1}) of alcoholic beverages

Beverage class	n	Methanol	Propan-1-ol	Butan-1-ol	Butan-2-ol	Isobutanol	2-Methylbutan-1-ol	3-Methylbutan-1-ol
Beer, b.f.	545	7 ± 3^a	13 ± 3	0	0	13 ± 4	13 ± 3	52 ± 12
Beer, t.f.	102	1–19	10–73	0	0	9–90	10–49	37–124
Red wine	282	104 ± 30	30 ± 7	0–7	0–1	47 ± 15	33 ± 6	137 ± 26
White wine	460	29 ± 16	31 ± 8	0–8	0	56 ± 18	27 ± 6	112 ± 25
Rosé wine	16	12–41	15–30	0	0	24–99	4–73	34–314
Champagne	53	16 ± 8	31 ± 5	0–9	0	53 ± 15	30 ± 7	126 ± 28
French cognac	25	273 ± 97	184 ± 23	0–1	0–6	385 ± 56	125 ± 33	764 ± 86
Wine brandy	25	272 ± 76	130 ± 22	0–4	1–18	252 ± 38	77–186	482 ± 961
Williams	18	3783 ± 983	1382 ± 686	211 ± 148	609 ± 479	210 ± 71	65 ± 21	307 ± 131
Cherry brandy	19	2202 ± 355	$2218 \pm 1\,227$	1–17	121 ± 30	151 ± 36	60 ± 15	307 ± 80
Plum brandy	16	3697 ± 881	1039 ± 688	53 ± 33	64 ± 56	230 ± 96	62 ± 18	341 ± 38
Slivovitz	15	1513–4037	326–1506	7–145	26–187	58–301	28–72	139–386
Caribbean rum	27	6–74	34–3633	0–1	0–126	8–455	0–219	0–788
Blended Scotch	50	112 ± 19	171 ± 29	0	0	263 ± 36	59 ± 12	239 ± 44
Scotch malt	23	159 ± 9	131 ± 16	0	0	376 ± 34	118 ± 10	486 ± 40
Irish whiskey	6	6–110	170–205	0	0	284–413	72–89	288–338
US whiskey	22	196–328	50–193	0	0	388 ± 99	271 ± 53	1059 ± 188
Canadian whiskey	8	70–90	13–82	0	0	20–50	26–55	102–197
Gin	14	12–1359	0–885	0–1	0	0–7	0–19	0–53
Vodka	27	1–170	0–16	0	0	0	0	0
Dutch Genever	8	38–95	0–74	0	0	0–106	0–67	0–138

b.f., bottom fermented; t.f., top fermented.
^{a}Mean $\pm$ SD.

(*Illicium verum*), and fennel (*Foeniculum vulgare*). Extracts of these herbs are used to make ouzo, raki, and the German aniseed liqueur "Küstennebel." Consumption of these products does give rise to detectable anethole in serum (maximum blood concentration—C_{max} 5–18 ng ml^{-1}) at about the same time as alcohol concentrations peak following consumption of low to moderate amounts of the beverage.

Absinthe contains the monoterpenoid ketone thujone and is found in *Artemisia absinthium* and *Artemisia pontica*. Thujone content of all the commercial products are at or below the mandated 35 mg kg^{-1}.

Methods

These volatile congeners including ethanol itself are invariably detected by temperature-programmed headspace-gas chromatography (GC). However, the detection limits are far lower than those used for conventional assays for ethanol. It is uncommon to measure ethanol blood concentrations <0.01 g/100 ml (0.1 g l^{-1}). The blood concentrations of congeners are over 1000 times lower. Consequently, the required minimum detection limits for congeners are at least: 0.5 mg l^{-1} for methanol, 0.05 mg l^{-1} for 1-propanol, and 0.02 mg l^{-1} for the butanols and for methyl ethyl ketone.

This is achieved by the use of larger volumes of blood (1 ml or more) and the use of salts (i.e., sodium sulfate) to increase

headspace concentrations (increases vapor pressure) in the vial. Higher chain alcohols are freed from glucuronic acid by prior digestion with beta-glucuronidase, and to reduce viscosity, water is added to dilute samples. Ultrasonication and/or ultrafiltration can also be used to break up cells. The use of small headspace vials increases sensitivity further.

The net effect of this is to have complex chromatograms. Capillary columns improve the separation of the constituents to the point of using even two columns of different polarity (e.g., CP-Sil-19 and CP-Wax-52); however, the use of capillary columns is difficult when injecting relatively large headspace volumes without high-pressure valves to regulate flow rates.

The best technique is to use cryofocusing in which a short capillary column is inserted before the injector through which refrigerated gaseous nitrogen is passed in the opposite direction to the carrier gas flow. This allows the volatiles to be trapped in the capillary and pressure injected into the analytic columns in a short burst.

While flame ionization detectors can be used to detect the eluting components, the use of mass spectrometry (MS) to identify these components is advisable in modern analytic toxicology. MS avoids the need to use two columns and can with use of retention time allow identification of congeners with much more certainty.

It is recommended to store blood samples in a frozen state at −20 °C until analysis to avoid loss of congeners and to reduce other changes that might occur, that is, putrefaction, although in sealed tubes, the stability of ethanol and congeners is quite good for at least a few months when stored at 4 °C. Putrefactive changes will lead not only to a discoloration of the blood but also to the formation of 1-propanol, 1-butanol, acetaldehyde, and other substances that elute in the chromatogram.

For the analysis of actual alcoholic beverages, similar GC methods can be employed using the headspace; however, more sophisticated methods have been employed using solid-phase microextraction fibers and GC–MS including two-dimensional GC with time-of-flight MS (GC–TOF–MS).

Disposition

All congeners appear to be well absorbed when consumed in alcoholic beverages; however, their distribution in the body increases as their solubility in fatty tissues increases. For example, ethanol is distributed to the water content of the body whereas the higher chain alcohols are distributed into the nonwater compartments of cells and consequently have a higher volume of distribution, often as much as double that of ethanol.

The higher chain alcohols are also conjugated with glucuronic acid. For example, 1-propanol is conjugated to about 30%, 1-butanol is conjugated to about 40%, and 2- and 3-methylbutan-1-ol are almost completely conjugated. There is some conjugation of ethanol; indeed, ethyl glucuronide can be used as a marker of alcohol exposure as it has a longer elimination half-life than ethanol itself, and its presence in blood and hair is used to assess the degree of chronic alcohol exposure. In some European countries, it is used to assess abstinence to ethanol and to provide an objective measure to regrant a driving license following loss of license for alcohol-related driving offenses.

The elimination of these congeners is complex. All alcohols are substrates for alcohol dehydrogenase (ADH); hence, the overall oxidation of the alcohols will depend on the overall quantity and type of the alcohols. As the ethanol concentration will usually be much greater, the amount of ethanol will affect the rate of metabolism of other substances by this route (**Table 2**).

There are differences in the concentration of congeners between blood and serum (plasma); hence, it is necessary to standardize on the specimen being analyzed.

Methanol

Methanol is an endogenous compound found in humans not consuming alcoholic beverages, particularly in persons consuming fruit, but it does not appear to be limited to this food source. Background serum concentrations in unexposed persons are usually well below 3 mg l^{-1}, with an average of around 1 mg l^{-1} or lower.

Consumption of methanol-free ethanol can cause significant rise in serum methanol concentrations at a rate of 0.1–

0.5 mg l^{-1} per hour. The net increase depends on the length of exposure to ethanol. This increase occurs because oxidation to formaldehyde by ADH is effectively blocked by the presence of ethanol at concentrations above 0.2 g l^{-1}. However, methanol is also removed by other processes, particularly through breath, hence its pharmacokinetics, as with all congeners, is complex.

Most alcoholic beverages contain small amounts of methanol, which further increase the serum methanol concentrations. In chronic alcoholics, methanol concentrations can easily exceed 10 mg l^{-1}. The presence of significant amounts of methanol in blood (10 mg l^{-1} or greater) can be used as a guide to suggest chronic alcohol abuse; however, the drinking pattern and type of alcohol consumed will affect the methanol concentration.

2-Propanol

Background concentrations of 2-propanol (isopropanol) in nondrinkers are usually <0.1 mg l^{-1}. Acetone, its major metabolite, has much higher endogenous concentrations at about 1–3 mg l^{-1}. Concentrations in people who drink alcohol rise substantially and exceed 10 mg l^{-1}; however, mean concentrations are closer to 1 mg l^{-1}. Corresponding acetone concentrations are about fivefold higher. Acetone is also found in persons with diabetic ketoacidosis. There is some evidence of formation of 2-propanol from acetone as well. Some absorption of this alcohol occurs from skin swabs containing this alcohol.

1-Propanol

This alcohol is not present normally in serum but is apparently produced in small amounts when pure ethanol is consumed. This congener is commonly present in alcoholic beverages with contents ranging from near zero for vodka and gin to over 1000 mg l^{-1} in fruit brandies. In beer and wine, the content is about 10 and 30 mg l^{-1}, respectively. Consequently, significant increases in the concentration of this alcohol occur in persons consuming alcoholic beverages containing this congener.

The concentration ratio of 1-propanol with 2-methyl-1-propanol (isobutanol) has been used to determine the source of the alcoholic beverage. Beer drinkers tend to have serum concentration ratios of these two alcohols in the order of 3:1 even though the content of these two alcohols in this type of product is similar, whereas wine drinkers tend to have similar serum concentrations. As 2-butanol concentrations decrease more quickly than 1-propanol, higher concentrations of 1-propanol suggest that some time has elapsed since consumption.

Isobutanol (2-Methyl-1-Propanol)

This alcohol is not present endogenously and is usually associated with 1-propanol. It is metabolized in the gastric mucosa

Table 2   Source, metabolic pathway, and some pharmacokinetic parameters of selected congeners

Congener	Source	Metabolism	Volume of distribution (l kg^{-1})[a]	Elimination half-life (h)[b]
Methanol	Endogenous, all alcoholic beverages	Oxidation to formaldehyde and formic acid	0.5	1.5–3
1-Propanol	Alcoholic beverages, particularly fruit brandies	Oxidation to propionaldehyde and propionic acid, and propyl glucuronide	0.7	1–2
2-Propanol	Endogenous, alcoholic beverages	Oxidation to acetone, and 2-propyl glucuronide	~0.7[c]	1–3
2-Methyl-1-propanol (isobutanol)	Alcoholic beverages except vodka; highest in fruit brandies	Aldehyde and acid, and glucuronide	1.3	1–3
1-Butanol	Bacterial formation in putrefaction; fruit brandies	Butyric aldehyde and butyric acid, and glucuronide	~1[c]	n.a.
2-Butanol	Fruit brandies	Methyl ethyl ketone	~1[c]	n.a.
2-Methyl-1-butanol	All beverages except vodka	Corresponding glucuronide, aldehyde, carboxylic acid, propionic acid, acetic acid	>1[c]	n.a.
3-Methyl-1-butanol	All beverages except vodka	Corresponding glucuronide, aldehyde, carboxylic acid, acetoacetic acid, acetic acid	>1[c]	n.a.

n.a., not available.
[a]These are approximate only and are only meant to reflect overall penetration into tissues.
[b]These half-lives will increase when metabolism is affected by other substances that compete with their breakdown.
[c]Data unavailable, estimates only.

and much of it is metabolized in the liver during the first pass; therefore, it has a short elimination half-life. Consequently, concentrations of this congener are less than that of 1-propanol even when similar amounts are present in beverages (see also previous paragraph).

2-Butanol

This alcohol is not present endogenously; however, it is present in fruit brandies and is often associated with 1-butanol. 2-Butanol is metabolized in part to methyl ethyl ketone, which can also be used to monitor exposure to beverages containing these congeners.

Isomeric Amyl Alcohols

Both 2-methyl-1-butanol (active amyl alcohol) and 3-methyl-1-butanol (isoamyl alcohol) are present almost exclusively in fruit brandies; however, their concentrations in serum are low following consumption of these drinks.

Toxicity of Congeners

As a general rule, while congeners are present in most alcoholic beverages, it is the ethanol that contributes most, if not all, of the toxicity. Ethanol depresses the central nervous system and disrupts many cellular activities including many biochemical pathways. Alcohol-induced acidosis is common and in some situations (e.g., liver disease, poor nutrition) can lead to abnormal glucose metabolism and ketoacidosis. In most cases,

toxicity is reversible once ethanol has cleared the body and fluids have been replaced.

Chronic abuse of alcoholic beverages leads to long-term tissue damage particularly erosive gastritis and ulceration of the stomach, liver cirrhosis, peripheral nerve disorders, and various forms of brain dysfunction including loss of memory and dementia, and fetal alcohol syndrome.

Methanol is arguably the most toxic congener primarily through its metabolites formaldehyde and formic acid. However, endogenous concentrations of methanol rarely exceed 1.5 mg l^{-1}, and it is unlikely that the methanol content of the beverages will itself become poisonous unless the beverage is consumed in massive amounts, or the drinker is an alcoholic and the methanol accumulates. Alcoholics are known to accumulate methanol that derives from the beverage consumed and from endogenous formation.

Hip Flask Defense

The hip flask defense relates to the consumption of alcohol after a traffic-related crime before apprehension by police. The detection and quantification of congeners in blood has been used to assist courts in establishing the accuracy of claims made by the defendant in drinking alcohol after driving, although this has been mainly used in Germany. The detection of congeners is useful only when the type of alcohol consumed after the collision is significantly different from that consumed before, there are no congeners in the alcoholic beverage (other than methanol) consumed postcollision, and there has not been more than a few hours' interval. There are various factors that influence the amount of congeners. This applies particularly to understanding the complex pharmacokinetics of the congeners in conjunction with often complex time courses of drinking.

The most useful application of pharmacokinetic calculation is the determination of the likely ethanol content. This requires knowledge or assumed knowledge of the drinking pattern before and after the collision. Unless the drinking pattern before the collision is witnessed and is reasonably reliable, such calculations can be easily criticized. Above all, such calculations require consideration of the likely range of absorption time, elimination rates, and even volume of distribution. For example, the elimination rate of ethanol can vary from 0.01 g/100 ml per hour (%/h) to well over 0.025%/h. This is dependent on a number of factors, particularly the blood alcohol concentration (BAC) and the regularity of alcohol consumption (induction of enzymes occurs with regular use).

In a 70-kg male person, the consumption of five glasses of red wine over 4 h can lead to BAC estimates of between (approximately) 0.4 and 1.0 g l^{-1} depending on the alcohol content per glass, elimination rate and absorption rate, and extent of ethanol. Consumption of food can significantly lower the BAC. If this person had a motor vehicle collision and left the scene before a BAC could be performed (usually by breath analysis) and consumed further alcohol (four glasses of wine) before being apprehended by the police 2 h later, it will be very difficult to prove he was over the legal limit of 0.5 g l^{-1} at the time of the collision even when the BAC at this point is just over the legal limit. The analysis of congeners is not useful since they will derive from alcohol consumed before and after the collision. However, if vodka was consumed after the collision then the relative absence of congeners (other than methanol) could prove that it was more likely than not that the allegation was true (i.e., he did drink vodka after the collision).

Due to individual variability, the complex pharmacokinetics, and likely differences in the contents of drinks, congener analysis can be useful only if the amounts of congeners in the possible scenarios are quite different.

See also: **Toxicology/Alcohol:** Blood; Breath Alcohol; Metabolites of Ethanol; Urine and Other Body Fluids.

Further Reading

Bilzer, N., Schmutte, P., Jehs, M., Penners, B.M., 1990. Kinetics of aliphatic alcohols (methanol, propanol-1 and isobutanol) in the presence of alcohol in the human body. Blutalkohol 27 (6), 385–409.

Bonte, W., 1987. Begleitstoffe alkoholischer Getränke. Max Schmidt-Römhild, Lübeck.

Bonte, W., Russmeyer, P., 1984. Normal distribution of congeners in alcoholic beverages. Beiträge zur Gerichtlichen Medizin 42, 387–394.

Charry-Parra, G., Dejesus-Echevarria, M., Perez, F.J., 2011. Beer volatile analysis: optimization of HS/SPME coupled to GC/MS/FID. Journal of Food Science 76 (2), C205–C211. Epub 2011 January 19. http://dx.doi.org/10.1111/j.1750-3841.2010.01979.x.

Gonzalez-Arjona, D., Lopez-Perez, G., Gonzalez-Gallero, V., Gonzalez, A.G., 2006. Supervised pattern recognition procedures for discrimination of whiskeys from gas chromatography/mass spectrometry congener analysis. Journal of Agricultural and Food Chemistry 54 (6), 1982–1989.

Gullberg, R.G., Jones, A.W., 1994. Guidelines for estimating the amount of alcohol consumed from a single measurement of blood alcohol concentration: Re-evaluation of Widmark's equation. Forensic Science International 69 (2), 119–130.

Haffner, H.T., Wehner, H.D., Scheytt, K.D., Besserer, K., 1992. The elimination kinetics of methanol and the influence of ethanol. International Journal of Legal Medicine 105 (2), 111–114.

Iffland, R., Balling, P., Oehmichen, M., Lieder, F., Norpoth, T., 1989. Methanol, iso-propanol, n-propanol–endogenous formation affected by alcohol? Blutalkohol 26 (2), 87–97.

Iffland, R., Jones, A.W., 2003. Evaluating alleged drinking after driving – The hip-flask defence. Part 2. Congener analysis. Medicine, Science, and the Law 43 (1), 39–68.

Iffland, R., Staak, M., Lieder, F., 1989. Ethanol and isopropanol consumption. Beiträge zur Gerichtlichen Medizin 47, 369–378.

Jones, A.W., Lowinger, H., 1988. Relationship between the concentration of ethanol and methanol in blood samples from Swedish drinking drivers. Forensic Science International 37 (4), 277–285.

Jungmann, L., Grosse Perdekamp, M., Bohnert, M., Auwarter, V., Pollak, S., 2011. Complex suicide by ethanol intoxication and inhalation of fire fumes in an old lady: Interdisciplinary elucidation including post-mortem analysis of congener alcohols. Forensic Science International 209 (1–3), e11–e15. Epub 2011 April 15.

Kimball, A.W., Friedman, L.A., 1992. Alcohol consumption regression models for distinguishing between beverage type effects and beverage preference effects. American Journal of Epidemiology 135 (11), 1279–1286.

Kraut, J.A., Kurtz, I., 2008. Toxic alcohol ingestions: Clinical features, diagnosis, and management. Clinical Journal of the American Society of Nephrology 3 (1), 208–225.

Majchrowicz, E., Mendelson, J.H., 1971. Blood methanol concentrations during experimentally induced ethanol intoxication in alcoholics. Journal of Pharmacology and Experimental Therapeutics 179 (2), 293–300.

Martensson, E., Olofsson, U., Heath, A., 1988. Clinical and metabolic features of ethanol–methanol poisoning in chronic alcoholics. Lancet 1 (8581), 327–328.

Robinson, A.L., Boss, P.K., Heymann, H., Solomon, P.S., Trengove, R.D., 2011. Development of a sensitive non-targeted method for characterizing the wine volatile profile using headspace solid-phase microextraction comprehensive two-dimensional gas chromatography time-of-flight mass spectrometry. Journal of Chromatography A 1218 (3), 504–517.

Rohsenow, D.J., Howland, J., 2010. The role of beverage congeners in hangover and other residual effects of alcohol intoxication: A review. Current Drug Abuse Reviews 3 (2), 76–79.

Sprung, R., Bonte, W., Rudell, E., 1983. Determination of congener substances of alcoholic beverages and their metabolites in blood and urine samples. Beiträge zur Gerichtlichen Medizin 41, 219–222.

Zuba, D., Piekoszewski, W., Pach, J., Winnik, L., Parczewski, A., 2002. Concentration of ethanol and other volatile compounds in the blood of acutely poisoned alcoholics. Alcohol 26 (1), 17–22.

Relevant Websites

http://what-when-how.com/forensic-sciences/congener-analysis/ (accessed 13 December 2011).

http://www.who.int/substance_abuse/publications/global_alcohol_report/msbgsruprofiles.pdf (accessed 27 November 2011).

Herbal Psychoactive Substances

J Beyer, Monash University, Southbank, VIC, Australia

Abbreviations

BCE	Before common era
CB$_1$	Cannabinoid receptor subtype 1
CB$_2$	Cannabinoid receptor subtype 2
GC–MS	Gas chromatography–mass spectrometry
HPLC	High-performance liquid chromatography
LC–MS	Liquid chromatography–mass spectrometry
LSD	Lysergic acid diethylamide
THC	Δ^9-Tetrahydrocannabinol

Introduction

Plants have been used by humans for their mind-altering properties for a long time. Products taken for such nonmedical reasons are called drugs of abuse. Most commonly abused substances that are extracted from or based on natural products are the classical drugs of abuse such as cannabis products, morphine, or cocaine.

In addition to these classical drugs, the so-called herbal or natural drugs consist of plant material with psychoactive properties. In recent years, the herbal drugs of abuse have become increasingly popular among drug abusers, largely due to publicity on the Internet.

The publicity has also sparked a development of synthetic drugs being introduced under the banner of "herbal" or "legal" highs. To sell psychoactive products, synthetic cannabinoids have been sprayed on nonpsychoactive plant mixtures.

However, as in the case of classical drugs of abuse, abuse of plants or plant ingredients may cause psychiatric problems such as addiction or chronic illnesses. Depending on the pharmacological activity of the contained active ingredients, they may even cause serious acute intoxication and poisoning, especially in overdose situations.

This chapter describes common herbal drugs of abuse in monographs. The monographs contain descriptions of the plants, their pharmacologically active compounds, and the current knowledge of their pharmacological properties.

Traditional Drugs of Abuse of Herbal Origin

Cannabis and Tetrahydrocannabinol

Cannabis is derived from *Cannabis sativa* L, an herbaceous annual plant. The species *C. sativa* can be divided into a number of subspecies and varieties. The plant is highly recognizable: the leaves are typically separated into five or more serrated leaflets. The stem of the plant is extremely fibrous and is therefore a popular source of fabric fiber.

Chinese medical records report the use of cannabis as far back as 2 737 before common era (BCE). The plant was also known on the Indian subcontinent and the Arabian Peninsula, before the start of the common era as an herbal remedy. Medical records show that cannabis was used as an antimalarial and antirheumatic drug, a narcotic, an aphrodisiac, a carminative, and as a remedy to treat nausea and headache.

Different varieties have become popular as commonly used drugs of abuse. Sinsemilla is a seedless, more potent form produced from the unfertilized flowering tops of female cannabis plants, often found in the United States. Other forms of cannabis include Thai sticks, hashish (resin), and oil (hash oil). Modern names used to describe cannabis include "weed," "grass," "dope," "dagga," and "pot."

The plant prefers a warm humid climate, although it will grow in most climates. However, indoor and glasshouse cultivation are required for the cooler climates. The cannabis plant is dioecious, with male and female flowers borne on separate plants.

The pharmacologically active compounds contained in cannabis are the cannabinoids, a group of at least 66 substances. The most psychoactive cannabinoid in cannabis is Δ^9-tetrahydrocannabinol (THC).

All parts of the plant contain THC, including flowers, leaves, seeds, and stalks. Oil is produced from the seeds and flower heads. The female plant is known to be more robust, produces larger flowers, and, importantly, contains a higher THC content.

Cannabis as a drug of abuse is used mainly by smoking in the form of cigarettes (joints) or using cold-water pipes (bongs). Baking "cookies" with the use of hash oil is also widespread. Procannabinoids that can be found in the plant material are converted to THC by heat.

When smoked, common single doses of cannabis are 50–100 mg. The rapid onset of action (within 10 min) assists in the dosage of cannabis and additional intakes are smoked until the desired effect is achieved. The total duration of action of smoked cannabis is 1–4 h.

Pharmacological effects of THC include an increase in heart rate, blood pressure, and body temperature. More importantly, the ingestion of THC-containing smoke produces a range of cognitive and psychomotor effects associated with a transient euphoric effect that is usually perceived as a "high." Short-term memory loss can occur particularly with repeated use.

The cannabinoids are ligands of the cannabinoid G-protein-coupled receptors. Evidence for the existence of a human cannabinoid receptor was found in the mid-1980s, and the cannabinoid receptor subtype 1 (CB_1) receptor was confirmed by cloning in 1990. A second cannabinoid receptor, the cannabinoid receptor subtype 2 (CB_2) receptor, was confirmed by cloning in 1993. The CB_1 receptor is predominantly found at central and peripheral nerve terminals, whereas the CB_2 receptor is mainly distributed in immune cells.

With the discovery of cannabinoid receptors, the question arose as to whether these receptors had endogenous ligands or whether they were targets only for THC and other plant cannabinoids. The first endogenous cannabinoid was described in 1992. The substance was identified as arachidonoyl ethanolamide and named anandamide. So far, five endogenous cannabinoid receptor agonists have been described.

Coca and Cocaine

Coca is a plant from the genus *Erythroxylum* and is native to northwestern South America. The use of coca has a long tradition in South America. The first European description of coca is from Amerigo Vespucci from 1 499; he described how South American aborigines would chew the leaves to overcome fatigue and hunger.

The most important alkaloid in the coca plant is cocaine, first isolated in 1859 by Albert Niemann, a German chemist. The leaves contain up to 2% cocaine in a dried state. Although the genus *Erythroxylum* includes several hundred species, only *Erythroxylum coca* and *Erythroxylum novogranatense* contain significant amounts of cocaine. Trace amounts of cocaine have recently been detected in 23 species of *Erythroxylum*, but with content below 0.001%.

In 1863, the Italian chemist Angelo Mariani introduced a coca extract in sweet wine as a tonic, the so-called Vin Mariani. This tonic was copied in 1884 in the United States by John Pemberton. One year later, Pemberton responded to the American Prohibition legislation by developing a nonalcoholic carbonated coca extract called Coca-Cola, which contained an estimated amount of 9 mg of cocaine and was on the market until 1903.

The use of coca leaves as a local anesthetic was first proposed by Samuel Percy in 1856. After the isolation of cocaine, the Austrian pharmacologist Karl Damian Ritter described narcotic effects after application on the skin. About 25 years later, cocaine was used in clinical practice as a local anesthetic in ophthalmic surgery. The advantage of cocaine as a local anesthetic is its unique combination of local anesthesia and intense vasoconstriction. Therefore, cocaine is still used for topical anesthesia by otorhinolaryngologists.

The safe maximum dosage as a local anesthetic for a cocaine-naive person is reported to be 200 mg or 2–3 mg kg^{-1}; however, this is based on anecdotal observations rather than controlled studies. Cocaine doses as low as 20 mg can cause adverse reactions if rapidly absorbed.

The onset of cocaine action is very fast and the half-life of cocaine is less than 1 h; therefore, combined with a strong reinforcing action, cocaine causes a rapid psychological dependence.

The anesthetic effects are pharmacologically caused by blocking of sodium channels, whereas the vasoconstriction is caused by sympathetic activation. Cocaine inhibits the reuptake of catecholamines, which increases the activity of sympathetic synapses. This stimulation also occurs in the brain; therefore, cocaine causes euphoria, garrulousness, and increased motor activity. Cocaine also decreases fatigue and is abused as a stimulant.

Poppies and Opiates

Poppies include a number of attractive wildflower species, of which many species are also grown in gardens. Of all the different poppy plants, the opium poppy or *Papaver somniferum* is pharmacologically the most important. *P. somniferum* is an annual plant with a simple or only slightly branching stem. The leaves are ovate-oblong and of gray-blue greenish color. The flower can vary in color; pink varieties are the most common. Incisions made in the unripe capsules of *P. somniferum* release white latex that quickly hardens and turns brown after contact with oxygen. The hardened brown latex is called raw opium; each capsule releases ∼20–50 mg.

The main active alkaloid in opium and other parts of *P. somniferum* is morphine, which was first isolated in 1806 by the German pharmacist Friedrich Sertuerner. He called the isolated alkaloid "morphium" after the Greek god of dreams, Morpheus. It was not only the first alkaloid to be extracted from opium, but the first alkaloid ever to be isolated from any plant. With the invention of the hollow needle and the syringe, morphine was used in the treatment of postoperative and chronic pain, and as an adjunct to general anesthetics.

Unfortunately, morphine had as much potential for abuse as opium. Looking for a safer and nonaddictive opiate, Felix Hofmann synthesized diacetylmorphine in 1898. From 1898 to 1910, diacetylmorphine was marketed by Bayer under the brand name heroin. The drug was promoted as a nonaddictive morphine substitute and cough medicine for children.

The abuse of opioids was common in the late nineteenth century, leading to the International Opium Commission meeting in 1909 (in Shanghai) as the first step toward international drug prohibition. Based on this meeting, the first international drug control treaty, the International Opium Convention, was signed in 1912 at The Hague. This convention went into force globally in 1919, when it was incorporated into the Treaty of Versailles. Today, opium and opiates are controlled by the International Narcotics Control Board of the United Nations under Article 23 of the Single Convention on Narcotic Drugs, and subsequently under the Convention on Psychotropic Substances. Opium-producing nations are required to designate a government agency to take physical possession of illicit opium crops as soon as possible after harvest and conduct all wholesaling and exporting through that agency.

Emerging and Popular Herbal Drugs of Abuse

Nightshades

Atropa belladonna

The perennial plant *Atropa belladonna* is commonly known as deadly nightshade. Other common names such as dwale, death's herb, or witch's berry give an impression of its toxicity and use in the Middle Ages. The pharmacological effects of the plant are part of the etymology of the botanical name. The genus *Atropa* is named after the goddess Atropos, who is known in Greek mythology to cut the life thread. The species name *belladonna* is Italian for beautiful lady, and originates from its historical use of the berry juice by women to dilate their pupils.

All parts of *A. belladonna* contain psychoactive tropane alkaloids. The main alkaloids present in *A. belladonna* are L-hyoscyamine and L-scopolamine. Even though only L-hyoscyamine is present in the plant, L-hyoscyamine is converted to a racemic mixture of 50% L-hyoscyamine and D-hyoscyamine. This conversion is either a result of extraction or release after ingestion. This racemic mixture is called atropine.

Atropine acts pharmacologically via blocking acetylcholine receptors of the muscarine subtype. The blockage of these receptors causes symptoms such as tachycardia, dilated pupils, decreased gastrointestinal motility, and dry hot skin and dry mouth due to decreased sweat and saliva production. Apart from these peripheral effects, atropine also affects the central nervous system and causes agitation, disorientation, and hallucinations, which explain the common abuse of the herb.

Commonly abused parts of the plant are leaves and berries in doses of approximately 0.2 g of dried matter. The abuse has often been described as an unpleasant experience when the dose was too high. The plant is described to show a long duration of effects, often up to 36 h when untreated.

Datura stramonium

The annual plant *Datura. stramonium*, which is often found in nutrient-rich soils, grows to a height of up to 1 m. This plant of the nightshade family is commonly known as thorn apple, jimsonweed, or angel's-trumpet. The large flowers of *Datura* are white, erect, and tubular. The tubular shape and its psychoactivity are related to the name angel's-trumpet. The name thorn apple is related to the fruits which are spiky, large, green capsules containing numerous black seeds. The plant is distributed generally throughout the temperate and subtropical regions. Similar to *Datura* in botanical appearance are the *Brugmansia* species, which are often cultivated in pots as house plants.

All parts of *Datura* and *Brugmansia* contain the psychoactive tropane alkaloids as already described for *A. belladonna*. The increasing misuse has forced a prohibition by law in Florida of planting angel's-trumpets.

Commonly abused parts of *Datura* are the dried flower petals (smokes) or the seeds (oral ingestion). Dosage, effects, and duration of effects are similar to those after the ingestion of *Atropa*.

Kath (*Catha edulis*)

The evergreen shrub *Catha edulis*, which is native to tropical East Africa and the Arabian Peninsula, is known as khat or qat. In these countries, therapeutic and recreational khat use has been an integral part of local culture for centuries. In the second part of the twentieth century, the consumption changed to an uncontrolled abuse and spread throughout other continents. In 1980, the World Health Organization classified khat as a drug of abuse capable of causing dependence.

The main psychoactive alkaloids of khat are cathinone and its metabolite cathine, also known as norpseudoephedrine. Cathinone was found to have a pharmacological profile closely resembling that of amphetamine. Cathinone acts as a central nervous system stimulant and shows sympathomimetic effects on releasing catecholamines from presynaptic storage sites. Experiments have shown that cathine acts like cathinone, but is less effective. Both are controlled substances in many countries due to khat abuse.

The fresh leaves are chewed as soon as possible after harvesting. Khat has been used traditionally as a stimulant in Ethiopia by older men in conjunction with religious rites. Today, khat leaves are chewed by men and women of all ages, mostly in countries where khat is grown. But in other countries too, emigrants try to maintain this habit. Therefore, large quantities of fresh leaves are illegally imported to other countries. Common doses are in excess of a few grams of fresh leaves and are chewed over a prolonged period of time.

In recent years, designer drugs based on the chemical structure of cathinone have emerged in the illicit drug market. Methcathinone was the first cathinone derivative which was synthesized in 1928 as an intermediate of the synthesis of D,L-ephedrine. Shortly after, mephedrone (4-methylmethcathinone, 4-MMC) was synthesized by a French chemist Saem de Burnaga Sanchez in 1929, but the compound was later considered to be an obscure chemical product. Prior to the widespread abuse of cathinone derivatives, some substances, namely bupropion, amfepramone, and metamfepramone, were marketed as appetite suppressants and, in the case of bupropion, as a drug for smoking cessation. To date, these substances are still prescribed and also abused as anorectic drugs.

Salvia (*Salvia divinorum*)

Salvia divinorum is an herbaceous plant, native to the Mazatec region of the Sierra Madre Oriental in the Mexican state, Oaxaca. This plant has been used in traditional spiritual practices by Mazatec aborigines in a manner very similar to magic mushrooms (*Psilocybe* spp.). The plant and its use were discovered by the West in 1962 by Gordon Wasson, followed by the first botanical description by Carl Epling and Carlos Játiva-M. in the same year. Shortly after the first botanical description of the plant and its psychoactive properties, Albert Hofmann tried to discover the active constituents by analyzing the juice pressed from the plant. His analysis was unsuccessful, and it took until 1982 to isolate the diterpenes salvinorin A and salvinorin B. So far, 14 diterpenes have been isolated from *S. divinorum*, but salvinorin A seems to be the major active compound. Even though the plant is closely related to common sage (*Salvia. officinalis*), neither an essential oil nor thujone, common in other *Salvia* species, has been detected in *S. divinorum*.

In 1994, Daniel Siebert showed that the leaves of *S. divinorum* have psychoactive effects when the ingredients of the juice are absorbed via oral mucosa. The plant material was inactive when swallowed as quickly as possible to bypass the oral mucosa. In this study, the author also showed that salvinorin A produced the same psychoactive effects as the plant juice. Some years later, in 2002, salvinorin A was found to be a potent and the first nonnitrogenous agonist of the κ-opioid receptor, whereas salvinorin B is inactive at this receptor. In recent times, the availability of the plant has increased rapidly, partially due to Internet trading. Within a few years, *S. divinorum* has become a popular herbal drug of abuse.

The unique pharmacology of salvinorin A as the first nonnitrogenous opioid receptor agonist and its popularity as a drug of abuse has substantially increased researchers' interest in it.

Dried leaves of *S. diviniorum* or concentrated extracts are commonly smoked, leading to a rapid onset of action. The peak of effects is experienced after 1–5 min, and the experience is described to have a duration of less than 15 min.

Iboga (*Tabernanthe iboga*)

The perennial rainforest shrub *Tabernanthe iboga*, commonly known as iboga, is native to central western Africa. The plant reaches about 1.5–2 m in height and has yellowish or pinkish flowers that turn into sweet fruits which do not contain psychoactive alkaloids. The plant is a sacrament and symbol of power in the Bwiti religion, with the roots used in religious ceremonies as a "bridge to the ancestors." In small amounts (up to 5 mg kg^{-1}), the root is chewed by locals to reduce hunger and fatigue, but larger amounts (10 mg kg^{-1} or greater) will cause hallucinations and have even caused death.

The root bark contains about 6% indole alkaloids: primarily ibogaine (12-methoxyibogamine), and also tabernanthine, ibogaline, and ibogamine.

Ibogaine is a noncompetitive antagonist at α3β4 nicotinic receptors and a sigma$_2$ receptor agonist, increases ribonucleic acid expression of glial cell line–derived neurotrophic factor, is a weak agonist on the serotonin 5HT2A receptor, and is a weak N-methyl-D-aspartate receptor antagonist. The major metabolite, noribogaine (12-hydroxyibogamine), is a potent serotonin reuptake inhibitor and is also a moderate kappa and weak mu opioid receptor full agonist. Ibogaine has also been used to treat dependency on alcohol and illicit drugs, although its efficacy is questionable.

Morning Glory and Lysergic Acid Amide

Morning glory is a common name for over 1 000 species of plants in the family *Convolvulaceae*. If morning glory is abused, the plant is probably either *Ipomea tricolor* or *Rivea corymbosa*. Both plants are perennial twinning lianas native to Central and South America. The seeds of both plants have been used by Native Americans for their hallucinogenic properties. The seeds of *I. tricolor* have been called *tlilitzin* by Aztecs, meaning "the very black," while the seeds of *R. corymbosa* were named *ololiuqui*, which is translated as "that which causes turns." Nowadays, the most commonly used term for the seeds of *I. tricolor* is badoh negro, and for the seeds of *R. corymbosa*, badoh blanco.

The fresh or dried seeds are ground and mixed with water and ingested orally. After ingestion, the seeds produce psychedelic effects similar to those of *Psilocybe* mushrooms or lysergic acid diethylamide (LSD). The hallucinogenic effects of a cold water extract are not exactly the same as those of LSD, but visions of "small people" are typical. Eating the seeds can cause side effects such as nausea and vomiting, probably induced by nonwater-soluble alkaloids.

In 1960, Albert Hofmann isolated ergot alkaloids like lysergic acid amide from *R. corymbosa*. The psychoactive effects of lysergic acid amide, also called ergine, were assessed by Albert Hofmann by self-administration back in 1947, well before this was discovered to be a natural compound. He described a tired, dreamy state with an inability to maintain clear thoughts after intramuscular administration of 500 mg of ergine.

Lophophora williamsii

The small spineless cactus *Lophophora williamsii* is commonly known as peyote. This cactus grows extremely slowly and flowers sporadically. In the wild, it takes up to 30 years to reach the size of a golf ball, and to produce the first flowers. The small pink fruits of peyote are sweet-tasting and delicate. The cactus is native to southern United States and Mexico, but is cultivated all over the world.

A recent study has shown prehistoric use of peyote by native North Americans. A radiocarbon study dated dried cacti, so-called mescal buttons, to the time interval 3 780–3660 BCE. Because psychotropic alkaloids were present in these dated buttons, it was concluded that they were used for their psychoactive effects.

The main reason for the psychoactive effects of peyote is the presence of the phenethylamine alkaloid mescaline. The effects of peyote and mescaline in humans are well studied. Native peyote cults used the cactus because it produces rich visual hallucinations. These effects were also used in psychiatric studies as a chemically induced model of mental illness. The mechanism of action is similar to that of LSD or psilocin. These substances act as partial agonists at 5-hydroxytryptamine receptors.

The abuse of peyote is mainly by oral ingestion of the dried cacti. Although the acute toxicity of peyote or mescaline is not as high as other herbal alkaloids, fatalities are described. Due to the strong hallucinations, fights among drug abusers or self-harm situations are not uncommon.

Piper methysticum

The common English name for the western pacific plant *Piper methysticum* is kava. Other names for the plant are "awa," used in Hawaii or "yaqona," common in Fiji. Kava is an evergreen bush growing up to 3 m tall, with heart-shaped leaves up to 20 cm in length. The plant is closely related to black pepper (*Piper nigra*) and also has a spicy taste. Kava is psychoactive, indicated by the scientific species name *methysticum*, which is Greek for intoxicating. Kava is consumed on many western pacific islands and in Australia. Traditionally, kava is prepared by grinding or chewing the rhizome, which is mixed with water or coconut milk. The effects after consumption of kava are talkative and euphoric behavior, anxiolytic effects, a sense of

well-being, clear thinking, and relaxed muscles. The plant contains a mix of kavalactones and kavapyrones. Extracts of the plant were introduced into modern medicine as a mild anxiolytic. After the report of some deaths due to its medicinal use, kava medicines were banned. Kava-containing medicine causes acute liver failure. The traditional use of kava by Pacific Islanders and by some aboriginal communities is not believed to be associated with liver damage. A recent study has shown that kava fed to rats does not cause liver damage. Further investigations are necessary to demonstrate the long-term safety of kava preparations.

Traditional kava ingestion uses dried kava root powder suspended in water, and common doses are 15–25 g of the dried root.

Analytical Methods

Because of the diversity of the psychotropic compounds in plants, a general laboratory screening procedure is not possible. Therefore, various specific methods for detection have been developed.

Methods for detection of naturally occurring psychoactive compounds include high-performance liquid chromatography (HPLC), liquid chromatography–mass spectrometry (LC–MS), and gas chromatography–mass spectrometry (GC–MS). The use of HPLC is common for detection of compounds such as the ingredients of kava, for example, kavalactones and kavapyrones. The modern and more sensitive LC–MS technique has been applied to many naturally occurring substances, especially if low concentrations have to be detected. The use of GC–MS technique is applicable if the substances are thermostable and it provides a powerful tool for detection of alkaloids such as atropine, cathinone, and mescaline. While GC–MS techniques are useful, LC–MS techniques are preferred for the detection of low concentrations in blood.

A postmortem detection of the toxic substances is often challenging. Determination of these is best conducted in urine (**Table 1**).

Summary and Conclusion

Psychoactive plants can be divided into two main categories: the classical psychoactive plants of abuse and the emerging drugs of abuse of herbal origin. The classical herbal plants of abuse have been known for their psychoactive properties for centuries and the isolated active ingredients have developed into the most common drugs of abuse in modern times. In recent years, it has become more and more common to abuse novel drugs of abuse, mainly due to publicly available knowledge communicated over the Internet.

Table 1   Herbal drugs of abuse listed by their common and scientific names, common routes of ingestion and most important active compounds

Common English name	Scientific name	Common abuse	Active compound (most important)
Coca	Erythroxylum coca	Smoking, intravenous abuse, snorting (free base)	Cocaine
Iboga	Tabernanthe iboga	Oral ingestion (eating roots)	Ibogaine
Kath	Catha edulis	Oral ingestion (chewing leaves)	Cathinone
Kava	Piper methysticum	Oral ingestion (drinking infuse), oral ingestion (herbal pills)	Kavapyrone
Marijuana	Cannabis sativa	Smoking, oral ingestion (eating cookies)	Δ^9-Tetrahydrocannabinol
Morning glory	Rivea corymbosa, Ipomea tricolor	Oral ingestion (drinking infuse), oral ingestion (eating seeds)	Ergine
Nightshades	Atropa belladonna, Datura stramonium, Brugmansia spp.	Oral ingestion (drinking infuse), oral ingestion (eating berries)	Atropine, scopolamine
Opium poppy	Papaver somniferum	Intravenous abuse, oral ingestion (tablets), smoking (common in Asian cultures)	Morphine, codeine
Peyote	Lophophora williamsii	Oral ingestion (drinking infuse), oral ingestion (eating)	Mescaline
Salvia	Salvia divinorum	Smoking, oral ingestion (chewing leaves)	Salvinorin A

The detection of novel drugs of abuse of herbal origins has become a very challenging part of forensic science, especially in analytical toxicology.

> *See also:* **Toxicology:** Herbal Medicines and Phytopharmaceuticals – Contaminations; Methods of Analysis – Confirmatory Testing; Methods of Analysis – Initial Testing; Pharmacology and Mechanism of Action of Drugs; **Toxicology/ Drugs of Abuse:** Blood.

Further Reading

Boumba, V.A., Mitselou, A., Vougiouklakis, T., 2004. Fatal poisoning from ingestion of *Datura stramonium* seeds. Veterinary and Human Toxicology 46 (2), 81–82.

DiSilvestro, R.A., Zhang, W., DiSilvestro, D.J., 2007. Kava feeding in rats does not cause liver injury nor enhance galactosamine-induced hepatitis. Food and Chemical Toxicology 45 (7), 1293–1300.

El-Seedi, H.R., De Smet, P.A., Beck, O., Possnert, G., Bruhn, J.G., 2005. Prehistoric peyote use: Alkaloid analysis and radiocarbon dating of archaeological specimens of Lophophora from Texas. Journal of Ethnopharmacology 101 (1–3), 238–242.

Frohne, D., 2005. In: Frohne, D., Pfaender, H.J. (Eds.), Poisonous Plants: A Handbook for Doctors, Pharmacists, Toxicologists, Biologists and Veterinarians, second ed. Manson Publishing, London.

Giannini, A.J., Castellani, S., 1982. A manic-like psychosis due to khat (*Catha edulis* Forsk.). Journal of Toxicology – Clinical Toxicology 19 (5), 455–459.

Kava Kava May Cause Irreversible Liver Damage. South African Medical Journal 92(12): 961.

Musshoff, F., Madea, B., Beike, J., 2000. Hallucinogenic mushrooms on the German market – Simple instructions for examination and identification. Forensic Science International 113 (1–3), 389–395.

Raetsch, C., 2005. The Encyclopedia of Psychoactive Plants: Ethnopharmacology and Its Applications. Park Street Press, Rochester, VT.

Rang, H.P., 1987. In: Rang, H.P., Dale, M.M. (Eds.), Pharmacology, second ed. Churchill Livingstone, Edinburgh; New York, pp. 547–567.

Toennes, S.W., Harder, S., Schramm, M., Niess, C., Kauert, G.F., 2003. Pharmacokinetics of cathinone, cathine and norephedrine after the chewing of khat leaves. British Journal of Clinical Pharmacology 56 (1), 125–130.

Relevant Website

http://www.erowid.org/psychoactives/psychoactives.shtml.

Herbal Medicines and Phytopharmaceuticals—Contaminations

W-C Cheng, C-S Ng, and N-L Poon, Government Laboratory, Hong Kong Special Administrative Region

Abbreviations

AAS	Atomic absorption spectrophotometry		ICP	Inductively coupled plasma
AChE	Acetylcholinesterase		LC	Liquid chromatography
AES	Atomic emission spectroscopy		MS	Mass spectrometry/spectrometer
DAD	Diode array detection		NPD	Nitrogen phosphorus detection
ECD	Electron capture detection		OES	Optical emission spectroscopy
GC	Gas chromatography		TCM	Traditional Chinese medicines
GUS	General unknown screening			

Introduction

Written historic records such as *Shennong Bencao Jing* in China, *Ebers Papyrus* of the ancient Egyptians, and a treatise called *Sushruta Samhita* of Indian Ayurveda provide evidence of the long history of the use of plant materials either alone or in combination with other plant(s) for medicinal purposes. Although the use of herbal medicines declined in favor of pharmaceuticals in the nineteenth century due to an emergence of synthetic pharmaceuticals, there has been an upward trend in the usage of herbal medicines and/or phytopharmaceuticals (a pharmaceutical agent of plant origin) in both developed and developing countries in recent years.

Many people have the perception that the use of plant materials for medicinal purposes is safe and rarely causes adverse toxic effects. However, incidental poisonings with serious or even fatal consequences have been reported from time to time. Apart from those caused by the use of toxic herbs with intended purpose(s), many of them are due to contamination or adulteration, which could happen either accidentally or intentionally. Such contaminations/adulterations can have important clinical and toxicological consequences and are particularly worrying because they are unpredictable, and often remain undetected unless they can be connected with health issues.

Sources of contamination can be originated from the environment. For example, toxic metals or other naturally occurring radionuclides may be absorbed during the growth of a plant; intentional or accidental usage such as pesticides or toxic pollutants emitted from factories that contaminate the nearby medicinal plants; and the presence of microbial and fungal growth resulting in microbial toxins such as aflatoxins, which are known to be highly toxic and carcinogenic.

Contamination with toxic herbs can occur either as a mix-up with other plants growing in the vicinity that are nontoxic or sometimes during the herbal preparation process due to poor quality control. Accidental herbal intoxication can also occur as a result of using the wrongly identified herbs either as a single plant or mixed with other herbs in compound formulations. Although there are numerous medicinal plants widely used today, significant numbers of the reported poisoning cases are confined only to a few types of toxic herbs. For instance, aconitine, gelsemine, and tropane alkaloids such as atropine and scopolamine are some of the typically toxic substances found that have caused poisonings or even deaths.

With the belief that herbal remedies can boost an individual's health and alleviate disease in an "all natural" way and be free from other side effects, poisonings have also been reported in many countries due to intake of herbal remedies that were later found to contain undeclared conventional drugs that are added intentionally in order to exert the claimed therapeutic effects.

Overall, many poisoning cases can be traced back to the use of poor-quality herbal medicines. Unlike most prescription drugs that required testing for safety, quality, and efficacy before putting into the market, herbal medicinal products are usually sold as dietary supplements or natural remedies, which in many countries are not subject to rigorous testing.

In view of the wide diversity of substances that may require toxicological examination in this context, some of the analyses may not be covered in routine toxicological screening procedures. As such, different strategies may be applied to deal with the analytical concerns for cases of intoxication related to herbal medication, and it is often useful if more detailed background information about the case is available.

Common Forms of Contamination/Adulterants

Heavy Metals

Heavy metals are commonly present in our environment. Apart from the accumulation during cultivation of soil, other possible sources of heavy metals found in herbal medicines are the accidental contamination from processing machinery or intentional addition to achieve the desired properties. The most commonly encountered heavy metals in herbal medicines include arsenic, lead, and mercury. The use of toxic heavy metals as mineral drugs has long been prescribed in some traditional medicines such as calomelas (as mercurous chloride) and realgar (as arsenic disulphide) in traditional Chinese medicines (TCM), and Talaka (as arsenic trisulphide), Naga bhasmas (as lead sulfide), and Makardhwaja (as mercuric sulfide) in Indian Ayurvedic medicines. To date, many countries have restrictions on the content of heavy metals. For instance, in Singapore, limits of 20 ppm lead, 5 ppm arsenic, and 0.5 ppm Hg were imposed on herbal medicines. The Hong Kong *Chinese Materia Medica Standards* also lists the general recommended limits of lead, mercury, and arsenic being 5.0, 0.2, and 2 mg kg^{-1}, respectively, in raw herbs. Despite various regulatory measures, herbal preparations containing heavy metal ingredients may still be sold illegally as health products. Intoxications due to intake of high levels of heavy metals in herbal preparations have been reported and some examples are shown in **Table 1**.

The natural presence of arsenic in herbal medicines should be no different from its wide occurrence in foods. In most cases, the inorganic trivalent form such as arsenious acid (arsenite) is more toxic than the pentavalent form. Arsenic levels can be measured in blood and urine. As arsenic is eliminated fairly quickly from the blood (about 2–4 h after exposure), the use of urine, which can detect arsenic within few days of exposure, can be considered. An abnormal arsenic level in blood for adults is greater than 100–200 µg l^{-1}.

Mercury intoxication can be due to either contamination or the intentional addition at high levels, as often seen without labeling in cosmetic ointments for whitening of skin. Blood and urine are suitable samples to be used for determining recent exposure to mercury. Liver and kidney function tests are also useful in severely exposed persons. The concentrations of mercury in normal subjects are usually less than 10 µg l^{-1} in blood.

Lead contamination can induce many adverse health effects such as mental retardation, and cognitive and behavioral problems, particularly in children. It has a half-life of a few months. When a subject presents with symptoms consistent with lead toxicity, blood testing is necessary. Symptoms of lead poisoning in adults may appear when the concentration in blood exceeds 8 µg l^{-1}. For children, a blood level as low as 3 µg l^{-1} can cause health problems.

Pesticides

Although the intake of herbal medication that causes serious pesticide intoxication is rarely noted, herbal medicines, like other plants, are liable to contain pesticide residues at levels that may be unsafe to humans. Similar to other agricultural products, pesticides can accumulate during cultivation from standard agricultural practices and administering of fumigants during storage. Commonly encountered pesticides in herbal drugs include a variety of insecticides such as organochlorines, organophosphorus, carbamates, and pyrethroids, and herbicides such as paraquat. Permissible or recommended limits of pesticide residues in herbal medicines are usually listed in some pharmacopeias/standards such as the *European Pharmacopoeia* and the Hong Kong *Chinese Materia Medica Standards*.

Table 1 Examples of intoxication cases with heavy metals in herbal products

Countries	Herbal products	Findings
Singapore	Antiasthmatic herbal preparations	Arsenic: 25–107 000 mg kg^{-1}
United States	Traditional Chinese herbal balls	Arsenic: 0.1–36.6 mg per ball
		Mercury: 7.8–621.3 mg per ball
United Kingdom	Herbal products for homeopathic remedies	Lead: 6.5–7.5 mg per tablet
United States	Ayurvedic herbs	Lead: 5–37 000 mg kg^{-1}
		Mercury: 28–104 000 mg kg^{-1}
		Lead: 37–8 130 mg kg^{-1}

Sources: Tay, C.H., Seah, C.S., 1975. Arsenic poisoning from anti-asthmatic herbal preparations. Medical Journal of Australia 2 (11), 424–428; Espinoza, E.O., Mann, M.J., Bleasdell, B., 1995. Arsenic and mercury in traditional Chinese herbal balls. The New England Journal of Medicine 333 (12), 803–804; Olujohungbe, A., Fields, P.A., Sandford, A.F,, Hoffbrand, A.V., 1994. Heavy metal intoxication from homeopathic and herbal remedies. Postgraduate Medical Journal 70, 764; Saper, R.B., Kales, S.N., Paguin, J., Phillips, R.S., 2004. Heavy metal content of ayurvedic herbal medicine products. Journal of the American Medical Association 292 (23), 2868–2873.

Pesticides, once deposited into the human body, will undergo various biotransformations. For organophosphorus and carbamate pesticides, they are metabolized rapidly and are excreted mainly as metabolites. Certain organochlorine pesticides may pass through the human body intact but due to their fat solubility will deposit in adipose tissue such that the parent compounds and the associated metabolites may also be detected in blood/serum and adipose tissue. In this regard, it would sometimes be necessary to analyze the metabolites together with the unchanged pesticides to provide clues for the types of poisoning. **Table 2** shows some examples of common pesticides with relevant metabolites.

The analysis of pesticides in body fluids is complicated as certain pesticides may be decomposed by acid or alkali. For instance, organophosphorus and certain carbamate pesticides are susceptible to hydrolysis in alkaline medium while some carbamate pesticides such as carbosulfan are unstable in acid. Relevant analytical procedures have been published by the World Health Organization and the *European Pharmacopoeia* for the analysis of pesticide residues in herbal medicines.

Toxic Herbs

Some toxic herbs that are considered to be dangerous in the Western community are often used for treatment of diseases in other parts of the world either in parallel with conventional medications or in situations where modern medicines are considered inadequate for the problem. *Callilepis laureola* (contains atractyloside) has been used in folk medicine in certain tribes of South Africa to serve as a multipurpose remedy including stomach problems, tapeworm infestations, impotence, and to induce fertility. In TCM, toxic herbs like *Radix*

Table 2 Selected pesticide metabolites/residues found in biological specimens

Pesticides	Metabolites
Organophosphorous	
Malathion	Dimethyldithiophosphoric acid (DMDTP) and dimethylthiophosphoric acid (DMTP)
Parathion	Diethylthiophosphoric acid (DETP), diethylphosphoric acid (DEP), and *p*-nitrophenol
Diazinon	Diethylthiophosphoric acid (DETP) and diethylphosphoric acid (DEP)
Chlorpyrifos	3,5,6-trichloro-2-pyridinol
Carbamates	
Carbofuran	Carbofuran phenol and 3-ketocarbofuran
Carbaryl	α-Naphthol
Organochlorines	
Aldrin/dieldrin	Dieldrin
Chlordane/ heptachlor	Nonachlor and oxychlordane

Aconiti Lateralis (contains aconitum alkaloids), which is used for the relief of pain, have been included in pharmacopeia and in compound formulation. The therapeutic use of these toxic substances is usually prescribed in small doses and the toxicity can be significantly reduced if they are properly processed and prescribed in combination with some other herbal constituents as "antidote". In view of the therapeutic usage of these toxic herbs in some herbal medicinal systems, it is not unreasonable to anticipate that the risk of contamination, mix-up, or misidentification would increase, in particular, when persons handling both toxic and nontoxic herbs are not properly trained and qualified.

Occasionally, consumption of nontoxic herbal medicines or remedies causes toxicity relevant to certain toxic herbal ingredients. The cause of poisoning is usually uncovered after review of the clinical presentation, supported by the analysis of the remnants of the herbal medicines, and analysis of biological specimens (such as urine) obtained from the victims. Toxic ingredients commonly encountered include aconitum alkaloids, gelsemine, and tropane alkaloids such as atropine and scopolamine.

A widely used nontoxic TCM called *Rhizoma Atractylodis* contaminated with other toxic herbs containing aconitum or tropane alkaloids has been identified to be the origin of several poisoning cases in Hong Kong. For instance, in one of the cases, morphological examination of *Rhizoma Atractylodis* revealed the presence of another species (**Figure 1**), which was later confirmed to contain tropane alkaloids.

Other examples reported include *Cassytha filiformis* (often used for alleviation of colds and fevers), which was mixed up or contaminated with other plants that grew around it such as *Gelsemium elegans* containing gelsemine; *Radix Strobilanthis Forrestii* contaminated with unknown atropine-containing species; and *Rhizoma Ligustici* contaminated with unknown aconitine-containing species.

Herbal medicines and phytopharmaceuticals are often prepared from one or many species of herbal materials. Misidentification in the handling of herbal materials with similar botanical features or nomenclature can sometimes occur and cause severe intoxication. For instance, the similarities in appearance and common name between *Stephania tetrandra* ("han fang ji") and the toxic *Aristolochia fangchi* ("guang fang ji") (containing aristolochic acid, a nephrotoxin) have been reported to be related to a number of intoxications resulting in nephropathy (**Figure 2**). Another example that caused a cluster of intoxication events in Hong Kong is the case in which *Flos Campsis*, a nontoxic herb, was substituted with *Flos Daturae Metelis*, a toxic herb containing atropine, in a decoction prescription due to their similar appearances (**Figure 3**). **Table 3** summarizes some reported incidents to be related to the mix-up or misidentification of toxic herbs.

Commonly confused species can be found in literature with detailed description of the morphological features of each

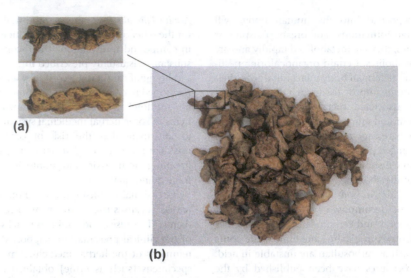

Figure 1   (a) An extraneous herb containing tropane alkaloids isolated from (b) a batch of *Rhizoma Atractylodis*.

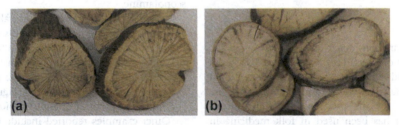

Figure 2   Appearance of (a) *Aristolochia fangchi* (guang fanji) and (b) *Stephania tetrandra* (han fanji).

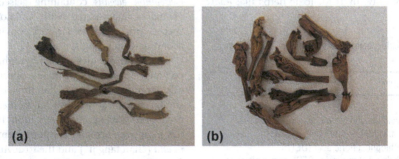

Figure 3   Appearance of (a) *Flos Daturae Metelis* and (b) *Flos Campsis*.

species. As such, identification of substitution of herbal materials can be achieved through morphological (macroscopic and microscopic) examination together with the chemical tests stipulated in various pharmacopeias if unused herbal remedies are available. However, difficulties arise if the herbal medicines concerned have been processed, for example, in powder form or as decoction (often with other ingredients); most, if not all, of the morphological characteristics will be lost and the chemical tests documented in pharmacopeias may no longer

be applicable. In this case, to assist in devising suitable toxicological analyses in relevant biological specimens obtained from the patient(s), the analyses of the toxic ingredients associated with the confused herbs or suspected herbs by chromatographic-based techniques are usually the method of choice. It would be prudent for toxicologists to have a better understanding of the types of toxic herbs, which may be region-specific and are likely to cause poisoning. **Table 4** lists some toxic ingredients of toxic herbs relevant to forensic toxicology.

Table 3   Incidents reported to be related to mix-up or misidentification of herbs

Nontoxic herbs	Toxic herbs (toxic ingredients) involved	Reasons for mix-up or misidentification	Consequences
Stephania tetrandra	Aristolochia fangchi (aristolochic acid)	Similar appearance and common name	Patients developed nephropathy and some required kidney transplants
Solanum lyratum	Aristolochia mollissima Hance (aristolochic acid)	Same common Chinese name "Pak Mo Tang"	Patient presented with kidney failure and cancer of the urinary tract
Mussaenda pubescens	Gelsemium elegans (gelsemine)	Similarity in appearance	Patients developed dizziness, generalized weakness, and even unconsciousness
Flos Campsis	Flos Daturae Metelis (tropane alkaloids)	Similarity in appearance	A number of anticholinergic poisonings
Radix Gentianae	Radix or Rhizoma Podophylli emodis (podophyllotoxin)	Similarity in appearance	Patients developed gastrointestinal symptoms followed by severe encephalopathy
Polygala Chinensis	Stephania rotunda (L-tetrahydropalmatine)	Proprietary medicine containing undeclared toxic herb	It caused life-threatening effect on central nervous system and respiratory depression in children and liver damage in adults

Sources: Nortier, J.L., Muniz-Matinez, M.C., Schmeiser, H.H. et al., 2000. Urothelial carcinoma associated with the use of Chinese herb (*Aristolochia fangchi*). New England Journal of Medicine 342 (2), 1 686–1 692; http://www.info.gov.hk/gia/general/200403/13/0313161.htm – Department of Health, Hong Kong – DH calls for suspension of the use of three Chinese herbs; Fung, H.T., Lam, K.K., Lam, S.K., Wong, O.F., Kam, C.W., 2007. Two cases of *Gelsemium elegans* Benth. poisoning. Hong Kong Journal of Emergency Medicine 14 (4), 221–224; http://www.chp.gov.hk/en/media/14/116.html – Centre of Health Protection, Department of Health, Hong Kong – Caution about substitution of Chinese herbal medicines Flos Campsis by Flos Daturae Metelis; Ng, T.H.K,, Chan, Y.W., Yu, Y.L. et al., 1991. Encephalopathy and neuropathy following ingestion of a Chinese herbal broth containing podophyllin. Journal of the Neurological Sciences 101 (1), 107–113; Horowitz, R.S., Dart, R.C. et al., 1993. Jin bu huan toxicity in children – Colorado. Morbidity and Mortality Weekly Report 42 (33): 633–636.

Table 4   Toxic ingredients of some common herbs relevant to forensic toxicology

Toxic alkaloids/ingredients	Scientific name	Common name
Aconitum alkaloids: aconitine, mesaconitine, and hypaconitine	Aconitum napellus	Monkshood
	Aconitum carmichaeli	"Chuan wu"
	Aconitum kusnezoffii	Wolfsbane, "Cao wu"
Scopolamine, atropine, hyoscyamine	Datura metel	"Yang jin hua"
	Datura stramonium	Jamestown weed
	Hyoscyamus niger	Henbane
	Atropa belladonna	Deadly nightshade
Gelsemine	Gelsemium elegans	"Gou wen"
	Gelsemium sempervirens	Carolina jasmine
Coniine	Conium maculatum	Poison hemlock
Harmine, harmaline	Banisteriopsis caapi	Caapi
Strychnine	Strychnos nux-vomica	"Maqianzi," Nux vomica, Ignatia
Matrine and oxymatrine	Sophora tonkinensis	Vietnamese Sophora
Aristolochic acids	Aristolochia fangchi	"Fang ji"
	Aristolochia clematitis	Birthwort
	Aristolochia reticulata	Red River snakeroot
Podophyllotoxin	Podophyllum emodi	"Guijiu," wild mandrake
	Podophyllum peltatum	Mayapple
Atractyloside and carboxyatractyloside	Atractylis gummifera	Chamaelon, birdlime
	Callilepis laureola	Impila
	Xanthium sibiricum	"Cang er zi"

Adulteration

Inferior products or extraneous materials

Many medicinal herbs are sold by weight. Therefore, direct or intentional adulteration with other inferior products or extraneous materials is often found. A noted example is soaking *Cordyceps sinensis*, a precious herbal medicine, in concentrated lead solution in order to increase its weight and increase earnings.

Conventional medications

The purpose of intentional adulteration of conventional medication(s) into herbal medicines is to disguise the belief that the use of such "natural" products can exert the claimed effects on improving health. However, incidents of toxicological concern due to intake of herbal remedies with undeclared conventional medications continue. A study in Taiwan revealed that 24% of 2609 market samples of TCM analyzed were found to have been adulterated with synthetic drugs of various pharmacological activities. One of the commonly encountered examples is the adulteration of phosphodiesterase type-5 inhibitors such as sildenafil and vardenafil (Western drugs for treatment of male erectile dysfunction) in sexual enhancement health products. In addition, there was an increasing trend for the use of analogs of drugs in virility products. These analogs are mimic chemicals of the original drugs by modifying their molecular structures to varying degrees. Unlike conventional medicines, drug analogs do not usually have proper safety evaluations and clinical study data, and are likely to pose a significant threat to health. Examples of analogs of sildenafil that had been found in herbal preparation are shown in **Figure 4**.

As adulterated ingredients are not declared in their packages with respect to identity and quantity, it may result in serious intoxications due to drug interactions and overdose. For instance, an outbreak of hypoglycemia in 68 patients resulted in three fatalities in Hong Kong. Sildenafil and glibenclamide were detected in the urine. Subsequent investigations confirmed that some of the patients had consumed sexual enhancement health products containing these undeclared drugs.

Another commonly encountered example is the adulteration of synthetic drugs in herbal slimming formulae. The drugs involved are anorexics (e.g., amfepramone, fenproporex,

sibutramine, fenfluramine, phentermine), anxiolytics (e.g., diazepam, clonazepam), and antidepressants (e.g., fluoxetine). This problem is widespread and occurs in many countries such as Hong Kong, Germany, and Brazil.

Analytical Strategy

As it is virtually impossible to screen for all toxic substances in every case, a rational case-specific analysis may be necessary. The presence of characteristic features of remnants and the symptoms exhibited by the patient may provide clues to the type of poisoning. Strategy for sampling and subsequently devising appropriate analytical methods for a case should be made with reference to the background history of the case, clinical or pathological features presented, and/or specific requests made by the relevant parties such as medical officers, pathologists, and/or the police. Herbal residues and/or herb samples, empty containers and/or packaging inserts suspected to have been taken by the person should be collected, as analysis of these items may be valuable for determining the types of analyses required on the biological specimens to substantiate the cause of poisoning.

For all suspected cases, the biological specimens usually available for analysis include blood/serum and urine. In the case of chronic exposure, additional specimens such as fingernails or hair may be useful. As the growth rate of hair is ~0.6–1.4 cm month^{-1}, hair provides a longer window of detection up to weeks or months. Other useful specimens such as stomach contents or vomit, if available, should also be taken. In postmortem cases, sections of liver or kidney are sometimes needed. Many toxic substances and their metabolites are present in liver at higher concentrations than that in blood. Consequently, liver may also be used to supplement the blood concentration data, in particular when it is the only specimen available in cases of advanced putrefaction. Kidney is sometimes useful in the investigation of heavy metal poisoning.

Table 5 summarizes the analytical methodology generally used for detection of some common contaminants/adulterants for their main toxic ingredients in biological specimens and herbal materials.

An example of an analytical scheme used for screening of contaminants/adulterants in biological specimens is shown in **Figure 5**.

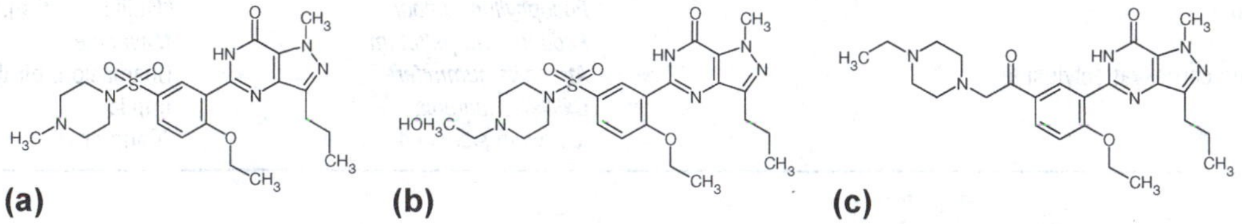

(a)   (b)   (c)

Figure 4 Chemical structures of sildenafil and analogs of sildenafil: (a) sildenafil, (b) hydroxyhomosildenafil, and (c) acetildenafil.

Table 5   Common detection methods for contaminants/adulterants in biological specimens and herbal products

Contaminants/ adulterants	Examples of common toxic ingredients	Sample preparation	Common detection methods
Heavy metals	Arsenic, lead, mercury	Digestion using mineral acid such as concentrated nitric acid	AES, atomic absorption spectrophotometry (AAS), ICP–AES, or ICP–MS
Pesticides	Organophosphorus, carbamates	Mixing with acetylthiocholine (AcTC) and Ellman's reagent, (dithionitrobenzoic acid)	Screening of organophosphorus and carbamates by measuring cholinesterase activity in blood
	Organophosphorus, carbamates, organochlorines, pyrethroids	Liquid–liquid extraction or solid-phase extraction	GC–ECD, GC–NPD, GC-MS, or LC-MS
Toxic herbs	Aconitine	Liquid–liquid extraction or solid phase extraction	GC-MS or LC-MS
	Atropine		
	Scopolamine		
	Gelsemine		
	Podophyllotoxin		
	Tetrahydropalmatine		
	Aristolochic acid		
Conventional medications	Sibutramine	Liquid–liquid extraction or solid phase extraction	GC-MS or LC-MS
	Fenfluramine		
	Glibenclamide		
	Sildenafil, tadalafil, vardenafil, and analogs		
	Phenolphthalein		
	Spironolactone		
	Dexamethasone		
	phenylbutazone		
	Piroxicam		

AAS, atomic absorption spectrophotometry; ECD, electron capture detection; NPD, nitrogen phosphorus detection.

Heavy Metal Analysis

There are various instrumental methods such as electrochemical, atomic absorption, and flame emission spectrophotometry, inductively coupled plasma (ICP) coupled with either atomic emission spectroscopy (ICP–AES) or mass spectrometry (ICP–MS) to analyze metals in biological specimens. An advantage of both ICP–AES and ICP–MS is that they can screen simultaneously many metals as well as conduct selective quantification of a single element at a very low detection limit. Digestion of the biological specimens can be achieved simply with a concentrated mineral acid such as nitric acid. The use of ICP–MS instrument equipped with either a double focusing sector for high-resolution application or a collision cell capable of removing polyatomic interference in the presence of a significant amount of matrix can further enhance its sensitivity and selectivity. As such, a much faster and simpler sample preparation, which involves a simple dilution of body fluid with a buffer consisting of a solution of Triton X-100, ethylenediaminetetraacetic acid, and ammonium hydroxide can be

considered. Accuracy can further be enhanced by an isotope dilution method as stable isotopes are available for most of the toxic metals.

Pesticide Analysis

In the analysis of pesticides in biological specimens, a combination of direct and indirect methods can be considered. For instance, if organophosphorus or carbamate pesticide poisoning is suspected, the cholinesterase activity of blood could be determined as the test can be conducted quickly.

Screening of blood cholinesterase activity

Organophosphorus and carbamate pesticides are well-known cholinesterase inhibitors. These pesticides inhibit the blood enzymes erythrocyte acetylcholinesterase (AChE), and the degree of enzyme inhibition is proportional to the amount of exposure such that AChE activities can be determined using a colorimetric method. The blood test is more effective for organophosphate exposure than for carbamate exposure

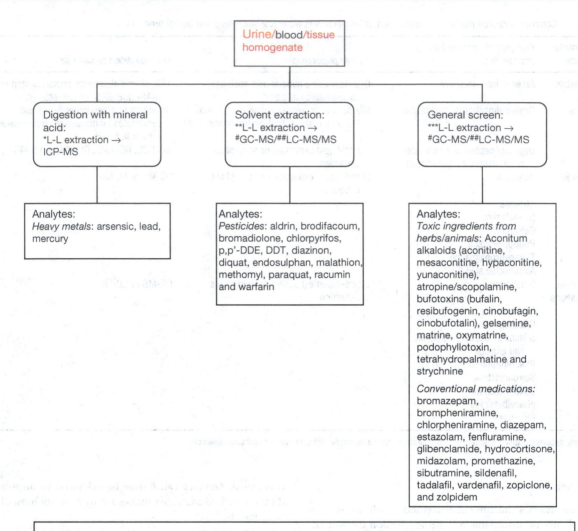

Figure 5   An example of a scheme for screening of contaminants/adulterants in biological specimens.

because the enzyme levels due to carbamate exposure may return to baseline levels within hours. Each person has a different normal baseline value of cholinesterase; therefore, due care should be exercised in the interpretation of results.

Chromatographic techniques

Depending on the chemical/physical properties of pesticides and/or their metabolites, a combination of suitably selected extraction methods involving liquid–liquid extraction using, for instance, hexane/acetonitrile under neutral or acidic condition and solid phase extraction such as C_{18} cartridges for sample preparation can be used. As some major metabolites of many pesticides are in forms of sulfate and glucuronide conjugates, enzymatic hydrolysis can be used prior to extraction to further improve the sensitivity.

Chromatographic techniques such as gas chromatography (GC) or liquid chromatography (LC) connected with various detectors can be employed to detect a wide range of pesticides with similar extraction properties, polarity, and detection characteristics. GC connected with specific detectors such as electron capture detector is particularly sensitive to organochlorine pesticides, while nitrogen phosphorus detector is sensitive for detection of organophosphorus pesticides. Low levels of pesticides both in herbal medicines and in biological specimens can also be analyzed using GC-MS. In addition to the retention time given by the corresponding GC techniques employed, the mass spectrometric detector allows sensitive detection (ppm to ppb) of a wide range of pesticides with structural information for confirmation purpose. As many pesticides are polar and thermally labile, derivatization such as methylation by diazomethane in methanol or acetylation using acetic anhydride in pyridine prior to GC analysis can increase the volatility and hence thermal stability for those pesticides that are not easily detected by GC. The additional mass gain by derivatization also improves the specificity of the mass spectral information.

Pesticides can also be analyzed using liquid chromatography-diode array detection (LC-DAD). The drawbacks of LC-DAD are the low chromatographic resolution compared with GC, and the low sensitivity of UV detection such that larger sample size, particularly in biological specimens, or derivatization may often be required. With the advancement of ultra-performance liquid chromatography (UPLC) using columns with sub-2 μ particles for higher separation efficiency coupled with triple quadruple mass spectrometer, methods can be readily developed for sensitive detection of a wide range of pesticides and related metabolites in various matrices.

Analysis of Toxic Herbs and Conventional Medications

As the contaminants/adulterants of poisonous alkaloids and conventional medicines can be very diverse and unpredictable, making it difficult to generate a comprehensive list that are relevant to toxicological analysis, the analytical detection of poisoning from unknown sources can be a challenge to toxicologists.

In the detection of drug analogs in herbal medications, because of the lack of structural information, reference spectrum, and reference standard of an analyte involved, a more fundamental approach would be necessary. Discovery of herbal preparation adulterated with drug analogs often involved

detection of subtherapeutic amounts of drugs with unknown spots or peaks by thin-layer chromatography or LC-DAD. Further investigation is then carried out by preparative chromatography to isolate the suspected active ingredient. The structures can be confirmed by techniques such as tandem mass spectrometry (MS/MS) and two-dimensional nuclear magnetic resonance spectroscopy. Other methods, such as setting up of a comprehensive scheduled selected reaction monitoring (SRM) built from the most probable ion fragment, precursor ion scanning of common ion fragment and accurate mass Fourier transform ion cyclotron resonance MS, can also be considered in the detection of analogs. The information obtained would be useful for devising or setting up methods for the toxicological screening of relevant drugs/metabolites in biological specimens.

While the majority of reported incidents in the context of contaminations/adulterations are confined to a limited number of toxic herbs and conventional medications, it is practical to devise specific multianalyte procedures to cover as many relevant analytes as possible based on available circumstantial information. Many well-known conventional drugs and some alkaloids found in toxic herbs can be covered by general unknown screening (GUS) procedures for screening of a wide spectrum of acidic, neutral, and basic organic drugs or poisons. As such, it is possible to incorporate those analytes that are compatible with the routine GUS procedures. For instance, toxic herbs with naturally occurring alkaloids are usually basic in nature and can be extracted by a carbonate buffer (pH 9) followed by extraction with a dichloromethane/toluene/isobutyl alcohol (3:6:1) mixture, which could also be used in routine GUS. Examples of alkaloids in the basic fraction include aconitum alkaloids (such as aconitine, mesaconitine, hypaconitine, and yunaconitine), gelsemine, atropine/scopolamine, tetrahydropalmatine, and beberine. In addition, the same basic fraction can also be used for the analysis of conventional medications such as glibenclamide, hypnotics and sedatives, benzodiazepines, antihistamines, appetite suppressants (e.g., sibutramine, fenfluramine), and drugs for treatment of erectile dysfunction (e.g., sildenafil, vardenafil, and tadalafil).

Similar to the analysis of pesticides, GC and high-performance liquid chromatography (HPLC)/UPLC, coupled with various detectors are common instrumentations for screening of a wide range of organic toxic substances in biological specimens. Using a combination of MS with either GC or HPLC/UPLC, confirmation and quantification can be simplified into one single analysis. GC-MS has been used for years in GUS for drugs and poisons with well-established techniques, and many useful spectral libraries relevant to toxicological screening are available. However, GC is not suitable for direct analysis of polar compounds although derivatization can partly solve the problem. With the use of multianalyte analytical protocol to cover over hundreds or even thousands of drugs and poisons, the use of LC-MS gained popularity in many toxicology laboratories to provide fast, selective, and sensitive method for GUS of organic drugs and poisons. In addition, the use of triple quadrupole LC-MS/MS with preset SRM could screen for as many relevant toxic ingredients/markers as possible even without any diagnostic information of a case. The time-of-flight or orbitrap MS coupled with LC or UPLC has provided another approach for comprehensive drug screening that provides a relatively high mass accuracy with resolution. Identification of drugs/metabolites is based on their accurate mass and confirmation could be achieved by comparison of retention time if a reference material is available and via drug metabolite patterns.

> *See also:* **Toxicology**: Herbal Psychoactive Substances; Methods of Analysis—Confirmatory Testing; Methods of Analysis—Initial Testing.

Further Reading

Beyer, J., Drummer, O.H., Maurer, H.H., 2009. Analysis of toxic alkaloids in body samples. Forensic Science International 185 (1–3), 1–9.

de Carcalho, L.M., Martini, M., Moreira, A.P.L., et al., 2011. Presence of synthetic pharmaceuticals as adulterants in slimming phytotherapeutic formulations and their analytical determination. Forensic Science International 204 (1–3), 6–12.

Espinoza, E.O., Mann, M.J., Bleasdell, B., 1995. Arsenic and mercury in traditional Chinese herbal balls. The New England Journal of Medicine 333 (12), 803–804.

Huang, W.F., Wen, K.C., Hsiao, M.L., 1997. Adulteration by synthetic therapeutic substances of traditional Chinese medicines in Taiwan. Journal of Clinical Pharmacology 37, 344–350.

Kumar, A., Nair, A.G.C., Reddy, A.V.R., Garg, A.N., 2006. Bhasmas unique ayurvedic metallic-herbal preparations, chemical characterization. Biological Trace Element Research 109, 231–254.

Kuo, C.H., Lee, C.W., Lin, S.C., et al., 2010. Rapid determination of aristolochic acids I and II in herbal products and biological samples by ultra-high- pressure liquid chromatography-tandem mass spectrometry. Talanta 80, 1672–1680.

Lacassie, E., Marquet, P., Gaulier, J.-M., et al., 2001. Sensitive and specific multi-residue methods for the determination of pesticides of various classes in clinical and forensic toxicology. Forensic Science International 121 (1–2), 116–125.

Mitchell-Heggs, C.A., Conway, M., Cassar, J., 1990. Herbal medicine as a cause of combined lead and arsenic poisoning. Human and Experimental Toxicology 9 (3), 195–196.

Moffat, A.C., 1986. Clarke's Isolation and Identification of Drugs in Pharmaceuticals, Body Fluids, and Post-mortem Material, second ed. Pharmaceutical Press, London.

Poon, W.T., Lam, Y.H., Lee, H.H.C., et al., 2009. Outbreak of hypoglycaemia: Sexual enhancement products containing oral hypoglycaemic agent. Hong Kong Medical Journal 15 (3), 196–200.

Saper, R.B., Kales, S.N., Paquin, J., Phillips, R.S., 2004. Heavy metal content of ayurvedic herbal medicine products. Journal of the American Medical Association 292 (23), 2868–2873.

Steenkamp, P.A., Harding, N.M., van Heerden, F.R., van Wyk, B.E., 2006. Identification of atractyloside by LC-ESI-MS in alleged herbal poisonings. Forensic Science International 163, 81–92.

Relevant Websites

http://www.tga.gov.au/industry/cm-argcm.htm—Australia Regulatory Guidelines for Complementary Medicines (ARGCM).

http://www.dh.gov.hk/english/main/main_cm/files/vol1/main.html—Department of Health: Hong Kong Chinese Materia Medica Standards, vol. I. Hong Kong (2005).

http://www.chp.gov.hk/files/pdf/poisoning_watch_vol3_iss1_eng.pdf—Department of Health: Slimming products – Are you aware of any serious adverse effects? (2010).

http://ods.od.nih.gov/About/DSHEA_Wording.aspx—Dietary Supplement Health and Education Act of 1994.

http://eng.sfda.gov.cn/WS03/CL0766/61638.html—Drug Administration Law of the People's Republic of China.

http://europa.eu/legislation_summaries/internal_market/single_market_for_goods/pharmaceutical_and_cosmetic_products/l21161_en.htm—European Pharmacopeia.

http://apps.who.int/medicinedocs/en/m/abstract/Js14878e/—WHO Guidelines for Assessing Quality of Herbal Medicines with Reference to Contaminants and Residues (2007).

http://www.who.int/mediacentre/factsheets/fs134/en/—WHO Traditional Medicine Fact Sheet N134, December 2008.

Key Terms

2,5-Phenethylamines, Acute-poisoning anesthetics, Acute-poisoning volatile compounds, Affinity, Agonist, Amphetamines, Anesthetic abuse, Antagonist, Atropa, Cannabinoids, Cannabis, Cathinones, Chromatographic analysis, Coca, Congeners, Contaminations, Datura, Dependence, Designer drugs, Drug of abuse, Dusting, Efficacy, Enzymes, Ethanol, Fentanyls, Fourier transform infrared spectroscopy, Fusel oils, Glue sniffing, G-protein-coupled receptors, Headspace gas chromatography, Heavy metals, Herbal, Herbal medicines, Huffing, Iboga, Inhalant abuse, Intracellular receptors, Ion channels, Isotope ratio mass spectrometry, Kath, Kava, Mass spectrometry, Methanol, Morning glory, Natural, Nuclear magnetic resonance, Pesticides, Peyote, Phencyclidines, Phytopharmaceuticals, Piperazines, Piperidines, Plants, Poppies, Potency, Presumptive testing, Psychoactive, Pyrrolidinophenones, Reuptake, Salvia, Semisynthetic drugs, Signal transduction, Solvent abuse, Source of alcohol, Steroids, Sudden sniffing death, Synthetic, Tachyphylaxis, Tolerance, Toluene abuse, Toxic herbs, Toxicology, Traditional Chinese medicines, Tryptamines, Volatile substance abuse (VSA), Volatile substance misuse.

Review Questions

1. What are the two species of *Papaver* known to produce opium?
2. What form of marijuana has the highest content of THC?
3. "Angel dust" is a term for what drug?
4. What are the potential sources for volatile inhalant substances? Are all of them illegal? Explain.
5. What is a "designer drug"? List at least five examples. How are they classified? Why can they be difficult to analyze?
6. Which designer drugs originally had a medical or pharmacological application and which are strictly derived for illegal consumption?
7. Which parts of a marijuana plant contain THC?
8. Where did LSD come from?
9. List the types of processes used in clandestine laboratories. How does each work and for which drugs are they used?
10. Why is the evidence seized from clandestine laboratories potentially difficult to analyze?
11. Historically, what is the most prevalent type of drug made in clandestine laboratories?
12. What are some of the safety precautions that should be taken at a clandestine laboratory scene?
13. What type of instrumental methods provide structural information about the drug's molecules?
14. How does isotope ratio mass spectrometry (IRMS) work?
15. Derivatization may be required for what chromatographic methods?
16. Beyond drug abuse, what other crimes or investigations may be required by the use of volatile substances and inhalants?
17. What is "spice"?
18. What forms can PCP take?
19. What is fentanyl? Why is it important historically?
20. Why are "date rape" drugs difficult to analyze in metabolites?

Discussion Questions

1. How are drugs classified? Why are they classified in this fashion? How else could they be classified?
2. Forensic toxicology not only addresses the drugs or poisons involved in the case but also their metabolism in the victim or decedent. How does the metabolism of these chemicals increase the complexity of toxicology? How does it make it different from drug chemistry?
3. Why are not all forensic toxicology laboratories the same? What factors influence the methods that are used and why?
4. Illicit drugs appear in a variety of forms, including tablets and capsules. What information can be derived from these forms that could not be from others, such as powders or liquids?
5. Do any of the drugs discussed in this section have a legitimate or medical use? Do the chemical or physical forms differ between licit and illicit use?

Additional Readings

Morelato, M., Beavis, A., Tahtouh, M., Ribaux, O., Kirkbride, P., Roux, C., 2013. The use of forensic case data in intelligence-led policing: The example of drug profiling. Forensic Science International 226 (1–3), 1–9.

Olaf, D., 2013. Forensic Drug Analysis. Future Science, Ltd., London.

Seely, K., Patton, A., Moran, C., Womak, M., Prather, P., Fantegrossi, W., Rodminska-Pandya, A., Endres, G., Channell, K., Smith, N., McCain, K., James, L., Moran, J., 2013. Forensic investigation of K2, Spice, and "bath salt" commercial preparations: A three-year study of new designer drug products containing synthetic cannabinoid, stimulant, and hallucinogenic compounds. Forensic Science International 233 (1), 416–422.

Section 4. Matrices

If "the dose makes the poison", then "the matrix makes the method" in toxicology. The various pathways of drugs and chemicals into the body influence the compound's absorption, distribution, metabolism, and excretion (ADME). The compound's levels and the kinetics of its exposure to the various tissues—and eventually matrices—influence the performance and pharmacology of the compound in the body's systems. The solubility of the drug, the time it takes for stomach contents to empty and the drug to travel through the intestines, and how easily the compound passes through the intestinal wall all matter for drugs taken orally, for example. Thus, given the suspected compound and its method of intake, the toxicologist must determine which matrix will provide the best chance for an accurate analysis and interpretation.

Blood

C Jurado, National Institute of Toxicology and Forensic Sciences, Sevilla, Spain

Glossary

Clearance A measure of the body's efficiency in eliminating drugs. Clearance is the volume of blood or plasma or mass of an organ effectively cleared of a substance by elimination (metabolism and excretion) divided by time of elimination.

Dose (of a substance) Total amount of a substance administered to, taken up, or absorbed by an organism, organ, or tissue.

Half-life The time required for the amount of a drug or other substance deposited in a living organism to be reduced to one half of its value by normal biological processes, when the rate of removal is approximately exponential.

Pharmacokinetics Process of the uptake of drugs by the body, the biotransformation they undergo, the distribution of the drugs and their metabolites in the tissues, and the elimination of the drugs and their metabolites from the body over a period of time.

Protein binding The process by which a drug binds to proteins in blood plasma. The amount of drug bound to protein determines how effective the drug is in the body. The bound drug is kept in the blood stream while the unbound components are pharmacologically active.

Route of administration Is the path by which a toxic agent gains access to an organism by administration through the gastrointestinal tract (ingestion), lungs (inhalation), skin (topical), or by other routes such as intravenous, subcutaneous, intramuscular, or intraperitoneal routes.

Volume of distribution A measure of the apparent space in the body available to contain the drug. Volume of distribution is the apparent (hypothetical) volume of fluid required to contain the total amount of a substance in the body at the same concentration as that present in the plasma, assuming equilibrium has been attained.

Introduction

The analysis of drugs of abuse in forensic toxicology can be performed using any biological specimen. Each one of them has particular characteristics, providing different information with various advantages and disadvantages. Nevertheless, drug analyses are most commonly performed using blood and urine and, more recently, hair.

One of the differences between specimens is the detection window. In blood samples, this time is very short, as most drugs of abuse disappear 8–24 h after consumption; consequently, these specimens can provide some information on the likely time since the last administration. Urine provides a longer detection time, which ranges from 6 h (for gamma hydroxybutyrate (GHB) for instance) to 2–3 days, with the exception of chronic users of cannabis in whom this time has been reported to reach up to 30 days. In hair, the detection window is dramatically increased, as drugs can be detected for months or years depending on the length of the lock of hair.

Blood samples are the specimens of choice when impairment of performance and behavior have to be established or when it is necessary to know if a person had been under the influence of drugs.

The aim of this chapter is to provide an overview of the analysis of drugs of abuse in blood. No reference is made either to the analytical methodologies for these types of cases or to the issues associated with the analysis of postmortem blood, as they are included in other chapters. The drugs of abuse covered in this chapter are the four main classes, amphetamines (APs), cannabis, cocaine (COC), and heroin, with a short reference to other drugs, such as lysergic acid diethylamide (LSD), ketamine, and phencyclidine (PCP). The most abused prescribed drugs, benzodiazepines, are also included.

Types of Blood Specimens

Whole Blood, Serum, and Plasma

Blood is a complex biological fluid consisting of a buffered clear liquid containing proteins, fats, solids, and suspended cells. Blood accounts for 8% of human body weight, with an average density of $\sim$1060 kg m^{-3}. An adult has a blood volume of $\sim$5 l, composed of plasma and several kinds of cells: erythrocytes (red blood cells), leukocytes (white blood cells), and thrombocytes (platelets). By volume, red blood cells constitute about 45% of whole blood, plasma about 54%, and white cells only about 0.7%.

If blood is allowed to stand without the addition of an anticoagulating agent, red cells will clot. The resultant fluid (serum) can be decanted. If anticoagulants are added to a tube of fresh blood, plasma can subsequently be prepared by spinning the tube in a centrifuge until the blood cells fall to the bottom of the tube. The total volume of plasma in an average person is 2.7–3.0 l. It is essentially an aqueous solution containing 92% water, 8% blood plasma proteins, and trace amounts of other materials.

Serum is, in most respects, similar to plasma except that it does not contain soluble factors that lead to blood clotting. In this sense, blood serum is blood plasma without fibrinogen or the other clotting factors.

The proportion of blood volume that is occupied by red cells is referred to as the hematocrit. It ranges from 35 to 54% in blood from healthy adults, being higher in men than in women. Most drugs are not equally distributed between the subcompartments of blood; consequently, the concentration in serum or plasma may differ from that in whole blood. The knowledge of blood to plasma concentration ratios is mandatory when the whole blood to plasma or serum levels have to be compared.

Plasma and serum samples are useless in a case where the compounds involved are known to be concentrated in the erythrocytes, such as phenothiazines, phenytoin, salicylic acid, chlorthalidone or imipramine, among others. Drugs of abuse, which are the compounds of interest in this chapter, do not show affinity for red blood cells; consequently, the three types of blood samples can be indistinctly used in their analysis. Nevertheless, drug analysis in forensic toxicology cases is usually performed on whole blood, whereas serum or plasma is preferably used in clinical studies.

Dried Blood Spot Samples

Dried blood spot (DBS) samples are becoming a significant tool in forensic toxicology. The first paper on DBS analysis for the estimation of blood glucose concentration was published in 1913 by Bang; however, the most prominent use of DBS dates back to the early 1960s when Robert Guthrie developed an assay for the detection of phenylketonuria. Recently, these samples have been successfully applied for the detection of illicit drugs in forensic cases whenever qualitative information is sufficient.

The collection of DBS samples is normally conducted by pricking the finger, heel, or toe with a lancet, and the blood drops are then spotted onto preprinted circles, ideally one drop per spot, on specially manufactured paper. Touching the circle area should be avoided, especially before the blood is applied and has completely dried. The blood sample can also be applied with a calibrated pipette onto the sampling paper, thus avoiding potential sampling errors. It is very important to dry blood spots completely before storage or transportation. In general, a minimum of 2–3 h drying in an open space at room temperature is recommended. However, the drying time depends on the type of paper and the blood volume applied.

Thus, after drying, the DBS samples should be protected against humidity and moisture. Humidity indicator cards should be included in the storage package. DBS samples protected in this manner may be stored at room temperature for many weeks, months, or years, depending on the analyte stability. Nevertheless, samples that contain unstable compounds should be stored at a lower temperature to enhance stability.

DBS is a useful tool in forensic toxicology, but it has not replaced conventional whole blood, plasma, or serum samples.

Table 1 Comparison between dried blood spot (DBS) samples with the conventional samples (whole blood, serum, and plasma)

	Conventional samples	DBS
Sampling method	Invasive	Less invasive
Storage	In freezer at -20 °C	At room temperature[a]
Infection risk	High	Minimum
Sample volume	>0.5 ml	<100 µl
Additional analysis	Possible	Not possible
Repetition of analysis	Possible	Not possible
Methods	Sensitive	Very sensitive

[a]In general, DBS samples may be stored at room temperature for many weeks, months, or years. However, samples that contain unstable compounds should be stored at a lower temperature to enhance stability.

Although DBS offers a number of advantages over conventional matrices, as shown in **Table 1**, it presents some challenges before it can be applied in routine practice, particularly stability and being able to provide quantitative results.

Drug Monographs

Amphetamines

These drugs are sympathomimetic phenethylamine derivatives possessing central and peripheral stimulant activity. They are used in the treatment of narcolepsy and attention deficit hyperactivity disorder. Recreationally, they are abused to increase alertness, relieve fatigue, control weight, treat mild depression, and for their intense euphoric effects, as well as psychedelic effects, as occurs with 3,4-methylenedioxymethamphetamine (ecstasy or MDMA), for example.

The most abused amphetamine (AP) compounds are amphetamines themselves, methamphetamine (MAP), MDMA, and 3,4-methylenedioxyamphetamine (MDA). They occur as structural isomers and stereoisomers. The S(+) or d-form possesses approximately three to four times the central activity of the isomer (enantiomer) R(−) or l-form. But enantiomers not only differ in pharmacological activity but also have different pharmacokinetic properties. The d-enantiomer of both AP and MAP are metabolized more rapidly than the l-enantiomer. The half-life for the d-isomer is 11–13 h, compared with a 39% longer half-life for the l-isomer. Consequently, knowledge of the enantiomer proportion can be helpful in the interpretation of analytical data.

Blood concentrations can generally be used to distinguish therapeutic MAP use from abuse. Concentrations of 0.02–0.05 mg l^{-1} are typical for therapeutic use, but up to 0.2 mg l^{-1} have been found in some cases. Normal concentrations in recreational use are 0.01–2.5 mg l^{-1} (median 0.6 mg l^{-1}), thus overlapping therapeutic concentrations.

MAP is metabolized to AP (also active), p-hydroxyamphetamine and norephedrine (both inactive).

Several other drugs are metabolized to AP and MAP and include benzphetamine, selegiline, and famprofazone. Peak plasma AP concentrations occur around 10 h after MAP use.

MDMA is metabolized to MDA with 65% of the dose excreted unchanged within 3 days. It is further metabolized to its 3-hydroxy-4-methoxy and 3,4-dihydroxy derivatives (HMA and HHA). Additional MDMA metabolites include 3-hydroxy-4-methoxymethamphetamine and 3,4-dihydroxymethamphetamine.

No clear correlation exists between MDMA blood concentrations and its effects. MDMA and MDA are the analytes detected in blood, with MDA concentrations typically only 5–10% of the corresponding MDMA concentrations. Higher MDA:MDMA ratios may indicate coadministration of MDA. Residual and unwanted effects are generally gone within 24 h, although confusion, depression, and anxiety may last several weeks.

Cannabis

The plant *Cannabis sativa* contains more than 60 cannabinoids or chemically related compounds, the most active of them being Δ^9-tetrahydrocannabinol (THC). Other compounds present in the plant in significant amounts are cannabidiol and cannabinol.

Most of the cannabinoids are psychoactive substances that produce pleasant feelings, drowsiness, and a decrease in cognitive and psychomotor performance. At the same time, they increase cardiac rate, blood pressure, and body temperature. Naïve consumers can experience anxiety, paranoia, or panic after smoking cannabis.

Although cannabis is usually smoked as a cigarette, oral ingestion also does occur. The data relating to the absorption of THC are shown in **Table 2**. The wide range in the bioavailability (18–50%) after smoking is a consequence of the large interindividual variability occurring during smoking dynamics. After oral administration, THC is also well absorbed, but peak plasma concentrations are much lower than after smoking and occurs much later.

Due to its fat solubility, THC is rapidly distributed into tissues and accumulates in adipose tissue. This distribution phase results in a rapid decline in blood plasma concentrations. The apparent half-life is ∼1 h, but in frequent users, the terminal half-life can reach 3–13 days.

THC metabolism is complex, with over 20 metabolites identified. The two monohydroxy metabolites 11-hydroxy-Δ^9-tetrahydrocannabinol (11-THC-OH) and 8-hydroxy-Δ^9-tetrahydrocannabinol (8-THC-OH) are active, with the former exhibiting similar activity and pharmacokinetics to THC, while the latter is less potent. Further oxidation of 11-OH-THC produces the inactive metabolite 9-carboxy-Δ^9-tetrahydrocannabinol (THC-COOH), which may be conjugated with glucuronic acid. Plasma THC concentrations generally fall

Table 2   Absorption parameters of the main drugs of abuse and drugs used for medicinal purposes

Compound	Route	Dose (mg)	C_{max} (ng ml^{-1})	T_{max} (h)
Amphetamines				
AP	Oral	10	35	2
MAP	Oral	10	30	1
MDMA	Oral	125	236	2.4
Cocaine	Oral	17–48	11–149	0.4–2
	Intranasal	32	40–88	0.39–0.85
	IV	32	310	0.08
	Smoking	50	230	0.75
Cannabis				
THC	Smoking	1.75%	50–130	0.25
	Oral	20	6	1-3
Heroin[a]				
Heroin	IV	200	1 530	0.02
6-MAM			4 620	0.02
Morphine			340	0.02–0.8
LSD	Oral	0.140	5	1
Ketamine	IV	175	1 000	0.2
PCP	Oral	1	2.7	1–4
Benzodiazepines				
Alprazolam	Oral	1	19	1.3
Diazepam	Oral	10	200–600	0.5–2
	IV	20	1 600	0.25
Nonbenzodiazepines				
Zolpidem	Oral	10	120	1.5–2.5
Zopiclone	Oral	7.5	76	1.1
Barbiturates				
Amobarbital	Oral	120	1800	2
Pentobarbital	IV	50	1 180	0.08
Phenobarbital	Oral	30	700	

C_{max}, peak concentration; *IV.*, intravenous; T_{max}, time to reach peak concentration.
[a]The data of MAM and morphine are obtained after the intravenous administration of 200 mg of heroin.

below 5 ng ml^{-1} less than 3 h after smoking, while in occasional users, concentrations rapidly fall below limits of quantitation within 8–12 h. The terminal half-life of THC-COOH in plasma is ~2–5 days, and it can be detected during a period of 12 days in the case of frequent consumers and during a period of 6 days in the case of nonfrequent users, respectively.

Sometimes it is necessary to ascertain if the person was under the influence of cannabis. The duration of action of cannabis is usually short, and it is related more to blood THC concentrations than to THC-COOH concentrations. The peak effect is experienced about 15–30 min after smoking, and the pharmacological effects often last for only 2–4 h.

Mathematical models, based on the THC:THC-COOH concentration ratios, have been developed to estimate the time of marijuana exposure within a 95% confidence interval. Knowing this elapsed time can then be used to predict impairment in concurrent cognitive and psychomotor effects based on data in the published literature.

Cocaine

Cocaine (COC) is one of the most potent of the naturally occurring central nervous system stimulants. It has been utilized in medicine as a local anesthetic and is still used in oral and nasal surgery. Recreationally, COC is used to increase alertness, relieve fatigue, feel strong, and be more decisive, and is abused for its intense euphoric effects.

The routes of administration of COC are different depending on the source of COC (leaves, sulfate salt, hydrochloride salt, and free base, known as crack), affecting not only its pharmacokinetic but also its pharmacological effects. COC is mainly inhaled through the nose (insufflation), but it is also smoked, used intravenously (IV), and even taken orally.

COC is rapidly absorbed following all the routes of administration. It is extensively metabolized to a variety of compounds: ~30–50% of COC is metabolized by hepatic esterases and plasma pseudocholinesterase to ecgonine methyl ester. Spontaneous nonenzymatic hydrolysis of another 30–40% results in benzoylecgonine. Both products are water soluble and inactive. Norcocaine is a very minor metabolite but is active and neurotoxic. The apparent half-life for COC is short, ~0.7–1.5 h, while the half-lives of benzoylecgonine and ecgonine methyl ester are 6–8 and 3–8 h, respectively.

Ethylbenzoylecgonine or cocaethylene, formed following concurrent ingestion of COC and alcohol, is also active and is equipotent to COC in blocking dopamine reuptake. Its metabolites are hepatotoxic.

During smoking of COC base (crack), anhydroecgonine methyl ester (AEME, methylecgonidine) is formed in large amounts as a pharmacologically active pyrolysis product of COC, and it is absorbed in the lungs. AEME is not produced when COC is snorted or used IV; consequently, it is a marker of COC smoking.

Typical concentrations in abuse range from 0 to 1 mg l^{-1}; however, concentrations up to 5 mg l^{-1} and higher have been reported in surviving chronic consumers. After single doses of COC, plasma concentrations typically average 0.2–0.4 mg l^{-1}. Repeated doses of COC may result in concentrations of >0.75 mg l^{-1}.

The faster the absorption, the more intense and rapid the peak effect, but the duration of action is shorter. Injecting COC produces an effect within 15–30 s. Smoking crack produces an almost immediate intense effect, which can last 5–15 min. Similarly, snorting COC produces effects almost immediately, and the resulting peak may last 15–30 min.

Heroin

Heroin (3,6-diacetylmorphine) is a semisynthetic opioid drug synthesized from morphine. The routes of administration are usually IV injection, subcutaneous injection, or nasal insufflation.

After administration, heroin is rapidly hydrolyzed by serum and liver esterases to 6-acetylmorphine (6AM) and then to morphine. Morphine undergoes glucuronidation into morphine-6-glucuronide (M6G) and morphine-3-glucuronide (M3G) by liver, kidney, and brain enzymes with an M6G:M3G ratio of ~0.15. Conjugation at the 6-hydroxyl position of morphine does not prevent binding to opioid receptors; hence, 6AM and M6G contribute to the narcotic effects of heroin, which has little affinity for opiate receptors itself.

Heroin blood levels decline very rapidly after IV drug administration and become undetectable after 10–40 min. Due to their short half-lives, heroin and 6AM are not usually found in blood samples, and their presence in blood indicates a very recent administration, while morphine and morphine glucuronides are detected over a longer period of time.

Pharmacokinetic data of heroin, 6AM, and morphine are summarized in **Tables 2 and 3**. Data on the M3G or M6G kinetics after heroin administration are scarce, mostly because in earlier times it was assumed that the morphine glucuronides were not relevant for the pharmacodynamic action of heroin. As M6G passes the blood–brain barrier with more difficulty than morphine, only a significant accumulation of M6G causes a pharmacodynamic effect. M3G lacks intrinsic opioid activity. After heroin administration, the terminal half-lives of morphine glucuronides (M3G and M6G) range from 2.0 to 6.4 h. The time to reach peak concentrations ranges from 0.7 to 5.1 h, which is comparable to the results obtained from controlled morphine pharmacokinetic studies. The half-lives of the morphine glucuronides do not depend on the route of administration.

Illegal heroin contains other opioids, one of them being acetylcodeine, which is present to the extent of 2–20% as a by-product and is not present in pharmaceutical preparations. Consequently, acetylcodeine is a useful marker to differentiate between legal and illegal heroin.

The development of tolerance to regular users makes interpretation of blood or plasma morphine concentrations extremely difficult.

Other Drugs

Lysergic acid diethylamide

Lysergic acid diethylamide (LSD) is an indole derivative. The d-isomer is one of the most potent hallucinogenic agents while the l-isomer is apparently inactive. LSD is an indirect serotonin antagonist, which produces sympathomimetic, parasympathomimetic, and neuromuscular effects (mydriasis, lacrimation, tachycardia, and tremor).

The oral route of administration is the most common, but nasal and parenteral routes can be used as well. LSD undergoes extensive biotransformation via N-demethylation and hydroxylation. In addition to N-desmethyl-LSD and hydroxy-LSD, other metabolites are 2-oxo-LSD and 2-oxo-3-hydroxy-LSD, all of them being inactive. Hydroxylated metabolites undergo glucuronidation to form water-soluble conjugates. The threshold toxic dose in humans has been reported to be 100–200 mg with associated blood concentrations of 2–30 ng ml^{-1}.

A common side effect of LSD is the unpredictable recurrence of hallucinations for weeks or months after the last dose. Hysterical behavior, hyperactivity, and life-threatening hyperthermia are exhibited in some cases.

The onset of effects is rapid within 5–10 min, with psychosis evident after 15–20 min. Peak effects occur 30–90 min after dosing, and they decline after 4–6 h. The duration of effects may be 8–12 h.

Ketamine

Ketamine is primarily used in veterinary applications as a tranquilizer. It is also used as an anesthetic induction agent

Table 3   Overview of pharmacokinetic parameters of the main drugs of abuse and drugs used for medicinal purposes

Compound	Half-life (h)	Clearance (ml min^{-1} kg^{-1})	BP ratio	V_D (l kg^{-1})	Protein binding (%)
Amphetamines					
AP	4–30^a		0.80	3–5	15–42
MAP	10–30		0.65	3–4	
MDMA	6–7		1.16	6	65
Cannabis					
THC	19–96	14	0.55	9–11	97
Cocaine	0.7–1.5	20–30	≈1.0	1.5–2	91
Heroin					
Heroin	0.03–0.12	30–461		25	40
6-MAM	0.1–0.42	134–144			
Morphine	2–3	21	1.02	1–6	35
LSD	3–4			0.3	65–90
Ketamine	2–4	17	1.7	3–5	20–50
Phencyclidine	7–46	0.14–0.77	≈1.0	5.3–7.5	60–80
Benzodiazepines					
Alprazolam	6–22	1.2		0.7–1.3	67–83
Diazepam	20–50	0.5	0.55	0.5–2.6	98–99
Nonbenzodiazepines					
Zolpidem	1.4–4.5	4.33		0.5–0.7	92
Zopiclone	3.5–6.5			1.3–1.6	45–80
Barbiturates					
Amobarbital	15–40	0.5		0.9–1.4	59
Pentobarbital	20–30	0.3–0.5	1.07	0.5–1.0	65
Phenobarbital	48–144	0.06	1.07	0.5–0.6	50

BP, blood to plasma concentration ratio; V_D: volume of distribution.
^{a}Half-life of amphetamine is pH dependent.

for diagnostic and surgical procedures in humans, prior to the administration of general anesthetics. Its recreational use is due to its psychedelic and dissociative effects.

The route of administration can be injection, snorting, oral ingestion, and rectal administration. In addition, and similarly to phencyclidine (PCP), ketamine can be added to tobacco or marijuana cigarettes and smoked.

Ketamine is rapidly distributed into the brain and other highly perfused tissues. It is metabolized to at least two active metabolites: first by N-demethylation to norketamine, which is then dehydrogenated to dehydronorketamine. Oral administration produces lower peak concentrations of ketamine, but increased amounts of the metabolites norketamine and dehydronorketamine. Norketamine produces depressant effects similar to those of ketamine. There are no significant differences between the pharmacokinetic properties of the S-(+) and R-(−)-isomers.

There is no direct correlation between ketamine concentrations and behavior. Drowsiness, perceptual distortions, and intoxication may be dose related in a concentration ranging from 50 to 200 ng ml^{-1}, and analgesia begins at plasma concentrations of about 100 ng ml^{-1}.

Adverse reactions include hallucinations, delirium, nausea, vomiting, respiratory stimulation, or depression. The drug has been abused by medical personnel for its hallucinogenic effects.

The onset of effects is within seconds if smoked, 1–5 min if injected, 5–10 min if snorted, and 15–20 min if orally administered. The effects generally last 30–45 min after injection, 45–60 min if snorted, and 1–2 h following oral ingestion.

Phencyclidine

PCP or 1-(1-phenylcyclohexyl) piperidine is a veterinary tranquilizer and, at the same time, a popular drug of abuse. It is structurally related to ketamine, and it acts as a hallucinogen, dissociative anesthetic, psychotomimetic, and sedative hypnotic.

It is self-administered by different routes (IV, nasal, oral), and it is well absorbed following all of them. It was first abused in the oral form, but later the smoked form gained popularity, in spite of ~50% of PCP in cigarette smoke being converted to an inactive thermal degradation product.

PCP binds with high affinity to sites located in the cortex and limbic structures of the brain. Due to its action on several systems, the physiological and behavioral effects of PCP are varied and depend on not only the dose but also the route of administration and chronicity of consumption.

Metabolism undergoes oxidation and hydroxylation to at least two inactive metabolites, which are later conjugated with glucuronic acid.

There is no direct correlation between PCP concentration and the degree of intoxication (behavioral or physical findings). PCP causes sedation, nystagmus, hypertension, ataxia, agitation, combativeness, seizures, coma, and respiratory depression.

Long-term users of PCP report feeling the effects within 2–5 min after smoking, with the peak effect after 15–30 min, and residual effects for 4–6 h, which can last up to 24 h in some cases. Long-term psychological effects are possible, and PCP may precipitate a psychotic reaction lasting a month or more that clinically appears like schizophrenia.

Abused Prescription Drugs

The difference between abuse and misuse is mainly based on the individual's intention or motivation. Drug abuse occurs when the medication is taken, usually at higher doses than prescribed, specifically in search of a pleasant or euphoric feeling; while misuse of a drug occurs when individuals are treating themselves, but not according to the directions of their health care providers.

Four major classes of drugs are mainly used for nonmedical purposes: (a) tranquilizers, such as benzodiazepines—including diazepam, alprazolam, etc.,—and nonbenzodiazepines—zolpidem, zopiclone, etc.; (b) sedatives, especially barbiturates; (c) stimulants—AP, methylphenidate, and MAP; and (d) pain relievers, particularly those containing opiates—hydrocodone, oxycodone, fentanyl, methadone etc.

Benzodiazepines

Benzodiazepines are among the most commonly abused prescribed drugs in forensic toxicology. Abuse is observed in two forms: persistent therapeutic use longer than generally recommended and illicit use, where the drug is self-administered without physician approval or supervision, which may involve use of high doses and clear indication of acute intoxication and impairment.

Benzodiazepines effect central depression on spinal reflexes, in part mediated by the brainstem reticular system. They are used as hypnotics since they have the ability to increase total sleep time. Cardiovascular effects are minimal, but heart rate is increased and cardiac output decreased. They are used recreationally as sedatives or to enhance the effects of alcohol or opioids.

All benzodiazepines demonstrate a wide range of absorption rates when orally administered and reach peak plasma concentrations within a few hours of oral administration. For example, single oral doses of 10 mg result in diazepam concentrations of 200–600 ng ml^{-1} at 0.5–2 h, while chronic doses of 30 mg produce steady state diazepam concentrations of 700–1 500 ng ml^{-1} and nordiazepam concentrations of 350–530 ng ml^{-1}.

There are significant differences in the bioavailability of the different compounds. For instance, diazepam and alprazolam have bioavailabilities of 100 and 90%, respectively; while triazolam bioavailability is around 40%.

The half-lives of benzodiazepines vary enormously, from 3 h for triazolam to over two days for nordiazepam. Benzodiazepines are extensively metabolized producing multiple metabolites, many of which share common pathways. The most common metabolites are hydroxylated and dealkylated analogs, which are often pharmacologically active. Diazepam is metabolized to nordiazepam, which is an active metabolite with a half-life of 40–99 h. Temazepam and oxazepam are minor active metabolites of diazepam.

Due to changing responses with repeated use and variability in response between persons, blood concentrations will not provide a good indication of likely behavioral effects. Additionally, the long half-life of some benzodiazepines may cause accumulation to occur with repeated use. Blood concentrations may be severalfold higher after chronic use compared to single use, and there are often significant increases in blood levels in the elderly. Therapeutic blood concentrations of diazepam typically range from 0.1 to 1.0 ng ml^{-1}. Plasma concentrations of 0.3–0.4 ng ml^{-1} are recommended for anxiolytic effects. Higher concentrations might suggest misuse or abuse.

In general, there is poor correlation between blood half-life of benzodiazepines and duration of action. In practice, low-potency benzodiazepines have a shorter duration of action compared with their half-lives, and high-potency benzodiazepines have a longer duration of action than predicted by their half-lives.

Nonbenzodiazepine drugs: zolpidem and zopiclone

Zolpidem and zopiclone are nonbenzodiazepine hypnotics used in short-term treatment of insomnia.

Zolpidem is an imidazopyridine derivative used as a hypnotic agent. In spite of its chemical structure being unrelated to benzodiazepines, it is, nevertheless, a type A gamma-aminobutyric acid receptor agonist and shares some of the pharmacological properties of benzodiazepines. Zolpidem shortens sleep latency and prolongs total sleep time in patients with insomnia but has little effect on the stages of sleep in normal subjects. It also has weak anticonvulsant properties.

Zolpidem is absorbed readily from the gastrointestinal tract and then is converted to inactive metabolites by oxidation and phenolic hydroxylation. Pharmacokinetic data are summarized in **Tables 2 and 3**.

Zopiclone is a cyclopyrrolone derivative, which has been clinically used as a hypnotic agent. It is metabolized via N-demethylation, N-oxidation, and ester hydrolysis. The N-oxide has some pharmacological activity.

Adverse effects after zolpidem and zopiclone consumption include dizziness, amnesia, headache, and nausea. Hallucinations may occur, especially in patients taking zolpidem together with antidepressant medication.

Barbiturates

Barbiturates exert hypnotic, sedative, anxiolytic, anticonvulsant, and anesthetic properties. The use of barbiturates as sedative–hypnotic agents has largely been replaced by the benzodiazepines; nevertheless, they maintain an important role as anticonvulsant and anesthetic drugs.

When utilized as sedative–hypnotics, barbiturates are orally administered, and they are rapidly and completely absorbed when used for the induction and maintenance of anesthesia. In the treatment of status epilepticus, they are administered IV.

Barbiturates are generally widely distributed throughout the body, and they are metabolized by oxidation and conjugation. The oxidation of substituents at the C5 position is the most important factor in terminating pharmacological activity.

See also: **Toxicology:** Interpretation of Results; Pharmacology and Mechanism of Action of Drugs; Postmortem Specimens; Postmortem Toxicology: Artifacts; **Toxicology/Drugs of Abuse:** Drugs in Hair; Postmortem Blood.

Further Reading

Baselt, R.C., 2002. Disposition of Toxic Drugs and Chemical in Man, sixth ed. Biomedical Publications, Foster City, CA.
Bogusz, M.J., 2000. Handbook of Analytical Separations. In: Forensic Science, vol. 2. Elsevier, The Netherlands.
Drummer, O.H., 2001. The Forensic Pharmacology of Drugs of Abuse. Arnold, London.
Karch, S.B., 1998. Drug Abuse Handbook. CRC Press, Boca Raton, FL.
Moffat, A.C., Osselton, M.D., Widdop, B. (Eds.), 2011. Clarke's Analysis of Drugs and Poisons, fourth ed. Pharmaceutical Press, London.

Relevant Websites

http://www.drugabuse.gov—National Institute on Drugs Abuse (NIDA).
http://store.samhsa.gov—Substance Abuse and Mental Health Services Administration (SAMHSA).
http://www.unodc.org—United Nations Office on Drugs and Crime (UNODC).

Urine and Other Body Fluids

A Stowell, Environmental Science and Research Limited, Porirua, New Zealand

Introduction

In forensic science practice, a satisfactory blood sample is not always available for alcohol analysis. In cases of severe trauma, the body may be completely exsanguinated. Even if a body is intact, the blood may be decomposing as a result of microbial growth. Yeasts produce alcohol, and many bacteria produce alcohol or break it down, so the presence or absence of alcohol in the blood of a decomposing body may not be good evidence of antemortem alcohol consumption or sobriety. When looking for evidence of antemortem alcohol intake, the ability to perform alcohol analysis on a range of other body fluids and tissues can often assist in the interpretation of questionable blood alcohol results. In some cases, it may also allow reasonable estimates of blood alcohol concentrations when no blood is available for analysis.

Alcohol exists almost exclusively in the body water and just as blood has high water content (~85% wt/vol or ~80% wt/wt), so do most of the body's soft tissues and organs, apart from those with a very high fat content. Therefore, once an alcohol dose has been fully distributed about the body by the blood, the concentration of alcohol in a soft tissue such as muscle, liver, brain, kidney, etc. will be proportional to the water content of that tissue. For example, if a tissue's water content is 10% higher than that of blood, the alcohol concentration of that tissue will usually be about 10% higher than that of blood. This is the basis for estimating blood alcohol concentrations from alcohol concentrations in other parts of the body.

An understanding of the processes of absorption, distribution, and elimination of alcohol is necessary when interpreting concentrations of alcohol in different parts of the body. These processes define the shape of the blood alcohol curve or the change in a person's blood alcohol concentration with time.

The blood alcohol curve, examples of which are shown in **Figures 1–3**, consists of three phases. The first is the absorption phase, where the rate of absorption into the blood is faster than the combined rate of metabolism and distribution. In this phase, the blood alcohol concentration rises. The second phase is the distribution, equilibration, or "plateau" phase, where absorption is coming to an end and is largely offset by the distribution of alcohol into the body water and removal of

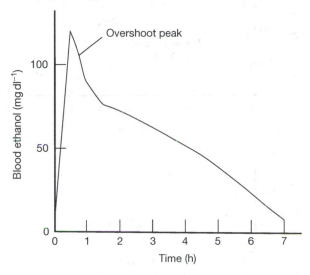

Figure 1 Alcohol absorption/elimination curve showing overshoot peak.

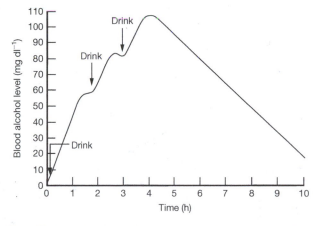

Figure 2 Alcohol absorption/elimination curve showing top-up peaks. Arrows indicate times at which alcoholic drinks were taken.

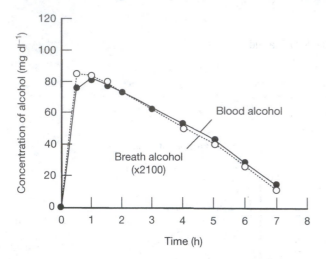

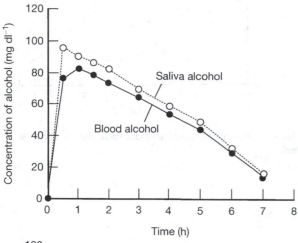

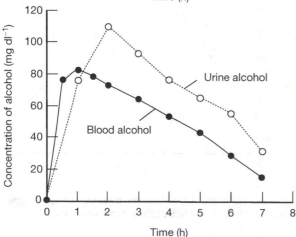

Figure 3 Comparability of alcohol levels between body fluids. Reproduced from Karch, S.B., (Ed.), 1998. Drug Abuse Handbook. CRC Press, Boca Raton, FL, p. 340.

alcohol from the body by metabolism. The length of this phase is highly variable, as is the shape of the blood alcohol curve during this phase. At one extreme, this phase is represented by a sharp peak and at the other by an essentially horizontal line. The third and final phase is the elimination or "clearance" phase, where absorption and distribution are complete, and the only factors influencing the blood alcohol concentration are metabolism and excretion. In this phase, the blood alcohol concentration is falling at an essentially constant rate until it reaches about 20 mg/100 ml. At this point, the rate of loss of alcohol from the blood changes from zero order to first order. In other words, the rate of loss becomes concentration dependent (exponential rate of loss).

Absorption

Absorption refers to the process by which alcohol passes from the gastrointestinal tract into the blood. Alcohol begins to move into the bloodstream within minutes of entering the stomach, but absorption of alcohol into the blood directly from the stomach is relatively slow. The stomach lining is not well adapted for absorption. It is adapted more for containment, to allow food to be homogenized and partly digested before delivery into the small intestine. The small intestine has a very thin wall and a large surface area compared with that of the stomach. It is well supplied with blood and is specifically adapted for nutrient absorption. It is in the small intestine where most absorption of alcohol takes place. Only in circumstances where release of stomach contents into the small intestine is unusually delayed, the rate of absorption of alcohol directly from the stomach will exceed the rate of absorption of alcohol from the intestine.

A valve called the pyloric sphincter separates the stomach from the small intestine. When this valve is closed, the stomach contents are blocked from reaching the small intestine. When it opens, the stomach contents flow into the small intestine, where further digestion and absorption takes place. Alcohol requires no digestion and is absorbed very rapidly without any expenditure of energy, flowing passively across the intestinal wall down a concentration gradient.

Therefore, the rate of absorption of alcohol into the blood mainly depends on how fast it travels through the stomach into the small intestine, a process called gastric emptying. The rate of gastric emptying is governed by many factors. Food in the stomach will generally slow it down. The alcoholic strength of a beverage can also influence gastric emptying, with strong spirits able to irritate the stomach, leading to closure of the pyloric sphincter and a delay in alcohol absorption. In some circumstances, the irritation can lead to prolonged closure of the sphincter, resulting in vomiting. This is a useful protective mechanism, where a dangerously high dose of alcohol has been consumed.

Prediction of alcohol absorption rates is very difficult. A single dose of alcohol can be almost fully absorbed and transported into the blood in less than half an hour, or it may take more than 2 h.

Following identical doses of alcohol, rapid absorption of alcohol into the blood will lead to a higher maximum or peak blood alcohol concentration than that will occur following slow absorption. Metabolism of alcohol begins as soon as alcohol enters the blood, and the longer it takes for full absorption to occur, the more alcohol is metabolized before the absorption is complete.

Rapid absorption of alcohol can sometimes lead to a sharp "spike" in the blood alcohol concentration, as illustrated in **Figure 1**. This is not common and only occurs when the rate of absorption of alcohol into the blood is much faster than the rate at which alcohol diffuses out of the blood into the body water. It is most likely to occur when drinking on an empty stomach and is unlikely to occur when drinking after or during a meal. When drinking occurs in a stepwise manner, the absorption phase of the blood alcohol curve can also rise in a stepwise manner, as shown in **Figure 2**.

Differences between alcohol concentrations in different parts of the body are greatest during the early stages of alcohol absorption. Once absorption is complete and the alcohol dose is relatively evenly distributed throughout the total body water, these differences are usually quite small for tissues and organs having a good blood supply. For example, during the first few minutes of drinking on an empty stomach, the alcohol concentration in the blood draining the small intestine will almost certainly be rising rapidly. At the same time, there will be essentially no alcohol in the urine and no alcohol in the venous blood returning from the arms and legs. The blood draining the small intestine quickly flows to the liver and then to the heart. From the heart, it will first pass into the lungs and then travel back to the heart to be pumped to all organs. Therefore, there is a clear order in which different parts of the body are exposed to the first "rush" of alcohol. The breath alcohol concentration closely reflects the alcohol concentration in lung tissue, which in the early stages of alcohol absorption will be higher than that in an arm or leg vein.

Distribution

The total blood volume is circulated in about 1 min; therefore, distribution of alcohol into the total body water is also quite rapid in spite of its large volume. The total body water volume is approximately nine times the volume of water in the blood, but a bolus dose of alcohol administered intravenously is fully distributed into the total body water in about half an hour. Alcohol moves freely from the blood into the extracellular and intracellular water, exposing cells of all tissues and organs to a concentration of alcohol similar to that existing in blood. This also applies to unborn children who are exposed to the maternal blood alcohol concentration.

However, it is important to recognize that with few exceptions, body fluids that are easily sampled for the purposes of alcohol analysis, either ante- or postmortem, are held in isolated compartments, for example, the urinary bladder (urine), gall bladder (bile), and the eye (vitreous and aqueous humor). The alcohol in the fluids within these compartments does not exchange rapidly with alcohol in the blood. Therefore, the alcohol content of urine, bile, and vitreous and aqueous humor always lags behind the alcohol content of blood.

Elimination

Elimination refers to the processes of metabolism and excretion. Metabolism is the transformation of alcohol to nontoxic breakdown products (mainly water and carbon dioxide). Metabolism occurs mainly in the liver and also in the kidneys and to a minor extent in other organs such as the stomach. Metabolism is mediated mainly by a family of enzymes called alcohol dehydrogenases that convert alcohol to acetaldehyde, a very toxic compound. Aldehyde dehydrogenases then rapidly convert this to acetate, which is much less toxic. The acetate is broken down into carbon dioxide and water in a complex sequence of enzyme-catalyzed reactions. A number of other pathways for alcohol metabolism exist, but they appear to be minor, including those leading to glucuronidation or sulfation of the alcohol molecule.

The rate of alcohol metabolism depends to a large extent on the dietary status. A 20–30% increase in the rate of metabolism may be seen when drinking occurs after a meal, compared with drinking after an overnight fast. But regardless of dietary status, alcohol doses consumed during social drinking sessions are usually more than enough to overload the capacity of the body to metabolize alcohol. This means that the body will metabolize alcohol at an essentially constant rate representing the maximum rate under any given circumstances. This rate will vary from person to person and from day to day for each individual, being dependent on a range of factors, including timing of food consumption before drinking and the degree of induction of the main enzyme systems responsible for alcohol metabolism. Metabolism rates are often expressed in terms of changes in the blood alcohol concentration per hour, during the elimination phase of the blood alcohol curve. For most healthy people who are not heavy drinkers, these rates are likely to be within the range of 10–20 mg per 100 ml per hour, but they could be considerably higher in heavy drinkers who have developed metabolic tolerance.

Excretion processes remove alcohol from the body in an unchanged state. The main excretion process involves removal of alcohol from the blood in the kidneys, via urine formation. But excretion of alcohol also occurs via the breath, perspiration, and any other process leading to removal of water from the body. Excretion usually accounts for less than 10% of the alcohol removed from the body, with the remainder removed by metabolism. However, when the blood alcohol concentration is very high, the proportion of alcohol removed by excretion increases because the alcohol contents of urine, breath, and sweat increase in direct proportion to the blood alcohol concentration. There is no such proportionate increase in the rate of alcohol metabolism.

Analysis of Urine and Other Body Fluids for Alcohol

It is usually appropriate to use the same methods employed for blood alcohol analysis when analyzing urine and other body fluids for alcohol content. A combined homogenization and dilution step will make sampling and analysis easier if the fluid is viscous or tissue is being analyzed.

With the exception of urine, oral fluid, sweat, and tears, the body fluids and tissues discussed in this chapter would only be taken from deceased persons for forensic alcohol analysis.

Urine

Because of its ease of collection and the volume usually available, urine is often sampled for forensic alcohol analysis. But as seen in **Figure 3**, at any point on the blood alcohol curve, the alcohol concentration in the urine is unlikely to closely reflect that in blood. In the absorption phase, the urine–blood alcohol concentration ratio is relatively low, while in the elimination phase, it is always much higher. Therefore, it is not surprising that this ratio has values ranging from close to zero to much greater than 10. It is not uncommon to find extremely high ratios in cases where alcohol is easily detected in the urine after being essentially eliminated from the blood. However, if urine sampling is carried out properly, it can be a useful indirect method of estimating the blood alcohol concentration.

The key to obtaining reliable blood alcohol estimates from analysis of urine is to first void the bladder, then void again as soon as practicable. Under these circumstances, the alcohol concentration in urine from the second void will reflect the average of the blood alcohol concentration over the period between voids. The shorter this period is, the closer the urine–blood alcohol concentration ratio will be to the ratio of the respective water contents of urine and blood, that is, between about 1.15 and 1.19. This range is appropriate if alcohol concentrations are expressed in terms of weight per volume, but where they are expressed in terms of weight per weight, the average ratio will be close to 1.25. In the remainder of this chapter, all body fluid–blood alcohol concentration ratios are based on weight/volume measurements.

Division of the urine alcohol concentration by 1.3 is often used to estimate a blood alcohol concentration based on a urine analysis. If the time between voids is less than an hour and sampling occurs well after drinking stops, this approach will usually give a reasonable (and conservative) estimate of the blood alcohol concentration at the time of urine sampling.

When both blood and urine samples are available, the urine–blood alcohol concentration ratio may be used to determine the phase of the alcohol curve at the time of sampling. A ratio of less than 1 or not more than 1.2 strongly suggests that the subject was in the absorption phase. A ratio of more than 1.3 strongly suggests that the subject was post-absorptive at the time of sampling. This interpretation applies to living and deceased subjects, provided decomposition processes have not set in before blood or urine sampling.

Saliva/Oral Fluid

Measuring the alcohol content of saliva is an excellent means of estimating the blood alcohol concentration. Saliva alcohol concentrations closely parallel the blood alcohol concentration, as seen in **Figure 3**.

The saliva–blood alcohol concentration ratio should be about 1.2 during the elimination phase of the alcohol curve, but in practice, it is much easier to obtain mixed oral fluid than pure saliva. Mixed oral fluid contains mucus secretions from the oral cavity in addition to saliva secreted from the parotid glands. The average oral fluid–blood alcohol concentration ratio is approximately 1.1, ranging from about 0.8 to 1.5, with surprisingly little dependence on either alcohol concentration or the phase of the blood alcohol curve.

Oral fluid is not commonly used for forensic alcohol analysis because of difficulties involved in obtaining substantial volumes and the possibility of contamination with high concentrations of alcohol after very recent drinking. Analysis of breath alcohol is much easier and serves the same purpose. However, satisfactory alcohol analysis can be performed with samples of less than 0.1 of a milliliter of oral fluid and residual alcohol resulting from recent drinking is usually completely cleared from the mouth within about 10 min by normal salivation and swallowing.

Vitreous Humor

Vitreous humor (VH) is a gel-like fluid obtained from the eye. Because it is in an isolated compartment well removed from the gut, putrefaction usually starts much later in the VH than it does in blood. Metabolism of alcohol in the VH is also minimal. For these reasons, the VH is often analyzed for alcohol when decomposition of the blood is suspected. If alcohol is found in VH, it may be used as evidence of ante-mortem alcohol consumption.

Approximately 2 ml of VH can usually be collected from each eye, providing enough material for alcohol analysis as well as for other drugs, if required. As for urine, the VH–blood alcohol concentration ratio is variable and dependent on the phase of the blood alcohol curve, low values occurring during the absorption phase and higher values occurring during the elimination phase. The average VH–blood alcohol concentration ratio ranges from about 0.9 to 1.3, with individual values covering a much wider range. As with urine, this variation occurs because the alcohol concentration of VH lags behind that of blood. Therefore, it is not possible to accurately determine a blood alcohol concentration from a single VH alcohol concentration. But as with urine, a conservative estimate of the minimum blood alcohol concentration existing sometime before death will be obtained if the alcohol concentration of the VH is divided by 1.3.

Cerebrospinal Fluid

Cerebrospinal fluid (CSF) provides cushioning for the brain and spinal column. Its volume in adults is about 125–150 ml and is continuously formed, circulated, and absorbed. It is not commonly sampled for alcohol analysis. In living subjects, it is sampled by lumbar puncture, a procedure requiring more skill and involving more risk than venous blood sampling. Even postmortem sampling of CSF is not common, as it is difficult to sample without contaminating it with blood. The CSF–blood alcohol concentration ratio lies within a range similar to that of the VH–blood ratio and is similarly dependent on the phase of the blood alcohol curve. But the minimum alcohol content of the blood sometime before death can be estimated from the CSF alcohol concentration in the manner described for the VH.

Synovial Fluid

Synovial fluid (SF) exists as a viscous lubricant in flexible joints such as the knee and elbow. If sourced from a knee, a sample of at least 0.5 ml may be obtained, that is, more than sufficient for alcohol analysis. The variability of the SF–blood alcohol concentration ratio may not be as great as that for urine, VH, or CSF, with the average SF–blood alcohol concentration ratio being close to 1. But in any individual case, the blood alcohol concentration could be between approximately half and twice the coexisting SF alcohol concentration.

As for urine, VH, and CSF, the SF–blood alcohol concentration ratio is dependent on the phase of the blood alcohol curve and the SF alcohol concentrations cannot be used to accurately predict blood alcohol concentrations, but they can be used to estimate the minimum blood alcohol concentration existing sometime before death using the method described for VH and CSF.

Bile

Bile and blood have similar water contents, and bile is often collected during autopsies for the analysis of alcohol and other drugs. It is manufactured in the liver and stored in the gall bladder, which often remains intact and free of contamination in cases of violent death. But where death occurs in the absorption phase, bile may be subject to contamination via postmortem diffusion of unabsorbed alcohol from the stomach. For autopsy specimens, values ranging from about 0.3 to 3 have been reported for the bile–blood alcohol concentration ratio, with an average close to 1. Division of the bile alcohol concentration by 1.1 should give a conservative estimate of the blood alcohol concentration sometime before death.

Liver and Other Tissues

Liver, brain, kidney, and muscle tissues usually have water contents of 75%–78%, so their alcohol contents in vivo should be a little less than the alcohol content of blood. The liver is a large organ and is easy to sample at autopsy, but it is not recommended for postmortem alcohol analysis. It is the main site of alcohol metabolism and although this stops very soon after death, the liver contains so much of the body's alcohol metabolizing "machinery" (enzymes and relevant cofactors) that it only has to continue functioning for a short time to have a major effect on the alcohol concentration within the liver tissue. Furthermore, the liver is rapidly exposed to microorganisms from the gastrointestinal tract after death and contains glycogen stores that act as a source of glucose, an ideal substrate for fermentation by yeasts and bacteria. Therefore, the liver–blood alcohol concentration ratio varies greatly, ranging from about 0.3 to 0.9, with an average of about 0.6, even when sampling occurs before obvious putrefaction has begun.

Kidney tissue is not recommended as suitable for postmortem alcohol analysis because it also has as a high capacity for alcohol metabolism.

The alcohol content of brain tissue is reported to vary greatly from region to region, making it unsuitable for sampling for alcohol analysis. In a study using the frontal lobe as the source of brain tissue, the brain–blood alcohol concentration ratio averaged 0.86 and ranged from 0.64 to 1.2.

Skeletal muscle should be the best tissue to sample when attempting to estimate the blood alcohol concentration from analysis of human tissues. Very little alcohol metabolism occurs in skeletal muscle, and large samples can be taken. The muscle–blood alcohol concentration ratio should be close to 0.86 and given the abundant blood supply to skeletal muscle, one might expect less variation in this ratio than is seen for body fluids in isolated compartments. However, significant variation is still seen, a range of 0.77–1.78 being found in one study, with the ratio dependent on the phase of the blood alcohol curve.

Bone marrow is well perfused with blood, is protected within the bone, and is well removed from potential contamination by either microorganisms or unabsorbed alcohol in the gastrointestinal tract. The variable fat content of marrow complicates alcohol analysis, but when the alcohol concentration of marrow tissue is normalized to a standard fat content, there appears to be a very strong correlation between the alcohol content of marrow and that of blood sampled at autopsy. However, this necessitates the analysis of marrow for its fat content. After such correction, the marrow–blood alcohol concentration ratio was found in one study to be within the approximate range of 0.6–1, averaging about 0.8 for human cadavers. The correction involved determining the fat content of the marrow and recalculating the alcohol content for its aqueous phase only. This specimen will not be useful in decomposing cases because of the volatility of ethanol. Microbial growth will be a much more important factor in cases of (especially advanced) decomposition, than the volatility of alcohol. The stability of alcohol in enclosed, essentially aqueous compartments is remarkably high.

Sequestered Hematomas

Analysis of blood clots may yield evidence of alcohol intoxication at the time of a traumatic incident when such evidence cannot be obtained from the analysis of blood or other body fluids. For example, head trauma may cause blood clots. When many hours pass between the time of their formation and the time of death, metabolism will cause the blood alcohol concentration to fall and may result in no alcohol being detected in postmortem blood. Alcohol in blood clots is at least partly protected from metabolism. Therefore, alcohol in a clot may still be detectable well after the alcohol is completely removed from the general circulation. But it is not possible to estimate the blood alcohol concentration at the time of injury from the alcohol content of the clot. Clots take variable times to form, and there will be at least some movement of alcohol into and out of the clot, during and after formation.

Stomach Contents

By itself, the concentration of alcohol in the stomach cannot be used to predict blood alcohol concentrations, but it can help determine the phase of the blood alcohol curve. During the absorption phase, the alcohol concentration of stomach fluid is likely to be much higher than blood alcohol concentrations compatible with life, that is, above 500 mg/100 ml. In the elimination phase, stomach fluid will usually have an alcohol content lower than this. Knowledge of the phase of the alcohol curve will always be useful when interpreting alcohol concentrations in other body fluids, narrowing the possibilities for fluid–blood ratios.

Putrefactive Blisters

Putrefactive blisters form on the skin of decomposing bodies. These may be gas or fluid filled. The fluid is mainly water and easily sampled and analyzed for alcohol. Although there is some correlation between the alcohol content of this fluid and that of postmortem blood, there will always be some difficulty in determining how much of the measured alcohol in both fluids was present before death and how much was formed or destroyed by microbial action after death. The presence or absence of other putrefactive alcohols such as n-propanol, isopropanol, and n-butanol may give an indication as to whether or not significant changes in the ethanol concentration have occurred after death, but these indicators are not completely reliable in that their absence does not necessarily rule out postmortem ethanol production.

Sweat

Sweat is formed as required by the eccrine glands and has a water content of about 98%. Therefore, the sweat–blood alcohol concentration ratio should be approximately 1.15. This is essentially what is found, and there is a strong correlation between venous blood and sweat alcohol concentrations, with somewhat less variability in the sweat–blood ratio than is seen for body fluids in isolated body compartments. However, sampling of sweat for alcohol analysis is not very common because of difficulties in sampling and the need to take special precautions to avoid alcohol losses.

Tears

Tears come from the lachrymal gland and have water content close to 100%. There is a strong correlation between tear and blood alcohol concentrations in all phases of the blood alcohol curve, with the measured tear–blood alcohol concentration ratio ranging from 1.08 to 1.20. This suggests that alcohol in blood rapidly equilibrates with tear fluid. Therefore, tears are close to an ideal medium for the estimation of coexisting blood alcohol concentrations. However, sampling will always pose ethical problems; an adequate supply of tears will not be forthcoming without some form of stress for the donor.

See also: **Toxicology/Alcohol:** Alcohol: Interpretation; Alcohol: Postmortem; Blood; Breath Alcohol.

Further Reading

Caplan, Y.H., Goldberger, B.A., 2003. Blood, urine and other fluid and tissue specimens for alcohol analyses. In: Garriot, J.C. (Ed.), Medicolegal Aspects of Alcohol, fourth ed. Lawyers & Judges Publishing Company, Inc, Tucson, pp. 149–161.

Garriot, J.C., 2003. Analysis for alcohol in post-mortem specimens. In: Garriot, J.C. (Ed.), Medicolegal Aspects of Alcohol, fourth ed. Lawyers & Judges Publishing Company, Inc, Tucson, pp. 163–176.

Jones, A.W., 2003. Disposition and fate of ethanol in the body. In: Garriot, J.C. (Ed.), Medicolegal Aspects of Alcohol, fourth ed. Lawyers & Judges Publishing Company, Inc, Tucson, pp. 47–112.

Kugelberg, F.C., Jones, A.W., 2007. Interpreting results of ethanol analysis in post-mortem specimens: A review of the literature. Forensic Science International 165, 10–29.

Blood

A Stowell, Environmental Science and Research Limited, Porirua, New Zealand

This chapter is a revision of the previous edition article by B. Hodgson, volume 1, pp. 74–80, © 2000, Elsevier Ltd.

Introduction

In most societies, alcohol (ethanol) is a legal drug used and abused for its mood-altering effects. It is a central nervous system depressant and as such inhibits many brain functions, leading to impairment of coordination, reaction time, and judgment. It also releases inhibitions by virtue of its depressant effect on inhibitory nerves. This may be at least partly responsible for the antisocial behavior displayed by many intoxicated people and may also be an important factor in criminal behavior.

In living subjects, the degree of alcohol-induced intoxication and performance impairment is best determined by mental and physical performance testing using a range of methods. Such testing is preferable to blood alcohol analysis because interindividual variations in tolerance to the effects of alcohol mean that different people will be impaired to different degrees at the same blood alcohol concentration. However, direct testing of impairment is reasonably time-consuming and often not practicable in a forensic context. It is not possible at all when the subject is deceased. Therefore, indirect methods such as blood and breath alcohol analysis have become the most common tools when assessing the degree of intoxication of living subjects. When dealing with the deceased, blood alcohol analysis is the best option.

In general, the alcohol-induced effects on human behavior are positively correlated with the blood alcohol concentration, and in most circumstances, the concentration of alcohol in blood taken from an arm vein will give a reasonable indication of the degree to which all organs and tissues of the body, including the brain, are exposed to alcohol. This follows from the fact that alcohol is very water soluble and distributes itself throughout the total body water. Blood is approximately 80% water and is an ideal vehicle for the transport of alcohol to all parts of the body.

Although blood from any part of the human circulatory system may be used for alcohol analysis, when dealing with living subjects, it is usually safest and most convenient to sample blood from an arm vein using a sterile hypodermic needle. Arteries are deeper and under higher pressure than veins so sampling of arterial blood is more likely to result in bruising and difficulty in stopping blood flow. If all that is required is a very small amount of blood (some analytical methods require only a few drops), the simplest approach is to use a sterile lancet to pierce a finger or thumb tip, allowing a few drops of blood to be squeezed from the minor puncture wound created.

Blood Collection

The most common method of collecting blood for alcohol analysis in a living person is by puncturing a cubital vein (near the surface of the arm on the inside of the elbow) with a hypodermic needle. The needle may be either attached to a syringe or double ended, with one end pushed through a rubber seal in an evacuated tube, once the vein has been pierced by the other end. Blood is drawn from the vein by virtue of the vacuum in the tube or by withdrawing the syringe plunger, thereby creating a partial vacuum in the syringe. Evacuated tubes are the method of choice where veins have good blood flow and are easily located. They have the advantage of allowing multiple tubes of blood to be collected from a single needlestick. However, where veins have weak blood flow and are prone to collapsing, an evacuated tube is usually not the best option. In this case, the standard syringe is more useful, allowing the operator (phlebotomist) to provide more gentle and variable suction when drawing blood from a "difficult" vein.

The volume of blood collected by either method is usually about 5–10 ml. This is more than enough for the blood alcohol analysis, including repeat analyses, if required. Modern forensic toxicology laboratories should be able to perform a full alcohol analysis on 0.5–1 ml of blood.

In the deceased, a wider selection of sites for blood collection is available, but this is counterbalanced by potential difficulties in the interpretation of differences between alcohol concentrations in blood from different sampling sites. In general, such differences are likely to be small in living people. But major trauma and postmortem changes can lead to large differences. Blood of uncertain origin (e.g., vein, artery, heart, or other ruptured organs and tissues) may gather in the chest and mix with the interstitial fluid that bathes the organs of the chest. This mixed fluid is often all that is readily available to the pathologist dealing with a body essentially exsanguinated as a result of gross trauma. If this mixed fluid is submitted as a "blood" sample for alcohol analysis, the analysis result will be difficult to interpret.

For example, if a person dies with a large amount of alcohol in their gastrointestinal tract, the difference between the alcohol concentration in blood from an arm vein and that in blood taken from the abdominal cavity may be very large if the abdominal cavity is contaminated with alcohol derived from a ruptured gut.

As for living people, venous blood taken from an arm or a leg of a deceased person, before significant decomposition starts, are the best samples for interpretative purposes. Such samples will best reflect the blood alcohol concentration at the time of death.

As in all other forensic work, collection of blood for alcohol analysis must involve steps to ensure the integrity and security of the sample, at least for the time necessary to transport it to the analytical laboratory and to perform the required analysis. This is particularly important when the result of the analysis is used to determine whether or not the sample donor was over or under a statutory blood alcohol limit.

In clinical settings, phlebotomists usually clean the skin at the sampling site with an alcoholic antiseptic solution, before blood sampling. Although swabs containing isopropanol are commonly used for this purpose, swabs containing ethanol are also available, and their use has the potential to elevate the blood alcohol concentration if the alcohol on the skin is not allowed to completely evaporate before blood sampling. Clearly, the cleansing agent should not be ethanol based. Even isopropanol could interfere with the analysis if it is used as an internal standard in the analytical procedure (see the section "Analysis") or if the analytical method cannot discriminate between ethanol and isopropanol.

Blood sampling without prior skin cleansing could potentially lead to contamination of the blood with a variety of microorganisms having the capacity to either produce or break down alcohol in the blood. But the risk of this occurring is effectively eliminated if the blood is drawn into evacuated tubes or placed in other clean receptacles containing sufficient preservative to inhibit microbial growth. An anticoagulant must also be used to maintain the blood in a liquid state. This facilitates the taking of homogeneous subsamples for analysis.

A wide range of evacuated blood sampling tubes exists for specific clinical purposes, but most of them are not suitable for forensic blood alcohol analysis. Therefore, in most jurisdictions, the law enforcement agencies are required to use blood sampling kits specifically designed to allow a clean blood sample to be taken and stored in a manner that prevents clotting and any other deterioration that might affect the measured blood alcohol concentration. The contents of a generic blood specimen collecting kit are pictured in **Figure 1**. It is self-contained and requires no additional equipment that might be open to question in terms of its cleanliness and alcohol-free status. The evacuated tubes contain both preservative and

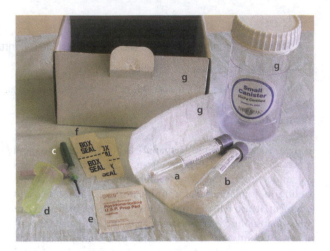

Figure 1   A generic blood specimen collection kit with two vacuum tubes (a, b), sterile needle (c), needle holder (d), nonalcoholic swab (e), seals (f), and packaging (g).

anticoagulant in quantities sufficient to be effective when the tube is filled with blood. Potassium oxalate in combination with 1% sodium fluoride is the preferred additive to collection tubes to stop blood from clotting, to inhibit microbial growth and to maintain the stability of blood alcohol concentrations as much as possible. Refrigeration at approximately 4 °C is also recommended for prolonged storage, especially where ambient temperatures are high.

It is important to recognize that it is impossible to stabilize blood alcohol concentrations completely over long periods. Many studies have shown that in properly preserved and well-sealed blood samples, the blood alcohol concentration falls slowly over a period of weeks and months. The cause is not completely understood but is probably due mainly to slow chemical oxidation. The rate of loss is very variable but could amount to 1–2 mg per 100 ml month^{-1} of refrigerated storage.

In many countries, whole blood is used for forensic alcohol analysis. In others, blood plasma or serum is used. In clinical laboratories, plasma or serum is often the material of choice for alcohol analysis because many other clinical tests are also performed on serum or plasma. This may seem a minor detail because serum and plasma are derived from and usually make up over 50% of whole blood. Nevertheless, the difference between the alcohol content of whole blood and that of serum or plasma is always significant. The alcohol content of all biological fluids is proportional to their water contents because alcohol is almost exclusively present in the water phase of these fluids. On the basis of the relative water content, the alcohol concentration in serum and plasma is approximately 11% higher on a weight per volume basis, than the alcohol concentration in whole blood from which the serum and plasma was derived. When the plasma: blood alcohol concentration ratio has actually been measured, a range of values have been found, with the average being closer to 1.15 than to the theoretical value of 1.11.

Any conversion of plasma or serum alcohol concentrations to whole blood concentrations must take into account the natural variations in water contents of these fluids. This will introduce an additional element of uncertainty in the analytical result.

Analysis

Chemical

The first useful methods for forensic blood alcohol analysis were chemical methods involving oxidation of the alcohol by a strong oxidizing agent. The most well known of these methods was developed by Eric Widmark, a Swedish pioneer in the field of alcohol metabolism. His method involved incubating small blood samples suspended over an acid dichromate solution in a sealed container. During an incubation period of many hours, the alcohol evaporated from the blood and was absorbed and completely oxidized by the acid dichromate mixture. The more alcohol oxidized, the less dichromate was left at the end of the reaction. The analysis was completed by measuring the residual dichromate in solution. This was usually performed using another chemical oxidation–reduction reaction that could be easily followed by an obvious color change when the reaction was complete. Although this procedure was robust and generally reliable, it was cumbersome compared with modern analytical methods and was subject to error if other oxidizable volatiles were present in the blood. In other words, the method was not specific to ethanol. Other common alcohols such as methanol and isopropanol would give a response similar to that of ethanol.

Methanol and isopropanol are common industrial solvents with many properties similar to those of ethanol. They may be consumed deliberately as substitutes for ethanol, or accidentally as contaminants or additives in illicit alcohol products.

Chemical methods for alcohol analysis are especially prone to error, where postmortem blood samples from decomposing bodies are being analyzed. Microorganisms produce a wide range of volatile oxidizable compounds, some of which are regarded as very good biological markers of putrefaction. It is obviously desirable to have analytical methods able to distinguish these compounds from each other as well as from ethanol, which may also be a product of putrefaction.

Biochemical

An analytical method still widely used in clinical laboratories involves oxidation of alcohol using the enzyme alcohol dehydrogenase (ADH). Although still not completely specific for ethanol, this method is simpler and quicker than chemical methods. The enzyme-catalyzed oxidation of ethanol to acetaldehyde requires the coenzyme nicotinamide adenine dinucleotide (NAD). For every molecule of ethanol oxidized, one molecule of reduced NAD is produced. Reduced nicotinamide adenine dinucleotide (NADH) is readily measured in solution by its absorption of ultraviolet light at a wavelength of 340 nm, using a relatively inexpensive spectrophotometer of the type used in some school laboratories. The degree of light absorption is directly proportional to the molecular concentration (molarity) of NADH, and this, in turn, is equivalent to the molecular concentration (molarity) of alcohol existing before the enzyme-catalyzed reaction started.

A number of variations of this method have been used and several commercial kits are available, either for small numbers of samples or for large numbers run using autoanalyzers of the type widely used in hospital laboratories.

Although such methods may still be used in forensic toxicology laboratories as screening methods, they are not adequate by themselves. ADH catalyzes the oxidation of a variety of alcohols in addition to ethanol. Therefore, there is no way of telling whether or not an apparent positive ethanol result is partly or even completely due to the presence of another alcohol such as methanol or isopropanol.

Gas Chromatography

The introduction of reliable gas chromatographs in the early 1950s significantly improved the forensic toxicologist's ability not only to distinguish ethanol from a variety of other low molecular weight volatile compounds but also to clearly distinguish between ethanol and other alcohols. This led to gas chromatography (GC) being the current method of choice for alcohol analysis in modern forensic toxicology laboratories.

In comparison with many other modern instrumental techniques, the GC is relatively inexpensive, simple, fast, and robust and provides the accuracy and precision necessary for reliable quantitative analysis.

A representation of the different components of a gas chromatograph is shown in **Figure 2**. The sample to be analyzed is injected into a heated injector port, where it is vaporized and carried by a stream of gas into a coiled tube (called a column) located in a thermostatted oven. The column is commonly made of metal or glass. It is either packed with a porous absorbent material or coated with a film of absorbent material on its inner surface. Modern GC columns are typically of the latter type and are many meters long, up to about 0.5 mm in diameter and made of very pure glass (fused silica) reinforced by an outer coating of tough plastic material.

The film of absorbent material is responsible for separating individual volatile components of the sample, as it passes through the column. The film will retain the volatile components to varying degrees depending on the degree of molecular

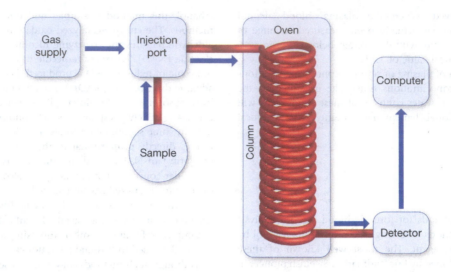

Figure 2   Schematic diagram of a gas chromatograph.

interaction between the film and each component. The degree and speed of separation of the components can be optimized by careful selection of the type of gas, gas flow rate, column temperature, column geometry, and the chemical nature of the absorbent film. A complete separation of common alcohols such as ethanol, methanol, and isopropanol can be commonly achieved in less than 2 min using a 20–30 m column.

As the different components emerge from the end of the column, they may be detected using a variety of different methods including mass spectrometry. However, most forensic toxicology laboratories find the common flame ionization detector more than adequate for blood alcohol analyses. These detectors are simple and very reliable. As the individual volatile components pass through a small flame, they are ionized, allowing them to be detected in the form of an analog electrical signal. The size of the signal is dependent on the amount of the detected component. This signal is then digitized to allow for easy quantitation.

The magnitude of the detector signal, by itself, is insufficient to determine the alcohol concentration of a sample. However, by comparing this signal with that produced by a sample of known alcohol concentration, the alcohol concentration of the unknown sample can be easily calculated because the detector response is directly proportional to the alcohol concentration. This, of course, is only true if the known and unknown samples are treated in exactly the same way before and during the analysis.

Although this is simple and robust methodology, its accuracy and precision can be affected by variations in the volume of sample injected onto the GC column. Consequently, a more reliable method designed to maximize accuracy and precision is almost always employed. This involves the use of internal

standardization, a widely used technique in analytical chemistry. It improves accuracy and precision and provides a powerful diagnostic tool if things go wrong with the analytical system. If an internal standard is used, the chances of a system failure going unnoticed are very low.

Internal standardization commonly involves diluting all blood samples and calibration standards with a fixed volume of a liquid containing another volatile compound that is readily detected by the analytical system, does not naturally occur in blood samples in readily detectable concentrations, and has a retention time clearly different from that of alcohol. Examples of such compounds are *n*-propanol and *t*-butanol, both volatile members of the alcohol family. If either of these internal standards is used and the analytical method is working well, the GC detector will produce, for every sample, a signal for the internal standard, which will be essentially the same size for every sample. Unusual variations in the internal standard signal could indicate poor precision of sample injection volume or poor control of the temperature of the GC column.

However, some variation in these parameters is inevitable, even with the best methods, using the best equipment. And without an internal standard, this would lead to variation in analytical results. Much of this variation is eliminated if calculation of the analytical results is based on the ratio of the alcohol signal to the internal standard signal. Precision of results is improved because variations in the alcohol signal are largely canceled by corresponding variations in the internal standard signal.

Figure 3 shows an automatic diluter used to take a fixed volume of blood and a fixed volume of an internal standard solution and dispense them into a sample container; in this case, a headspace vial used in headspace GC. The blood: internal

Figure 3 Apparatus for automatic sampling of blood (a) and automatic dispensing of the blood into a headspace sampling vial (b). An internal standard solution is mixed with the blood in step (b).

standard dilution ratio is commonly about 1:10, producing a solution that is much less viscous than whole blood and one that may be injected directly into the injection port of the GC. Although the diluted sample can be manually injected, this is labor intensive and has largely been replaced with automatic injectors. These are usually integrated with the gas chromatograph and extract small volumes of the diluted blood samples and inject them into the injector port of the GC at regular intervals.

Regardless of whether manual or automatic injection is used, the direct injection of diluted blood samples into the injector port tends to shorten the life of GC columns and necessitates frequent cleaning of the injector port. As a result, a cleaner method of introducing samples into the injector port is often preferred. Headspace injection is such a method and involves analysis of the air (headspace) in equilibrium with the diluted blood sample. In many ways, it is analogous to breath testing, whereby the blood alcohol level is determined by analysis of air in equilibrium with blood perfusing the lung tissue.

Reliable analysis using headspace GC requires the diluted samples to be incubated in sealed vials with large headspace volumes at controlled temperatures. The incubation period is usually chosen to allow full equilibration of alcohol and the internal standard between the diluted sample and the headspace air. **Figure 4** shows a typical computer-controlled headspace GC system. In this apparatus, the sample vials sit in a rack on the top of the GC before incubation and are each incubated for 12.5 min at 60 °C in a thermostatted shaker to the left of the sample rack, before analysis. All instrumental parameters such as column temperature, total analysis time, sample incubation temperature and time, gas flow rate, injector port temperature, and detector temperature are controlled by the computer. This system, in common with many others, has two analytical columns housed in the same oven. Each is connected to the same injection port but is

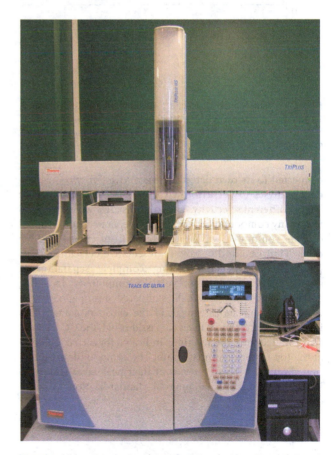

Figure 4 A headspace gas chromatograph complete with automatic headspace sampler. The sampler is fixed to the top of the gas chromatograph and includes a rack of headspace vials awaiting analysis.

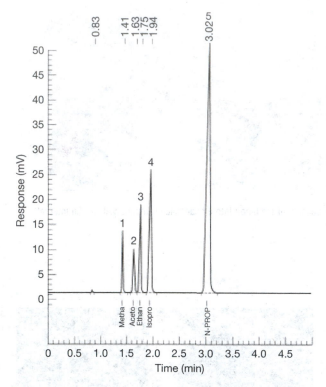

Figure 5 Flame ionization detector 1. Column: DB Wax × 0.32 mm × 10 m, 0.5 µm film; joined to DB-1 0.32 mm × 20 m, 5.0 µm film. 1, Methanol; 2, acetone; 3, ethanol; 4, isopropanol; 5, *n*-propanol (internal standard).

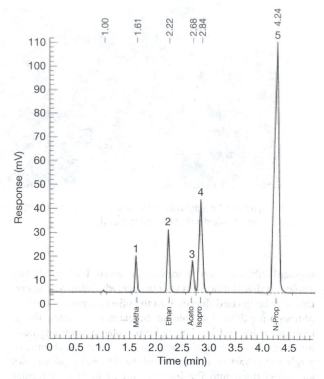

Figure 6 Flame ionization detector 2. Column: DB-1 0.32 mm × 30 m, 5.0 µm film. 1, Methanol; 2, ethanol; 3, acetone; 4, isopropanol; 5, *n*-propanol (internal standard).

connected to its own detector. This allows for two independent analyses to be performed simultaneously on columns having different selectivity. The columns are always chosen so that if any compound cannot be fully separated from ethanol on one column, it will be separated from ethanol on the other. **Figures 5 and 6** show representative detector outputs (chromatograms) demonstrating complete separation of a mixture of five different volatile compounds, including ethanol and the internal standard *n*-propanol. Each compound appears as a peak in the chromatogram and is identified by the time it takes to pass through the GC column. This is called the retention time, indicated for each compound at the top of each chromatogram. The compounds are quantitated on the basis of the size of their peak areas relative to known standards, using internal standardization as previously described.

Quality Assurance

Any laboratory conducting forensic alcohol analysis should have a documented quality management system involving both quality assurance and quality control. Quality assurance

involves maintenance and compliance with documented processes and procedures aimed at ensuring that the laboratory's output is fit for purpose. Quality control involves regular checking of the laboratory's output to demonstrate that it is fit for the purpose.

It is not necessary for all laboratories to conform to identical quality standards, as long as the standards are well defined and available to the laboratory's customers. However, there are many advantages in following internationally accepted quality standards. Standards such as ISO/IEC 17025:2005 have been written by experts in their field and provide solid guidelines for quality assurance in chemical testing laboratories, recognizing that there are often many satisfactory ways of complying with a standard.

In a blood alcohol testing laboratory, quality assurance measures will include proper validation of all analytical methods used in the laboratory, thorough documentation and dissemination of the laboratory's procedures and processes, maintenance of appropriate training programs for both technical and administrative staff, regular audits of the laboratory's quality system, and regular participation in interlaboratory collaborative trials and proficiency tests. It is common for laboratories to seek accreditation by a national or international body, accreditation being granted when the laboratory demonstrates that it complies with an international standard such as ISO/IEC 17025:2005.

Validation of a new method is easily achieved by comparing results obtained using the new method with those obtained using a previously validated method. If there is no statistical difference between methods in terms of results obtained, the new method is considered validated. If there is no previously validated method available, validation is usually performed by rigorous testing of the new method with standards having the same range of alcohol content and composition as the samples for which the method is being developed. Such testing should involve determination of accuracy, precision, and specificity over the relevant concentration range and should involve several analysts on several different days, ideally using several analytical instruments.

It is common to perform blood alcohol analysis using large batches of 25–50 samples, each sample being analyzed at least twice, with the average of replicate results being reported. Regardless of the quality of the method, this average result will always have some degree of uncertainty associated with it. Therefore, in many jurisdictions, an appropriate "margin for error" is deducted from this result before reporting. This deduction should not be arbitrary. It should be based on the actual precision and accuracy of the method, determined during validation studies and updated when necessary.

It is usually not appropriate to specify rigid performance criteria for an analytical method used by different laboratories in different countries. The quality and type of analytical equipment and infrastructure required to run this equipment will often determine the accuracy and precision of results. Nevertheless, most modern GC methods should allow a blood alcohol concentration of 100 mg per 100 ml (0.1%, w/v) to be determined with a standard deviation (SD) of about ± 1 mg per 100 ml (± 0.001%, w/v). If reliable calibration standards are used, the accuracy of modern methods should be very close to 100%. Therefore, the "margin for error" to be applied to any result should be determined largely by the precision of the method and the number of replicate analyses. The margin for error in the average of duplicate results is typically not more than about 2% of this average. If referring to "standard uncertainty" as defined in the ISO GUM, use of a coverage factor of ~ 2 will give a 95% confidence interval equivalent to the result of a single analysis ± 2 SD. But when multiple analyses are performed, the 95% confidence interval for the mean will be less than ± 2 SD.

In headspace GC methodology, calibration standards must be run in every batch to ensure a high degree of accuracy, and it is best practice to run additional quality control samples in each batch. These are samples of known concentration, usually made up to be close to relevant statutory limits or other important thresholds, for example, nonstatutory cutoff limits applied under workplace health and safety policies.

Each laboratory should set its own acceptance criteria for batches of samples and for the results of individual samples within those batches. These criteria will typically involve limits to the differences between replicate results for a particular blood sample; limits to how far results for quality control samples can deviate from the expected value; limits to the variation between internal standard peak areas, minimum standards for peak areas and peak symmetry; and limits to the variability of calibration factors. Once again, these criteria should not be arbitrary; they should reflect the actual characteristics of the method so will often vary between laboratories and may vary with time within laboratories.

Laboratories conducting forensic alcohol analysis should keep all documentation relating to the testing procedures for an appropriate time. This time is usually defined by statute and allows for all relevant evidence to be produced, if required, in any subsequent litigation. Furthermore, although the analysis of blood for alcohol content is a relatively simple procedure, and one which has become highly automated, the science behind it is not simple. Therefore, any laboratory engaged in forensic alcohol analysis should employ the services of at least one forensic scientist with appropriate expertise. Ideally, they should have broad knowledge of the laboratory's procedures relating to the receipt, identification, documentation, chain of custody, and secure storage for all blood samples and other items of evidence. They should also understand the behavior of alcohol in blood during long-term storage, the theory and practice of alcohol analysis, and how to make appropriate allowance for uncertainty in analytical results. Knowledge of human alcohol metabolism and the effects of alcohol are also useful and often expected, when engaged in blood alcohol litigation.

See also: **Toxicology/Alcohol:** Alcohol: Interpretation; Alcohol: Postmortem; Breath Alcohol; Urine and Other Body Fluids.

Further Reading

Anderson, W.H., 2003. Collection and storage of specimens for alcohol analysis. In: Garriot, J.C. (Ed.), Medicolegal Aspects of Alcohol, fourth ed. Lawyers and Judges Publishing Company, Inc, Tucson, AZ, pp. 237–248.

ISO/IEC 17025, 2005. General Requirements for the Competence of Testing and Calibration Laboratories, second ed. International Organization for Standardization/International Electrotechnical Commission, Geneva, p. 28.

Jones, A.W., 1996. Measuring alcohol in blood and breath for forensic purposes – A historical review. Forensic Science Reviews 8, 13–44.

Jones, A.W., Pounder, D.J., 2008. Update on clinical and forensic analysis of alcohol. In: Karch, S.B. (Ed.), Forensic Issues in Alcohol Testing. CRC Press, Boca Raton, FL, London & New York, pp. 21–64.

Jones, A.W., Schuberth, J., 1989. Computer-aided headspace gas chromatography applied to blood-alcohol analysis: Importance of online process control. Journal of Forensic Sciences 34, 1116–1127.

Kolb, B., Ettre, L.S., 1997. Static Headspace-gas Chromatography: Theory and Practice. Wiley-VCH, New York.

Breath Alcohol

JG Wigmore, Toronto, ON, Canada

This chapter is a revision of the previous edition article by R.G. Gullberg, volume 1, pp. 86–93, © 2000, Elsevier Ltd.

Abbreviations

BAC	Blood alcohol concentration	GC	Gas chromatography
BrAC	Breath alcohol concentration	IR	Infrared
BBR	Blood to breath ratio (for alcohol)	MAE	Mouth alcohol effect

Glossary

Gas chromatography (GC) A commonly used method in forensic toxicology for the separation, detection, and quantitation of the various components of a mixture of volatile substances. The separation is typically achieved by the use of a long narrow tube or column, in which the various components of the volatile mixture are sorted by their different affinities to the column.

Henry's law A physical law, which states that at equilibrium and at a fixed temperature there will be a fixed ratio between the concentration of a volatile substance dissolved in a liquid and the concentration of the volatile in the air above the liquid.

Infrared (IR) Electromagnetic radiation that has a wavelength longer than that of visible red light and shorter than that of radio waves (i.e., between 0.7 and 1000 μm).

Lambert–Beer law A physical law, which shows that the intensity of light in an absorbing medium is related exponentially to path length and the absorption coefficient of the media.

Introduction

Breath alcohol (ethyl alcohol, ethanol) testing is one of the oldest and most established areas of forensic toxicology. It is employed by many countries as the sole analytical method to enforce drunk driving laws as there are many advantages of breath compared to blood alcohol testing. They include the following:

- Breath alcohol testing is noninvasive and safe. No needles are required as in the collection of blood samples, and hence there is no possibility of injury or transmission of disease.
- Breath alcohol results are known immediately compared to the several days or weeks for blood alcohol concentrations (BACs) to be reported by forensic laboratories. Hence the police are immediately aware of what charge to lay and whether medical treatment may be required for the arrested drunk driver (e.g., alcohol poisoning).

- Continuity (chain of custody) is relatively easy to ensure as the breath sample is provided by the drunk driver directly into the breath alcohol testing instrument. No special blood tubes, swabs, identity seals, biohazard refrigeration, or special transportation is required as it is for blood samples.
- No medical staff or phlebotomists are required for breath alcohol testing. Breath tests can be conducted by trained police operators, which shorten the time between the arrest and testing.
- There is no problem with the drunk driver's real or alleged phobia of blood or needles if he/she is being breath alcohol tested.
- Breath alcohol correlates better with brain alcohol concentration (arterial blood) and will give a better indication of alcohol-related impairment on the rising BAC phase compared to venous blood samples, which are the samples collected from drunk drivers.

The major disadvantage of breath alcohol testing is that breath testing can be conducted only in cooperative, conscious subjects, whereas blood samples may be collected in hospital from injured unconscious drivers.

This chapter covers the historical, biological, and analytical aspects of forensic breath alcohol testing, one of the tests most commonly conducted in forensic toxicology.

Historical Aspects

The history of forensic breath alcohol testing is shown in **Table 1**. The main analytical technique for determining breath (and blood) alcohol concentrations for over 100 years has been the oxidation of alcohol by potassium dichromate and sulfuric acid (acid dichromate) as follows:

$$2K_2Cr_2O_7 + 8H_2SO_4 + 3CH_3CH_2OH \rightarrow 2Cr_2(SO_4)_3$$
$$+ 2K_2SO_4 + 8CH_3COOH + 11H_2O$$

This reaction could be measured by titration, or as in the case of breath alcohol testing, by measuring the color change, a decrease in the yellow color of potassium dichromate. As this method uses toxic chemicals and is slow and cumbersome and difficult to automate, it has been replaced by other analytical methods.

Alcohol in the Blood and Breath

Once an alcoholic beverage is consumed orally, the alcohol diffuses quickly from the stomach and small intestine into the blood. The blood is pumped by the heart throughout the body, and the alcohol is distributed to the various tissues according to their water content. The blood, which contains alcohol, is pumped by the right side of the heart via the pulmonary artery to the lungs. The lungs have approximately 250 million small pear-shaped sacs known as alveoli. As there is approximately 100 ml of blood in the lung capillaries, at any given time, in effect, a thin film of blood is spread over the large surface area of the lungs, which facilitates the rapid diffusion of volatile compounds (such as oxygen, carbon dioxide, and alcohol) from the blood into the breath. The diffusion of alcohol from the blood into the breath is based on Henry's law.

When the BAC is increasing, the arterial BAC is greater than the venous BAC. As breath alcohol concentrations (BrACs) are based on the arterial BAC in the lungs, and venous blood samples are generally collected from the cubital vein in the arm, the BrAC can be greater than the venous BAC during this period of time. However, the brain alcohol concentration (and hence alcohol-induced impairment) is related to the arterial BAC. BrACs, therefore, provide a more accurate indication of impairment than the venous BAC, when the BAC is increasing.

Table 1   Major historical developments in breath alcohol testing

Year	Development
1803	Henry's law that a fixed ratio occurs between a volatile in a liquid and air at equilibrium at a constant temperature was published. It is the basis of breath alcohol testing
1835	The oxidation of alcohol by acid dichromate is described by J. Liebig
1867	Breath alcohol concentrations were determined by F.E. Anstie using an acid dichromate solution. He first reported the mouth alcohol effect
1910	The applicability of Henry's law to the distribution of volatile substances between blood and alveolar breath was reported by A.R. Cushny
1927	E. Bogen first described the use of breath alcohol testing for medicolegal purposes and proposed a blood to breath alcohol ratio of approximately 2000:1
1931	R.N. Harger of Indiana University developed the first portable breath alcohol testing instrument to be used by the police
1954	R.F. Borkenstein of Indiana University developed the Breathalyzer®, which measured Breath alcohol concentration by a potassium dichromate/sulfuric acid method. It was the most successful and the most widely used breath alcohol testing instrument for law enforcement purposes. Approximately, 30 000 Breathalyzers® were manufactured worldwide until production ceased in 1997
1964	The Grand Rapids Study (a roadside survey), published by R.F. Borkenstein, determined by breath alcohol testing the increased risk of causing a motor vehicle collision with increasing blood alcohol concentration. A legal limit of 0.08 g/100 ml (17 mmol l^{-1}) was proposed. This study had a major impact on drinking and driving laws in North American, Europe, and Australia
1970	A small gas chromatograph for breath alcohol testing was developed by J.R. Penton and M.R. Forrester
1971	R.A. Harte described a portable infrared breath alcohol testing instrument called the Intoxilyzer®
1972	Fuel cell (electrochemical) based breath alcohol testing was described by H.W. Bay, K.F. Blurton, H.C. Lieb, and H.G. Oswin
2001	A portable mass spectrometer to determine breath alcohol concentrations was developed by P.F. Wilson et al.

During exhalation, the temperature of the breath decreases from body temperature (~37 °C) to breath temperature of approximately 34 °C. This occurs as the breath returns heat and moisture to the mucous lining of the upper respiratory tract (URT) in order to minimize water and heat loss during breathing. The interaction of alcohol in the breath with the URT causes the blood to breath alcohol ratio (BBR) to be approximately 2300–2400:1 during a forced exhalation.

There are three main phases of the BrAC curve during a forced exhalation. The first part of breath exhaled is the tidal phase, where the breath from the URT (dead space), which contains little alcohol, is exhaled. The BrAC then increases rapidly as the breath containing alcohol from the lungs is reached. Finally, an approximately level profile, or plateau, of the BrAC is obtained during the final stage of exhalation.

Hyperventilation can cause the BrAC to be lowered by approximately 10%, and likewise, hypoventilation can cause the BrAC to be increased by 10%. However, the effect of these breathing techniques on BrAC disappears virtually as soon as the person resumes normal breathing.

Body temperature may also affect the BrAC. In vitro testing using alcohol simulators has shown that a 1 °C increase in the temperature of the solution caused an approximately 6.5% increase in the vapor alcohol concentration. In vivo testing with drinking human subjects has shown that the change in BrAC is much less affected by body temperature.

Analytical Methods

Most of the breath alcohol testing instruments currently used for law enforcement purposes employ one of the following techniques.

Infrared Spectrophotometry

This is the most common analytical technique for evidential breath alcohol testers used by the police. The breath alcohol (CH_3CH_2OH) concentration is determined by the absorption of infrared (IR) light according to the Lambert–Beer law as follows:

$$I = I_0 e^{-abc}$$

where I is the final intensity of IR light (e.g., when end-expired breath sample is in the sample chamber); I_0, the initial intensity of IR light; e, the mathematical constant (2.71); a, the absorption coefficient of alcohol; b, the path length (the distance IR light travels through the sample chamber); and c, the concentration of alcohol vapor in the sample chamber.

In the 1970s when IR breath alcohol technology was first developed, the path length (b) of breath alcohol instruments was required to be several meters long in order to obtain the maximum change in intensity of IR light (I) for detection. With improvements in IR technology, the necessary path length has been reduced to centimeters and thus has reduced the size of these instruments.

Different IR wavelengths have been employed to increase the specificity of IR breath alcohol testing, such as:

3.39 µm: asymmetrical stretching vibration of the methyl group (–CH_3)
3.48 µm: symmetrical stretching vibration of the methyl group
9.4 µm: stretching vibration of the C–O bond

Other wavelengths have been employed to measure carbon dioxide and water vapor concentrations in the expired breath to assist in the determination of a uniform breath sample and potential mouth alcohol effects (MAEs).

2.77 and 4.26 µm: carbon dioxide
2.57 µm: water

Electrochemical (Fuel Cell)

The concentration of the alcohol in the end-expired breath sample is oxidized by an immobilized electrolyte, a working electrode, and a counter electrode to produce an electrical current. The electrochemical reactions are as follows:

$$CH_3CH_2OH + 3H_2O \rightarrow 2CO_2 + 12H^+ + 12e^-$$

at the working electrode, and;

$$3O_2 + 12H^+ + 12e^- \rightarrow 6H_2O$$

at the counter electrode.

The disadvantage of electrochemical analysis of breath alcohol compared to IR is that only the end-expiratory BrAC is determined (one data point), whereas IR measures the entire exhalation BrAC curve.

Dual IR/Electrochemical

IR and electrochemical techniques have been combined in some breath alcohol testing instruments. Typically, IR monitors the BrAC curve during exhalation and the end-expiratory BrAC is measured by the electrochemical technique. The two different types of sensors allow for greater specificity.

Gas Chromatography

The end-expiratory breath is passed through a column, which separates the alcohol from the various other components of breath and is then quantified with flame ionization or thermal conductivity detectors. This technique has not gained widespread use as gas chromatographs were typically larger and required compressed tanks of nitrogen, hydrogen, or helium. Newer miniature GCs, using scrubbed ambient air instead of pressurized gases in tanks, may increase the use of this technique by law enforcement agencies.

Types of Breath Alcohol Testing Instruments
Passive Alcohol Sensor

The passive alcohol sensor is designed to quickly and easily detect alcohol in the ambient air around the suspected drunk driver. It is the least accurate of types of breath alcohol testing instruments as end-expiratory breath is not tested directly and may be affected by ambient conditions around the tested driver.

Screening Device

As it is difficult for the police to detect alcohol impairment in alcohol-tolerant, heavy drinkers by physical observation alone, a handheld device, typically using an electrochemical sensor, which samples the end-expired breath of the suspected drunk driver, provides the police with grounds to demand an evidential breath alcohol test.

Alcohol Ignition Interlock Device

These devices are usually installed in an automobile as a result of a court order or conditional licensure for convicted drinking drivers. The driver is required to provide an end-expired breath sample into the alcohol ignition interlock device (AIID) before the automobile will start and additionally at random times throughout driving. A FAIL recorded by the AIID (typically at BACs of 0.02–0.04 g/100 ml (4–9 mmol l^{-1})) will result in the automobile not starting, the lights flashing, or the horn honking loudly. AIIDs when installed have been found to reduce the incidence of alcohol-related motor vehicle collisions.

Evidential Breath Alcohol Instruments

These instruments are the most reliable, sophisticated, and accurate of all types of breath alcohol testing instruments. Evidential breath alcohol testing instruments usually are based on multiple IR wavelengths or dual IR/electrochemical testing. A typical evidential breath alcohol testing sequence is shown in **Table 2**.

A 15–20 min pretest observation/deprivation period will prevent the MAE. Air blanks are conducted throughout the testing sequence to ensure that the ambient air is free of alcohol or other potential interfering volatile substances and that the evidential breath alcohol testing instrument has been cleared of any alcohol vapor from previous testing. A calibration check

Table 2   An example of an evidential breath alcohol testing sequence

Fifteen to twenty minute observation/deprivation period
Air blank
Calibration check
Air blank
First breath alcohol test
Air blank
Second breath alcohol test
Air blank
Results are automatically printed

(involving a wet-bath simulator or pressurized dry gas) of a known alcohol vapor concentration ensures that the instrument is measuring alcohol vapor accurately. Two breath tests with good duplication (usually within 0.02 g/100 ml (4 mmol l^{-1})) increases the reliability of breath alcohol testing of the drunk driver. The computerized, automatic breath alcohol testing sequence and printing of the results eliminates the possibility of any real or alleged manipulation of the evidential breath alcohol testing instrument by the police operator.

Forensic Issues

As several million evidential breath alcohol tests are conducted on suspected drinking drivers throughout the world every year, it is not surprising that many forensic issues have been raised in criminal court. The main three issues are as follows.

Blood to Breath Alcohol Ratio

Breath alcohol testing instruments in many countries are calibrated on the BBR of 2100:1. That is, 2100 ml (2.1 l) of end-expired breath is deemed to have the same amount of alcohol as 1 ml of blood. The BBR in drunk drivers has been found to be closer to 2300–2400:1. BBRs >2100:1 in a person will mean that the BAC is underestimated, and BBRs <2100 will mean the BAC is overestimated. Therefore, using breath alcohol instruments calibrated at 2100:1 will underestimate the BAC of drunk drivers by 10% or more on average.

A wide range of unrealistic BBRs have been used in criminal court to dispute the validity of breath alcohol testing. Most of the ranges have been due to the low BAC at which the BBR was determined. As with all ratios, the BBR has greater variability at lower BACs, as shown in **Table 3**.

A ±0.005 g/100 ml (1 mmol l^{-1}) variation in BrAC at a BAC of 0.012 g per 100 ml (3 mmol l^{-1}) can produce an apparently enormous BBR range of 1482–3600:1. The BBRs determined at these low BACs have been applied incorrectly at the typically high BACs (on average 0.150 g/100 ml (33 mmol l^{-1}) in most countries) found in drunk drivers.

Table 3   Apparent blood to breath alcohol ratios (BBRs) when breath alcohol concentration is within ±0.005 g/100 ml (1 mmol l^{-1}) of the blood alcohol concentration (BAC)

BAC (g/100 ml)	Breath alcohol concentration range (±0.005 of BAC)	Apparent BBRs
0.012 (3 mmol l^{-1})	0.007–0.017 (2–4 mmol l^{-1})	1482–3600:1
0.040 (9 mmol l^{-1})	0.035–0.045 (8–10 mmol l^{-1})	1867–2400:1
0.080 (17 mmol l^{-1})	0.075–0.085 (16–19 mmol l^{-1})	1976–2240:1
0.150 (33 mmol l^{-1})	0.145–0.155 (32–34 mmol l^{-1})	2032–2172:1

Field studies of evidential breath and blood alcohol testing in several countries have shown that instruments calibrated at a BBR of 2100:1 will only rarely (<1%) overestimate the actual BAC, and in those cases, the overestimate is usually <0.01 g per 100 ml (2 mmol l^{-1}). However, in order to avoid much needless legal arguments, most countries have now changed their drunk driving laws to include not only a per se BAC limit but also a BrAC. In the United States, the common BrAC limit is expressed in g/210 l of breath, which basically enshrines a BBR of 2100:1 by law.

Mouth Alcohol Effect

The BrAC can be falsely elevated if there is residual alcohol from a last alcoholic drink or an alcohol-containing fluid (such as mouthwash) remaining in the oral cavity at the time of the breath test. The MAE, however, disappears rapidly in an exponential decrease and will only cause false elevations in BrAC for 15–20 min at most. The MAE is less when the alcohol concentration of the beverage is low (such as beer at 5% v/v alcohol rather than liquor (40% v/v alcohol)), when the beverage is swallowed rather than gargled, when the subject opens his mouth and talks and when salivation is stimulated (such as when chewing gum). Dentures, chewing tobacco, or gum in the mouth do not significantly prolong the MAE.

As alcohol rapidly leaves the stomach and stomach concentrations are typically <1% alcohol v/v shortly after drinking has ceased, belching, burping or gastroesophageal reflux disease, or a hiatus hernia will not produce a significant, long-lasting MAE.

In addition, evidential breath testing procedures that include a 15–20 min deprivation or observation period before testing and two breath samples with good agreement will preclude a significant MAE occurring during routine evidential breath alcohol testing of drunk drivers by the police. Some evidential breath alcohol testing instruments (usually, IR) also have a mouth alcohol detection system as an additional safeguard against the MAE.

Specificity

In order for a nonalcohol compound to produce a false-positive breath alcohol test result, it must be a volatile organic compound that is relatively nontoxic. The main endogenous compound that could produce a false-positive BrAC is acetone. Acetone can be found in relatively high concentrations in the breath of uncontrolled diabetics, fasting individuals, and people on a high-protein low-carbohydrate diet. All current evidential breath alcohol testers, however, are not affected by acetone.

Exogenous compounds that could potentially cause a false-positive BrAC include mainly glues, paints, and solvents. These volatile compounds are eliminated from the breath exponentially in a similar manner as for the MAE, on exposure to fresh air. Solvents also tend to have significant toxicity and have characteristic odors. As a result, solvent inhalation would not be expected to remain undetected during routine evidential breath alcohol testing.

Conclusion

Breath alcohol testing has been of critical importance in the enforcement of laws against drunken driving in many countries and has greatly enhanced traffic safety by decreasing the incidence of drinking and driving. Several million evidential breath alcohol tests are conducted globally each year and have gained widespread public support. Such issues as the BBR, MAE, and specificity have little scientific merit in routine evidential breath alcohol testing involving proper scientific controls such as duplicate breath tests, a preliminary deprivation/observation period, and calibration checks as part of the breath alcohol testing procedure.

See also: **Chemistry/Trace/Drugs of Abuse:** Analysis of Controlled Substances; **Forensic Medicine/Clinical:** Traffic Injuries and Deaths; **Foundations:** History of Forensic Sciences; Principles of Forensic Science; **Foundations/Fundamentals:** Measurement Uncertainty; **Legal:** History of the Law's Reception of Forensic Science; **Methods:** Chromatography: Basic Principles; Gas Chromatography; Spectroscopic Techniques; Spectroscopy: Basic Principles; **Toxicology:** Toxicology: History; Volatile Substances and Inhalants; **Toxicology/Alcohol:** Alcohol: Interpretation; Blood; Urine and Other Body Fluids.

Further Reading

Borkenstein, R.F., Crowther, R.F., Shumate, R.P., Ziel, W.B., Zylman, R., 1974. The role of the drinking driver in traffic accidents (The Grand Rapids Study). Blutalkohol 11, 1–131.

Cowan, J.M., Burrin, J.M., Hughes, J.R., Cunningham, M.P., 2010. The relationship of normal body temperature, end-expired breath temperature and the BAC/BrAC ratio in 98 physically fit human test subjects. Journal of Analytical Toxicology 34, 238–242.

Garriot, J.C., 2008. Garriott's Medicolegal Aspects of Alcohol, fifth ed. Lawyers and Judges Publishing Company Inc, Tuscon, AZ.

Gullberg, R.G., 2000. Methodology and quality assurance in forensic breath alcohol analysis. Forensic Science Review 12, 49–68.

Gullberg, R.G., 2004. Common legal challenges and responses in forensic breath alcohol determination. Forensic Science Review 16, 91–101.

Jones, A.W., 1990. Physiological aspects of breath alcohol measurement. Alcohol, Drugs and Driving 6, 1–25.

Jones, A.W., 1996. Measuring alcohol in blood and breath for forensic purposes – A historical review. Forensic Science Review 8, 13–44.

Jones, A.W., 2000. Medicolegal alcohol determinations – Blood or breath alcohol concentrations? Forensic Science Review 12, 23–47.

Jones, A.W., Andersson, L., 2003. Comparison of ethanol concentrations in venous blood and end-expired breath during a controlled drinking study. Forensic Science International 132, 18–25.

Kechagias, S., Jonsson, K.-A., Franzein, T., Andersson, L., Jones, A.W., 1999. Reliability of breath-alcohol analysis in individuals with gastroesophageal reflux disease. Journal of Forensic Science 44, 814–818.

Langille, R.M., Wigmore, J.G., 2000. The mouth alcohol effect after a mouthful of beer under social conditions. Canadian Society of Forensic Science Journal 33, 193–198.

Lucas, D.M., 2000. Professor Robert F. Borkenstein – An appreciation of his life and work. Forensic Science Review 12, 1–21.

Stowell, A.R., Gainsford, A.R., Gullberg, R.G., 2008. New Zealand's breath and blood alcohol testing programs: Further data analysis and forensic implications. Forensic Science International 178, 83–92.

Wigmore, J.G., Langille, R.M., 2009. Six generations of breath alcohol testing instruments: Changes in the detection of breath alcohol since, 1930. An historical overview. Canadian Society of Forensic Science Journal 42, 276–283.

Wigmore, J.G., Wilkie, M.P., 2002. A simulation of the effect of blood in the mouth on breath alcohol concentrations in drinking subjects. Canadian Society of Forensic Science Journal 35, 9–16.

Relevant Websites

www.csfs.ca—Canadian Society of Forensic Science and the Alcohol Test Committee.

www.borkensteincourse.org—Indiana University Center for Studies of Law in Action-The Robert F. Borkenstein Course.

www.iactonline.org—International Association for Chemical Testing.

www.icadts.org—International Council for Alcohol, Drugs and Traffic Safety.

www.ncjrs.gov/index.html—National Criminal Justice Reference Service- US Department of Justice.

www.nhtsa.dot.gov—National (US) Highway Traffic Safety Administration.

Metabolites of Ethanol

J Beyer, Monash University, Southbank, VIC, Australia
SC Turfus, Victorian Institute of Forensic Medicine, Southbank, VIC, Australia

Abbreviations

BW	Body weight	EtS	Ethyl sulfate
EtG	Ethyl glucuronide	FAEE	Fatty acid ethyl ester
EtP	Ethyl phosphate	PEth	Phosphatidylethanol

Introduction

The main biotransformation product of ethanol (EtOH) is acetic acid, which is produced by the oxidative pathway catalyzed by alcohol dehydrogenase. Although it accounts for more than 95% of the dose, it is not useful for diagnostic purposes and will therefore not be considered in this chapter. With less than 5% of EtOH being excreted into urine unchanged, the metabolites described here collectively account for less than 1% of the dose. Nevertheless, they are very useful diagnostic markers for EtOH consumption.

EtOH undergoes metabolism by phase II processes. A small fraction of EtOH is conjugated by uridine diphosphate-glucuronyltransferase to ethyl glucuronide (EtG) or with activated sulfate to ethyl sulfate (EtS). Another phase II reaction was described in 1972 with the formation of ethyl phosphate (EtP) in the liver of rats pretreated with large doses of EtOH.

Formation of fatty acid ethyl esters (FAEEs) is another described nonoxidative EtOH metabolic pathway, mainly formed via the enzyme O-acyltransferase. Also of interest for the detection of alcohol consumption is the EtOH metabolite phosphatidylethanol (PEth), which was detected in tissues of EtOH-exposed rats in 1984 and characterized as a specific product mediated by the enzyme phospholipase D. Importantly, PEth is only formed in the presence of EtOH. The chemical structures of metabolites and their formation are depicted in **Figure 1**.

The detection of the metabolites EtG, EtS, EtP, FAEEs, and PEth can be relevant in forensic toxicology, particularly as the time frame for detection of these metabolites is longer than that of EtOH itself. EtOH may also be detected in decomposed specimens due to fermentation. Therefore, the detection of these direct metabolites of EtOH may assist in differentiating alcohol intake from its presence due to fermentation. Detection of EtG and the FAEEs in hair samples can also be used to determine the history and extent of alcohol consumption.

Because of their implication in forensic interpretation, several methods have been developed to determine EtOH metabolites in conventional matrices such as plasma/blood and urine, as well as in alternative matrices. Indeed, the concentrations obtained in various biological matrices are usually used together to determine the cause of a positive test result.

EtG

EtG is a stable, nonvolatile, and water-soluble direct metabolite of EtOH. Although the isolation of EtG in human urine dates back to 1967, its synthesis was not reported until 1995. Since then, it has become commercially available and the added availability of pentadeuterated EtG in 1997 has greatly facilitated investigations into the metabolism and fate of EtOH, and subsequently its detection in a number of biological matrices.

EtG in Urine

After acetylation of evaporated urine and detection by gas chromatography–mass spectrometry, EtG was first quantified in the urine from drunk drivers in 1995. An improvement of the sensitivity and selectivity of EtG determination was the use of silylation instead of acetylation and the implementation of deuterium-labeled EtG (EtG-d_5). The application of the improved method showed a detection time frame up to 75 h in the urine in alcohol-withdrawal patients. Since then, many methods for the determination of EtG have been published. The maximum concentration of EtG in urine has been reported as 1790 mg l^{-1} in a drunk driver. The implementation of more sensitive instruments such as liquid chromatography–tandem

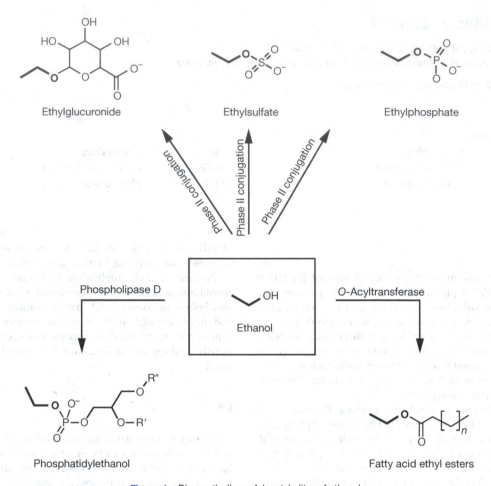

Figure 1 Diagnostically useful metabolites of ethanol.

mass spectrometry allows the detection of lower concentrations of EtG in urine by at least 10-fold. With the use of these sensitive instruments, very low concentrations of EtG in urine were described after the use of EtOH-containing hand sanitizers, mouthwashes, yeast, and sugar. These findings, in combination with low limits of detection, have led to many debates as to what cutoff should be used to determine intentional EtOH consumption with a current range of 0.1– 1.1 mg l^{-1}, with some laboratories recommending even higher cutoffs. A recent development has been the commercial availability of an immunoassay to detect EtG in urine. This now allows laboratories to adopt the convention of screening followed by confirmation of the presence of EtG in urine.

EtG in Blood or Serum

One year after the detection and quantification of EtG in urine, human blood concentrations were first described. Compared to urine, less data are available for blood and plasma concentrations. The maximum concentration of EtG in whole blood has been reported as 56 mg l^{-1}, which was found in postmortem blood. The ratio of EtG in serum/whole blood ranges from about 1.3 to 1.9.

EtG in Hair

The first publication for the determination of EtG in hair appeared in 2000. The advantages of testing for EtG in hair are well documented; hair is relatively noninvasively collected, is difficult to adulterate, and most importantly provides the best retrospective detection compared with other matrices, assuming there is specimen available for collection. Interestingly, the most concentrated hair sample was shown to contain 14 ng mg^{-1} of EtG, which was found in the hair of a socially acceptable alcohol user at autopsy, but the reason for this is unknown.

EtG in Other Specimens

EtG can be detected in various postmortem specimens such as vitreous humor, fat, liver, and bone marrow. Liver showed the highest concentration of EtG with up to 77 $\mu g\, g^{-1}$ tissue. The same study also showed the presence of EtG in bone marrow, which is often still available in cases of extensive decomposition and thus could be a useful tissue where other specimens are unavailable. Vitreous humor has also shown to be a more reliable matrix than blood, and concentrations of up to 9.4 $mg\, l^{-1}$ have been detected in this matrix. Vitreous humor is a reliable matrix as it is remote from gut bacteria, which can potentially produce or break down EtG. This phenomenon is complicated by the presence of an already high EtOH concentration in the matrix and/or a urinary tract infection. In addition, the presence of a high concentration of glucose, either due to the consumption of certain foods or the levels produced among diabetics, could potentially result in fermentation followed by the production of EtG from EtOH. The EtG in vitreous humor is far less susceptible to these effects. The average concentrations in cadavers are about 63, 4.3, and 2.1 $mg\, l^{-1}$ for urine, blood, and vitreous humor, respectively. Thus, although concentrations of EtG in vitreous humor are lower than in either blood or urine, it has been shown to be a more reliable matrix.

Interpretation of EtG Concentrations

The measurement of EtG as a marker for compliance in alcohol abstinence has resulted in many laboratories routinely testing for EtG in urine. Testing for selectivity and robustness are vital when methods are modified by other laboratories to avoid false positive results. The majority of positive samples usually have concentrations below 100 $mg\, l^{-1}$. Based on current knowledge, the formation of EtG is not possible without the presence of EtOH. Interpretation of low EtG concentrations (e.g., below 10 $mg\, l^{-1}$) should also factor the possibility of an intake of low amounts of EtOH, for example, in low alcoholic beverages. In cases where trace amounts of EtG (e.g., below 0.5 $mg\, l^{-1}$) are detected, the possibility of EtG formation due to the presence of EtOH from other sources (other than alcoholic drinks) should be considered.

Controlled drinking experiments have shown that after the intake of low amounts of EtOH, EtG was detectable in urine. An intake of 0.1 $g\, kg^{-1}$ body weight (BW) of EtOH showed peak concentrations of 0.2–8.4 $mg\, l^{-1}$ and an intake of 0.5 $g\, kg^{-1}$ BW showed maximum concentrations of 41–73 $mg\, l^{-1}$. In this study, EtG was detectable in urine for 30 h, whereas EtOH was detectable in urine for only 7 h. Maximum concentrations after an intake of EtOH of 0.2 $g\, kg^{-1}$ BW is about 0.7–2.9 $mg\, l^{-1}$. Due to interindividual differences in absolute EtG urine concentrations and the influence of several factors (e.g., dilution of urine),

it is not possible to estimate the amount of EtOH consumed based on EtG concentrations in urine.

Blood EtG concentrations are significantly lower than those in urine with the majority of published levels below 10 $mg\, l^{-1}$. These studies show no correlation between blood EtOH and blood EtG concentrations. Consequently, back calculations of the amount of EtOH consumed prior to sample collection are not possible if only EtG is present in the blood. Low blood concentrations of EtG can result from heavy drinking many hours prior to sample collection or resulting from the intake of small amounts of alcohol shortly prior to collection. Maximum EtG blood concentrations are about 0.3–0.5 $mg\, l^{-1}$ after intake of 0.5 $g\, kg^{-1}$ BW of EtOH. Maximum concentrations of EtOH are reached between 0.5 and 2 h after controlled intake of EtOH, whereas maximum EtG concentrations are reached between 3.5 and 5 h. The EtOH/EtG ratio in blood (EtOH in g l^{-1} vs. EtG in $mg\, l^{-1}$) is >1 in the first 2.5 h after ingestion, after which it drops to <1 until EtG is no longer detectable. Therefore, a ratio of EtOH/EtG < 1 may indicate that the alcohol had been ingested more than 2.5 h before sampling. Although a single intake of alcohol is relatively uncommon in communities where drinking is acceptable, this ratio could help to interpret alleged drinking after driving. For the interpretation of EtG concentrations in blood after multiple ingestions of alcohol, interpretation is not as straightforward and no simple rules are currently available.

For the interpretation of a person's history of alcohol abuse, hair analysis for EtG can be useful. However, false negative results also occur. In hair samples from social drinkers, the detection of EtG is uncommon. In 2005, EtG hair concentrations below 8 $pg\, mg^{-1}$ appeared to be suggestive of teetotalers and those containing above 25 $pg\, mg^{-1}$ suggested chronic alcohol abuse. However, concentrations above 25 $pg\, mg^{-1}$ of EtG in hair have been detected in social drinkers and, conversely, concentrations below 25 $pg\, mg^{-1}$ have been detected in hair samples from known alcoholics, suggesting that the use of such cutoffs in hair may not be appropriate to distinguish these groups.

In postmortem samples, the detection of EtG is a marker of antemortem alcohol consumption and can distinguish from postmortem formation of alcohol from microbial contamination or fermentation in the body after death. However, it has also been shown that EtG can be degraded by bacteria present during decomposition processes where fresh clinical urine specimens with confirmed bacterial growth showed a degradation of spiked EtG of 60–100% after 5 days of storage at room temperature. Other markers such as EtS or EtP may be useful for the determination of antemortem consumption. Based on current knowledge, the presence of EtG in postmortem samples indicates alcohol consumption antemortem in most cases. However, the absence of EtG does not exclude the possibility of alcohol consumption antemortem due to possible degradation.

EtS

EtOH undergoes conjugation with sulfates via the enzyme sulfatransferase. In 2004, EtS was found to be present in humans after ingestion of EtOH. Since the first reporting of EtS as a human metabolite, there are few data to suggest its presence in human urine from subjects either withdrawing from alcohol abuse or in postmortem tissues. In urine, the maximum concentration that has been found is 264 mg l^{-1}. As for EtG, the concentrations of EtS detected in urine also vary considerably, although there appears to be a weak correlation between EtG and EtS concentrations in postmortem urine samples.

In general, EtS is often not detected in blood samples from either social drinkers or alcoholics. Nevertheless, persons who had considerable exposure to EtOH had average concentrations of 55, 1.8, and 0.9 mg l^{-1} for urine, blood, and vitreous humor, respectively. Up to 4.1 mg l^{-1} of EtS can be detected in vitreous humor. Currently, no method for the detection of EtS in hair has been published. EtS may be a better marker for proof of antemortem alcohol consumption instead of EtG due to it being less prone to degradation by bacteria.

Both EtG and EtS have been found in wine with concentrations of EtS up to 10 times higher than concentrations of EtG.

EtP

EtP was first described in animal studies in 1972. The study reported the presence of EtP in the liver of rats pretreated with high doses of EtOH. The concentrations of EtP found in the postmortem urine specimens are substantially lower than EtG and EtS concentrations. A maximum concentration of 0.15 mg l^{-1} occurs 2 h after the ingestion of a single dose (0.2 g kg^{-1}) of EtOH. There are few other data on EtP concentrations and its potential use as a marker to detect alcohol consumption.

FAEEs

In the past, the detection of FAEEs was mainly used to explain organ damage caused by heavy EtOH consumption. In 1989, Laposata et al. demonstrated the use of FAEEs in adipose tissue as a possible marker for chronic EtOH ingestion. In the last years, these metabolites have been detected in various specimens for forensic medical purposes. Whole reviews are dedicated exclusively to the subject in different matrices, such as meconium and hair, and the interested reader is referred to these for more information.

FAEEs in Hair

In forensic toxicology, FAEEs are mainly detected and quantified in hair. More than 15 FAEEs have so far been detected, but only four esters—ethyl myristate, ethyl palmitate, ethyl oleate, and ethyl stearate—have been chosen as markers of EtOH consumption, as they have the highest concentrations in hair. The FAEEs are incorporated into hair mainly from sebum due to their high lipophilic properties. The sum concentrations of the four main FAEEs in hair can be up to 44 ng mg^{-1}, a concentration that was determined after autopsy.

FAEEs in Other Specimens

In addition to FAEEs detection in hair, these nonoxidative metabolites of EtOH have also been detected in meconium and various postmortem tissues. Concentrations between 0.065 and 174 ng mg^{-1} have been observed in the meconium of babies born to women abstaining from EtOH consumption. In the meconium of babies from nonabstaining women, the concentrations ranged from 0.124 to 1268 ng mg^{-1}.

FAEEs have also been determined in postmortem tissues. Due to the lipophilic properties of FAEEs, concentrations in postmortem tissues such as adipose, blood, brain, and liver have been reported. The highest concentrations of FAEEs were found in liver, where values were up to 569 pmol mg^{-1}.

Interpretation of FAEE Concentrations

FAEEs have been detected in specimens from teetotalers, nondrinkers, and children from women abstaining from alcohol consumption. It is therefore necessary for cutoff levels to be determined to avoid misinterpretation when using FAEEs as a marker for alcohol consumption.

In hair analysis, it is common to use the sum concentration of ethyl myristate, ethyl palmitate, ethyl oleate, and ethyl stearate as a marker of alcohol consumption. For chronic excessive alcohol consumption, a cutoff value of 0.5 ng mg^{-1} has been proposed.

Meconium analysis faces similar problems as hair in the interpretation of concentrations of FAEEs. Ethyl linoate appears to be the best marker in meconium analysis for differentiation between abstaining and nonabstaining women due to a sensitivity and specificity of this marker of 88% and 64%, respectively. This low specificity should be carefully considered in the interpretation of meconium analysis as false negative reports can occur.

PEth

The formation of PEth in rat organs after EtOH treatment was first described in 1984. The formation of PEth in various rat organs occurs via transphosphatidylation, which is catalyzed by the enzyme phospholipase D. Although PEth was already discussed in 1988 as a possible marker for alcoholism, blood concentrations of PEth were only first described in 1997. Alcoholics have a mean concentration of about 13 µmol l^{-1} of PEth at the first sampling, and PEth remains detectable for up to 14 days, in contrast with blood EtOH, which could not be detected the morning after admission. PEth concentrations are the highest in blood of alcoholics compared to other organs and body fluids. This marker can be produced postmortem in blood if EtOH is present in this matrix. It appears that humans do not have enzymes to break down PEth in blood, and PEth accumulates in the red blood cells but can be degraded in HepG2 cell lines. PEth is a specific marker of alcohol consumption to humans as it is only detectable after moderate drinking. PEth is not detected in the blood of healthy volunteers following the consumption of a single dose (32–47 g) of EtOH, although it can be detected in people who have ingested much higher doses. In contrast, 75% of students with prolonged alcohol consumption (average 48–102 g day^{-1} for 3 weeks) have detectable PEth.

PEth concentrations vary substantially between blood and plasma, with only 10–14% of the concentration in plasma as there is in blood. Considering the lipophilic properties of PEth, this marker may not be incorporated in hair in significant amounts.

Therefore, PEth may be considered an appropriate marker for alcohol consumption and abuse, but additional data are necessary to determine its sensitivity and specificity, especially in matrices other than blood.

Summary and Conclusion

Alcohol consumption may be determined not only by the detection of EtOH itself but also by the measurement of various direct metabolites. The detection of alcohol metabolites is of forensic interest in cases where EtOH is either not detectable or was possibly formed via postmortem decomposition.

The detection of minor metabolites of EtOH in biological matrices provides an ability to obtain more information on the possible consumption of EtOH. Postmortem detection of EtOH is not conclusive of antemortem alcohol consumption due to the possible EtOH formation as a result of microbial contamination or fermentation in the body after death. To avoid misinterpretation, EtG is used as the main direct biochemical marker of antemortem alcohol consumption in a number of biological matrices.

Different markers will have different purposes. For example, the detection of EtG in urine is suitable for the detection of alcohol intake a few days prior to collection and may be suitable for detecting a single dose. Hair analysis is useful for detecting drinking pattern and possibly monitoring abstention whereas detection of alcoholism.

See also: **Toxicology/Alcohol:** Alcohol Congeners and the Source of Ethanol; **Alcohol:** Interpretation; Blood; Breath Alcohol; Urine and Other Body Fluids.

Further Reading

Appenzeller, B.M., Agirman, R., Neuberg, P., Yegles, M., Wennig, R., 2007. Segmental determination of ethyl glucuronide in hair: A pilot study. Forensic Science International 173, 87–92.

Aradottir, S., Seidl, S., Wurst, F.M., Jonsson, B.A., Alling, C., 2004. Phosphatidylethanol in human organs and blood: A study on autopsy material and influences by storage conditions. Alcoholism, Clinical and Experimental Research 28, 1718–1723.

Bisaga, A., Laposata, M., Xie, S., Evans, S.M., 2005. Comparison of serum fatty acid ethyl esters and urinary 5-hydroxytryptophol as biochemical markers of recent ethanol consumption. Alcohol and Alcoholism 40, 214–218.

Borucki, K., Schreiner, R., Dierkes, J., et al., 2005. Detection of recent ethanol intake with new markers: Comparison of fatty acid ethyl esters in serum and of ethyl glucuronide and the ratio of 5-hydroxytryptophol to 5-hydroxyindole acetic acid in urine. Alcoholism, Clinical and Experimental Research 29, 781–787.

Bottcher, M., Beck, O., Helander, A., 2008. Evaluation of a new immunoassay for urinary ethyl glucuronide testing. Alcohol and Alcoholism 43, 46–48.

Doyle, K.M., Bird, D.A., al-Salihi, S., et al., 1994. Fatty acid ethyl esters are present in human serum after ethanol ingestion. Journal of Lipid Research 35, 428–437.

Drummer, O.H., Odell, M., 2001. The Forensic Pharmacology of Drugs of Abuse. Arnold, London.

Garriott, J.C., 2003. Medical-Legal Aspects of Alcohol, fourth ed. Lawyers & Judges Publishing Company, Inc, Tucson, AZ.

Hansson, P., Caron, M., Johnson, G., Gustavsson, L., Alling, C., 1997. Blood phosphatidylethanol as a marker of alcohol abuse: Levels in alcoholic males during withdrawal. Alcoholism, Clinical and Experimental Research 21, 108–110.

Helander, A., Beck, O., 2005. Ethyl sulfate: A metabolite of ethanol in humans and a potential biomarker of acute alcohol intake. Journal of Analytical Toxicology 29, 270–274.

Helander, A., Dahl, H., 2005. Urinary tract infection: a risk factor for false-negative urinary ethyl glucuronide but not ethyl sulfate in the detection of recent alcohol consumption. Clinical Chemistry 51, 1728–1730.

Helander, A., Olsson, I., Dahl, H., 2007. Postcollection synthesis of ethyl glucuronide by bacteria in urine may cause false identification of alcohol consumption. Clinical Chemistry 53, 1855–1857.

Hoiseth, G., Bernard, J.P., Karinen, R., et al., 2007. A pharmacokinetic study of ethyl glucuronide in blood and urine: Applications to forensic toxicology. Forensic Science International 172, 119–124.

Moffat, A.C., Osselton, M.D., Widdop, B., 2004. Clarke's Analysis of Drugs and Poisons, thirrd ed., vol. 1. Pharmaceutical Press, London.

Mueller, G.C., Fleming, M.F., LeMahieu, M.A., Lybrand, G.S., Barry, K.J., 1988. Synthesis of phosphatidylethanol – A potential marker for adult males at risk for alcoholism. Proceedings of the National Academy of Sciences of the United States of America 85, 9778–9782.

Musshoff, F., Albermann, E., Madea, B., 2010. Ethyl glucuronide and ethyl sulfate in urine after consumption of various beverages and foods – Misleading results? International Journal of Legal Medicine 124, 623–630.

Palmer, R.B., 2009. A review of the use of ethyl glucuronide as a marker for ethanol consumption in forensic and clinical medicine. Seminars in Diagnostic Pathology 26, 18–27.

Schmitt, G., Aderjan, R., Keller, T., Wu, M., 1995. Ethyl glucuronide: An unusual ethanol metabolite in humans. Synthesis, analytical data, and determination in serum and urine. Journal of Analytical Toxicology 19, 91–94.

Thierauf, A., Kempf, J., Perdekamp, M.G., et al., 2011. Ethyl sulphate and ethyl glucuronide in vitreous humor as postmortem evidence marker for ethanol consumption prior to death. Forensic Science International 210 (1–3), 63–68.

Tomaszewski, M., Buchowicz, J., 1972. Alcoholysis of the endogenous phosphate esters in rats treated with large doses of ethanol. Biochemical Journal 129, 183–186.

Yegles, M., Labarthe, A., Auwarter, V., et al., 2004. Comparison of ethyl glucuronide and fatty acid ethyl ester concentrations in hair of alcoholics, social drinkers and teetotallers. Forensic Science International 145, 167–173.

Relevant Website

http://etg.weebly.com/index.html.

Oral Fluid

OH Drummer, Monash University, Southbank, VIC, Australia

Glossary

Cutoff Concentration above which a positive result is reported.

pH The logarithm of the concentration of hydrogen ions of water; pH 7 refers to a neutral situation.

pK_a The pH at which half of the molecule exists in ionized form.

Introduction

Some parts of the community are known to misuse legal drugs, for example, sedatives and pain-relieving medications, for obtaining relief from pain and in case of ill health, while other persons use illegal drugs such as cannabis (marijuana), cocaine, and one or more of the amphetamines for recreational reasons. Persons who use drugs on a long-term basis have often increased their dose due to their developing tolerance and have also become dependent on them, making it very difficult to stop using them. This pattern of use leads to a pattern of addiction that not only controls their lives but is also associated with adverse symptoms and drug-seeking behaviors. Impaired cognition, and poorer reaction times and coordination skills can lead to an increased accident risk, whether it is at the workplace or while driving a motorized vehicle. The ability to screen persons rapidly for potential use of impairing drugs has become a significant safety issue.

For many years, drug tests using urine have been performed to determine if one or more of the targeted drugs of abuse are present in the body. For the most part, urine testing only provides information on past use, usually within 1–3 days of collection and can reveal very little about drugs being actually present in blood at the time of collection. While urine is still a useful specimen, there has been a trend to use oral fluid to test for drug use.

Drugs can be present in oral fluid, which can be collected without great inconvenience to the subject, whereas urine can be collected only in toilet facilities, and blood requires venipuncture by a specially trained person, which may be regarded as invasive by the subject when there may not be actual evidence of drug use by him/her.

This chapter provides an overview of the use of oral fluid in forensic toxicology.

What Is Oral Fluid?

Oral fluid is sometimes called saliva, but it is actually a composite of a number of fluids (including saliva) secreted into the oral cavity. These are secreted primarily by three glands: the parotid, submaxillary, and sublingual glands, as well as by other smaller glands. Oral fluid is of variable viscosity and pH depending on a range of physiological variables and can vary in flow from almost zero to several milliliters per minute.

The mechanism of drug transport from blood to oral fluid is largely by passive diffusion to non-protein bound and non-ionized molecules with a low molecular weight. Oral fluid contains predominantly the parent drug because the higher lipid solubility of parent drugs allows passive diffusion. Consequently, drugs with high lipid solubility tend to have higher concentrations. There are also differences in the concentration of drugs in the various secretions, and as these secretions are dependent on variable factors, the overall concentration of drug is not easy to predict.

Collection of Oral Fluid

The most common way to collect fluids in the mouth is the use of a material that absorbs fluids on and around the tongue similar to a cotton bud. This is allowed to be in the mouth for a few to several minutes until sufficient fluid has been absorbed. This is then added to a diluent (aqueous buffered solution) that dilutes the oral fluid and makes it more amenable to analysis.

Neat oral fluid is also used. This involves expectoration or spitting a sample into a plain collection tube. While this provides neat (undiluted) oral fluid, it is relatively viscous and can make accurate sampling difficult. As it may also be contaminated with food and other debris from the mouth, it will, therefore, require filtration or centrifugation.

If only initial testing is required, a simple swab of fluid on the tongue or the inside of the cheek can provide sufficient sample for a rapid drug test. However, if this test is positive, there is no oral fluid for any second or confirmatory test. This will then require a second collection.

Hunger will stimulate production of oral fluids, while inadequate hydration and certain drugs such as the amphetamines and cannabis can reduce production.

When oral fluid content and/or flow is suboptimal, it will require a much longer collection time to collect a small volume of oral fluid. It may take several minutes to collect <1 ml of oral fluid.

One of the potential pitfalls related to the use of absorbent swabs in the collection of oral fluid is that there may be some loss of drug on the swab itself. There have been many examples in the past of severe losses of drug on this surface leading to false-negative results (i.e., drug was present, but the test was negative). Hence, it is good practice to test for recovery of drugs as quickly as possible after use and ensure that the testing process is sufficiently reliable and sensitive.

Factors Affecting Drug Presence in Oral Fluids

Drugs in oral fluid are for the most part in equilibrium with drug in the blood, particularly drug in blood plasma that is not bound to proteins (so-called free fraction). The concentration of drug in oral fluid is also dependent on the respective pH of the two fluids and the pK_a of the drug in question.

For example, the oral fluid to plasma concentration ratio (O/P) for a basic drug with pK_a and free fraction from protein binding in plasma (f_p) and oral fluid (f_o), at the respective pH of the fluids (pH_o and pH_p) is given by the following equation:

$$O/P = \frac{1 + 10^{(pH_o - pK_a)}}{1 + 10^{(pH_p - pK_a)}} \times \frac{f_p}{f_o}$$

Drugs with high pK_a are usually unionized at pH around 7 (e.g., amphetamines) and will, therefore, have a relatively high concentration in oral fluid compared to drugs with a low pK_a (i.e., acidic drugs such as the benzodiazepines).

The normal pH of oral fluids is between 6.2 and 7.4; however, this can vary depending on time of day, food, age, health, and the use of certain drugs. Oral fluid production is stimulated by the use of lollies that contain citric acid, chewing gum, or other agents. When this occurs, the concentration of basic drugs such as cocaine, codeine (and probably other opiates), and the amphetamines drops substantially due to the lowering of the pH affecting the equilibrium between oral fluid and plasma.

In practice, the oral fluid/plasma (blood) concentration ratio is not constant because the pH of oral fluid changes and for some drugs, local absorption in the mucosa of the oral cavity results in oral fluid concentrations that are higher than expected. This latter effect is particularly pronounced for Δ^9-tetrahydrocannabinol (THC) as the drug is usually smoked and being fat soluble, it is absorbed into the mucosal membranes and slowly released over several hours. However, for some drugs, there is a weak correlation between a blood/plasma concentration and an oral fluid concentration and the degree of impairment. Hence oral fluid is favored as alternative for blood/plasma since it is much more likely to indicate recent use and likely impairment whereas urine does not have this association. Table 1 provides an indication of the oral fluid to blood concentration ratios for selected drugs of abuse.

A number of drugs affect the secretion of oral fluid including amphetamines, sedating antihistamines, antipsychotic drugs, anticholinergic drugs, and a number of antidepressants, and cannabis. There are a few drugs that increase flow including β_2 bronchostimulants (e.g., salbutamol).

Mouth rinsing with water will reduce the concentration temporarily by leaching out some drug in the mucous membranes, but the equilibrium will reestablish with 10–15 min. The use of commercial products designed to act as adulterants (e.g., mouth washes) have been shown to have little effect after 30 min.

Applications of Oral Fluid Drug Testing

One of the largest applications for oral fluid has been testing drivers suspected of using drugs. In Australia, for example, most states and territories have widespread mass screening programs to test drivers at the roadside without cause in order to deter

Table 1   Average oral fluid to blood concentration ratios for selected drugs of abuse

Drug (type)	Average oral fluid to blood concentration ratio
Alcohol (ethanol)	1.07
Amphetamines (e.g., methamphetamine, amphetamine, 3,4-methylenedioxymethamphetamine)	2–20
Barbiturates (e.g., amobarbital, pentobarbital)	0.1–0.5
Benzodiazepines (e.g., alprazolam, diazepam)	<0.05
Cocaine	2–5
Opiates (e.g., codeine, morphine, methadone)	2–5
Tetrahydrocannabinol	10–20

The average ratios are indicative figures and will change depending on a number of factors.

drivers using illicit drugs, particularly methamphetamine, ecstasy, and cannabis. Similar testing is being trialed in Europe. In this process, the initial test is a swipe on the tongue while the driver is still behind the steering wheel after having passed a breath test for alcohol. If this test is positive for one of the targeted drug classes, the police require the driver to leave his/her vehicle and submit to a collection of oral fluid at a neighboring facility, usually a specially outfitted van or bus parked nearby. If a further test for these drug classes is positive using another screening device, the remaining specimen is sent to a forensic laboratory for confirmatory testing, and the driver is not allowed to continue driving. A confirmed positive results in a penalty.

Oral fluid testing is also used at workplaces in safety critical industries such as transportation (road, rail, and aviation), mining, construction, and petrochemical industries. It can also be used on prisoners and on persons suspected of a crime and who are also suspected of being under the influence of a drug.

However, it should not be seen as a replacement or a substitute for urine testing. Urine testing can usually provide a longer window of detection than oral fluid, although for some drugs with a high oral fluid to blood ratio, the detection window may be similar if low detection limits in oral fluid are used. It is recommended that detection limits in oral fluid, usually referred to as cutoffs, are sufficiently low to detect reasonable use of drug but not too low to detect beyond a time when a person might be adversely affected by the drug.

For example, confirmatory testing limits of THC in oral fluid of 10 ng ml^{-1} reflect use of cannabis for several hours, whereas lowering the cutoff to 2 ng ml^{-1} may allow detection for at least 24 h.

Oral fluid has been used in clinical settings to monitor use of therapeutic drugs. These have been used for some anticonvulsant drugs, digoxin, methadone, some anticancer drugs, and a number of steroids. Even ethanol (alcohol) can be measured in oral fluid as a quick screening method if breath testing is not possible.

Analytical Testing Methods

Field testing, point-of-care testing, or on-site testing is commonly employed. A number of devices are available for such use and include handheld cartridges for visual assessment of test results to small instruments that automate the process and can provide an electronic reading of the test result. At this point, there is no consistency in the specifications applied to these devices including sensitivity and detection limit (or cutoff), and specificity. This means that at the present moment, there is no easy way to assess the performance of these devices or cartridges without personal evaluation.

Currently, these devices are largely based on lateral flow immunoassay; hence, they will not detect all members of a drug class equally. For example, for the amphetamine and benzodiazepine classes the required sensitivities will be different for the various members of these classes and their individual concentrations are quite different to that of blood. For example, benzodiazepines have much lower concentrations in oral fluid compared to blood, and only the lower potency members can be detected in oral fluid with any frequency.

Laboratory-based testing using commercial kits based on enzyme-linked immunosorbent assay technology is much more reliable than on-site testing and will produce a lower false-positive and false-negative rate. Laboratory testing can be done under more controlled conditions including temperature control and use of appropriate standards and quality controls.

All initial tests need to be confirmed by mass spectral methods. These may include gas chromatography–mass spectrometry or liquid chromatography–mass spectrometry. Numerous methods have been published, some in which multiple analytes can be confirmed in one analytical schema. The choice of method is largely dependent on its availability in a laboratory and the sample volume. Low sample volumes (under 0.5 ml) may require the more sensitive tandem mass spectrometry methods.

Unfortunately, there are no agreed laboratory methods for this form of testing with each jurisdiction applying different cutoff concentrations. This is largely reflected by the relative immaturity of this form of testing. This is likely to change as experience in the use of this specimen in forensic toxicology increases.

See also: **Toxicology:** Methods of Analysis—Confirmatory Testing; Methods of Analysis—Initial Testing; **Toxicology/Drugs of Abuse:** Drugs in Hair; Postmortem Blood; Urine.

Further Reading

Allen, K.R., 2011. Screening for drugs of abuse: Which matrix, oral fluid or urine? Annals of Clinical Biochemistry 48, 531–541.

Aps, J.K., Martens, L.C., 2005. Review: The physiology of saliva and transfer of drugs into saliva. Forensic Science International 150 (2–3), 119–131.

Bosker, W.M., Huestis, M.A., 2009. Oral fluid testing for drugs of abuse. Clinical Chemistry 55 (11), 1910–1931.

Caplan, Y.H., Goldberger, B.A., 2001. Alternative specimens for workplace drug testing. Journal of Analytical Toxicology 25 (5), 396–399.

Choo, R.E., Huestis, M.A., 2004. Oral fluid as a diagnostic tool. Clinical Chemistry and Laboratory Medicine 42 (11), 1273–1287.

Drummer, O.H., 2005. Review: pharmacokinetics of illicit drugs in oral fluid. Forensic Science International 150 (2–3), 133–142.

Drummer, O.H., 2008. Introduction and review of collection techniques and applications of drug testing of oral fluid. Therapeutic Drug Monitoring 30 (2), 203–206.

Kadehjian, L., 2005. Legal issues in oral fluid testing. Forensic Science International 150 (2–3), 151–160.

Vearrier, D., Curtis, J.A., Greenberg, M.I., 2010. Biological testing for drugs of abuse. EXS 100, 489–517.

Verstraete, A.G., 2004. Detection times of drugs of abuse in blood, urine, and oral fluid. Therapeutic Drug Monitoring 26 (2), 200–205.

Walsh, J.M., de Gier, J.J., Christopherson, A.S., Verstraete, A.G., 2004. Drugs and driving. Traffic Injury Prevention 5 (3), 241–253.

Relevant Websites

http://www.ncbi.nlm.nih.gov.
http://www.parliament.uk/documents/post/postpn228.pdf.
http://www.samhsa.gov.
http://www.standards.org.au.

Drugs in Hair

P Kintz, X-Pertise Consulting, Oberhausbergen, France

Glossary

Anabolic steroids Steroids with anabolic properties.
Beta-adrenoceptor agonists Agonists of the beta-adrenergic receptors.
Corticoids Gluco- and mineralocorticoids.
ELISA Enzyme immunoassay.

GC–MS Gas chromatography coupled to mass spectrometry.
MS Mass spectrometry.
RIA Radioimmunoassay.
Tandem MS Triple quadrupole mass spectrometry.

Introduction

Using hair as a medium to analyze drug exposure has received increased attention in recent times because of the less embarrassing circumstances of collection, its long drug detection window, and because it does not decompose like other body tissues after death.

In 1979, Baumgartner and colleagues published the pioneering report on using radioimmunoassay to detect morphine in the hair of heroin abusers. Today, chromatographic procedures, especially those coupled with mass spectrometry (MS) or tandem MS, represent the gold standard for the identification and quantification of drugs in hair, owing to their higher sensitivity and specificity.

Hair analysis is now routinely used as a tool for detection of xenobiotics (drugs of abuse, pharmaceuticals, environmental contaminants, doping agents, etc.) in forensic science, traffic medicine, occupational medicine, and clinical toxicology.

This chapter summarizes and discusses some applications and methods used in hair analysis.

Biology of Hair

Hair is a product of differentiated organs in the skin of mammals composed of protein (65–95%, keratin essentially), water (15–35%), lipids (1–9%), and minerals (<1%). The hair shaft consists of an outer cuticle that surrounds a cortex. In some types of hair, a central medulla surrounds the cortex. The hair shaft develops in a follicle closely associated with the sebaceous and apocrine glands. The growth of hair occurs in cycles, alternating between periods of growth (*anagen* phase) and periods of quiescence (*catagen* and *telogen* phases). About the 1 million hair follicles of the adult scalp, comprising approximately 85% of the hair, are in the growing phase and the remaining 15% is in a quiescent stage. Hair is produced during 4–8 years for head hair (<6 months for nonhead hair) at a rate of approximately 0.22–0.52 mm day^{-1} or 0.6–1.42 cm month^{-1} for head hair. The growth rate depends on type of hair, physiological factors, and the anatomical location.

The exact mechanism by which chemicals are bound in hair is not known, but it is generally considered that xenobiotics can enter hair by at least three mechanisms: from the blood during formation of hair in the follicle, from transfer of substances in sweat and sebum, and from the external environment.

Hair is best collected from the area at the back of the head, called the *vertex posterior*. Compared with other areas of the head, this area has less variability in the hair growth rate, the number of hairs in the growing phase is more constant, and the hair is less subject to age- and sex-related influences. Pubic hair, arm hair, and axillary hair are possible alternative sources for drug detection when scalp hair is not available; however, interpretation is more complex.

Hair Analysis

The most crucial issue facing hair analysis is the avoidance of false-positive results caused by passive exposure to the drug. In most laboratories, hair analysis starts with a wash step to remove external contamination.

Hair analysis involves at least five steps:

1. decontamination of the hair;
2. preparation of the hair: pulverization, segmentation into short segments;

3. incubation: in methanol, acid, sodium hydroxide, buffer
4. extraction: liquid/liquid, solid phase, solid-phase micro-extraction; and
5. analysis: enzyme-linked immunosorbent assay (ELISA) and/or chromatography (gas, liquid) coupled to mass spectrometry (tandem MS).

Cutoff concentrations from the Society of Hair Testing (SoHT) and expected concentrations in hair for drugs of abuse are presented in **Table 1**.

These cutoffs were established to avoid false-positive results due to external contamination. They are used both for ELISA screening and chromatographic confirmations in workplace drug testing. In most cases, they are not applied in forensic cases, where sometimes a single exposure has to be demonstrated.

ELISA technique, daily used by numerous laboratories to screen xenobiotics in hair, requires hair decontamination, followed by a thin grinding of the specimen and its incubation in methanol. After evaporation of the solvent, appropriate buffer is added to the dry extract and ELISA is performed following the procedures (same as for blood and urine) of the manufacturers.

Applications

Verification of History of Drug Use

By providing information on exposure to drugs over time, hair analysis may be useful in verifying self-reported histories of drug use in any situation in which a history of past rather than recent drug use is desired. During controlled studies, a drug user is not able to hide their drug abuse as the window of detection is often so long, that is, months. Urine or blood tests are not useful to detect drug use when drugs are consumed every few days even when the tests are repeated.

The advantages and disadvantages of drug detection in urine and hair are presented in **Table 2**.

Hair analysis can also provide a retrospective calendar of an individual's drug use. For this, multisectional analysis is

Table 1 Society of Hair Testing cutoff concentrations (when tested by gas chromatography (GC)/mass spectrometry (MS) and expected concentrations for drugs of abuse in hair

Drug	GC/MS cutoff concentration	Expected concentrations
Heroin	0.2 ng mg^{-1} of 6-acetylmorphine, morphine	0.5–100 ng mg^{-1}, in most cases <15 ng mg^{-1}
Cocaine	0.5 ng mg^{-1} of cocaine and 0.05 ng mg^{-1} of benzoylecgonine and cocaethylene	0.5–100 ng mg^{-1}, in most cases <50 ng mg^{-1}, in crack abusers >300 ng mg^{-1} is possible
Amphetamine, MDMA	0.2 ng mg^{-1} for each drug	0.5–50.0 ng mg^{-1}
Cannabis	0.1 ng mg^{-1} for THC	THC: 0.05–10 ng mg^{-1}, in most cases <2 ng mg^{-1}
	0.2 pg mg^{-1} for THC-COOH	THC-COOH: 0.5–50 pg mg^{-1}, in most cases <5 pg mg^{-1}

MDMA, 3,4-Methylenedioxymethamphetamine; THC, Δ^9-tetrahydrocannabinol; THC-COOH, Tetrahydrocannabinol-11-oic-acid.

Table 2 Main characteristics and performance of analyses in urine and hair

	Urine	Hair
Drugs of abuse and pharmaceuticals detected[a]	All	All
Main compounds	Metabolites	Parent drugs and metabolites
Detection time window	2–3 days	Months, years
Analytical techniques	Immunoassays, followed by chromatography/mass spectrometry	Immunoassays, followed by chromatography/mass spectrometry
Specificity	Pharmacological group identification, then specific confirmation	Pharmacological group identification, then specific confirmation
Analysis duration	+	+++
Type of measurement	Incremental	Cumulative
Sample collection	± Invasive	Noninvasive
Adulteration	Possible	Unlikely[b]
Preservation	−20 °C	Ambient temperature

[a]Only doping hormones (erythropoietin, growth hormone, etc.) are not incorporated in hair.
[b]Cosmetic treatment will reduce concentrations.

required and involves taking a length of hair and cutting it into sections to measure drug use during shorter periods of time. The hair must be cut as close as possible to the scalp and particular care is also required to ensure that the individual hairs in the cutoff tuft retain their original orientation.

The most extensive study on sectional analysis for drugs of abuse has involved patients in rehabilitation centers. Segmental hair analysis is used to verify both their previous drug history and their recent enforced abstinence. To verify abstinence, the lowest drug concentration is found in the segments nearest the root.

The differentiation of heroin users from individuals exposed to other sources of morphine-based alkaloids can be achieved by identifying directly heroin or its metabolite, 6-acetylmorphine.

Hair analysis is suitable for accurately monitoring relative changes in drug intake in the same individual. In several studies (although there is a lot of variability from one person to another), it has been shown that a doubling of drug dose in the same individual results in an approximate doubling of the drug content in the hair, which is not always the case for blood and urine drug level. Patients who received constant methadone doses under close supervision should show some constancy in their methadone levels in hair.

Several studies have suggested that the hair color (or the melanin content) may be the major determinant of drug binding and, consequently, may result in color bias in hair testing. Researchers have demonstrated that different hair types incorporate differing amounts of drugs when exposed under identical conditions. The higher accumulation of alkaline substances (such as cocaine or heroin) in black hair when compared with blond hair will need to be addressed (or controlled) in order not to discriminate specific ethnic groups due to hair color.

Alcohol Abuse

Considering the large scale of alcohol-associated problems, the diagnosis of excessive alcohol consumption is an important task from a medical and legal point of view. Major markers of ethanol consumption in hair are ethyl glucuronide (EtG) and fatty acid ethyl esters (FAEEs). Detection of EtG in hair is associated with excessive alcohol consumption, whereas a negative result does not unambiguously exclude the alcohol abuse. Investigations on the FAEE can also be used to monitor excessive alcohol consumption. FAEEs are formed in the presence of ethanol and free fatty acids, triglycerides, lipoproteins, or phospholipids by an FAEE synthase found in liver and also in hair roots. FAEE determination is of interest as they appear responsive to alcohol-induced organ damage. Four FAEEs (ethyl myristate, ethyl palmitate, ethyl oleate, and ethyl stearate) are the most suitable markers for the detection of heavy alcohol consumption and show differential concentrations in

hair of children, adult teetotalers, and social drinkers in comparison with FAEE concentrations found in hair of alcoholics.

The SoHT provides guidelines for hair testing for chronic excessive alcohol consumption. The cutoff for EtG in hair to strongly suggest chronic excessive alcohol consumption is proposed at 30 pg mg^{-1} scalp hair measured in the 0–3 up to 0–6 cm proximal segment. The cutoff for the sum of the four FAEEs in hair to strongly suggest chronic excessive alcohol consumption is proposed at 0.5 ng mg^{-1} scalp hair measured in the 0–3 cm proximal segment. If the proximal 0–6 cm segment is used, the proposed cutoff is 1.0 ng mg^{-1} scalp hair. In both cases, if samples less than 3 cm are used, the results should be interpreted with caution. At this time, there is no consensus on how to determine abstinence.

Verification of Doping Practices

Athletes use both endogenous and exogenous anabolic steroids as they increase lean body mass and strength, as well as aggressiveness, and result in shorter recovery time between workouts.

The greatest use of hair in this context is investigating false negatives results in negative test results on blood or urine, particularly if banned substances have been used more than a few days before the competition. Hair can also indicate the history and frequency of drug intake as repetitive use can be demonstrated by segmental analysis along the hair shaft.

Unlike testosterone in urine, the interpretation of concentrations in hair can be difficult. The range between physiological concentrations of testosterone and those found in abusers is small. Therefore, to complement testosterone determination, the identification of unique testosterone esters in hair enables an unambiguous determination of doping because the esters are exogenous substances and therefore could not come from endogenous testosterone.

Another advantage of hair analysis is the possible discrimination between nandrolone and abuse of other 19-norsteroids (norandrostenedione and norandrostenediol), which lead to the same urinary metabolites (norandrosterone and noretiocholanolone). This is obviously not possible in urine as hair can identify the identity of the parent compounds.

In case of longitudinal surveys of athletes, hair analysis appears as the solution of choice to document doping practices.

Beta-adrenoceptor agonists are banned in competition sports because of their sympathomimetic properties (stimulant effects) and their activity as anabolic agents at higher dosages. However, salbutamol is permitted to be used by inhalers only and must be declared prior to the competition. As the drug is permitted for specific therapeutic purposes, together with a medical prescription, it is relatively easy to evade a positive urine test (by having a urine concentration below the positive cutoff, such as for salbutamol or corticoids). Again, segmental hair analysis would document unambiguously doping by the athletes, when the drug (such as a corticoid or an anabolic compound) is found in several consecutive hair sections. This can also be controlled in case of long-term abuse of corticoids.

Regranting of Driving Licenses

The major practical advantage of hair testing compared with urine and blood testing for drugs is its larger detection window, which is weeks to months depending on the length of the analyzed hair shaft, against a few days for urine for most drugs. There is a reasonable agreement that the qualitative results obtained from hair analysis are valid provided that contamination cannot be excluded and that hair can provide long-term histories of drug use. In some countries, persons whose driving license has been refused, revoked, or suspended for addiction to psychoactive drugs or for driving "under the influence" can obtain a license after a medical committee has confirmed complete abstinence from illicit drugs by hair testing and has excluded any additional risk of future relapse of drug abuse (use of both clinical evaluation and hair testing). To provide objective evidence of abstinence from drugs with an acceptable chronological window in order to support the clinical decision of this medical committee, hair analysis has been included in a panel of clinical and laboratory tests, aimed at determining any drug-associated behaviors of subjects. When hair analysis and urine analysis results are compared, hair shows a much higher diagnostic sensitivity for repeated use of drugs.

Drug-Facilitated Crimes

The use of a drug to modify a person's behavior for criminal gain is not a recent phenomenon. However, the recent increase in reports of drug-facilitated crimes (sexual assault, robbery, incapacity, etc.) has caused alarm in the community. Drugs involved can be pharmaceuticals, such as benzodiazepines (flunitrazepam, lorazepam, etc.), other hypnotics (e.g., zopiclone, zolpidem), sedatives (neuroleptics, some sedating antihistamines, etc.), or anesthetics (gamma-hydroxybutyrate, ketamine), or drugs of abuse, such as cannabis, ecstasy, or N,N-diethyllysergamide (LSD), or more often ethanol. Surreptitious administration into beverages such as coffee, soft drinks (cola), or even better alcoholic cocktails is relatively simple.

Most of these substances possess amnesic properties, particularly the benzodiazepines, and therefore the victims are less able to accurately recall the circumstances under which the sexual offense occurred. As they are generally short-acting, they impair an individual rapidly but only for some hours. In these situations, blood or even urine testing may not be suitable as the substance has been removed by the body. Hence, hair testing can provide evidence of prior exposure. The use of tandem MS now allows the detection of a single dose of most sedatives.

The discrimination between a single exposure and long-term use can be documented by multisectional analysis. With the concept of absence of migration along the hair shaft, a single point of exposure must be present in the segment corresponding to the period of the alleged event, using a growth rate for hair of 1 cm month^{-1}. As this growth rate can vary from 0.7 to 1.4 cm month^{-1}, the length of the hair section must be calculated accordingly. A delay of 3–5 weeks between the offense and hair collection for sectional analysis (2-cm segments) is recommended to allow the relevant hair shaft to externalize. The hair must be cut as close as possible to the scalp. Particular care is also required to ensure that the individual's hair in the strand retains the correct orientation.

Recent Trends about Contamination

Numerous applications have been described in the literature where hair analysis was used to provide evidence of either single dose or chronic drug administration and surreptitious administration of drugs to commit a crime while a person is under the influence of a drug.

The most crucial issue facing hair analysis is the avoidance of technical and evidentiary false positives. Technical false positives are caused by errors in the collection, processing, and analysis of specimens, while evidentiary false positives are caused by passive exposure to the drug. Contamination of hair through environmental exposure also has the potential to cause a false-positive result to be obtained. There are various approaches to avoid evidentiary and technical false positives. The proper washing process will not only remove surface contamination but also can provide useful information on the source of drug uptake in hair, that is, from growing hair follicle or from surface bodily fluids.

There is no consensus or uniformity in the washing procedures; however, most have similar characteristics. The agents used in washing are detergents such as shampoo, surgical scrubbing solutions, surfactants such as 0.1% sodium dodecyl sulfate, phosphate buffer, or organic solvents such as acetone, diethyl ether, methanol, ethanol, dichloromethane, hexane, or pentane of various volumes and various contact times. A single washing step is the most common procedure, although a second identical wash is sometimes performed. If external contamination is found by analyzing the wash solution, the washout kinetics of repeated washing can demonstrate that external contamination is rapidly removed. The concentration of drug in the hair after washing should exceed the concentration in the last wash by at least a factor of 10. One method involves washing hair 3 times with phosphate buffer prior to analysis to remove any possible external contamination and that the total concentration of any drug present in the three phosphate washes should be greater than 3.9 times the concentration in the last wash. Washing (rinsing hair) can remove drug from the interior as well as from the exterior surface of hair during the decontamination procedure.

However, it is not possible to distinguish a drug-contaminated subject from an active user. Thus, while a negative result excludes both chronic use and contact with drugs, a positive result cannot be interpreted as a sure sign of drug addiction.

The detection of drug metabolite(s) in hair, whose presence could not be explained by hydrolysis or environmental exposure, establishes that internal drug exposure has occurred. Cocaethylene and norcocaine metabolites of cocaine meet these criteria as these metabolites are seldom found in illicit cocaine samples, and hence would not be present in hair as a result of environmental contamination. This procedure can be extended to other drugs, such as the carboxy metabolite of cannabis (THC-COOH). However, not all drugs have specific metabolites that can be detected in hair.

The presence of similar concentrations of drug in consecutive segments can be considered as indicative of potential contamination from an individual's body fluids or tissues or other forms of contamination unless it can be shown that the person was in treatment with this substance over the period represented by segments.

Whatever the result, a proper interpretation of hair results is critical and should be done ideally with other information available, for example, medical history, witness statements, and available circumstances of the matter.

Results from a single segment of hair cannot be used to discriminate long-term exposure to a drug from single exposure. This means that segmental testing is needed if a history of drug exposure is required.

It is also not possible to determine the dose of drug from a hair analysis result.

Conclusion

The value of hair analysis for the identification of drug exposure in a person is steadily gaining recognition. This can be seen from its growing use in preemployment screening, in various forensic science applications, and in clinical applications. Hair analysis may be a useful adjunct to conventional (urine, blood) drug testing in toxicology. Specimens can be more easily obtained with less embarrassment, and hair can provide a more accurate history of drug use. Gas chromatography and liquid chromatography–MS are the methods of choice for hair analysis including use of tandem MS for detection of low-dose compounds. There are still controversies on how to best interpret the results, particularly concerning external contamination, cosmetic treatments, ethnic bias, and source of drug incorporation.

See also: **Toxicology:** Methods of Analysis—Confirmatory Testing; Methods of Analysis—Initial Testing; **Toxicology/Drugs of Abuse:** Postmortem Blood; Urine.

Further Reading

Baumgartner, W.A., Hill, V.A., 1992. Hair analysis for drugs of abuse: Decontamination issues. In: Sunshine, I. (Ed.), Recent Developments in Therapeutic Drug Monitoring and Clinical Toxicology. Marcel Dekker, New York, pp. 577–597.

Baumgartner, W.A., Hill, V.A., Blahd, W.H., 1989. Hair analysis for drugs of abuse. Journal of Forensic Sciences 34, 1433–1453.

Baumgartner, A.M., Jones, P.F., Baumgartner, W.A., Blank, C.T., 1979. Radioimmunoassay of hair for determinating opiate-abuse histories. Journal of Nuclear Medicine 20, 748–752.

Goldberger, B.A., Caplan, Y.H., Maguire, T., Cone, E.J., 1991. Testing human hair for drugs of abuse. III. Identification of heroin and 6-acetylmorphine as indicators of heroin abuse. Journal of Analytical Toxicology 15, 226–231.

Kintz, P. (Ed.), 1996. Drug Testing in Hair. CRC Press, Boca Raton, FL, pp. 1–293.

Kintz, P. (Ed.), 2006. Analytical and Practical Aspects of Drug Testing in Hair. CRC, Taylor & Francis, Boca Raton, FL, pp. 1–382.

Kintz, P., 2007. Bioanalytical procedures for detection of chemical agents in hair in the case of drug-facilitated crime. Analytical and Bioanalytical Chemistry 388, 1467–1474.

Kintz, P., Cirimele, V., Jeanneau, T., Ludes, B., 1999. Identification of testosterone and testosterone esters in human hair. Journal of Analytical Toxicology 23, 352–356.

Kintz, P., Cirimele, V., Ludes, B., 2000. Discrimination of the nature of doping with 19-norsteroids through hair analysis. Clinical Chemistry 46, 2020–2022.

Kintz, P., Evans, J., Villain, M., Cirimele, V., 2010. Interpretation of hair findings in children after methadone poisoning. Forensic Science International 196, 51–54.

Madea, B., Musshoff, F. (Eds.), 2004. Haaranalytik. Deutscher Artze-Verlag (in German), Germany, pp. 1–305.

Politi, L., Morini, L., Leone, F., Polettini, A., 2006. Ethyl glucuronide in hair: Is it a reliable marker of chronic high levels of alcohol consumption? Addiction 101, 1408–1412.

Pragst, F., Rothe, M., Moench, B., Hastedt, M., Herre, S., Simmert, D., 2010. Combined use of fatty acid ethyl esters and ethyl glucuronide in hair for diagnosis of alcohol abuse: Interpretation and advantages. Forensic Science International 196, 101–110.

Romano, G., Barbera, N., Lombardo, L.I., 2001. Hair testing for drugs of abuse: Evaluation of external cocaine contamination and risk of false positives. Forensic Science International 123, 119–129.

Saitoh, M., Uzaka, M., Sakamoto, M., Kobori, T., 1969. Rate of hair growth. In: Montana, M., Dobson, T. (Eds.), Advances in Biology of Skin: Hair Growth. Pergamon Press, Oxford, pp. 183–194.

Stout, P.R., Ropero-Miller, J.D., Baylor, M.R., Mitchell, J.M., 2006. External contamination of hair with cocaine: Evaluation of external cocaine contamination and development of performance-testing materials. Journal of Analytical Toxicology 30, 490–500.

Stramesi, C., Polla, M., Vignali, C., Zucchella, A., Groppi, A., 2008. Segmental hair analysis in order to evaluate driving performance. Forensic Science International 176, 34–37.

Relevant Websites

http://www.ftc-muenchen.de—FTC (Germany).
http://www.psychemedics.com—Psychemedics (USA).
http://www.roarforensics.com—ROAR Forensics (UK).
http://www.soht.org—Society of Hair Testing.
http://www.x-pertise.com—X-Pertise Consulting.

Postmortem Blood

D Gerostamoulos, Monash University, Southbank, VIC, Australia

This chapter is a revision of the previous edition article by M.D. Osselton, volume 2, pp. 646–650, © 2000, Elsevier Ltd.

Glossary

Chain of custody Ensuring evidence is secure and traceable at all times.

Postmortem redistribution Recognized toxicological phenomenon of changes in drug concentration after death.

Postmortem toxicology Analysis of drugs/poisons in specimens from deceased persons.

Introduction

The application of routine toxicology to coroners/medical examiner cases is essential in any case of a sudden or unexpected death to understand if drugs and/or poisons may have contributed to the cause of death or whether the deceased may have been under the influence of drugs at the time of death.

The suitable collection of specimens is vital to ensure that the laboratory has access to the most appropriate specimens. The interpretation of toxicology results is often the most difficult task due to variations in response from one person to another, in tolerance that develops with repeated use and as postmortem concentrations of substances often change. Time delay between death and collection of specimen results in likely changes in concentration of drugs or poisons. The inherent chemical stability of a drug may result in that drug being transformed after death, leading to different concentrations to those just before death. Microbial or bacterially mediated changes may also result in drugs being changed after death.

This chapter explores these issues and provides guidance on the best practice to interpret postmortem blood concentrations.

Sample Collection and Chain of Custody

Following a sudden or unexpected death, the forensic toxicologist is recommended to undertake toxicological analysis. The common circumstances where analysis may be requested are

- after a suspected drug overdose or poisoning;
- in accident investigation—to determine whether drugs may have been a contributory factor to an accident;
- in homicide investigations—to determine whether drugs may have led to behavioral changes prior to death;
- in deaths where drugs are suspected of being misused or where compliance has led to a possible adverse drug reaction, for example, deaths in hospital.

In order to screen or quantify the concentration of a drug or poison, an appropriate specimen needs to be collected at autopsy for toxicological analysis. The choice of specimen is often dictated by the type of case being investigated as well as the condition of the body. Routine specimen collection protocols should be established by the requesting laboratory for suitable toxicology. It is the duty of the toxicologist to ensure that the pathologist is provided with advice concerning the most appropriate samples and containers required. Whenever possible, the laboratory should provide a sample collection kit containing suitable containers, labels, and packaging to enable the pathologist to collect and submit a full range of samples and also to ensure chain of custody. It is better to collect more samples than that may be required at the first postmortem examination, rather than having to try to go back for more later.

A general outline concerning blood as a tool for toxicological analysis is presented here; however, the reader is referred to the section dealing with postmortem specimens for details of other specimens that can be collected. There are, however, a number of significant considerations that must be borne in mind when analyzing postmortem tissues that are unique to these postmortem specimens; a different approach to interpretation is warranted than that which is applied to blood samples obtained from living subjects.

It is vital that any specimen collected must be labeled, sealed, collected, and bagged separately in tamperproof containers as soon as practicable after collection. The label must include as a minimum the case number and name of deceased; additional details may include age, gender, or case type. The label must be placed over the side of the specimen (tube or pot). All specimens pertaining to a case must be collected and bagged separately in tamperproof containers. Unique numbered seals must be used for each case. The chain of custody must be preserved at all times for court purposes. Seal numbers must be recorded, and appropriate sampling information pertaining to each case must be available for court purposes. If the continuity of evidence is compromised, this can result in the evidence not being admitted in court.

The identification used for all items should be retained throughout the life of the item in the laboratory. The identification system must be designed and operated to ensure that all items cannot be confused physically or when referred to in records or other documents, as well as accommodating a subdivision of groups of items and the transfer of items within and from the laboratory. A chain of custody record must be maintained by the laboratory that provides a comprehensive history of each evidence transfer such that the analysis of these specimens can be satisfactory for court purpose.

Toxicology Testing

The forensic toxicologist is primarily concerned with the analysis of biological samples from deceased persons to assist a forensic pathologist/coroner in the determination of the cause of death. The analysis of postmortem samples can be challenging, as there is often a lack of information in terms of signs or symptoms prior to the death of the individual. The type of analysis can also be compounded by little circumstantial evidence prior to the death (e.g., deceased found at home, nil suspicious circumstances, etc.). The testing of biological fluids and/or tissues for drugs and other substances is a complex process requiring sophisticated instrumentation and specialized training for staff. The request for "toxicology" leads to series of tests, usually on blood, for a large range of over-the-counter, prescription, and illicit drugs as well as alcohol (strictly speaking ethanol). When urine is available, tests are also conducted for the presence of drugs of abuse. (These include amphetamines such as dexamphetamine, methamphetamine, ecstasy (MDMA), and several other designer amphetamines; cannabis products; cocaine; benzodiazepines; and the heroin metabolite 6-acetylmorphine.) The drugs typically included in testing, but not limited to, are shown in **Table 1**. A list of the most common drugs detected should be included as part of the toxicology report. Routine testing, that is, testing without specific indication of a particular substance, covers the common drugs but it does not include all drugs. Those drugs or poisons not tested require specific requests to the toxicology laboratory. Some examples of the drugs that may not be routinely tested but that can be relevant to cases are GHB (gamma-hydroxybutyrate), volatile substances (e.g., propane), barbiturates, and LSD (lysergic acid diethylamide).

Determination of carbon monoxide (CO) poisoning will be required when a known source of CO, such as coal gas, burnt

Table 1   Drugs that should be included in routine forensic toxicology investigations

Alcohol: Chemically known as ethanol. Test also includes methanol and acetone[a]

Amphetamines: for example, (dex)amphetamine, methylamphetamine, 3,4-methylendioxymethamphetamine (ecstasy), etc.

Antidepressants: for example, citalopram, sertraline, mirtazapine, etc.

Antipsychotics: for example, risperidone, olanzapine, chlorpromazine, clozapine, etc.

Benzodiazepines: for example, diazepam, temazepam, alprazolam, etc.

Cannabis: Δ^9-tetrahydrocannabinol in blood and its metabolite in urine

Cocaine: cocaine and its metabolites

Narcotic analgesics: for example, codeine, methadone, pethidine (meperidine), morphine, oxycodone, etc.

[a]Acetone can be derived from abnormal body metabolism in diabetic ketoacidotic states.

charcoal, or automobile exhaust, is located at the scene. This is done by the measurement of CO binding to hemoglobin (as carboxyhemoglobin saturation) in blood. On the other hand, it would be of forensic interest to determine whether a fire victim had died because of CO poisoning or had already died before the fire had started. It is not possible to measure carboxyhemoglobin in severely decomposed cases or cases where blood is not available.

Poisons are sometimes an issue in death investigations. This can occur through recreational exposure by inhalation of "solvents" (often hydrocarbons such as butane lighter fluid or fuels) or plant-derived substances (e.g., scopolamine from Angel's trumpets), accidental exposure to a substance used in the workplace, or suicidal ingestion of a poison such as strychnine, organophosphate pesticides, cyanide salts, and so on. These all require specialist tests for their detection in blood and require the laboratory to be alerted to their possible usage.

Endogenous substances such as insulin (in cases of suspected overdose), glucose (poorly controlled diabetics—vitreous humor is used for glucose measurements when a significant interval from death to sampling occurs), tryptase (marker of anaphylactic reactions), potassium (from administration errors in hospital), and so on also need to be specifically requested usually for serum analysis. Serum can only be obtained in "fresh" bodies due to postmortem autolysis of blood. Collection of blood on admission gives a much greater likelihood of a successful collection of serum (i.e., when the body first arrives at the mortuary).

There is no universal test for all drugs or poisons. So, when the availability of tissue/samples is limited, the analysts should have all the information available to assist in conserving valuable samples for the most appropriate analyses. Access to a full case history may not only help to save valuable samples but can also save considerable time and expense in carrying out unnecessary tests. The investigating officer should therefore be required to submit as much information about the case as possible, as this may influence the type and extent of analysis undertaken as well as the interpretation of analytical results. Submitting officers should be required to provide, at a minimum, the following information:

- name of deceased;
- age;
- occupation;
- race (Caucasian, Chinese, African-American, etc.);
- date/time of discovery of body;
- date/time of death;
- date/time of postmortem;
- time between death and postmortem (postmortem interval);
- full details/case history and circumstances surrounding/leading to death;
- details of any signs or symptoms noted prior to death (e.g., diarrhea, loss of weight, delirium, drunkenness, convulsions, hallucinations, etc.);
- temperature of body surroundings/environment where body was found;
- medical history of deceased;
- availability to deceased or relatives of drugs/medicines/poisons;
- known dosages of prescription medication;
- whether deceased was a known or suspected drug user;
- whether the body was embalmed prior to autopsy;
- if death occurred following admission to hospital, the survival period between admission and death;
- the treatment/drugs/resuscitation procedures carried out before death;
- if death occurred in hospital, details of any antemortem blood samples collected (if any of these are available, they should be requested for analysis); and
- whether the stomach was washed out on admission to hospital (if so, access to the stomach wash, if it is available, should be requested).

All too often a seemingly straightforward and uncomplicated death can turn into a serious case that will culminate in some form of criminal proceedings. It is far better to have all the information at hand while planning how to manage the case than to have to revisit it in hindsight or at the request of the defense lawyer. The more information that is at hand before undertaking any work, the more reasoned is the approach to analysis and interpretation will be. With the increasing availability of sensitive benchtop mass spectrometry to almost all laboratories in recent years, there has been a trend toward undertaking blood analysis alone in many cases, rather than performing analysis on a range of tissues. Historically, blood, stomach contents, liver, and urine were all used to provide a composite picture in postmortem toxicology cases. This was partly necessitated because analytical methods were relatively insensitive and necessitated a plentiful supply of material for drug extraction. In more recent years, however, toxicologists have been able to develop analytical methods that enable blood analyses to be undertaken for a wide range of drugs in small blood samples, often at concentrations significantly lower than in liver, stomach content, and urine. During recent years, the knowledge concerning what happens to drugs during postmortem, between death and the time of sampling, has grown and led many forensic toxicologists to view with caution the way that analytical results are used. If blood samples could be collected within minutes of death, the philosophy that a postmortem blood sample provides a "snapshot" of the blood concentration of a drug at the time of death might be supportable. In reality, however, it is usually impossible to collect blood samples within minutes of death. In most cases, a considerable amount of time elapses between the moment of death and postmortem blood sampling. In the majority of cases encountered by the forensic toxicologist, the time of death and the interval elapsing between death and sampling is unknown.

Postmortem Changes in Drug Concentration

The body of a living person comprises millions of microscopic cells grouped together as tissues or organs, each with specific functions to perform. Each cell is a highly organized structure of chemical membranes, containing and controlling numerous complex chemical processes. The cells are bathed in the interstitial fluid, which provides link with the circulating blood, the function of which is to transport oxygen and essential substances around the body for the cells and to carry waste products and toxins away from the cells to specific sites in the body from where they may be eliminated (e.g., liver and kidneys). When death occurs, the mechanisms for controlling the chemical reactions within the cells cease to function. Failure of the heart to circulate blood deprives the body tissues of oxygen and other nutrients and leads to the accumulation of waste materials in and around the cells, resulting, within a short time, in cell death. Cell death is characterized by chemical disorganization, failure of cell metabolism and cell function, and eventually a disintegration of the cell structure. As the cell walls begin to lose integrity, leakage of the cell contents into the surrounding environment takes place and out-of-control enzymes, formerly contained within the cells, start to destroy the cells and tissues in a self-destructive process known as autolytic decomposition.

After death, the temperature at which the body is stored can alter the rate of decomposition. In a body stored under refrigerated conditions, the process of autolysis and decomposition is slowed down, whereas a body maintained at an elevated temperature will be likely to decompose at a faster rate. After death, the processes that combat and protect the body from microbial infection become ineffective; hence, microbial action also contributes to the process of decomposition. As decomposition advances, drugs may be released from tissues and intracellular binding sites and diffuse from areas of higher concentration to areas of lower concentration. This offers an explanation as to why postmortem heart blood concentrations may be several orders of magnitude higher than the blood collected from the femoral vein in the upper leg. Following the consumption of a drug overdose, the liver concentrations of drugs can become very high, as this organ is one of the principal organs in the body where drugs are metabolized in preparation for their elimination. Likewise, capillary-rich lung tissue containing lipoproteins may also accumulate high concentrations of drugs. After death, drugs diffuse from the lung, liver, and other tissues where they are present in high concentrations into the pulmonary artery and vein and also into the vena cava. The diffusion process continues over time, resulting in significant variations in blood drug concentrations.

The observation that drugs are found in different concentrations at different sites in the body after death was first recorded in 1960. This observation prompted the recommendation that, ideally, peripheral blood samples should be used for toxicological analyses. It was not, however, until the mid- to late 1980s that toxicologists really began to realize the full significance of postmortem change. Several groups published a number of significant observations that have led toxicologists to express caution in interpreting postmortem blood drug concentrations. One group demonstrated that postmortem redistribution of basic drugs can occur rapidly after death and that attempts to resuscitate a corpse using cardiac massage, or even movement of the body from the site of death to the postmortem room, may influence drug distribution. As a result of their observations, the authors judged that it is unsafe to attempt to apply pharmacokinetic calculations, based on the results of a single postmortem blood analysis, to deduce the quantity of drug taken. It is also unsafe to assume that blood drawn from a peripheral site is unaffected by postmortem redistribution. Recent work has shown that drug concentrations increase after death even if collected from a peripheral site. Pathologists or mortuary technicians must be aware that simply taking blood down the femoral vein may result in drawing blood drawn from the major vessels in the torso, such as the vena cava, where the process of diffusion from the liver or heart may be well advanced.

The ability to obtain a satisfactory peripheral blood sample at postmortem may be affected by the state of the body and blood vessels. Ideally, the femoral vein should be dissected and cut and the portion closest to the abdomen tied off with a ligature. Blood should then be collected from the leg portion of the vein, either by using a syringe or by gently massaging the vein along the leg. Many pathologists prefer to collect blood samples from the vein in the upper arm rather than the leg.

However, since the subclavian vein is much closer to the heart and pulmonary blood vessels than the femoral vein, there is an increased chance that blood drawn from this site may have been affected by postmortem diffusion from the heart.

The heart is often a source of a plentiful supply of blood. However, if heart blood is collected and analyzed, peripheral blood samples must also be collected and analyzed to demonstrate whether significant differences in concentrations are present. The lungs are served with a plentiful supply of blood that can contain drugs in very high concentrations. After death, diffusion of drugs may occur from the lung into the left ventricle, resulting in blood drug concentrations in the left ventricle that are up to 10 times higher than those in the right ventricle. Particular caution should be exercised in the interpretation of results when blood samples have been collected from babies. In small infants, the volume of available blood may be limited because of the body size. There is also an increased risk that samples may contain blood drawn from the major blood vessels in the torso, where the risk of contamination by hepatic blood is high. In these cases, consideration must be given to the fact that hepatic blood may contain drugs in concentrations that are orders of magnitude higher than that in peripheral blood samples.

This reinforces the necessity for toxicologists to insist that all samples are clearly labeled with respect to the site and time of sampling. Where the site of sampling is in doubt, this should be stated in the toxicology report and the interpretation should be covered by appropriate caveats. Fluid scooped from the body cavity is occasionally submitted under the description of "blood." Such a sample is unsuitable for interpretative purposes, as it is seldom an authentic blood sample and there is a high probability that it is contaminated with stomach content, pooled abdominal blood, bile, urine, and intestinal contents. Significant variations in drug concentrations are encountered in blood drawn from different sites of the body. Reference tables of blood drug concentrations rarely provide detailed case histories and many of these were compiled before the extent of the implications of postmortem change were realized. Those tasked with interpreting postmortem blood concentrations should therefore exercise extreme caution before expressing their views in a report or before a court of law. Caution must also be exercised when, in the case of an extremely decomposed or exhumed body, no blood is available and tissue drug concentrations are used for interpretative purposes. The practice of attempting to deduce a postmortem blood drug concentration from a tissue concentration by using tissue: blood ratios published in data collections is scientifically unsound and should not be undertaken.

Postmortem artifacts may also influence the ratios of metabolites to their parent drug in blood. For example, it has been suggested that the ratios of unconjugated to conjugated morphine might assist in indicating whether death had occurred within a short time of the entry of the drug into the body. This philosophy proposed that if death occurred rapidly after entry of morphine or heroin into the body, the concentration of unconjugated morphine present in blood would be higher than the conjugated morphine concentration. The volume of distribution of morphine is, however, large compared with that of morphine glucuronides. Hence, while only a small proportion of morphine is present in the circulating blood, a significant proportion of the morphine glucuronides are present in blood. Any factors that could change the distribution of morphine, or cause the conversion of some or all the morphine glucuronides back into morphine, could grossly affect the interpretation of results based on morphine:morphine glucuronide ratios and subsequently provide an erroneous conclusion with respect to time of dosing in relation to death.

There are many compilations of postmortem blood drug data that have been associated with fatal poisoning. However, it must always be remembered that in many cases, blood drug concentrations cannot be interpreted in isolation, and the task of interpretation should only be undertaken after full discussion has taken place between the toxicologist and the pathologist.

Most experienced toxicologists will have encountered cases where the so-called "fatal blood concentrations" have been measured in a deceased person, but the cause of death was not directly associated with the drug detected. Drug addicts and palliative care patients can build up considerable tolerance to drugs such as opiates and appear to behave relatively normally, while the concentrations of opiates in their blood would be capable of causing death in a nontolerant subject. It is also well known that in many cases, the cause of death may be directly attributed to gunshot wounds, stabbing, or road traffic accidents, but concentrations of drugs in blood fall within the range of concentrations associated with fatal poisoning. Our knowledge of postmortem change and the effects that may be associated with it is still far from being complete. However, an awareness that such phenomena exist should provide a warning to toxicologists and pathologists that the process of interpreting postmortem blood results is not simple. Because of the problems associated with drug tolerance and postmortem movement of drugs, all that can be safely deduced from a blood drug concentration alone is that the drug or its metabolites are present. A more elaborate interpretation should only be reached after all the factors in a case have been drawn together, including the histological evidence, the gross pathology, the known circumstances of the case, and the medical history of the deceased.

See also: **Toxicology:** Pharmacology and Mechanism of Action of Drugs; Postmortem Specimens; Postmortem Toxicology: Artifacts; Toxicology: Overview and Applications; **Toxicology/ Drugs of Abuse:** Blood; Drug-Facilitated Crimes; Drug-Impaired Driving.

Further Reading

Baselt, R.C., 2011. Disposition of Toxic Drugs and Chemicals in Man, ninth ed. Biomedical Publications, Foster City, CA.

Cooper, G., Paterson, S., Osselton, D.M., 2010. The United Kingdom and Ireland association of Forensic Toxicologists Forensic Toxicology Laboratory Guidelines (2010). Science & Justice 50, 166–176.

Dinis-Oliveira, R.J., Carvalho, F., Duarte, J.A., et al., 2010. Collection of biological samples in forensic toxicology. Toxicology Mechanisms and Methods 20 (7), 363–414.

Drummer, O.H., 2007. Post-mortem toxicology. Forensic Science International 165 (2–3), 199–203.

Drummer, O.H., Gerostamoulos, J., 2002. Postmortem drug analysis: Analytical and toxicological aspects. Therapeutic Drug Monitoring 24 (2), 199–209.

Flanagan, R.J., 2008. Interpretation of postmortem toxicology: More complicated than it might seem – Part 1. Adverse Drug Reaction Bulletin 249, 955–958.

Flanagan, R.J., Connally, G., Evans, J.M., 2005. Analytical toxicology: Guidelines for sample collection postmortem. Toxicological Reviews 24 (1), 63–71.

Jones, G.R., Peat, M.A., 1999. Forensic toxicology laboratory guidelines. Journal of Analytical Toxicology 23 (7), 636.

Moffat, A.C., Osselton, D.M., Widdop, B., Watts, J. (Eds.), 2011. Clarke's Analysis of Drugs and Poisons, fourth ed. Royal Pharmaceutical Society, London.

Skopp, G., Lutz, R., Ganssmann, B., Mattern, R., Aderjan, R., 1996. Postmortem distribution pattern of morphine and morphine glucuronides in heroin overdose. International Journal of Legal Medicine 109 (3), 118–124.

Urine

M-C Huang, B-L Chang, and **CH Liao,** Department of Health, Taipei, Taiwan
RH Liu, University of Alabama, Birmingham, AL, USA

This chapter is reproduced from the previous edition, volume 2, pp. 651–662, © 2000, Elsevier Ltd.

Introduction

Analyses of drugs of abuse in biological media have been mainly associated with death investigation and criminal prosecution of those accused of driving under the influence of alcohol. In the United Sates of America (US), urine drug testing has recently become widely used as a deterrent tactic in combating drug abuse: in the military, the criminal justice system, and later in the workplace. In the aviation industry, urine drug testing is a common practice worldwide. As a result of the North American Free Trade Agreement, workplace urine drug testing is now extended beyond the US border. Recently, the government of Taiwan has also implemented urine drug testing programs in schools, the workplace, and in the criminal justice system. These practices have dramatically increased the number of tests and the use of urine as the test specimen.

The *Mandatory Guidelines for Federal Workplace Drug Testing Program*, published by the US Department of Health and Human Services on 11 April 1988, and its updated versions, formulated the mechanisms by which the National Laboratory Certification Program oversees civilian drug testing activities in the United States. These guidelines, and previously established military directives, adopt urine as the routine specimen for testing the following drug categories: amphetamines, barbiturates, benzodiazepines, cannabis, cocaine, lysergic acid diethylamide, methadone, methaqualone, opiates, phencyclidine, and propoxyphene. (To the authors' knowledge, no random urine drug testing program included all of these drug categories.)

Test methodologies adopted by these testing programs normally include an immunoassay (preliminary or initial test), followed by confirmatory gas chromatography–mass spectrometry (GC-MS) analysis of the drug tested positive by the immunoassay. In a workplace drug testing program, test results are initially considered (within the laboratory) presumptive "positive" or "negative"—terms that do not hold the same meanings as commonly defined in the laboratory for scientific measurements. Universal administrative cutoff values, rather than scientific and statistical detection limit data established by individual laboratories, are used as the basis for determining whether a specimen is (presumptive) positive or negative (of the preliminary test). Those considered positive are further tested using a GC-MS protocol, again using a universal administrative cutoff concentration of the targeted analyte as the basis for deciding whether a specimen can be reported as positive. Cutoff values adopted by the US workplace and the military drug testing programs are shown in **Table 1**.

Urine Specimen Characteristics and Specimen Integrity

Specimen Characteristics

Compared with blood, urine is relatively free of protein, thus making it possible for direct extraction. Urine also contains high concentrations of metabolites and provides a longer detection time for most drugs. Thus, urine is a preferred specimen for monitoring drug exposure (within a certain time window) of a large population on a regular basis.

Since certain drugs may not be found (or detected in low levels) in urine, while found in liver and blood samples in intoxicated concentrations, urine screen alone may not be sufficient for systematic toxicological analysis. Furthermore, blood is a better specimen for impairment or toxicological assessment purposes, as it is most closely related to drug concentrations at the effector sites.

Urine drug testing results depend on factors such as the time lapse between specimen collection and drug intake, and urine pH. For example, diet that causes urine pH changes may significantly alter the excretion patterns of certain drugs. Thus, weakly basic drugs (such as amphetamine) are more efficiently excreted in acid urine, whereas weakly acidic drugs (such as barbiturates and salicylates) are more efficiently excreted in alkaline urine.

Specimen Integrity

Factors that may compromise specimen integrity, thus affecting test results, include the following:

- substitution of a nonurine liquid or urine from a different person;
- addition of an adulterant rendering the specimen unsuitable for certain test methodologies;

Table 1   Cutoffs[a] of immunoassay and GC/MS test adopted by the US certification programs

Drug	Immunoassay (ng ml⁻¹)			GC-MS(ng ml⁻¹)		
	Analyte targeted	DoD	HHS	Analyte targeted	DoD	HHS
Amphetamines	Amphetamines	–	1000			
	Amphetamine	500	–	Amphetamine	500	500
	Methamphetamine	500	–	Methamphetamine	500	500[a]
Barbiturates	Secobarbital	200	–	Amobarbital	200	–
				Butalbital	200	–
				Pentobarbital	200	–
				Secobarbital	200	–
Cocaine	Benzoylecgonine	150	300	Benzoylecgonine	100	150
Marijuana	9-THC-COOH	50	15	9-THC-COOH	50	15
Opiates	Morphine	300	300	Codeine	2000	2000
				Morphine	4000	2000[b]
				6-MAM	10	10[b]
Phencyclidine	Phencyclidine	25	25	Phencyclidine	25	25
LSD	LSD	0.5	–	LSD	0.2	–

6-MAM, 6-monoacetylmorphine; DoD, US Department of Defense drug testing program; HHS, US Department of Health and Human Services, National Laboratory Certification Program; 9-THC-COOH, 11-nor-Δ⁹-tetrahydrocannabinol-9-carboxylic acid; LSD, lysergic acid diethylamide.
[a]For administrative purposes, a sample is considered negative if the concentration of the target analyte is lower than the listed "cutoff" value. It is also commonly practiced that a sample is considered positive only if ≥200 ng/ml amphetamine is also present.
[b]Testing of 6-MAM is required only when the concentration of morphine is ≥2000 ng ml⁻¹.
Courtesy of the American Association for Clinical Chemistry.

- the presence of certain characteristics associated with the specimen container or storage conditions.

Implementation of proper chain-of-custody procedures can best safeguard the integrity of a specimen. Laboratory procedures described later are often used to evaluate specimen integrity; they are, however, not always effective.

Specimen origin identification

Analysis of blood group antigens and polymorphic proteins may help exclude a specific person as the specimen donor. These approaches are often ineffective owing to their low discrimination power and the large sample size required.

DNA-based technologies can be more effective. Squamous and transitional epithelial cells from the urinary tract often provide adequate DNA for specimen identification purposes. Since restriction fragment length polymorphism methods require larger DNA fragments and sample size, methods based on polymerase chain reaction offer higher success rates. Various genotypes of six markers that can be determined by a commercial kit are shown in **Table 2**.

Specimen adulteration and evaluation parameters

Specimens can be adulterated in vivo through the use of diuretics (or simply a large volume of liquid), pH-altering liquids, or materials that cause the excretion of test-interfering substances. In vitro adulterations using household

Table 2   Genetic markers and allele frequencies[a] using the PM + DQA1 typing kit

Marker	Allele	Frequency[a]
HLA DQA1	1.1	0.158
	1.2	0.190
	1.3	0.073
	2	0.145
	3	0.192
	4.1	0.214
	4.2/4.3	0.028
Low-density lipoprotein receptor (LDLR)	A	0.448
	B	0.552
Glycophorin A (GYPA)	A	0.530
	B	0.470
Hemoglobin G gammaglobin (HGBB)	A	0.537
	B	0.450
	C	0.013
D7S8	A	0.610
	B	0.390
Group specific component (GC)	A	0.275
	B	0.178
	C	0.547

[a]Data for US Caucasian males. Data taken from the reagent package insert (Perkin-Elmer, Foster City, CA).
Courtesy of Dr Alan HB Wu and Forensic Science Review.

products are most widely reported events. These products often affect immunoassay test results. Some adulterants may actually destroy analytes, resulting in negative GC-MS test results.

It is often difficult to distinguish between an adulterated urine specimen and a genuine one that responds marginally toward tests implemented to monitor parameters indicative of adulteration, such as specific gravity, pH, and creatinine level. Selecting appropriate cutoff values of these parameters, which can best identify presumptive positive adulteration specimens for further confirmatory identification of adulterant, is no trivial matter. For example, adopting 1.007–1.035 specific gravity range and >45 mg dl^{-1} creatinine content as integrity criteria resulted in 69 (47.9%) out of the 144 highly suspicious urine specimens evading detection.

Obviously, the most effective evaluation parameter varies with the adopted method of adulteration. Indicative parameters include temperature, color and smell, pH, and contents of additional substances, including diuretics, household items, and chemicals such as nitrite and glutaraldehyde, reportedly being specifically formulated for urine adulteration purposes.

Analyte stability

Stability of the analytes during the postcollection period may affect the quantitative data and the interpretation of these results. Important factors affecting the stability of an analyte include pH variations caused by intrinsic and extrinsic specimen characteristics; container properties, and other storage conditions such as light and temperature; and the presence of oxygen, preservatives, and other foreign substances.

Application of Immunoassays to Urine Drug Testing

Immunoassays are adopted as the "official" preliminary test method in workplace urine drug testing programs because they are sensitive (without requiring pretreatment), can be automated, and are based on an underlying principle that is different from the confirmatory GC-MS methods.

Common Immunoassays

Most immunoassay procedures adopt the competitive binding principle in which the antibody is allowed to react with a mixture of labeled (control) and unlabeled (sample) drugs. The presence and the quantity of a drug in the sample is evaluated on the basis of the quantities of the labeled drug in the reacted or unreacted forms. The control drugs are labeled in different ways, each requiring different methods of detection and quantification. For example, radioactive isotopes, such as ^{125}I, are used for labeling in radioimmunoassay methods; active enzymes, which are capable of converting (indirectly) nicotinamide adenine dinucleotide to its reduced form (NADH), are coupled to the drug in enzyme-multiplied

immunoassay techniques (EMIT); fluoresceins are coupled to the drug used in fluorescence polarization immunoassay; and particles are attached to the drug in particle immunoassay.

An immunoassay system is considered heterogeneous if a phase-separation step is needed prior to detection. The detection process is designed to measure the extent of the labeled antigen linked (directly or indirectly) to the antibody, thus reflecting the amount of the test drug (unlabeled antigen) in the sample. Methodologies based on the measurement of radioactivity are heterogeneous because the detecting device cannot differentiate the source of the radioactivity (free or bound labeled antigen). Therefore, a separation step is required.

Methodologies based on a change in optical intensities do not require the separation step if these properties are modified through the substrate's linkage (directly or indirectly) to the antibody. They are considered homogeneous immunoassays. Both heterogeneous and homogeneous immunoassays are used for workplace drug urinalysis.

Interferences and Cross-Reactivity

Interference can be broadly defined as the cause for a test result that does not provide the intended diagnostic finding reflecting the true status of the specimen. The following conditions may generate test results leading to incorrect interpretation of the specimen status:

- the presence of the targeted analyte derived from sources other than the targeted drugs of abuse;
- the presence of cross-reacting compounds with known or unknown structures;
- specimen conditions that cause nonspecific binding or interfere with the assay's detection mechanism;
- the presence of adulterants that degrade the analytes or alter their interacting characteristics.

Targeted analytes from legal sources

Some of the analytes targeted as indicators of drug abuse may derive from unintended exposure, food consumption, or licit medication. For example, it is well known that morphine and codeine may be observed in urine specimens collected from individuals consuming food items with poppy seeds or prescriptions containing morphine or codeine. Methamphetamine and amphetamine can derive from the use of Vicks nasal inhaler and a substantial number of licit drugs.

Cross-reacting compounds

Cross-reacting compounds are widely reported and many are listed in reagent inserts or documentation provided by the manufacturers. Identities of most reported cross-reacting compounds are known, while others are not. For example, it has been reported that unknown metabolites of chlorpromazine, brompheniramine, and labetalol caused EMIT d.a.u. monoclonal amphetamine/methamphetamine assay to generate false positive results. Metabolites, not the parent drugs, are believed to be the responsible cross-reacting compounds because

- these drugs were prescribed for urine specimen donors;
- these parent drugs were present in the urine specimens;
- studies on control samples with various concentrations of the parent drugs *alone* failed to generate a positive result.

Since reference metabolites of these drugs are not available, the exact cross-reacting metabolites cannot be identified.

Nonspecific binding

Many postmortem urine specimens reportedly produced absorbance change values lower than those resulting from negative calibrators and specimens collected from healthy persons. This is attributed to the presence of nonspecific interacting materials that cause a higher initial absorbance value.

Detection mechanism

Enzyme immunoassay methods are most likely to suffer spectrometric interference caused by other substances present. Listed below are some examples:

- p-Nitrophenol (a metabolite of methyl parathion) and tolmetin (a nonsteroidal antiinflammatory drug) and its metabolites can absorb strongly in the 340 nm region at pH 8.0 and thus cause interference.
- The presence of metronidazole or mefenamic acid causes excessively high initial absorbance values, thus preventing the assessment of EMIT test data.
- Salicyluric acid (the principal metabolite of aspirin) interferes with the EMIT test methodology by reducing the molar absorptivity of NADH at 340 nm.

Adulterants

Adulterants may actually destroy the targeted drugs, thus rendering the specimen "truly" negative, while most adulterants cause nonspecific binding or create interference to the targeted antibody–antigen reaction or the detection mechanism.

Many household products are known to affect the responses of common immunoassays. Results from an exemplar study are shown in **Table 3**. Most interference studies did not compare the effects of adulterants on various immunoassays under the same conditions; it is therefore difficult to make general statements concerning the robustness of one methodology over the others. It seems to be clear, however, that cannabinoid assays are more susceptible to the interfering effects of adulterants.

Numerous mechanisms have been proposed to account for the observed interference, but exact causes are generally unknown. It has been proved, however, that bleach actually causes the degradation of 9-THC-COOH. Visine was believed to increase the adhesion of 9-THC-COOH to the borosilicate glass specimen containers, thereby reducing the availability of 9-THC-COOH in antibody-based assays.

Application of GC-MS in Urine Drug Testing

Confirmatory test procedures for drugs of abuse in biological media often include acid, base, or enzyme hydrolysis; liquid–liquid or solid-phase extraction; and often with derivatization. Selective ion monitoring (SIM) GC-MS protocols are used almost universally for the analysis of the limited number of drugs/metabolites targeted by workplace drug testing programs.

Sample Pretreatment

Many free drugs (and their metabolites) have a strong affinity to proteins, whereas most conjugates are highly hydrophilic and not amenable to extraction by organic solvents. Thus, pretreatment procedures generally include the hydrolysis of drug conjugates (if present), the removal of the binding proteins, and the extraction of the drugs from the resulting reaction mixture. Since urine has limited protein content, protein removal is generally not a critical step.

Acid and enzyme hydrolysis of conjugated drugs

Both acid hydrolysis and enzyme digestion have their merits. For example:

- β-glucuronidase is known to release intact benzodiazepines from their glucuronide conjugates without converting to their corresponding benzophenones, which is a typical product of acid hydrolysis.
- Compared to β-glucuronidase, acid hydrolysis of morphine glucuronide is less time-consuming and can achieve a higher recovery rate. However, this process tends to cause the decomposition of acid-labile compounds in the matrix, leaving a dirty reaction mixture.

Enzyme hydrolysis may be preferred when the analyte is acid-labile and high recovery is not an important factor, i.e., when sensitive detection and quantification methodologies are incorporated in the overall protocols.

Extraction

An extraction step typically removes interfering materials and concentrates the analyte (through reconstituting the extraction residue into a small volume of suitable solvent prior to final instrumental analysis).

Liquid–liquid extraction systems are designed to have the analyte partition preferably into the organic phase in its

Table 3   Effect of various adulterants on immunoassays for drugs of abuse

Adulterant	Amphetamines	Barbiturates	Benzodiazepines	Cocaine	Opiates	Phencyclidine	Marijuana
Ammonia							+R
Ascorbate							−R
Bicarbonate	−R	−R			−E	−F	
Bleach	−R; −E; −F; −C	−C	−E; −C	−C	−R; −E; −F; −C	−R; −E; −F; −C	−E; −F; −C
Detergent	−C	+F; −C	−C	+F; −C	−C	−C	
Drano	−E; −C	−E; −C	−E; −C	−R; −E; −F; −C	−E; −C	−C	−R; −E; −C
Golden seal	−C		−F				−R; −E; −C
Hand soap	+F	+F	−E				−R; −E
Joy	+F	+F	+R; −E;+F		−E		+R; −E;+F
Lime	−R				−R		−R
Peroxide			−E;+F				
Phosphate				−R−F	−F	−R	
Salt (NaCl)	−E	−E	−E	−E	−E	−E	−E
Vanish	−R				−R		−R
Vinegar							−E; −F
Visine			−E				−R; −E; −C

Adulterant reduces (−) or increases (+) response to drug listed by methodology. C, cloned enzyme donor immunoassay; E, enzyme multiplied immunoassay technique; F, fluorescence polarization immunoassay; R, radioimmunoassay.
Courtesy of Dr Alan HB Wu and Forensic Science Review.

unionized form or as an ion pair. The analyte may also be "salted out" of the aqueous phase into the organic one by greatly increasing the ionic strength of the former using a high concentration of electrolytes. pH adjustment of the sample or the addition of a proper counterion may be used to facilitate a favorable partitioning of the drug in its unionized form or as an ion pair, respectively.

In a solid-phase extraction process, separation is performed with a solid additive or column material using hydrophilic, hydrophobic, or ionic groups attached to silica. Solid-phase extraction approaches offer the following advantages over conventional liquid–liquid procedures:

- less organic solvent usage;
- no foaming problems;
- shorter sample preparation time;
- ease of incorporation into an automatic operation process.

Solid-phase extraction procedures now widely adopted for the analysis of drugs of abuse in urine, include four basic operational steps: conditioning, loading, rinsing, and eluting. The first solvent for conditioning should be as strong as, or stronger than, the elution solvent. The second conditioning solvent should be the same as, or as close to the strength of, the loading solvent as possible. The solvent used for loading should be as weak as possible to produce the tightest or narrowest band of adsorbed sample on the sorbent. A solvent that is slightly stronger, or of the same strength as the loading solvent, is used as the rinse solvent. The rinse will elute unwanted sample components that are not as strongly retained as the analytes, and also wash down small droplets of loading solvent adhering to the walls of the tube to ensure that all sample come in contact with the sorbent. An ideal eluting solvent should elute the analytes within 5–10 bed volumes. The optimal amount of solvent to elute the analytes from a 500 mg cartridge is about 0.6–1.2 ml. Using a solvent that is too strong will result in the elution of unnecessary sample components that are more strongly retained than the analytes, whereas a solvent that is too weak will result in excessive elution solvent volumes, which negate the advantage of reducing solvent consumption with solid-phase extraction cartridges. Sometimes, a desired solvent strength may have to be obtained by blending appropriate amounts of miscible solvents.

If a water-immiscible eluant is selected and the final analysis is to be performed with GC, a "drying" procedure should be applied between the rinsing and the eluting steps. It has been reported that the combination of vacuum and a small amount of methanol can produce a "dry" eluate without causing a substantial loss of drugs.

Chemical Derivatization

Many drugs/metabolites are derivatized, prior to the measurement step, to bring the analytes to the chemical forms that are compatible with the chromatographic environment or to maximize their chromatographic separation and detection efficiencies. For example, derivatizations are carried out to improve the analyte's volatility; to eliminate active functional groups that may cause undesired interactions with the chromatographic components, resulting in peak loss (due to irreversible adsorption) or peak tailing (caused by reversible adsorption); and, through the use of a chiral agent, to achieve resolution of enantiomeric components.

Derivatization is also an effective approach to achieve higher detection or quantification efficiency or to facilitate analyte structure elucidation. For example, the hydroxy group in oxazepam is derivatized to prevent ring contraction that may occur at elevated temperatures. In GC-MS applications, mass shifts in the spectra produced by different derivatizing agents can reveal valuable information concerning the functional groups in the analyte.

Qualitative Analysis

Serving as a chromatograph detector, a master spectrometer (MS) provides valuable "fingerprint" information by resolving and displaying charged particles originated from chromatograph eluates. Together with the chromatographic retention data, the MS detection provides test results that are normally considered conclusive for analyte identifications. MS detector also facilitates adoption of an isotopic analog of the analyte as the internal standard in an analytical protocol.

Serving as an internal standard, an isotopic analog of the analyte incorporated at the very early stage of the analytical process serves as a model compound that, through its detection at the final step, provides a mechanism to prove successful completion of the entire analytical protocol. (Verifying a successful protocol is essential when the targeted analyte is not detected in the test sample.) Internal standards also provide intrasample retention time and ion intensity data that help analyte identification and quantification.

In general, fully credible qualitative analysis (as opposed to target-compound analysis) requires operating the MS in full-scan mode. The resulting spectra are then compared with those in the database or with an in-house standard; together with the GC retention data, analyte identification is often conclusive.

Data collection using SIM mode can provide enhanced sensitivity and is commonly used as an integral part of a well-designed target compound analysis (qualitative and quantitative) scheme. Without the benefits of complete spectra, the use of SIM data for qualitative determination purposes should be exercised with extreme caution. For example:

- As many ions that are characteristic of the analyte should be selected. Ideally, the molecular ion should be used if it exists with a reasonable intensity. If the analyte is derivatized with a derivatizing reagent prior to the GC-MS analysis, at least one of the ions selected should include the complete or a characteristic moiety of the analyte. The exclusive use only of ions that are derived from the derivatizing reagent is not acceptable.

- The intensity ratios of the selected ions should be closely monitored and compared with the corresponding ratios obtained from a standard (or control) that is analyzed under identical conditions.

- The retention times of all ions monitored for the analyte should be coincidental. In addition, the retention time and ion intensity ratios of the internal standard should be compared to the corresponding data of the analyte. This "intrasample" information further improves the certainty of an identification.

- This approach should only be applied to well-studied systems in which isotopic analogs of the analytes are normally available and incorporated in the analytical process. Furthermore, GC operational conditions should be optimized so that closely related compounds are chromatographed with distinguishable retention data.

Considering the fact that the identified analyte has also survived the chemical processes (hydrolysis, extraction, and derivatization) designed for the targeted drug and proven effective for the internal standard (often a deuterated analog with chemical properties practically identical to the analyte), the above identification criteria should not reach an incorrect conclusion if executed by an able analyst.

Quantitative Determination

Although MS by itself is not necessarily the most quantitative detector for a chromatographic system, the use of an isotopic analog as the internal standard alleviates the effects of many variations in the analytical process, thus often providing the best overall quantitative result.

Internal standard

Deuterated analogs of the analytes are now commonly used internal standards for the quantification of drugs in biological matrices. However, not all deuterium-labeled isotopic analogs (of the analyte) are effective. Since the analyte and the internal standard are rarely separated adequately, the proposed isotopic analog must generate at least one (preferably two or three) ion relatively free of cross-contribution by the analyte. There must also be at least three ions designated for the analyte that are relatively free of cross-contribution by the proposed internal standard. If these requirements are not met, quantitative results and the ion intensity ratio data (which are commonly used as important parameters for analyte identification) may become unreliable.

Calibration approaches

A typical quantitative GC-MS protocol involves monitoring several selected ions from the analyte and the isotopic analog. Quantification is achieved by comparing a selected analyte-to-isotopic analog ion intensity ratio observed from the test

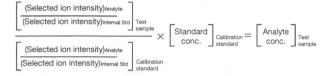

Figure 1 Formula for the calculation of the analyte concentration using a one-point calibration protocol. Courtesy of Central Police University Press.

specimen and the same ratio observed from the calibration standard. The calibration standard contains the same amount of the internal standard and a known amount of the analyte and is processed in parallel with the test specimen. The analyte concentration in the test specimen can be calculated using a one-point calibration approach, as shown in **Figure 1**.

This procedure can be used to determine directly the analyte concentration in a test specimen (one-point calibration) and has proven highly effective when the concentration of the analyte is in the immediate vicinity of the single calibrator's concentration. Alternatively, the ion intensity ratio data can be used to determine the responses of a set of standards from which a calibration curve is established and used for analyte concentration determination in a test specimen (multiple-point calibration). Multiple-point calibration approaches can be implemented with different regression models, including linear or nonlinear; weighted or unweighted; and whether or not to force the regression through the point of origin.

It has been shown that multiple-point nonlinear calibration can provide a wider calibration range. Empirical studies also indicate that one-point calibration quantification results for pentobarbital were actually inferior to those obtained for the other three barbiturates—even though d_5-pentobarbital was used as the single internal standard for all analytes. Factors that should be carefully evaluated include the following:

- cross-contribution of quantification ions selected for the analyte and the internal standard;
- selection of an appropriate calibration model to take into account the cross-contribution interference—a common phenomenon.

Instrumental parameters

For best accuracy and precision of SIM measurements, instrumental parameters such as instrument resolution, ion-monitoring position, threshold setting, and dwell time must also be carefully considered. Instrument drift from the peak center and the fluctuations in intensities of the selected ion beams will affect measurement precision, mainly because of the greater variation in the intensities of the weaker signals detected. Improper threshold settings will also affect the weaker signals to a greater extent. To achieve the best results, the signal level of the internal standard should be comparable to that of the analyte.

For GC-MS applications, problems associated with differences in ion residence time in the ion source must also be addressed. To assure adequate accuracy, the number of data points that define an ion chromatographic peak must be sufficient, preferably about 20. Because ions are sequentially monitored, the number of data points for a GC peak depends not only on the chromatographic peak width but also on the ion-monitoring cycle time. The cycle time depends on the number of ions monitored, the time spent on monitoring each ion (dwell time), and the "overhead time" needed by the system for effective switches.

Application Examples

The implementation of workplace testing programs prompted the development of many robust extraction–derivatization GC-MS procedures for routine and large-scale analysis of targeted drugs in urine specimens. Examples of these protocols are summarized in **Figure 2**. Evaporated residues are reconstituted and analyzed using GC-MS parameters shown in **Table 4**. Qualitative and quantitative determination criteria described in earlier sections are used for these procedures.

Correlation of Immunoassay and GC-MS Test Results

Conventional immunoassay reagents are typically not very specific. In fact, cross-reactivity to drugs with similar structures can be advantageous in general applications. It is, however, a significant disadvantage when used in workplace drug testing programs in which a positive result is reported only if the GC-MS result (of a targeted drug/metabolite) is at or above a cutoff concentration, and the prior immunoassay screen test result is also at or above an identical or higher cutoff level. Thus, manufacturers often strive to reduce a reagent's cross-reacting characteristics and improve the detection mechanism so that immunoassay test results can be more comparable with GC-MS, thereby improving the overall test efficiency. The ideal situation is that all samples screened positive are confirmed to contain the target drug/metabolite at or above the GC/MS cutoff level, while those screened negative contain no (or below GC/MS cutoff) targeted drug/metabolite.

Because immunoassay reagents are not absolutely specific, the ideal situation can never be realized. One can hope, however, for an immunoassay to respond sensitively toward variations of the analyte content, especially in the vicinity of the selected cutoff concentration. Furthermore, the immunoassay responses should correlate reasonably with the GC-MS results. The appropriate relationship between the cutoffs set for these two tests depend on the metabolite's distribution pattern of the drug and the cross-reactivity characteristics of the adopted immunoassay.

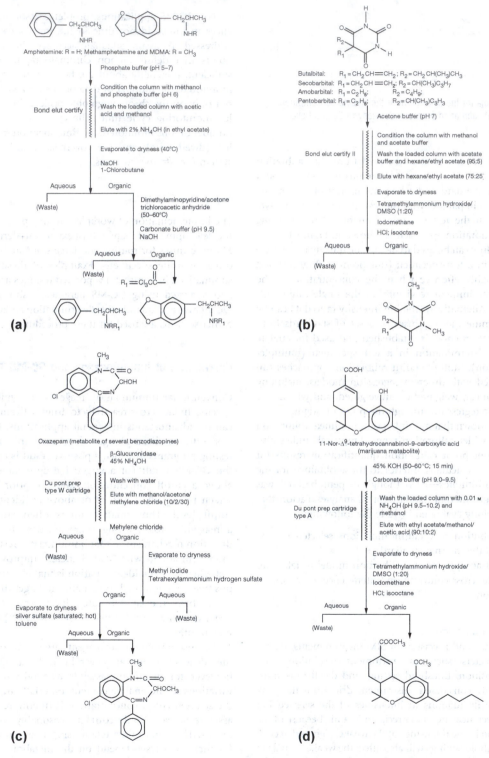

Figure 2   Specimen pretreatment procedures for GC-MS analysis of selected drugs in urine: (a) amphetamines; (b) barbiturates; (c) oxazepam; (d) 11-nor-Δ^9-tetrahydrocannabinol-9-carboxylic acid; (e) benzoecgonine; (f) phencyclidine; (g) methadone; and (h) opiates. Courtesy of the American Chemical Society.

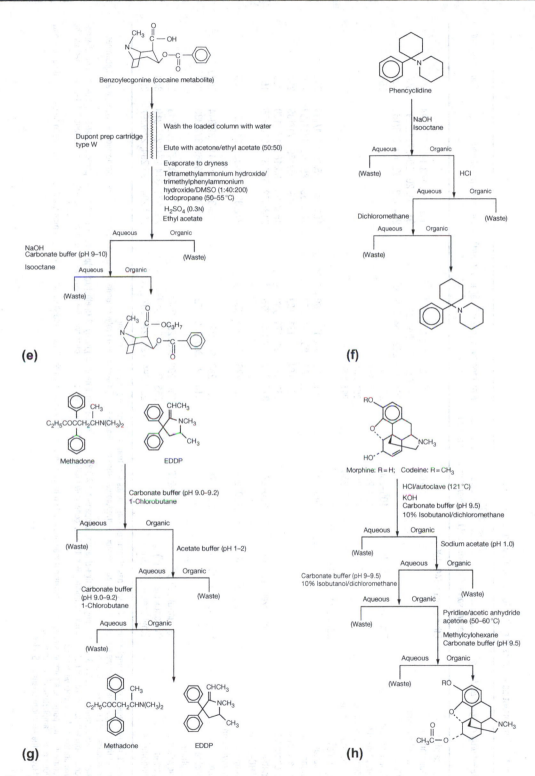

Figure 2 (Continued)

Table 4   Important parameters for SIM GC–MS analysis of targeted drugs

Targeted drug category and drug[a]	Targeted GC		Ions monitored (m/e)[b] analyte; Int. Std[c]	Ion ratios monitored	Cutoff[d] (ng ml⁻¹)
	Recon. solvent (approx. vol.)	Oven temp. range (°C)			
Amphetamines					
Amphetamine	Ethyl acetate (40–100 µl)	150–200	118, 188, *190*, 123, *194*	118/190, 188/190; 123/194	500
Methamphetamine			91, 202, *204*, 209, 211	91/204, 202/204; 211/209	500
MDMA			*204*, 162, 202; *164*, 208	204/162, 202/162; 208/164	500
l-Amphetamine	Ethyl acetate (10 µl)	100–250	*237, 241*		500
d-Amphetamine		100–250	*237, 241*		
l-Methamphetamine		100–250	*251; 258*		
d-Methamphetamine		100–250	*251; 258*		
Barbiturates					
Butalbital	Ethyl acetate (20 µl)	140–190	181, 195, *196*; 171, *189*	181/196, 195/196; 171/189	200
Amobarbital			169, 184, *185*; 171, *189*	184/169, 185/169; 171/189	200
Pentobarbital			169, 184, *185*; 171, *189*	184/169, 185/169; 171/189	200
Secobarbital			181, 195, *196*; 171, *189*	153/168, 195/168; 171/189	200
Cannabis					
9-THC-COOH	Cyclohexane (20 µl)	220–270	313, 357, *372*; 360, *375*	313/372, 357/372; 360/375	15
Cocaine					
Benzoylecgonine	Cyclohexane (20 µl)	190–240	210, 226, *331*; 213, 334	210/331, 226/331; 213/334	150
Opiates					
Codeine	Ethyl acetate (20 µl)	200–270	229, 282, *341*; 232, 344	229/341, 282/341; 232/344	2000
Morphine			310, 327, *369*; 330, 372	310/369, 327/369; 372/330	2000
Phencyclidine	Methanol (20 µl)	170–210	186, *200*, 243; 205, 248	186/243, 200/243; 205/248	25
Oxazepam	Cyclohexane (20 µl)		255, 271, *314*; 276, 319	255/271, 314/271; 276/319	300
Methadone	Ethyl acetate (20 µl)		223, 294, *295*; 226, 297	223/294, 295/294; 226/297	300

MDMA, 3,4-methylenedioxymethamphetamine; GC-MS, gas chromatography–mass spectrometry; SIM, selective ion monitoring.
[a]Some of these drugs/metabolites were analyzed as derivatives using methodologies shown in **Figure 1**.
[b]Italic ions are used for quantification.
[c]1-Phenyl-2-aminopropane-1,2,3,3,3-d_5, 1-phenyl-2-(methyl-d_3-amino)propane-1,2,3,3,3-d_6, 1-(3,4-methylene-dioxy)phenyl-2-(methylamino)pro-pane-1,2,3,3,3-d_6, pentobarbital-5-ethyl-d_5, 11-nor-Δ^9-tetra-hydrocannabinol-9-carboxylic acid-5'-d_9, benzoylecgonine-N-methyl-d_3, codeine-N-methyl-d_3, morphine-N-methyl-d_3, phencyclidine-phenyl-d_5, oxazepam-phenyl-d_5, and methadone-1,1,1-d_3 are used as the internal standards for respective analytes.
[d]For administrative purpose, a sample is considered negative if the concentration of the target analyte is lower than the listed "cutoff" value. It is also common practice for a sample to be considered positive only if ≥200 ng ml⁻¹ amphetamine is also present.
Courtesy of the American Chemical Society.

Testing for marijuana use serves as an excellent example to illustrate the importance of cutoff selection when using an immunoassay as the preliminary test for GC-MS analysis. With a specific cutoff adopted for the GC-MS test, overall positive rate varies with the cutoff level adopted for the immunoassay. Immunoassay cutoffs that best correspond to a specific GC-MS cutoff varies with the type, the manufacturer, and the lot of the adopted immunoassay.

Issues in the Interpretation of Urine Drug Testing Results

It has been widely publicized that urine specimens tested positive for opiate and amphetamine may actually be caused by the use of licit medication or food items. For the opiate drug category, it is possible to confirm heroin use if 6-monoacetylmorphine is detected. Concentrations of morphine and codeine and their ratio can also provide useful, but often inconclusive, information.

Detection of methamphetamine as an analytical artifact has been attributed to the presence of high level of ephedrine or pseudoephedrine in urine specimens. It is thus recommended that a urine specimen cannot be reported positive for methamphetamine without the presence of amphetamine.

Amphetamine and methamphetamine may derive from the use of Vicks nasal inhaler and other medicines. For example, amphetamine is available as Dexedrine, which consists solely of dextroamphetamine (*d*-amphetamine), and benzphetamine, which consists of equal amounts of *d*-amphetamine and racemic (*d,l*-) amphetamine. Amphetamine and methamphetamine may also be present as metabolites of other drugs (precursors), such as amphetaminil, benzphetamine, clobenzorex, deprenyl, dimethylamphetamine, ethylamphetamine, famprofazone, fencamine, fenethylline, fenproporex, furfenorex, mefenorex, mesocarb, and prenylamine. Since amphetamine and methamphetamine derived from these drugs have certain enantiomeric composition characteristics, enantiomeric analysis can often provide valuable information, but not always with definite conclusions.

Unintended passive inhalation of marijuana and cocaine can also result in the detection of the metabolites normally monitored to indicate the abuse of these drugs. The detection of cocaine metabolite has also been attributed to drinking Health Inca Tea, handling of cocaine-containing currency, and skin absorption for those who are exposed to cocaine at their work environment. Analyte concentrations resulting from drug exposure are generally low; claims should be evaluated carefully on a case-by-case basis. Opinions are often offered; definite conclusions are not always achievable based on test results alone.

Acknowledgments

We are grateful to the Taiwanese National Science Council for providing a visiting appointment (NSC87-2811-B-043A-0001) to Ray H Liu, which greatly facilitated the preparation of this publication.

See also: **Chemistry/Trace/Drugs of Abuse:** Classification; **Methods:** Mass Spectrometry; **Toxicology/Drugs of Abuse:** Blood; Drug-Facilitated Crimes; Drug-Impaired Driving; Drugs in Hair; Oral Fluid; Postmortem Blood.

Further Reading

Department of Health and Human Services, Substance Abuse and Mental Health Services Administration, 1994. Mandatory guidelines for federal workplace drug testing programs: Notice. Federal Register 59, 29908–29931.

Edwards, C., Fyfe, M.J., Liu, R.H., Walia, A.S., 1993. Evaluation of common urine specimen adulteration indicators. Journal of Analytical Toxicology 17, 251–252.

Liu, R.H., 1994. Elements and Practice in Forensic Drug Urinalysis. Central Police University Press, Taipei.

Liu, R.H., Gadzala, D., 1997. Handbook of Drug Analysis: Application in Forensic and Clinical Laboratories. American Chemical Society, Washington, DC.

Liu, R.H., Goldberger, B.A., 1995. Handbooks of Workplace Drug Testing. American Asso ciation for Clinical Chemistry, Washington, DC.

Liu, R.H., McKeehan, A.M., Edwards, C., et al., 1994. Improved gas chromatography/mass spectrometry analysis of barbiturates in urine using centrifuge-based solid-phase extraction, methylation, with d_5-pentobarbital as internal standard. Journal of Forensic Science 39, 1501–1514.

Wu, A.H.B., 1998. Integrity of urine specimens for toxicological analysis: Adulteration, mechanism of action, and laboratory detection. Forensic Science Review 10, 47–65.

Postmortem Specimens

GR Jones, Alberta Medical Examiners Office, Edmonton, AB, Canada

Introduction

In theory, modern analytical techniques allow most drugs and poisons to be measured in almost any biological fluid or tissue. However, the practical choice of which human fluids or tissues to use comes down to two main factors—what is available and the interpretive value of the results. For a body that has been outside for weeks or months, bone, and possibly bone marrow, may be all that is available as the remainder of the body has decomposed and may also have been devoured by insects and scavengers. In order to interpret the results, there must be a body of knowledge that allows sense to be made of drug concentrations. This applies to both drugs (prescribed or illicit) taken by humans or substances they may be exposed to (e.g., pesticides). For reasons largely beyond the scope of this section, reliance on a single measurement of a drug in a single specimen is best avoided because of a possible overlap of so-called therapeutic and toxic ranges. Measurement of drug concentrations in more than one specimen type can increase the reliability of interpretation. The following section outlines some of the advantages and disadvantages of various specimens for postmortem toxicology.

Blood, Serum, and Plasma

The term "blood" usually refers to whole blood as it would be drawn from a vein or artery. If the red and white cells are spun down by centrifugation, the clear straw-colored fluid on top is the plasma. If whole blood is allowed to clot and the clot is separated by centrifugation, the clear straw-colored fluid is called serum. For forensic toxicology purposes, plasma and serum are usually regarded as equivalents.

With some exceptions, blood is regarded as the primary specimen for forensic toxicology. During life, blood is a living fluid that circulates to, and is in equilibrium with, virtually all tissues, including the receptors where many drugs have their site of action. However, after death, blood cells die and the cells lyse, the red cells releasing large amounts of hemoglobin. Therefore, most postmortem toxicology testing relies not on serum or plasma (as for most clinical toxicology testing) but on whole, hemolyzed blood. Despite the processes that occur after death, postmortem blood is typically a dark red fluid containing numerous microclots, which, with some care, may be measured by pipette. After the blood circulation ceases,

sedimentation occurs, where the red blood cells gradually settle to the lowest point in an organ or tissue. Therefore, the hemoglobin concentration of any given blood sample can vary considerably, depending on where it was drawn from. Where the difference in drug concentration between red cells and plasma is more or less even, sedimentation should not have a significant effect on interpretation. However, where the concentration of a drug is significantly different in red cells versus plasma, interpretation may be markedly affected.

Collection Site

Blood is most conveniently collected from the area of the largest pool in the body—the heart and the major vessels connected to it. However, blood in the heart and other central organs (e.g., lungs, liver) is subject to postmortem redistribution (PMR). Drugs that are highly protein-bound tend to concentrate in the major organs such as the lungs, liver, and heart. PMR is the process whereby drugs that concentrate in organs and tissues outside of the blood volume during life are released from those tissues after death, causing blood concentrations of many drugs to markedly increase after death. Not all drugs are subject to PMR, but in varying degrees, a large number are. In general, the extent of PMR will generally be less the farther from the central organs blood is drawn. It is therefore good practice to collect at least some volume of blood (e.g., 5–10 ml) from a site remote from the central organs, such as the femoral veins. The volume of blood required for comprehensive postmortem toxicology may exceed 20 ml, especially if several drugs need to be quantitated; therefore, a sample of subclavian or cardiac blood may be collected for the purpose of qualitative drug screening.

Blood should always be collected with a clean (unused) disposable syringe and needle (typically 16 G or larger) from a clearly identified blood vessel rather than a "blind stick." A "blind stick" to the chest can result in the inadvertent collection of pulmonary blood, pericardial fluid, or pleural fluid. Care is particularly important in cases of death involving trauma where the major organs have moved or ruptured and where chest fluid or, worse, bloody abdominal fluid may be drawn.

It is good practice to ligate (tie off) peripheral blood vessels prior to sampling blood. This is to prevent drawing blood from the larger central vessels that may be subject to PMR—for example, when drawing blood from the groin area (i.e., near the iliac–femoral junction). However, there is growing evidence that for at least some drugs, even a properly collected femoral blood sample may be subject to PMR from surrounding skeletal muscle.

Blood Clots

Many cranial injuries are caused by intoxication with alcohol or drugs. The collection of a blood clot from a subdural hematoma can provide evidence of an alcohol or drug concentration closer to the time of the original injury. Blood that leaks from a damaged blood vessel as a result of such injuries will clot in the subdural space and no longer be subject to normal circulation and clearance. If death is delayed, for example, due to medical treatment, an elevated subdural clot alcohol or drug concentration may provide useful information. Unfortunately, the drug concentration will not persist indefinitely but will diminish over a period of hours or days due to diffusion from the clot into surrounding tissue.

Containers, Preservative

It is good practice to collect at least 5–10 ml postmortem blood into a container that results in a sodium or potassium fluoride concentration of 1–2%. Fluoride inhibits ethanol formation from microbiological metabolism of glucose and similar substrates. However, fluoride also inhibits the action of esterases and will therefore impede the breakdown of some drugs such as cocaine. It should be noted that most gray stopper clinical blood collection tubes only contain sodium fluoride equivalent to 0.25%.

However, a much larger blood sample (e.g., 30–80 ml) may be collected into a plain screw-capped container with no preservative. Addition of an anticoagulant is usually not necessary because the blood-clotting system is no longer vital after death and the extent of clotting is relatively limited.

Blood collected for the analysis of volatile solvents or gases should be collected into a glass container with tight sealing cap with polytetrafluoroethylene or similar liner.

Trauma, Medical, and Other Artifacts

Caution must be exercised during the collection of blood from areas of the body where significant trauma has occurred or drug administration has taken place. Trauma may result in rupture of the stomach, causing contamination of the entire abdominal cavity, including the area adjacent to the junction of the femoral and iliac veins. Rupture of the stomach and diaphragm can cause spillage of gastric contents into the chest cavity, especially after falls from a height or motor vehicle accidents. The integrity of such chest cavity specimens is always extremely suspect and susceptible to contamination.

Antemortem Blood and Serum

In cases where death after an intoxication, poisoning, or other event has been delayed due to medical treatment, postmortem drug concentrations will be an inaccurate measure of the drug present at the time of the event (if indeed the drug is still present at all when death occurs). Blood, serum, or plasma collected on first admission to an emergency department can therefore provide valuable toxicological evidence. Even if the death occurs fairly quickly after medical treatment is initiated, antemortem specimens are of value because, by definition, specimens collected right before or around the time of death will not be subject to PMR.

Urine

The main advantages of urine over blood are that the concentrations of many drugs in urine are considerably higher than the corresponding concentrations in blood, and urine is much easier and "cleaner" to deal with analytically than postmortem blood.

A disadvantage of urine is that the parent drug is sometimes absent due to extensive metabolism, placing reliance on identification of metabolites. Further, there is virtually no correlation between urine drug concentrations and pharmacological effect. Attempted "normalization" of urine drug concentrations to creatinine does little to improve their usefulness. Ethanol is one of the few exceptions, where measuring urine concentrations can serve as a corroborative finding of a positive blood concentration (absent glucose in a poorly controlled diabetic).

However, while urine may sometimes be a useful specimen for postmortem toxicology screening, laboratories should not rely on it since the bladder may spontaneously empty during the process of dying.

Vitreous Humor

Vitreous humor is the primary fluid that makes up much of the interior volume of the eyeball—about 3 ml per eye—and is composed of 98–99% water. Vitreous humor is useful for the postmortem measurement of alcohol because it remains sterile for days after death and is therefore not subject to artifactual alcohol formation (unlike postmortem blood). Due to the higher water content of vitreous compared to whole blood, at equilibrium, vitreous alcohol concentrations are typically 10–15% higher.

Vitreous fluid has also been used for the measurement of drugs. However, its use is limited by two factors. First, the volume available is usually limited to about 6 ml, even if both eyes are used. The second factor is that vitreous drug concentrations can be very different from the corresponding whole blood or plasma concentrations. Concentrations of highly lipid soluble or highly protein-bound drugs tend to be much lower in vitreous fluid, due to the relative absence of lipid material and much lower protein content than whole blood.

The measurement of drugs in vitreous fluid has also been touted as a way of avoiding the complexity of interpretation when using whole blood, as the eyes are remote from the major abdominal and chest organs thought to be responsible for PMR. However, these assumptions should be viewed cautiously as PMR from the brain is at least a theoretical possibility.

Bile

In a person whose gall bladder has not been surgically removed for medical reasons, the volume of bile available typically ranges from about 5 to 20 ml, but can be larger. Bile tends to concentrate many drugs, in particular those that form glucuronide and other conjugates, such as morphine. However, that apparent benefit is no longer useful, because modern methodology can detect and measure even subtherapeutic concentrations of most drugs in blood using gas chromatography/mass spectrometry (GC/MS) and liquid chromatography/mass spectrometry (LC/MS) methodologies.

However, bile, like urine, is not a circulating fluid and therefore not in constant equilibrium with blood. Bile is also likely subject to the postmortem diffusion of drugs from the liver.

The Liver

The liver has long been used as one of the primary specimens for drug measurement and interpretation. It is a large organ that tends to concentrate many drugs and is relatively easy to homogenize. Most importantly, the literature contains a substantial amount of data regarding liver concentrations of drugs in various types of postmortem cases. Care must be taken to differentiate high liver drug concentrations resulting from an acute ingestion or overdose from high concentrations resulting from impaired metabolism or clearance. Some regard the liver as a more useful specimen than postmortem blood for drug measurement because, with one exception, it is not subject to PMR. The exception is that high concentrations of drug in the stomach can diffuse across the stomach wall and causes local increases in the lobes of the liver that are the closest (e.g., left lobe).

It is important that efficient homogenization occur using a high-efficiency blender that uses shearing and sometimes ultrasonic action. It is also important that the whole homogenate be used for quantitative analysis and not just the supernatant. That is because a large proportion of drug will be bound to the cell wall and other cellular structure and would result in a disproportionally low result if only the supernatant were used.

The Brain

The brain is a potentially useful tissue for postmortem drug analysis. Many drugs tend to concentrate in the brain relative to blood, and it is a very easy specimen to homogenize. Being remote from the stomach, it is not subject to postmortem diffusion or PMR from any other organs. The database of brain drug concentrations in the literature is considerably smaller than for the liver. However, the brain is a particularly useful organ for the measurement of drugs that are subject to rapid enzymatic hydrolysis in whole blood, due to esterases (e.g., cocaine, heroin, or 6-acetylmorphine).

Some practitioners are also reluctant to homogenize and analyze brain samples routinely, because of the small but serious risk of exposure to Creutzfeldt–Jakob disease.

Lungs

The use of pulmonary tissue typically has little or no advantage over the liver or brain for measuring drug concentrations. Also, pulmonary tissue is more fibrous than liver and an adequate database of known drug concentrations is lacking that might aid interpretation. Lung tissue has been collected for the analysis of volatile poisons (e.g., solvents, gases). However, unless death occurs very quickly, much of the volatile agent may be absorbed into the body or lost to the atmosphere before the autopsy occurs.

The Kidney

Kidney tissue has also periodically been collected and analyzed in postmortem cases. As a tissue for measuring drug concentrations, it has little if any advantage over liver and the database of blood drug concentrations is considerably smaller than for liver. The kidney has been most often used for measuring concentrations of heavy metals, especially where long-term toxicity is suspected (as compared to acute poisoning).

Skeletal Muscle

Skeletal muscle is the largest mass of soft tissue in the body and is usually the last to survive the process of putrefaction and decomposition. Skeletal muscle tends to be more fibrous than liver or brain. It is moderately well perfused, suggesting the possibility of a reasonably good relationship between skeletal muscle and blood drug concentrations. Again, the disadvantage of skeletal muscle is lack of a good database of "normal" (i.e., "therapeutic") or toxic concentrations, although extremes of concentration may be easier to interpret. The limited data that have been published on skeletal muscle drug concentrations suggest that there is at least some site-to-site variation.

Other Tissues and Fluids

Gastric Contents

Gastric (stomach) contents can be useful for helping to determine if an overdose has been consumed, or even simply for the detection of drugs. Analysis of gastric contents is most useful where ingestion of an overdose is possible. In these circumstances, considerable dilution of the stomach contents may be necessary, therefore diluting out the potential matrix effect of a large amount of food. In evaluating the results of gastric drug concentrations, it is critical to keep in mind that it is the total amount of drug present that is important, not the concentration of drug. It should also be kept in mind that stomach contents are rarely homogeneous as a specimen, and may contain wholly or partially digested pills. Therefore, to maximize accuracy, the entire stomach contents should be collected and homogenized prior to analysis. If this is not practical, then a best effort to mix the stomach contents should occur prior to sampling at autopsy, and the total volume that is present recorded. It should also be borne in mind that the presence of only a small amount of drug in the gastric contents does not preclude the possibility of oral consumption of an overdose. Death of a drug overdose victim can take several hours, during which time the stomach may be largely emptied of drug.

Cerebrospinal Fluid

Cerebrospinal fluid (CFS) is similar in composition to vitreous fluid, containing a high water content (98–99%). While CSF can be used for alcohol and drug analysis, it is more difficult to collect after death and can be contaminated with blood. The published data for drug concentrations in CSF are considerably more limited than for vitreous fluid, making interpretation challenging.

Pericardial Fluid

Pericardial fluid is a clear, colorless to straw-colored fluid that is contained in the pericardial sac that bathes and surrounds the heart. Some toxicologists have advocated using pericardial fluid for drug quantitation. However, very few data exist in the literature to aid with interpretation of the results obtained.

Due to its intimate proximity to the heart, pericardial fluid is almost certainly subject to postmortem diffusion from the heart and lungs. Moreover, little is known about how quickly pericardial fluid drug concentrations would equilibrate with the blood.

Chest Fluid and Pleural Cavity Fluid

Pleural cavity fluid is analogous to pericardial fluid, in that it is the fluid in the pleural sac that bathes the lungs. After death, pleural fluid can easily become contaminated with blood, and it will be affected by postmortem diffusion from the lungs. "Chest fluid" is regarded as any fluid found within the chest cavity. It is sometimes collected when blood is difficult to obtain from a specific vessel such as the femoral or subclavian vein. Chest or pleural cavity fluid may be contaminated with blood or, worse, stomach contents if the diaphragm and stomach have ruptured. In other words, pleural cavity and chest fluid should be regarded as poor-quality specimens and any quantitative drug concentration derived from those fluids interpreted with extreme caution.

Heart Tissue

Myocardial tissue offers little advantage over other organ tissue for the routine analysis of postmortem drug concentrations. It tends to be more fibrous than some other tissues and a very limited database of published myocardial tissue drug concentrations exists to aid interpretation.

The Spleen

The primary reason spleen tissue has been collected is for the high concentrations of red blood cells it contains. For example, in some fire deaths, the heat produced may denature most or all of the readily available blood that might otherwise be collected. However, spleen tissue, partially protected inside the abdominal cavity, may contain enough red blood cells to allow measurement of carboxyhemoglobin (indicating the extent of inhalation of carbon monoxide and other products of combustion into the body during a fire).

Hair, Nails, Bone, Bone Marrow, and Cartilage

Hair is occasionally useful in postmortem toxicology for differentiating chronic from acute drug use, especially in criminal cases. Traditionally, head hair grows at a rate of about 1–1.5 cm month^{-1}. By careful collection and segmental analysis, it is possible to estimate when drug use started or finished, or whether the drug detected resulted from an acute dose shortly before death (because of its absence in the hair). However, analytical toxicology testing of hair is not widely performed, other than for a small range of drugs of abuse, and is rarely performed on postmortem cases except in specific, typically criminal, cases.

Nails can also be used to analyze for drugs, but it seldom has any advantage over other specimens. The analytical protocols used for nail clippings would be similar to those used for hair.

In certain types of postmortem cases, hair, nails, bone, and possibly bone marrow may be all that remains of a body. If the body is not discovered for several weeks, animal activity may consume all of the internal organs, and eventually all skeletal muscle, leaving only skeletal remains (bone, bone marrow, and perhaps cartilage). Bone can be analyzed for the presence of drugs, much as nails or hair can. Bone needs to be thinly shaved or ground to a powder in order to be extracted and analyzed. If death of the person was rapid, due to an acute poisoning or overdose, detection will depend on how well perfused the specimen was. In theory, detection in bone marrow stands a fair chance of success because bone marrow is well perfused during life. However, detection of a drug resulting from a single acute dose in a poorly perfused specimen like bone may stand only a poor chance of success.

Injection Sites

Suspected injection sites may be excised and submitted for toxicology testing, although pathologists and toxicologists must be careful about interpretation of the results. Most drugs are widely distributed through the body, including all of the major organs, muscle, and, not least, skin. Therefore, a drug would be expected to be found in any skin sample, regardless of the route of ingestion into the body. It is therefore critical that if analysis of a suspected injection site is to be undertaken, a corresponding skin sample must be collected from a "control" site on the opposite side of the body where injection is not suspected to have occurred. A good example is testing for a possible insulin overdose.

Maggots

Several papers have been published describing the collection and analysis of maggots from a dead body. Putrefaction of a body can complicate the detection of drugs. A body lying unattended for more than a few hours will attract flies that will lay eggs on the body. The eggs will mature into larvae, the resulting maggots that will feed on the body, and so ingest drugs that are present in body tissues and fluids. The maggots can be collected and analyzed in the same manner as any other tissue or fluid. The problem is that maggots metabolize drugs. Failure to detect a drug does not necessarily mean that the drug was not present in the body at the time of death. Therefore, the analysis of maggots for the presence of drugs is largely regarded as being of limited forensic value.

Special Considerations

Putrefaction

The decomposition of a human or animal body after death causes proteins, fats, and other substances to break down into smaller molecules. That process is partially caused by naturally autolytic enzymes such as lysozymes (contained within each cell), and similar enzymes contained in bacteria. The net effect on postmortem drug concentrations is to make analysis of body fluids and tissues difficult due to greatly increased amounts of putrefactive amines and lipids. Nonetheless, from the perspective of postmortem specimen collection, there is little that can be done except than to rely on the use of tissue from the major organs. Successful testing relies on good design of the analytical method. The majority of drugs are amine-like in character, and so they are relatively easy to separate from fats. However, if putrefaction is advanced, separation of amine-like drugs from putrefactive amines during the extraction step becomes next to impossible and so highly specific analytical methods such as mass spectrometry must be used. Despite the problems that putrefaction causes, collection of the available postmortem specimens may still allow meaningful analysis an interpretation for some drugs.

Embalmed Bodies

The embalming process creates special problems. Embalming fluid, containing formaldehyde, methanol, isopropanol, detergents, dyes, and other substances, is forced into the body through the major blood vessels and also introduced directly into the major organs and body cavity. In the process, much of the blood in the body is flushed out or diluted with embalming fluid. Tissues are "fixed," causing the organs to harden. In an embalmed body, the collection of blood is usually not possible. Vitreous fluid in the eye is somewhat protected from the embalming process, and may be collected. However, at the very least, methanol from embalming fluid will usually penetrate the eye as embalmers typically take special care to perfuse the facial area in order to preserve the "look" of the person.

The collection and analysis of major organs such as the liver may be valuable. However, the toxicologist should be careful to take into account the potential dilution effect of embalming fluid, as well as the fact that formaldehyde can react with some drugs causing the concentration to decrease or to disappear.

Labeling

All specimens, particularly blood, must be properly labeled with a unique case identifier (usually case number and decedent name), the name of the specimen, and, where appropriate, the location the specimen was collected from (e.g., for blood, whether femoral, subclavian, and aorta). If two containers are collected of the same specimen type (e.g., two tubes of femoral blood), it is important to uniquely label each tube (e.g., #1, #2, #3, or A, B, C). This is particularly important for postmortem blood because it is not a homogeneous fluid; sequentially drawn specimen from the same site may contain different concentrations of drug. It is important that the exact site of draw must be indicated, and not simply terms like "peripheral" or "central." For example, to some, "peripheral" simply means any blood vessel outside of the heart itself and may, erroneously, be interpreted to include subclavian, inferior vena cava, and aorta blood.

Chain of Custody

The requisition accompanying the specimen to the laboratory should contain the necessary demographic information, as well as sufficient information for the laboratory to decide which specific tests should be performed on a specimen or case. Unless specimens are being transported internally, they should be either individually sealed or the bag or box containing multiple specimens from a single case sealed as part of the chain of custody. The requisition should also be signed and dated by the person responsible for collecting and releasing the specimens for transfer or transport, and should be signed and dated by the person accepting receipt of the package in the laboratory. In most jurisdictions, documentation of courier transportation is accepted as part of the intermediate transport chain of custody (i.e., the courier is not required to sign the requisition as part of the chain of custody documentation).

See also: **Toxicology:** Interpretation of Results; Pharmacology and Mechanism of Action of Drugs; Postmortem Toxicology: Artifacts; **Toxicology/Drugs of Abuse:** Drugs in Hair; Postmortem Blood.

Further Reading

ABFT (American Board of Forensic Toxicology), 2002. Forensic Toxicology Laboratory Accreditation Manual. American Board of Forensic Toxicology, Colorado Springs, CO. http://www.abft.org/files/ABFTLaboratoryManual.pdf (accessed 28 June 2011).

Dinis-Oliveira, R.J., Carvalho, F., Duarte, J.A., et al., 2010. Collection of biological samples in forensic toxicology. Toxicology Mechanisms and Methods 20, 363–414.

Flanagan, R.J., Connally, G., Evans, J.M., 2005. Analytical toxicology: Guidelines for sample collection post-mortem. Toxicological Reviews 24, 63–71.

Hepler, B.R., Isenschmid, D.S., 2006. Specimen selection, collection, preservation, and security. In: Karch, S., Druid, H. (Eds.), Handbook of Drug Abuse, second ed. CRC Press, Roca Raton, FL, pp. 975–991.

Jones, G.R., 2004. Post-mortem toxicology. In: Moffat, A.C., Osselton, M.D., Widdop, B. (Eds.), Clarke's Analysis of Drugs and Poisons, third ed. Pharmaceutical Press, London, pp. 94–108.

NAME (National Association of Medical Examiners), 2011. NAME Accreditation and Inspection Checklist. http://thename.org/index.php?option=com_docman&task=cat_view&gid=45&Itemid=26 (accessed 28 June 2011).

Skopp, G., 2004. Preanalytic aspects in post-mortem toxicology. Forensic Science International 142, 75–100.

Skopp, G., 2010. Post-mortem toxicology. Forensic Science, Medicine, and Pathology 6, 314–325.

SOFT/AAFS (Society of Forensic Toxicologists/American Academy of Forensic Sciences), 2006. Forensic Toxicology Laboratory Guidelines. Society of Forensic Toxicologists/American Academy of Forensic Sciences, New York. http://www.soft-tox.org/files/Guidelines_2006_Final.pdf (accessed 28 June 2011).

Behavioral Toxicology

D Gerostamoulos, Monash University, Southbank, VIC, Australia

The ability of drugs, both prescription and illicit drugs, to cause behavioral changes is arguably one of the most common issues confronting forensic practitioners. The consumption of new designer drugs as well as combinations of alcohol and prescription drugs can lead to behavioral changes in persons, often resulting in violent crime. Victims of crime can also be subject to the effects of drugs through either covert or overt administration of substances in recreational or domestic settings. Sudden or unexpected behavioral changes resulting from the consumption of drugs can lead to adverse events, which include self-harm and death. Indeed, the risk of death, including homicide and suicide, is well documented with the use of alcohol, illicit drugs, and some prescription drugs. These dangers are confined not only to individuals using drugs themselves but also to those people living with drug-using persons but who themselves do not abuse alcohol or drugs (e.g., children).

Drugs of most concern include alcohol, all of the amphetamine class of drugs (including a range of designer stimulants, e.g., methcathinones), cocaine, benzodiazepines and related sedatives (e.g., zolpidem), and hallucinogens such as ketamine and phencyclidine (PCP), although many other illicit and prescription drugs can have profound behavioral effects directly or can modify the behavioral effects of other drugs. Newer drugs such as gammahydroxybutyrate (GHB) and other similar depressant drugs are often used in drug-facilitated sexual assault, rendering a victim incapacitated or unconscious.

Prevalence of drugs capable of causing behavioral changes is significant. Among the victims of homicide, the most common is alcohol, followed by benzodiazepines, cannabis, opiates, and stimulant drugs. This chapter explores the notion of behavioral toxicity and its relevance to forensic medicine and also provides some of the most common examples to illustrate the significance of this phenomenon.

What Is Behavioral Toxicity?

This is a term used to define changes in behavior that impact adversely on rational thought and actions that may predispose to violence or other behaviors and have been caused by the effects of chemical substances. Most typically, these substances are illicit drugs, but this can also be caused by the inhalation of volatile substances (e.g., petroleum products, solvents, etc.), the use of natural products that contain psychoactive compounds, or the misuse of prescribed medications. The net effect of these behaviors is often the association with criminal acts.

This phenomenon is illustrated by excessive alcohol consumption, in which a person becomes disinhibited, leading to an outburst of aggression following an argument, resulting in harm to another person. While the actions cannot be blamed on the drug itself, the drug has modified the person's behavior to increase the propensity to violence and often also the severity of the violence. This is a well-known association with excessive alcohol use; however, with some drugs (e.g., benzodiazepines), changes in behavior are not so predictable and can depend upon frequency and dose as well as other factors.

Mechanisms of Action

Chemical substances may act on receptors in the brain or bind to membranes affecting cellular functions in the brain, modifying normal nerve function. The transmission of signals by nerves involves the use of chemicals known as neurotransmitters. These neurotransmitters include substances such as norepinephrine (noradrenaline), serotonin (5-hydroxy tryptamine or 5-HT), dopamine, N-methyl-D-aspartic acid (NMDA), and gamma-aminobutyric acid (GABA).

Interference in the actions of neurotransmitters can occur either by blocking the effects of these substances on receptors located on adjacent tissue (postsynaptic sites) or the nerve ending itself (presynaptic sites) or by modifying the release, reuptake, or metabolism of these substances. For example, cocaine inhibits the reuptake of norepinephrine and dopamine and thereby effectively prolongs the effects of released neurotransmitters. Reuptake is essentially a process to recycle neurotransmitters in which active processes exist within nerve terminals to reabsorb the released neurotransmitter. Amphetamines can increase the amount of neurotransmitter released by the nerve ending, thereby increasing the actions of the nerve impulse.

Benzodiazepines block the effects of released GABA. The binding of benzodiazepine on this receptor has a net effect of increasing the movement of chloride through ion channels in membranes. This process reduces the stimulation of areas in the brain involved in regulating a range of behaviors and physiological functions, including those involving emotions and memory.

Some drugs increase the actions of the neurotransmitter by inhibiting the enzyme responsible for metabolizing excess neurotransmitter, monoamine oxidase (e.g., the antidepressants moclobemide, phenylzine, etc.).

Alcohol

Alcohol, or more accurately termed as ethanol, is by far the most common drug affecting behavior. Alcohol is a complex drug in terms of its mechanism of action. It is a central nervous system (CNS) depressant and acts to depress various functions in the brain and nervous systems generally. It resembles the volatile anesthetics such as chloroform, ether, and the modern halogenated anesthetics. Alcohol not only affects membrane function nonspecifically but also affects a number of excitatory and inhibitory amino acid transmitters such as GABA, glutamate, dopamine, and serotonin (5-HT).

Blood ethanol concentrations (BAC) in excess of 0.02% adversely affect coordination skills and cognitive function. These symptoms become quite obvious at BAC of 0.1%, causing slurred speech, unsteadiness on the feet, poor judgment, and decision-making. Disinhibition is most apparent over 0.1% BAC and is associated with aggression and with loud and outrageous behavior, risk-taking, and criminal activity. A high proportion of homicide cases (more than one-third) involve alcohol often at blood concentrations greater than 0.1%. In drug-facilitated crime cases, alcohol is the most common drug involved typically at blood concentrations of 0.10–0.15%, rendering a person incapable of responding to normal stimuli.

Stimulants (Amphetamines and Cocaine)

This group of strong stimulants typically includes (dex) amphetamine, methamphetamine, and the designer amphetamines such as 3,4-methylenedioxy-methamphetamine (ecstasy, (MDMA)), 3,4-methylenedioxyamphetamine (eve, (MDA)), N-methyl-benzodioxazoyl-butanamine (MBDB), and p-methoxy-amphetamine (PMA). They all act as strong stimulants of the CNS and, depending on the drug, elevate heart rate, increase anxiety, improve mood, and reduce the effects of fatigue. Ecstasy and some of the other designer amphetamines increase empathy and are often used in nightclubs to increase socialization. Owing to the stimulatory effects of these drugs on the CNS, persons become agitated and talkative. Other behavioral manifestations of strong stimulants include rapid or confused speech and aggressive behavior. The term "excited delirium" has been used to describe symptoms of bizarre and/or aggressive behavior, shouting, paranoia, violence toward others, unexpected physical strength, and hyperthermia. This agitated behavioral state is more likely to be observed in persons abusing cocaine, engaged in repeated binge use of the drug.

Newer designer stimulant drugs, such as cathinones and methcathinones (e.g., mephedrone, methdrone), and their derivatives have become increasingly popular largely because of having similar behavioral properties as amphetamine. Even though not as potent as the traditional amphetamines, these derivatives have the potential to induce feelings of irritability, restlessness, and lack of concentration—important observations particularly in motor vehicle accidents.

Persons driving cars or motorcycles using these stimulants display less vigilance and are less able to properly respond to multiple inputs (i.e., display impaired divided attention tasks). These drivers are also likely to drift out of the lane of travel, show erratic driving, and are associated with high-speed collisions. Prolonged use of amphetamines and cocaine can cause long-lasting or even permanent damage to dopamine- and serotonin-containing nerves in the brain, leading to stereotyped behaviors and psychoses. Consequently, it should be of no surprise that these drugs are associated with violence, particularly assault, occasioning harm including homicides.

Anabolic Steroids

Anabolic steroids are the drugs related to the male sex hormone testosterone and have androgenic activity, or an ability to increase muscle mass and tone. Numerous drugs are available in this group, mostly illicit, as solutions for injection, although some are taken orally. These steroids include stanozolol, nandrolone, methenolone, metandienone, oxymetholone, and trenbolone to name but a few. These drugs can be taken as small doses of two or more steroids, larger doses in cycles lasting 1–3 months, or as ever-increasing doses as demanded. The net effect is a larger buildup of muscle mass compared to a drug-free situation for a given amount of body building.

A well-recognized side effect associated with the use of anabolic steroids is the appearance of mood disorders, irritability, and aggression. Controlled studies in athletes show a significant number of steroid users reporting major mood disorders, including mania, hypomania, and major depression. Psychoses, delusions, aggressive, and violent behavior are also strongly associated with active steroid users. Reports of fits of anger, assault, and attempted murder are also linked to steroid use.

Personality profiles of men using anabolic steroids also show enhanced physical and verbal aggression and disinhibition.

Hallucinogens

Hallucinogens produce an altered perception of reality and include lysergic acid diethylamide (LSD), often sold as "trips" or "tabs." LSD users are often confused and exhibit illogical actions and may result in bizarre behaviors and paranoid delusions. PCP and its analogues, thienyl cyclohexyl piperidine (TCP), phenyl cyclohexylpyrrolidine (PHP), phenyl cyclopentyl piperidine (PCPP), and cyclohexamine (PCE), produce an altered conscious state leading to hallucinations, dysphoria, symptoms of dissociation, and distortion of visual and other sensory signals. PCP shows some actions similar to LSD. Ketamine shares similar properties with PCP and is used widely by veterinary surgeons. PCP is sold as powder, flakes, or liquid. In any of these forms, it can be impregnated in tobacco or cannabis cigarettes, or leaf material. Street doses of PCP range from 1 to 10 mg. Ketamine is sold as solutions for injection, powder, or tablet form. Ketamine is also commonly cut with other illicit drugs such as amphetamine, cocaine, and heroin.

Users of PCP can experience acute psychotic episodes leading to reckless and dangerous actions and it is not surprising that this drug is also associated with violence and dissociated behavior. In some persons, excessive PCP can lead to lethargy/stupor, acute brain syndrome, or even coma; however, surprisingly, many can be alert and oriented. Other common hallucinogens include plant alkaloid mescaline and active ingredient in "magic mushrooms" psilocin/psilocybin. These substances produce physiological and psychological changes including anxiety, compulsive movements, and antisocial behavior (see Poisons: Detection of Naturally Occurring Poisons).

Benzodiazepines

Benzodiazepines are a large class of minor tranquilizers that are legally available, but are abused either by themselves or in combination with other drugs, often alcohol, amphetamines, and heroin. They include alprazolam, clonazepam, diazepam, flunitrazepam, and temazepam. The drugs sedate and reduce anxiety and, in sufficient doses, produce unsteady gait, slurred speech, and disorientation. They often affect retention of events when under the influence of the drugs, for example, cause anterograde amnesia. Benzodiazepines have adverse effects on driving skills through impairment of psychomotor and cognitive skills such as increased reaction times, poor lane control and poor lane tracking, and impaired divided attention tasks. In some subjects, disinhibition may be observed with the excessive use of the drug either alone or in combination with other CNS active drugs. Alcohol is a commonly associated drug that intensifies these behavioral changes. Disinhibition of normal control mechanisms results in aggression and bizarre behavioral changes. These reactions, although not common, can produce disturbing changes when benzodiazepines are abused. In extreme cases, subjects may not have any conscious control over their actions (see Benzodiazepines).

Cannabis

Cannabis is the fourth most common recreational drug used around the world behind caffeine, alcohol, and nicotine. The psychoactive component of cannabis, delta-9-tetrahydrocannabinol (THC), is responsible for the majority of the drug's effects. The most pronounced behavioral impairments include disruption of memory, particularly impairment of attention as well as distortions of perception and judgment. Psychomotor impairment for the duration of intoxication includes impairment of muscle control, manual dexterity, simple and complex reaction time, and performance of divided attention tasks. A high proportion of unexpected deaths involve the use of cannabis (e.g., suicides, homicides, and motor vehicle accidents). The detrimental effects of the drug can result in poor judgment and slower responses, which may cause harm or death, particularly in motor vehicle drivers who are under the influence of cannabis.

Psychoses

Aggression can occur even without the direct effects of drugs, particularly in psychiatrically disturbed persons. Several psychotic disorders, including schizophrenia, may be associated with symptoms of acute agitation and aggression. Cannabis intoxication can also cause acute psychotic episodes. Drug treatment can play an important role in the management of agitated persons. For example, short-acting antipsychotic medications can be used for the treatment of agitation and aggressive behavior of patients experiencing an acute psychotic phase. Benzodiazepines including clonazepam or lorazepam are also often given by injection to achieve rapid results.

Tolerance and Withdrawal

Users of essentially all of the drugs aforementioned will exhibit tolerance or neuroadaptation if the drugs are used regularly. This applies particularly to the amphetamines and cocaine, although users of cannabis and other CNS depressants can show significant signs of drug dependence and tolerance if the drugs are constantly being misused. Chronic use of alcohol will also lead to dependence and tolerance. Tolerance occurs as the human body becomes accustomed to the pharmacological and physiological effects of the drug, causing drug users to compensate by consuming larger amounts of drug. They will consume doses severalfold higher during their active phase than when they first started using the drug. Tolerance can occur after days to weeks of use. Drug-dependent persons will, by definition, not only exhibit drug-seeking behavior but also show signs of withdrawal following drug abstinence. Withdrawal symptoms can often be more profound than the direct effects of drug. For strong stimulants, abstinence symptoms are often severe and will be associated with behavioral changes. This includes fatigue (hypersomnolence or rebound fatigue following excessive stimulation of the CNS), depression, and suicidal behavior. Paranoid psychoses and other mood disorders can occur and can be particularly troublesome.

See also: **Toxicology:** Toxicology: Overview and Applications; **Toxicology/Alcohol:** Alcohol: Interpretation; Blood; **Toxicology/Drugs of Abuse:** Drug-Facilitated Crimes; Postmortem Blood.

Further Reading

Darke, S., 2010. The toxicology of homicide offenders and victims: A review. Drug and Alcohol Review 29 (2), 202–215.

Darke, S., Duflou, J., Torok, M., 2009. Drugs and violent death: Comparative toxicology of homicide and non-substance toxicity suicide victims. Addiction 104 (6), 1000–1005.

Drummer, O.H., Odell, M., 2001. The Forensic Pharmacology of Drugs of Abuse. Oxford University Press, London.

Logan, B.K., 2001. Amphetamines: An update on forensic issues. Journal of Analytical Toxicology 25 (5), 400–404.

Logan, B.K., Fligner, C.L., Haddix, T., 1998. Cause and manner of death in fatalities involving methamphetamine. Journal of Forensic Sciences 43 (1), 28–34.

Moffat, A.C., Osselton, D.M., Widdop, B., Watts, J. (Eds.), 2011. Clarke's Analysis of Drugs and Poisons, fourth ed. Royal Pharmaceutical Society, London.

Patorno, E., Bohn, R.L., Wahl, P.M., et al., 2010. Anticonvulsant medications and the risk of suicide, attempted suicide, or violent death. JAMA: The Journal of the American Medical Association 303 (14), 1401–1409.

Pollanen, M.S., Chiasson, D.A., Cairns, J.T., Young, J.G., 1998. Unexpected death related to restraint for excited delirium: a retrospective study of deaths in police custody and in the community. Canadian Medical Association Journal 158 (12), 1603–1607.

Pope, H.G., Katz Jr., D.L., 1994. Psychiatric and medical effects of anabolic–androgenic steroid use. A controlled study of 160 athletes. Archives of General Psychiatry 51, 375–382.

Rivara, F.P., Mueller, B.A., Somes, G., Mendoza, C.T., Rushforth, N.B., Kellermann, A.L., 1997. Alcohol and illicit drug abuse and the risk of violent death in the home. JAMA: The Journal of the American Medical Association 278 (7), 569–575.

Steele, T.D., McCann, U.D., Ricaurte, G.A., 1994. 3,4-Methylenedioxymethamphetamine (MDMA, "Ecstasy"): pharmacology and toxicology in animals and humans. Addiction 89 (5), 539–551.

Takeuchi, A., Ahern, T.L., Henderson, S.O., 2011. Excited delirium. The Western Journal of Emergency Medicine 12 (1), 77–83.

Stomach Contents Analysis

WM Schneck, Spokane, WA, USA

Glossary

Alternate light source (ALS) An instrument that delivers a high intensity light of an adjustable wavelength.

Cotyledons Botanically, a food storage organ in seeds. The embryos of flowering plants usually have either one cotyledon or two. Seeds of gymnosperms, such as pines, may have numerous cotyledons. In some seeds, the cotyledons are flat and leaflike; in others, such as the bean, the cotyledons store the seed's food reserve for germination.

Dichotomous plant cell key A dichotomous key is a method for determining the identity of something (e.g., the name of a plant cell) by going through a series of choices that lead the user to the correct name of the item. Dichotomous means "divided in two parts."

Entomology (ical) The scientific study of insects.

Formaldehyde An organic compound with the formula CH_2O with a characteristic pungent odor. An aqueous solution of formaldehyde can be used as a disinfectant and preservative as it kills most bacteria and fungi including spores.

Histology The study of the microscopic anatomy of cells and tissues of plants and animals. It is performed by examining a thin section of tissue using a light microscope or electron microscope. Histological stains are often used to visualize and identify microscopic structures.

Masticate Chewing, crushing, and grinding of food in the mouth prior to swallowing.

Neolithic Period A period in the development of human technology, beginning about 9500 BCE.

Polarized light microscope A specialized type of light microscope employing a set of polarizing filters typically set below and above a round specimen stage. When an object is viewed in polarized light, observable optical properties inherent within the object are used in characterization and identification.

Titanium dioxide A white inorganic material, TiO_2, that occurs naturally as the mineral anatase and rutile and is used extensively in industrial applications and sometimes as a food colorant.

The process of digestion begins in the mouth, where enzymes in saliva begin to break down starch products as food is chewed. Food is then swallowed and travels to the stomach, where the physical action of peristalsis churns and kneads the food into a semisolid amorphous mass called chyme. Gastric juices secreted from the walls of the stomach add hydrochloric acid, mucus, and the gastric enzymes pepsin and rennin. These enzymes start the break down of proteins into amino acids. Food normally resides in the stomach for up to 6 h; although when an individual becomes ill or is violently attacked, physiologic reactions may occur that discharge food from the stomach and out through the mouth.

One of the earliest recorded scientific experiments involving gastric contents and digestive processes occurred in 1822. William Beaumont, M.D., a surgeon stationed at Fort Mackinac, performed the first experiments on gastric digestion on an unfortunate individual by the name of Alexis St. Martin, a Canadian voyageur. An accidental discharge from a shotgun lacerated St. Martin's diaphragm and perforated his stomach, reportedly with stomach contents oozing into the wound site. Dr Beaumont dressed his wounds and after 3 years of convalescence began conducting digestion experiments on St. Martin's still open stomach wound. Beaumont inserted different foods directly into St. Martin's stomach in cloth sacks with an attached string and recorded the time taken for the food to digest in his stomach. In 1833, Beaumont published, *Experiments and Observations on the Gastric Juice and the Physiology of Digestion*, a book based on his experiments on St. Martin. His observations laid the groundwork for future study on the human stomach and the digestive process.

Procedures for the Examination of Gastric Contents and Vomit Stains

The stereomicroscope, polarizing light microscope (PLM), and the scanning electron microscope (SEM) are the instruments used to characterize and identify food traces. The identification

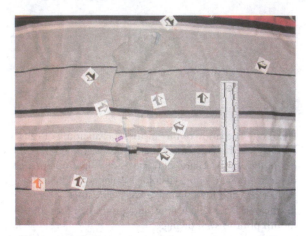

Figure 1   Gastric content stains on a shirt. Arrows point to stains. Note the scale in the photograph to document the size of stains.

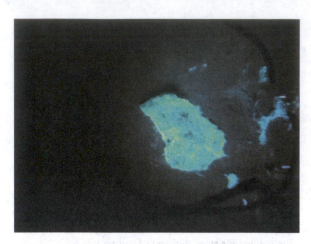

Figure 3   Ultraviolet fluorescence of a vomit stain on a shoe.

of vomit stains is based on the characterization of partially digested and masticated food ingredients and the presumptive presence of gastric enzymes. Samples submitted to the forensic laboratory may include stomach contents from postmortem examinations, dried stains collected at crime scenes, or stains found on materials such as clothing. The presence of drips, projected patterns, and transfer stains are important to document in sketches and photographs (**Figures 1 and 2**). Large vomit stains are recognized by the all too familiar gross appearance and attendant unpleasant odor. When stain size is small, further microscopical and enzymatic tests are conducted to identify the stain as vomit. Dried stains can be collected by scraping and particle picking with forceps to a small paper envelope. In the laboratory, suspected vomit stains can be

examined visually and documented as part of a routine clothing or materials examination. An alternate light source or a handheld long-wave/short-wave ultraviolet (UV) lamp can be used to search for stains. Many vomit stains glow, allowing rapid detection using the UV lamp (**Figure 3**). This type of illumination may have deleterious effects on nucleated cells useful in deoxyribonucleic acid (DNA) analysis as well as the DNA itself; therefore, consultation with DNA scientists is required prior to its use. When a stain has been located, a stereo binocular microscope is used to magnify the area up to approximately 100 times. Individual particles within the stain can be particle picked to a microscope slide for further analysis by PLM. A portion of the stain can be removed and tested for the presence of gastric enzymes common in gastric fluids.

Microscopic Examinations

When autopsy specimens of gastric contents are received, a small amount of formaldehyde may be added as a disinfectant and preservative. If the vomit or gastric contents are received in the liquid state, a representative portion can be wet sieved through a variety of fine, progressively smaller screens, catching food particles of known size ranges on the various screens. The screened particles can be identified directly on the screen or applied to a microscope slide by gently smearing a small quantity across the slide with a drop of distilled water. If a dry vomit stain is received, a portion of the stain can be gently particle picked to a microscope slide and resuspended in distilled water or a variety of other mounting media such as Norland Optical Adhesives, Cytoseal™, Cargille refractive index liquids, or Permount®. Stains can be used to improve contrast and aid in the identification of food products. Some of the more common stains used in the examination of food

Figure 2   Food particles embedded on the outsole of a restaurant worker's shoe.

products include toluidine blue, aqueous iodine solutions, safranin, trypan blue, and Oil Red "O" (**Figure 4(a)–(d)**).

The microscopist should have available dichotomous plant cell keys, commercially prepared microscope slide sets, and prepared food standards (e.g., starches and spices) prior to undertaking the identification of food particles. Vomit may contain food particles from meat, grains, vegetables, dairy products, fruits, nuts, candy, and fats. Large fragments of food, such as seeds, pieces of meat, and leafy vegetables, often can be identified visually and with a stereo binocular microscope. The stereo binocular microscope can also be used to examine vomit stains in situ, showing the relationship of food particles as they were applied to the substrate.

Smaller food particles may contain particles such as starch grains that require closer scrutiny using PLM. Starch is a carbohydrate storage product and is common in many foods. Starch occurs as insoluble granules stored primarily in the roots, tubers, and seeds of plants but may also occur in the leaves and stems. Important commercial sources of starch are derived from the cereals (corn, wheat, and rice) and the root tubers (potato and cassava-tapioca). The starch granule develops stratified layers that are formed around a nucleus, called the hilum. The size of starch grains can be readily measured and compared to known standards of starch using the PLM. The shape of starch grains can vary from near perfect spheres to polygons, flattened spheroids, elongated disks, and many others. In crossed-polarized light, unprocessed starch grains have a characteristic "Maltese cross" extinction pattern, with the hilum often near the center of the cross (**Figure 5**). The size and shape of each starch grain is characteristic of the plant from which it is derived.

At elevated temperatures in the presence of water, starch undergoes a process called gelatinization. This process can be observed microscopically beginning with granule swelling and progressing at higher temperature to the loss of the Maltese cross-birefringence pattern observed in polarized light. The stain trypan blue is recommended for the examination of processed starch. Trypan blue will only stain damaged or cooked grains, leaving the intact uncooked grains clear.

The informative textbooks *Food Microscopy*, *Identifying Plant Food Cells in Gastric Contents for Use in Forensic Investigations: A Laboratory Manual*, *The Particle Atlas*, and the *Atlas of Microscopy*

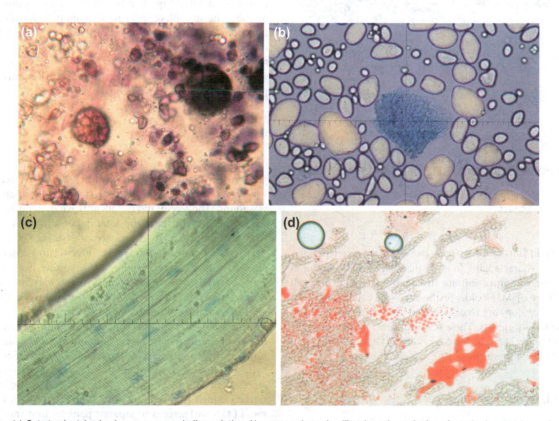

Figure 4 (a) Oat starch stained using an aqueous iodine solution. Unprocessed starch will stain various shades of purple. Image taken using plane polarized light microscopy. (b) Processed starch is stained blue using trypan blue, whereas the unprocessed potato starch is unaffected by the stain. Image taken using plane-polarized light microscopy. (c) Skeletal muscle stained blue–green using toluidine blue. The cell nuclei are stained blue. Image taken using plane-polarized light microscopy. (d) Lipids are stained red using Oil Red O. Image taken using plane-polarized light microscopy.

Figure 5 Using crossed-polarized light microscopy, intact starch grains show a black a "Maltese cross" pattern. This image is potato starch.

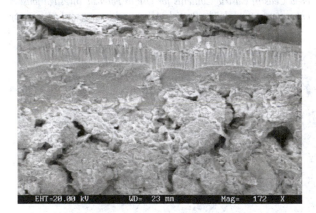

Figure 6 Cell wall structure of a pinto bean is shown by using scanning electron microscopy.

of Medicinal Plants Culinary Herbs and Spices are excellent references when characterizing food particles. SEM is also useful in the characterization of minute structural features such as cell walls (**Figure 6**). Many older textbooks in the field of analytical vegetable histology are recommended for anyone interested in studying food products. These textbooks include *The Structure and Composition of Foods*, *The Microscopy of Vegetable Foods*, and *The Microscopical Examination of Foods and Drugs*.

Gastric Enzyme Screening Test

The literature contains only a few references concerning the identification of gastric fluid and in particular vomit stains. Simon describes a test for the presence of gastric enzymes. If

a specific quantity of gastric juice coagulates in the presence of milk, the enzymes chymosin (also known as rennin) and chymosinogen are present. Lee et al. modified these clinical assay procedures to test for the pepsin and rennin-like activity on gastric fluid and stains of gastric fluid. This author repeated some of Lee et al.'s work by testing physiological fluids (including saliva, semen, urine, feces, whole blood, etc.) for the presence of coagulation in whole milk. None of the tested materials coagulated whole milk. Pepsin is a proteolytic enzyme found in the gastric secretions of many vertebrates. Proteolytic enzymes hydrolyze, or break down, proteins or peptides into simpler more soluble products during the digestion process. The presence of gastric enzymes in a stain indicates that it originated from a mammal but not necessarily a human. A quick screening test for the presence of gastric fluid can be used to identify stains that are suspected to be vomit. Known vomit samples as small as 0.75 mm in diameter have tested positive using this procedure. A small portion of the suspected stain is removed to a black porcelain spot plate along with a dried recently obtained vomit control. Several drops of whole cow's milk are pipetted into each well. The spot plate is placed in a humidity chamber at 38 °C for approximately 30 min. The spot plate wells are then examined with a stereo binocular microscope. The occurrence of coagulation or curdling indicates that gastric enzymes are present in the sample (**Figure 7(a) and (b)**). The known vomit sample should also exhibit the same reaction. The reactions on the spot plate should then be documented.

Case Studies

Case 1: The frozen well-preserved remains of an elderly gentleman were recovered in a wheat field. A suspect vehicle was searched, and a date and time stamped restaurant receipt was found. The receipt did not identify what menu items were selected, but it did have the total dollar amount purchased. Due to the absence of entomological evidence, the time of death could not be determined. The investigators requested the examination of gastric contents to determine if the stomach contents would reveal food from the victim's last meal and if it could be the food from the restaurant on the receipt. If so, an approximate time of death could be determined.

The stomach contents consisted of approximately one-fourth of a cup of viscous semiliquid material with a light brown solid component. Approximately 60 ml of formaldehyde solution was added to the mass as a preservative. A representative portion of the gastric contents was stirred and sieved through 12 mesh (1.7 mm), 20 mesh (850 μm), and 40 mesh (425 μm) screens to separate particles into varying sizes for examination. The particles were rinsed with alcohol and placed into a petri dish for stereomicroscopic examination (**Figure 8**). Selected particles were transferred to microscope

Figure 7   (a) Spot plate well with whole cow's milk and a known dried vomit control sample prior to incubation. (b) Spot plate as seen in (c) after 30 min incubation showing curdling, a positive test for the presence of gastric enzymes.

slides for examination and identification via light microscopy with magnification up to 400 times. Additional particles were selected and characterized using SEM.

The author visited the restaurant and narrowed down the menu choices from the receipt and purchased a crisp taco shell with refried brown pinto beans, lettuce, chopped red tomatoes, and yellow shredded cheese and "Mexi-fries". Samples of soft and hard taco shell, crisp burrito shell, and four varieties of salsa condiments were sampled. Packets of "hot" and "original" sauce were also collected. A portion of the refried bean component was chewed and discharged into a separate petri dish for comparison to the gastric contents. In addition, one yellow bell pepper was purchased to microscopically compare the distinctive yellow food particles found in both the gastric contents and the "hot" and "original" sauce packets for similarities.

Identifiable food particles in the gastric contents consisted primarily of light brown pinto beans showing outer shell/seed coat with a double-walled (~50 μm) columnar structure. Internal bean cotyledons containing starch were white in color and prune-like in structure (**Figure 9**). The outer skin of yellow bell pepper, light reddish-brown red pepper particles, pepper seeds, corn starch, and wheat starch were identified in the gastric contents. Other menu choices at the restaurant contained skeletal muscle/meat, red tomato, green spices, and yellow cheese. These items were not seen in the gastric contents.

Food products purchased at the suspected chain restaurant contained refried pinto beans in many of their meals. Yellow bell pepper particles, pepper seeds, and possible red pepper were found in the "original" and "hot" sauce packets. Wheat and corn starch flour were used in their soft taco shells. Menu items that can be purchased with primarily refried pinto beans were half a pound soft taco (beans only), an original crisp

Figure 8   Screened gastric stomach contents.

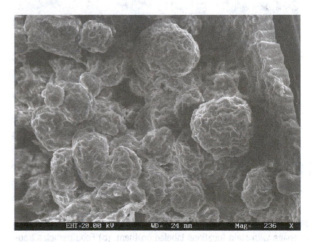

Figure 9   Pinto bean cotyledons imaged using a scanning electron microscope.

(bean) burrito, and a soft (bean) burrito. The food ingredients found in the victim's stomach probably originated from a nonmeat, bean taco or burrito, with an added condiment such as "original" or "hot" sauce. The food was found to be consistent with a Mexican-style meal and could have been the one purchased at the date and time stamped on the receipt, thus indicating the approximate time of his demise within 1 day.

Case 2: During dinner and drinks at an upscale restaurant, a patron broke an arm in several locations as she reportedly slipped and fell in the restroom. This action initiated a civil lawsuit against the establishment. Opposing experts found a small oil stain on the back of her pants; unfortunately they missed the vomit stains on her shoes, pants, and blouse (**Figure 10(a) and (b)**). The food particles in the stains matched the food ingredients that comprised the dinner she was eating. Further investigations revealed that she historically

Figure 10   (a) The back of a pair of ladies' slacks showing clear film overlays with stain locations labeled on them. (b) Food particles trapped within the fabric of the slacks are imaged using a stereomicroscope.

had an adverse reaction to alcohol—projectile vomiting. She likely slipped on her own vomit and fell in the restroom. The plaintiff dropped the case when confronted with the evidence.

Case 3: A parent left his infant unattended in a car seat for 20 min. On arrival, the infant was lifeless and unresponsive. The autopsy was inconclusive and cause of death determined as unknown. The infant's and the father's clothing were examined for physical evidence. Several minute red stains were observed on the infant's and the father's clothing, which were not blood. The stains were similar to each other containing sucrose, titanium dioxide, red pigment, and a positive gastric enzyme test. Further investigations recovered a red candy ball under the front driver's seat, which exhibited similar color and ingredients as the stains on the clothing of the infant and father and car seat straps. The infant likely choked on the candy and obstructed his airway. During the resuscitation attempt and subsequent removal from the car seat by his father, the candy may have been expelled from his trachea.

Case 4: The Ice Man (also known as Otzi), a 5 200-year-old well-preserved mummy was discovered in 1991 in the Tyrolean Alps at the Austrian/Italian border. Microscopic examination of the Iceman's last meal was reconstructed from a tiny piece of transverse colon dissected from the mummy. Particles of semidigested einkorn, an important agricultural wheat of the Neolithic Period, were discovered by particle analysis. It was determined that the einkorn was ground to a fine meal and was probably eaten like a cracker. Electron microscopy revealed charcoal attached to the einkorn bran. The presence of charcoal was thought to represent remnants of a baking process.

See also: **Methods:** Analytical Light Microscopy; Microscopy (Electron).

Further Reading

Varriano–Marston E, polarization microscopy. In: Bechtel, D.B. (Ed.), 1983. Applications in Cereal Science, Ch. 3, pp. 71–108.

Bisbing, R.E., Schneck, W.M., 2006. Particle analysis in forensic science. Forensic Science Review 24 (2), 119–143.

Bock, J.H., Lane, M.A., Norris, D.O., 1988. Identifying Plant Food Cells in Gastric Contents for the Use in Forensic Investigations: A Laboratory Manual. U.S. Department of Justice, National Institute of Justice, Washington, DC.

Dickson, J.H., Oeggl, K., Holden, T.G., Handley, L.L., O'Connell, T.C., Preston, T., 2000. The omnivorous Tyrolean iceman: colon contents (meat, cereals, pollen, moss, whipworm) and stable isotope analysis. Philosophical Transactions of the Royal Society of London 355, 1843–1849.

Edwards, M. (Ed.), 2004. Detecting Foreign Bodies in Food. CRC Press LLC, Boca Raton, FL.

Essery, R.E., 1922. The value of fish scales as a means of identification of the fish used in manufactured products. The Analyst 47, 163–165.

Fast, R.B., Caldwell, E.F. (Eds.), 2000. Breakfast Cereals and How They Are Made, second ed. American Association of Cereal Chemists, St Paul, MN.

Flint, O., 1984. Applications of light microscopy in food analysis. The Microscope 32, 133–140.

Flint, O., 1994. Food Microscopy: A Manual of Practical Methods, Using Optical Microscopy. Microscopy Handbooks 30. Bios Scientific Publishers, Oxford, UK.

Gantner, G.E., Dwyer, J.D., Lynch, E., 1976. Identification of Food Materials in Gastric Contents (Emphasizing Microscopic Morphology). Forensic Science Foundation.

Greenish, H.G., 1923. The Microscopical Examination of Foods and Drugs. Blakiston's Son and Co, Philadelphia, PA.

Hanausek, T.F., 1907. The Microscopy of Technical Products. Wiley, New York.

Hood, L.F., Liboff, M. Starch ultrastructure. In: New Frontiers in Food Microstructure. American Association of Cereal Chemists, St. Paul, MN, pp. 341–370. Ch. 11.

Jackson, B.P., Snowdon, D.W., 1990. Atlas of Microscopy of Medicinal Plants, Culinary Herbs and Spices. CRC Press, Boca Raton, FL.

Lee, H.C., Gaensslen, R.E., Galvin, C., Pagliaro, E.M., 1985. Enzyme assays for the identification of gastric fluid. Journal of Forensic Sciences 30, 97–102.

Makowski, J., Vary, N., McCutcheon, M., Veys, P. (Eds.), 2010. Microscopic Analysis of Agricultural Products. AOCS Press, Urbana, USA.

McCrone, W.C., Delly, J.G., 1973. The Particle Atlas, vol. II. Ann Arbor Publishers, Ann Arbor, MI.

McCrone, W.C., Delly, J.G., Palenik, S.J., 1979. The Particle Atlas, vol. V. Ann Arbor Publishers, Ann Arbor, MI.

Platek, S.F., Crowe, J.B., Ranieri, N., Wolnik, K.A., 2001. Scanning electron microscopy determination of string mozzarella cheese in gastric contents. Journal of Forensic Sciences 46, 131.

Radley, J.A., 1976. Examination and Analysis of Starch and Starch Products. Applied Science Publishers LTD, England.

Schneck, W.M., 2004. Cereal murder in spoken. In: Houck, M. (Ed.), Trace Evidence Analysis, More Cases in Mute Witnesses. Elsevier Academic Press Chapter 6, Burlington, MA, pp. 165–190.

Schoch, T.J., Maywald, E.C., 1956. Microscopic examination of modified starches. Analytical Chemistry 28, 382–387.

Simon Charles, E., 1897. A Manual of Clinical Diagnosis by Means of Microscopic and Chemical Methods, for Students, Hospital Physicians, and Practitioners. Lea Brothers and Co., Philadelphia, pp. 141–146.

Vaughan, J.G. (Ed.), 1979. Food Microscopy. Academic Press, London.

Whistler, R.L., Bemiller, J.N., Paschall, E.F. (Eds.), 1984. Starch: Chemistry and Technology, second ed. Academic Press, Orlando, FL.

Winton, A.L., Winton, K.B., 1932. The Structure and Composition of Foods, vol. 1. Wiley, New York, NY.

Winton, A.L., Moeller, J., Winton, K.B., 1916. The Microscopy of Vegetable Foods. Wiley, New York, NY.

Yahl, K.R., 1984. Starch pasting for industrial applications and some problems. The Microscope 32, 123–140.

Yahl, K.R., 1992. Utilization of a polarization color technique for the identification of starch composition. The Microscope 40, 247–250.

Key Terms

Addiction, Advantages of breath alcohol testing, Alcohol, Alcohol abuse, Alcohol ignition interlock devices, Amphetamines, Analysis, Antemortem, Autopsy, Behavior, Benzodiazepines, Bile, Blood, Blood to breath alcohol ratio, Bone, Bone marrow, Breath alcohol testing history, Breathalyzer®, Calibration, Cannabis, Cerebrospinal fluid, Chain of custody, Circumstances, Cocaine, Collection site, Confirmatory tests, Containers, Contamination, Court, Cut-offs, Death, Death investigation, Detection, Digestion, Doping, Driving license review, Drugs, Drugs of abuse, Electrochemical, Embalming, Enzyme, Ethanol, Ethyl glucuronide (EtG), Ethyl phosphate (EtP), Ethyl sulfate (EtS), Evidence, Evidential breath alcohol testingGas chromatography, Fatty acid ethyl esters (FAEE), Food, Forensic science, Forensic toxicology, Gastric, Gastric contents, Gastroesophageal reflux disease, Hair, Headspace gas chromatography, Heart, Henry's law, Heroin, Histology, Homicide, Immunoassays, Infrared spectrophotometry, Initial tests, Ketamine, Labeling, Lambert–Beer law, Liver, LSD, Lung, Maggots, Metabolism, Microscopy, Mouth alcohol effect, Muscle, Nail, Nonoxidative metabolism, On-site drug testing, Opioids, Oral fluid, Passive alcohol screeners, Pericardial, Phencyclidine, Phosphatidylethanol (PEth), Plant food cells, Plasma, Pleural, Poison, Polarized light microscope, Postmortem, Preservative, Putrefaction, Quality assurance, Quality control, Ratio, Redistribution, Saliva, Sampling, Scanning electron microscope, Serum, Sexual assault, Specificity, Specimens, Spleen, Staining, Stereo binocular microscopy, Suicide, Sweat, Synovial fluid, Tears, Testing, Toxicology, Uncertainty, Urine, Urine: Vitreous humor, Violence, Vitreous humor, Vomit, Workplace drug testing.

Review Questions

1. How is ethanol classified as a drug? Why?
2. Why are veins a preferred location for drawing blood from a living person?
3. Who was Eric Widmark?
4. What makes urine a good matrix for blood alcohol analysis?
5. What is vitreous humor?
6. When might a blood clot be used for evidence of intoxication?
7. What is the main analytical technique for determining breath and blood alcohol concentrations?
8. What is Henry's Law?
9. What is a metabolite?
10. What is ethyl glucuronide? Why is it toxicologically important?
11. What is phosphatidylethanol? What is it useful for in toxicology?
12. What is the difference between serum and plasma?
13. Can dried blood be used in forensic toxicology?

14. What is MDMA? How is it classified?
15. What is the blood–brain barrier? Why is it important?
16. What is ketamine? What is its primary application?
17. What is the composition of hair?
18. Why do most toxicological analyses of hair start with a wash step?
19. What is behavioral toxicology?
20. How are gastric contents examined? What can they determine?

Discussion Questions

1. List the advantages of using breath as a matrix for blood alcohol analysis. What are the weaknesses of it? Do the strengths outweigh the weaknesses? Why or why not?
2. What are the issues relating blood alcohol concentrations to breath alcohol concentrations? What factors can influence this relationship?
3. Police conduct traffic stops and administer standardized field sobriety tests (SFST). In essence, this means that nontechnical people use subjective evaluations and a scientific detection system to make a field-based judgment. How do you think this affects the results? How accurate do you think the SFSTs are? Now read Hlastala et al., 2005. Do you still have the same opinion?
4. How do you think drug–drug interactions confound toxicology? What about in hospital patients? The elderly? Professional athletes? What other groups can you think of?
5. In Schneck's article on gastric contents, reread Case 4 about The Ice Man. Archaeologists used "forensic" methods to determine Otzi's last meal. Does this legitimize forensic science? If so, how? Could the argument be made that this example proves that forensic science is nothing but a "bunch of methods"?

Additional Readings

Bévalot, F., Cartiser, N., Bottinelli, C., Guitton, J., Fanton, L., 2016. State of the art in bile analysis in forensic toxicology. Forensic Science International 259, 133–154.

Hlastala, M.P., Polissar, N.L., Oberman, S., 2005. Statistical evaluation of standardized field sobriety tests. Journal of Forensic Science 50 (3), 1–8.

Metushi, I.G., Fitzgerald, R.L., McIntyre, I.M., 2016. Assessment and comparison of vitreous humor as an alternative matrix for forensic toxicology screening by GC–MS. Journal of Analytical Toxicology. http://dx.doi.org/10.1093/jat/bkw009.

Meyer, G.M., Maurer, H.H., Meyer, M.R., 2016. Multiple stage MS in analysis of plasma, serum, urine and in vitro samples relevant to clinical and forensic toxicology. Bioanalysis 8 (5), 457–481.

Palermo, A., Botrè, F., de la Torre, X., Fiacco, I., Iannone, M., Mazzarino, M., 2016. Drug-drug interactions and masking effects in sport doping: influence of miconazole administration on the urinary concentrations of endogenous anabolic steroids. Forensic Toxicology 34 (2), 386–397.

Section 5. Interpretation

Because of its close relationship with medicine (both ante- and postmortem), toxicology has several levels of interpretation it can provide. At the case or individual level, its results can assist with determining cause and manner of death. At the jurisdictional level, it can provide regional information about trends or patterns, such as drug prevalence or new drugs emerging in the area. Finally, at the national or epidemiological level, toxicology can contribute to a better understanding of large-scale demographic patterns and changes in use or victims over time (See Figure 24). Knowing that a major shift has occurred in deaths from heroin from more urbanized areas to less urbanized ones and from blacks and Hispanics to whites is important for medicine, law enforcement, social services, and many other government agencies.

Like other forensic disciplines, toxicology must *infer* its results because the compound in question has been ingested and metabolized. This may complicate the interpretation because sometimes the metabolites have a stronger pharmacological effect on the body than the original drug. The emphasis, therefore, is on validation, calibration, and a solid understanding of measurement uncertainty.

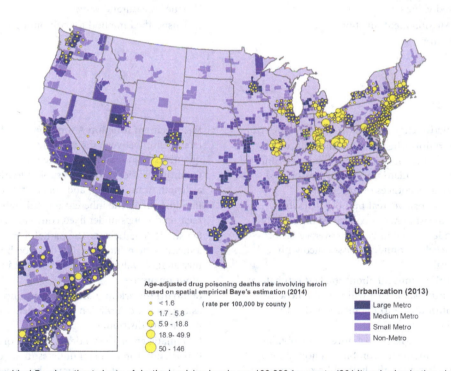

Figure 24 Spatial empirical Baye's estimated rate of deaths involving heroin per 100 000 by county (2014) and urbanization classification (2013). From Dart, R.C., Surratt, H.L., Cicero, T.J., Parrino, M.W., Severtson, S.G., Bucher-Bartelson, B., J.L., 2015. Trends in opioid analgesic abuse and mortality in the United States. New England Journal of Medicine, 372 (3), 241–248.

Measurement Uncertainty

Ted Vosk, Criminal Defense Law Firm, Kirkland, WA, USA

Nomenclature

b_{ias} Bia

$\overline{\gamma}_c$ Bias corrected mean measured value

Y_b Best estimate of "true" measurand value

μ_c Combined uncertainty

k Coverage factor

U Expanded uncertainty

X Input quantities

ε_m Maximum total error

$\overline{\gamma}$ Mean measured value

$f(X_1,X_2,...,X_N)$ Measurement function

ε Measurement error

γ Measured value

$Y_{99\%}$ Measurand value with 99% level of confidence

ε_{ran} Random error

μ_r Relative standard uncertainty

$\partial f/\partial x_i$ Sensitivity coefficients

σ Standard deviation

μ Standard uncertainty

ε_{sys} Systematic error

Y "True" measurand value

⊞ Unspecified method for combining ε_{sys} and ε_{ran}

Glossary

Bias The quantitative characterization of systematic error.

Combined uncertainty The standard uncertainty associated with the final measurement result determined by "adding" up the standard uncertainties associated with each of the individual sources of uncertainty.

Coverage factor A positive, real number that when multiplied by a measurement's combined uncertainty yields the expanded uncertainty. The coverage factor determines the level of confidence associated with a coverage interval.

Coverage interval An interval about the best estimate of a measurand's "true" value that will contain those values believed to be attributable to the measurand with a specified level of confidence.

Expended uncertainty Measure of uncertainty obtained by multiplying a measurement's combined uncertainty by a coverage factor. It defines the half width of a coverage interval.

Level of confidence The probability, defined as a degree of belief, that the "true" value of a measurand lies within the range defined by a coverage interval.

Measurand The quantity whose value is sought to be determined by a measurement.

Measurement function A function that describes the relationship between the measurand value and those quantities required to determine it.

Quantity Physical properties subject to measurement, such as length, time, weight, and concentration.

Random error The inherent unpredictable fluctuation in measured values under fixed conditions.

Sensitivity coefficients The partial derivatives of a measurement function that describe how the measurand's value varies with changes in the values of the input quantities.

Standard uncertainty Measurement uncertainty expressed as the standard deviation of a frequency or belief-based probability distribution.

Systematic error The tendency of a set of measurements to consistently (on average) underestimate or overestimate the "true" value of a measurand by a given value or percentage.

Uncertainty The quantitative characterization of the dispersion of values that, based on one's universe of information concerning a measurement, are believed to be reasonably attributable to a measurand.

Measurement

Measurement constitutes a specific category of scientific investigation. It is an empirical process whereby a researcher seeks to determine the numerical magnitude attributable to some physical/phenomenological quantity of interest referred to as the "measurand." Many naively consider measurement to be a mechanical process whereby the quantity of interest is sensed/probed by a measuring instrument yielding directly the value attributable to the measurand. This mechanical activity is simply one step in the overall measurement process, however. Alone, it does not tell us what we want to know about the value(s) attributable to a measurand. Rather than a passively mechanical process of probing and discovery, measurement is more completely understood as an empirically grounded, information-based inference requiring active input from the researcher before any value can be attributed to a measurand. Measurement uncertainty identifies in an explicit, quantitatively rigorous manner the limitations governing the rational inferences that can be made concerning the value(s) attributable to a measurand based on the results of measurement.

Measurement to Meaning

Measurement Error and Error Analysis

What does a measurement result mean? In other words, given a measured value y, what value(s) can actually be attributed to a measurand. Lay people often interpret the value reported by a measurement as representing the singular "true" value attributable to a measurand (**Figure 1**):

$$Y = y \qquad [1]$$

Science has long realized, however, that "error" is an inherent characteristic of measurement distinguishing measured values from the "true" quantity values sought to be determined (**Figure 2**).

Error analysis is the traditional approach to the interpretation of measurement results. It is based on the premise that if the error associated with a measurement can be determined then a measurand's "true" value can also be determined:

$$Y = y - \varepsilon \qquad [2]$$

There are two types of errors associated with every measurement: random and systematic. Systematic error is the tendency of a method/instrument to yield values that are consistently (on average) artificially inflated or depressed with respect to the "true" values of the quantities being measured. It is quantitatively characterized as bias (**Figure 3**).

The identification of systematic error can be one of the most difficult aspects of the measurement process. The reason is that if one is measuring an unknown quantity, the measured values themselves provide no basis for concluding that they are systematically offset from the measurand's "true" value. Thus, one can never know whether all systematic errors associated with a measurement have been identified. Some sources of systematic error can be identified and quantified through measurement of reference materials. Even when rigorously determined in this manner, however, the magnitude of the bias can never be exactly known.

Random error is the unpredictable/random fluctuation in measured values under fixed conditions. It introduces inherent variability into the measurement process placing a fundamental limitation on the repeatability of measured results. For many common situations, the random variation in a measurement's results can be approximately characterized by a Gaussian (normal) distribution (**Figure 4**).

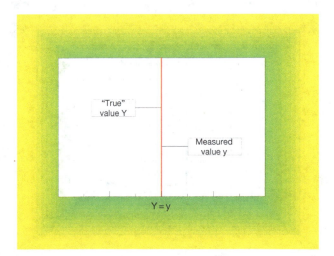

Figure 1 Measurement as singular "True" value.

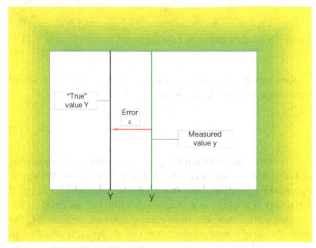

Figure 2 Measurement in reality inherent error.

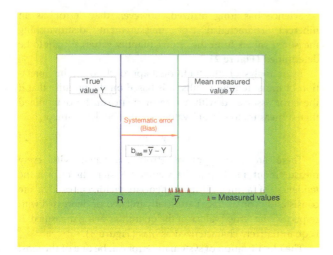

Figure 3 Systematic error and bias.

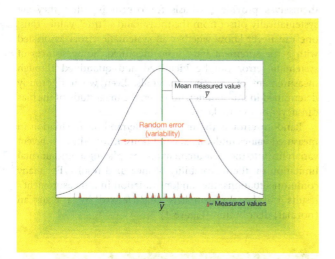

Figure 4 Random error and variability.

Random error is quantitatively characterized by a set of measurement's standard deviation:

$$\sigma_y = \sqrt{\frac{\sum_{i=1}^{n}(y_i - \bar{y})^2}{n - 1}} \qquad [3]$$

The standard deviation provides a measure of the variability of individually measured values about their mean. If there is significant variability, the standard deviation will be large. If variability is slight, the standard deviation will be small.

Systematic and random errors describe aspects of the *physical state of a measurement*. It is not always clear whether an error should be categorized as systematic or random, and the determination may be context dependent. Taken together, they

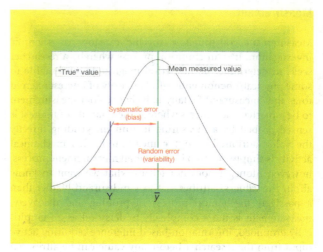

Figure 5 Measurement error.

constitute what is formally known as "measurement error" (**Figure 5**).

The total error associated with a measurement can never be absolutely determined, that is, it is unknowable. As a result, error analysis can never supply a measurand's "true" value. Instead, the goal of error analysis is to identify, minimize, and eliminate *as best as possible* all identifiable sources of error so as to provide an estimate of a measurand's value that is *as close as possible* to its "true" value (**Figure 6**).

This requires some method for combining systematic and random components of error to obtain a characterization of a measurement's total error:

$$\varepsilon = \varepsilon_{\text{sys}} \boxplus \varepsilon_{\text{ran}} \qquad [4]$$

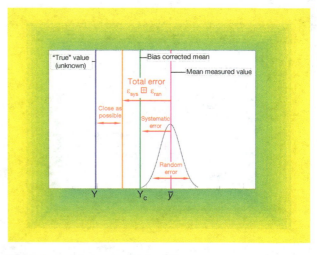

Figure 6 Error analysis estimate as close as possible.

To understand where this leads, one must have an idea of the mathematical underpinnings of error analysis. Error analysis is ground in frequentist statistical theory. Frequentist theory defines probability in terms of relative frequency of occurrence. This means that the probability that a particular condition will be found to exist is determined by how frequently it occurs within the universe of all possible events. Although these probabilities can seldom be known because the universe of all possible events can seldom be completely known, they can be "objectively" estimated as the relative frequency of occurrence over sample data sets. What is critical is that in error analysis, the estimation of probabilities is "objectively" based solely on statistical sampling according to the frequentist paradigm.

The analysis of random error fits well within the frequentist paradigm. On the other hand, except in limited circumstances, the evaluation of systematic error does not. Because systematic and random errors are different in nature, each requires distinct treatment. There is no rigorously justifiable manner within the frequentist paradigm by which systematic and random errors can be combined to yield a statistically meaningful estimate of a measurement's total error.

Due to the frequentist underpinnings of error analysis, the best it can provide is an upper limit on a measurement's total error. This bounded error is often expressed as some linear combination of the bias and standard deviation associated with a measurement:

$$\varepsilon_m = b_{ias} + 3\sigma \qquad [5]$$

This places a bound on the maximum separation expected between a measured and "true" value. It does not, however, denote how close together the two values are *actually* expected to lie. In other words, it tells us the worst a measurement result could be without any indication of how good it actually is. Moreover, the meaning of this bounded error is vague, as it fails to tell us how probable it is that a measured value lies within the prescribed range of the measurand's "true" value. Given a measured value y, the best error analysis provides is an incompletely defined estimate of the maximum separation between a measured value and a "true" value. It cannot tell us the values that are likely to be attributable to the measurand given a particular measured value.

The Meaning of Meaning

A significant epistemological question surrounds any scientific proposition: Is a scientific proposition intended to describe some physical state of the universe itself or simply to describe our state of knowledge about such a physical state? If it is the former, the direct object of the proposition is an external fully independent reality. If it is the latter, the direct object of the proposition is an internal cognitive position that is information dependent. Many claim that if scientific propositions are to be objectively meaningful, they must fall into the first category. Others counter that regardless of the objective content of scientific propositions, they necessarily reside in the second category as all we can ever actually claim to know is our internal cognitive state, not some independent external reality.

Although seemingly esoteric, the position adopted can have practical implications. It may change not only the interpretation of scientific statements but also the manner in which they can be investigated. And so it is with scientific measurement. When a measurement result is reported, is it to be interpreted as a statement about the physical state of a measurand? Or, is it simply an expression of our state of knowledge about the measurand's physical state? And what are the practical implications of the choice made?

Measurement error is an aspect of the *physical state* of a measurement. It is related to a measurand through error analysis that purports to convey the bounds of its actual *physical state* through the determination of a bounded error. Where a precise estimate of a measurand's actual value is not critical, the bounded error may provide a result with sufficient meaning to be useful. Where a measurand's actual value is important, however, this level of meaning may be inadequate. If possible, one would like to understand the meaning of a measured value in terms of how it maps into those values that are *likely* to be attributable to the measurand.

Measurement Uncertainty

The New Paradigm

Measurement uncertainty addresses the shortcomings of error analysis by fundamentally redefining the way measurement is interpreted and providing a quantitative metric for mapping measured values into those believed to be reasonably attributable to a measurand. In this new paradigm, error is replaced as the focus of analysis by a new entity: uncertainty. This is not a matter of mere semantics. Uncertainty and error are completely distinct concepts. While measurement error concerns the actual *physical state of* a measurand, measurement uncertainty relates to the *state of knowledge about* the measurand.

This does not mean that those phenomena formerly understood as systematic and random errors are ignored. To the contrary, they are fully encompassed within the uncertainty framework. What they represent, however, has been reconceptualized to overcome the limitations inherent in frequentist philosophy. Central to the uncertainty paradigm is the alternative Bayesian notion of probability as a degree of belief. That is, probability is defined by how strongly one believes a given proposition. This formulation permits consideration of information about a measurand beyond that cognizable in frequentist theory and provides a common basis for its analysis whether statistically or nonstatistically based.

In the uncertainty paradigm, as in error analysis, a measurand's "true" value is unknowable. However, this is not due to the physical phenomenon of irreducible error, but due to the impossibility of our ever possessing perfect knowledge concerning a measurand's state. Uncertainty focuses on this limitation interpreting a measurement result as a probability distribution that characterizes one's state of knowledge about a measurand's value. While measurement error as a physical phenomenon is as unknowable as a measurand's "true" value, the characterization of a result as a probability distribution in this manner permits a result's uncertainty to be rigorously determined.

When a measurement is performed, it always takes place against a backdrop of existing information about the measurement to be made and the measurand itself. Some of this information may be in the form of statistically obtained data, while some may be based on other sources such as general knowledge of the behavior and properties of relevant materials, methods, and instruments. When a measurement is performed, the discrete value obtained adds to our universe of information and updates our state of knowledge concerning the measurand. Because our information is necessarily incomplete, our knowledge concerning the measurand remains fuzzy. Given the information possessed, the discrete value obtained represents a packet of values dispersed about the measured result, all of which are believed to be attributable to the measurand with relative degrees of conviction (**Figure 7**).

It is the identification of probabilities as degrees of belief that transforms this packet of values into a probability distribution. In this context, the meaning of a measured value

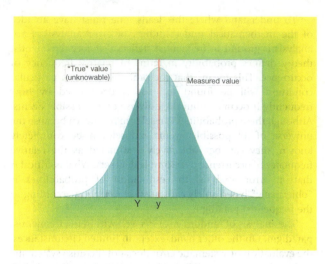

Figure 8   Measurement as probability distribution.

corresponds to a probability distribution characterizing the relative likelihood of the values believed to be attributable to a measurand based on the totality of currently available information (**Figure 8**).

This distribution completely specifies our state of knowledge concerning the values attributable to a measurand. Moreover, it delineates in a mathematically rigorous manner how a measured value, y, maps into those values believed to be attributable to a measurand. By doing so, it also determines the inferences that can be made concerning a measurand's value based on the values measured.

As an example, given a measured value, the distribution permits one to determine the probability that a measurand's value lies within any given range of values. In this context, one can think of the probability associated with the distribution as being equal to the area under the curve representing it. The probability that a measurand's value lies within a specified range is given by the proportion of the area under the curve spanning the range in question to the total area under the curve (**Figure 9**).

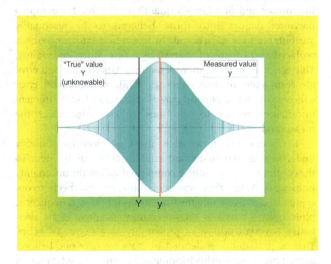

Figure 7   Measurement as packet of values.

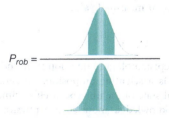

$$P_{rob} = \frac{}{}$$

Figure 9   Probability = ratio of areas under curve.

Given a measured value, y, the question of what values can *reasonably* be attributed to a measurand involves two competing considerations. First, we want to exclude values that, although possible, are highly improbable. Second, we need to include enough values so that there is a significant probability that the measurand's value is actually among those considered. The measurement's probability distribution provides a conceptually straightforward way of accomplishing this. Simply slice off the tails of the distribution while including enough of its middle so that the area of the remaining region represents a significant probability that the measurand's value lies within it (**Figure 10**).

From this, we can obtain a range of values reasonably attributable to a measurand, along with an associated probability that the value of the measurand lies within it. This defines the uncertainty of a measurement. Measurement uncertainty is the quantitative characterization of the dispersion of values that, based on the universe of information concerning a measurement, are believed to be *reasonably* attributable to a measurand. The half-width of this range of values is known as a result's expanded uncertainty, U (**Figure 11**).

The expanded uncertainty defines what is known as a "coverage interval" about a measured value. The coverage interval conveys the set of quantity values reasonably attributed to the measurand along with the specific probability that its "true" value actually lies within this range. The

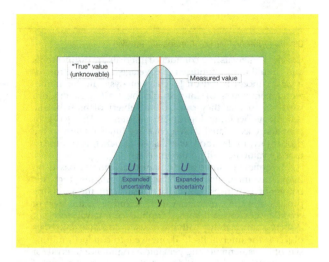

Figure 11 Expanded uncertainty.

probability is referred to as the interval's associated "level of confidence." Coverage intervals having an associated level of confidence between 95% and 99.7% are typically selected (**Figure 12**):

$$\text{Coverage interval}$$
$$y - U < Y_{99\%} < y + U \qquad [6]$$

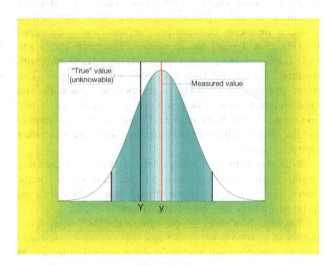

Figure 10 Values reasonably attributable to measurand.

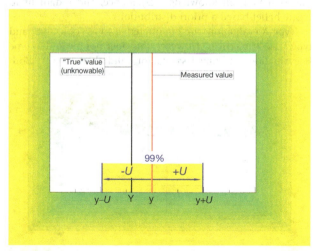

Figure 12 Coverage interval.

Coverage Interval versus Confidence Interval

Coverage intervals and confidence intervals are distinct tools and should not be confused. A coverage interval is a metrological concept based on Bayesian analysis. In this framework, parameters of interest can be treated as random variables so that they can be the subject of probabilistic statements without logical inconsistency. The level of confidence associated with a coverage interval refers to the probability, understood as a degree of belief, that a measurand's value lies within the interval.

A confidence interval is a statistical concept based on frequentist methodology. In this framework, the stochastic nature of the investigation lies entirely in the sampling process, not the parameter value. Accordingly, the level of confidence associated with a confidence interval does not associate a probability with the measurand value. Rather, its object is the interval itself. If one were to conduct multiple sets of measurements and generate a confidence interval for each set, the level of confidence tells you the proportion of these intervals that would be expected to cover/overlap a measurand's value (**Figure 13**).

There are two types of uncertainties: type A and type B. Unlike the two types of errors, type A and type B uncertainties are not distinguished by the nature of their source. Instead, they are defined by the manner in which they are determined. Type A uncertainty refers to the uncertainty that has been determined by statistical (frequentist) methods utilizing observed frequency distributions. Type B uncertainty refers to the uncertainty that has been determined by nonstatistical means relying on knowledge, experience, and judgment to create belief-based a priori distributions.

Type A evaluations are often referred to as "objective" and type B as "subjective." However, this does not mean that type B evaluations are any less real or valid than type A. Both evaluations rely on accepted notions of probability. Nor is one approach necessarily superior to the other. Whether type A or type B analysis yields better results is context dependent.

Regardless of the approach employed to determine them, a foundational tenant of this paradigm is that the uncertainties themselves do not differ in nature. Once determined, all distributions are interpreted in the Bayesian manner, representing models of our state of knowledge quantified according to degree of belief. This permits type A and type B uncertainties to be treated on equal footing as standard deviations of the distributions they are based on, providing rigorous justification for their combination into a "combined uncertainty" using traditional methods of analysis.

The importance of this lies in the fact that a measurement's uncertainty is usually made up of the combination of uncertainties from several distinct sources. To understand the significance, recall the inability of error analysis to combine systematic and random errors in a rigorously justifiable manner to determine a measurement's total error. To avoid confusion, in the context of uncertainty, systematic errors are referred to as "systematic effects." For pedagogical purposes, systematic effects were not included in the above discussion. Nonetheless, the determination of uncertainty assumes that every measurement has been corrected for significant systematic effects.

What the uncertainty paradigm permits us to do, regardless of the nature of a systematic effect or how it has been quantified, is to treat it as a probability distribution. When this is done, the distribution's expectation yields the required systematic correction (hereinafter referred to as bias) and its standard deviation characterizes the uncertainty associated with the bias. Treated in this manner, systematic effects and their associated uncertainties are placed on equal footing with measured values and their associated uncertainties, so that those phenomena formerly understood as systematic and random errors can now be combined in a logically consistent and rigorously justifiable manner. In general, the evaluation of the uncertainty arising from systematic effects may be either type A or type B.

Returning to the above discussion, it can now be seen that the uncertainty paradigm naturally incorporates systematic effects into the mapping of measured values to those believed to be attributable to a measurand (**Figure 14**).

The correction shifts the position of the probability distribution along the axis of values while the uncertainty associated with the correction will modify the shape of the distribution. As would be expected, this will shift the coverage interval in the direction of the correction as well.

Something that must be considered at this point is that given the inherent variability of measured values, it is seldom acceptable to base the determination of a measurand's value on a single measurement. Good practice requires acquisition of multiple measured values combined to determine their mean.

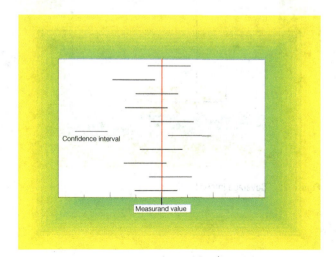

Figure 13   Interpretation of a confidence interval.

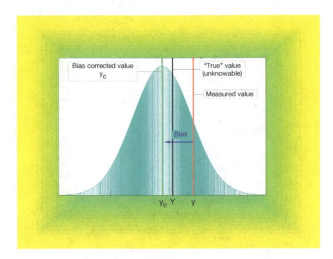

Figure 14 Mapping measurement to "reality."

The *best estimate* of a measurand's "true" value is then given by the *bias corrected mean* of the measured values:

$$\text{Best estimate} = \text{bias corrected mean}$$
$$Y_b = \bar{y}_c \qquad [7]$$

It is a fundamental principle of measurement that where the actual value of a measurand is important, a result is not complete and cannot be properly interpreted unless it has been corrected for bias and is accompanied by a quantitative statement of its uncertainty. Accordingly, a complete measurement result consists of the best estimate of the measurand's "true" value accompanied by its uncertainty:

$$\text{Measurement result} = \text{best estimate} \pm \text{uncertainty}$$
$$Y_{99\%} = Y_b \pm U \qquad [8]$$

$$\text{Coverage interval}$$
$$Y_b - U < Y_{99\%} < Y_b + U \qquad [9]$$

Measurement Uncertainty: A Forensic Example

The value of a measurand can be critical to the determination of certain criminal matters. For example, some states define the offense of driving under the influence of alcohol (DUI) by an individual's "true" breath alcohol concentration (BrAC). The measurement of BrAC, like any other scientific measurement, is accompanied by uncertainty. Thus, by themselves, the values reported by a breath test machine tell us little about an individual's "true" BrAC and whether they have actually committed a crime. Consider tests administered to two different individuals on different instruments in a state where DUI is defined by a BrAC of 0.08 g/210 L (**Figures 15 and 16**).

Blank test	.000
Internal standard	Verified
Subject sample	.084
Blank test	.000
External standard	.082
Blank test	.000
Subject sample	.081
Blank test	.000

Figure 15 Identical measurement results, different measurement meaning: Breath analysis.

Blank test	.000
Internal standard	Verified
Subject sample	.084
Blank test	.000
External standard	.079
Blank test	.000
Subject sample	.081
Blank test	.000

Figure 16 Breath analysis.

Each test reports identical BrAC values in excess of the state's per se limit with a mean value of 0.0825 g/210 L. Without more, these "breath test tickets" clearly seem to indicate that the BrACs in question exceed the legal limit. Moreover, given that the external standard readings are both reading true, there is actually no way to distinguish between these two tests.

The two tests' uncertainties reveal a different picture though. Despite identically measured values, the uncertainty of each, expressed as coverage intervals, is different (**Figures 17 and 18**).

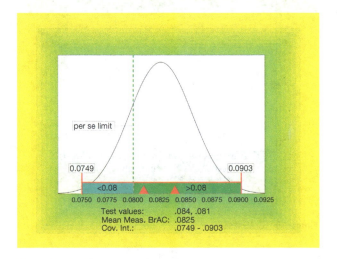

Figure 17 BrAC test 1.

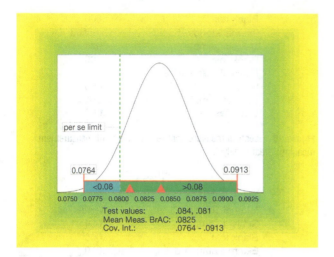

Figure 18 BrAC test 2.

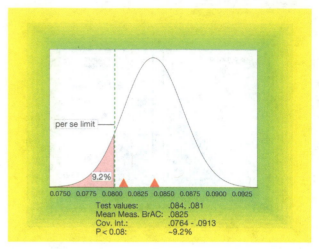

Figure 20 BrAC test 2.

Clearly, the computed uncertainty associated with test 1 is greater than that associated with test 2. Moreover, further examination reveals that the likelihood that each individual's BrAC is actually less than 0.08 g/210 L is nearly 20% and 10% for tests 1 and 2, respectively (**Figures 19 and 20**).

Thus, not only do these "identical" tests not have identical meanings but each represents a sizeable likelihood in the context of reasonable doubt that the BrACs in question are less than the relevant limit. Proper interpretation of these results clearly requires knowledge of their uncertainty.

Determining Measurement Uncertainty

There are several different methods for determining a measurement's uncertainty. The first step in each is to identify and quantify all systematic effects and appropriately correct for each.

The second step is typically the identification of relevant sources of uncertainty. A common way to document these is through a cause and effect diagram, which depicts each source of uncertainty and their relationship to each other and the final result (**Figure 21**).

When all the quantities on which a measured value depends can be varied simultaneously, a result's uncertainty can be determined, directly using statistical methods. Except for simple measurements, however, this approach is typically not practical.

Generally, then, the next step is to determine the magnitude of each of the relevant uncertainties. Each is quantified as a standard deviation and referred to as a "standard uncertainty:"

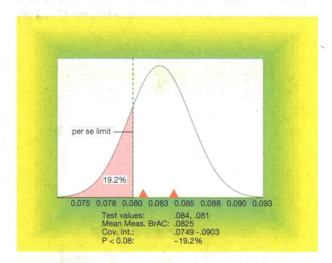

Figure 19 BrAC test 1.

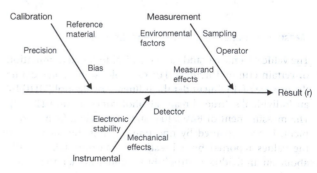

Figure 21 Cause and effect diagram.

Standard uncertainty

$$\mu \equiv \sigma \qquad [10]$$

The relative standard uncertainty is the ratio of the standard uncertainty to the best estimate of the measurand value. It can be useful when combining or comparing uncertainties of separate measurements:

Relative standard uncertainty

$$\mu_{r_y} = \frac{\mu_y}{|Y_b|} \qquad [11]$$

For some measurements, each source of uncertainty may be associated with the measurement as a whole and manifest itself independently as a direct effect on the final result. Such is the case with direct measurements. In these circumstances, a result's "combined uncertainty," μ_c, is given by the root-sum-square (rss) of the standard uncertainties:

$$\mu_C = \sqrt{\sum_{i=1}^{n} \mu_i^2} \qquad [12]$$

Most measurements are indirect in nature, determining a measurand's value through its relationship to other measured quantities. The most common method of determining uncertainty in these circumstances is discussed in the *Guide to the Expression of Uncertainty in Measurement* (the *GUM*). Application of the *GUM* requires that a measurement be modeled as a mathematical function, referred to as the Measurement Function:

Measurement function

$$Y = f(X_1, X_2, \ldots, X_N) \qquad [13]$$

This function describes the relationship between the measurand value and those quantities required to determine it. For example, if the measurand is the volume of a cylinder, the measurement function might be given as

$$V(r, h) = \pi r^2 h \qquad [14]$$

The combined uncertainty of the measurand is determined by "adding" up the individual standard uncertainties using the method of *Propagation of Uncertainty*:

$$\mu_c = \sqrt{\sum_{i=1}^{N} \left(\frac{\partial f}{\partial x_i} \cdot \mu_{x_i}\right)^2 + 2\sum_{i=1}^{N-1}\sum_{j=i+1}^{N} \frac{\partial f}{\partial x_i} \cdot \frac{\partial f}{\partial x_j} \cdot \mu_{x_i x_j}} \qquad [15]$$

If each of the input quantities is independent, the expression simplifies to

$$\mu_c = \sqrt{\sum_{i=1}^{N} \left(\frac{\partial f}{\partial x_i} \cdot \mu_{x_i}\right)^2} \qquad [16]$$

For the volume of a cylinder, the combined uncertainty would be given by the expression

$$\mu_{cv} = \sqrt{(2\pi r h \mu_r)^2 + (\pi r^2 \mu_h)^2} \qquad [17]$$

Propagation of Uncertainty: Applied to Measurement Functions with Independent Input Quantities

1. Measurement function:

$$Y = a \cdot X \qquad [18]$$

$$Y_b = a \cdot X_b \qquad [19]$$

$$\mu_y = a \cdot \mu_x \qquad [20]$$

2. Measurement function:

$$Y = X^n \qquad [21]$$

$$Y_b = x_b^n \qquad [22]$$

$$\mu_{r_y} = \frac{\mu_y}{|Y_b|} = |n| = \frac{\mu_x}{|x_b|} \qquad [23]$$

3. Measurement function:

$$Y = X - W + \cdots + Z \qquad [24]$$

$$Y_b = x_b - w_b + \cdots + z_b \qquad [25]$$

$$\mu_y = \sqrt{\mu_x^2 + \mu_w^2 + \cdots + \mu_z^2} \qquad [26]$$

4. Measurement function:

$$Y = \frac{X \times \cdots \times W}{Z \times \cdots \times Q} \qquad [27]$$

$$Y_b = \frac{x_b \times \cdots \times w_b}{z_b \times \cdots \times q_b} \qquad [28]$$

$$\mu_{r_y} = \frac{\mu_y}{|Y_b|}$$

$$= \sqrt{\left(\frac{\mu_x}{x_b}\right)^2 + \left(\frac{\mu_w}{w_b}\right)^2 + \cdots + \left(\frac{\mu_z}{z_b}\right)^2 + \left(\frac{\mu_q}{q_b}\right)^2} \qquad [29]$$

The expanded uncertainty is obtained by multiplying the combined uncertainty by a coverage factor, k:

$$\text{Expanded uncertainty}$$
$$U = k\mu_c \qquad [30]$$

The coverage factor determines the coverage interval's level of confidence. It is commonly based on a t-distribution. Where a measurement's degrees of freedom are sufficiently large, the level of confidence bestowed by a given coverage factor is approximately that associated with a Gaussian distribution (**Figure 22**).

The coverage factor is typically chosen to yield a level of confidence of 95% or greater. For the volume of a cylinder, the expanded uncertainty yielding a 99% level of confidence would be given by the expression

$$U = 2.576\sqrt{(2\pi rh\mu_r)^2 + (\pi r^2\mu_h)^2} \qquad [31]$$

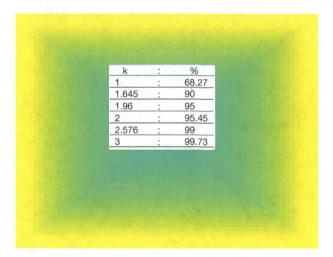

k	:	%
1	:	68.27
1.645	:	90
1.96	:	95
2	:	95.45
2.576	:	99
3	:	99.73

Figure 22   Coverage factors and levels of confidence: Gaussian distribution.

For the *GUM* to apply, the distribution characterizing a final result must not depart appreciably from normality. Where this is not the case, or where a measurement function is complicated or unknown, a more general approach to the determination of uncertainty is based on the *propagation of distributions*. Instead of determining the standard uncertainty of each input quantity and combining them, the distributions characterizing the quantity value of each input quantity are directly combined to construct the distribution characterizing our state of knowledge of the measurand's value (**Figure 23**).

The standard deviation of the final distribution yields a result's standard uncertainty. It should be noted that the resultant distribution and, hence, its uncertainty (coverage interval) need not be symmetric about the mean. The Monte Carlo method, a computer-based iterative simulation process, is an example of this approach.

A final approach to the determination of uncertainty is the top-down method, called so because it focuses on the measurement process as a whole instead of its detailed breakdown into distinct sources of uncertainty. It utilizes overall reproducibility estimates, based on measurement trials, as a direct estimate of the uncertainty associated with a measurement method. This approach is often utilized where a measurement function is complicated or unknown. Although each has its advantages, in certain circumstances, the *GUM* and top-down approaches can be used together to determine the uncertainty of a measurement where desirable.

Meaning Requires Uncertainty

Scientific measurement provides a powerful tool for investigating physical phenomena. No matter how good a measurement is, we can never know the "true" value of the quantity of interest. Error analysis focuses on the measurand itself, with the intent of providing a value that is as close as possible to

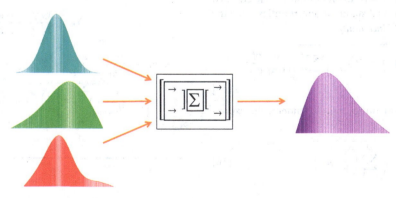

Figure 23   Propagation of distributions.

its "true" value. What it actually provides is an ill-defined upper limit on a measurement's total error, revealing the worst a measured value might be without conveying how good it actually is. Uncertainty analysis focuses on our state of knowledge about a measurand, providing a quantitative mapping of measured values into those values believed to be actually and reasonably attributable to the quantity of interest. This conveys the meaning of a result by rigorously defining and constraining the inferences that can be drawn from it. Accordingly, where the actual value of a measurand is important, a result is not complete and cannot be properly interpreted unless it is accompanied by a quantitative statement of its uncertainty.

> *See also:* **Foundations:** Statistical Interpretation of Evidence: Bayesian Analysis; The Frequentist Approach to Forensic Evidence Interpretation; **Legal:** Legal Aspects of Forensic Science; **Methods:** Chemometrics; **Toxicology:** Interpretation of Results; **Toxicology/Alcohol:** Breath Alcohol.

Further Reading

Ehrlich, C., Dybkaer, R., Wöger, W., 2007. Evolution of philosophy and description of measurement. Accreditation and Quality Assurance 12, 201–218.

Estler, W.T., 1999. Measurement as inference: fundamental ideas. CIRP Annals 48 (2), 611–631.

EURACHEM, 2000. Quantifying Uncertainty in Analytical Measurement. QUAM:2000.1.

EURACHEM, 2007. Measurement Uncertainty Arising from Sampling: A Guide to Methods and Approaches.

ISO, 2004. Guidance for the Use of Repeatability, Reproducibility and Trueness Estimates in Measurement Uncertainty Estimation. ISO/TS 21748.

JCGM, 2008. Evaluation of Measurement Data – Guide to the Expression of Uncertainty in Measurement (GUM). JCGM 100.

JCGM, 2008. Evaluation of Measurement Data – Supplement 1 to the 'Guide to the Expression of Uncertainty in Measurement' – Propagation of Distributions Using a Monte Carlo Method. JCGM 101.

JCGM, 2008. International Vocabulary of Metrology – Basic and General Concepts and Associated Terms (VIM). JCGM 200.

JCGM, 2009. Evaluation of Measurement Data – an Introduction to the 'Guide to the Expression of Uncertainty in Measurement' and Related Documents. JCGM 104.

Kacker, R., Sommer, K., Kessel, R., 2007. Evolution of modern approaches to express uncertainty in measurement. Metrologia 44, 513–529.

Kirkup, L., Frenkel, B., 2006. An Introduction to Uncertainty in Measurement: Using the GUM (Guide to the Expression of Uncertainty in Measurement). Cambridge University Press, New York.

NIST, 1994. Guidelines for Evaluating and Expressing the Uncertainty of NIST Measurement Results. NIST 1297.

Vosk, T., 2010. Trial by numbers: uncertainty in the quest for truth and justice. The NACDL Champion 56, 48–56 (Reprinted with permission in The Voice for the Defense 40 (3), 24–33 (2011).

Postmortem Toxicology: Artifacts

G Skopp, University Hospital, Heidelberg, Germany

Glossary

Accumulation Progressive increase in concentration following repeated doses of a drug.

Acidosis A blood pH value below 7.4.

Adipose tissue Body tissue containing stored fat.

Alkalosis A blood pH value above 7.4.

Antemortem Done or occurring before death.

Arterial Of or being in an artery (blood vessel carrying blood high in oxygen content).

Autopsy Examination of a corpse to determine or confirm the cause of death.

Biochemical conversion Structural change of a drug involving chemical processes occurring in living organisms.

Cell membrane The outer covering of cells.

Cholinesterase An enzyme that catalyzes the hydrolytic cleavage of the acyl group from various esters of choline and some related compounds.

Dalton Atomic mass unit.

Diffusion Movement of drugs along a concentration gradient.

Dissociation constant Equilibrium constant for the reaction in which a weak acid is in equilibrium with its corresponding base in aqueous solution.

Embalming To treat a corpse or a part of it with preservatives such as formaldehyde so as to prevent decay.

Enzyme induction Increase of drug metabolism by drugs or chemicals.

Enzyme inhibition Decrease of drug metabolism by drugs or chemicals.

Equilibration Development or maintenance of equilibrium.

Eschweiler–Clarke reaction Chemical reaction whereby an amine is methylated (reductive amination).

Excretion Physical removal of a substance (drug) from the body.

Extraction efficiency Ratio of the detector response of an analyte from an extracted sample to the detector response of the analyte from an unextracted sample (solution) containing the same amount of analyte that was added to the extracted sample.

Formulation A medicinal preparation used in a special form such as a tablet.

Glucuronidase An enzyme that catalyzes the hydrolysis of various glucuronides.

Hemolytic Destruction of red blood cells leading to the release of hemoglobin.

Heterocyclic ring Cyclic compound which has atoms of at least two different elements.

Homogenization To make, for example, a tissue specimen uniform in consistency.

Hydrolysis Reaction of a substance with water in order to be changed into one or more other substances.

Immunoassay A laboratory technique that makes use of the binding between an antigen and its homologous antibody in order to identify (and quantify) drug classes or—less often—a single substance.

Interaction The action of one drug to the effectiveness or toxicity of another one.

Interference Errors in the analytical results of chemical, physical, instrumental, but also of human origin.

Lipid solubility Ability of a compound to dissolve in fat or nonpolar lipids.

Media A fluid or tissue in which a substance is present or can be analyzed from.

Metabolism Enzymatic or biochemical transformation of a substance (drug) to metabolic products.

Methanolysis Reaction of a substance with methanol in order to be changed into one or more other substances.

Methylation Addition of a methyl group to a molecule.

Organophosphorous Organic compounds containing carbon–phosphorus bonds.

Oxidation Gain of oxygen and/or loss of electrons.

pH value Logarithm of the reciprocal of hydrogen ion concentration.

Physicochemical Relating to both physical and chemical properties.

Propellant A compressed gas that acts as a vehicle for discharging the contents of an aerosol container.

Rate-limiting step The slowest step in a metabolic pathway or series of chemical reactions which determines the overall rate of the other reactions in the pathway.

Redistribution (postmortem) Process of drugs diffusing from tissues into blood along a concentration gradient between death and time of specimen collection.

Reduction Loss of oxygen and/or gain of electrons.

Stability-indicating assay Validated analytical procedure that accurately and precisely measures active ingredients—drug substance or metabolite—free from potential interferences like degradation products, components from the particular matrix, or other potential impurities.

Sulfatase Enzyme that catalyzes the hydrolytic cleavage of inorganic sulfate from sulfate esters.

Therapeutic range Range of concentrations in blood at which a drug is effective with minimal toxicity to most individuals.

Transport mechanisms Mechanisms that enable cells to move materials into or out of a cell.

Trauma, traumatic An injury to living tissue.

Venous Of or being in a vein (blood vessel carrying blood low in oxygen content).

Vitreous humor Clear gelatinous substance that fills the eyeball.

Introduction

The question that is usually asked if a death case is suspected of poisoning is: "Did a drug cause or contribute to the death?" Although the answer is likely to come from combined analysis of the medical history, the circumstances surrounding death, the manner of death, and the measured concentration of the respective drug, the answer may not be straightforward or, in some cases, remain uncertain. Even if extensive background information is available, there are many uncertainties relating a concentration found postmortem to the concentration before death, and from the putative antemortem level to the severity of poisoning.

A major difficulty which has to be dealt with in a post-mortem toxicology investigation is artificial changes related to the media, the drug, and its concentration; such artifacts are not naturally present in the corpse but can occur already during the process of dying, pretreatment of the corpse (such as embalming), the postmortem time period, as well as the collection, storage, processing, and analysis of postmortem specimens. Artifacts may produce qualitative as well as quantitative changes. These artifacts remaining an inherent part of postmortem toxicology, it is essential to be aware of them and to be able to identify situations where they occur.

This chapter gives a short summary on artifacts that can occur during the prefinal phase and the period until the autopsy is performed, including changes that may occur in the quality of the specimens and the amount of drugs present, and those artifacts caused by the analytical procedure.

The Prefinal Phase

In any drug-related case, it is necessary to state whether a drug concentration in blood is compatible with overdose or is more in accord with therapeutic use. Pharmacokinetic concepts describing the time course of drug absorption, distribution, metabolism, and excretion can provide an estimate of the quantitative relationship between the dose of a drug and the observed blood or tissue concentration. Although an accurate measurement of the blood concentration can be accomplished in most cases, the interpretation of the analytical result is not straightforward.

For example, a considerable overlap occurs in the concentrations seen in clozapine-, morphine-, or methadone-related deaths following deliberate self-poisoning and in subjects who had died with no evidence of drug misuse. Factors likely to contribute to the uncertainty of published reference ranges for drugs prior to death are summarized in **Table 1**.

The rate and extent of a drug's absorption is largely dependent on its physicochemical properties, the formulation, and the physiologic factors. Blood flow is the rate-limiting step in drug distribution. Accordingly, rapid distribution of lipid-soluble drugs is observed between the blood and lungs, liver, heart, and brain. Less rapid equilibration is found in skeletal muscle, bone, and adipose tissue, which receive a smaller volume of blood per unit mass per minute. Drugs with a molecular mass of up to 600 Da quickly diffuse out of the vascular system into the interstitial fluid bathing the cells. Lipid-soluble molecules penetrate the cell membrane itself while water-soluble molecules such as pregabaline are dependent on special transport mechanisms. The more lipophilic the compound, the faster is its distribution into tissues. In acute poisoning cases, death can occur before steady state has been reached, resulting in appreciably higher arterial than venous blood concentrations. For example, maximum arterial plasma concentrations of amitriptyline, heroin, 6-acetylmorphine, and morphine were 4, 2.4, 5.4, and 1.4 times higher, respectively, than maximum venous concentrations during the absorption/distribution phase.

Table 1   Factors likely to affect a drug's reference range already during the prefinal phase

Antemortem influence	General remarks	Example(s)
Changes of pharmacokinetic parameters	Immobilization; drop in blood pressure; decreased tissue perfusion and tissue hypoxia; impaired ventilation and acidosis; progressive dehydration; hepatic and renal failure; disease state	Respiratory depression due to accumulation of the active metabolite morphine-6-glucuronide in renal insufficiency or decreased clearance and lower volume of distribution of morphine in trauma and fire victims; about fourfold increase of the half-life of diazepam in alcoholic cirrhosis; inflammation increases drug penetration
Interactions	Pharmacokinetic and pharmacodynamic interactions: drug–drug, drug–alcohol, drug–nutrient, and drug–herb interactions	Golden seal—inhibition of CYP2D6; increase of the area under the curve for amitriptyline and nortriptyline in the presence of ethanol
Tolerance	Acquired tolerance due to decreased efficacy at the receptor site or increased metabolism due to induction of enzyme activities; cross-tolerance, for example, between opioids may also occur	Cocaine, heroin, methadone
Treatment in hospital	Intravenous fluids; resuscitation measures; devices, which automatically deliver medication by the parenteral route	Decreased or nondetectable amounts of alcohol and drugs; intubation-related lidocaine artifacts; locally elevated drug levels due to fentanyl patches

Drug metabolism, which refers to the biochemical conversion of a drug to another chemical form, can be considerably altered by induction or inhibition of enzyme activities. There is clear evidence that smoking cessation increases blood concentrations of drugs such as warfarin, olanzapine, or clozapine, which also have narrow therapeutic concentration range. Smoking cessation causes smoking-induced CYP1A2 levels to return to normal. Drug–drug interactions are widely recognized and are listed in databases and texts. Far less, however, is known on drug–nutrient or drug–herb interactions. Activities of CYP3A4, 2C9, and 1A2 may be increased by St. John's wort, whereas inhibition of CYP3A4, 2D6, and 1A2 has been observed by kava. Drugs with the relative elimination rate being slower at higher than at lower concentrations in blood may also present a problem. For example, a 50% increase in the daily dose of aspirin has been observed to produce a 300% increase in salicylate in the blood. Moreover, plasma concentrations of gabapentin, methylenedioxymethamphetamine (Ecstasy), and propanolol do not increase proportionally with increasing dose.

Renal excretion playing a major role in drug elimination, considerable accumulation of drug metabolites can be observed in subjects suffering from renal insufficiency. Therefore, determination of active metabolites, such as morphine-6-glucuronide or oxypurinol, the active metabolite of allopurinol, is of utmost importance. Usually, a high ratio of parent drug to metabolite concentration has been taken as an indication that death had occurred rapidly, and vice versa. However, such ratios may be misleading as genetic factors contribute substantially to the large differences among people in metabolic clearance of drugs.

Besides these pharmacological considerations, the context in which the subject was found must be considered in interpreting analytical data. Acidosis or alkalosis can markedly alter the disposition of a drug. Acidosis produces a shift of weak bases, including most drugs, from the blood or extracellular fluid to the cellular space. These shifts occur in all tissues including the brain. Extended blood loss, for example, caused by traumatic bleeding, results in an increased heart rate, peripheral vasoconstriction, and transfer of extracellular fluid into the blood circulation. Therefore, the blood drug concentration in a trauma victim may differ from the concentration present at the time of trauma. In addition, treatment during hospitalization or resuscitation may produce artifacts (see **Table 1**).

There are many additional and unique aspects causing postmortem changes of the corpse, the sample, and the analyte therein, which will subsequently be discussed.

The Corpse

Postmortem changes affect the micro- and macroenvironment of the foreign substances and refer to all processes by which their movement between body fluids and tissues takes place. This phenomenon is gathered under the generic term of postmortem redistribution. Currently, there are no accepted biomarkers available to indicate the magnitude of postmortem changes likely to influence drug distribution in blood.

Decomposition of circulating proteins and membrane macromolecules that bind drugs, destruction of biological membranes that delineate drug compartments, loss of energy-dependent gradients and postmortem acidosis that influence the local concentration of drugs during the early postmortem period all contribute to changes postmortem.

Many drugs are sequestered antemortem in organs or may be still present in the gastrointestinal tract in acute poisoning; they can be redistributed either by the vascular pathway depending on the fluidity of the blood, by passive diffusion through the blood vessels, or from the lumen of a body cavity toward surrounding organs. Inflammation may promote drug penetration into tissues. If a vomit containing a large amount of drug is aspirated into the trachea, postmortem diffusion into heart blood should be considered; examples of this are ethanol, toluene, and lidocaine. Although postmortem diffusion of a drug from the urinary bladder is rare, it can take place in the case of a large amount of urine containing a high content of drug. Therefore, femoral blood should not be used as a single specimen for drug analysis when the substance is a likely cause of death.

Tissue redistribution of drugs after death is determined by some of the same factors governing distribution (see earlier); it is more common for basic drugs and has largely been attributed to the physicochemical properties of a drug including molecular size, dissociation constant, lipid solubility, tissue binding, and the environmental pH value. Lipophilic drugs often have a high tissue concentration and are more likely to be redistributed. It appears that an apparent distribution volume >3 l kg^{-1} facilitates postmortem redistribution, such as for the antidepressant amitriptyline. The apparent distribution volume is simply a proportionality constant relating the plasma concentration to the total amount of drug in the body; in man, it can vary from 0.04 (plasma volume) to 20 l kg^{-1} or more. Atomoxetine may be an exception inasmuch as the drug apparently undergoes postmortem redistribution despite a relatively low distribution volume of 0.85 l kg^{-1}.

A longer period of time between death and sample collection may give more potential for postmortem changes. Nevertheless, the most important quantitative changes in drug concentration occur within a few hours following death. In animal studies, the concentration of dothiepin steadily increases to reach about 400% of the original concentration at 8 h postmortem. Fluctuating blood concentrations of fluoxetine and norfluoxetine in a dog model could be observed up to 2 h after the animals had been sacrificed with no significant differences between the 2-h and 12-h samples. However, the time period (e.g., up to 24 h) may not necessarily correlate with the ante/postmortem concentration ratios, and some drugs have lower postmortem levels than antemortem levels (e.g., phenobarbital, phenytoin, carbamazepine, and its 10,11 epoxide metabolite, as well as tetrahydrocannabinol).

Additional factors that have not been studied in detail but are likely to contribute to postmortem redistribution are (1) the position of the body when found, which may result in blood draining from central to peripheral sites if blood has remained sufficiently fluid, and (2) the storage temperature of the body, with a greater potential of changes at a higher temperature.

Body fluids, tissues, and drugs present in these specimens are subject to fundamental changes. Enzymes naturally present in the body cause autolysis, while putrefaction is due to destruction by microorganisms. The pH value in blood immediately drops up to 5.5 after death has occurred, and a decrease in water content can often be observed. Hemolysis is seen with most blood specimens, which can be either fluid, clotted, or partially clotted. In addition, hypostasis occurs due to gravity. Overall, the composition of the postmortem blood sample, which is most commonly used to test for actual impairment or acute overdose, substantially differs from that taken from a living subject.

For any drug that exhibits an unequal distribution between the liquid and cellular components of blood, drug measurement may be influenced by the profound changes of the medium. Distribution ratio may differ not only between drugs but also between the parent drug and major metabolites. Ratios determined from spiked or authentic samples—the latter procedure should be favored over in vitro partition experiments—can be useful for a gross estimation, keeping in mind that the distribution range may scatter over a wider range in postmortem samples as has been shown for cannabinoids.

Parallel or opposed effects to that resulting from postmortem redistribution may arise from the formation of totally new entities, an artificial raise of the drug concentration, or degradation of labile compounds. A most prominent example is ethanol, which may be produced by a wide range of microorganisms penetrating from the intestines or from the skin as part of postmortem degenerative processes. Generally, postmortem produced levels may be lower than 0.07%, but may reach significant concentrations up to 0.22% if conditions are optimal. Formation of ethanol may be more pronounced after severe trauma and at an elevated temperature. If the body is kept refrigerated, no ethanol is usually produced within 24 h; however, its formation can occur if the body is not refrigerated within 4 h of death. It is important that determination of ethanol is corroborated by analyses from other fluids, such as vitreous humor, which is well protected from microbial infiltration after death.

Artificial formation has also been observed with gamma hydroxybutyrate (GHB), cyanide, and carbon monoxide. Fatalities mostly involved gamma butyrolactone and 1,4-butandiol, which are readily available precursors of GHB. In postmortem peripheral blood, endogenously formed GHB could reach 200 mg l^{-1}, which overlaps with those of reported fatalities. Although GHB cutoff values of 30 or 50 mg l^{-1} blood or analysis of additional samples such as urine and vitreous humor have been proposed, appraisal of postmortem concentration is challenging. The amount of carbon monoxide in blood may increase due to postmortem formation by decomposition of hemoglobin and myoglobin during putrefaction, especially in cases of drowning. As smoking may be a common source of carbon monoxide hemoglobin, a cutoff value of 10% is useful.

A number of compounds are unstable in whole blood, such as all volatile compounds, N- and S-oxide metabolites, ester-type drugs, molecules with a nitro group, N-sulfate and N-glucuronide metabolites, acyl glucuronides, sulfhydryl-containing drugs, alkyl nitrites, and peroxides. Instability in postmortem fluids and tissues is largely due to chemical or metabolic instability. Cocaine and heroin are the most notable examples, which are broken down in an aqueous solution and enzymatically. The nitrobenzodiazepines (e.g., flunitrazepam, clonazepam, and nitrazepam) are also known to degrade after death to the corresponding 7-amino form. Conversion of morphine glucuronides, which are stable in freshly drawn blood from living subjects, to morphine is attributed to residual or bacterial glucuronidase activities.

An embalming procedure can cause dilution of the blood, leading to a partial or complete loss of the drug present at the time of death. Embalming fluids contain formaldehyde, which is a highly reactive chemical agent, and also alcohols including ethanol. Most likely pathways of drug changes are through hydrolysis or methylation via the Eschweiler–Clarke reaction depending on time, pH, and concentration of formaldehyde. For example, amitriptyline has been formed from nortriptyline, methamphetamine from amphetamine, and N,N-dimethylamphetamine from methamphetamine. Conversion of bupropion to the respective N-methyl derivative is more efficient than for olanzapine with its secondary amino group being embedded in the heterocyclic ring. Denaturation of body fluids and tissues may also render specimens more difficult to extract.

The Sample

Specimens that are routinely collected include blood from peripheral sites such as the femoral or subclavian veins as well as heart blood, urine, gastric contents, and organs, particularly liver. Further samples may be taken, depending on the case (see **Table 2**). Incorrect or insufficient sampling will severely affect a postmortem investigation. The nature and integrity of a sample submitted for analysis largely define the reliability and relevance of any analytical result. Although availability is often dictated by the case, selection of the sample is far more important than in other branches of forensic toxicology. In addition, the use of appropriate containers and preservatives can be critical for identifying a substance.

How samples should be collected from the corpse has not been detailed here but is described elsewhere. Some guidelines have been published for collecting the most appropriate specimens for analysis. Sampling should be standardized to minimize site-to-site variability and to ensure comparability of the analytical results. Contamination being the most common cause of artifacts, sampling should be performed before the autopsy is started, if appropriate.

Peripheral blood such as femoral blood is suggested to be subject to redistribution from muscle and fat only. Nevertheless, at least a specimen taken from another site should be analyzed for a proper interpretation of the blood concentration. In the case of ethanol, vitreous humor is an appropriate second specimen, and liver has been the most common second specimen for drug analysis. Liver may also be helpful to diagnose intoxication with an antidepressant; for example, the ratio of amitriptyline to nortriptyline concentrations has been suggested to differentiate acute intoxication from therapeutic use.

To analyze postmortem specimens will be useless if intoxication has been survived for a few hours or days in a hospital; samples collected during the stay should preferably be analyzed instead. Evidence collected at the scene such as drug paraphernalia or containers with remaining liquid or solid remains can provide additional information; such information may drive analysis forward in the right direction in some instances, whereas in others suspected substances may not be implicated in the fatality at all.

An appropriate and clean container has to be used for each sample to maintain its integrity. If a container is partially filled, evaporation of volatiles and oxidative loss of drugs may occur, whereas the container or the lid may break upon freezing if it is filled to a minimum headspace. The best material is glass, which is recommended whenever solvent abuse or an anesthetic death is suspected. A teflon- or aluminum foil-lined lid should then be used. Disposable plastic tubes or bottles are appropriate provided that breakage upon freezing or adsorption of the drug does not occur. Plasticizers, particularly phthalates, may originate from plastic bags. Testing of the material before routinely collecting specimens will reduce sampling artifacts.

There is no obligatory requirement for specimen preservation, which affects blood specimens in particular. Generally, anticoagulants are not recommended. Formation of ethanol and degradation of cocaine may be slowed, preserving the sample with fluoride. Nevertheless, in vitro formation of ethanol has been observed in samples containing fluoride. In cocaine-containing specimens, an accumulation of methyl ecgonine has been observed in the presence of fluoride. Therefore, summing up the concentrations of cocaine and its three hydrolysis products to estimate the cocaine concentration in blood at death has been suggested. Preservation with fluoride at a final concentration of 1–5% is also recommended for analysis of cyanide, carbon monoxide, and GHB. It also stabilizes lorazepam and oxazepam by approximately 13% compared to unpreserved samples. However, fluoride should not be added when organophosphorous compounds are involved. Acidification may stabilize cocaine and N-glycosides; and ascorbic acid may reduce losses of substances such as apomorphine. Ascorbic acid, however, may lead to a reduction

Table 2   Samples that should be taken prior to autopsy or during autopsy, if appropriate

Sample	Acquisition/Amount	Purpose	Challenge
Samples that should be taken prior to autopsy			
Femoral venous blood; alternative: another peripheral specimen	By preparation and ligation of the blood vessel; 10–25 ml	Quantitative analysis	Insufficient amount, results may not be used in isolation; the specimen is not beyond postmortem redistribution
Urine	By puncture of the abdominal wall; up to 50 ml	Drug screening; exposure toward volatiles (e.g., metabolites of toluene, xylene)	Availability; no evidence of acute exposure; failure in very acute poisons or if a drug is not cleared by the kidneys
Liquor cerebrospinalis; vitreous humor	Suboccipital puncture/aspiration by suction; respective total volume	Biochemical markers such as glucose, lactate, urea, and nitrogen in suspected renal failure; ethanol	Small volume; there are different opinions whether specimens from both eyes may be combined
Hair, nails	Preferably from the posterior vertex, fixed by a string; a pen-sized bundle of hair; nail clippings as far as available	Long-term changes in pattern of drug use; noncompliance; discrimination between single or chronic exposure; exposure by a third party; crime under the influence of drugs; heavy metal poisoning	Hair soaked with body fluids or vomits; small database for the interpretation of results determined from nails
Samples that can be taken during autopsy			
Heart blood	After opening of the pericardial sack; up to 20 (50) ml	Drug screening	Subject to postmortem diffusion/redistribution; not for quantification
Gastric contents or vomited material	Separation of tablets or suspected materials; total volume if inhomogeneous or 50 ml	Drug screening	Documentation of the total volume; inhomogeneous specimen; a small amount of drug present may not be assigned to oral intake, but does not rule out an overdose
Bile bladder fluid	Aspiration or squeezing into a container; total volume	Previous/chronic exposure	Rather chronic than acute use; concentrations may be significantly higher than in blood; highly variable blood/bile ratios
Tissue such as liver, muscle, kidneys, lungs, and brain	Sampling at an early stage of autopsy; ~50 g	Whenever body fluids are not available	Recording of organ weight; substantial site-to-site variability; liver: tissue from deep within the right lobe
Entomological species	As much as available	In case of putrefaction	Qualitative result; larvae rapidly eliminate drugs when removed from the corpse
Bone or bone marrow	3 cm of the long bones; or as much as available	In case of skeletonization or heavy metal poisoning	Qualitative result

of *N*-oxides, resulting in an increase in the concentration of the parent drug, and chlorpromazine and clozapine can be cited as an example.

The Compound

Postmortem changes must be considered for all but a few drugs. Basically, instability of a drug substance depends on its structure, physicochemical properties, the matrix, the storage container, temperature, and time. Stability is defined as the capability of the sample material to retain the initial value of

a measured quantity for a defined period within specific limits when stored under defined conditions. Such consideration can inevitably not start until the time of sampling and covers the time until analysis. Some of the degradation mechanisms seen during storage are similar to those that have been observed during the postmortem interval (see earlier). Often, the particular matrix has not been considered, and stability of drugs in tissues has very rarely been reported.

Experimental investigation on time- and temperature-dependent changes may give information on the reaction type involved in drug degradation and on potential degradation products. It should be considered that postmortem degradation may differ from a drug's instability observed in biological fluids obtained from living subjects. For example, morphine is primarily affected by oxidation in freshly drawn blood, whereas in postmortem samples kept at the same conditions, hydrolysis of morphine glucuronides is the predominant reaction, the degradation rate being dependent on the particular glucuronidase activities of the specimen.

Sometimes, metabolites or breakdown products are far more stable than the parent compound. The poor stability of cocaine, benzoylecgonine, and methyl ecgonine, as well as of heroin and 6-acetylmorphine, is well documented. Alternate analysis for ecgonine and morphine as rather stable breakdown products is recommended. Ethyl glucuronide (EtG) has been suggested as a marker of antemortem ingestion of alcohol in cases where postmortem production of ethanol is questioned. EtG being unstable in blood, however, a negative result may also arise from degradation of the phase-II metabolite. As ethyl sulfate is more stable due to the lack of sulfatases in bacteria, its determination along with EtG has been recommended. The breakdown of many benzodiazepine-type compounds has been studied in more detail. Interestingly, the long-term stability of the benzodiazepines estazolam and alprazolam has been attributed to the triazolo rings in their structures, which make these compounds more resistant to hydrolysis.

Approaches to maintain stability such as pH adjustment, addition of inhibitors, or antioxidants have already been addressed earlier. The storage of analytes in blood dried on filter paper is an upcoming technique to adequately stabilize labile compounds. A commonly encountered condition in the forensic laboratory is lowering of the temperature, which will decrease all changes occurring through neoformation, hydrolysis, oxidation or reduction, and enzyme activities. For example, the cholinesterase activity in blood almost does not decline 3 weeks after storage at room temperature. The highest enzyme activities are present in liver, but can also be found in other tissues such as the kidneys and the brain. As degradation takes place even at 4 °C, immediate freezing of specimens is recommended. The majority of analytes in blood is sufficiently stable when stored at -20 °C for about 12 months except 7-aminonitrazepam, tetrahydrocannabinol, and zopiclone, for example. Postmortem testing of inhalants, aerosol propellants such as propane and butane, fuels, chlorinated solvents, and amyl nitrite is difficult not only as a result of their volatility but also of their instability. A loss of up to 25% of blood toluene has been observed in sealed glass tubes stored at room temperature for 7 days. Hair samples, however, should be stored at room temperature protected from humidity and light to avoid drug loss. Methemoglobin levels rise as an apparent effect of frozen storage, whereas storage at -80 °C is most desirable for a reliable determination of carbon monoxide in blood.

The Analytical Assay

Although the history of a sample appears to be most relevant to the production of artifacts, artifacts may also occur during the isolation and determination of a drug. Appropriate procedures in postmortem drug analysis have been sufficiently covered by recent reviews.

False positives are common with immunoassays, and interactions are not limited to matrix effects or the structural similarity of compounds. Insufficiency of some assays for high-potency benzodiazepines is well known, and a hydrolysis step prior to analysis may overcome this problem.

Often, a special pretreatment or homogenization according to the specimen's nature and/or a more sophisticated cleanup extraction of putrefied or embalmed materials is required for all forms of chromatography. The lack of suitability of routinely applied isolation methods may result in poor recovery and coextraction of interferences, leading to signal overlap and ion suppression or enhancement.

The chemical properties of a reagent used for sample preparation can give rise to chemical reactions of the solvent itself, an impurity, or a stabilizer that it may contain. For example, phosgene in chloroform reacts to form carbamate derivatives during extraction of tricyclic antidepressants; and formation of methochloride adducts is known for clozapine, olanzapine, and ofloxacine when treated with dichloromethane. Artifactual formation of 4-androsten-3,17-dione and androsterone from the internal standards $[16,16,17-d_3]$-testosterone and $[16,16,17-d_3]$-5α-androstane-3α,17β-diol through enzymatic oxidation of the 17β-hydroxyl function to a 17-keto function by 17β-hdroxysteroid dehydrogenate, and deuterium–hydrogen exchange at C16 during the methanolysis deconjugation step have been observed. Glucuronidase/arylsulfatase used for cleavage of phase-II metabolites has been suggested as a source of a cyclodipeptide, which has been assigned as a possible dihydroergotamine artifact in a screening procedure.

As the extraction efficiency of a drug or metabolite from a postmortem specimen may vary depending on the sample matrix, validation of the analytical procedure is needed on all types of specimens. If it varies from case to case, or even from site to site within the same corpse, the standard addition method may be applied provided that a sufficient amount of specimen is available.

It is now recognized that determination of major or active metabolites and degradation products along with the parent drug is essential to avoid misinterpretation of the data due to artifacts. Such a stability-indicating assay is one that can accurately and selectively differentiate the intact drug from its potential decomposition products.

Conclusions

Each death is unique, and the factors that may alter the effects on and the concentration of a drug in the body are not known in detail in most cases. It must be accepted that artifacts as an integral part of postmortem toxicology frequently interfere with a straightforward interpretation of the analytical results.

The conclusion that death was caused by intoxication should be based on three pillars: a concentration that is typically encountered in such fatalities, the history and the circumstances surrounding death must be consistent with poisoning, and exclusion of diseases or injuries that are inconsistent with life at the postmortem examination.

In addition, a thorough understanding of the kinetics and instability of a drug is imperative. Appropriate sampling techniques and measures to maintain the sample integrity will minimize further artifactual formation of both the analyte and the matrix following acquisition of the specimen. Investigation of samples taken from different sites may ease concerns related to postmortem redistribution. Analysis of tissue samples can be of value if a sufficiently large database exists. Often, a routinely applied analytical assay has to be modified; in this case, a thorough evaluation of the analytical procedure is mandatory. Application of a method that covers determination of the target analyte as well as its possible metabolites and degradation products will improve the informative value of such an assay.

> *See also:* **Anthropology/Odontology:** Postmortem Interval; **Forensic Medicine/Pathology:** Estimation of the Time Since Death; **Investigations:** Collection and Chain of Evidence; **Toxicology/Drugs of Abuse:** Drugs in Hair; Postmortem Blood.

Further Reading

Andresen, H., Aydin, B.E., Mueller, A., Iwersen-Bergmann, S., 2011. An overview of gamma-hydroxybutyric acid: Pharmacodynamics, pharmacokinetics, toxic effects, addiction, analytical methods, and interpretation of results. Drug Testing and Analysis 3 (9), 560–568. http://dx.doi.org/10.1002/dta.254.

Baselt, R.C., 2011. Disposition of Toxic Drugs and Chemicals in Man, ninth ed. Biomedical Publications, Seal Beach, CA.

Boy, R.G., Henseler, J., Ramaekers, J.G., Mattern, R., Skopp, G., 2009. A comparison between experimental and authentic blood/serum ratios of 3,4- methylenedioxymethamphetamine and 3,4-methylenedioxyamphetamine. Journal of Analytical Toxicology 33, 283–286.

Chen, J., Hsieh, Y., 2005. Stabilizing drug molecules in biological samples. Therapeutic Drug Monitoring 27, 617–624.

Cook, D.S., Braithwaite, R.A., Hale, K.A., 2000. Estimating antemortem drug concentrations from postmortem blood samples: The influence of postmortem redistribution. Journal of Clinical Pathology 53, 282–285.

Drummer, O.H., 2007a. Post-mortem toxicology. Forensic Science International 165, 199–203.

Drummer, O.H., 2007b. Requirements for bioanalytical procedures in postmortem toxicology. Analytical and Bioanalytical Chemistry 388, 1495–1503.

Drummer, O.H., 2008. Postmortem toxicological redistribution. In: Rutty, G.N. (Ed.), Essentials of Autopsy Practice. Springer, London.

Drummer, O.H., 2010. Forensic toxicology. EXS 100, 579–603.

Flanagan, R.J., 2008. Fatal toxicity of drugs used in psychiatry. Human Psychopharmacology 23, 43–51.

Flanagan, R.J., Conally, G., Evans, J.M., 2005. Analytical toxicology: guidelines for sample collection postmortem. Toxicological Reviews 24, 63–71.

Garcia Boy, R., Henseler, J., Mattern, R., Skopp, G., 2008. Determination of morphine and 6-acetylmorphine in blood with use of dried blood spots. Therapeutic Drug Monitoring 30, 733–739.

Garside, D., Ropero-Miller, J.D., Riemer, E.C., 2006. Postmortem tissue distribution of atomoxetine following fatal and nonfatal doses – three case reports. Journal of Forensic Sciences 51, 179–182.

Giroud, C., Menetrey, A., Augsburger, M., Buclin, T., Sanchez-Mazas, P., Mangin, P., 2001. Delta(9)-THC, 11-OH-delta(9)-THC and delta(9)- THCCOOH plasma or serum to whole blood concentrations distribution ratios in blood samples taken from living and dead people. Forensic Science International 123, 159–163.

Gurley, B.J., Swain, A., Hubbard, M.A., et al., 2008. Clinical assessment of CYP2D6-mediated herb–drug interactions in humans: Effects of milk thistle, black cohosh, goldenseal, kava kava, St. John's wort, and Echinacea. Molecular Nutrition & Food Research 52, 755–763.

Hachad, H., Ragueneau-Majlessi, I., Levy, R.H., 2010. A useful tool for drug interaction evaluation: the University of Washington metabolism and transport drug interaction database. Human Genomics 5, 61–72.

Hammett-Stabler, C.A., 2008. The pre-analytical phase of drug-testing. In: Dasgupta, A. (Ed.), Handbook of Drug Monitoring Methods – Therapeutics and Drugs of Abuse. Humana Press, Totowa, NJ, pp. 87–96.

Hearn, W.L., Walls, H.C., 2007. Introduction to post-mortem toxicology. In: Karch, S.B. (Ed.), Drug Abuse Handbook, second ed. CRC Press, Boca Raton, FL, pp. 965–975.

Hoiseth, G., Karinen, R., Christophersen, A., Morland, J., 2010. Practical use of ethyl glucuronide and ethyl sulfate in postmortem cases as markers of antemortem alcohol ingestion. International Journal of Legal Medicine 124, 143–148.

Hoiseth, G., Kristoffersen, L., Larssen, B., Arnestad, M., Hermansen, N., Morland, J., 2008. In vitro formation of ethanol in autopsy samples containing fluoride ions. International Journal of Legal Medicine 122, 63–66.

Izzo, A.A., Ernst, E., 2009. Interactions between herbal medicines and prescribed drugs. Drugs 69, 1777–1798.

Kintz, P., 2004. Value of hair analysis in postmortem toxicology. Forensic Science International 142, 127–134.

Kugelberg, F.C., Alkass, K., Kingbäck, M., Carlsson, B., Druid, H., 2006. Influence of blood loss on the pharmacokinetics of citalopram. Forensic Science International 161, 163–168.

Kugelberg, F.C., Jones, A.W., 2007. Interpreting results of ethanol analysis in postmortem specimens: A review of the literature. Forensic Science International 165, 10–29.

Kwok, W.H., Leung, D.K.K., Leung, G.N.W., et al., 2008. Unusual observations during steroid analysis. Rapid Communications in Mass Spectrometry 22, 682–686.

May, T., Jürgens, U., Rambeck, B., Schnabel, R., 1999. Comparison between pre-mortem and postmortem serum concentrations of phenobarbital, phenytoin, carbamazepine and its 10,11-epoxide metabolite in institutionalized patients with epilepsy. Epilepsy Research 33, 57–65.

Meyer, M.R., Maurer, H.H., 2011. Absorption, distribution, metabolism and excretion pharmacogenomics of drugs of abuse. Pharmacogenomics 12, 215–233.

Mohammadi, A., Amini, M., Hamedani, M.P., Torkabadi, H.H., Walker, R.B., 2008. Study of the formation of artifacts following dichloromethane reaction with some nitrogenous drugs. Asian Journal of Chemistry 20, 5573–5580.

Moriya, F., Hashimoto, Y., 2004. Tissue distribution of intubation-related lidocaine in brain-dead patients. American Journal of Forensic Medicine and Pathology 25, 351–354.

Musshoff, F., Madea, B., 2007. Analytical pitfalls in hair testing. Analytical and Bioanalytical Chemistry 388, 1475–1494.

Pelissier-Alicot, A.L., Gaulier, J.M., Marquet, P., 2003. Mechanisms underlying postmortem redistribution of drugs: A review. Journal of Analytical Toxicology 27, 533–544.

Peters, F.T., 2007. Stability of analytes in biosamples – An important issue in clinical and forensic toxicology? Analytical and Bioanalytical Chemistry 388, 1505–1519.

Rentsch, K.M., Kullak-Ublick, G.A., Reichel, C., Meier, P.J., Fattinger, K., 2001. Arterial and venous pharmacokinetics of intravenous heroin in subjects who are addicted to narcotics. Clinical Pharmacology and Therapeutics 70, 237–246.

Sato, K., 2005. II.1.1 Carbon monoxide. In: Suzuki, O., Watanabe, K. (Eds.), Drugs and Poisons in Humans. A Handbook of Practical Analysis. Springer, Berlin, Heidelberg, New York, pp. 91–99.

Schaffer, S.D., Yoon, S., Zadensky, I., 2009. A review of smoking cessation: Potentially risky effects on prescribed medications. Journal of Clinical Nursing 18, 1533–1540.

Shakleya, D.M., Kraner, J.C., Kaplan, J.A., Gannett, P.M., Callery, P.S., 2006. Identification of N, N-dimethylamphetamine formed by methylation of methamphetamine in formalin-fixed liver tissue by multistage mass spectrometry. Forensic Science International 157, 87–92.

Skopp, G., 2004. Preanalytic aspects in post-mortem toxicology. Forensic Science International 142, 75–100.

Skopp, G., 2009. Postmortem toxicology: Artifacts. In: Jamieson, A., Moenssens, A. (Eds.), Wiley Encyclopedia of Forensic Science. Wiley, Chichester, pp. 1–22.

Suma, R., Kosanam, H., Prakash, P.K.S., 2006. Stability of bupropion and olanzapine in formaldehyde solution. Rapid Communications in Mass Spectrometry 20, 1390–1394.

Tenore, P.L., 2010. Advanced urine toxicology testing. Journal of Addictive Diseases 29, 436–448.

Theobald, D.S., Peters, F.T., Beyer, J., Ewald, A.H., Maurer, H.H., 2005. GC-MS detection of dihydroergotamine artifact – Proof of ingestion of dihydroergotamine? Toxichem Krimtech 72, 81–84.

Wallace, K.L., Curry, S.C., 2002. Postcollection rise in methemoglobin level in frozen blood specimens. Clinical Toxicology 40, 91–94.

Yarema, M.C., Becker, C.E., 2005. Key concepts in post-mortem drug redistribution. Clinical Toxicology 43, 235–241.

Relevant Websites

http://www.atsdr.cdc.gov—Agency for Toxic Substances and Disease Registry.
http://www.ababour.net—Alan Barbour's Forensic Toxicology Page.
http://www.soft.org—Society of Forensic Toxicologists.
http://www.tiaft.org—The Association of Forensic Toxicologists.

Interpretation of Results

GR Jones, Alberta Medical Examiners Office, Edmonton, AB, Canada

This chapter is a revision of the previous edition article by W.L. Hearn, volume 3, pp. 1391–1397, © 2000, Elsevier Ltd.

Abbreviations

DRE	Drug recognition expert		PMR	Postmortem redistribution
FUDT	Forensic urine drug testing		SAMHSA	Substance Abuse and Mental Health Services Administration (US)
MRO	Medical review officer			

Glossary

Cutoff The administrative concentration of a drug above which the test is considered "positive."

Introduction

Forensic toxicology concerns the analysis of biological specimens (fluids and tissues) for the presence and, often, the concentration of drugs and poisons. The results of the analyses must be correlated with the circumstances of the case to determine what role, if any, the detected substances played. This correlative function is commonly called interpretation. This chapter will examine the three major subspecialties of forensic toxicology and the various factors that enter into the interpretation process in each.

The forensic toxicology laboratory exists for the sole purpose of providing interpretable analytical data. Therefore, the analytical strategy is designed with anticipation of the need for later interpretation. The most appropriate specimens should be analyzed by sensitive, specific, and quantitatively accurate and precise techniques to yield reliable data upon which to base opinions. The toxicologist must be absolutely certain that the analytical data are accurate. Furthermore, the samples must be properly preserved and clearly traceable to the subject of the investigation by an unbroken chain of custody, and handled and stored with a level of security sufficient to preclude tampering.

The choice of specimen(s) and the scope of analysis are determined largely by the purpose of the investigation. Modern forensic toxicology can be divided into three major categories:

forensic urine drug testing (FUDT), human performance toxicology, and postmortem toxicology. FUDT seeks evidence of illegal drug use by current or prospective employees; human performance toxicology attempts to determine whether the subject was impaired or intoxicated at some specific time by analyzing specimen(s) collected later; and postmortem toxicology investigates the role of drugs and poisons in causing or contributing to the subject's death. Each presents specific requirements and challenges for the interpreting toxicologist.

Forensic Urine Drug Testing

FUDT, also known as workplace drug testing, has as its goal the minimization of drug abuse in the workplace. This goal is accomplished by intimidating potential drug users through fear of detection and by elimination of drug users from the workforce through treatment or discharge. As most employees are not suspected of any wrongdoing, the sampling process is designed to be minimally intrusive. Urine is usually the specimen of choice, although hair and sweat are sometimes used. To control the cost of analysis, FUDT programs restrict the scope of analysis to the drugs deemed most dangerous by virtue of their addictive nature, illegality, abuse liability, or potential harm to the employees' health or productivity. The most commonly included drugs are methamphetamine, amphetamine, cocaine, marijuana, opiate narcotics (morphine, codeine, heroin), and phencyclidine (PCP). Effective October 2010, methylenedioxyamphetamine, methylenedioxymethamphetamine ("Ecstasy"), and methylenedioxyethylamphetamine were added to the list of substances that must be tested for under US-regulated Substance Abuse and Mental Health Services Administration and Department of Transport drug testing. For nonregulated drug testing, other drugs such as barbiturates, benzodiazepines (e.g., diazepam and alprazolam), and lysergic acid diethylamide (LSD) may be added if desired or their use is perceived to be common in a particular geographic area.

In workplace drug testing, the only issue is whether or not the subject of the test illegally used a controlled drug. The drug testing is usually performed on urine. If a drug or drug metabolite(s) is conclusively identified in a properly collected sample, at a concentration that is equal to or greater than the cutoff for the assay, then the person who provided the urine is presumed to have used the drug. However, legitimate questions may be raised about whether ingestion was intentional or took place unknowingly. Such questions are often referred to a physician trained in interpretation of drug testing reports, a medical review officer (MRO), but they may also be asked of the toxicologist. The toxicologist or the MRO may be able to comment on the reasonableness of arguments offered in defense of one who tested positive for a drug. Above all, unbiased interpretation must include consideration of alternative explanations for apparently incriminating findings.

First, the toxicologist or MRO must be aware of circumstances that can produce positive tests in a person who has not abused the drug (Table 1). For example, research has shown that passive exposure to marijuana smoke does not yield urinary concentrations of Δ^9-tetrahydrocannabinol metabolites above 40 ng ml^{-1}. However, taking dietary supplements containing hemp seed oil or eating hemp seed confections can cause readings over 200 ng ml^{-1}. Poppy seeds contain traces of morphine sufficient to cause a positive drug test if poppy seed

pastries are eaten. Moderately high urine morphine concentrations have been obtained in controlled experiments in which human volunteers provided urine samples for opiate analysis after consuming poppy seed pastries. Testing for the alkaloid, thebaine, derived from poppy seeds, may help distinguish food from pharmaceutical morphine. Several pharmaceuticals contain, or are metabolized to, the "L" isomer of methamphetamine, (i.e., L-deoxyephedrine; e.g., in Vick's Inhaler™), rather than the controlled "D" isomer. Routinely applied confirmatory tests cannot distinguish between optical isomers, but chiral separation columns or derivatives can. Such definitive testing may be required if someone challenges a positive urine test for methamphetamine. Another commonly reported explanation for positive urine drug test results is the subject's unknowing consumption of a food or beverage containing a drug that someone else added surreptitiously (e.g., marijuana brownies). The testing methods are sufficiently sensitive to detect excretion products from doses of drug that may be too small to produce observable symptoms. The possible motivation for someone to administer the drug should be considered, as well as the opportunity to do so without detection. Women sometimes allege that they were exposed to a drug such as cocaine through transfer of semen from a drug-using sex partner; however, the amount of cocaine in semen of a user has been measured and is insufficient to produce a positive urine test if ingested. Some people have suggested that their cocaine-positive drug test resulted from handling contaminated money. The amount of cocaine found in US currency is too small to cause a positive test by dermal absorption, but a single cocaine particle falling into the sample container from the subject's hand could produce a positive result. To prevent contamination, test subjects are often required to wash their hands before providing a urine sample.

Human Performance Toxicology

Human performance toxicology deals with the effects of alcohol and other intoxicating substances on a subject's ability to drive a motor vehicle or engage in other potentially hazardous activities. When impairment, rather than use, is the issue, more information is needed for interpretation. The presence of drug or metabolites in urine is useless for demonstrating impairment. At best, finding an intoxicating substance in urine can explain the source of obvious symptoms of impairment. The concentration of drug and its active metabolites(s) in blood is important, but other factors must also be considered. Individual variability and tolerance can affect the degree of impairment at any given blood drug concentration. Combinations of drugs can interact to increase or decrease impairment. For most drugs, a relationship between drug concentration and performance impairment has not been established. Therefore, evidence for interpretation

Table 1   Innocent causes of positive urine drug tests

Drug	Source
Marijuana	Hemp seed oil or hemp seed confections
Cocaine	Coca tea, maté de coca, may be imported from South America and has been available in health food stores in the past
Morphine, codeine	Poppy seed pastry—contains morphine and codeine
Amphetamine	Metabolism of medications, for example, clobenzorex
Methamphetamine	Nasal inhalers: L-deoxyephedrine—methamphetamine; metabolism of medications, for example, deprenyl—selegiline

should include the subject's blood concentrations of all drugs capable of causing impairment, as well as evidence that the subject was impaired. The toxicologist familiar with the behavioral effects of drugs may be able only to offer an opinion that the observed symptoms are consistent, or not consistent, with the effects of the detected drugs. However, to infer that because a drug was present, regardless of concentration, the subject must have been impaired without having evidence of symptoms of intoxication is speculation, not objective interpretation.

The extent to which drug testing is performed on drivers varies considerably, depending on the particular jurisdiction. For many police forces, testing may be limited to breath alcohol measurement. Where testing for drugs is performed (driving under the influence of drugs programs), urine or blood has traditionally been collected. The problem with urine is that some drugs can be detected for days after last use and it is difficult or impossible to relate positive results to impairment without the corroboration of observed behavior. Blood is more useful, but testing is more difficult to perform and the collection of blood is considered "invasive." For those reasons, the collection and analysis of saliva have become common in many countries. Although there are analytical challenges for the analysis of saliva, it is relatively easy to collect (there are commercial kits available), and in most instances, a positive drug finding can be more easily related to recent use.

Drug Recognition Expert Programs

Drug recognition expert (DRE) programs, such as that sponsored by the US National Highway Traffic Safety Administration, can provide valuable documentation of intoxication. In DRE programs, trained observers examine subjects suspected of being intoxicated and record their observations in a standardized format. The examination includes physiological symptoms (e.g. pulse, respiration, pupil responses, and others), physical tests of coordination and balance, and tests of mental agility, memory and perception. Finally, an algorithmic approach is applied to the observations to place symptom patterns into eight categories: not impaired, or impaired by sedative, stimulant, narcotic, hallucinogen, marijuana, PCP-like, or volatile inhalant substances. If the subject is examined while symptoms are present, the documentary evidence can be evaluated in conjunction with results of toxicological analyses. The forensic toxicologist may then be able to offer opinions on the cause-and-effect relationship of the observed behavior or symptoms and the detected intoxicants. Research has shown accuracy rates in the range of 50–80% for DRE examinations, depending upon the drug category and the examiner's training and experience. Therefore, DRE reports must always be confirmed by laboratory analysis before any punitive action, such as conviction for driving while intoxicated, can be justified.

Postmortem Toxicology

Because of their variety and complexity, postmortem toxicological investigations provide the greatest challenges for the interpreting toxicologist. The questions that may be raised in a death investigation may be the same as those involved in workplace drug testing or human performance toxicology, but often the postmortem toxicologist must deal with far more complicated issues. To do so requires not only a familiarity with principles of pharmacology, physiology, biochemistry, and anatomy but also an awareness of pathological changes associated with toxicity and postmortem changes affecting drug concentrations. Knowledge of factors such as the behavioral effects of drugs and the lifestyle of drug-using subcultures can help in understanding and explaining some aspects of a case.

In postmortem toxicology, interpretation is a thought process that begins with the initial case review and guides the analytical strategy that culminates with the toxicologist forming opinions regarding the involvement of drugs or other substances in the death of an individual. The first question that must be addressed is what, if anything, was ingested by the deceased? The answer lies in the outcome of a thorough toxicological analysis that is capable of detecting relevant (i.e., therapeutic or subtherapeutic) concentrations of any substance that could realistically be present. The extent of the search is governed, in part, by the other aspects of the investigation. If there is a strong suspicion of a drug or poison, then the toxicologist must search more diligently than if there is no such suspicion. A negative result must be interpreted from an understanding of the sensitivity of the analytical method. It implies that the analyte targeted by the test was not present or, if present, was at a concentration below the detection limit. If methods of sufficient sensitivity are used, negative findings mean that either nothing was ingested or something outside the scope of analysis was involved. Knowledge of the chemical properties of various drugs and poisons and of the capabilities and limitations of available analytical techniques is essential to the determination of whether the analysis is capable of detecting all targeted substances.

When drugs or other toxic substances are detected in body fluids or tissues, the toxicologist must gather additional data in an effort to determine what role, if any, the detected substances played in the events leading to death. In some cases where the cause of death is manifestly obvious, such as accidental, the result of assault, or self-inflicted trauma, the issue becomes one of the impairing or intoxicating effects of drugs, including alcohol (behavioral toxicity). Substances lacking psychoactivity are usually incidental to the investigation, unless they could have affected survivability. In cases of death attributable to natural disease, the toxicologist is concerned with substances that can exacerbate preexisting illness. Examples include cocaine and other sympathomimetic agents with heart disease or berry aneurysms, and nonselective β-adrenergic blocking agents in patients with asthma. Other potential issues for the toxicologist include adverse interactions of therapeutic drugs and unsuspected intentional overdose in an otherwise seriously ill person. In some cases, such as death from epileptic seizures, it may be important to document whether the deceased was compliant with life-sustaining therapy.

When a toxic mechanism of death is suspected from the findings of the investigation and autopsy, the toxicologist is asked to identify the offending substance(s) and, insofar as possible, to determine the route and mode of entry. Was ingestion accidental or intentional? Was enough drug or poison present to cause death, and was it ingested acutely or cumulatively? If multiple substances are detected, do they possess additive or synergistic toxic activity?

Drug Interactions

If multiple substances are identified, some may be unrelated to the cause of death, whereas others may have interacted, resulting in fatal consequences. Drugs with similar toxic mechanisms, such as respiratory depression or cardiovascular stimulation or depression, can be expected to contribute additively or synergistically to the net toxic effect. For example, ethanol, benzodiazepines, and opiates all have respiratory depressant activities at toxic concentrations. In combination, they can produce serious or fatal respiratory depression, even when the individual drugs are present in subtoxic concentrations. The calcium channel blocker, verapamil, and β-adrenergic antagonists, such as propranolol or timolol, may both be prescribed for migraine headaches or to lower blood pressure. When combined, verapamil and beta blockers can sometimes lead to fatal cardiogenic shock and can even cause the heart to stop beating. It is sometimes apparent that one drug exerted the predominant effect, without which the death would not have occurred. This is often the case with heroin toxicity. Other drugs, such as alcohol, benzodiazepines, cocaine, or other opiates, if present, would be expected to contribute to toxicity, but usually would not be lethal without the addition of heroin.

Postmortem Changes Affecting Toxicology

During life, drugs are differentially concentrated in the various organs to levels that may be orders of magnitude higher than that in blood. By definition, the higher the proportion of a drug that is sequestered outside of the blood volume, the higher is the "volume of distribution" of that particular drug. The liver, heart, and lungs are among the tissues known to sequester various drugs. After death, the physiological and chemical conditions that maintain the differential begin to degrade, causing such changes as a decrease in blood pH. These physiological changes cause protein binding to decrease, allowing drugs to diffuse out of tissues into blood—a process often

referred to as postmortem redistribution (PMR). Drugs with a relatively high volume of distribution are substantially more affected by PMR than drugs like benzodiazepines that have a volume of distribution closer to 1. Therefore, blood collected from the vena cava is likely to contain excess drug released by the liver, as well as any drug freshly absorbed from the gastrointestinal tract. Heart blood, "chest cavity blood," or aorta blood may contain drug released by the heart tissue, lungs, and liver and, potentially, may be contaminated by stomach contents. A therapeutic concentration of drug can quickly rise into the "toxic" or "lethal" range on tables derived from clinical observations of living subjects. Large differences in drug concentrations are often found when blood from these visceral sites is compared with blood from a peripheral site, such as femoral or subclavian vein. It is now recognized that analysis of peripheral (e.g., femoral) blood provides data that are closer to the blood concentration that existed at the moment of death. Nonetheless, there is growing evidence that for some drugs, even properly collected peripheral blood may be subject to significant PMR. Therefore, the toxicologist cannot simply compare a drug's concentration in blood with published clinical data of therapeutic, toxic, and lethal concentrations. To do so would probably lead to erroneous conclusions. Postmortem drug concentrations should be compared with postmortem data on the same site from cases of known drug toxicity and from cases where toxicity was not involved. Such an approach will often help to distinguish elevated from normal drug levels. Analysis of tissue such as liver frequently reveals very high concentrations of many drugs in overdose cases. However, care must be taken to differentiate acute ingestion of an overdose from accumulation (buildup) of a drug in the body due to impaired metabolism or excretion. Measuring the total amount of unabsorbed drug remaining in the stomach after death can support the conclusion of toxicity due to ingestion of an acute overdose if a quantity representing more than a normal dose is found. Finding a trace of drug in the stomach does not prove an oral route of administration, because most drugs diffuse from the blood into the stomach. The same is true when cocaine is detected in a sample obtained by swabbing the nasal passages. A small amount of cocaine will pass from blood to the nasal secretions regardless of the route of administration. Only if a relatively large amount of cocaine is found can one conclude that it was taken intranasally.

While PMR may elevate drug concentrations in blood, some drugs continue to be metabolized after death. Enzymes, especially esterases, that do not require oxygen or consume energy remain active and hydrolyze susceptible drugs, including cocaine, heroin, and a heroin metabolite, 6-monoacetylmorphine. The net effect of the competing processes, redistribution and metabolism, on drug concentrations in postmortem specimens is unpredictable.

Ethanol can be produced by fermentative microorganisms during putrefaction so that concentrations in specimens from a decomposing body are not representative of the blood alcohol concentration at the time of death. In many cases where ethanol is found in a decomposed body, it may be said that the deceased probably consumed some alcohol before death, but when ethanol concentrations are lower than $0.1\,\mathrm{g\,dl^{-1}}$ in a severely putrefied body, the alcohol may have been entirely produced by postmortem fermentation. Even higher values of postmortem ethanol production (over $0.2\,\mathrm{g\,dl^{-1}}$) have been reported. If available, analysis of vitreous humor (eye fluid) for ethanol may help determine whether the person consumed ethanol while they were alive. Vitreous humor can remain sterile for several days after death, and therefore fermentation due to the action of microorganisms cannot occur.

Putrefaction can also affect interpretation of carbon monoxide measurements in postmortem blood. The percent of total hemoglobin combined with carbon monoxide (i.e., carboxyhemoglobin) is usually measured spectrophotometrically. A decomposition product, sulfmethemoglobin, has an absorption spectrum that overlaps that of carboxyhemoglobin. Putrefaction will elevate the carbon monoxide reading with most methods, but may depress it with others. Therefore, the toxicologist must understand the effects of sulfmethemoglobin on the method whose result is being interpreted to know whether the reading is artifactually high or low in a decomposed sample. In severely decomposed blood, it may not be possible to obtain a usable carboxyhemoglobin measurement. While direct measurement of carbon monoxide in a sample is possible using some methods, the problem remains that interpretation of the concentration needs to be related back to the percentage saturation of carbon monoxide in hemoglobin. In a decomposed or heat-denatured blood sample, the hemoglobin may be all but destroyed.

Correlative Information

The presumption of toxicity must be further evaluated, taking other physical and factual evidence into consideration. The terminal events, medical and social history, and autopsy findings must be correlated with drug concentration data. Tolerance from chronic use of a drug such as morphine can raise the threshold for therapeutic effect into a range that would be lethal to a nontolerant individual. Although not specific, pulmonary edema and congestion revealed by autopsy can lend support to a suspicion of drug toxicity due to respiratory depression. Even though many pathological changes in the body are not specifically associated with drug toxicity, their presence is supportive, whereas their absence would indicate that drug toxicity was not responsible for the death. Some diagnoses, such as sudden infant death syndrome, and some cardiac deaths are justified only after other causes, including poisoning, are excluded.

Observations from the death scene, such as a body posture that restricts respiration or a plastic bag over the head, can explain why some people die with drug concentrations that, while elevated, would not normally be expected to cause death. Drug intoxication in these cases would be one factor that prevents the victim from restoring normal respiratory exchange. Elevated body temperature measured at a death scene can be related to a disturbance in thermoregulatory homeostasis that is often associated with toxicity due to cocaine, amphetamines, neuroleptics, and some other drugs.

Witnesses to a death can sometimes provide valuable information about the behavior of the deceased and the terminal symptoms. Reports of bizarre and violent behavior followed by sudden death are evidence of excited delirium, which may be attributable to cocaine or amphetamines if supported by analytical documentation of their presence. Concentrations are usually below the range considered to be lethal, so the behavioral evidence may be critical in arriving at a correct conclusion. Drug paraphernalia found at a death scene raises or supports a suspicion of drug toxicity, which can be confirmed by autopsy and toxicological analysis.

When a hospitalized victim of trauma or poisoning dies in spite of treatment, medical records documenting the progression of symptoms can sometimes be correlated with postmortem toxicology data. The mechanism of toxicity of the drugs or poison, such as the electrocardiographic abnormalities caused by tricyclic antidepressants, should be manifest in the reported symptoms and observed physical findings. This becomes especially important when life support efforts delay the terminal event, allowing the responsible toxin to be eliminated to a point that postmortem concentrations are too low to be detected or, if detected, to be considered toxic without the additional supporting evidence. In some jurisdictions, the postmortem toxicology laboratory obtains specimens of blood, urine, and stomach contents collected soon after the patient's arrival at the hospital. These antemortem specimens sometimes yield the only reliable evidence of the state of intoxication of the deceased at the time of admission. For example, drugs administered by physicians, including morphine, haloperidol, lignocaine (lidocaine), atropine, and others, will not usually be found in admission specimens, whereas drugs taken prior to hospitalization will.

Drug Metabolism (Biotransformation)

Whenever a foreign substance is introduced into the body, drug-metabolizing enzymes act upon it to accelerate its elimination. Cytochromes of the P_{450}-class, esterases, and other hydrolases introduce polar functional groups, such as hydroxyl, carboxyl, or amino, and conjugating enzymes, including glucuronyl transferases and sulfotransferases, and link the polar functional groups to highly water-soluble polar molecules, glucuronic acid, or sulfate, in order to form water-soluble conjugates that are readily excreted.

Biotransformation of drugs and poisons is a factor that is frequently considered in the interpretation process. Drug metabolites are often pharmacologically inactive, but some retain activity or possess activity different from the parent drug. In some cases, such as aromatic amines (2-naphthyl amine, 4-aminobiphenyl), halogenated hydrocarbons (chloroform, carbon tetrachloride), and acetaminophen, metabolism yields toxic products. Some biotransformation reactions are subject to induction or inhibition by certain drugs so that the rate of metabolism of other drugs or poisons is increased or decreased. Thus, if an inhibitor of a specific enzyme is present, concentrations of that enzyme's substrate can rise to toxic levels, or an inducer can cause accumulation of a toxic metabolite or can lower a drug's concentration to an ineffective level. An awareness of metabolic interactions and biotransformations can help the toxicologist distinguish between intentional and accidental intoxication.

The postmortem toxicology laboratory often quantifies both parent drug and its principal metabolite(s). The ratio of parent drug to metabolite concentrations can indicate whether ingestion was chronic or acute. Metabolites of many drugs accumulate in the body with chronic administration. Conversely, an acute overdose may yield only a small amount of metabolite before death occurs. Furthermore, drugs such as propoxyphene and meperidine that are converted to toxic metabolites may produce toxicity by virtue of accumulation of the metabolite during chronic administration.

Pharmacokinetics

The science of pharmacokinetics describes the time course of drug action in terms of the processes of absorption, distribution, and elimination. The onset of drug action is determined, first, by the rate of distribution to the site of action. The action is terminated by the elimination of the drug via metabolism and excretion.

Although the concentration of drug in the postmortem blood, tissues, or urine cannot usually be related to pharmacokinetic parameters determined in living humans, the clinical data are still valuable to the postmortem toxicologist. For example, a drug's elimination rate can usually be expressed in terms of its half-life ($t\frac{1}{2}$ elim.), which is the length of time required for the concentration to decline to half of its initial value in a process following first-order kinetics (i.e., the rate of elimination is proportional to drug concentration at any time point). Approximately 99% of the drug will be eliminated by 6–7 half-lives after its distribution is complete. Usually absorption and distribution occur much faster than elimination. Therefore, if a drug is detected in postmortem blood, it was probably taken within 6–7 half-lives prior to death.

The distribution pattern between blood and other biofluids and tissues can also be useful for interpretation.

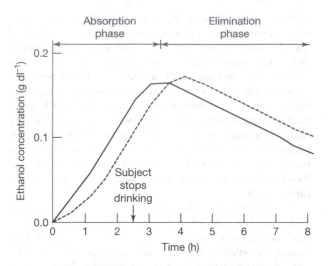

Figure 1 Hypothetical pharmacokinetic curves for ethyl alcohol in blood (—) and vitreous humor (- - - -). Note that the vitreous alcohol concentration is lower than that in the blood during the absorption phase, but it exceeds the blood alcohol concentration during elimination.

Probably the drug whose pharmacokinetic behavior is best understood is ethanol. In postmortem toxicology laboratories, ethanol is usually measured in different body fluids from the same individual to facilitate interpretation. At or near equilibrium, the concentration of ethanol in vitreous humor (eye fluid) is usually about 15–20% higher than that in whole blood. If both fluids are analyzed and blood has higher ethanol concentration than vitreous, then by the pharmacokinetics of ethanol (**Figure 1**), the individual was in the absorption phase, or the sample was contaminated with ethanol from stomach contents or putrefaction. Conversely, if the vitreous ethanol concentration is much higher than the blood, the blood sample may have been diluted, and the toxicologist should consider the site of collection and whether intravenous fluids were administered prior to death. To resolve discrepancies, other samples may be analyzed, including blood from another site, bile, brain tissue, urine, and stomach contents. A pattern should emerge from the data to explain the pharmacokinetic state at the time of death.

Behavioral Toxicity

Psychoactive drugs, both licit and illicit, can cause alterations in perception, judgment, coordination, mood, and information processing. In cases involving violence or accidental trauma, when such drugs are detected in the body of the deceased, questions inevitably arise regarding the role of the drug(s) in precipitating the fatal event. The issues are similar to those in human performance toxicology, except that specimens are usually collected postmortem rather than from a living subject. Therefore, drug concentrations must be considered in light of postmortem changes, and impairment or intoxication must be deduced from factual evidence (eyewitnesses) and physical evidence available at the scene where the fatal incident occurred. For example, a motor vehicle crash investigation may discover evidence of driver error, and later toxicological analysis reveals elevated blood alcohol or a high concentration of a drug with the potential to cause impairment. Similarly, when a person becomes excited, violent, and irrational, then disrobes, breaks objects, struggles with police, and suddenly becomes unresponsive and dies, a finding of even a few hundred nanograms per milliliter of cocaine in the blood of the deceased suggests that the death or behavior can be attributed to cocaine-induced excited delirium. This opinion is supported by a documented high postmortem body temperature and a post-mortem blood benzoylecgonine concentration of several thousand nanograms per milliliter.

Because of the many factors affecting measured postmortem drug concentrations, such data can rarely serve as the sole basis for interpretation. They must be correlated with evidence from the autopsy and with information gathered by police, and other investigators. Conversely, inferences and suspicions derived from autopsy and investigation must be refined and confirmed through toxicological studies. Only then can reliable opinions be formulated regarding the role of drugs or poisons in a death investigation.

See also: **Toxicology/Alcohol:** Alcohol: Interpretation; Blood; Urine and Other Body Fluids.

Further Reading

Baselt, R.C., 2011. Disposition of Toxic Drugs and Chemicals in Man, ninth ed. Chemical Toxicology Institute, Foster City, CA.

Baxter, K. (Ed.), 2010. Stockley's Drug Interactions, ninth ed. Pharmaceutical Press, London.

Druid, H., Holmgren, P., 1997. A compilation of fatal and control concentrations of drugs in postmortem femoral blood. Journal of Forensic Sciences 42, 79–87. View Record in Scopus | Cited By in Scopus (101).

Ellenhorn, M.J., Schonwald, S., Ordog, G., Wasserberger, J., 1997. Ellenhorn's Medical Toxicology: Diagnosis and Treatment of Human Poisoning, second ed. Williams and Wilkins, Baltimore, MD.

Garriott, J.C. (Ed.), 2008. Medicolegal Aspects of Alcohol Determination in Biological Specimens, fifth ed. Lawyers and Judges Publishing Company, Phoenix, AZ.

Green, K.B., Isenschmid, D.S., 1995. Medical review officer interpretation of urine drug test results. Forensic Science Review 7, 41–60.

Karch, S.B. (Ed.), 2006. Drug Abuse Handbook, second ed. CRC Press, Boca Raton, FL.

Klaassen, C.D., 2001. Casarett and Doull's Toxicology: The Basic Science of Poisons, sixth ed. McGraw-Hill, New York.

Moffat, A.C., Osselton, M.D., Widdop, B. (Eds.), 2011. Clarke's Analysis of Drugs and Poisons, fourth ed. Pharmaceutical Press, London.

O'Hanlon, J.F., de Gier, J.J., 1986. Drugs and Driving. Taylor and Francis, London.

Olson, K.R. (Ed.), 2006. Poisoning and Drug Overdose, fifth ed. Appleton and Lange, Norwalk, CT.

Ropero-Miller, J., Goldberger, B. (Eds.), 2008. Handbook of Workplace Drug Testing, second ed. AACC Press, Washington, DC.

Methods of Analysis—Initial Testing

PD Felgate, Forensic Science Centre, Adelaide, SA, Australia

Abbreviations

0.1 M acetic acid	0.1 Molar acetic acid	mm	Millimeter
CH_2Cl_2	Dichloromethane	Na	Sodium
EtOH	Ethanol	NH_3	Ammonia
iPrOH	Isopropanol	nm	Nanometer
m	Meter	rpm	Revolutions per minute
m/z	Mass-to-charge ratio	μl	Microliter
mg/ml	Milligrams per milliliter	μl/min	Microliters per minute
ml/min	Milliliters per minute	μm	Micrometer

Glossary

Carboxy-THC Carboxy metabolite of THC.
DUI Driving under the influence (of drugs).
GC/ECD Gas chromatography with electron capture detection.
GC/MS Gas chromatography with mass spectrometric detection.
GC/NPD Gas chromatograph with nitrogen–phosphorus detector.
LC/DAD Liquid chromatography with photodiode array detection.

LC/MS Liquid chromatography with mass spectrometric detection.
LC/MS/MS Liquid chromatography with tandem mass spectrometric detection.
RT Retention time.
SPE Solid-phase extraction.
SPME Solid-phase microextraction.
STA Systematic toxicological analysis.
THC Delta9-tetrahydrocannabinol.

Introduction

Toxicological analysis, be it forensic, clinical, environmental, workplace, drug abuse, or doping control, principally involves the detection of chemical substances potentially harmful to living organisms. Chemical analysis is used to detect the presence of these substances, measure their concentrations, and interpret this in relation to their relative toxicity. Paracelsus (1493–1541) said:

> All things are poison and nothing is without poison, only the dose permits something not to be poisonous. (Wikipedia)

Our society is surrounded by a large number of compounds that are potentially poisonous (including chemicals, drugs, pesticides, common household products, etc.) and the task of the toxicologist is a formidable one to attempt to cover as many of these substances as possible in a toxicology screen.

Forensic toxicology involves the use of a number of analytical techniques, which can include or exclude the presence of these compounds. For most laboratories that may be analyzing hundreds or thousands of samples per year, it is not practical to try and cover all of these compounds and an appropriate approach is to screen for the common drugs of abuse, prescription and nonprescription drugs in the first instance, and then carry out any specific analyses that may be indicated by the case history. In most forensic toxicology laboratories, a general drug screen includes a range of immunoassay tests, alcohol analysis (either by direct liquid injection or headspace gas chromatography (GC)), and a broad-based GC or high-performance liquid chromatography (HPLC) procedure as shown in **Figure 1**.

Laboratories would then have a suite of specific methods for the detection of nonroutine compounds (e.g., headspace analysis for volatile organic compounds, pesticides, and rodenticides) and drugs not covered by their general screen due to sensitivity (e.g., lysergic acid diethylamide (LSD) or buprenorphine) or specific extraction techniques (e.g., quaternary ammonium compounds). Thin layer chromatography may also be used in some laboratories, but has largely been replaced with other forms of chromatographic separation. Nitrogen–phosphorus detectors (NPDs) are commonly used in GC screening as the large majority of drugs contain nitrogen, whereas many endogenous compounds (fatty acids, cholesterol, and other lipids) are nonnitrogenous. Electron capture detectors (ECDs) have also been used for the screening of halogenated compounds (e.g., many benzodiazepines contain halogens) and provide an extremely sensitive detection method.

Similarly, HPLC systems are often coupled to an ultraviolet (UV) detector or to a photodiode array detector (DAD). With the improvement in technology and the decrease in costs, mass spectrometer (MS) detectors are now increasingly replacing NPD and ECD in GC systems, and UV and DAD in HPLC systems. There are a number of articles in the literature relating to systematic toxicology analysis (STA).

Sample Selection

It is important in forensic toxicology that the appropriate sample is selected for screening as this will have significant relevance for the interpretation of the results. In cases where it is necessary to only show that a subject has used a drug, it would be more suitable to analyze urine or hair as these samples are more likely to show past exposure to a drug. However, if the presence of a drug is necessary to show the involvement of that drug in the behavior of the subject involved in criminal activity, that is, cause of death, driving under the influence (DUI), then the best samples for analysis would be blood or oral fluid. In postmortem cases, it is also preferable to analyze peripheral blood as this is the least likely site to experience any postmortem changes in drug concentrations and represent more closely the concentration of the drug at the time of death. Some laboratories may choose to screen heart blood as this will contain higher concentrations of the drug and make their detection easier; however, it is important that any further quantitative analysis is carried out on peripheral blood for interpretation purposes. Interpretation of these drug levels should still be made with caution as even in peripheral blood, there may be significant changes in some drug concentrations after death.

A simple guide for sample selection is shown in **Table 1**.

Immunoassays

Immunoassay in forensic toxicology is primarily used to screen biological samples for presence of drugs or drug classes. It offers a rapid and convenient way of screening large numbers of samples from a variety of different matrices (blood, urine, oral fluid, etc.) for a number of drugs and drug classes.

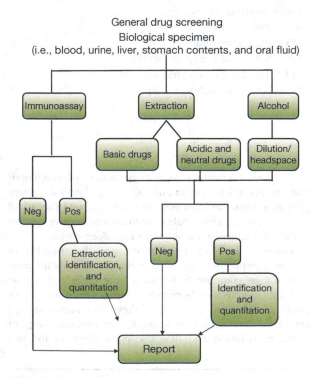

General drug screening
Biological specimen
(i.e., blood, urine, liver, stomach contents, and oral fluid)

Figure 1 Flowchart showing common screening procedures.

Table 1 Time frame for drugs in different biological specimens

Specimen	Drug(s) present	Time frame	Interpretation
Blood	Parent/metabolites	Hours	Recent use
Oral fluid	Parent	Hours	Recent use
Urine	Metabolites	Hours/days	Use
Hair	Parent/metabolites	Months	Use

A negative immunoassay result avoids the need for more complicated and expensive analytical procedures. It requires little or no sample preparation, although some techniques may require pretreatment of blood or tissue specimens. Any size laboratory can use immunoassay with methods that range from on-site testing for the analysis of a single sample to fully automated systems capable of handling thousands of samples per day. Immunoassays are based on the interaction of the target compound (antigen) with the corresponding antibody. For drug testing, the immunoassay uses an antibody specific for the nominated drug or drug class and a labeled form of the same drug or of the antibody to produce a measurable signal.

Although immunoassays are extremely useful in screening large numbers of samples, they cannot be used as confirmation of the drug or drug class, and any positive results should always be confirmed by a more specific technique (gas chromatography–mass spectrometry (GC–MS) or liquid chromatography–mass spectrometry (LC–MS)) that produces an unequivocal identification of the compound.

The basic immunoassay technique involves the competition of a fixed amount of labeled drug with an aliquot of the sample for the specific binding sites on a fixed quantity of antibody. At equilibrium, the proportion of labeled drug molecules bound is inversely proportional to the number of unlabeled drug molecules as shown in **Figure 2**.

Immunoassays can be divided into two types.

1. Homogeneous immunoassays:

These are assays that do not require separation of the antibody-bound drug from the unbound (free) drug before measurement of the signal. They include assays that rely on optical change (e.g., UV absorption, fluorescence, or luminescence) where there is a difference between the signals from the bound and the unbound labeled drug. Examples of this type of immunoassay are EIA (enzyme immunoassay), CEDIA (cloned enzyme donor immunoassay), FPIA (fluorescence polarization immunoassay), and microparticle methods.

2. Heterogeneous immunoassays:

These assays require separation of the antibody-bound drug and the unbound drug before measurement of the signal. This is required as there is no difference in the signals from the antibody-bound and the unbound drugs. Examples of this type of immunoassay are ELISA (enzyme linked immunosorbent assay), RIA (radioimmunoassay), and chemiluminescence immunoassays.

There are two distinct advantages of the heterogeneous immunoassays over the homogeneous type. The first advantage is that as they employ a wash step, this removes any potential endogenous interfering compounds, which may be produced by whole blood or highly discolored urine. This also means that there are no preliminary sample extraction steps required. The second advantage is that these assays have lower limits of detection. This is best illustrated by being able to use whole blood in heterogeneous assays, whereas extraction of the blood sample is often required for homogeneous assays.

Specificity and Cross-Reactivity

It is important with any immunoassay technique to determine how the assay responds to other drugs relative to the drug used as a calibrator. The cross-reactivity of the assay is important as it will determine the suitability of the test. For example, determining *Cannabis* use by the analysis of a urine sample requires the immunoassay to have good cross-reactivity with the major urinary metabolite, Carboxy-tetrahydrocannabinol (THC). However, by contrast, the assay needs to have good cross-reactivity to THC if the samples to be analyzed are oral

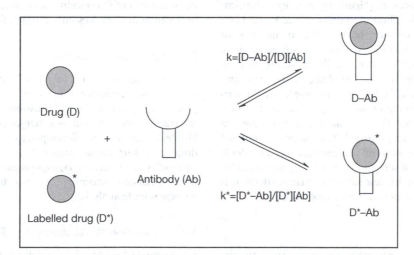

Figure 2 Competitive binding process in immunoassay.

fluid or hair as the relative parent drug concentration is greater than metabolite in these specimens.

There are many commercial immunoassay kits available and specifications as to their sensitivity and specificity should be available for each kit, so that the laboratory can determine if the test meets its requirements.

Enzyme Immunoassay

EIA can be either homogeneous (Enzyme Multiplied Immunoassay technique or EMIT) or heterogeneous (ELISA) immunoassays.

EMIT is a liquid-phase assay based on the enzyme activity of a drug-labeled enzyme, and antibodies raised against the drug of interest modulate the activity of the enzyme. In the presence of glucose-6-phosphate, the enzyme reduces nicotine adenine dinucleotide (NAD) to NADH and the resulting increase in absorbance is measured spectrophotometrically at 340 nm. As the amount of drug in the sample increases, there will be a corresponding increase in enzyme activity and an increase in the rate of NADH production, which will be measured spectrophotometrically by monitoring the λ_{max} at 340 nm.

As EMIT relies on a color change in the solution, it is not suitable for samples such as blood or highly discolored urine without sample pretreatment. Another limitation of the technique as well as interference from other cross-reacting compounds is that, any compound in the matrix that may inhibit the enzyme activity will also affect the result.

ELISA is probably the most commonly used immunoassay in most forensic toxicology laboratories. Commercial ELISA kits are supplied as a dry 96-well microplate with each well precoated with the antidrug antibodies.

ELISA is a heterogeneous, solid-phase assay that requires the separation of reagents. The most common ELISA technique is the competitive immunoassay (**Figure 3**). In antigen competitive assays, the antibody is bound to the well, and labeled and unlabeled antigens compete for the limited number of antibody-binding sites. After the incubation period, an immune complex is formed from the antigen–antibody binding and any unbound antigen is removed by washing. A substrate and chromogen is then added to the immune complex and a reaction between the enzyme and the substrate causes the chromogen to become colored. The more antigen (drug) present in the sample, less the color produced. The reaction is stopped after a preset time by the addition of dilute acid and the color is measured at the λ_{max} at 450 nm. ELISA is a more sensitive technique than EMIT and is less subject to matrix effects. It is regularly used to analyze postmortem blood samples.

Radioimmunoassay

RIA was one of the first heterogeneous immunoassays and the most common type is the antibody-coated tube utilizing

γ-emitting I^{125}-labeled antigen. Separation of the bound and free antigen is accomplished by simply decanting the liquid leaving the bound fraction coated to the tube and the resulting radiation measured with a gamma radiation counter. The technique has been largely replaced by the EIA methods as they avoid using radioisotopes.

Cloned Enzyme Donor Immunoassay

CEDIA is a more recent homogeneous immunoassay that uses the binding of an antibody to change the activity of genetically engineered fragments of β-galactosidase from *Escherichia coli* as the enzyme label. The enzyme is present as two inactive fragments, the enzyme acceptor (EA) and the enzyme donor (ED). ED contains a small portion of enzyme missing from the larger EA fragment. Antibodies that bind to the hapten that is conjugated to the ED fragment prevent the reassociating of the enzyme and reduces the enzyme activity. As the amount of drug increases, the amount of bound antibody to the ED fragment decreases resulting in an increase in enzyme activity due to the reassociation of EA and ED. The enzyme hydrolyzes chlorophenol red-β-galactoside to chlorophenol red and galactoside and the enzyme activity can be measured spectrophotometrically.

Fluorescence Polarization Immunoassay

FPIA is also a heterogeneous immunoassay technique that uses fluorescein-labeled antigen. The labeled antigen can rotate freely when not bound to an antibody; however, when it is bound, its ability to rotate is dramatically reduced. Light at the excitation wavelength of fluorescein is passed through a polarized filter and as the drug present in the sample competes with the fluorescein-labeled antigen for the antibody, there is a reduction in the amount of fluorescein bound and, therefore, a reduction in the amount of fluorescence through the polarized filter.

Chemiluminescence Immunoassay

This technique is similar to other heterogeneous assays but offers greater sensitivity using chemiluminescence. The signal produced is generated by the emission of light during a chemical reaction and captured by a charged coupled device camera. This technique has been developed to assay a range of different drugs and drug classes achieved by attaching specific drug antibodies to discrete test regions on the biochip, which allows the simultaneous screening for many drugs or drug classes in a single sample analysis.

Kinetic Interaction of Microparticles in Solution

Kinetic interaction of microparticles in solution is a homogeneous immunoassay in which the labeled compound is

Antibody coated well

Sample added and labelled antigen

Unbound antigen and enzyme
labelled antigen removed by
washing leaving only bound antigen
and enzyme labelled antigen

Substrate and chromatogen added

Enzyme–substrate reaction results in
colour development of chromatogen.
More the drug present, less the
color.

Figure 3 Competitive immunoassay process.

Key to diagram

Y Antibody

o Enzyme labelled antigen

● Antigen in sample

◁ Chromogen

∿ Substrate

---

a microparticle with several drug molecules attached. If the sample being analyzed is drug free, then the microparticle with the drug molecules attached conjugates with several antibody molecules and aggregates to form a larger particle, which will scatter transmitted light, and as the reaction proceeds, the abundance will increase. If drug molecules are present in the sample, they will compete with the conjugates bound to antibodies and result in a decrease in the rate of absorbance increase in proportion to the concentration of drug present.

Sample Extraction

There are two major methods for sample extraction:

Solvent Extraction (Liquid–Liquid Extraction)

This is the most frequently used separation technique in toxicology laboratories worldwide. Most drugs have some degree of polarity and so it is important to select a solvent that will maximize the extraction of the target drugs but minimize the extraction of endogenous compounds. By adjusting the pH of the specimen, drugs can be separated into basic and acidic drugs.

Making the specimen basic (pH 9) by the addition of ammonia or sodium borate buffer will favor the extraction of weakly basic drugs. Buffering the specimen to pH 4 by the addition of an acidic buffer (potassium dihydrogen phosphate) will allow the extraction of acidic and neutral drugs. Basic drugs comprise the majority of drugs found in forensic cases and are often present at low concentrations in blood. To improve the detection of these drugs, it may be necessary to incorporate a cleanup step (or back extraction) in the extraction scheme to remove more of the endogenous compounds and still retain the drugs of interest. This can be particularly important when analyzing postmortem blood specimens that can often contain a multitude of endogenous compounds formed postmortem. Once the specimen has been extracted at basic pH into an appropriate solvent (such as butyl chloride), it is back extracted into aqueous acid solution (usually 0.1 M sulfuric acid), and the acidic and neutral compounds will remain in the organic layer. The acidic layer is separated from the organic layer and is then made alkaline (sodium hydroxide) and reextracted into organic solvent, which is then separated from the aqueous and concentrated, usually under a stream of nitrogen. Care should be exercised in the evaporation step as some of the more volatile compounds can be lost if subjected to heat; amphetamine and methylamphetamine are prime examples.

The concentrated extract can now be analyzed using the appropriate chromatographic technique. A typical basic/neutral drug extraction scheme is shown in **Figure 4**.

Acidic drugs of forensic interest tend to be present in much higher concentrations than basic drugs and the need for a cleanup step in the extraction is generally not required. If a cleanup step is required, it can be achieved by the partitioning between immiscible solvents of differing polarities. The more lipid-soluble endogenous compounds (sterols and fatty acids) will partition into the less-polar solvent (e.g., petroleum ether), whereas the more polar drugs will partition into the more polar solvent (e.g., acetonitrile). A typical extraction scheme for acidic and neutral drugs is shown in **Figure 5**.

Solid-Phase Extraction

Solid-phase extraction (SPE) techniques have become more common in forensic toxicology laboratories because of their better extraction efficiencies, particularly with more polar drugs, and the ability to automate the extraction using liquid handling systems. Initial difficulties with postmortem samples, which often contain large amounts of particulate material, are often clotted, and in the past could easily plug the fine SPE absorbent packing, have now been overcome by better sample preparation techniques (sample dilution and centrifugation) and improved SPE column technology.

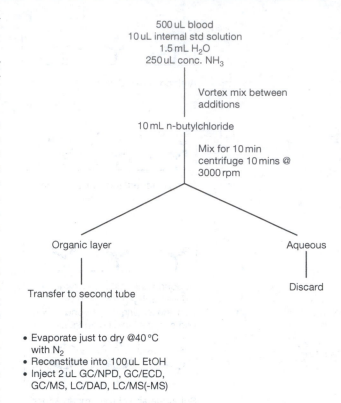

Figure 4   Extraction scheme for basic and neutral drugs.

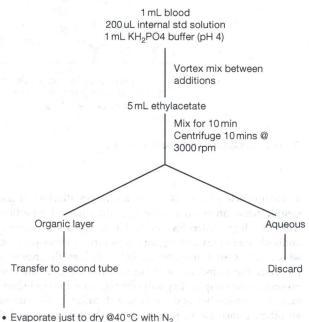

Figure 5   Extraction scheme for acidic/neutral drugs.

There are predominantly three different mechanisms for the retention of compounds, which are retained by the sorbent:

1. Reverse phase—Polar liquid phase and nonpolar solid phase. Compounds are retained by hydrophobic interactions (nonpolar–nonpolar interactions, dispersion forces).
2. Normal phase—Nonpolar liquid phase and polar solid phase. Compounds are retained by hydrophilic interactions (polar–polar interactions, hydrogen bonding).
3. Ion exchange—Electrostatic attraction of charged group on the compound and charged group on the sorbent.

Table 2 shows the characteristics of solvents commonly used in SPE.

The basic procedure for SPE is a five-step process as shown in **Figure 6**, and a typical SPE using a combination of a strong cation exchange and a C8 sorbent for the analysis of opiates in blood is shown in **Figure 7**.

Solid-Phase Microextraction

An alternative technique to liquid–liquid extraction and SPE is the solid-phase microextraction (SPME). It has been developed for the analysis of volatile and some nonvolatile compounds. This technique incorporates sample extraction, concentration, and sample introduction in one step and is fast, requires no solvents, is reusable, and can be adapted to any GC. It consists of a fused silica fiber coated with a stationary phase that is attached to a stainless steel plunger. After inserting the plunger through a septum into a vial containing the sample, the fiber is exposed to either the headspace or the liquid for 20–30 min.

The equilibration time can be reduced by increasing the ionic strength of the sample, stirring, or heating the sample. After equilibration, the fiber is retracted back into the plunger and inserted into the GC injection port where it is desorbed by exposing the fiber again (see **Figure 8**).

This also serves to recondition the fiber, which can be reused for up to 100 further analyses. The fiber may also be reextracted into an organic solvent and analyzed by liquid chromatography (LC). There are a number of different stationary phases available to suit the type of analysis.

Screening by GC

GC has been one of the most widely used techniques in forensic toxicology laboratories. If a drug has sufficient volatility for it to exist in the vapor phase at temperatures up to 350 °C without decomposing, then there is a high probability that it can be analyzed by GC. Sample extracts can be separated into their components by introducing an aliquot of the extract (sample injection) onto a column that contains a stationary phase that has a continuous flow of an inert gas (e.g., helium) through it. This column is contained in an oven with controlled temperature. The components within the extraction mixture will spend differing periods of time in the stationary phase depending upon their affinity for it and the time for the molecules to reach the end of the column will vary (retention time). For molecules that have a greater affinity, the time will be longer as they will spend longer time immobilized in the stationary phase compared with those that have a lesser affinity. As the components elute from the end of the column,

Table 2 Characteristics of commonly used solvents in Solid-phase extraction

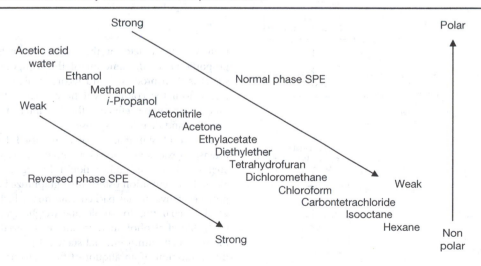

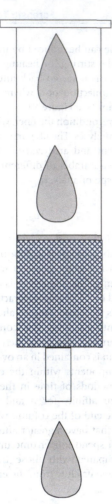

1. Select the appropriate SPE cartridge-capacity, bed weight and sorbent type

2. Condition the cartridge. Use an appropriate solvent or aqueous buffer to wet the sorbent material and allow the sample to come into contact with the packing. Do not allow the SPE packing to dry between conditioning and sample addition as there will be uneven contact between sample and packing resulting in non-reproducible efficiency and drug recoveries.

3. Add the sample. Pass the sample solution slowly through the column using either vacuum or positive pressure at a flow rate of ~2mL min^{-1}.

4. Wash the column. Remove un-retained and unwanted compounds from the column using the same solution that the sample was dissolved in or solvents of sufficient polarity that will not remove the compound(s) of interest.

5. Elute the compound(s). The compound(s) of interest are eluted using a solvent of sufficient polarity to recover the analyte(s) but leave any un-wanted compounds that have not been removed by the wash step

Figure 6 Solid-phase extraction sequence.

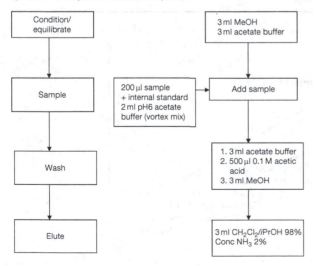

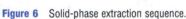

Figure 7 Analysis of opiates using mixed-mode SPE (a combination of a strong cation exchange and a C8 sorbent. UCT XTRACT®, 200 mg/3 ml).

there will be a detector that will produce a signal that is proportional to the amount of the compound present, the signal is then processed and recorded. Each compound that elutes from the column will have a characteristic retention time, which can be defined as the time interval between sample injection and detector response.

Few solid stationary phases are used for screening in forensic toxicology; however, many forensic laboratories analyze blood and other liquid biological specimens for alcohol concentration using either graphitized carbon black or polymer conventional packed columns, which are extremely good at separating low-molecular weight hydrocarbons (C1–C10). Blood alcohol analysis can be achieved by dilution of the specimen within internal standard (e.g., n-propanol) and direct injection of an aliquot of the aqueous mix (**Figure 9**). Another technique is to add an internal standard to an aliquot of the sample and seal the vial, which is then heated to ~60 °C,

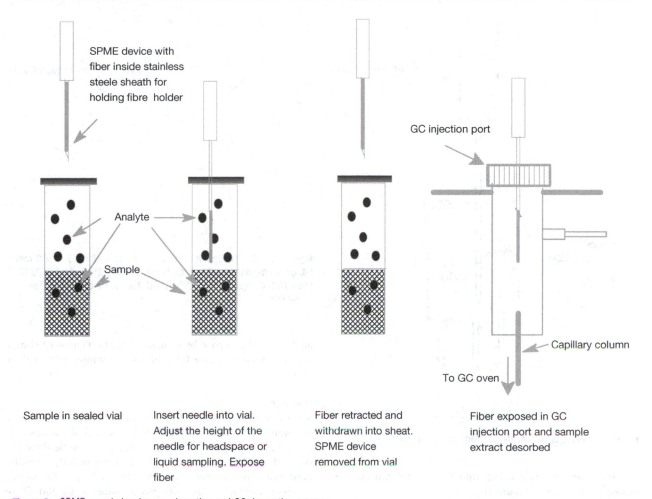

Sample in sealed vial

Insert needle into vial. Adjust the height of the needle for headspace or liquid sampling. Expose fiber

Fiber retracted and withdrawn into sheat. SPME device removed from vial

Fiber exposed in GC injection port and sample extract desorbed

Figure 8 SPME sample headspace adsorption and GC desorption process.

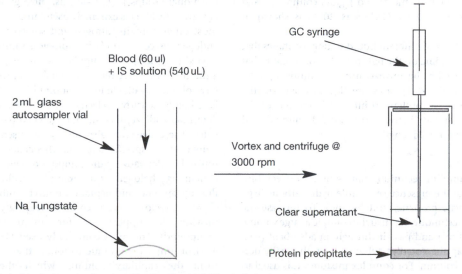

Figure 9 Blood alcohol analysis—sample preparation for direct injection technique.

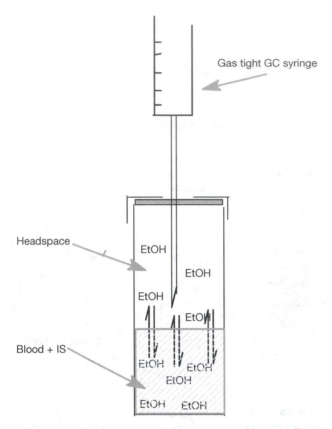

Figure 10   Blood alcohol analysis: headspace technique.

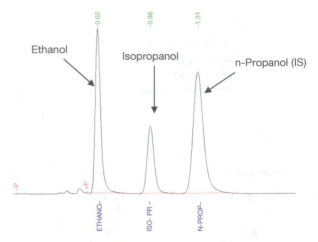

Figure 11   Chromatogram of ethanol analysis in blood: 2 m × 2 mm i.d. glass column packed with Carbopak C with 0.2% Carbowax 20 M. Oven 100 °C, injection port 220 °C, FID 220 °C, He carrier gas flow 30 ml min⁻¹.

and the headspace is injected onto the GC column via the heated injection port (**Figure 10**).

A typical chromatogram of ethanol analysis using a 2 m × 2 mm internal diameter (i.d.) glass column packed with Carbopak C with 0.2% Carbowax 20 M is shown in **Figure 11**.

There are a number of different liquid stationary phases that can be utilized depending on the nature of the compounds that require separation with the most common comprising poly-siloxanes. These stationary phases are liquids coated to the inside of a fused silica capillary column. Dimensions of the capillary column can vary between 0.1 and 0.32 mm i.d. and can be from 10 to 60 m in length.

Headspace analysis

The headspace sampling technique can be used to screen biological samples for the presence of volatile hydrocarbons (e.g., petroleum products, propane, and butane). To increase the sensitivity of this technique, it is usual to sample a large volume of headspace (50 ml) and pass it through an adsorbent (e.g., Porapak Q) to trap the volatiles, which is then thermally desorbed onto a GC column. For complex mixtures, it is usual to

analyze the headspace by capillary GC/MS. **Figure 12** shows a typical total ion trace for a headspace sample of petrol in blood.

Detectors

Some detectors, for example, flame ionization detectors (FID), are nonspecific in nature and will respond to almost all compounds that pass through the GC column while there are others that will specifically respond to compounds that contain particular atoms. For example, the NPDs will detect compounds that contain nitrogen or phosphorus and EPDs will detect compounds that have electron-capturing atoms or functional groups (e.g., halogens, nitro groups, and carbonyl groups). The NPD is extremely useful in drug screening because most drugs contain nitrogen and solvents and many of the endogenous compounds in biological samples that are coextracted (e.g., fatty acids, lipids, and sterols) do not. There are a number of relative retention databases using standard capillary columns available for compound identification. The ECD is a highly sensitive selective detector particularly useful to detect benzodiazepines and halogenated pesticides and herbicides. These detectors also offer greater sensitivity and selectivity over nonspecific detectors. This greater sensitivity can be utilized by derivatizing the compounds with functional groups containing halogen, for example, trifluoroacetic, pentafluoropropionic, and heptafluorobutyric anhydrides.

MS detectors have become increasingly popular as they provide the opportunity for unique identification of compounds. The most commonly used MS detector uses an electron impact technique to ionize the compounds eluting from the capillary column, which then fragments in

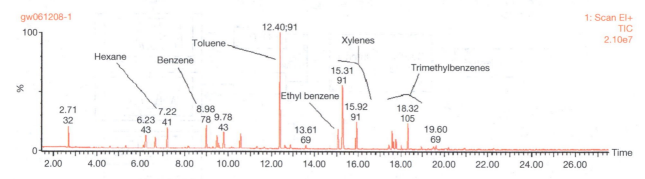

Figure 12 Total ion chromatogram of a headspace sample containing petrol: 60 m × 0.25 mm i.d. BP-1 capillary (film thickness 1 μm), oven temperature 45 °C (6 min) to 260 °C at 10 °C min^{-1}.

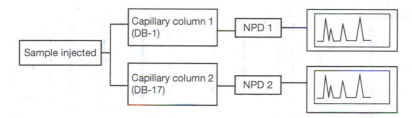

Figure 13 Sample injection split between two different columns.

a characteristic and reproducible way. These fragments are focused and accelerated into a mass filter (quadrupole or ion trap), which rapidly scans for masses, usually in the range up to about 1000 amu. The characteristic mass spectrum produced can be searched against a number of commercial mass spectral libraries (e.g., PMW (Pfleger, Maurer, Weber), MPW (Maurer, Pfleger, Weber), NIST, and Wiley libraries) as well as in-house user-generated libraries. The advances in computer technology allow the searching of vast library data extremely fast.

For added sensitivity, the quadrupole MS can be operated in the selected ion mode (SIM) where only preselected masses for the compounds of interest are collected. This is a useful technique for targeted screening of drugs but is limited for general unknown screening.

The ion trap detector offers similar sensitivity when operated in either the full scan or the SIM mode due to its longer ion collection period. Mass spectra produced by the two different mass detectors are sometimes quite different as they are characterized by the conditions under which they are run, and this can make comparison between different instruments difficult.

Dual detector systems

It is not uncommon in forensic toxicology laboratories to use a dual detector screening system. There are several different combinations that can be used, and the sample can be split at the injection port and two columns of differing polarity used to separate the drugs in the extract (**Figure 13**) or the effluent from the column can be split between two different detectors (**Figure 14**).

When using the single-injection dual column approach, the effluent from both columns will be detected by the same type of detector (usually NPD or ECD) and a relative retention time (RRT) database can be set up for both columns (e.g., DB-1 and DB-17). Searching the RRT of unknown peaks in the two chromatograms will provide better discrimination as to the identity of the unknown than if data from a single chromatogram was used (**Figure 15**). A much more common configuration is to split the effluent from the end of the column to two detectors, one being an NPD and the other, an MSD. By using the NPD chromatogram to identify peaks of interest (many endogenous peaks will not produce an NPD response), the mass spectrum of the peak at the corresponding retention time can be obtained from the MS total ion chromatogram (TIC) (**Figure 16**).

Gas Chromatography–Mass Spectrometry

The use of GC–MS to screen biological samples for drugs is also a popular technique. However, because extracts from biological samples often contain many endogenous compounds, the

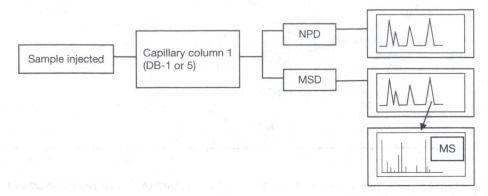

Figure 14   Column effluent split between two detectors.

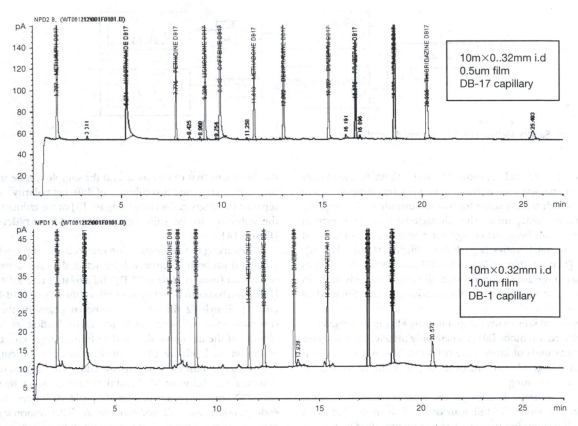

Figure 15   Dual column NPD chromatogram. Column oven 100 °C (0.5 min)–280 °C (8 min) at 10 °C min⁻¹, injection port 250 °C, detector 325 °C, He carrier 4.9 ml min⁻¹, splitless injection.

technique requires an extensive sample preparation before GC–MS analysis if a general drug screen is required. TIC-containing endogenous compounds can often mask low concentrations of drugs. An alternative technique is to use selected ion extraction for characteristic ions of drugs of interest, and these extracted ion chromatograms can show the presence of drugs even if the TIC does not. Unfortunately, this technique can limit the number of drugs that can be screened for but is very good for selective drug screening. **Figure 17** shows a TIC and extracted ion chromatogram of a blood extract.

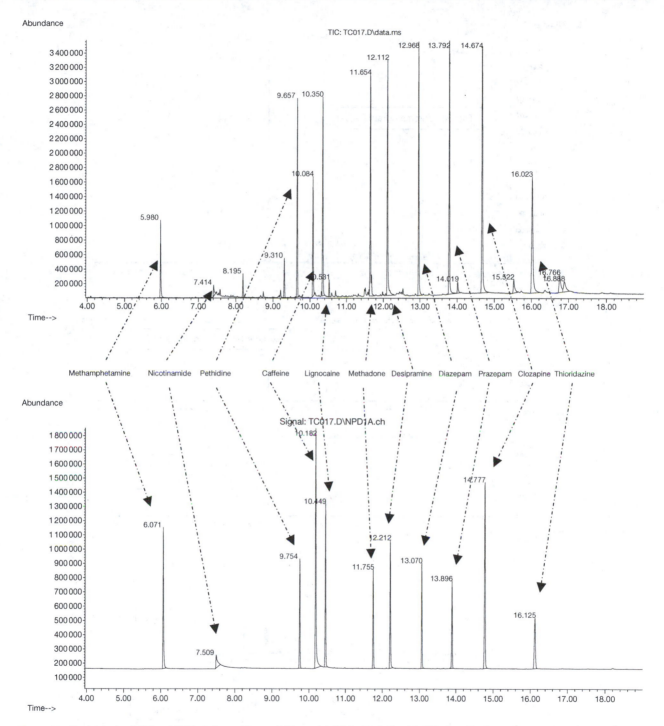

Figure 16 Dual detector (MSD and NPD). Column: 30 m × 0.25 mm i.d. HP-5: 60 °C (2 min)–300 °C at 20 °C min⁻¹, He carrier 4 ml min⁻¹, injection port 280 °C, NPD 280 °C, MSD transfer line 260 °C.

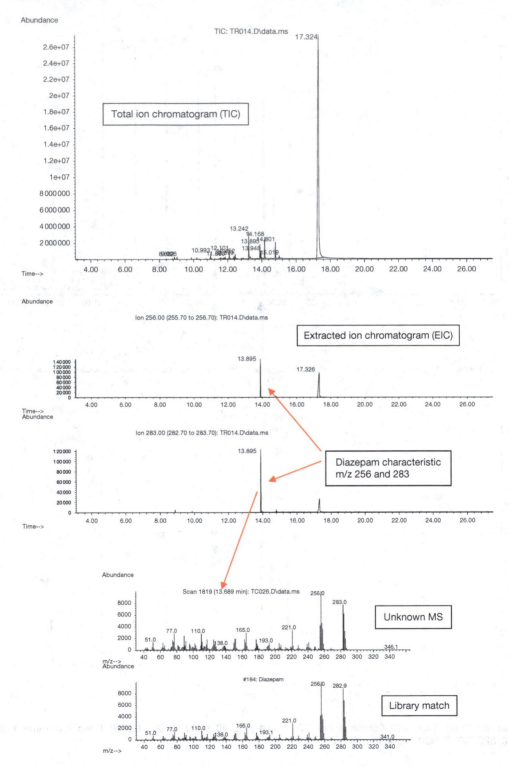

Figure 17 (Top) Total ion chromatogram of blood extract. (Center) Extracted ion chromatogram (*m/z* 256 and 283). (Bottom) Mass spectrum—Diazepam with library match.

Screening by Liquid Chromatography

HPLC with Photodiode Array Detector

At one time, HPLC was only used for the analysis of compounds that could not be analyzed by GC (nonvolatile thermally unstable compounds). Since the introduction of the photodiode array detector (DAD) in the mid-1980s, the ability to produce a UV spectrum has dramatically increased the use of HPLC systems for routine drug screening. The identification of drugs is based on the combination of retention time and UV spectrum as shown in **Figure 18**.

LC is the separation of components in a mixture based on the selective partitioning of compounds between a liquid mobile phase and a stationary phase. The sample is introduced through an injection port into the mobile phase stream, delivered by the high-pressure pump, and moves through the column where the separation takes place. They are then detected at the column outlet with a flow-through detector or are transferred into a MS.

The selection of the stationary phase and mobile phase is important as alterations to one or the other can lead to improved compound separation particularly when there are endogenous compounds present.

LC–MS and Liquid Chromatography–Tandem Mass Spectrometry

Over the last decade, the use of LC–MS and liquid chromatography–tandem mass spectrometry (LC–MS/MS) has become increasingly important in drug screening because of the high selectivity of MS detection and the possibility of analyzing aqueous samples and polar, thermally labile, and nonvolatile analytes. The application of single-stage quadrupole or ion trap mass spectrometers for screening is limited due to coeluting compounds and high matrix burden. Methods for STA using triple-stage quadrupole or hybrid triple-quadrupole linear ion trap mass spectrometers have solved these problems. Instruments have been greatly improved and a new screening technique based on high-resolution MS with benchtop time-of-flight (TOF) has been recently developed.

Recent developments of LC-MS-based screening procedures have covered hundreds of toxicologically important compounds and can be divided into three general approaches.

Multitargeted Screening

This method uses triple-stage quadrupole or hybrid triple-quadrupole linear ion trap mass spectrometers and relies on the mass spectral information of the analytes of interest being included in the method. The number of compounds that can be included is limited by the minimum dwell time for each multireaction monitoring (MRM) transition included in the one measurement cycle. This was a limitation to the number of compounds that could be screened for; however, software development has allowed for the scheduling of MRM's within-time windows for transitions monitored by the survey scan

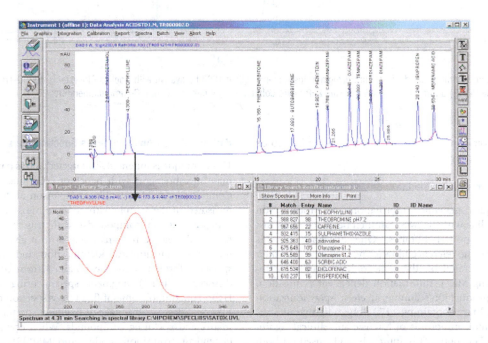

Figure 18 HPLC/DAD chromatogram of a drug mix showing the UV spectra and library search of theophylline. Agilent Zorbax SB-C18 (5 μm, 2.1 × 150 mm) with XDBC8 guard column (5 μm, 4.6 × 12.5 mm).

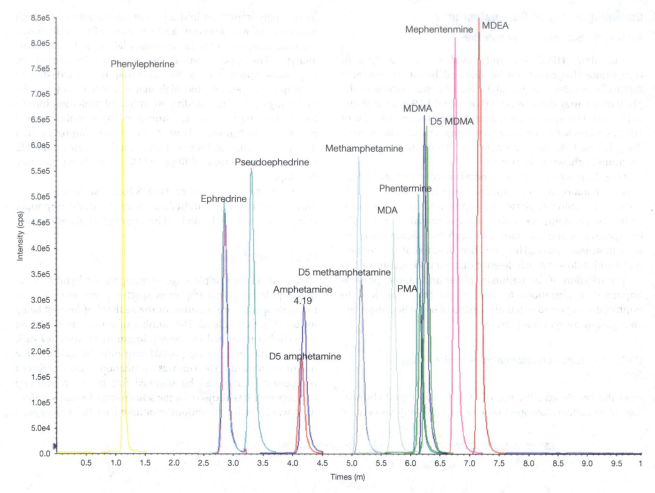

Figure 19 ESI amphetamines product ion chromatogram: Instrument: Agilent 1200 LC system with Applied Biosystems 4000Q-Trap MS. Column: Phenomenex Luna PFP(2) 3 μm 50 mm × 4.6 mm with PFP guard column 5 μm 4 mm × 2.0 mm. Column temperature: 25 °C.

allowing the overall number of transitions in a method to be increased dramatically.

Ion Trap or Triple-Quadrupole Mass Spectrometers

These techniques generate information-rich product ion spectra, which, like with GC/MS, can then be searched against reference mass spectral libraries. One drawback of this technique is that the reference libraries need to have had their mass spectra generated on the same or very similar instrumentation. Using MRM, information dependent acquisition, and enhanced product ion scanning, an electrospray ionization (ESI)–MS/MS library containing 1253 drugs, pharmaceuticals, and toxic organic compounds of forensic and clinical significance has been generated. This approach can be used for both targeted and untargeted screening.

High-Resolution Accurate Mass Spectrometers

This technique is inherently untargeted and is based on accurate mass measurements with benchtop TOF mass spectrometers. Compounds are identified by comparison of the accurate mass measured in the sample with accurate mass databases of toxicological relevant compounds. With this approach, accurate mass and isotopic patterns alone do not give sufficient information for unequivocal identification and more structural-specific information can be obtained from collision-induced dissociation (CID) fragment spectra using in-source CID. Hybrid quadrupole time-of-flight mass spectrometry (LC-QTOF-MS) provides the advantage of fragment spectra not affected by matrix and coeluting compounds. When operated in a data-dependent acquisition mode (auto MS/MS) where the presence of a nominated ion triggers an MS/MS of the compound, it

Table 3 Precursor ions and major product ions for each of the amphetamines in **Figure 19**

ID	Q1 Mass	Qualifier masses	RT (min)
Amphetamine	136	119, 91, 65	4.0
Paramethoxyamphetamine (PMA)	166	149, 121, 91	6.1
Ephedrine	166	148, 133, 117	2.7
Pseudoephedrine	166	148, 133, 117	3.2
Methyenedioxyamphetamine (MDA)	180	163, 105, 133	5.6
Methylenedioxyethyamphetamine (MDEA)	208	163, 133, 105	7.1
Methylenedioxymethamphetamine (MDMA)	194	163, 133, 105	6.2
Methamphetamine	150	119, 91, 65	5.1
Phenylephrine	168	150, 109, 91	1.1
Phentermine	150	91, 133, 105	6.1
Mephentermine	164	91, 133, 105	6.7
D5-MDMA	199	165	6.1
D5-Methamphetamine	155	121	5.0
D5-Amphetamine	141	93	4.0

combines the advantage of TOF-MS for comprehensive data collection with the measurement of accurate CID fragment spectra from all relevant compounds.

Mass Spectrometer Inlet Systems

There are two main interfaces that allow the introduction of a liquid effluent from the LC column at atmospheric pressure into the high-vacuum mass spectrometer system: ESI and atmospheric pressure chemical ionization (APCI). In ESI, the column effluent is formed into charged droplets using a strong electrical field with ions produced from evaporating solution droplets. In APCI, the effluent is first nebulized and then heated with ions produced by gas-phase ion–molecule reactions. A series of low-pressure chambers and ion-focusing lenses is used to optimally transport the ions into the MS. Both ESI and APCI produce limited spectral information compared to electron impact mass spectra and for identification purposes, it is often necessary to perform secondary fragmentation (MS/MS). **Figure 19** shows the separation of amphetamines in blood using LC-ESI/MS/MS. **Table 3** shows the selected precursor ions $[M + H]^+$ and the resultant fragment ions used for the identification of the compounds.

One problem that is commonly encountered in LC-MS is ion suppression. Matrix effects can either reduce the response of the compound of interest (ion suppression) or increase it (ion enhancement). Both can seriously compromise the accuracy of quantitation and in a worst case scenario, ion suppression could lead to a false negative result. For this reason, experiments on matrix effects are an essential part of LC-MS(MS)-based method validation, sample preparation should reduce the amount of endogenous compounds in the matrix extract that can lead to ion suppression, and the effect of other compounds used in the analysis (salts, drugs, metabolites, and

deuterated internal standards) should be evaluated before using this technique routinely.

See also: **Methods:** Chromatography: Basic Principles; Gas Chromatography; Gas Chromatography–Mass Spectrometry; Liquid and Thin-Layer Chromatography; Liquid Chromatography–Mass Spectrometry; **Toxicology:** Methods of Analysis—Confirmatory Testing; Volatile Substances and Inhalants.

Further Reading

Allen, K.R., Azad, R., Field, H.P., Blake, D.K., 2005. Replacement of immunoassay by LC tandem mass spectrometry for the routine measurement of drugs of abuse in oral fluid. Annals of Clinical Biochemistry 42, 277–284.

Annesley, T.M., 2003. Ion suppression in mass spectrometry. Clinical Chemistry 49, 1041–1044.

Baselt, R., 2008. Disposition of Toxic Drugs and Poisons in Man, eighth ed. Biomedical Publications, CA.

Broecker, S., Herre, S., Wust, B., Zweigenbaum, J., Pragst, F., 2010. Development and practical application of a library of CID accurate mass spectra of more than 2,500 toxic compounds for systematic toxicological analysis by LC-QTOF-MS with data-dependent acquisition. Analytical and Bioanalytical Chemistry 400, 101–117.

Dresen, S., Gergov, M., Politi, L., Halter, C., Weinmann, W., 2009. ESI-MS/MS library of 1,253 compounds for application in forensic and clinical toxicology. Analytical and Bioanalytical Chemistry 395, 2521–2526.

Fernandez, M.D., Wille, S.M., Samyn, N., Wood, M., Lopez-Rivadulla, M., De Broeck, G., 2009. High-throughput analysis of amphetamines in blood and urine with online solid-phase extraction-liquid chromatography–tandem mass spectrometry. Journal of Analytical Toxicology 33, 578–587.

Ferrer, I., Thurman, E.M. (Eds.), 2009. Liquid Chromatography Time-of Flight Mass Spectrometry. John Wiley & Sons, NJ.

Flanagan, R.J., Taylor, A., Watson, I.D., Whelpton, R., 2007. Fundamentals of Analytical Toxicology. John Wiley & Sons, West Sussex, England.

Herrin, G.L., McCurdy, H.H., Wall, W.H., 2005. Investigation of an LC-MS-MS (QTrap^W) method for the rapid screening and identification of drugs in post-mortem toxicology whole blood samples. Journal of Analytical Toxicology 29, 599–606.

Jansen, R., Lachatre, G., Marquet, P., 2005. LC-MS/MS systematic toxicological analysis: comparison of MS/MS spectra obtained with different instruments and settings. Clinical Biochemistry 38, 362–372.

Johnson, R.D., Botch, S.R., 2011. The screening of forensic blood, urine, and tissue specimens for xenobiotics using ion-trap liquid chromatography–tandem mass spectrometry. Journal of Analytical Toxicology 35, 65–74.

Langel, K., Gunnar, T., Ariniemi, K., Rajamaki, O., Lillsunde, P., 2011. A validated method for the detection and quantitation of 50 drugs of abuse and medicinal drugs in oral fluid by gas chromatography–mass spectrometry. Journal of Chromatography B 879, 859–870.

Liu, H.-C., Liu, R.H., Lin, D.-L., Ho, H., 2010. Rapid screening and confirmation of drugs and toxic compounds in biological specimens using liquid chromatography/ion trap tandem mass spectrometry and automated library search. Rapid Communications in Mass Spectrometry 24, 75–84.

Lynch, K.L., Breaud, A.R., Vandenberghe, H., Wu, A.H.B., Clarke, W., 2010. Performance evaluation of three liquid chromatography mass spectrometry methods for broad spectrum drug screening. Clinica Chimica Acta 411, 1474–1481.

Maurer, H.H., 1999. Systematic toxicological analysis procedures for acidic drugs and/ or metabolites relevant to clinical and forensic toxicology and/ or doping control. Journal of Chromatography B 733, 3–25.

Maurer, H.H., 2000. Screening procedures for simultaneous detection of several drug classes used for high throughput toxicological analyses and doping control. A review. Combinatorial Chemistry & High Throughput Screening 3, 467–480.

Maurer, H.H., 2005. Advances in analytical toxicology: current role of liquid chromatography–mass spectrometry (LC-MS or LC-MS/MS) relevant to clinical and forensic toxicology. Analytical and Bioanalytical Chemistry 381, 110–118.

Maurer, H.H., 2007. Current role of liquid chromatography–mass spectrometry in clinical and forensic toxicology. Analytical and Bioanalytical Chemistry 388, 1315–1325.

Maurer, H.H., 2010. Perspectives of liquid chromatography coupled to low-and high-resolution mass spectrometry for screening, identification, and quantification of drugs in clinical and forensic toxicology. Therapeutic Drug Monitoring 32, 324–327.

McMaster, M.C., 2007. HPLC a Practical User's Guide. John Wiley & Sons, NJ.

Moffat, A.C., Osselton, M.D., Widdop, B., 2004. Clarke's Analysis of Drugs and Poisons, third ed., vols 1 and 2. Pharmaceutical Press, London, UK.

Mosaddegh, M.H., Richardson, T., Stoddart, R.W., McClure, J., 2001. Application of solid-phase micro-extraction technology to drug screening and identification. Annals of Clinical Biochemistry 38, 541–547.

Muller, C., Schafer, P., Stortzel, M., Vogt, S., Weinmann, W., 2002. Ion suppression effects in liquid chromatography-electrospray-ionisation transport-region collision induced dissociation mass spectrometry with different serum extraction methods for systematic toxicological analysis with mass spectra libraries. Journal of Chromatography B 773, 47–52.

Niessen, W.M.A., 2003. Progress in liquid chromatography–mass spectrometry instrumentation and its impact on high-throughput screening. Journal of Chromatography A 1000, 413–436.

Ojanpera, S., Ojanpera, I., 2005. Forensic drug screening by LC-MS using accurate mass measurement. LC-GC Europe 18, 607–614.

Peters, F.T., 2011. Recent advances of liquid chromatography–(tandem) mass spectrometry in clinical and forensic toxicology. Clinical Biochemistry 44, 54–65.

Polettini, A., 2006. Applications of LC-MS in Toxicology. Pharmaceutical Press, IL.

Pragst, F., Herzler, M., Erxleben, B.-T., 2004. Systematic toxicological analysis by high-performance liquid chromatography with diode array detection (HPLC-DAD). Clinical Chemistry and Laboratory Medicine 42, 1325–1340.

Rittner, M., Pragst, F., Bork, W.-R., Neumann, J., 2001. Screening method for seventy psychoactive drugs or drug metabolites in serum based on high-performance liquid chromatography-electrospray ionization mass spectrometry. Journal of Analytical Toxicology 25, 115–124.

Sauvage, F.L., Saint-Marcoux, F., Duretz, B., Deporte, D., Lachatre, G., Marquet, P., 2006. Screening of drugs and toxic compounds with liquid chromatography-linear ion trap tandem mass spectrometry. Clinical Chemistry 52, 1735–1742.

Sharp, M.E., 2001. A comprehensive screen for volatile organic compounds in biological fluids. Journal of Analytical Toxicology 25, 631–636.

Stimpfl, T., Jurenitsch, J., Vycudilik, W., 2001. General unknown screening in post-mortem tissue and blood samples: A semi-automatic solid-phase extraction using polystyrene resins followed by liquid–liquid extraction. Journal of Analytical Toxicology 25, 125–129.

Strano-Rossi, S., Molaioni, F., Botre, F., 2005. Application of solid-phase micro-extraction to antidoping analysis: determination of stimulants, narcotics, and other classes of substances excreted free in urine. Journal of Analytical Toxicology 29, 217–222.

Telepchak, M.J., August, T.F., Cahnet, G., 2004. Forensic and Clinical Applications of Solid Phase Extraction. Humana Press, NJ.

Thieme, D., Sachs, H., 2003. Improved screening capabilities in forensic toxicology by application of liquid chromatography–tandem mass spectrometry. Analytica Chimica Acta 492, 171–186.

Viette, V., Guillarme, D., Mylonas, R., et al., 2011. A multi-target screening analysis in human plasma using fast liquid chromatography-hybrid tandem mass spectrometry (part 1). Clinical Biochemistry 44, 32–44.

Vinesse, N., Marquet, P., Duchoslav, E., Dupuy, J.L., Lachatre, G., 2003. A general unknown screening procedure for drugs and toxic compounds in serum using liquid chromatography-electrospray-single quadrupole mass spectrometry. Journal of Analytical Toxicology 27, 7–14.

Weinmann, W., Gergov, M., Goerner, M., 2000. MS/MS-libraries with triple quadrupole-tandem mass spectrometers for drug identification and drug screening. Analusis 28, 934–941.

Weinmann, W., Wiedemann, A., Eppinger, B., Renz, M., Svoboda, M., 1999. Screening for drugs in serum by electrospray ionization/collision- induced dissociation and library searching. Journal of the American Society for Mass Spectrometry 10, 1028–1037.

Yawney, J., Treacy, S., Hindmarsh, K.W., Burczynski, F.J., 2002. A general screening method for acidic, neutral, and basic drugs in whole blood using the Oasis MCX[W] column. Journal of Analytical Toxicology 26, 325–332.

Methods of Analysis—Confirmatory Testing

A Polettini, University of Verona, Verona, Italy

Abbreviations

GC	Gas chromatography	MDEA	3,4-Methylenedioxyethylamphetamine
HRMS	High-resolution mass spectrometry	MDMA	3,4-Methylenedioxymethylamphetamine
IP	Identification points	MRIC	Minimum required identification criteria
IS	Internal standard	MRQC	Minimum required quantification criteria
ISO	International Organization for Standardization	MS	Mass spectrometry
		RRT	Relative retention time
LC	Liquid chromatography	RT	Retention time
LLOQ	Lower limit of quantification	SIM	Selected ion monitoring
LRMS	Low-resolution mass spectrometry	SRM	Selected reaction monitoring
		ULOQ	Upper limit of quantification
MDA	3,4-Methylenedioxyamphetamine		

Glossary

Confirmatory test An analytical test capable of identifying a xenobiotic, presumptively detected in a sample by a first-level (screening) test.

Measurement uncertainty Measurement of the cumulative effect of all possible sources of variability resulting from the application of a given analytical method.

Method validation Set of tests carried out in order to assess the ability of an analytical method to achieve the objectives it has been developed for. They typically include evaluation of specificity, lower limit of detection and of quantification (LLOQ), upper limit of quantification (ULOQ), absolute recovery, matrix effect, calibration range, accuracy, and precision within the same analytical session and between different sessions (at LLOQ and at least another level), analyte stability, robustness, and applicability of dilution.

Minimum required identification criteria Criteria that must be met at least in order to properly identify a compound in a sample. They may be specific of the analytical technique or set of analytical techniques adopted, and must be established in advance.

Principles of Confirmatory Testing

In a forensic setting, truth must be established beyond any reasonable doubt in order to guarantee the rights of all parties. This obvious but nevertheless essential principle, when transferred to analytical toxicology, requires unequivocal identification of a xenobiotic in a sample. The identification of a drug (most commonly a xenobiotic) in a sample is quite often a critical step in a forensic investigation, proving the link between drug use and a judicially relevant event. These events could be drug dealing, driving under the influence, a workplace accident, a drug-facilitated sexual assault, or even a homicide.

In forensic toxicology, it is generally accepted that identification must be accomplished through the use of at least two analytical techniques based on different chemical and physical principles, supporting the results of each other. Therefore, whenever a presumptive identification is obtained, a second confirmatory test must be applied producing an analytical result as independent as possible from that of the first-level (screening) test. The rational behind this principle is that the chance that both tests (screening and confirmatory) may give a false positive identification must be as low as possible. Therefore, a confirmatory method based on a detection principle very similar to that of the screening test is unacceptable (e.g., confirmation of an immunochemical result with another immunochemical method). The use of a chromatographic technique to confirm a result obtained by chromatography is acceptable only if the two separation techniques produce different results (i.e., significantly different retention behavior for the same analyte). The introduction of hyphenated chromatographic and spectroscopic techniques (e.g., liquid chromatography (LC) combined with ultraviolet-visible spectrophotometry or gas chromatography (GC)/LC combined to mass spectrometry (MS)) has somewhat changed this picture, as these involve the application of two different analytical techniques within a single test. While the use of hyphenated chromatographic and spectroscopic techniques for confirmatory purposes is correct in principle, it must be clear that it is viable only if it does exclude the possibility of a false positive result due to contamination during sample processing and/or instrumental analysis (i.e., by including the analysis of reagent blanks and sample blanks within the batch of samples).

The confirmatory test must be characterized by a higher analytical selectivity, and therefore better specificity (expressed as the ratio of true negatives/(true negatives + false positives)) and at least equal, but preferably better, sensitivity (true positives/(true positives + false negatives)) than the first-level (screening) test. Quite often, the screening test does not discriminate between related substances (either parent compound and metabolites, e.g., heroin and its phase I and phase II metabolites, or a group of structurally related compounds, e.g., ecstasy and derivatives), whereas the confirmatory test enables the specific detection and identification of each single compound/metabolite. Therefore, the sensitivity of the screening method is often referred to the drug class (e.g., opiates, ecstasy, and derivatives), while that of the confirmatory test is referred to each single compound/metabolite (morphine, 6-acetylmorphine, codeine, or 3,4-methylenedioxymethylamphetamine, 3,4-methylenedioxyamphetamine, 3,4-methylenedioxyethylamphetamine, etc.). In such a case, by definition, the sensitivity of the confirmatory test must be better than that of the screening test (as a rule of thumb, the cutoff for a compound in the confirmatory test should be at least one half of the cutoff for the drug class in the screening test).

Whenever a large number of samples needs to be tested for forensic purposes (e.g., in workplace drug testing), the application of the confirmatory testing responds also to cost-efficiency reasons. It is economically efficient to perform a rapid, automated, and low-cost screening test (e.g., a colorimetric, enzymatic, or immunochemical test) providing adequate sensitivity (i.e., low rate of false negatives) and submit all presumptive positive results to confirmation, which typically requires more expensive, complex, and time-consuming tests.

Analytical procedures used in confirmatory testing must not only be standardized and available in written form but also be fully validated according to an internationally accepted standard. The laboratory should be also accredited according to the International Organization for Standardization (ISO) 17 025 requirements. In addition, they must provide all the necessary details, specifications, and criteria for the execution, verification, and interpretation of results. A parameter deserving particular attention in the validation of a confirmatory testing is analytical selectivity. This is typically verified either through the separate analysis of different blank samples ($n = 6$–10) and through the analysis of samples containing the most frequently encountered exogenous compounds within the geographical area or the particular setting of the samples to be confirmed. In both cases, the absence of any interference to the target analyte's detection must be proved.

Although it is beyond the scope of the present chapter, it must be realized that, in order to establish a link between the use of a drug or poison and a crime, not only a proper analytical strategy—including an adequate confirmatory testing—must be implemented but also, and equally importantly, a proper chain of custody ensuring the authenticity, integrity, and traceability of the sample needs to be ensured. In addition, if not already established by specific regulations, it is advisable, whenever possible, to collect a further sample aliquot (sample B or revision sample) identical to that used for screening and confirmatory purposes (sample A) that must be properly stored in a sealed container and kept available for further testing (counter or revision analysis) in case of disputes on the results obtained on sample A.

Certified Reference Standards

Proper identification of an analyte for forensic purposes requires that, whenever feasible, the reference standard be examined under identical analytical conditions of the unknown, providing results that fulfill all the required identification criteria discussed later in this chapter. Therefore, whenever a reference standard of certified purity (within the expiry date) may be obtained, definitive identification must be achieved by direct comparison with the reference standard. If a certified reference standard is not available, another standard may be used. In cases when neither is available, reference analytical data (e.g., reference relative retention time (RRT) or retention index or reference mass spectrum contained in a database) may be used provided that their origin and quality are verified and that the instrumental conditions used to obtain them match those used for the analysis of the unknown.

MS in Confirmatory Testing

The application of MS in confirmatory testing, owing to the intrinsic analytical selectivity of this technique (MS provides an absolute measure of the mass/charge ratio of the molecular or pseudomolecular ion and of specific fragment ions). It is generally accepted that, whenever its application is feasible, MS is the technique of choice for confirmation purposes. However, recent developments in MS have led to a spread of MS-based analytical techniques, including single, tandem MS (MS–MS) and multiple configurations (MS^n), at low-resolution MS or high-resolution MS (HRMS) mass resolution, alone or in combination with one or more chromatographic separation techniques (e.g., GC, LC, coupled column LC, and LC–LC). As a result, minimum required identification criteria (MRIC) for each of these techniques and their combinations have still to be determined (see the section "Minimum Required Identification Criteria").

Internal Standardization

In all cases where the instrumental technique makes it feasible and appropriate, it is strongly advisable to use an internal standard (IS) in confirmatory testing. The addition of one or more ISs increases the certainty of identification and quantification. The IS provides higher precision and accuracy to the measurement of chromatographic retention (RRT = analyte retention time/IS retention time) of the analyte and to its quantification as well (by correcting for volume errors, variability in extraction efficiency, and instability of the detection system). Alternatively, other more complex means of standardization of chromatographic retention may be adopted (e.g., Kovats retention indices). The IS must be added to samples and controls as early as possible during the sample preparation procedure, that is, before any treatment of the sample. Hair—and other solid and nonhomogeneous substrates—represents an exception to this rule as the added IS might be removed during sample treatment (e.g., washing) preceding extraction. Therefore, it is advisable to add the IS after washing, cutting/powdering, and weighing of the hair sample. Whenever an MS technique is involved, the use of deuterated or other isotope-labeled ISs (with a mass difference ≥ 3 from the unlabeled analyte) should be considered as their behavior, in terms of chromatographic retention and MS fragmentation, is *nearly* identical to that of the corresponding unlabeled analyte, yet it allows the MS differentiation from the unlabeled analyte. The use of other unlabeled compounds as IS is a viable alternative when an isotope-labeled IS is not available, provided that the presence of the compound in the sample has been excluded, and its MS separation from the target analyte is ensured, particularly in the case of (even partial) coelution with the target analyte.

When LC–MS is adopted as the instrumental technique, it is advisable to adjust chromatographic conditions in order to make the target analyte and the IS to elute as close as possible to each other in order to account for matrix effects phenomena (e.g., ion suppression). The amount of isotope-labeled standard added to samples should be properly selected in order to avoid any significant effect on ionization efficiency (e.g., due to competition for ionization) or quantification (e.g., due to isotopic contributions) of the analyte. The stability of the IS during sample preparation and storage in the autosampler must be verified during the method validation.

Minimum Required Identification Criteria

For any analytical techniques or combinations applied to confirmatory testing, MRIC can be established and adopted following the directions and suggestions of relevant regulations, guidelines of scientific associations, reference literature, and general principles accepted by the scientific community. These criteria must be properly assessed in order to achieve the identification of an analyte in a sample.

Table 1 shows typical MRIC adopted for the most common analytical techniques.

For gas chromatographic analysis, the absolute retention time (RT) or the RRT to an IS should be within $\pm 1\%$ and $\pm 2\%$, respectively, of that obtained for the standard analyte in the positive control for capillary GC. For LC, a wider tolerance window is acceptable ($\pm 2\%$ and $\pm 4\%$ for RT and RRT, respectively).

When full scan MS analysis is adopted, a preliminary identification may be achieved by comparing the MS spectrum of the unknown and that of the reference analyte using one of the available MS library search algorithms. To this purpose, as mass spectra obtained from biological extracts are sometimes affected by chemical noise, it is strongly advised to adopt reverse-search algorithms instead of forward-search ones. Reverse-search algorithms look for the presence of fragment ions of the reference mass spectrum in the unknown mass spectrum, whereas forward-search algorithms do the opposite. Therefore, the presence of any interference fragment ions in the unknown mass spectrum will not affect the matching result of the reverse-search as they do when a forward-search algorithm is applied. Owing to the ability of reverse-search algorithms to identify mass spectra in the presence of chemical noise, at least to some extent, it is also recommended to avoid background subtraction of the unknown mass spectrum, in order to prevent any distortion of relative mass abundances of the fragment ions specific to the unknown analyte, thus affecting the matching result.

Another essential requisite of confirmatory testing by full scan MS is the appropriate selection of the scan range. The upper limit of the acquisition range should be at least 30 mass

Table 1   Typical minimum required identification criteria adopted for the most widespread analytical techniques

Analytical technique	Minimum required identification criteria
Capillary gas chromatography	Absolute RT of the unknown within ±2% (or RRT within ±1%) of the reference analyte
Liquid chromatography	Absolute RT of the unknown within ±4% (or RRT of within ±2%) of the reference analyte
MS analysis in full scan mode	(1) All fragment ions of the reference spectrum with a relative abundance higher than 10% of the base peak must be present in the unknown, not background subtracted, mass spectrum
	(2) The relative abundance of these ions in the unknown spectrum must be within ±20% of that of the corresponding ions in the reference analyte spectrum
MS analysis in selected ion monitoring (SIM) mode	(1) At least three fragment ions
	(2) Ion ratios for the unknown spectrum within ±20% of those of the reference analyte (if fragment ions with ≤10% relative abundance in the full scan spectrum of the reference analyte are selected, a ±50% tolerance is acceptable)
MS/MS analysis in product ion full scan mode	(1) All fragment ions of the reference product ion spectrum with a relative abundance higher than 10% must be present in the unknown, not background subtracted, product ion mass spectrum
	(2) The relative abundance of these ions in the unknown spectrum must be within ±20% of that of the corresponding ions in the reference analyte spectrum
	(3) The surviving precursor ion should be present in the product ion spectrum with a relative abundance ≥5%
MS/MS analysis in selected reaction monitoring (SRM) mode	(1) At least two precursor-to-product transitions
	(2) The relative abundance of the two product ions must be within ±25% of the corresponding value obtained for the reference analyte

RT, absolute retention time; RRT, retention time relative to an internal standard.

units higher than the mass of the reference compound, in order to account for the formation of possible adducts, and the lower limit should equal that used for the acquisition of mass spectra of the reference database (typically m/z 50). However, it must be noted that for some compounds, for example, amphetamine-like drugs and tricyclic antidepressants, the lower limit should be reduced to m/z 30 or 40 in order to include the base mass peak ($[CH_4N]^+$, m/z 30; $[C_2H_6N]^+$, m/z 44) and to increase selectivity of detection as well. After preliminary identification by library search, proper identification should be accomplished by verifying that all criteria listed in **Table 1** for identification in MS full scan mode are fulfilled.

Whenever the confirmation of a target analyte must be achieved, MS analysis in selected ion monitoring (SIM) mode may be adopted instead of full scan. In such a case, at least three fragment ions per compound should be monitored. These should include the molecular ion or adduct, depending on the ionization technique used, and exclude isotopic peaks and nonspecific losses (e.g., loss of water). The ratios between fragment ion peaks (heights or, preferably, areas) should be within ±20% of those obtained for the analyte in the positive control. However, for fragment ions whose relative abundance is lower than 10% in the full scan reference spectrum, a ±50% tolerance may be accepted.

For tandem MS analysis (MS–MS) of product ions in full scan mode (i.e., product ion scan), the same criteria described for full scan single MS analysis apply. In addition, the molecular or pseudomolecular ion should be selected as precursor ion, and the product ion spectrum should include the surviving precursor ion with a relative abundance of at least 5%.

Confirmatory analysis in MS–MS selected reaction monitoring (SRM) mode should be performed by monitoring at least two precursor-to-product transitions. The precursor ions of the transitions monitored should be either the molecular/pseudomolecular ion, or an adduct (depending on the ionization technique applied), or another structurally specific ion, and the product ions should not result from nonspecific losses (e.g., loss of water). In addition, the ratio of the two product ion peaks (heights or, preferably, areas) should be within ±25% of the corresponding value obtained for the positive control.

Exceptions to these MRICs may be adopted only if they are justified by the physical–chemical and/or structural characteristics of the analyte, or by the limitations in the instrumental technique used. Reasons justifying any deviations from the MRIC discussed earlier must be reported in the corresponding standardized operating procedure of the confirmatory test.

Alternatively, in order to avoid deviations from MRIC, a modification in the chromatographic behavior and/or in the fragmentation pattern of an analyte may be obtained by means of derivatization techniques. In addition, as a general rule, the identification of specific metabolic products or precursors of an analyte in the sample may be used in order to further support the identification of the analyte.

If analytical techniques or combinations other than those listed earlier are used, no generally accepted MRIC are usually available. However, a general validity procedure for setting specific identification criteria may be adopted, such as the so-called ad hoc confirmation package widely used in the veterinary area. This procedure is based on the principle that any analytical technique possesses a certain discrimination power of its own. Therefore, a definite number of identification points (IPs) may be attributed to each analytical technique. IPs resulting from the application of different techniques in either an online or offline combination may be summed up, the total number of IPs corresponding to the sum of each IP contribution derived from each individual technique. An example of this approach is the IP system established by the European Commission Decision 2002/657/EC (12 August 2002) implementing Council Directive 96/23/EC concerning the performance of analytical methods and interpretation of results. According to this system, the identification of an unknown compound is achieved with sufficient selectivity when, through the application of an analytical technique or more analytical techniques in either online or offline combination, a total of at least 4 IPs are reached. **Table 2** shows some examples of the total number of IPs relative to different combinations of MS ions acquired with different instrumental techniques. For example, a chromatographic/mass spectrometric analysis in SIM mode with three ions monitored would provide a total of 4 IPs: 1 IP from chromatographic separation and one for each of the ions monitored, provided that the MRIC described in **Table 1** for the corresponding techniques are all met. A tandem mass spectrometric analysis where two transitions from the same precursor ion are monitored would also provide a total of 4 IPs: 1 IP from the monitoring of the precursor ion, and 1.5 IPs for each of the two product ions (again, MRIC for tandem MS analysis in SRM described in **Table 1** need to be met). If a chromatographic separation is placed before MS–MS analysis, the total number of IPs rises up to 5. The use of HRMS allows a considerable gain in the number of IPs per ion, owing to the much higher selectivity of the technique (see **Table 2**).

Minimum Required Quantification Criteria

Frequently, a confirmatory test may be used also for quantification purposes. Therefore, in addition to minimum identification criteria, minimum required quantification criteria (MRQC) should also be adopted and satisfied. If the method is used for qualitative confirmation purposes with reference to a predetermined cutoff, the measurement uncertainty in correspondence to this value must be evaluated and subtracted from the measured value; a positive result shall be reported only in case the measured value, subtracted from the measurement uncertainty, falls above the confirmation cutoff. The result of a qualitative confirmatory test should be reported exclusively as a positive/negative or inconclusive result, the latter applying to cases where any of the batch or sample validation criteria are not met.

Whenever a confirmatory method is used for quantification purposes, its quantification performance must be thoroughly validated through the assessment of the overall measurement uncertainty, the lower limit of quantification, the upper limit of quantification (ULOQ), and the calibration range. The applicability of dilution to samples with an expected analyte's concentration falling above the ULOQ should also be validated. The quantification procedure shall include, among the MRQC, the quantification of an adequate number of negative and positive quality controls within a predefined tolerance. The result of a quantitative analysis must be expressed in a uniform measurement unit, preferably accepted by the International System of Units, avoiding any doubtful interpretation, and directly comparable to the measurement unit of reference values, if available.

Table 2 Number of identification points (IPs) relative to different combinations of MS ions acquired with different instrumental techniques

Analytical technique	Number of ions monitored	IP
Low-resolution MS (LRMS)	N	N
LC/LRMS or GC/LRMS	N	$N+1$
LRMS^n (precursor ion)	1	1
LRMS^n (product ion[a])	N	$1.5N$
High-resolution MS (HRMS)	N	$2N$
HRMS^n (precursor ion)	1	2
HRMS^n (product ion[a])	N	$2.5N$

[a]The same number of IPs applies to MS^3 or higher ions.
Source: The International Association of Forensic Toxicologists (TIAFT) (2001) Systematic Toxicological Analysis: Laboratory Guidelines. http://www.tiaft.org/node/82 (accessed June 2011).

See also: **Toxicology:** Methods of Analysis – Initial Testing; Toxicology: Overview and Applications.

Further Reading

De Zeeuw, R.A., 2004. Substance identification: The weak link in analytical toxicology. Journal of Chromatography B 811, 3–12.

Drummer, O.H., 2001. The Forensic Pharmacology of Drugs of Abuse. Arnold, London, p. 463.

European Commission, 2002. European Commission Decision 2002/657/EC (12 August 2002) implementing Council Directive 96/23/EC concerning the performance of analytical methods and interpretation of results. Official Journal of the European Union 221, 8–36.

Fenton, J.J., 2002. Confirmatory tests in toxicology. In: Fenton, J.J. (Ed.), Toxicology: A Case Oriented Approach. CRC Press, Boca Raton, FL, pp. 359–402.

International Organization and for Standardization, 2005. General Requirements for the Competence of Testing and Calibration Laboratories (UNI CEI EN ISO/IEC 17025:2005). ISO, Geneva.

Kovats, E., 1958. Gas-chromatographische Charakterisierung organischer Verbindungen. Teil 1: Retentionsindices aliphatischer Halogenide, Alkohole, Aldehyde und Ketone. Helvetica Chimica Acta 41, 1915–1932.

Lee, S., Choi, H., Kim, E., Choi, H., Chung, H., Chung, K.H., 2010. Estimation of the measurement uncertainty by the bottom-up approach for the determination of methamphetamine and amphetamine in urine. Journal of Analytical Toxicology 34, 222–228.

Moffat, A.C., Osselton, M.D., Widdop, B., 2004. Forensic toxicology. In: Moffat, A.C., Osselton, M.D., Widdop, B. (Eds.), Clarke's Analysis of Drugs and Poisons, third ed., vol. 1. Pharmaceutical Press, London, pp. 80–93.

Moffat, A.C., Owen, P., Brown, C., 1978. Evaluation of weighted discrimination power calculations as an aid to the selection of chromatographic systems for the analysis of drugs. Journal of Chromatography 161, 179–185.

Penders, J., Verstraete, A., 2006. Laboratory guidelines and standards in clinical and forensic toxicology. Accreditation and Quality Assurance 11, 284–290.

Peters, F., 2006. Method validation using LC-MS. In: Polettini, A. (Ed.), Applications of LC-MS in Toxicology, first ed. Pharmaceutical Press, London, pp. 71–96.

Peters, F.T., Drummer, O.H., Musshoff, F., 2007. Validation of new methods. Forensic Science International 165, 216–224.

Polettini, A., 2006. Application of LC-MS in Toxicology. Pharmaceutical Press, London, p. 256.

Rivier, L., 2006. Identification and confirmation criteria for LC-MS. In: Polettini, A. (Ed.), Applications of LC-MS in Toxicology, first ed. Pharmaceutical Press, London, pp. 97–110.

Sanderson, K., 2009. Big Interest in Heavy Drugs. Nature News. http://www.nature.com/news/2009/090316/full/458269a.html (accessed June 2011).

Society of Forensic Toxicologists/American Academy of Forensic Sciences, 2006. Forensic Toxicology Laboratory Guidelines. Version. http://www.soft-tox.org/files/Guidelines_2006_Final.pdf (accessed June 2011).

The International Association of Forensic Toxicologists (TIAFT), 2001. Systematic Toxicological Analysis: Laboratory Guidelines. http://www.tiaft.org/node/82 (accessed June 2011).

US Food and Drug Administration, 2001. Guidance for Industry: Mass Spectrometry for Confirmation of the Identity of Animal Drug Residues. Draft Guidance 118. US FDA, Rockville, MD. http://www.fda.gov/downloads/AnimalVeterinary/GuidanceComplianceEnforcement/GuidanceforIndustry/UCM052658.pdf (accessed June 2011).

World Anti-Doping Agency, 2010. Identification Criteria for Qualitative Assays, WADA Technical Document – TD2010IDCR. http://www.wada-ama.org/Documents/World_Anti-Doping_Program/WADP-IS-Laboratories/WADA_TD2010IDCRv1.0_Identification%20Criteria%20for%20Qualitative%20Assays_May%2008%202010_EN.doc.pdf (accessed June 2011).

Chemometrics

A Mendlein, C Szkudlarek, and JV Goodpaster, Indiana University Purdue University Indianapolis, Indianapolis, IN, USA

Introduction

The statistical methods that are used for measurements involving a single variable are easily calculated by hand, using a calculator, or with a spreadsheet. However, these statistical methods are not robust enough for comparing data from spectroscopy, chromatography, or mass spectrometry, where one sample (observation) has many data points at different wavelengths, times, or ions (variables). In chemometrics, multivariate chemical data (i.e., data sets containing more than one variable) are often thought of as collections of matrices where each row corresponds to a number of measurements of a single sample or single experiment. Each column represents the measurements on a single variable, such as that of a wavelength along a spectroscopic peak. By using multivariate statistical methods, the statistical significance of the differences in these patterns can be established. Chemometric methods are typically applied to reducing data, sorting and grouping, investigating the dependence among variables, prediction, or hypothesis testing. Overall, chemometrics can reduce the complexity of a large data set and make predictions about unknown samples. Chemometrics can also be used to interpret the results of forensic analyses, especially those involving pattern recognition. When using multivariate statistical techniques, replicate sample measurements should be made to allow for experimental uncertainty and determine the significance of between-sample differences.

Multivariate statistics has proven valuable for many years and numerous standard texts are available for study (see Further Reading). In fact, the underlying principles of some of these statistical methods have been known for nearly a century. For instance, the idea of principal component analysis (PCA) as a dimension reduction and data display technique originated with Pearson in 1901. In 1933, Hotelling detailed algorithms for computing principal components (PCs). The multivariate distance bearing Mahalanobis' name was introduced by him in 1936, and linear discriminant analysis (LDA) was first developed by Fisher that same year.

As it stands today, forensic scientists often rely upon visual comparisons of chromatograms and spectra when making determinations of whether known and unknown samples might have come from the same source. As a result, there is no statistical basis for determining the evidentiary value of these comparisons. Given the recent challenges to the reliability of these trace evidence comparisons, many laboratories are seeking to find ways to compare samples in a more quantitative manner. For example, multivariate statistics could address the relevance and reliability issues raised in *Daubert v. Merrell Dow Pharmaceuticals*. Chemometrics could also help with the implementation of the recommendations from the National Academy of Sciences (NAS) report on strengthening forensic science, which was issued in 2009. Specifically, Recommendations 3 and 5 can be addressed in part by the use of chemometrics. Recommendation 3 deals with issues of accuracy and reliability in the various forensic science disciplines, and Recommendation 5 seeks to address issues of human observer bias and sources of human error (e.g., visual versus chemometric analysis of data).

Fortunately, the use of multivariate statistical analysis is a growing practice in forensic chemistry. Forensic scientists often have to identify patterns and interpret differences in data. Chemometrics makes this task more accurate, objective, and manageable. It is especially useful when the scientist is presented with large quantities of data. For example, comparing hundreds of spectra, chromatograms, etc. by inspection was never a valid scientific technique, but was widely used (and sometimes still is) until the adoption of multivariate statistical techniques by increasing numbers of forensic chemists. Multivariate statistics has been used on many types of forensic trace evidence, including accelerants, inks, fibers, smokeless powder, glass, and paint.

In general, a chemometric approach to a large data set follows a number of distinct steps:

1. Acquire data of the highest quality possible.
2. Carry out data preprocessing to remove any systematic (and unimportant) differences between samples.
3. Utilize unsupervised chemometric methods to visualize the underlying structure of the data (e.g., the number of classes).
4. Utilize supervised chemometric techniques to predict the class membership of unknown samples.

Although these steps are not always followed in all cases, they will serve as a useful outline for the discussion that follows.

Preprocessing Techniques

Preprocessing is the preparation of data before the application of chemometric algorithms. It is often required before performing multivariate statistical analyses. Preprocessing can remove noise and variation that might complicate data interpretation. However, some preprocessing can negatively impact the data, so techniques must be chosen and applied carefully.

The signal-to-noise ratio can be increased and unnecessary noise can be removed by data smoothing. Unfortunately, smoothing can cause distortions in peak height and width, can impair resolution of peaks, and can result in the loss of some features. Most smoothing methods involve creating a "window" of a specified number of data points and using the data values within the window to estimate a "noise-free" value for the point in the center of the window. Depending on the method used, the "noise-free" value may be the mean or median of the values in the window, or a predicted value from a polynomial fit to the data. Respectively, these methods are called mean smoothing, median smoothing, and running polynomial smoothing. The most common method of smoothing is running polynomial smoothing, including the Savitzky–Golay algorithm. This method is well documented and often used in instrument software.

Background correction is employed to keep varying background levels from confusing interpretation. For instance, fluorescence interference may dominate the background of a Raman spectrum. Background correction can be accomplished by subtracting a straight line or polynomial from the baseline in a spectrum. It can also be done by replacing sample vectors with their first derivative. A Savitzky–Golay algorithm exists for background correction as well, replacing each data point with the derivative of the smoothing polynomial at that point.

Normalization of spectra eliminates variations due to sample size, concentration, amount, and instrument response. It is typically conducted after smoothing and background correction have been completed. Normalization divides the values of the variables by a constant value, scaling them to a constant total (e.g., 1 or 100). The sample values may be divided by the sum of the absolute values of all intensities, normalizing the sample to unit area. The sample values may also be divided by the square root of the sum of squares of the intensities, normalizing to unit vector length.

Mean centering shifts the origin of the coordinate system to the center of the data. It eliminates constant background without changing differences in variables. It involves subtracting the mean of each variable from the related elements of the sample vectors. It essentially calculates the mean spectrum for the data set and subtracts that "centroid" from each spectrum. Mean centering is often inappropriate for use in signal analysis, because the concern is variability above a baseline rather than around an average. This centering loses information about the origin of the factor space, relative magnitudes of eigenvalues, and relative errors.

Autoscaling is the use of variance scaling and mean centering. It multiplies all of the spectra in the data set by a scaling factor for each wavelength. Autoscaling is done to either increase or decrease the influence on the calibration of each wavelength. It is recommended when variables have different units of measurement or show large differences in variance. However, it can negatively impact the precision or calibration. Also, if absolute intensities are important (e.g., correspond to concentration of a sample component), autoscaling should not be used.

Agglomerative Hierarchical Clustering

The purpose of cluster analysis is to determine whether individual samples fall into groupings and what those groupings might be. No prior knowledge of groupings is known. Therefore, cluster analysis is considered an unsupervised technique in that the algorithm does not rely on any inputs from the user. Cluster analysis has been applied to a number of different evidence types ranging from inks to tapes to photocopy/printer toners.

Cluster analysis involves determining the similarities or dissimilarities between objects (i.e., distances). The items that are deemed most similar will be clustered together. The distance between objects can be measured using different approaches. The first is Euclidean distance or ruler distance. Based on the Pythagorean theorem, it is calculated as the "ruler distance" between two points in an n-dimensional space. Another method is the Manhattan distance. If the Euclidean distance represents the length of the hypotenuse of a right triangle, Manhattan distance represents the distance along the two other sides of the triangle. It is generally greater than Euclidean distance. The Mahalanobis distance is an additional method for measuring similarity and dissimilarity. This method accounts for the fact that some variables may be correlated and uses the inverse of the variance–covariance matrix as a scaling factor.

Hierarchical clustering looks for the most similar or dissimilar pair of objects or clusters, then combines or divides them at each step, until all of the objects have been appropriately clustered. The information is then displayed in a two-dimensional plot called a dendrogram. There are two main types of hierarchical clustering: agglomerative hierarchical clustering (AHC) and divisive hierarchical clustering. AHC takes every object to be in its own individual cluster at first. The objects are then grouped into larger clusters, such that those in each group are more closely related than those in different groups. The most similar objects are clustered first, then those clusters are further grouped according to similarity until as few clusters as possible exist. Divisive clustering, on the other hand, starts with one group containing all of the objects and divides them based on their dissimilarity.

AHC can utilize several linkage methods. These methods include nearest neighbor, furthest neighbor, and centroid, among others. Nearest neighbor linkage, also called single linkage, joins clusters or objects based on the smallest distance between an object in the old cluster and the other objects or clusters. Furthest neighbor, or complete linkage, is the opposite of nearest neighbor and uses the greatest distance to link clusters or objects. Finally, the centroid method links clusters based on the distance between the calculated centroids of clusters rather than nearest or furthest neighbors. This method is more sensitive to outliers, as they can negatively impact the calculation of the centroid of a group.

An example of a simple two-dimensional data set containing five observations is shown in **Figure 1**. This data set is then processed using single-linkage clustering and the dendrogram it would produce is shown.

In general, AHC is an excellent tool for initial data analysis. It allows users to examine large sets of data for both expected and unexpected clusters. However, AHC does not give any indication of which variables have the greatest influence on the clustering. And while the dendrogram is simple and standardized, and represents the entirety of the data set, it is the only view of the data available using this method. There is no way to interactively view and manipulate the dendrogram so that the user may exploit human pattern-recognition abilities.

A more realistic example is shown in **Figure 2**. In this example, the data set consists of 50 visible spectra (400–700 nm) of various cotton fibers dyed with reactive dyes, all of which are a shade of red/pink. In this dendrogram, there are two distinct clusters that contain the spectra from dyes C (Reactive Red 123) and D (Reactive Red 195). The remaining cluster contains the more difficult to distinguish spectra from dyes B (Reactive Red 120), E (Reactive Red 2), and F (Reactive Red 228).

Principal Component Analysis

PCA is a dimensionality reduction technique that condenses the original variables to a smaller number of significant PCs. PCA is possibly the most widely used multivariate chemometric technique as it can be used for any multivariate data set such as spectra or chromatograms.

The information gained by PCA can be visually represented in a couple of ways. The first, and most traditional form, is the scores plot. This plots the score of one PC against the score of another for each sample. Those objects that cluster closely together are similar to one another, while objects that are far apart on a scores plot are dissimilar to one another. The second method of visualizing PCA is the loadings plot. Factor loadings are plotted against each variable (e.g., wavelength). The factor loadings represent the cosines of the angle between the PC and each variable. Where the cosines are positive, the variables are positively correlated. Where the cosines are negative, the variables are negatively correlated. Areas where the cosine is nearly zero, the variables have no correlation.

The possible number of PCs is the smaller of the number of variables or the number of samples. To find the first PC, the axis that minimizes the orthogonal sum of squares of the data points must be found. This PC will account for the greatest amount of variance in the data set. The second PC accounts for the next greatest amount of variance in a direction perpendicular to the first PC. Each successive PC captures less of the remaining variability in the data set. Significant PCs will have larger eigenvalues, or the sum of squares of each PC or score. The sum of the eigenvalues over all PCs is equal to the number of variables present in the data set (e.g., measured wavelengths).

PCs have eigenvalues associated with them that reflect the variance, percent variance, and cumulative variance for the PC. A number of PCs must be selected to represent the data set and put through discriminant analysis (DA) if desired. If too many PCs are used, the "noise" from extra PCs may interfere with the formation and verification of classes. To choose the correct number, one of three methods can be employed. The first method involves choosing a cumulative variance that must be met, such as 95%, and using the number of PCs that exceeds that percentage. The second method, introduced by Cattell in 1966, uses a scree plot, which plots eigenvalues against factor number. Where a sudden break in the plot occurs, this location indicates the number of significant PCs. To the right of this location is "factorial scree," or debris. The third method uses the Kaiser criterion, proposed by Kaiser in 1960, to determine the number of PCs. All eigenvalues that are greater than one would be considered significant.

An example of PCA is shown in **Figure 3**, where the clustering of elemental data is shown (as obtained by X-ray fluorescence of the backing of electrical tapes). The extent to which variance in the data set is successfully depicted in two

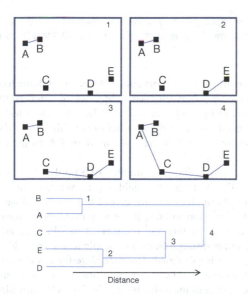

Figure 1 Single linkage clustering using Euclidean distance as a measure of similarity.

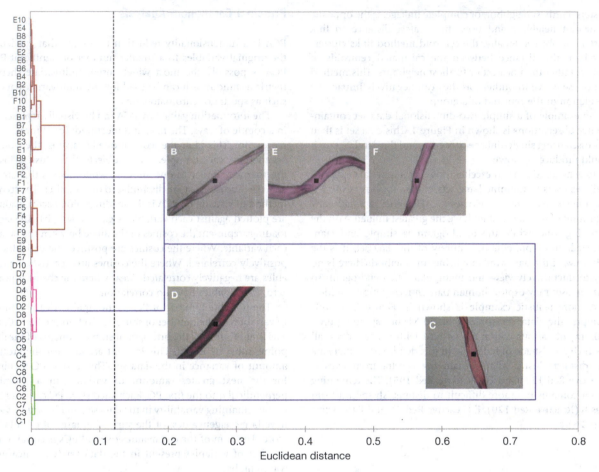

Figure 2 An AHC Dendrogram showing the degree of similarity between UV–visible spectra for the dyed cotton fibers shown. Note that fibers with highly similar colors also will cluster together. Ideally, the replicates from a given sample will cluster together, as is the case with fibers C and D.

dimensions is reflected in the total amount of variance captured by the first two PCs. In this case, almost 85% of the variance can be represented in a simple 2D scatter plot. This implies that the remaining PCs are relatively unimportant as they only account for approximately 15% of the total variance.

Discriminant Analysis

LDA is another dimensionality reduction technique. DA defines the distance of a sample from the center of a class, and creates a new set of axes to place members of the same group as close together as possible, and move the groups as far apart from one another as possible. These new axes are discriminant axes, or canonical variates (CVs), that are linear combinations of the original variables. DA is a form of supervised pattern recognition, as it relies upon information from the user in

order to function. In particular, DA requires knowledge of group memberships for each sample. DA is often applied to the same sample types as is PCA, where the latter technique can be used to reduce the number of variables in the data set and the resultant PCs are then used in DA to define and predict classes.

DA requires that the number of samples (i.e., spectra) exceeds the number of variables (i.e., wavelengths). If the number of samples does not exceed the number of variables, the DA calculation will fail; this is why PCA often precedes DA as a means to reduce the number of variables. Finally, the Mahalanobis distance from the sample to the centroid of any given group is calculated. The procedure for DA is somewhat analogous to that of PCA. However, instead of maximizing the sum of squares of the residuals as PCA does, DA maximizes the ratio of the variance between groups divided by the variance within groups.

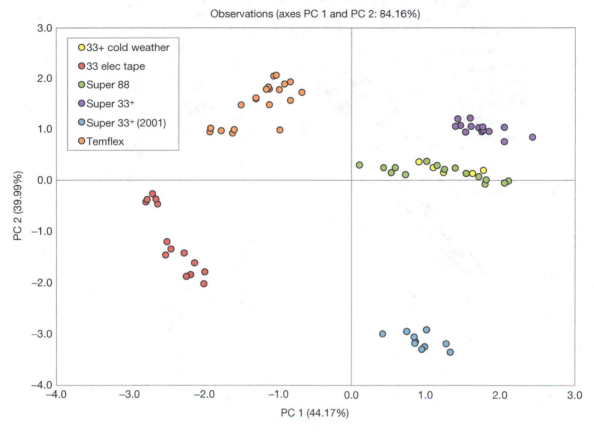

Figure 3 PCA of elemental data obtained via X-ray fluorescence of electrical tape backings. Note that the six brands form five distinct clusters in a two-dimensional representation of the data.

Once this procedure has been followed and the new samples have been classified, cross-validation is performed to test the classification accuracy. There are a number of methods available for cross-validation. Resubstitution uses the entire data set as a training set, developing a classification method based on the known class memberships of the samples. The class membership of every sample is then predicted by the model, and the cross-validation determines how often the rule correctly classified the samples. Resubstitution has a major drawback, however. Since it uses the same data set to both build the model and to evaluate it, the accuracy of the classification is typically overestimated. When the classification model is applied to a new data set, the error rate would likely be much higher than predicted. Another method of cross-validation is the hold-out method. This method separates the data set into two parts: one to be used as a training set for model development, and a second to be used to test the predictions of the model. Separating the data used to train the model from the data used to evaluate it creates an unbiased cross-validation. However, in situations where data are limited,

this may not be the best approach, as all of the data are not used to create the classification model. Also, acquiring enough data to have appropriately sized training and test sets may be time-consuming or difficult due to resources.

One final method for cross-validation is the leave-one-out method. In this method, a sample is removed from the data set temporarily. The classification model is then built from the remaining samples, and then used to predict the classification of the deleted sample. This process continues through all samples, treating each sample as an unknown to be classified using the remaining samples. More than one sample can also be left out at a time. For example, 20% of the samples may be temporarily removed while the model is built using the remaining 80%. The leave-one-out method uses all available data for evaluating the classification model. It is time-consuming, but usually preferable.

It is common for PCA and DA to work together by first reducing the dimensionality and noise level of the data set using PCA and then basing DA on the factor scores for each observation (as opposed to its original variables). **Figure 4**

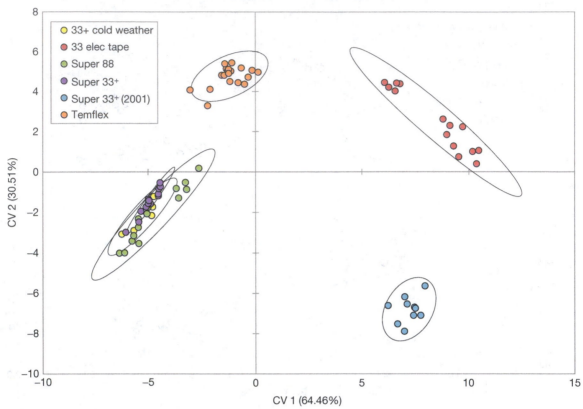

Figure 4   Results of discriminant analysis of the data presented in **Figure 3**. Ellipses represent the 95% confidence limits for each of the classes. Classes that are superimposed in two dimensions (e.g., Super 33+, Super 33+ cold weather, and Super 88) are more likely to be confused with one another (see **Table 1**).

shows the results of such a treatment on the same set of data shown in **Figure 3**. The extent to which DA is successful at discriminating between highly similar observations can be expressed as a "confusion matrix" where the observations are tallied in terms of their original classification and the resulting classification from DA (see **Table 1**).

Conclusions

The field of chemometrics is in constant flux as new methodologies are developed and eventually tested on data sets of amazing complexity. As such, the forensic application of chemometrics will also continue to evolve. Although chemometrics has not made its grand debut into the courtroom as of this writing, the reliance of forensic scientists on databases and comparisons of known and unknown samples makes this inevitable. This is particularly true given the increasing demand

for quantitative measures when expressing scientific opinions. Barriers to the full implementation of chemometric techniques in forensic science include lack of training among forensic scientists in mathematics and statistics and the need for specialized software packages to carry out calculations. Furthermore, forensic scientists must be able to explain to a jury and/or judge what the statistical procedure entailed and, most importantly, what it means. These barriers are coming down steadily, however, through education and training of forensic scientists and increasing availability of software that is either a stand-alone program or embedded within familiar spreadsheet applications. The Web sites for several of these software packages are listed below. Overall, the marriage of statistics with forensic examinations is perfectly natural, but on the other hand, it is a major change in the way forensic scientists think and work. Ultimately, it remains to be seen how this partnership will develop, but its potential impact is indisputably large.

Table 1 A "confusion matrix" resulting from leave-one-out cross validation of the data in **Figure 4**

From	To								
	Super 33+ (cold weather)	33	Super 88	Super 33+	Super 33+ (2001)	Temflex	Total	% correct
Super 33+ (cold weather)	0	0	5	0	0	0	5	0.00
33	0	14	0	0	0	0	14	100
Super 88	2	0	13	0	0	0	15	87
Super 33+	0	0	0	14	0	0	14	100
Super 33+ (2001)	0	0	0	0	10	0	10	100
Temflex	0	0	0	0	0	20	20	100
Total	2	14	18	14	10	20	78	91

Note that those classes that are most confused are Super 88 and 33+ cold weather.

See also: **Foundations:** Statistical Interpretation of Evidence: Bayesian Analysis; The Frequentist Approach to Forensic Evidence Interpretation.

Miller, J., Miller, J., 2005. Statistics and Chemometrics for Analytical Chemistry, fifth ed. (England: Pearson Education Limited).

Morgan, S., Bartick, E., 2007. In: Blackledge, R. (Ed.), Forensic Analysis on the Cutting Edge: New Methods for Trace Evidence Analysis. Wiley, New York.

National Research Council, 2009. Strengthening Forensic Science in the United States: A Path Forward. National Academies Press, Washington, DC.

Further Reading

Beebe, K.R., Pell, R.J., Seasholtz, M.B., 1998. Chemometrics: A Practical Guide. Wiley, New York.

Brereton, R.G., 2007. Applied Chemometrics for Scientists. Wiley, West Sussex, England.

Johnson, R., Wichern, D., 1982. Applied Multivariate Statistical Analysis. Prentice Hall, Englewood Cliffs, NJ.

Kramer, R., 1998. Chemometric Techniques for Quantitative Analysis. Marcel Dekker, New York.

Relevant Websites

www.chemometrics.com—Applied Chemometrics.

www.chm.bris.ac.uk/org/chemometrics/chemometrics.html—Bristol Centre for Chemometrics.

www.camo.com—Camo.

www.infometrix.com—Infometrix.

www.mathworks.com—Mathworks.

www.xlstat.com—Statistics package for Excel—XLSTAT.

Interpretation

DH Kaye, Penn State School of Law, University Park, PA, USA

Glossary

Bayes' factor The ratio of the odds in favor of a hypothesis given data divided by the odds of the hypothesis prior to considering the data. The Bayes' factor equals the likelihood ratio.

Bayes' rule An individual may start with a subjective probability (the "prior") that expresses a degree of belief about a hypothesis. Bayes' rule gives a procedure for combining this prior with evidence to compute the "posterior" probability, which expresses the investigator's or fact finder's belief about the hypothesis given the evidence. In its simplest form, Bayes' rule states that the posterior odds in favor of the hypothesis are the product of its prior odds and the likelihood ratio for the hypothesis.

Likelihood A measure of the degree to which data support a hypothesis about the process that produced the data. The likelihood for a hypothesis is proportional to the probability of observing the data assuming that the hypothesis is true.

Likelihood ratio The ratio of the likelihoods of two competing hypotheses. Numerically, it equals the ratio of the conditional probability of data given one hypothesis to the conditional probability of the data given the other hypothesis.

Odds The probability that an event will occur (or that a hypothesis is true) divided by the probability that it will not (or that the hypothesis is false). For example, if the chance of rain tomorrow is 2/3, then the odds on rain are $(2/3)/(1/3) = 2/1$, or 2 to 1; the odds against rain are 1 to 2.

P-value The p-value is the probability of getting data as extreme as (or more extreme than) the observed data under the "null hypothesis" that the data arise purely from random variation. A statistical hypothesis test asks whether the data are outside the range that reasonably would be expected under this null hypothesis. Large p-values are consistent with the null hypothesis; small p-values undermine this hypothesis. However, p itself does not give the probability that the null hypothesis is true.

Introduction

Natural and social scientists collect and interpret data, and they develop and apply theories about the phenomena that produce the data. Measurements of the 3° cosmic background microwave radiation, for example, permit inferences about the nature of the early universe, ruling out some theories and supporting others. Likewise, forensic scientists make measurements, interpret them, and evaluate certain theories in light of them. Their theories tend to be particular rather than general: This white powder contains D-cocaine; these grains of pollen originated from plants in this geographic area; these striations on a bullet resulted from this gun (or one remarkably like it); these bloody fingerprints were deposited by this finger (or one remarkably like it); and so on. Many theories in other fields of science, such as inferences about the features of the early universe, are also particular rather than universal.

Forensic science differs from all other branches of science, however, because forensic scientists perform one unusual set of tasks. They present and explain their findings not only to fellow scientists, but also to investigators, lawyers, and judges or juries. They must do so in a way that helps people who do not possess scientific expertise make practical decisions. Ultimately, the task of the forensic scientist is to supply accurate and useful information to legal investigators and decision makers. This chapter concerns the task of translating laboratory measurements into statements that will assist legal fact finders in evaluating hypotheses about the events that are relevant in legal disputes.

For concreteness, the discussion refers to the interpretation of trace evidence—primarily DNA and fingerprints—but the analysis applies to a broad range of forensic evidence. The next section outlines a general, probabilistic perspective on moving from data to hypotheses. The final section examines common interpretive practices from this perspective and in light of the needs of the legal system.

A Framework for Inference

Measurements Are Not Necessarily True Values

Associating a trace with its source involves two logical steps: (1) ascertaining the similarities and differences between two samples and (2) assessing the significance of the measurements. The measurements pertain to properties of the material or mark—the refractive index of glass, the color of hair, the sizes of DNA fragments, the concentrations of elements, and so on. Let X be a variable (a scalar or a vector) whose possible values x depend on these properties. For instance, if X is the color of a hair fiber and the measurements are visual observations, then categories such as white, gray, blond, red, brown, and black are values x of X. A continuous variable such as a refractive index has an infinite number of possible values. An analyst comparing two items measures values m_1 for item 1 and m_2 for item 2. Because of inherent or other limitations in the measurement process, these values almost always differ from the true values. How should the analyst interpret m_1 and m_2? What can and should the analyst say in written reports or in courtroom testimony about the origin of the two samples in light of the measured values?

Likelihoods Indicate Relative Support

Statistically, the information from the measurement phase can be expressed in terms of likelihoods. Likelihoods are proportional to the conditional probabilities of the data given in different states of the world. They indicate the degree of support that the measurements lend to claims about these states. The underlying idea is that measurements that would arise more frequently or with a greater probability under one hypothesis than another support the former hypothesis more than the latter. For instance, looking out of a window and seeing that it is dark supports the hypothesis that it is midnight much more than it supports the hypothesis that it is midday. Darkness at noon can occur (during a total solar eclipse), but these events are rare, whereas darkness at midnight is common.

A little notation is helpful in spelling this out in the forensic context. If S is the hypothesis that the pair of samples originated from the same source, then the likelihood for S is (within an arbitrary multiplicative constant) just the conditional probability $P(m_1 \& m_2|S)$. (Here, "|" means "given" or "conditioned on.") Similarly, if D is the hypothesis that the pair came from different sources, then the likelihood for D is $P(m_1 \& m_2|D)$ (multiplied by the same constant). The ratio of the two likelihoods is thus:

$$LR_m = \frac{L(S; m_1 \& m_2)}{L(D; m_1 \& m_2)} = \frac{P(S|m_1 \& m_2)}{P(D|m_1 \& m_2)} \quad [1]$$

Note that when the data are equally probable under each hypothesis, they are of no value in deciding which competing

hypothesis is true. In this situation, LR_m is 1, and the results of the forensic examination are inconclusive.

If the data are 100 times more probable when the samples come from the same source than from different ones, then the likelihood ratio for the hypotheses is $LR = 100$. The data support S 100 times more strongly than they support D.

Likelihood ratios of 10^{15} (and more) have been quoted for DNA evidence in the United States. These ratios are not conditioned strictly on the basis of the measurements m_1 and m_2. The actual measurements are reflective fluorescence units as the DNA fragments flow past a detector. Software converts them into a graph (an electropherogram). Distinct peaks rising far enough above the level of background noise indicate alleles of different lengths. A good deal of interpretation already has taken place in deducing the allele lengths. Likewise, with friction ridge skin comparisons, deciding what features to compare and how similar the features are is an interpretative activity in the measurement phase.

The large DNA likelihood ratios apply to the inferred genotypes, not to the original measurements. To be clear about this, let g stand for the pair of genotypes inferred from the measurements m_1 and m_2 and write $LR_g = P(g|S)/P(g|D) = 10^{15}$. If the interpretation of the peaks is correct, then $LR_m = LR_g$, but even a small probability that the true genotypes are not those inferred from the electropherograms reduces the likelihood ratio (i.e., $LR_g < LR_m$).

Bayes' Rule Gives Probabilities of Hypotheses

With likelihood ratios like 10^{15}, DNA analysts sometimes report that the source of the known sample is the source of the questioned sample. Fingerprint analysts also make such source attributions, although traditionally they have had no quantified likelihood ratios to quote and have relied instead on a difficult-to-validate theory of "universal, general uniqueness" of all pairings of the unknown mark with all marks that could be derived from all possible reference samples on earth. A definite source attribution expresses the analyst's conviction that out of all the people or objects that conceivably might be the source of the questioned sample, only the one that generated the "matching" known sample is a realistic possibility.

Source attribution can be overtly probabilistic. The "probability of paternity" used in courts for the last 30 or 40 years is the best known example. Suppose that only a small, degraded sample of DNA is available from the limited remains of a body that might be the child of two parents who reported a missing child. The likelihood ratio for the hypotheses of the child belonging to these parents versus a randomly selected set of parents, considering only the genotypes of the DNA samples from the remains and the two putative parents, might be 100. (To keep things simple, this overlooks the possibility that the remains are those of a child of one but not of both the putative parents.) To move to the probability of the hypothesis of parentage, however, Bayes' rule is needed. A simple version of the formula indicates the impact that the likelihood ratio of 100 would have on any set of prior odds for parentage. Let S be the hypothesis that the remains are those of the offspring of the putative parents, G the genotypes of the trio, and N the nongenetic evidence about S and general background information, the formula states that

$$\text{Odds}(S|G\&N) = \text{LR} \times \text{Odds}(S|N)$$
$$= 100 \times \text{Odds}(S|N) \qquad [2]$$

Allowing the nongenetic information N to be implicit gives the more common, shorter formula

$$\text{Odds}(S|G) = \text{LR} \times \text{Odss}(S) \qquad [3]$$

Thus, if the nongenetic evidence established prior odds of 1:10 (a probability of $1/11 = 0.09$), the reported genotypes (if accurately ascertained) would raise the odds to $100:10 = 10:1$ (probability $= 10/11 = 0.91$). Bayesian statisticians thus can describe the likelihood ratio as the ratio of the posterior odds to the prior odds ("Bayes' factor"). But one need not believe that it is justifiable to assign probabilities to hypotheses to take the narrower view that the likelihood ratio expresses the relative support that the evidence gives to one hypothesis over another.

Bayesian Decision Theory Selects between Hypotheses

In principle, an analyst can reach a conclusion about the source hypotheses by selecting the one that maximizes the analyst's expected utility. For example, an analyst might feel 9 units of regret for declaring a common source when, in fact, the samples come from different sources (endorsing S when D is true); 1 unit of regret for endorsing D when S is true; and be unmoved (feel 0 units of regret or satisfaction) for correct decisions. If the analyst declares S, then the expected regret is $9 \times P(D|m_1 \& m_2)$; if the analyst declares D, the expected regret is $1 \times P(S|m_1 \& m_2)$. Since $P(D|m_1 \& m_2) = 1 - P(S|m_1 \& m_2) = 1 - p$, the analyst minimizes expected regret by endorsing S whenever $9(1 - p) < p$, that is, whenever $p > 9/10$. A risk-neutral analyst who is still more distressed by false identifications relative to false exclusions should not declare S unless the source probability crosses an even higher threshold.

Current Practices and Possible Improvements

The previous section sketched a framework for moving from measurements m_1 and m_2 on a pair of samples to statements about the implications of these measurements. The ideas shed light on how an analyst can and should present the findings.

Reporting an Exclusion, Match, or Inconclusive Result

Reports from examiners who compare samples based on training and experience normally begin with a statement about the degree to which the measurements on the samples agree. Phrases such as "match," "consistent with," "identical," "similar in all respects tested," and "cannot be excluded as the source of" merely express a finding that the observed features in the two samples show a high degree of correspondence and no great differences (compared to what the examiner expects for marks from the same source). By themselves, these terms are relatively uninformative. The significance of the consistency can be high (as it usually is with fingerprints or DNA), moderate (with more common feature sets), or low or even unknown (as some commentators argue is the case for hair and bite marks).

When the observations do not correspond well, an examiner may testify to an "exclusion." An exclusion means that, according to the examiner's knowledge base, the measurements are so different that they would almost never arise when the items have a common source, while the measurements could easily be this different when the items come from different sources. In other words, an exclusion means that the perceived likelihood ratio is close to 0.

Finally, a forensic analyst may decline to classify or characterize the pair of samples, as when a fingerprint examiner decides that a latent print is not even worth comparing ("not suitable") or a DNA analyst finds that the quality and quantity of the DNA is unacceptable. Or, the analyst may give it a try but then discover too little useful information to say more than "inconclusive."

When the measurements lie on a continuous scale, as with the refractive index of glass, the nomenclature of "match" versus "exclusion" is artificial. A numerical likelihood ratio indicates the probative value of the degree of correspondence directly. There is no need for an intermediate step of forcing the continuous variable into discrete categories. Nonetheless, speaking of "matches" or "inclusions" and then describing their significance may be more familiar and comprehensible to judges or jurors. When this terminology is used, it is important to explain the intended meaning.

Reporting Random-Match Probabilities and Frequencies

The most common way of explaining the significance of a DNA match is to report a random-match probability (RMP) or estimated frequency in major population groups. Finding a match in unusual traits obviously is more probative than a match for common traits. This intuition is justified by the fact that the RMP is the denominator in $\text{LR}_g = P(g|S)/P(g|D)$. Reducing the RMP by a factor of 10 therefore increases the likelihood ratio by this same factor. Although the RMP is only part of the full likelihood picture (a fact that makes its use inappropriate in cases of mixed DNA stains), its use is comparable to the statistician's p-value as a gauge of probative value. The statistician may reject a null hypothesis when, under the null hypothesis, the probability of finding an outcome as extreme as (or more extreme than) the one observed is small. The underlying logic is that if the match is unlikely to arise under this hypothesis, then the match is unlikely to be merely coincidental.

Of course, rejecting the hypothesis that the suspect is unrelated to the source of the crime-scene sample but just happens to have the same genotype leaves open various explanations. For example, the crime-scene DNA might not be the suspect's because of an error in inferring the genotypes or labeling the samples. Or the crime-scene DNA might be the suspect's, but someone other than the suspect might have deposited it there.

With any type of evidence for which RMPs are available, care also must be taken to avoid naively transposing the conditional probabilities. An RMP of 0.1%, for example, should not be misreported or misconstrued as a 99.9% chance that the trace originated from the defendant. The extent to which naive transposition is in error depends on both the probability of the match given D and the prior probability of S, since these factors also determine the posterior odds. Although transposition may sometimes be harmless error, it is always a conceptual error that can lead to problems in courtroom presentations.

Reporting Likelihood Ratios Quantitatively or Qualitatively

We have seen how likelihoods determine the strength of the evidence in favor of a particular hypothesis. One way to present a likelihood ratio is to say that it tells the number of times it is more probable to see a match when the samples originate from the same source than when they come from difference sources. Analogies can be made to clinical medicine. For example:

> The match here is like the symptoms of a disease. The symptoms appear LR times more often when patients have the disease than when they do not. They do not establish for certain that the patient has the disease, but they make the odds LR times greater that he does.

As with the match probability, in a quantitative presentation, care is required to avoid the fallacy of the transposed conditional (also called the prosecutor's fallacy in legal circles). An LR of 1000, for instance, does not mean that S is 1 000 times more likely than D (making the probability of S is 1 000/ 1 001 = 0.999). To a Bayesian, it means that whatever the odds of S may have been, they have gone up by a factor of 1 000. If the rest of the case against a defendant is very weak—imagine, for example, that a similar case could have been brought against 500 other people—then the posterior odds on S are roughly 1 000 × 1:500 = 2:1, corresponding to a posterior probability of only 2/3 = 0.667.

A number of authors propose expressing the likelihood ratio as a qualitative statement about the strength of the evidence. One table recommends expressions ranging from "limited evidence to support" $(1 < \text{LR} \leq 10)$ to "very strong evidence to support" $(\text{LR} > 10\ 000)$. Indeed, such phrases may be the best that can be made when adequate sampling and modeling to estimate how many matching items there would be in the relevant population have not been conducted. Although jurors may be hard-pressed to appreciate the difference between gradations such as "moderately strong evidence" and "strong evidence," this approach confines the analyst to opening on the power of the evidence. Supporters of the approach see this as a great strength, but other experts would prefer to address hypotheses like S and D more explicitly. Trying to do so quantitatively raises legal issues.

Reporting Posterior Probabilities Quantitatively

Testifying about posterior probabilities has produced a contentious literature with a disorderly array of judicial opinions. A major difficulty with incorporating Bayesian computations of source probabilities into forensic work is that the forensic expert is not normally well situated to estimate prior odds that depend on nonscientific evidence in the case. Several procedures have been discussed or used in particular cases: (1) applying a uniform prior distribution across the suspect population; (2) assuming that the prior probability is one-half; and (3) producing a list of posterior probabilities for a range of priors.

First, in some cases, it may be possible to enumerate a small suspect population. In *State v. Klindt*, 389 N.W.2d 670, the prosecution sought to prove that a torso found in the Mississippi River was the remains of a woman named Joyce Klindt. Four women had been reported missing in four nearby states. A statistician computed likelihoods based on immunogenetic markers and other information about these women. He assumed that each woman was equally likely to be the one whose body was found. At the murder trial of Joyce Klindt's husband, the statistician testified that "the probabilities were over 99% that the torso was Joyce Klindt's rather than any of the other three" (Id. at 671). The court did not discuss the statistician's assumption that the prior probability with respect to each woman was 1/4.

Even when the suspect population is indeterminate, one could start with a prior probability assuming that everyone (or every object) in some geographic region is equally likely to be the source and then adjust it in light of the scientific evidence. Suppose the LR for a DNA match to a bloodstain in New York City is 1 000 000. If all residents of New York City (now ~8 000 000) were equally likely to have left the stain, then the prior odds of S to D would be 1:8 000 000, and the posterior odds would be 1 000 000 times that, or 1:8. The prosecutor then would have to point to other evidence to raise the posterior odds into the beyond-a-reasonable-doubt range. Unlike eqn [2], which requires conditioning on all the nonscientific evidence in the case, this computation tries to ignore all such evidence by regarding the matching test result as the first item of evidence to consider.

This approach resembles the suggestion of the English Court of Appeals in *R. v. Doheny* (1997), 1 Cr. App. R. 369, 374, that a DNA expert should "say how many people with the matching characteristics are likely to be found in the United Kingdom – or perhaps in a more limited subgroup, such as, for instance, the Caucasian sexually active males in the Manchester area." A few commentators with similar ideas have cautioned against "speculation" and urged that any "guess" take the form of an "interval … set wide enough to have a high probability of including the actual number that might be in the pool" (Saks and Koehler, 2004, p. 217). Mathematically, there is not much difference between quoting a posterior probability of $1/n$ and reporting that there are n or so equally likely suspects or objects that could not be excluded. However, framing the evidence as the number of individuals who could not be excluded by exhaustive testing invites the jury to think about these many alternatives to the prosecution's theory and the fact that the state has not tested many other possible sources. Some research suggests that this creates a weaker impression on the jury than giving a posterior probability that focuses their attention on the defendant.

A second approach to the prior probability of S is to assume that its value is one-half. This assumption is made in so-called one-man paternity cases. In these cases, the competing hypothesis usually is taken to be that a "random man" is the father and to have half the initial probability mass. Testimony as to the resulting posterior probability, with or without disclosure of the prior odds of 1:1, usually was admitted with little appreciation of the nature of the computation, but more recent criminal and civil court cases on the admissibility of Bayesian presentations with these artificial priors reach conflicting results.

In the third and final procedure that could be applied to Bayes' rule explicitly in court, the expert clearly communicates that the prior odds are for the judge or jury to ascertain. Jurors then can be invited to select the prior probability on the basis of the other evidence in the case, and advised to use the trace evidence according to Bayes' rule to deduce a posterior probability. A better solution might be to present a table of prior and posterior probabilities to demonstrate the power of the matching trace evidence. This variable-prior-probability method does not force jurors to articulate the prior odds, and this avoids certain logistical, psychological, and jurisprudential difficulties that confront the juror-choice-of-prior-probability method.

Categorical Source Attribution

For most types of trace evidence, probability models for feature sets are not well established and frequency data are limited. What is a forensic scientist to do? In some fields, the

convention is to eschew interpretation by merely reporting consistency of features or an inability to exclude. Of course, this leaves the fact finder uninformed about the importance of the match, but if nothing more is known and research establishes that the analysis of the features has some discriminating power, then a candid recitation of these facts may be better than nothing.

At the other extreme, pattern-matching experts, such as latent fingerprint examiners, have long claimed the ability to attribute a mark to the single source from which it came because there is (or so they postulate) no chance of any other possible source producing exemplars as similar to the crime-scene mark as the one they have for comparison. But the theory of unique identification, as opposed to a highly probable identification, is all but impossible to validate. As a result, there is movement toward the less dogmatic view that a fingerprint match based on a sufficiently clear and extensive latent print makes it very likely that an examiner's positive identification is correct for suspect populations of realistic sizes. Although it might be preferable merely to describe the results of the comparison as providing very strong evidence for S, offering a specific source attribution is scientifically defensible if its probabilistic nature is made clear and controlled experimentation demonstrates the ability of analysts to distinguish reliably and accurately between appropriate samples from the same source and samples from different sources.

> *See also:* **Foundations**: Forensic Intelligence; Overview and Meaning of Identification/Individualization; Interpretation/The Comparative Method; Semiotics, Heuristics, and Inferences Used by Forensic Scientists; Statistical Interpretation of Evidence: Bayesian Analysis.

Further Reading

Aitken, C., Roberts, P., Jackson, G., 2010. Fundamentals of Probability and Statistical Evidence in Criminal Proceedings. Royal Statistical Society, London.

Aitken, C., Taroni, F., 2004. Statistics and the Evaluation of Evidence for Forensic Scientists, second ed. John Wiley & Sons, Chichester.

Balding, D.J., 2005. Weight-of-Evidence for Forensic DNA Profiles. John Wiley & Sons, Chichester.

Barnett, V., 1999. Comparative Statistical Inference, third ed. John Wiley & Sons, Chichester.

Edwards, A.W.F., 1972. Likelihood: An Account of the Statistical Concept of Likelihood and its Application to Scientific Inference. Cambridge University Press, Cambridge.

Evett, I.W., Weir, B.S., 1998. Interpreting DNA Evidence. Sinauer Associates, Sunderland.

Kaye, D.H., 1989. The probability of an ultimate issue: The strange cases of paternity testing. Iowa Law Review 75, 75–109.

Kaye, D.H., 2009a. Identification, individuality, and uniqueness: What's the difference? Law, Probability and Risk 8, 85–94.

Kaye, D.H., 2009b. False, but highly persuasive: How wrong were the probability estimates in McDaniel v. Brown? Michigan Law Review First Impressions 108, 1–7.

Kaye, D.H., 2009c. Rounding up the usual suspects: A legal and logical analysis of DNA database trawls. North Carolina Law Review 87, 425–503.

Kaye, D.H., 2010. The Double Helix and the Law of Evidence. Harvard University Press, Cambridge, MA.

Kaye, D.H., 2012. Latent Print Examination and Human Factors: Improving the Practice through a Systems Approach. NIST, Gaithersburg.

Kaye, D.H., Bernstein, D.E., Mnookin, J.L., 2011. The New Wigmore, a Treatise on Evidence: Expert Evidence, second ed. Aspen Publishers, New York.

Koehler, J.J., 2001. The psychology of numbers in the courtroom: How to make DNA-match statistics seem impressive or insufficient. Southern California Law Review 74, 1275–1306.

National Research Council Committee on Identifying the Needs of the Forensic Science Community, 2009. Strengthening Forensic Science in the United States: A Path Forward. National Academy Press, Washington, DC.

Robertson, B., Vignaux, G.A., 1995. Interpreting Evidence: Evaluating Forensic Science in the Courtroom. John Wiley & Sons, Chichester.

Royall, R.M., 1997. Statistical Evidence: A Likelihood Paradigm. Chapman & Hall/CRC, London.

Saks, M., Koehler, J.J., 2008. The individualization fallacy in forensic science. Vanderbilt Law Review 61, 199–219.

Taroni, F., Bozza, S., Biedermann, A., et al., 2010. Data Analysis in Forensic Science: A Bayesian Decision Perspective. John Wiley & Sons, Chichester.

Thompson, W.C., Taroni, F., Aitken, C.G., 2003. How the probability of a false positive affects the value of DNA evidence. Journal of Forensic Sciences 48, 47–54.

Walker, R. (Ed.), 1983. Inclusion Probabilities in Parentage Testing. American Association of Blood Banks, Arlington.

Key Terms

Agglomerative hierarchical clustering (AHC), Analytical artifacts, Bayes' rule, Bayesian, Bias, Chemometrics, Cluster analysis, Clustering, Confidence interval, Confirmation, Confirmatory analysis, Corpse, Coverage interval, Cutoff, Data analysis, Degradation and formation of drugs, Degree of belief, Detection, Drug screening, Evidence, Forensic toxicology, Frequentist, Gas chromatography, GUM, Half-life, Identification, Identification criteria, Immunoassay, Impairment, Inference, Interactions, Interpretation, Likelihood ratio, Linear discriminant analysis (LDA), Liquid chromatography, Liquid/liquid extraction, Mass spectrometry, Measurement, Measurement error, Metabolism, Method validation, Pattern recognition, Pharmacokinetics, Postmortem, Postmortem changes, Principal components analysis (PCA), Probability, Probability distribution, Propagation of distributions, Propagation of uncertainty, Random error, Redistribution, Screening, Sensitivity, Solid-phase extraction, Solid-phase microextraction, Specificity, Specimen selection/collection, Stability during storage, Systematic error, Tolerance, Toxicity, Trace evidence, Type A uncertainty, Type B uncertainty, Uncertainty.

Review Questions

1. What is a measurand?
2. What is error? How can it be defined?
3. What is the difference between Type A and Type B uncertainties?
4. What is an artifact? How does it relate to a toxicology analysis?
5. What is postmortem redistribution?
6. Why would incorrect or insufficient sample affect a postmortem investigation?
7. What does the instability of a drug depend on?
8. Why are test subjects required to wash their hands before providing a urine sample?
9. What is the accuracy rate of drug recognition expert programs (DRE)?
10. How could circumstances of the death scene, such as body position, influence a toxicological analysis?
11. What is pharmacokinetics?
12. List methods that may be used for initial toxicology testing.
13. What is an immunoassay?
14. What are the two major methods for sample extraction?
15. What is headspace?
16. What are sensitivity and specificity? How are they defined?
17. What is a certified reference standard?
18. What does ULOQ stand for? What does it mean?
19. What does MRQC stand for? What does it mean?
20. List at least five drugs that increase impairment when combined with alcohol.

Discussion Questions

1. Re-read Vosk's entry on measurement uncertainty, especially his forensic example of DUI measurements. What are the implications for DUI arrests given the potential error rate? What does this mean for the toxicology laboratory?

2. What does Vosk mean when he says, "Meaning requires uncertainty"?
3. What factors contribute to tissue redistribution of drugs after death? How could these change a toxicologist's analysis or interpretation?
4. Explain how the Widmark factor works. What role does it play in toxicological interpretations?
5. What are the longer term effects of alcohol on the body? How does this influence a toxicological investigation? What indicators would suggest to a toxicologist that they are dealing with someone who has used or abused alcohol chronically?

Additional Readings

Castillo-Peinado, L.S., de Castro, M.L., 2016. Present and foreseeable future of metabolomics in forensic analysis. Analytica Chimica Acta 925, 1–15.

Meyer, G.M., Maurer, H.H., Meyer, M.R., 2016. Multiple stage MS in analysis of plasma, serum, urine and in vitro samples relevant to clinical and forensic toxicology. Bioanalysis 8 (5), 457–481.

Saks, M.J., Koehler, J.J., 2005. The coming paradigm shift in forensic identification science. Science 309 (5736), 892–895.

Wallace, J., 2016. Reliability of measurement uncertainty estimates for forensic analyses: evidence from recent proficiency tests. Accreditation and Quality Assurance 21 (3), 211–219.

Zamengo, L., Frison, G., Tedeschi, G., Frasson, S., 2016. Forensic-metrological considerations on assessment of compliance (or non-compliance) in forensic blood alcohol content determinations: A case study with software application. Forensic science international 265, 144–152.

Section 6. Professional Issues

Toxicologists face the same professional issues as other forensic experts, and then some. Their testimony can be involved and complex, their reports are nearly indecipherable (imagine a nonscientist reading "lysergic acid diethlyamide adulterated with 25I-NBOMe, an *N*-benzyl derivative of the phenethylamine molecule 2C-I formed by adding a 2-methoxybenzyl (BnOMe) onto the nitrogen (N) of the phenethylamine backbone"). Beyond that, like DNA experts, they work with potentially infectious body tissues (that may contain poisons or other harmful chemicals).

Drug-facilitated crimes, such as sexual assault, are more prevalent in some areas than others, requiring forensic toxicologists to learn about specific drugs, such as 4-hydroxybutanoic acid (GHB). Prescription drugs can also be a complicating factor, especially for those under the care of multiple doctors who may not coordinate medications or doses. Finally, drug testing for the workplace and for sports falls into the purview of the toxicologist, especially if there is an accident, health issue, or death.

Crime Scene to Court

K Ramsey and E Burton, Greater Manchester Police Forensic Services Branch, Manchester, UK

Glossary

T1/2/3 CSI Skill tiers defined for Crime Scene Investigation officers, with 1 being the most basic level of training (usually volume crime offenses only), 2 being the range of volume, serious and major crime investigations, and 3 being trained in crime scene management/the coordination of complex investigations.
CBRN Chemical, biological, radiation, and nuclear incidents.
L2 Level 2 investigations, specific skills required for, e.g., covert operations, deployment and substitution of items, forensic markers.
CCTV Closed circuit television (cameras or evidence from).

HTCU Hi-tech crime unit (examination of hardware/software/data/images from any system or device).
VSC/ESDA Video Spectral Comparison—the analysis of inks, primarily in fraudulent documents; Electro Static Detection Analysis—the examination of (writing) indentations on paper.
NaBIS National Ballistic Intelligence Service (UK).
LCH Local Clearing House (firearms).
NCA National Crime Agency (UK).
CPS Crown Prosecution Service (UK).
NOS National Occupational Standards.
CPD Continuous Professional Development.

Introduction

A multitude of disciplines evolved within forensic science during the twentieth century, resulting in highly specialized fields of evidential opportunities to support criminal investigations. Many of the more traditional disciplines, for example,

footwear analysis and blood pattern interpretation, now have well-established principles and methodologies that have been proven in a criminal justice context; developments in these areas are largely confined to technical support systems and information sharing through databases. The very rapid rate of development of DNA profiling techniques during the 1980s and 1990s led to the emergence of national and international DNA databases; however, the pace of change has now significantly reduced. Conversely, the end of the twentieth century and the early part of the twenty-first century have seen an explosion of new forensic evidence types that are less established in court—disciplines such as CCTV, mobile phone, computer analysis, and the use of digital images and social media are collectively referred to as e-forensics.

Owing to the highly specialized nature of each forensic discipline and the varied rate of evolution, forensic science effectively represents a composite of interrelated, and often distinct, opportunities to support criminal investigations.

Most current models of forensic service delivery, especially where part of a wider organization, for example, police forces and enforcement agencies, have arisen over time by bolting on additional elements and clustering together within related fields. If the current capability of forensic science was to be designed from scratch as an effective entity, it is certain that a more integrated, and hence effective, structure would be proposed.

In addition, there has been a professionalization of forensic science in the workplace and increasing requirements for regulation; as recently as the 1980s, crime scene investigation, for example, was widely undertaken by police officers and was largely restricted to recording/recovering visible evidence; this was used in a limited capacity to support that particular investigation without scope for wider intelligence development. Now, crime scene investigation is predominantly undertaken by specialist staff employed to exclusively undertake these duties.

To practice in a forensic discipline, specialized training, qualifications, and competency levels are required. The range of evidence types that have potential to support investigations has widened considerably. Some disciplines lend themselves to cross-skilling.

Public expectations of what forensic science can deliver have been heightened by highly popular mainstream television programs, both documentary and fictional. Often, the expectation of what can be delivered exceeds what is either possible or financially sensible. This leads to a requirement on service providers and users to make informed (evidential and financial) decisions regarding the best use of forensic evidence in support of investigations.

This chapter considers options to optimize the use of forensic evidence types recovered from crime scenes in the context of the different models available to criminal justice systems; the concept of integrated case management is outlined and discussed.

Task

To bring together all potential forensic evidential opportunities, holistically review their significance to the investigation, prioritize the progression of work, deliver the best evidence to the court for testing (complying with all continuity, integrity, and quality requirements), and ensure the best value for money when determining spend on forensic evidence.

Internationally, there are variable constraints and opportunities due both to the different criminal justice models and the commercial market situation at state/regional and country levels.

Models

1. All forensic evidence sourced within a law enforcement agency, for example, a police laboratory.
2. All forensic evidence provided by external specialists contracted to a law enforcement agency.
3. Composite of (1) and (2).

Forensic Strategies

The recovery of evidence from the crime scene is only the start of the forensic process. Once the evidence has been collected, packaged, and preserved, it needs to be analyzed in order to provide meaningful information to the investigation and subsequently the courts.

Forensic examinations are carried out in order to implicate or eliminate individuals and also in order to establish what has occurred during the commission of an offense or incident.

Deciding what analysis is required can be a complex process. Some of the issues for consideration include the following:

- Is it necessary to examine all the evidence that is recovered?
- Should every possible test be carried out?

In an ideal world, it would be preferable to carry out every possible analysis; however, in reality, it is likely that this will be neither practicable nor financially viable. In addition, carrying out every possible analysis would overload forensic laboratories.

When making decisions about what forensic analysis should be carried out, it is vitally important that consideration is given to both the potential prosecution and defense cases. An impartial approach must be taken to assessing examination requirements. It is often not necessary to carry out an examination of every item of evidence recovered, but examinations should be directed to where value could potentially be added to an investigation.

A forensic strategy should be developed around every case where forensic evidence plays a part, and may relate to an overall case or to an individual item of evidence. A forensic strategy should be developed in a holistic manner taking into account all potential evidence types and should direct and coordinate the forensic examinations/analyses that are required.

Forensic strategies can be developed in different ways by one or more of the following:

- Investigating officer
- Crime Scene Investigator (CSI) or Crime Scene Manager
- Forensic Scientist/Forensic Specialist
- Forensic Submissions Officer (Forensic Submissions Officer is a role that can be variably named; this role relates to an informed individual within a Police Force or Law Enforcement Agency who uses knowledge and expertise to advise on forensic analysis and who has decision-making authority and control of the budgetary spend. May also be known as Forensic Advisor, Scientific Support Manager, etc.)
- Legal Representative
- Pathologist

Forensic strategies are generally initially developed and applied by individuals involved in the prosecution aspects of a crime. Although this is the case, it is vitally important that a balanced and unbiased approach is taken to the development of a strategy and consideration given to information that may support the defense case as well as the prosecution case. Examinations that are likely to add value or provide information to an investigation (irrespective of whether it will support or weaken the prosecution case) should be carried out and all results must be disclosed to the defense team. Defense should also be given the opportunity to carry out any review of strategies, examination processes, and/or results that they require and be provided with access to any items of evidence that they want to examine themselves in order to build the defense case.

In order to develop the forensic strategy and make appropriate decisions about which forensic examinations will be of value to the investigation, the following are necessary:

- To be able to gather as much information as possible about the circumstances of the case
  - circumstances of evidence recovery
  - accounts given by victim(s), witnesses, suspect(s), etc.
- To have an understanding and knowledge of forensic science and its application to investigations

A forensic strategy meeting is a useful way of ensuring that all relevant parties are aware of the full circumstances of the case and enables a "multiagency" discussion about the processing of all exhibits to optimize evidential potential in a comprehensive and coordinated manner.

It can often be the case that police officers do not have a full understanding or knowledge of forensic science, likewise forensic scientists historically have had a relatively poor understanding of police and investigative processes; this can lead to miscommunication and confusion in relation to the application of forensic science to meet investigative needs. A joint approach to the development of forensic strategies helps to improve the communication and understanding on a case-by-case basis.

A formal forensic strategy meeting is often required only in more serious cases; however, the general approach can be applied to any investigation. Even in the most simple cases, it is often beneficial for discussions to take place between the investigating officer, the CSI, the forensic advisor/budget holder/decision maker, and the prosecutor. Alternatively, generic strategies can be implemented, for example, for a particular crime type or *modus operandi*.

When making an assessment regarding the potential examination of a particular item and the development of a forensic strategy, the requirements of the investigation are the primary concern and consideration should be given to the following issues:

- The type and nature of the item/exhibit
- The context of the item
  - Exactly where and when it was recovered
  - Condition of the item, that is, wet, damaged, etc.
- The integrity of the item
  - Has it been appropriately recovered, handled, packaged, and preserved?
  - Is the security and continuity of the item intact?
- The potential evidence that may be obtained from the item, for example, DNA, fingerprints, fibers, footwear marks
- The information these evidence types may provide to the investigation
- Whether this potential information is likely to add value to the investigation
  - Is it possible that new information will be provided?
  - Is it possible that an account given by a witness, victim, or suspect will be supported or refuted?
  - Will the information help to establish what has occurred?
- Whether there is a conflict between potential evidence types, and if so, which evidence type will be of most value under the circumstances
  - For example, swabbing/taping for DNA may damage fingerprints, but where the DNA is likely to be at low levels and requires specialized low-template DNA analysis, the presence of DNA may not necessarily prove contact with an item, whereas fingerprints will always prove that contact has occurred
- The chances of success, that is, obtaining a result/information of value to the investigation (this may be inclusive or exclusive)

Much work has historically been completed in relation to developing and understanding the success rates relating to DNA profiling; however, relatively little work has been undertaken to fully understand the success rates associated with other forensic evidence. This is largely due to the fact that other evidence types, such as fibers, gunshot residue, footwear marks, etc. are generally more complex to interpret than DNA. In relation to DNA profiling, success rates are generally based on the chances of obtaining a DNA profile; however, with the other evidence types, the value of the outcome is very much dependent on the circumstances of the investigation. For example, when searching an item of clothing taken from a suspect for glass, the absence of glass or the presence of glass could both be of value to the investigation depending on the circumstances. The presence of glass on the clothing that matches control sample(s) from the crime scene is only of value if its presence cannot be accounted for in any legitimate way; conversely, the absence of glass on the item of clothing may lead to a conclusion that the suspect was not involved in the offense, depending on the circumstances of the offense and arrest.

In addition to being able to understand and evaluate the chances of being able to obtain a meaningful result, it is also vital that the value of the overall contribution to the entire case is understood. This involves being able to understand the value and contribution of the forensic examination to the detection of the offense as well as the outcome of the court process. This is an even more difficult issue to evaluate and understand than the chances of being able to obtain a forensic test result.

Because the value of forensic evidence is so dependent on the individual case circumstances, decisions about examinations must be made on an individual case basis. There have been recent developments in some agencies/Forces to better understand the chances of success of different types of forensic evidence and the value to investigations; this will help to better inform decisions about evidential potential and examination viability as well as assisting to achieve value for money. This approach is best described as *forensic effectiveness*.

The forensic strategy should also take into account the timescales associated with the investigative process and the criminal justice system, and it should be ensured that forensic analysis can meet the requirements of the criminal justice process, including court dates and any requirements to disclose appropriate information to the defense team(s).

Each police force/law enforcement agency will have its own approach to the submission of exhibits for forensic examination/analysis; irrespective of whether the analysis is carried out in an internal police laboratory, external commercial company, or government owned laboratory, these approaches can be applied to all examinations and all evidence types.

These approaches help to ensure that decisions are made based on scientific knowledge, viability, and evidential value taking into account all aspects of the investigation. They will help to ensure that the best evidence is obtained while considering value for money and that it can be applied to any investigation irrespective of the seriousness of the offense or the scale of the investigation.

Integrated Case Management

The concept and use of forensic strategies in directing investigations is not new, but is often limited by the evolved structure of forensic disciplines within investigative agencies. Classically, DNA and fingerprint evidence from volume crimes will be independently submitted at the same time by different routes and this often results in wasted effort/spends and duplicated results. The development and use of forensic intelligence has been variable. Emerging thinking includes organizational redesign of forensics to better integrate with related functions such as intelligence collection, targeted deployment of resources, and prioritized forensic submissions.

The concept of integrated case management draws together informed operational deployment (e.g., of CSIs) followed by a more holistic approach to submissions for testing. The strategy takes greater account of supporting intelligence and desired outcomes. Regular reviews and trigger points are included for the staged submission of potential evidence, and communication with investigators is enhanced so allowing for a more responsive and directed investigation.

Ultimately, the production of *intelligent identifications* can be better achieved by having an integrated process that links the enforcement priorities, available resources, potential forensic evidence, intelligence, and prosecutor requirements; this model provides flexibility to respond to changing demands and gives an increased likelihood of efficient and effective spend on forensic support to investigations. There is no single way to achieve this, but an illustration of how to rethink some of the traditional silo-based forensic disciplines is provided in **Figure 1**.

Summary

The single biggest challenge to the forensic science community during the twenty-first century is to modernize delivery of integrated services in support of investigations. This must:

● build on the previous development of each discipline;
● accommodate the new and emerging technological disciplines;
● meet the regulatory requirements;
● reflect the changing workforce and skills;
● deliver the best evidence to courts in support of investigations.

See also: **Foundations:** Forensic Intelligence; History of Forensic Sciences; Principles of Forensic Science.

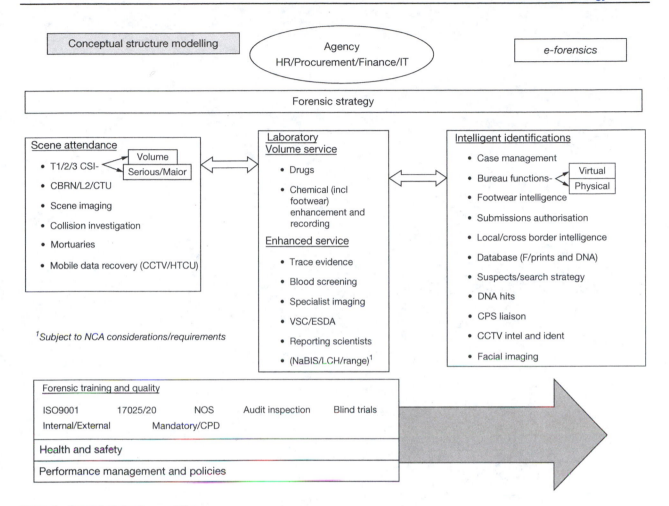

Figure 1 Conceptual structure modeling.

Further Reading

Faigman, et al., 2006. Modern Scientific Evidence: The Law and Science of Expert Testimony.

Fisher, B.A.J., Fisher, D.R., 2012. Techniques of Crime Scene Investigation, eighth ed. CRC, Boca Raton, FL.

Houck, M., Crispino, F., McAdam, T., 2013. The Science of Crime Scenes. Elsevier.

Innocence Project, 2011. http://www.innocenceproject.org/Content/Facts_on_PostConviction_DNA_Exonerations.php (accessed 10 March 2011).

Kirk, P.L., 1974. In: Thornton, J.L. (Ed.), Crime Investigation, second ed. Wiley, New York. (1985 reprint edn. Malabar, FL: Krieger Publishing Company).

NAS, 2009. Strengthening Forensic Science in the United States: A Path Forward. NAS Report: Committee on Identifying the Needs of the Forensic Sciences Community. National Academies Press, Washington, DC.

White, P., 2010. Crime Scene to Court: The Essentials of Forensic Science. Royal Society of Chemistry, Cambridge, ISBN 978-1-84755-882-4.

Forensic Laboratory Reports

J Epstein, Widener University School of Law, Wilmington, DE, USA

There is no precise formula, dictated by law or science, as to what a forensic laboratory report must contain when it reports test results or analysis outcomes. Its content may be determined by the individual examiner's predilections, internal laboratory policy, the law of the jurisdiction, accreditation organization standards, or the reason(s) for its production. What can be said with certainty is that by understanding the current criticism of the practice of producing forensic laboratory reports and trends in standards for reports, and by considering the use to which the report may be put in the court process and the legal and ethical commands regarding reporting and, more generally, the duties of the forensic scientist, a model for forensic laboratory reports can be identified.

Before discussing these factors, it bears mention that the term "report" itself lacks clarity, as it may refer to the complete case file documenting the examination or just to the compilation of results. For this chapter, the term "report" denotes the latter—the document prepared for the consumer [the investigator, counsel, or court official who directed that the examination and testing be conducted]. Even this report may vary in degree of detail, as there can be the summary report advising the requesting party of the outcome; a more formal report prepared for disclosure to the court or opposing counsel as part of pretrial discovery; an amplification of the initial discovery-generated report when it is determined that the expert will in fact testify; and a report that will be presented in lieu of actual testimony. Additional documentation may include an administrative or dispositional report detailing the receipt or return of the item(s) sent for analysis.

What must also be acknowledged is that the expert's role in the adjudicative process is in some ways defined by whether the system is adversarial, with the expert being called by the party seeking to establish a point, as in the United States; or inquisitorial/"common law," where the expert is a court witness, presumed to be neutral, and without allegiance to a particular party, as in France, Belgium, and Germany. These demarcations are not always adhered to, as American law permits a trial judge to appoint and take testimony from a "court" expert under Federal Rule of Evidence 706, and in some cases involving offenses of fraud and falsification, France permits competing experts. These differing roles, however, do not alter the necessary components of a forensic laboratory report (and, as is detailed below), both ethical and legal considerations as well as a commitment to the role of science may require the report to be neutral and to acknowledge any limitations and/or weaknesses.

Contents of a Report: A "Science" Standard

At least in the United States, there has been substantial criticism of forensic laboratory reporting. This is found in *Strengthening Forensic Science: A Path Forward*, the 2009 report of the National Research Council of the National Academy of Sciences. After reporting that forensic laboratory reports lack precise terminology, it concluded that most laboratory reports do not meet the standard it proposed:

> As a general matter, laboratory reports generated as the result of a scientific analysis should be complete and thorough. They should describe, at a minimum, methods and materials, procedures, results, and conclusions, and they should identify, as appropriate, the sources of uncertainty in the procedures and conclusions along with estimates of their scale (to indicate the level of confidence in the results). Although it is not appropriate and practicable to provide as much detail as might be expected in a research paper, sufficient content should be provided to allow the nonscientist reader to understand what has been done and permit informed and unbiased scrutiny of the conclusion.

This criticism does not stand in isolation. A 2011 British court decision also expressed concern over the sufficiency of detail and documentation in a forensic [latent print] prosecution. After noting the failure of the examiner to contemporaneously record "detailed notes of his examination and the reasons for his conclusions[,]" the court added that [t]he quality of the reports provided by the Nottinghamshire Fingerprint Bureau for the trial reflected standards that existed in other areas of forensic science some years ago, and not the vastly improved standards expected in contemporary forensic science.

The NRC standard is more detailed than that of various forensic organizations. ASCLD/LAB, for example, requires that only written reports be generated for "all analytical work" and must contain conclusions and opinions and a clear communication of "the significance of associations made…"

Other standards address the need for full documentation, but do not distinguish between a laboratory's bench notes and the final product. For example, International Organization for

Standardization's ISO/IEC Standard 5.10.5 requires that "the laboratory shall document the basis upon which the opinions and interpretations have been made" without specifying where that information is to be recorded. Similar language is used for ballistics reports, as recommended by the Scientific Working Group on firearms [SWGGUN] requiring that "[w]hen opinions and interpretations are included, the laboratory shall document the basis upon which the opinions and interpretations have been made. Opinions and interpretations shall be clearly marked as such in the test report."

Yet, the more detailed mandate urged by the NRC Report is not unique. Scholars and agencies have articulated similar or at least substantial standards. A publication of *The Royal Society of Chemistry* in 2004, suggested the following information as appropriate for inclusion in an expert report:

- A summary of the event to contextualize the scientific test(s)
- An outline of the scientific work conducted
- A listing of items examined
- Description of the work performed
- A statement interpreting the findings
- An overall conclusion

The RSC text also urges that the report identify the assistants in the testing and the role each played and include appendices with tables or similar displays of test results.

For DNA analysis, the Federal Bureau of Investigation's standards for DNA laboratories require reports to include a description of the evidence examined and of the technology, results and/or conclusions, and a "quantitative or qualitative interpretative statement."

One final scientific issue regarding the contents of a report is the concern over bias. Research has shown that information received by the analyst might affect his/her judgment, as when the examiner receives domain-irrelevant information such as the fact that the suspect whose fingerprints are being examined "confessed to the crime" or when the verification is not "blind." Documentation of such information in a laboratory report (or the bench notes) is one responsive action, as is an internal laboratory policy to reduce analyst or verifier exposure to potentially biasing information.

Contents of a Report: Legal Standards

That which science requires is to some extent mirrored in legal requirements for expert reports. These vary from nation to nation, and within nations when states or regions have their own authority to legislate criminal practice.

In the United Kingdom, Rule 33.3, Criminal Procedure Rules 2010 mandates contents of a full report, that is, one for submission in court, as follows:

1. the findings on which they have relied in making the report or statement;

2. details of which of the findings stated in the report or statement are within their own knowledge, which were obtained as a result of examinations, measurements, tests, etc. carried out by another person and whether or not those examinations, measurements, tests, etc. were carried out under the expert's supervision;

3. the identity, qualifications, relevant experience, and any certification of the person who carried out the examination, measurement, test, etc.;

4. details of any statements of fact, literature, or other information upon which they have relied, either to identify the examination or test requirements, or which are material to the opinions expressed in the report or statement or upon which those opinions are based;

5. a summary of the conclusions and opinions reached and a rationale for these;

6. a statement that if any of the information on which their conclusions or opinions are based on changes then the conclusions or opinions will have to be reviewed;

7. where there is a range of opinion on the matters dealt with in the report or statement, a summary of the range of opinion, and reasons for the expert's own opinion;

8. any information that may cast doubt on their interpretation or opinion; and

9. if the expert is not able to give an opinion without qualification, what the qualification is.

Much less specific is the legislated mandate for federal criminal prosecutions in the United States. Under Federal Rule of Criminal Procedure 16, the Government must permit the defense to inspect and to copy or photograph the results or reports of any scientific test or experiment and must produce before trial a written summary of any proposed expert testimony that describes the witness's opinions, the bases and reasons for those opinions, and the witness's qualifications. Defense counsel in criminal cases has a reciprocal disclosure requirement. Despite the seeming generality of these terms, American courts have at times interpreted them to require some greater detail in the reports, such as underlying documentation.

In the United States, an additional requirement derived from the Constitution's guarantee of Due Process of Law may affect what must be included in a laboratory report issued by a police or other government agency. The prosecution must disclose information that is "favorable to the accused" and "material either to guilt or to punishment" as well as "evidence that the defense might have used to impeach the Government's witnesses by showing bias or interest." This extends to "evidence affecting credibility[.]" This information is generally denominated "Brady material."

The applicability of these rules to official [police or state] laboratories is settled. The US Supreme Court has held that the disclosure obligation extends to police agencies working with the prosecution, and this has been extended to forensic examiners. Hence, in a report or some other communication, a forensic examiner in government employ must ensure that "Brady material" is disclosed.

What remains to be defined are the terms "exculpatory" or "impeachment" information. The core of each is easily described. Evidence is "exculpatory" if it tends to reduce the degree of guilt or question proof of culpability; "impeachment" information is proof of a bias or interest, or otherwise information that could be used to contradict or attack the credibility of the analyst or report. This type of disclosure parallels that of forensic laboratory reports imposed by the United Kingdom's evidence code. The code requires inclusion in the report of "a summary of the range of opinion and reasons for the expert's own opinion; [] any information that may cast doubt on their interpretation or opinion; and if the expert is not able to give an opinion without qualification, what the qualification is."

Reports: Stand-Alone Evidence or Support for a Testifying Expert

Whether a laboratory report may stand on its own as evidence in a trial, or instead must be accompanied by testimony of the forensic analyst, is a function of the law of the jurisdiction in which the case is tried. In the United States, a prosecution expert's report may not be admitted on its own, as this is deemed to violate the defendant's right to confront adverse witnesses. The Supreme Court in Melendez-Diaz versus Massachusetts held that a certificate of analysis fell within the core class of testimonial statements because it was a solemn "declaration or affirmation made for the purpose of establishing or proving some fact." In the 2011 follow-up of the Melendez-Diaz decision, the Court further held that another lab analyst may not come in to testify to the report's contents, at least where the other analyst neither supervised nor observed the initial testing. [This applies only to prosecution expert reports, as in the United States only the defendant has a guarantee of the right to confront witnesses. Admissibility of a defense forensic report without examiner testimony would be determined by the state's rules of evidence, but is generally unheard of.]

At the same time, the confrontation right does not mean that the analyst must testify. A state may create a notice and demand statute under which the prosecution notifies the defendant of its intent to use an analyst's report as evidence at trial, after which the defendant has a specified period of time in which to demand the expert's live testimony. A defendant's failure to "demand" waives the need for the analyst's presence and allows use of the report. As well, an accused may always agree to stipulate to the report's content, eliminating the need for any live testimony.

The Melendez-Diaz approach is not followed uniformly on an international basis. Canada permits proof by means of an expert report, without live testimony, where the proponent of the report has provided it to the opposing party and the trial court recognizes the author as a legitimate expert. The court retains discretion to mandate the expert's appearance for cross-examination. Australia's Evidence Act of 1995 similarly authorizes expert proof by certificate, but the opposing party may require the offering side to "call the person who signed the certificate to give evidence." In the United Kingdom, expert reports are themselves admissible as evidence, subject to the judge's discretion in requiring the analyst or examiner to appear.

Ethical Considerations and Forensic Reports

The decision of what to include in a forensic laboratory report, beyond that required by law or by science, may be informed by ethical considerations. Forensics organizations often have ethical codes, but they may be silent as to the particulars of report writing. Illustrative is the Code of the American Board of Criminalistics, which only asserts general obligations such as "[e]nsure that a full and complete disclosure of the findings is made to the submitting agency[.]" Other codes may not mention reporting at all but instead address only the delivery of information without distinguishing between the written report and a courtroom presentation of evidence. An exception is that of the Australian and New Zealand Forensic Science Society, Inc., which requires that a report be nonpartisan when results are ambiguous. "Where test results or conclusions are capable of being interpreted to the advantage of either side in a legal proceeding, each result or conclusion should be given weight according to its merit."

Ethical considerations may also be imposed by law. In the United Kingdom, the expert is deemed to hold only one allegiance, that to the court, regardless of the party who retained the individual. Specific ethical obligations are imposed for written reports. First, where there is a range of opinion, the expert must summarize the various positions. Second, if the opinion rendered cannot be given without qualification, the expert must disclose that and state the qualifying aspects or concerns.

Conclusion

Within and across nations, there is no clear standard for forensic reports intended for court use, except where prescribed by law. What should be manifest is that the more detailed the report, and thus the more it is capable of rigorous assessment by an independent expert evaluator, the more credibility will be attributed to both the results and the examiner.

See also: **Legal:** History of the Law's Reception of Forensic Science; Legal Aspects of Forensic Science; Legal Systems: Adversarial and Inquisitorial; **Management/Quality in Forensic Science:** *Sequential Unmasking:* Minimizing Observer Effects in Forensic Science; **Professional:** Ethics.

Further Reading

Codes of Practice and Conduct for Forensic Science Providers and Practitioners in the Criminal Justice System 44–45 (United Kingdom). http://www.homeoffice.gov.uk/publications/police/forensic-science-regulator1/quality-standards-codes-practice?view=Binary.

Dror, I.E., Cole, S., 2010. The vision in 'blind' justice: Expert perception, judgment and visual cognition in forensic pattern recognition. Psychonomic Bulletin & Review 17 (2), 161–167.

Dror, I.E., Rosenthal, R., 2008. Meta-analytically quantifying the reliability and bias-ability of forensic experts. Journal of Forensic Sciences 53 (4), 900–903.

National Research Council, 2009. Strengthening Forensic Science in the United States: A Path Forward. National Academies Press, Washington, DC. http://www.ncjrs.gov/pdffiles1/nij/grants/228091.pdf.

Quality Assurance Standards for Forensic DNA Testing Laboratories, Standard 11.2. http://www.cstl.nist.gov/strbase/QAS/Final-FBI-Director-Forensic-Standards.pdf.

Reviewing Historical Practices of Forensic Science Laboratories, 29 September 2010. http://www.ascld.org/.

Rothwell, T., 2004. Presentation of expert forensic evidence. In: White, P. (Ed.), Crime Scene to Court: The Essentials of Forensic Science, second ed. RSC, Cambridge, pp. 430–432. Ch. 15.

Spencer, J.R., 2002. Evidence. *European Criminal Procedures.* Cambridge University Press, New York, pp. 632–635. Ch. 15.

Relevant Websites

http://www.criminalistics.com/ethics.cfm—American Board of Criminalistics, Rules of Professional Conduct.

http://www.afte.org/AssociationInfo/a_codeofethics.htm—Association of Firearms and Toolmarks Examiners, AFTE Code of Ethics.

http://www.ascld.org/—The American Society of Crime Laboratory Directors.

http://www.ascld-lab.org/—The American Society of Crime Laboratory Directors Laboratory Accreditation Board.

http://www.anzfss.org.au/code_of_ethics.htm—Australian and New Zealand Forensic Science Society.

http://www.forensicdna.com/Media/Bias_FS.htm—An Extended List of Articles on the Issue of Bias in Forensic Examinations.

http://www.iso.org/iso/home.html—International Organization for Standardization.

http://www.swggun.org/swg/index.php?option=com_content&view=article&id=25:transition-from-ascldlab-legacy-to-isoiec-17025&catid=10:guidelines-adopted&Itemid=6—SWGGUN, Transition from ASCLD/LAB Legacy to ISO/IEC 17025.

http://webarchive.nationalarchives.gov.uk/+/;   http://www.justice.gov.uk/criminal/procrules_fin/contents/rules/part_33.htm—United Kingdom, Criminal Procedure Rules 2010.

Health and Safety

N Scudder and B Saw, Australian Federal Police, Canberra, ACT, Australia

Glossary

Clandestine laboratory ("Clan Labs") Setting up of equipment or supplies for the manufacture of illegal compounds such as drugs or explosives.

Confined space An enclosed or partially enclosed space that is not intended or designed primarily for human occupancy, within which there is a risk of one or more of the following: (1) an oxygen concentration outside the safe oxygen range; (2) a concentration of airborne contaminant that may cause impairment, loss of consciousness, or asphyxiation; (3) a concentration of flammable airborne contaminant that may cause injury from fire or explosion; (4) engulfment in a stored free-flowing solid or a rising level of liquid that may cause suffocation or drowning.

Dynamic risk management The continuous assessment of risk in the rapidly changing circumstances of an operational incident, in order to implement the control measures necessary to ensure an acceptable level of safety.

Hazard The potential for a substance to cause adverse effects.

Hierarchy of control measures Ranking of measures taken to prevent or reduce hazard exposure according to effectiveness, from the most effective measures that eliminate hazards to the least effective measures that achieve only limited protection.

OHS policy A policy document indicating an organization's commitment to OHS, its intentions, objectives, and priorities and identifying roles and responsibilities.

Risk The likelihood of injury or illness arising from exposure to any hazard(s) and the magnitude of the adverse effect.

Occupational Health and Safety Policy

The legislation in many countries places the onus of responsibility on employers to provide a healthy and safe working environment under occupational health and safety (OHS) legislation and common law. Employers should ensure that all managers, supervisors, and staff are aware of their OHS responsibilities. Management leadership can positively influence OHS outcomes for an organization.

Workplace health and safety is an ongoing process. Subject to the legislative requirements of each jurisdiction, in most instances a documented OHS policy is required. The development of such a policy requires the commitment of both staff and management. Once commitment has been achieved, the OHS policy should be developed with involvement from all stakeholders, and promulgated.

The OHS policy should:

- articulate the organization's commitment to OHS;
- indicate that sufficient resources (both financial and personnel) will be provided to promote and maintain OHS standards and meet OHS requirements;
- outline the organization's intentions, objectives, and priorities OHS;
- describe in broad terms the means by which the objectives will be met;
- identify the roles and responsibilities of management, supervisors, and staff in meeting OHS requirements; and
- be signed off by the most senior manager of the organization, reflecting the importance of the policy.

The OHS policy should be reviewed periodically to ensure its currency.

The OHS policy is, however, only one part of an appropriate OHS strategy for a forensic organization. The OHS policy must be underpinned by risk assessments and incident/accident reports that enable the organization to assess its OHS exposure, to meet legislative requirements such as reporting obligations, and to respond to risks appropriately.

An organization can develop a list of the main hazards that its staff are likely to be exposed to in the course of their duties, utilizing OHS reports, incident/accident reports, and previous risk assessments. Prioritizing the main health and safety issues allows the organization to develop appropriate action plans to meet the objectives of its OHS policy.

Forensic organizations may consider integration of some OHS requirements with their quality assurance system. Many laboratories effectively use their quality system to embed OHS requirements in their documented procedures, to review OHS hazards as part of a periodic audit program or to manage elements of their OHS action plans through their corrective action system. OHS, like quality, can then be viewed as an important yet integrated component of an effective management system.

Risk Assessments

Once potential OHS hazards have been identified, forensic organizations should evaluate the likelihood of injury from the interaction to the hazard and the magnitude of the adverse effect. The process of risk assessment will be very useful for managing potential OHS hazards within the facility and the expected external work environment. The purpose of the risk assessment process is to ensure that all workplace hazards have been identified, recorded, assessed, controlled, and reviewed. The desired outcome of this process is to eliminate, as far as practicable, the risk of injury or illness to personnel, damage to property, and damage to the environment. The process of developing risk assessment is often better suited to the known work environment. An OHS assessment of an office or laboratory can quickly identify specific hazards that may require attention. Obviously, this works well for the office and laboratory environment within one's control; however, each external scene will be different.

It is important that the range of potential hazards in external crime scenes and work environments is considered. While some risks can be grouped and managed collectively, the specific hazard and risk mitigation and control will vary from scene to scene given the circumstances. Given this, forensic practitioners should have an ability to undertake dynamic risk assessments, or "risk on the run" as it is known in some jurisdictions.

Dynamic Risk Management

Dynamic risk assessments are conducted by a forensic practitioner as part of the attendance and examination process. In some instances, such as attendance at a clan lab, a person may be designated as the Site Safety Officer and have carriage of this as well as health and safety for all personnel at the site. Practitioners should be trained to assess the risk given the circumstances at the time, considering the actual hazards present at a crime scene.

A designated forensic practitioner or Site Safety Officer should undertake a quick reconnaissance of the crime scene to ensure the safety of forensic practitioners and others working at the scene. A review of the scene should be repeated whenever the situation at the scene changes. This could involve a visual inspection without entering the crime scene, and asking a number of questions. For example:

- Does the crime scene involve structures that are now unstable?
- Has confirmation been obtained from the Fire Brigade or other emergency responders that power, gas, and water to the site have been turned off?
- Is there adequate shelter so that practitioners can rest without succumbing to environmental stressors such as heat, cold, wind, or rain?

It is important to close the loop, and incorporate any strategic elements of each dynamic risk assessment in OHS policy and planning. After each incident, any relevant information obtained during the dynamic risk assessment should be recorded and collated for strategic analysis.

Hierarchy of Control Measures

Within OHS, there is a "hierarchy of control" designed to mitigate or resolve a risk deemed unacceptably high.

The hierarchy of control is a sequence of options that offer a number of ways to approach the hazard control process. Various control options may be available. It is important to choose the control that most effectively eliminates the hazard or minimizes the risk in the circumstances. This may involve a single control measure or a combination of different controls that together provide the highest level of protection that is reasonably practicable.

1. Eliminate the hazard. If this is not practical, then:
2. Substitute the hazard with a lesser risk. If this is not practical, then:
3. Isolate the hazard. If this is not practical, then:
4. Use engineering controls. If this is not practical, then:
5. Use administrative controls, such as safe work practices, instruction, and training. If this is not practical, then:
6. Use personal protective equipment (PPE), such as gloves, eye protection, boots, and respirators.

It is important that management and staff discuss and consult, where possible, during all phases of the hazard identification, risk assessment, and risk control process.

Examples

1. If an organization is considering purchasing a piece of analytical equipment and two products have the same capabilities but substantially different noise levels during operation, the organization may consider the noise level of the equipment during procurement and opt for the quieter system. This example demonstrates the principle of eliminating the hazard at source, which is the most effective control measure, when compared to training and provision of PPE such as hearing protection.

2. In the case of a fire scene of a building, applying a hierarchy of control approach, it is first necessary to consider the elimination or substitution of hazards. In a fire scene, this is not possible. It is, however, possible to isolate the scene to prevent danger to the public and to maintain the integrity of the scene. Power, water, and gas to a building should be disconnected prior to entering the site. A structural engineer's opinion may be necessary prior to entry to the building. Safe entry and exit to the site can be established. Other administrative controls, such as briefing practitioners and maintaining records of the entry and exit of personnel, may be applied. Finally, practitioners can be prevented from entering the fire scene unless utilizing the appropriate PPE.

Specific Laboratory Hazards

The likely hazards within a laboratory environment include the following.

Chemicals

Chemical exposure may occur through inhalation, skin absorption, or direct ingestion and, once absorbed, are either stored in a particular organ or tissue, metabolized, or excreted. The effect of a chemical on a person is dependent on a number of factors such as duration and frequency of exposure, concentration of the chemical, and an individual's metabolism. A synergistic effect may occur when the undesirable effects of one substance are intensified if exposure has occurred to another substance.

Some nanomaterials exhibit different chemical properties compared to what they exhibit on a macroscale. As this is a relatively new field, there is insufficient knowledge regarding the hazards posed by nanomaterials. The potential hazards associated with nanomaterials may include increased reactivity because of their increased surface-area-to-volume ratio, the ability to cross some of the body's protective mechanism, and the lack of the body's immunity against such small particles. Because of this lack of knowledge, the suggested control strategy to be used when working with nanomaterials should be "as low as reasonably achievable" (ALARA) approach to reduce exposure.

The effects of chemicals on the body may be categorized:

- poisonous or toxic chemicals are absorbed into the body and exert either an acute or short-term effect, such as headache, nausea, or loss of consciousness, or a long-term effect such as liver or kidney damage, cancer, or chronic lung disease;
- corrosive chemicals burn the skin, eyes, or respiratory tract;
- irritants can inflame the skin or lungs, causing conditions such as dermatitis or bronchitis;

- sensitizers may exert long-term effects, especially to the skin (such as contact dermatitis) and to the respiratory tract (such as occupational asthma) by inducing an allergic reaction; and
- explosive or flammable substances pose immediate danger of fire and explosion, causing damage to the body through direct burning, or through inhalation of toxic fumes emitted during combustion.

Safety Data Sheets (SDS), also known as Material Safety Data Sheets (MSDS), are designed to provide relevant information regarding the identity, physical characteristics, safe storage, use, disposal, first-aid treatment, and spill management of substances that are handled in the workplace. The information includes whether the substance is deemed to be a hazardous and/or a dangerous goods item. At a minimum, the SDS should be consulted before the first use of a chemical or other substance within a laboratory, or if practitioners are unfamiliar with the product. Copies of SDS should be retained according to legislative requirements. In some jurisdictions, electronic SDS management systems can allow an efficient way of accessing up-to-date SDS information.

Sharps

Sharps are objects that have sharp edges or points that have the potential to cut, scratch, or puncture the skin. Sharps can cause physical injury and have the potential to introduce infectious and toxic agents through the wounds created in the skin. Examples include hypodermic syringes and needles, knives, or broken glassware.

All forensic practitioners have a responsibility to handle and package sharps safely. Particular care should be given to ensuring that sharps are appropriately labeled when packaged. Sharps such as knives could, for example, be packaged in clear plastic tubes, making it easier for a person opening the item to identify the contents and the direction the sharp items is facing. Forensic Labs should be encouraged to develop policies that encourage forensic practitioners and others that submit items to develop safe-packaging procedures.

Biological Material

Examples of "biological material" commonly encountered in forensic examinations include body tissue, blood, and body fluids (urine, saliva, vomit, pus, seminal fluid, vaginal fluid, and feces). Biological material is potentially hazardous as it may contain infectious agents such as viruses, bacteria, fungi, and parasites that cause a variety of communicable diseases.

Hair, fur, and items of clothing that have been in close contact with humans or animals may also harbor parasites such as fleas or nits.

When examining plant material such as cannabis, consideration should be given to the presence of *Aspergillus* sp. mold. If the *Aspergillus* spores are inhaled into the lungs, a serious, chronic respiratory or sinus infection can result. If mold is visible, the cannabis should be treated as a biological and respiratory hazard.

It is impossible to determine the prevalence of infectious or communicable diseases in the environment in which forensic practitioners work. Consequently, practitioners should adhere to recommended procedures for handling biological material and adopt an approach known as the "standard precautions." This approach requires practitioners to assume that all biological material is a potential source of infection, independent of diagnosis or perceived level of underlying risk.

Vaccinations should be offered for practitioners. The types of vaccinations given may depend on whether work is confined to the laboratory or whether work is performed in the field, as well as whether forensic practitioners are likely to be deployed overseas where other diseases may be more prevalent.

Firearms

Forensic practitioners may retrieve firearms from crime scenes. All personnel who may be required to handle firearms, either in the field, in the laboratory, or in support roles such as property or exhibit stores should be trained in how to render a firearm safe. As with the "standard precautions," it is important to consider all firearms as potentially loaded, and adopt the practice of never pointing a firearm in the direction of another person, even after it has been rendered safe.

Firearms examiners, who undertake firearms investigations including test firing and bullet recovery, will be exposed to hazards such as noise and lead. They should have their hearing and blood lead levels monitored on a regular basis, to ensure that hearing protection is being worn and is functioning correctly, and any exposure to lead from the firearms is quickly identified and addressed.

Computer Forensics Laboratory

Computer forensic examiners specialize in obtaining, analyzing, and reporting on electronic evidence stored on computers and other electronic devices. Crimes involving a computer can range across the spectrum of criminal activity, from child pornography to theft of personal data to destruction of intellectual property. Potential hazards involve static postures, occupational overuse, and stress from viewing graphic images.

Some suggestions to minimize the stress from viewing graphic images are as follows:

- psychological assessment before and after viewing graphic material, and periodically;
- exposure to only one medium, for example, visual material only, rather than examining both sound and visual material simultaneously;

- specifying limits as to the amount of time spent examining explicit material in a day; and
- ceasing any examination of explicit material at the end of their shift, to allow themselves time to refocus attention away from this stressor.

Electrical/Machinery

Forensic laboratories use a wide range of electrical equipment and machinery. Practitioners need to ensure that any inherent risk from electric shock is mitigated. The use of residual current devices (safety switches) is an appropriate strategy, as is visual inspection and periodic testing and tagging of power cords, to detect obvious damage, wear, and other conditions that might render it unsafe by a person qualified to do so under the legislation in effect in the jurisdiction.

Fume Cupboards

Fume cupboards are integral to minimizing the risk of exposure to chemical and biological hazards. Not all fume cupboards are suitable for all hazards. Fume cupboards should be maintained and inspected periodically. During maintenance, attention should be given to the following:

- The fume cupboard itself, including flow rates and replacement of absorbents or filters.
- In the case of externally vented fume cupboards, the ductwork and location of external vents. This is particularly important during any building maintenance or refurbishment.

Fume cupboards must be used for all operations that have the potential to release hazardous fumes, mists, or dusts.

- Before commencement of work, ensure that the fume cupboard is clean and free from contamination.
- Ensure the minimum of equipment is stored in the fume cupboard and is placed toward the back of the cupboard to reduce disturbance to the air flowing into the fume cupboard.
- Lower the sash as far as practicable during use to improve fume containment.

Recirculating fume cabinets rely on filtration or absorption to remove airborne contaminants released in the fume cabinet before the exhaust air is discharged back into the laboratory. They are suitable for light to moderate use with a known range of substances. The range of substances for which each cabinet can be used is limited by the need for compatibility with the chemicals in use as well as with the particular type of absorbent or filter fitted to the cabinet.

Robotics

The introduction of automated robotic platforms has significantly enhanced the efficiency of forensic analysis. The use of robotics is becoming more common and is very useful for a range of repetitive laboratory tasks. Besides saving time, robotics overcomes the need for repetitive work involved in pipetting, eliminating musculoskeletal injuries.

Hazards associated with robotics include the risk of exposure to the chemicals used in the work, electrocution, and cutting, stabbing, or shearing from the moveable parts of the robot. The interlocks on the robots should not be bypassed.

X-rays

X-rays are used in analytical and imaging instrumentation. Potential exposure to X-rays is generally localized to specific parts of the body, usually the hands or fingers. Depending on the X-ray energies delivered, effects may range from erythema (redness) at point of exposure, blood changes, cancer through to death. Depending on the legislative requirement in each country, practitioners working with X-ray equipment may be required to use dosimeters to assess radiation dose.

Lasers

Lasers span the visible and nonvisible electromagnetic spectrum and have many applications in forensic science, including Raman spectroscopy. Lasers are generally classified according to the level of risk they represent. Damage from laser beams can be thermal or photochemical. The primary sites of damage are the eyes and skin. Hazards associated with laser work may include:

- fire,
- explosion,
- electrocution, and
- inhalation of contaminants from laser interactions.

  Precautions for use of lasers include as follows:

- Display the class of laser in use.
- Appropriate protective eye wear with side protection and appropriate attenuation for the wavelength(s) in use must be worn.
- Interlocks on the laser should not be bypassed.
- Keep the laser beam path away from eye level whether one is seated or standing.

High-Intensity Light Sources

High-intensity light sources such as the Polilight® provide a range of colored light bands and white light for forensic work.

- Care should be taken that high-intensity white light is not directed onto any object at short distances from the end of the light guide, as this can cause severe heat damage to the object, and may result in a fire.
- The light beam should never be directed at eyes as the light can cause permanent damage.

Manual Handling

Manual handling refers to any activity that involves lifting, lowering, carrying, pushing, pulling, holding, restraining, or the application of force. Only a very small number of manual handling injuries are caused by the lifting of heavy weights alone. Actions such as reaching, twisting, bending, or maintaining static postures contribute to injury affecting the muscle or skeletal systems of the body. These musculoskeletal injuries predominantly involve the neck, back or shoulder or arm muscle, tendon, ligament, or joints.

Injuries may be caused from activities such as maintaining static postures while working at fume cupboards, repetitive keyboard and mouse work, pipetting, prolonged use of comparison microscopes.

Some preventative strategies include as follows:

- Seeking further assistance to have the activities assessed to minimize the manual handling risks inherent in the activity.
- Planning tasks so that rest breaks are scheduled.
- Choosing the best tools for the tasks.
- Alternate hands while using a mouse, if possible.

There is a move to make instruments smaller and more portable for use at crime scenes. While this has significant benefits, including potentially reducing the number of exhibits collected, moving equipment can also raise manual handling concerns.

General Laboratory Management

Housekeeping is important in laboratories. It is important to maintain clear passageways, have proper labeling of chemicals, clean and uncluttered work areas, and appropriate storage. The handling of powders is a potentially hazardous operation and good housekeeping can help minimize airborne contamination from spilled materials. Having a planned preventative maintenance program and regular inspections of the workplace, plant, and equipment are essential for the smooth running of the laboratory.

Handling of Exhibits in Court

Each evidential item must be appropriately packaged and sealed, if this is not already the case, before it is exhibited in court. Items such as clothing, which are normally stored in paper, may need to be repackaged in clear plastic allowing the item to remain sealed and minimizing the risk of cross contamination when handled in court. Caution should be exercised against opening exhibits in court, in case any hazards such as mold or irritant fumes are released.

Hazards in the Field

Forensic practitioners are often required to work or train in the field. Consideration should be given to managing hazards that may affect practitioners, including:

- environmental hazards such as heat, cold, humidity or wet weather, the terrain, and fauna or flora at the scene;
- the type of operation, for example, working in a clandestine laboratory often involves quite specific hazards;
- the possible presence of offenders or other security risks such as booby traps at a scene; and
- the availability of first aid and emergency response domestically and overseas.

The risks from these hazards should be considered within the scope of the exercise or operation. Some possible responses to hazards, which may be considered in a dynamic risk assessment, include as follows:

- Designating a location for emergency equipment, such as a crime scene vehicle, and ensuring that disinfectants, antiseptics, and a first-aid kit are easily accessible.
- Planning an emergency exit from the scene and ensuring that this is communicated to all personnel present.
- Establishing a decontamination point if there is exposure to chemical or biological material.
- The use of appropriate PPE including sunglasses, sunscreen, and hats when working outdoors.
- Depending on the external temperature, work activity, duration, and PPE worn, practitioners should have access to shade for rest and adequate fluids if required during hot weather to prevent heat stress. The wearing of PPE including chemical suits and respirators requires longer and more frequent periods of rest break for recovery in hot temperatures and humid environment.
- In cold weather, provision should be made to have adequate warm clothing and a sheltered area.
- The risk of animal or dog bites while attending a crime scene should not be discounted. If practitioners are searching in vegetated areas, the risk of snake or tick bites should be considered, along with possible exposure to plants such as poison ivy or stinging nettles.

Confined Spaces

Forensic practitioners may have to enter confined spaces. Due to the high risks associated with entering the confined space,

many jurisdictions mandate that entry into a confined space must not be made until a confined space permit has been issued. Practitioners must receive specific training before work or entry into confined spaces.

Chemical, Biological, Radiological, and Nuclear Incidents

Forensic practitioners may be required to attend a chemical, biological, radiological, and nuclear (CBRN) incident. CBRN incidents where forensic practitioners may attend and conduct examinations include:

- chemical (warfare agent, toxic industrial chemical);
- biological (weaponized agent, natural disease);
- radiological (discrete, or wide area contamination); and
- nuclear.

Depending on the response agency protocol in place, forensic practitioners may be working closely with the Fire Brigade and other emergency first responders. Entry must not be made into the "warm" or "hot" zone of the scene without consultation with the other emergency first responders.

Clan Labs

Clan labs pose a significant threat to the health and safety of police officers, forensic practitioners, the general public, and the environment. There are many hazards associated with clan labs including:

- flammable materials and/or explosive atmosphere;
- acutely toxic atmospheres;
- leaking or damaged compressed gas cylinders; and
- traps and hazards deliberately set to cause injury or death to police and other responders.

As a result of the frequency at which clan labs are encountered and the severe and variable risks associated with the investigation, many jurisdictions have developed specific policies and procedures concerning clan lab investigations.

For forensic practitioners to deal with clan labs requires a high level of fitness as well as technical expertise. Practitioners have to understand:

- illicit drug chemistry;
- how to neutralize the risks of explosions, fires, chemical burns, and toxic fumes;
- how to handle, store, and dispose of hazardous materials; and
- how to treat medical conditions caused by exposure.

Practitioners must also wear full protective equipment including respirators and may be required to move equipment at the clan lab in the process of collecting evidence. The storage and handling of unknown chemicals from clandestine laboratories or seizures should also be considered.

Preliminary identification should take place, before its storage or disposal.

When unknowns such as "white powders," chemicals (in liquid, solid, or gas state) or biological materials are encountered in the field, it is prudent to be cautious and obtain up-to-date intelligence to shed more light on what is at the scene. It may be an explosive material or contain anthrax spores or ricin or something as innocuous as talc.

Some precautions include:

- wearing the appropriate level of protective clothing/equipment for the activity;
- avoiding direct contact with the substance, even if only in small quantities;
- not smelling or tasting anything from the scene;
- noting physical characteristics such as color, form, and consistency;
- where it is safe to do so, looking for hazard symbols on packaging or labels if available; and
- seeking specialist advice if unable to identify the substance.

Potential Hazards during an Overseas Deployment

Forensic practitioners can be required to work overseas to assist with large-scale disasters. An example was the Thailand Tsunami Victim Identification process involving forensic practitioners from 30 countries working to recover and identify bodies. Forensic practitioners need to be mindful of hazards likely to be encountered during an overseas deployment depending on the location, magnitude of the operation, and how many practitioners are deployed. Some hazards to be considered include:

- climatic demands;
- remote and sometimes dangerous terrain;
- different cultural sensitivities;
- security requirements;
- different levels of infrastructure support at the locality;
- logistics, including the transport of large quantities of equipment, manual handling, setting up, and packing up;
- different hygiene levels;
- diseases that can be transmitted by insect and or animal vectors;
- the possibility of infectious diseases; and
- asbestos and other hazards in buildings.

Work-Related Stress

Practitioners at work may experience work-related stress. There are some specific stressors unique within forensic work. Forensic practitioners may experience workplace-related stress

due to their attendances at morgues, violent crime scenes, Disaster Victim Identification or from requirements to view explicit or graphic material or images.

Indicators of stress include changes in eating habits, tiredness due to changes in sleep patterns, frequent absences from work, reduced productivity, concentration, motivation, and morale. Physical symptoms may include headaches, abdominal pains, diarrhea, constipation, high blood pressure, insomnia, anxiety state, and depression.

Many organizations offer programs to provide assistance to employees, including counseling to help practitioners to deal with work-related stress or resilience training to manage work–life balance.

> *See also:* **Management/Quality in Forensic Science:** Principles of Quality Assurance; Risk Management; Principles of Laboratory Organization.

Further Reading

Clancy, D., Billinghurst, A., Cater, H., 2009. Hazard Identification and Risk Assessment – Understanding the Transition from the Documented Plan to Assessing Dynamic Risk in Bio Security Emergencies. World Conference on Disaster Management, Sydney, Australia. http://www.humansafety.com.au/getattachment/da338cb7-29b0-4d3a-8a06-d7dc0b569a87/C20.aspx.

Furr, K., 2000. Handbook of Laboratory Safety, fifth ed. CRC Press, Florida.

Green-McKenzie, J., Watkins, M., 2005. Occupational hazards: Law enforcement officers are at risk of body fluid exposure. Here's what to expect if it happens to you. Law Enforcement Magazine 29 (9), 52–54, 56, 58.

Hanson, D., 2007. Hazardous duty training officers to tackle hazmat emergencies. Law Enforcement Technology 34 (4), 80–85.

Haski, R., Cardilini, G., Bartolo, W., 2011. Laboratory Safety Manual. CCH Australia Ltd, Sydney.

Horswell, J., 2000. The Practice of Crime Scene Investigation. CRC Press, Florida.

Jackel, G., 2004. The high cost of stress. AUSPOL: The Official Publication of the Australian Federal Police Association and ALAJA 1, 4–37.

Mayhew, C., 2001a. Occupational health and safety risks faced by police officers. Australian Institute of Criminology. Trends and Issues in Crime and Criminal Justice 196, 1–6.

Mayhew, C., 2001b. Protecting the occupational health and safety of police officers. Australian Institute of Criminology. Trends and Issues in Crime and Criminal Justice 197, 1–6.

Rothenbaum, D., 2010. Exposed: An officer's story. Clan Lab Safety Alert 7 (2), 1–2.

Smith, D., 2005. Psychosocial occupational health issues in contemporary police work: A review of research evidence. Journal of Occupational Health and Safety, Australia and New Zealand 21 (3), 217–228.

Tillman, C., 2007. Principles of Occupational Health and Hygiene: An Introduction. Allen & Unwin, Crows Nest.

Whitman, M., Smith, C., 2005. The culture of safety: No one gets hurt today. Police Chief LXXII (11), 20–24, 26–27.

Winder, C., 2011. Hazard Alert: Managing Workplace Hazardous Substances. CCH Australia Ltd, Sydney.

Witter, R., Martyny, J., Mueller, K., Gottschall, B., Newman, L., 2007. Symptoms experienced by law enforcement personnel during methamphetamine lab investigation. Journal of Occupational and Environmental Hygiene 4, 895–902.

Relevant Websites

http://www.ccohs.ca/oshanswers/occup_workplace/labtech.html—Canadian   Centre
for Occupational Health and Safety (CCOHS).
http://www.cdc.gov/niosh/—Centers for Disease Control and Prevention (CDC).
http://www.forensic.gov.uk/html/company/foi/publication-scheme/health-and-
safety/—Forensic Science Service, Health and Safety.
http://www.hse.gov.uk/services/police/index.htm—Health and Safety Executive (HSE).

http://www.londonhealthandsafetygroup.org/archive.html—London Health and Safety
Group.
http://www.osha.gov/—Occupational Safety & Health Administration.
http://www.police.qld.gov.au/Resources/Internet/rti/policies/documents/
QPSForensicServicesHealth_SafetyManual.pdf—Health and Safety Manual, Police
Forensic Services, Queensland Police.
http://www.ccohs.ca/oshanswers/occup_workplace/police.html—What do Police do?.

Postmortem Specimens

GR Jones, Alberta Medical Examiners Office, Edmonton, AB, Canada

Introduction

In theory, modern analytical techniques allow most drugs and poisons to be measured in almost any biological fluid or tissue. However, the practical choice of which human fluids or tissues to use comes down to two main factors—what is available and the interpretive value of the results. For a body that has been outside for weeks or months, bone, and possibly bone marrow, may be all that is available as the remainder of the body has decomposed and may also have been devoured by insects and scavengers. In order to interpret the results, there must be a body of knowledge that allows sense to be made of drug concentrations. This applies to both drugs (prescribed or illicit) taken by humans or substances they may be exposed to (e.g., pesticides). For reasons largely beyond the scope of this section, reliance on a single measurement of a drug in a single specimen is best avoided because of a possible overlap of so-called therapeutic and toxic ranges. Measurement of drug concentrations in more than one specimen type can increase the reliability of interpretation. The following section outlines some of the advantages and disadvantages of various specimens for postmortem toxicology.

Blood, Serum, and Plasma

The term "blood" usually refers to whole blood as it would be drawn from a vein or artery. If the red and white cells are spun down by centrifugation, the clear straw-colored fluid on top is plasma. If whole blood is allowed to clot that is separated by centrifugation, the clear straw-colored fluid is called serum. For forensic toxicology purposes, plasma and serum are usually regarded as equivalent.

With some exceptions, blood is regarded as the primary specimen for forensic toxicology. During life, blood is a living fluid that circulates to, and is in equilibrium with, virtually all tissues, including the receptors where many drugs have their site of action. However, after death, blood cells die and the cells lyse, the red cells releasing large amounts of hemoglobin. Therefore, most postmortem toxicology testing relies not on serum or plasma (as for most clinical toxicology testing), but on whole, hemolyzed blood. Despite the processes that occur after death, postmortem blood is typically a dark red fluid containing numerous microclots, which, with some care, may be measured by pipette. After the blood circulation ceases,

sedimentation occurs, where the red blood cells gradually settle to the lowest point in an organ or tissue. Therefore, the hemoglobin concentration of any given blood sample can vary considerably, depending on where it was drawn from. Where the difference in drug concentration between red cells and plasma is more or less even, sedimentation should not have a significant effect on interpretation. However, where the concentration of a drug is significantly different in red cells versus plasma, interpretation may be markedly affected.

Collection Site

Blood is most conveniently collected from the area of the largest pool in the body—the heart and the major vessels connected to it. However, blood in the heart and other central organs (e.g., lungs, liver) is subject to postmortem redistribution (PMR). Drugs that are highly protein bound tend to concentrate in the major organs such as the lungs, liver, and heart. PMR is the process whereby drugs that concentrate in organs and tissues outside of the blood volume during life are released from those tissues after death, causing blood concentrations of many drugs to markedly increase after death. Not all drugs are subject to PMR, but in varying degrees, a large number are. In general, the extent of PMR will generally be less the farther from the central organs blood is drawn. It is therefore good practice to collect at least some volume of blood (e.g., 5–10 ml) from a site remote from the central organs, such as the femoral veins. The volume of blood required for comprehensive postmortem toxicology may exceed 20 ml, especially if several drugs need to be quantitated; therefore, a sample of subclavian or cardiac blood may be collected for the purpose of qualitative drug screening.

Blood should always be collected with a clean (unused) disposable syringe and needle (typically 16 G or larger) from a clearly identified blood vessel rather than a "blind stick." A "blind stick" to the chest can result in the inadvertent collection of pulmonary blood, pericardial fluid, or pleural fluid. Care is particularly important in cases of death involving trauma where the major organs have moved or ruptured and where chest fluid or, worse, bloody abdominal fluid may be drawn.

It is good practice to ligate (tie off) peripheral blood vessels prior to sampling blood. This is to prevent drawing blood from the larger central vessels that may be subject to PMR—for example, when drawing blood from the groin area (i.e., near the iliac–femoral junction). However, there is growing evidence that for at least some drugs, even a properly collected femoral blood sample may be subject to PMR from surrounding skeletal muscle.

Blood Clots

Many cranial injuries are caused by intoxication with alcohol or drugs. The collection of a blood clot from a subdural hematoma can provide evidence of an alcohol or drug concentration closer to the time of the original injury. Blood, which leaks from a damaged blood vessel as a result of such injuries, will clot in the subdural space and no longer be subject to normal circulation and clearance. If death is delayed, for example, due to medical treatment, an elevated subdural clot alcohol or drug concentration may provide useful information. Unfortunately, the drug concentration will not persist indefinitely but will diminish over a period of hours or days due to diffusion from the clot into surrounding tissue.

Containers, Preservative

It is good practice to collect at least 5–10 ml postmortem blood into a container that results in a sodium or potassium fluoride concentration of 1–2%. Fluoride inhibits ethanol formation from microbiological metabolism of glucose and similar substrates. However, fluoride also inhibits the action of esterases and will therefore impede the breakdown of some drugs such as cocaine. It should be noted that most gray-stopper clinical blood collection tubes only contain sodium fluoride equivalent to 0.25%.

However, a much larger blood sample (e.g., 30–80 ml) may be collected into a plain screw-capped container with no preservative. Addition of an anticoagulant is usually not necessary because the blood-clotting system is no longer vital after death and the extent of clotting is relatively limited.

Blood collected for the analysis of volatile solvents or gases should be collected into a glass container with tight sealing cap with polytetrafluoroethylene (PTFE) or similar liner.

Trauma, Medical, and Other Artifacts

Caution must be exercised during the collection of blood from areas of the body where significant trauma has occurred or drug administration has taken place. Trauma may result in rupture of the stomach, causing contamination of the entire abdominal cavity, including the area adjacent to the junction of the femoral and iliac veins. Rupture of the stomach and diaphragm can cause spillage of gastric contents into the chest cavity, especially after falls from a height or motor vehicle accidents. The integrity of such chest cavity specimens is always extremely suspect and susceptible to contamination.

Antemortem Blood and Serum

In cases where death after an intoxication, poisoning, or other event has been delayed due to medical treatment, postmortem drug concentrations will be an inaccurate measure of the drug present at the time of the event (if indeed the drug is still present at all when death occurs). Blood, serum, or plasma collected on first admission to an emergency department can therefore provide valuable toxicological evidence. Even if the death occurs fairly quickly after medical treatment is initiated, antemortem specimens are of value because, by definition, specimens collected right before or around the time of death will not be subject to PMR.

Urine

The main advantages of urine over blood are that the concentrations of many drugs in urine are considerably higher than the corresponding concentrations in blood, and urine is much easier and "cleaner" to deal with analytically than postmortem blood.

A disadvantage of urine is that the parent drug is sometimes absent due to extensive metabolism, placing reliance on identification of metabolites. Further, there is virtually no correlation between urine drug concentrations and pharmacological effect. Attempted "normalization" of urine drug concentrations to creatinine does little to improve their usefulness. Ethanol is one of the few exceptions, where measuring urine concentrations can serve as a corroborative finding of a positive blood concentration (absent glucose in a poorly controlled diabetic).

However, while urine may sometimes be a useful specimen for postmortem toxicology screening, laboratories should not rely on it since the bladder may spontaneously empty during the process of dying.

Vitreous Humor

Vitreous humor is the primary fluid that makes up much of the interior volume of the eyeball—about 3 ml per eye—and is composed of 98–99% water. Vitreous humor is useful for the postmortem measurement of alcohol because it remains sterile for days after death and is therefore not subject to artifactual alcohol formation (unlike postmortem blood). Due to the higher water content of vitreous compared to whole blood, at equilibrium, vitreous alcohol concentrations are typically 10–15% higher.

Vitreous fluid has also been used for the measurement of drugs. However, its use is limited by two factors. First, the volume available is usually limited to about 6 ml, even if both eyes are used. The second factor is that vitreous drug concentrations can be very different from the corresponding whole blood or plasma concentrations. Concentrations of highly lipid soluble or highly protein-bound drugs tend to be much lower in vitreous fluid, due to the relative absence of lipid material and much lower protein content than whole blood.

The measurement of drugs in vitreous fluid has also been touted as a way of avoiding the complexity of interpretation when using whole blood, as the eyes are remote from the major abdominal and chest organs thought to be responsible for PMR. However, these assumptions should be viewed cautiously as PMR from the brain is at least a theoretical possibility.

Bile

In a person whose gall bladder has not been surgically removed for medical reasons, the volume of bile available typically ranges from about 5 to 20 ml, but can be larger. Bile tends to concentrate many drugs, in particular those that form glucuronide and other conjugates, such as morphine. However, that apparent benefit is no longer useful, because modern methodology can detect and measure even subtherapeutic concentrations of most drugs in blood using gas chromatography–mass spectrometry (GC–MS) and liquid chromatography–mass spectrometry (LC–MS) methodologies.

However, bile, like urine, is not a circulating fluid and therefore not in constant equilibrium with blood. Bile is also likely subject to the postmortem diffusion of drugs from the liver.

The Liver

The liver has long been used as one of the primary specimens for drug measurement and interpretation. It is a large organ that tends to concentrate many drugs and is relatively easy to homogenize. Most importantly, the literature contains a substantial amount of data regarding liver concentrations of drugs in various types of postmortem cases. Care must be taken to differentiate high liver drug concentrations resulting from an acute ingestion or overdose from high concentrations resulting from impaired metabolism or clearance. Some regard the liver as a more useful specimen than postmortem blood for drug measurement because, with one exception, it is not subject to PMR. The exception is that high concentrations of drug in the stomach can diffuse across the stomach wall and causes local increases in the lobes of the liver that are the closest (e.g., left lobe).

It is important that efficient homogenization occur using a high-efficiency blender that uses shearing and sometimes ultrasonic action. It is also important that the whole homogenate be used for quantitative analysis and not just the supernatant. That is because a large proportion of drug will be bound to the cell wall and other cellular structure and would result in a disproportionally low result if only the supernatant were used.

The Brain

The brain is a potentially useful tissue for postmortem drug analysis. Many drugs tend to concentrate in the brain relative to blood, and it is a very easy specimen to homogenize. Being remote from the stomach, it is not subject to postmortem diffusion or PMR from any other organs. The database of brain drug concentrations in the literature is considerably smaller than for the liver. However, the brain is a particularly useful organ for the measurement of drugs that are subject to rapid enzymatic hydrolysis in whole blood, due to esterases (e.g., cocaine, heroin, or 6-acetylmorphine).

Some practitioners are also reluctant to homogenize and analyze brain samples routinely, because of the small but serious risk of exposure to Creutzfeldt–Jakob disease.

Lungs

The use of pulmonary tissue typically has little or no advantage over the liver or brain for measuring drug concentrations. Also, pulmonary tissue is more fibrous than liver and an adequate database of known drug concentrations is lacking that might aid interpretation. Lung tissue has been collected for the analysis of volatile poisons (e.g., solvents, gases). However, unless death occurs very quickly, much of the volatile agent may be absorbed into the body or lost to the atmosphere before the autopsy occurs.

The Kidney

Kidney tissue has also periodically been collected and analyzed in postmortem cases. As a tissue for measuring drug concentrations, it has little if any advantage over liver and the database of blood drug concentrations is considerably smaller than for liver. The kidney has been most often used for measuring concentrations of heavy metals, especially where long-term toxicity is suspected (as compared to acute poisoning).

Skeletal Muscle

Skeletal muscle is the largest mass of soft tissue in the body and is usually the last to survive the process of putrefaction and decomposition. Skeletal muscle tends to be more fibrous than liver or brain. It is moderately well perfused, suggesting the possibility of a reasonably good relationship between skeletal muscle and blood drug concentrations. Again, the disadvantage of skeletal muscle is lack of a good database of "normal" (i.e., "therapeutic") or toxic concentrations, although extremes of concentration may be easier to interpret. The limited data that have been published on skeletal muscle drug concentrations suggest that there is at least some site-to-site variation.

Other Tissues and Fluids

Gastric Contents

Gastric (stomach) contents can be useful for helping to determine if an overdose has been consumed, or even simply for the detection of drugs. Analysis of gastric contents is most useful where ingestion of an overdose is possible. In these circumstances, considerable dilution of the stomach contents may be necessary, therefore diluting out the potential matrix effect of a large amount of food. In evaluating the results of gastric drug concentrations, it is critical to keep in mind that it is the total amount of drug present that is important, not the concentration of drug. It should also be kept in mind that stomach contents are rarely homogeneous as a specimen, and may contain wholly or partially digested pills. Therefore, to maximize accuracy, the entire stomach contents should be collected and homogenized prior to analysis. If this is not practical, then a best effort to mix the stomach contents should occur prior to sampling at autopsy, and the total volume that is present recorded. It should also be borne in mind that the presence of only a small amount of drug in the gastric contents does not preclude the possibility of oral consumption of an overdose. Death of a drug overdose victim can take several hours, during which time the stomach may be largely emptied of drug.

Cerebrospinal Fluid

Cerebrospinal fluid (CSF) is similar in composition to vitreous fluid, containing a high water content (98–99%). While CSF can be used for alcohol and drug analysis, it is more difficult to collect after death and can be contaminated with blood. The published data for drug concentrations in CSF are considerably more limited than for vitreous fluid, making interpretation challenging.

Pericardial Fluid

Pericardial fluid is a clear, colorless to straw-colored fluid that is contained in the pericardial sac that bathes and surrounds the heart. Some toxicologists have advocated using pericardial fluid for drug quantitation. However, very few data exist in the literature to aid with interpretation of the results obtained. Due to its intimate proximity to the heart, pericardial fluid is almost certainly subject to postmortem diffusion from the heart and lungs. Moreover, little is known about how quickly pericardial fluid drug concentrations would equilibrate with the blood.

Chest Fluid and Pleural Cavity Fluid

Pleural cavity fluid is analogous to pericardial fluid, in that it is the fluid in the pleural sac that bathes the lungs. After death, pleural fluid can easily become contaminated with blood, and it will be affected by postmortem diffusion from the lungs. "Chest fluid" is regarded as any fluid found within the chest cavity. It is sometimes collected when blood is difficult to obtain from a specific vessel such as the femoral or subclavian vein. Chest or pleural cavity fluid may be contaminated with blood or, worse, stomach contents, if the diaphragm and stomach have ruptured. In other words, pleural cavity and chest fluid should be regarded as poor-quality specimens and any quantitative drug concentration derived from those fluids interpreted with extreme caution.

Heart Tissue

Myocardial tissue offers little advantage over other organ tissue for the routine analysis of postmortem drug concentrations. It tends to be more fibrous than some other tissues and a very limited database of published myocardial tissue drug concentrations exists to aid interpretation.

The Spleen

The primary reason spleen tissue has been collected is for the high concentrations of red blood cells it contains. For example, in some fire deaths the heat produced may denature most or all of the readily available blood that might otherwise be collected. However, spleen tissue, partially protected inside the abdominal cavity, may contain enough red blood cells to allow measurement of carboxyhemoglobin (indicating the extent of inhalation of carbon monoxide and other products of combustion into the body during a fire).

Hair, Nails, Bone, Bone Marrow, and Cartilage

Hair is occasionally useful in postmortem toxicology for differentiating chronic from acute drug use, especially in criminal cases. Traditionally, head hair grows at a rate of about 1–1.5 cm month^{-1}. By careful collection and segmental analysis, it is possible to estimate when drug use started or finished, or whether the drug detected resulted from an acute dose shortly before death (because of its absence in the hair). However, analytical toxicology testing of hair is not widely performed, other than for a small range of drugs of abuse, and is rarely performed on postmortem cases except in specific, typically criminal, cases.

Nails can also be used to analyze for drugs, but its seldom has any advantage over other specimens. The analytical protocols used for nail clippings would be similar to those used for hair.

In certain types of postmortem cases, hair, nails, bone, and possibly bone marrow may be all that remains of a body. If the body is not discovered for several weeks, animal activity may consume all of the internal organs, and eventually all skeletal muscle, leaving only skeletal remains (bone, bone marrow, and perhaps cartilage). Bone can be analyzed for the presence of drugs, much as nails or hair can. Bone needs to be thinly shaved or ground to a powder in order to be extracted and analyzed. If death of the person was rapid, due to an acute poisoning or overdose, detection will depend on how well perfused the specimen was. In theory, detection in bone marrow stands a fair chance of success because bone marrow is well perfused during life. However, detection of a drug resulting from a single acute dose in a poorly perfused specimen like bone may stand only a poor chance of success.

Injection Sites

Suspected injection sites may be excised and submitted for toxicology testing, although pathologists and toxicologists must be careful about interpretation of the results. Most drugs are widely distributed through the body, including all of the major organs, muscle, and, not least, skin. Therefore, a drug would be expected to be found in any skin sample, regardless of the route of ingestion into the body. It is therefore critical that if analysis of a suspected injection site is to be undertaken, a corresponding skin sample must be collected from a "control" site on the opposite side of the body where injection is not suspected to have occurred. A good example is testing for a possible insulin overdose.

Maggots

Several papers have been published describing the collection and analysis of maggots from a dead body. Putrefaction of a body can complicate the detection of drugs. A body lying unattended for more than a few hours will attract flies that will lay eggs on the body. The eggs will mature into larvae, the resulting maggots that will feed on the body, and so ingest drugs that are present in body tissues and fluids. The maggots can be collected and analyzed, in the same manner as any other tissue or fluid. The problem is that maggots metabolize drugs. Failure to detect a drug does not necessarily mean that the drug was not present in the body at the time of death. Therefore, the analysis of maggots for the presence of drugs is largely regarded as being of limited forensic value.

Special Considerations

Putrefaction

The decomposition of a human or animal body after death causes proteins, fats, and other substances to break down into smaller molecules. That process is partially caused by naturally autolytic enzymes such as lysozymes (contained within each cell), and similar enzymes contained in bacteria. The net effect on postmortem drug concentrations is to make analysis of body fluids and tissues difficult due to greatly increased amounts of putrefactive amines and lipids. Nonetheless, from the perspective of postmortem specimen collection, there is little that can be done except than to rely on the use of tissue from the major organs. Successful testing relies on good design of the analytical method. The majority of drugs are amine-like in character, and so they are relatively easy to separate from fats. However, if putrefaction is advanced, separation of amine-like drugs from putrefactive amines during the extraction step becomes next to impossible and so highly specific analytical methods such as mass spectrometry must be used. Despite the problems that putrefaction causes, collection of the available postmortem specimens may still allow meaningful analysis an interpretation for some drugs.

Embalmed Bodies

The embalming process creates special problems. Embalming fluid, containing formaldehyde, methanol, isopropanol, detergents, dyes, and other substances is forced into the body through the major blood vessels and also introduced directly into the major organs and body cavity. In the process, much of the blood in the body is flushed out or diluted with embalming fluid. Tissues are "fixed," causing the organs to harden. In an embalmed body, the collection of blood is usually not possible. Vitreous fluid in the eye is somewhat protected from the embalming process, and may be collected. However, at the very least, methanol from embalming fluid will usually penetrate the eye as embalmers typically take special care to perfuse the facial area in order to preserve the "look" of the person.

The collection and analysis of major organs such as the liver may be valuable. However, the toxicologist should be careful to take into account the potential dilution effect of embalming fluid, as well as the fact that formaldehyde can react with some drugs, causing the concentration to decrease or to disappear.

Labeling

All specimens, particularly blood, must be properly labeled with a unique case identifier (usually case number and decedent name), the name of the specimen, and, where appropriate, the location the specimen was collected from (e.g., for blood, whether femoral, subclavian, and aorta). If two containers are collected of the same specimen type (e.g., two tubes of femoral blood), it is important to uniquely label each tube (e.g., #1, #2, #3, or A, B, C). This is particularly important for postmortem blood because it is not a homogeneous fluid; sequentially drawn specimen from the same site may contain different concentrations of drug. It is important that the exact site of draw must be indicated, and not simply terms like "peripheral" or "central." For example, to some, "peripheral" simply means any blood vessel outside of the heart itself and may, erroneously, be interpreted to include subclavian, inferior vena cava, and aorta blood.

Chain of Custody

The requisition accompanying the specimen to the laboratory should contain the necessary demographic information, as well as sufficient information for the laboratory to decide which specific tests should be performed on a specimen or case. Unless specimens are being transported internally, they should be either individually sealed or the bag or box containing multiple specimens from a single case sealed as part of the chain of custody. The requisition should also be signed and dated by the person responsible for collecting and releasing the specimens for transfer or transport, and should be signed and dated by the person accepting receipt of the package in the laboratory. In most jurisdictions, documentation of courier transportation is accepted as part of the intermediate transport chain of custody (i.e., the courier is not required to sign the requisition as part of the chain of custody documentation).

See also: **Toxicology:** Interpretation of Results; Pharmacology and Mechanism of Action of Drugs; Postmortem Toxicology: Artifacts; **Toxicology/Drugs of Abuse:** Drugs in Hair; Postmortem Blood.

Further Reading

ABFT (American Board of Forensic Toxicology), 2002. Forensic Toxicology Laboratory Accreditation Manual. American Board of Forensic Toxicology, Colorado Springs, CO. http://www.abft.org/files/ABFTLaboratoryManual.pdf (accessed 28 June 2011).

Dinis-Oliveira, R.J., Carvalho, F., Duarte, J.A., et al., 2010. Collection of biological samples in forensic toxicology. Toxicology Mechanisms and Methods 20, 363–414.

Flanagan, R.J., Connally, G., Evans, J.M., 2005. Analytical toxicology: guidelines for sample collection post-mortem. Toxicological Reviews 24, 63–71.

Hepler, B.R., Isenschmid, D.S., 2006. Specimen selection, collection, preservation, and security. In: Karch, S., Druid, H. (Eds.), Handbook of Drug Abuse, second ed. CRC Press, Roca Raton, FL, pp. 975–991.

Jones, G.R., 2004. Post-mortem toxicology. In: Moffat, A.C., Osselton, M.D., Widdop, B. (Eds.), Clarke's Analysis of Drugs and Poisons, third ed. Pharmaceutical Press, London, pp. 94–108.

NAME (National Association of Medical Examiners), 2011. NAME Accreditation and Inspection Checklist. http://thename.org/index.php?option=com_docman&task=cat_view&gid=45&Itemid=26 (accessed 28 June 2011).

Skopp, G., 2004. Preanalytic aspects in post-mortem toxicology. Forensic Science International 142, 75–100.

Skopp, G., 2010. Post-mortem toxicology. Forensic Science, Medicine, and Pathology 6, 314–325.

SOFT/AAFS (Society of Forensic Toxicologists/American Academy of Forensic Sciences), 2006. Forensic Toxicology Laboratory Guidelines. Society of Forensic Toxicologists/American Academy of Forensic Sciences, New York. http://www.soft-tox.org/files/Guidelines_2006_Final.pdf (accessed 28 June 2011).

Drug-Facilitated Crimes

KS Scott, Arcadia University, Glenside, PA, USA

Abbreviations

CNS	Central nervous system	MDMA	3,4-Methylenedioxymethylamphetamine
DFC	Drug-facilitated crime	mg%	mg (ethanol) per 100 mL of blood or plasma
DFSA	Drug-facilitated sexual assault		
GABA	Gamma-aminobutyric acid	UNODC	United Nations Office of Drugs and Crime
GHB	Gamma-hydroxybutyrate	WHO	World Health Organization

Introduction

A drug-facilitated crime (DFC) takes place when illegal activity occurs against a person, while they are incapacitated because of the effects of a drug or drugs in their body. If the literature on this topic is searched, the majority of resulting scientific papers and Web sites refer solely to drug-facilitated sexual assault (DFSA), a crime that is very much at the forefront of the media. However, DFCs include a wide range of offenses, including blackmail, theft, and extortion, and in some cases, may involve combinations of various crimes. The administration of drugs to dependents in order to sedate them is also considered a DFC.

Specific advertizing campaigns now exist as a deterrent to young adults with a focus on the overuse of alcohol or binge drinking on nights out. Despite media hype that the pub and club scenes are rife with drink-drug spiking, the majority of journal articles reviewing the types of drug found in DFSA cases conclude that in the majority of cases, alcohol is the main drug found in alleged victims. This, however, does not negate the fact that in some cases drugs are involved.

Definitions

DFC or DFSA is a term used to refer to all forms of nonconsensual activity undertaken when the victim of the activity is profoundly intoxicated. Legally, there are three main ways by which the intoxication can occur as follows:

1. self-ingestion of an incapacitating or disinhibiting substance;
2. forced or covert administration of an incapacitating or disinhibiting substance;
3. self and forced or covert administration of an incapacitating or disinhibiting substance.

The incapacitating or disinhibiting drugs may be illicit or medicinal drugs, and in many cases, a combination of drug types and alcohol are found. Operation Matisse has recommended that DFSA is redefined as either Proactive DFSA, where the victims are drugged either by force or covertly, or Opportunistic DFSA, where the victims are intoxicated by their own actions.

Drug-Facilitated Sexual Assault

Sexual assaults in general are underreported to the authorities. The British Crime Survey (2001) reported that only 12% of subjects who admitted undergoing a serious sexual assault reported the crime to the police. In 2004, there were 2689 prosecution of rape with less than 30% of these cases resulting in conviction. The World Health Organization (WHO) has evaluated the use of drugs by not only victims of crime but also the perpetrator of these crimes. A strong link between interpersonal violence (including sexual offenses) and drug use has been shown.

Of all subjects who stated that they had been sexually assaulted vaginally or anally, 5% stated that they had been drugged, and 15% stated that they had been unable to consent because of alcohol intoxication. For other penetrative offenses, 6% stated that they had been assaulted while drugged and 17% of them had been unable to give consent because of alcohol intoxication. Regardless of the date, country, or governing body, who has produced these statistics, the picture is the same worldwide and DFSA is a crime that warrants investment at a government level.

The low-reporting rates for sexual offenses are further decreased in DFCs because of feelings of guilt or shame due to self-administered drugs and alcohol, particularly, when the drug ingestion is illicit; confusion and uncertainty because of memory impairment due to the drugs' effects regarding what happened; and reluctance to make accusations without personal knowledge, or memory, of the circumstances leading to the assault.

Typical Drugs in DFC

The types of drug found or utilized in DFC are varied in their effects and cover the whole range of drugs investigated in a Forensic Toxicology laboratory. Although one might think that DFC drugs should be central nervous system (CNS) depressant in nature, CNS stimulants are also encountered. In general, CNS depressants slow down the activity of the CNS and the transmission of messages going between the brain and the body, and CNS stimulants speed these processes up and may contribute to the impairment from a CNS depressant. Both types of drugs can have fatal consequences if misused or combined with other drugs or alcohol.

Drugs that are taken by the victim himself or herself tend to be disinhibiting in nature, resulting in a fortuitous or opportunistic event, where the potential victim is taken advantage. Both CNS stimulants and depressants are found in these types of cases. Some substances with CNS stimulant activity, including amphetamine-type stimulants, may cause disinhibition, leading to inappropriate risk-taking behavior resulting in nonconsensual sexual activity.

In contrast, the type of drug forced or administered to a potential victim is more likely to be incapacitating in nature and likely to be preplanned. These drugs are more likely to be CNS depressants and have effects as noted below.

The ideal candidate drugs for DFC are likely to exhibit some or all of the following properties: odorless, colorless, easily dissolvable in liquid, amnesic, fast acting at low doses, short lived, producing disinhibition, and relaxation to incapacitate the victim.

The amnesic effect of candidate drugs is an important property, as this results in delayed presentation and therefore loss of associated evidence. In some cases, anterograde amnesia may be so profound that the victim is never aware of the events that took place and therefore will never report the crime.

The high potency, low dose, and short half-life of these drugs result in further complications to the investigation, as even if the victim does present within a reasonable time frame, some of the drugs will no longer be present or detectable in the toxicological samples taken for analysis.

Within the media in the previous decade, there have been two favorite drugs that may or may not have been successfully utilized in these crimes. These two drugs are discussed in more detail below along with potential issues relating to their detection in biological samples.

Gamma-Hydroxybutyrate

The first of the drugs and possibly the most complicated is gamma-hydroxybutyrate (GHB). One of the reasons why GHB is problematic in terms of toxicology is that it occurs naturally in the brain. It is a precursor and metabolite of gamma-aminobutyric acid (GABA). As a drug, it was first manufactured in the 1960s, and it has been used as a general anesthetic, as a sleep aid, and in the treatment of alcoholism. In the 1980s, it was marketed as a supplement for body builders, as it increases the episodic secretion of growth hormone. More recently, it is being prescribed for sleep disorders, including narcolepsy. For many years, it has been popular on the club scene, because of production of feelings of mild euphoria and alcohol-like symptoms. GHB is now illegal in most countries because of its unwanted side effects and allegations of use in DFC.

As a DFC drug, GHB ticks many of the boxes, it is odorless, colorless, quite water soluble, and thereby can be surreptitiously slipped into a drink. It also acts fast with a relative short duration of action. In solution, it is mildly saline and therefore has a slightly salty taste; however, if diluted into the drink of a subject, it is possible that they would not notice this.

As with other drugs, the effects (and side effects) of GHB depend on the weight, height, and health of the subject on whether they have other drugs or alcohol in their system and whether they have used GHB before. GHB has a steep dose response curve and therefore small increases in dose could have a significant effect on the intensity of the effects and the onset of CNS depression. This makes it particularly dangerous to the naive user, particularly, when it has been given to them without their knowledge.

The reported effects of GHB include mild euphoria (at low doses), amnesia, intoxication, drowsiness, dizziness, nausea, visual hallucinations (at higher doses), hypotension, bradycardia, severe respiratory depression, and possibility of coma and death if too high a dose is taken or given.

Although GHB has been reported to have a short half-life of approximately 30–50 min, it is now believed that like ethanol, GHB has no true half-life and exhibits zero-order kinetics with a proposed elimination rate of 18 mg l^{-1}. It does, however, like ethanol, have a terminal half-life that fits with the previously denoted half-life. This would in part account for the short detection half-life, which is also complicated by the fact that all blood and urine samples contain GHB because of the endogenous presence of GHB. GHB levels of up to 490 mg l^{-1} have been reported for Hospital Emergency patients. At this level, GHB would be detected for over 24 h; however, only a tolerant individual would survive this.

Owing to the endogenous nature of GHB, laboratories are required to use cut-offs for reporting positive results. Endogenous levels in the living are below 10 mg l^{-1} in blood and recommended cutoff values are 10 mg l^{-1} for blood and

5 mg l^{-1} for urine. A further compounding issue with GHB is that its metabolites are other endogenous compounds that culminate in the production of water and carbon monoxide. Thus, proof of use via metabolite detection in urine is not an option.

Flunitrazepam

The second commonly noted DFC drug is the benzodiazepine flunitrazepam. As noted above, flunitrazepam has a reasonable half-life (16–35 h); however, it is effective at low doses. Flunitrazepam is characterized as a short-acting benzodiazepine. Benzodiazepines are sedative-hypnotic drugs that are used to treat anxiety, insomnia and sleep disorders, and seizure disorders. Some of them are also used as skeletal-muscle relaxants as premedication for hospital procedures. Flunitrazepam is ten times more potent than diazepam, and while commonly prescribed for anxiety and sleep disorders in Europe, Latin America, and elsewhere, it was never approved for use or sale in the United States. In the United Kingdom, it is now classified as a Schedule 3 drug under the Misuse of Drugs Act (1971) meaning that it, along with temazepam, is more restricted in terms of prescription than other benzodiazepines.

Effects and side effects of flunitrazepam include disinhibition, amnesia and memory impairment, excitability or aggressive behavior, decreased blood pressure, drowsiness, visual disturbances, lack of consciousness, dizziness, confusion, and stomach disturbances. As with GHB, many of the boxes associated with "good" DFC drugs are ticked. The drug is odorless, tasteless, and colorless; however, following allegations of its use in DFC cases, the producers introduced a blue dye into the tablets and lowered the tablet strength to 1 mg.

Despite the allegations of its use in DFCs when statistics from toxicology laboratories across the world are evaluated, other benzodiazepines are much more commonly encountered, for example, in a UK study, there were 84 cases where benzodiazepines were detected and reported; in a Canadian study, 20 cases were reported; and in a Swedish study, 147 cases were reported. In the UK and Canadian studies, no flunitrazepam was detected; however, in the Swedish study, flunitrazepam was detected in seven cases and metabolites of flunitrazepam was detected in a further seven cases. A further case from Japan in 2006 found the primary metabolite of flunitrazepam, namely, 7-amino-flunitrazepam to be present in the urine of the victim, which had been collected 24 h postingestion. The victim claimed loss of memory and memory impairment for a period of approximately 19 h postingestion.

More recently, single-dose studies for flunitrazepam in the urine of 16 volunteers have indicated that metabolites can be detected up to and exceeding 10 days postdose. This advocates the use of urinalysis in late-reporting DFC cases. The study also warns against reliance on immunoassay screening in DFC. Guidelines on recommended maximum cutoff concentrations

in urine have been issued by the Society of Forensic Toxicologists (SOFT) for both parent drugs and metabolites. The recommendation for metabolite testing also highlights the need for hydrolysis, in particular, with drugs that form conjugated metabolites (e.g., benzodiazepines).

Alcohol in DFC

By far, alcohol is the most commonly encountered drug in all DFSA studies. The percentage of cases in which alcohol was detected ranged from 37% to 69%. The main reason for the prevalence of alcohol is its wide availability, its acceptability in society, and the fact that most cases of alleged DFSA occur when the victim is socializing. In studies, up to 77% of the evaluated cases claimed to have consumed alcohol.

The effects of alcohol are well documented and understood as is its pharmacology. Unlike other drugs measured in toxicological samples, it is possible to extrapolate back from the results of a blood–alcohol result and estimate the level of alcohol, which would have been present at the time of the offense. This is an extremely important piece of forensic evidence as a reasonable opinion regarding the likelihood of the victim being unable to provide informed consent is possible. It has been estimated that the average alcohol concentration in casework is around 220 mg% with a range of <100 to >400 mg%. This raises the issue of capacity to give informed consent and the legal consequences of this.

In 2006, the association of alcohol-induced blackouts and grayouts to blood–alcohol concentrations was evaluated. This information is useful in DFC as knowledge of the likelihood of an amnesic episode is a supportive courtroom tool. If a subject has a blood alcohol of 305 mg% or above, they are more likely to be telling the truth regarding a blackout.

The Role of the Forensic Medical Examiner/Forensic Nurse in DFC Cases

When an alleged victim does report to the police, it is important that forensic protocols be strictly adhered to in order that if a prosecution is brought forward, the forensic evidence is suitable for admission to court. Once the subject has undergone initial interview, a qualified medic (medical examiner, forensic nurse, or equivalent) is introduced to them in order to evaluate them and collect any evidence that may be present depending on the crime that has been committed. If the subject appears to be intoxicated or makes an allegation of drink spiking, it is of upmost importance to obtain blood and urine samples as soon as possible following protocols for whatever jurisdiction the subject is in. Failure to take these samples in a timely manner may result in insufficient evidence being available for prosecution.

In sexual assault cases, the subject will be asked to consent to a full forensic examination, and therefore consent is required before this can commence. If the examiner feels that the subject is under the influence of drugs or alcohol, a sleeping off period may be required until the examiner feels that the subject is consenting of free will. As with drug driving, the examiner may form an opinion as to what type of drugs are in the system of the subject at the time of the examination. This may assist the laboratory in their analysis, particularly where samples are time limited, as is the case with certain drugs even if the subject reports the day after the alleged offense.

In other types of DFC, although a full body examination may not be required, there may be other types of evidence that can be collected, including hairs and fibers and control samples from the subject for elimination purposes. The same criteria regarding the collection of samples for toxicological analysis apply, and these samples must be collected as soon as possible after the alleged crime has been reported.

Samples Types in DFC

In many jurisdictions, it still remains a standard practice to only take urine samples in DFC cases, particularly, if the crime is reported after more than 24 h have passed. With urine, "at time" intoxication is impossible to prove and if drugs are still in the system, the expert testimony of the police officers and medical staff who interacted with the alleged victim will be critical. Although toxicological evidence is still required on urine, the interpretation provided by the toxicologist for drugs will be limited.

However, many drugs, including prescription and illicit drugs, may still remain in the blood stream for up to and

exceeding 24 h. This is dependent on the plasma elimination half-life of the drug. In addition, many of the drugs utilized have active metabolites that may have longer half-lives and therefore prolong the effects of the drug. All drugs, however, have metabolites and an understanding of the metabolic profile of a drug is an important consideration for a reporting forensic toxicologist and for toxicology laboratories when they are designing analytical protocols. For example, diazepam has a plasma half-life of 16–40 h, but its primary metabolite desmethyldiazepam has a half-life of 40–100 h. The metabolite is therefore detected not only for a longer period of time but also shows a much higher degree of interindividual variation. A selection of the drugs detected in alleged cases of sexual assault in the United Kingdom between January 2000 and December 2003 are summarized in **Table 1** along with their usual elimination half-lives.

Recently, the United Nations Office of Drugs and Crime (UNODC) has produced guidelines for the forensic analysis of drugs in DFC, including advice on the timely collection of blood, urine, and hair samples; instrumentation requirements; and interpretation of results.

Although as noted above, some of the drugs have long half-lives, the dose required for effect also has to be taken into consideration when evaluating the toxicological evidence. In addition, drugs with similar half-lives need not be detected for the same length of time because of differences in dosing and in other pharmacological parameters including volume of distribution. An example of this regarding parent drugs is for diazepam and flunitrazepam. Diazepam has a half-life of between 16 and 40 h, and flunitrazepam has a half-life of 20–40 h. The half-lives of the drugs are comparable. However, diazepam is usually dosed at 5–20 mg, whereas flunitrazepam is effective at doses of only 1–2 mg meaning a method for the therapeutic

Table 1   Selected DFC drugs from the UK casework and their half-lives

Drugs (number of cases/spikings)	Half-life [range (mean)]	Drugs (number of cases/spikings)	Half-life [range (mean)]
Diazepam (44/3)	20–40 h	Dihydrocodeine	~4 h
Temazepam (24/6)	8–15 h	Methadone	10–25 h (15 h)
Lorazepam (5/1)	9–24 h (14 h)	Amitriptyline	9–36 h
Nitrazepam (4/1)	18–38 h (28 h)	Mirtazapine	20–40 h
Chlordiazepoxide (3)	5–30 h (15 h)	Procyclidine	8–16 h (12 h)
Lormetazepam (1/1)	~10 h	Promethazine	10–15 h
Flurazepam	2–3 h[a]	Thioridazine	10–36 h
Clobazam	10–58 h (25 h)	Phenobarbitone	90–100 h
Zopiclone	3.5–6.5 h	MDMA (47/3)	6–7 h
GHB	20–50 min (18 mg l^{-1})	Cannabis (260)	~2 h
Chlorpheniramine	(2–43 h)[b]	Cocaine (110)	0.7–1.5 h
Diphenhydramine	2.4–9.3 h	Amphetamine (23)	4–8 h
Codeine/morphine	2–4 h	Heroin (12)	2–3 h (morphine)
Dextropropoxyphene	8–24 h (15 h)	Ketamine (3)	2–3 h

[a]N-Desalkylflurazepam has a half-life of 2–5 days.
[b]Shorter half-life in children.

detection of flunitrazepam needs to be much more sensitive than a method for diazepam.

Detection of drugs in blood close to the time of the offense gives the best forensic evidence that a DFC may have taken place; however, this on its own cannot prove that a crime has occurred. Toxicological evidence is only a small part of a much bigger picture, which the law enforcement agencies and forensic scientists must put together in order to secure a conviction, if it is to be shown that a crime has been committed.

In later reporting cases, that is, cases reporting more than 48 h, although there may be drugs remaining in the subject's system, for most single-dose drugs, the levels remaining are likely to be below the detection limits of many laboratories, and therefore urine becomes the primary evidential sample. It is critical here that suitable sample preparation techniques are carried out, including hydrolysis for laboratories that do not carry out direct analyses of phase II metabolites (glucuronides and sulfates). The hydrolysis process cleaves the drug or metabolite from its conjugate allowing for direct analysis of the total drug or metabolite present in the sample. In DFC cases, this is particularly important for urinalysis of benzodiazepines.

The final sample that must be included in any discussion of DFC is hair. By their very nature, DFCs warrant hair analysis as in many cases reporting of the crime is late and conventional samples are of little or no use. Even in cases where the victim reports within 24 h of the offense, hair samples must be considered.

For hair analysis, the reporting of DFCs can be classified into three categories: immediate (within 24 h), intermediate (up to 1 week), and delayed (more than 1 week). In immediate cases, a hair sample can be taken by the medic present at the initial evaluation. This is particularly important where GHB is suspected by the victim or as a result of the initial enquiry. Assuming that all other toxicological tests are negative, this sample, along with a second sample taken 4 weeks after the initial sample, should be tested for GHB. The first sample acts as a control as GHB is an endogenous drug and endogenous levels vary from person to person with reported endogenous GHB levels from 0.35 to 1.86 ng mg^{-1}. The second sample can therefore be compared to this to evaluate the presence of GHB in this sample. The UNODC guidelines state that a hair sample should be obtained at least 4 weeks after the alleged offense to ensure any drug ingested at the time of the offense is cleared from the scalp are before collection.

In intermediate cases, again the first sample acts as a control for GHB. Hair specimens in living persons are taken by cutting close to skin at the vertex region of the scalp. As newly forming hairs take 7–10 days to reach the surface of the scalp, samples taken before 1 week postincident should not contain the drugs ingested at the time of the incident.

Drugs are incorporated into hair directly from the blood stream or from the sweat, sebaceous, and apocrine glands around the hair follicle. Thus, any drug that is present in the blood should be detectable in hair. Factors affecting the detectability of the drugs include the physicochemical properties of the drug, drug treatments (e.g., bleaching and dying), hygienic washing, the amount of drug ingested, and the time from ingestion to sample collection.

A controlled study to evaluate if GHB could be detected in hair following a single exposure showed that it was possible to determine an elevated level of GHB in the hair of the subject corresponding to the time of ingestion using 3 mm segments of hair. Similarly, documented exposure to GHB via hair analysis has since been shown and highlights the importance of a control sample when GHB ingestion is suspected.

The third category of hair is not as useful for the analysis of GHB unless enough segments of hair are available in order to evaluate the baseline level of GHB in the individual's hair. Hair in these cases is the main sample that can be utilized in order to indicate ingestion of a drug around the time of the offense. However, for all drugs that have been administered as a single dose, there is a risk of washout, and therefore the evidential value of hair is decreased. Where a drug is detected, because of interindividual variation in the growth rate, the longer the time lapse between incident and hair collection the wider the estimated time of a positive result will be.

Controlled studies to evaluate the detectability of single exposure to a drug are of paramount importance in this area of forensic toxicology. Such reports exist for a variety of drugs, including GHB, flunitrazepam, clonazepam, diazepam, alprazolam, triazolam, ketamine, and a variety of metabolites. However, the real challenge lies in the detection of single exposures to drugs, where the target drug is unknown. Several case studies regarding this are available, and the types of cases discussed include sexual assault, drink spiking, robbery, poisoning, and child neglect cases. The results indicated that the majority of drugs utilized were sedative in nature, including benzodiazepines (flunitrazepam, lorazepam, alprazolam, clonazepam, and bromazepam); GHB; zolpidem; and antidepressant, including citalopram and methadone. The only stimulant drug detected was 3,4-methylenedioxymethylamphetamine (MDMA) that fits in the category of disinhibiting CNS stimulants discussed above.

Analytical Issues in DFC

The investigation of a DFC should involve a full toxicological investigation. Screening techniques for the full range of drugs of abuse should be carried out as per the laboratories' protocols and confirmation of each positive result. Obtaining suitable samples of suitable volume is therefore critical, and in some cases, sufficient blood may not be available for complete testing and therefore analyses need to be prioritized. The medical history of the victim is therefore important, for example, if they are prescribed a benzodiazepine. It may not be necessary to carry out a benzodiazepine confirmation analysis unless there is a potential for this to contribute to the impairment of another drug, for example, alcohol.

With the increase in sensitivity and selectivity of analytical instrumentation, laboratories are becoming increasingly able to detect drugs and their metabolites for longer periods of time. The usefulness of the toxicological component of DFC investigation is therefore extending in time with drug metabolites being detected more than 10 days postincident. This information should be made public so that victims of these crimes realize that it may still be useful to report, and the investigators can encourage victims to provide samples for longer time frames than the 24–48 h currently utilized in many jurisdictions.

Interpretation of Toxicological Results in DFC

Of final note is the importance of correct interpretation of data obtained. Reporting toxicologists must have an awareness of the pharmacology of the drugs involved and remember that absence of evidence does not always equate to lack of a crime. By understanding how long a drug is present in a sample along with the limitation of the instrumentation available, a fair interpretation of the data should be possible.

Regarding hair analysis, the limitations regarding precision of time frame, issues regarding washout, etc. should be acknowledged.

However, the toxicologist should also remember they cannot prove who administered the drug and the exact time that it was administered. It is possible that an alleged victim could have taken a sedating drug in order to fool the system and wrongly incriminate someone or in order to calm their nerves following an actual offense. The toxicologist can only report the results they have found and provide an interpretation based on the facts available to them at the time of reporting.

Conclusion

Drug-facilitated crimes need to be investigated in terms of both the reported crime, for example, sexual assault and the toxicological evidence. Owing to the sedating and amnesic properties of many of the drugs found in these crimes, they can be late-reporting cases, and thus, an understanding of the properties of the drugs and the limitations of analytical instrumentation are important considerations. Worldwide studies indicate that the most prevalent drug in cases of this type is alcohol and that a wide range of sedative drugs can be used and are found in toxicological samples. The use of hair in these

cases is becoming of increased importance and therefore this matrix should be collected where possible.

> *See also:* **Toxicology/Alcohol:** Alcohol: Interpretation; **Toxicology/Drugs of Abuse:** Drug-Impaired Driving; **Toxicology:** Behavioral Toxicology; Methods of Analysis—Confirmatory Testing; Methods of Analysis – Initial Testing.

Further Reading

Baselt, R.C., 2008. Disposition of Toxic Drugs and Chemicals in Man, eighth ed. Biomedical Publications, Foster City.

Beynon, C.M., McVeigh, C., McVeigh, J., Leavey, C., Bellis, M.A., 2008. The involvement of drugs and alcohol in drug-facilitated sexual assault: A systematic review of the evidence. Trauma, Violence & Abuse 9 (3), 178–188.

Brown, K., 2001. Forensic examination of sexual assault victims. In: Hazelwood, R.R., Burgess, A.W. (Eds.), Practical Aspects of Rape Investigation, third ed. CRC Press, Boca Raton, FL, pp. 365–398.

Cooper, G.A.A., 2011. Hair testing is taking root. Review article. Annals of Clinical Biochemistry 48, 515–530.

Drummer, O.H., 2001. The Forensic Pharmacology of Drugs of Abuse. Arnold, London.

Forsman, M., Nyström, I., Roman, M., et al., 2009. Urinary detection times and excretion patterns of flunitrazepam and its metabolites after a single dose. Journal of Analytical Toxicology 33, 491–501.

Goulle, J.P., Cheze, M., Pepin, G., 2003. Determination of endogenous levels of GHB in human hair. Are there possibilities for the identification of GHB administration through hair analysis in cases of drug-facilitated sexual assault? Journal of Analytical Toxicology 27, 574–580.

Hall, J., Goodall, E.A., Moore, T., 2005. Alleged drug facilitated sexual assault (DFSA) in Ireland from 1999 to 2005. A study of blood alcohol levels. Journal of Forensic and Legal Medicine 15 (8), 497–504.

Jones, A.W., Eklund, A., Kronstrand, R., 2009. Concentration-time profiles of gamma-hydroxybutyrate in blood after recreational doses are best described by zero-order rather than first-order kinetics. Journal of Analytical Toxicology 33 (6), 332–335.

Kintz, P., Cirimele, V., Jamey, C., Ludes, B., 2003. Testing for GHB in hair by GC/MS/MS after a single exposure. Application to document sexual assault. Journal of Forensic Sciences 48 (1), 1–6.

Kronstrand, R., Scott, K., 2006. Drug incorporation into hair. In: Kintz, P. (Ed.), Analytical and Practical Aspects of Drug Testing in Hair Forensic Science Series. CRC Press, Boca Raton, FL, pp. 1–24.

LeBeau, M., 2008. Guidance for improved detection of drugs used to facilitate crimes. Therapeutic Drug Monitoring 30 (2), 229–233.

Moffat, A.C., Osselton, M.D., Widdop, B. (Eds.), 2004. Clarke's Analysis of Drugs and Poisons, third ed. Pharmaceutical Press, London.

Scott, K.S., 2009. The use of hair as a toxicological tool in DFC casework. Science & Justice 49, 250–253.

Scott-Ham, M., Burton, E.C., 2006. A study of blood and urine alcohol concentrations in cases of alleged drug-facilitated sexual assault in the United Kingdom over a three-year period. Journal of Clinical Forensic Medicine 3 (13), 107–111.

Relevant Websites

http://www.homeoffice.gov.uk/publications/alcohol-drugs/drugs/acmd1/drug-facilitated-sexual-assault/ACMDDFSA.pdf?view=Binary—Advisory Council on the Misuse of Drugs. Drug Facilitated Sexual Assault. 2007.

http://www.druginfo.adf.org.au/drug-facts/ghb—Australian Drug Foundation.

http://www.ncjrs.gov/pdffiles1/nij/grants/212000.pdf—Estimate of the incidence of drug facilitated sexual assault in the US.

http://www.unodc.org/unodc/en/publications.html—Guidelines for the forensic analysis of drugs facilitating sexual assault and other criminal acts.

http://www.homeoffice.gov.uk/rds/crimstats04.html—Home Office Criminal Statistics 2004 England and Wales.

http://www.cesar.umd.edu/cesar/drugs/rohypnol.pdf—Maryland University, Center for Substance Abuse Misuse (CESAR).

www.soht.org—Society of Hair Testing.

www.soft-tox.org—Society of Forensic Toxicologists.

http://www.who.int/violenceprevention/interpersonal_violence_and_illicit_drug_use.pdf—World Health Organisation: Interpersonal violence and illicit drugs.

Drug-Impaired Driving

A Verstraete and S-A Legrand, Ghent University, Ghent, Belgium

Glossary

BAC Blood–alcohol concentrations
DRE Drug recognition evaluation
DRUID Driving under the influence of alcohol, drug, and medicines
DUID Driving under the influence of drugs
GBL Gamma-butyrolactone
GC–MS Gas chromatography–mass spectrometry
GHB Gamma-hydroxybutyrate
LC–MS Liquid chromatography–mass spectrometry
OF Oral fluid
SNRI Selective serotonin–norepinephrine reuptake inhibitor
SSRI Selective serotonin reuptake inhibitors
THC Tetrahydrocannabinol

Introduction

The road transport system is one of the most hazardous and most expensive in terms of human lives lost in the world. The consumption of psychoactive substances such as alcohol, drugs, and certain medicines is likely to endanger the driver's ability to drive safely. Impaired driving is still one of the major causes for road accidents or road deaths in Europe and elsewhere in the world. Driving is a complex task, requiring the cooperation of several different cognitive and psychomotor functions at once. Crashes can be the consequence of many different factors, which can be classified into three categories: the road, the vehicle, and the driver. A crash is rarely attributable to only one factor; therefore, it is very difficult to precisely determine the contribution of alcohol and/or drugs in a collision.

Influence of Drugs on Performance

Research on the effects of drugs on performance can be broadly separated into experimental and epidemiological studies. In experimental research, different doses of a certain drug are administered to volunteers, and the effects on performance are measured and compared to those of a placebo and on a positive control. Epidemiological studies give information concerning the effects associated with the use of drugs by examining the incidence of drugs in various populations.

The possible effects of several drug classes are described (see **Table 1**). The reader should keep in mind that the effect and the duration depend on many factors such as the dose, the route of administration, and the individual characteristics and susceptibility of the user.

Alcohol

Alcohol is a central nervous system depressant. Many studies have already been performed to determine the effects of acute alcohol ingestion on cognitive functions and driving performance. These studies found that numerous driving-related skills are degraded beginning at low blood–alcohol concentrations (BACs). With increasing BAC, reaction time is increased and coordination is decreased. The main effects of alcohol on the driving skills are slowed reaction time, poor judgment, impaired vision and hearing, poor coordination, and a false sense of confidence. Its toxic effects vary considerably from person to person and are influenced by variables such as gender, body weight, rate of consumption (time), and total amount consumed. When a certain tolerance has developed, despite feeling unaffected by alcohol, a person may be over the $0.5 \, g \, l^{-1}$ limit and have slowed reactions, resulting in impaired driving skills.

Cannabis

Cannabis has both hallucinogenic and central nervous system-depressant properties. Cannabis acutely reduces some cognitive and psychomotor skills, such as equilibrium, coordination, tracking ability, perception, motor impulsivity, and vigilance, and slows reaction time. These effects are mostly dose dependent. Cannabis can also have an effect on behavior. The results of experiments in laboratory settings are contradictory, while in some driving studies (with rather low doses) users are aware of the impairment and often compensate their driving style by driving more slowly, overtaking less, or keeping longer distances from other vehicles. Nevertheless, the driver is still

Table 1   Influence of drugs on performance.

| | Side effect | | |
	Acute	Chronic	Combination
Alcohol	Slowed reaction time, poor judgment, impaired vision and hearing, poor coordination and a false sense of confidence, risk-taking behavior.	Slowed reflexes, slower information processing, significant loss of cognitive functions. When drinking regularly, one will be able to drink larger quantities before feeling or appearing intoxicated (tolerance).	The sedative effects of both alcohol and sedative medications can enhance each other. Various combinations definitely impair the driving performances.
Cannabis	Mydriasis, dry mouth, anxiety, decrements in cognitive and psychomotor functions, impairment of the road tracking ability (accuracy to steer a car), hazard perception, increase in lateral position variability.	Defects in cognitive functions and psychomotor functions, amotivational behavior.	Additive or even synergistic relation with negative effects of alcohol. In combination with cocaine: additional impairment compared to the use of cannabis or cocaine alone. Cannabis tends to increase the intensity of the performance impairment produced by alcohol.
Stimulants	Lack of coordination, sensory disturbances, disorientation, restlessness, lapses of attention, fatigue, difficulty reacting appropriately to safely control a vehicle, increased risk taking, overconfidence in driving skills, drowsiness, or rebound fatigue (as the effects wear off). Positive effects and negative effects on cognition and psychomotor performance.	Defects in cognitive functions, increased impulsivity, and depression.	Alcohol reinforces negative effects and can cause some additional defects. Some effects of alcohol can be diminished.
Narcotic analgesics	Miosis, analgesia, psychomotor and cognitive decrements, euphoria ("rush"), impaired judgment coordination, visual disturbances or dizziness, blurred vision, impaired visual fields and nighttime vision, drowsy driving.	Cognitive and psychomotor decrements, depression, anxiety.	Combination of narcotic analgesics and other CNS depressants (including alcohol) has additive depressant effects.
Central nervous system depressants	Impairment of mental and motor functions, drowsiness and light-headedness, sedation, and anticholinergic effects. The level of impairment varies from person to person and between different medications within the same therapeutic class.	Withdrawal symptoms, adverse effects on mood, and cognitive functions.	Alcohol can have an additive effect on sedation and psychomotor impairment.
GHB	Signs of impairment are consistent with those of a CNS depressant, including erratic driving (weaving, swerving, ignoring road signs), confusion, slowed reaction time, increased risk taking, unresponsiveness, tunnel vision, lack of balance, unsteady coordination, and varying states of wakefulness.	The long-term effects of GHB use are unclear. As the effects of GHB are similar to those of sedative drugs, it is possible for the user to become physically and psychologically dependent.	The adverse effects of GHB may be greatly increased by the use of alcohol. Alcohol is particularly dangerous in combination with GHB, as it can be difficult to control the dose.

unable to completely compensate for the loss of capability in some psychomotor skills. When combined with alcohol, the effects appear to be considerably greater than would be expected. Other studies have found that tetrahydrocannabinol (THC) consumption significantly impairs the subjects' performance in driving tests at whatever dose used. Some research suggested that perceptual motor speed and accuracy, two very important parameters of driving ability, seem to be impaired only immediately after cannabis consumption, while other studies found data suggesting a more lasting toxic effect on the central nervous system, which persists even after all drug residues have left the system.

Stimulants (Amphetamine, Methamphetamine, and Cocaine)

Stimulants produce a number of effects on drivers, which range from the acute phase (shortly after drug consumption) to the postacute phase, when drug withdrawal or abstinence can be an issue. Stimulants cause a strong central stimulation and euphoria. The user thinks he can do everything and will take more risks, but after some time (hours or days depending on the pattern of use), the subject is exhausted and falls asleep (crash phase). Tests in driving simulators revealed that the intake of amphetamine causes an overall decrease in the accuracy of simulated driving by inducing problems such as incorrect signaling, failing to stop at a red traffic light, and slow reaction times. During the crash phase following the use of amphetamines, the subject feels very tired, unable to combat sleep, and depressed. This phase can last for several days. The desired effects of cocaine are similar to those of the amphetamines, but the onset is slower and the duration is longer. The use of a combination of alcohol and cocaine decreases psychomotor impairment and improves performance on cognitive tests when compared to the use of alcohol alone. However, cocaine also decreases the subjective feeling of drunkenness caused by alcohol and can reinforce detrimental effects of other drugs such as cannabis. The combination of cannabis and cocaine causes additional impairment to the use of cannabis or cocaine alone. Conversely, alcohol can reinforce the negative effects of the stimulants and can cause some additional defects.

Narcotic Analgesics

The narcotic analgesics include the drugs heroin, methadone, and morphine. Narcotic analgesics are used in medicine as strong analgesics, for relief of severe or chronic pain. Some, for example, methadone, are also used to treat addiction to opioids. When these substances are used occasionally under the guidance of a physician, they can be a safe and effective pain reliever. Regular use of narcotic drugs can be addictive, causing withdrawal symptoms. The user of narcotic analgesics generally feels intense euphoria ("rush") accompanied by

a warm flushing of the skin, dry mouth, and heavy extremities, and alternates between a wakeful and drowsy state. Tolerance to the effects of opioids is well documented, and there is some evidence that people who become stabilized on moderate doses of opioids have tolerance to some of the impairing effects of the drugs.

Central Nervous System Depressants

This category includes drugs such as benzodiazepines (e.g., diazepam and temazepam), sedative hypnotics (e.g., zolpidem and zopiclone), some antidepressants, muscle relaxants, and some antihistamines. These substances have a legitimate therapeutic use. Discussing the potential effect of these substances on the driving abilities becomes difficult because sometimes, in some individual cases, poor compliance of the above-mentioned therapeutic substances can lead to even more dangerous situations on the road than when the substance/medicine is used properly. For example, some studies showed that a depressed driver, treated with an impairing drug such as an antidepressant, is a better driver than an untreated driver.

Benzodiazepines are used primarily for rapid relief of anxiety, muscle relaxation, sedation, and hypnosis (sleeping aid), and for their anticonvulsant effects. The most frequently encountered adverse effects are impairment of mental and motor functions, drowsiness, and light-headedness. Benzodiazepines cause impairment ranging from mild to substantial depending on the half-life of the drug and their use. Studies have shown that short-acting benzodiazepines without active metabolites are less impairing than long-acting benzodiazepines since the effects do not persist much longer than several hours. When combined with other substances, especially alcohol, the risk of being involved in a (serious or fatal) collision is increased. It should be noted that with regular use, tolerance develops reducing the degree of impairment.

Antihistamines are drugs used to treat allergic reactions. Depending on the distribution of the drug in the body, the adverse effects can include sedation, digestive tract troubles, and anticholinergic effects. The antihistamines are divided into first-generation and second-generation histamines. The second-generation drugs are generally nonsedating, although exceptions exist. Alcohol can have an additive effect on sedation and psychomotor impairment, particularly when combined with more sedating first-generation drugs such as diphenhydramine, doxylamine, and the pheniramines.

Antidepressants are substances commonly prescribed for mood disorders, anxiety, and sometimes pain. There are first- and second-generation antidepressants and an atypical group. The second-generation drugs, selective serotonin reuptake inhibitors (SSRIs) or selective serotonin–norepinephrine reuptake inhibitor (SNRI), are associated with fewer adverse effects compared to the first generation ones, mainly because of greater selectivity. Adverse effects encountered with first-generation antidepressants are anticholinergic effects (blurred vision) and sedation, while second-generation antidepressants seem not to cause major impairment of cognition or psychomotor skills. Consequently, SSRIs and SNRIs are generally regarded as behaviorally safe drugs, whereas first-generation antidepressants are classified as impairing, particularly because of their sedative effects.

New Psychoactive Designer Drugs

The popularity of this group of relatively new drugs, such as mephedrone, piperazines, gamma-butyrolactone (GBL) or gamma-hydroxybutyrate (GHB), and synthetic cannabinoids, has increased over the past years. Except for those on GHB, very few data are available to establish the prevalence of these new drugs as well as to consider the effect of these drugs on driving or road safety in general. From what is known of the chemical structures of the drugs, the effects of these new drugs on road safety may be inferred by reference to research on similar drugs.

Chronic Effect of Drugs

Chronic use refers to regular (often daily) use over some days to weeks. The effects of drugs on performance can not only be the consequence of the acute effects of the drugs (including the "crash" phase after drug use) but also of the impairment caused by withdrawal or by chronic use.

The effects of cannabis usually last for some hours, but in high users, they can last for up to 24 h, indicating that a person using cannabis in the evening can still experience residual impairment the following day. Chronic use of cannabis also affects driving performance, even when intoxication is no longer present. Very heavy chronic use of marijuana is associated with persistent decrements in neurocognitive performance even after 28 days of abstinence.

The chronic use of amphetamines causes depression and has obvious negative effects on cognitive and psychomotor skills, which last longer than the period of intoxication and are often correlated to the severity of use. It is also linked to psychiatric problems, such as depression, hallucinations, schizophrenia, and paranoia. The use of 3,4-methylenedioxy methylamphetamine (MDMA) (ecstasy) can cause a decrease in attention, short-term and long-term memory, verbal memory, visuospatial skills, executive functioning, and prediction of object movement under divided attention. Chronic ecstasy use can lead to higher impulsivity.

Chronic use of cocaine can lead to significant cognitive deficits, such as impaired psychomotor performance, impulsive behavior, and even psychosis.

Finally, the withdrawal symptoms of certain medicines (e.g., venlafaxine and paroxetine (antidepressants)) can cause serious impairment due to adverse effects on mood and cognitive functions.

Epidemiology and Crash Risk

Prevalence of Drugs in the General Driving Population or in a Subset of Drivers

The prevalence of drugs in the general driving population can be estimated by means of roadside surveys, in which samples of randomly stopped drivers are analyzed. About 1–6% of drivers stopped during roadside surveys in Europe tested positive for drugs in oral fluid (OF). Large differences in prevalence between countries exist. Despite differences in methodology in studies, cannabis is the most frequently detected drug followed by benzodiazepines. The combination of alcohol and drugs is found in about 0.3–1.3% of the general driving population. The latest National Roadside Survey of Alcohol and Drug use conducted in 2007 in the United States found a prevalence of 16% drug-positive at night when either OF or blood tests were used.

Studies have shown that drugs are found in 19–50% of drivers injured in a traffic crash, 6–35% of drivers killed in a traffic crash, and 55–99% of drivers suspected of driving under the influence of drugs (DUID). These figures vary widely due to regional differences and variations in methodology. For example, in some studies, blood was analyzed, while others used urine or OF. The variation in detection times in these matrices can influence the results. Furthermore, there are differences in the types of drugs analyzed and the kind (and sensitivity) of analysis method used. A large-scale epidemiological study called DRUID (driving under the influence of alcohol, drug, and medicines) recently analyzed the prevalence of alcohol and other psychoactive substances in seriously injured drivers in six different European countries with a standardized study design. Alcohol ($\geq 0.1\,\mathrm{g\,l^{-1}}$) was the most common finding, with a range between 18% (Lithuania) and 42% (Belgium), followed by THC (range 0.5%—Lithuania and 7.6%—Belgium) and benzodiazepines (0%—The Netherlands and 10%—Finland). Again, the most prevalent drug found was cannabis. Other important drugs were amphetamines, benzodiazepines, and opiates.

Risks Associated with DUID

Crash risk can be determined by comparing the prevalence of a certain drug in the general driving population to the prevalence in drivers who were involved in a traffic crash. Several studies have already shown that an increasing BAC is associated with increasing crash risk. Other studies have calculated the crash risk associated with other psychoactive substances. The impaired motorists, methods of roadside testing, and assessment for licensing study in the Netherlands revealed that drivers under the influence of benzodiazepines alone have a relatively higher risk for an accident, which is three times greater than the risk of a drug-free driver. The highest risk was associated with the use of drugs in combination with alcohol ($\geq 0.8\,g\,l^{-1}$), namely, a 179 times higher risk! A study in Canada, for example, showed that the crash risk associated with driving under the influence of cocaine, benzodiazepines, and cannabis is, respectively, 5, 2.5, and 2.2 times higher than that of a person who has not consumed these drugs.

Some studies have estimated the risk of being responsible for a traffic crash while DUID. The results indicate that increasing BACs are associated with increasing crash risk. They also show that driving under the influence of cannabis increases the risk of being responsible for a crash. The risk increases with increasing cannabis concentration in blood, indicating a causal relationship between cannabis and crashes. In a French study on cannabis intoxication and fatal road crashes, cannabis detection was associated with increased risk of responsibility (odds ratio = 3.32, 95% confidence interval 2.63–4.18). The risk of being responsible for a fatal accident when driving under the influence of cannabis and alcohol is approximately equal to the multiplication of the risks when driving under the influence of cannabis or alcohol alone. Responsibility analyses have also shown that benzodiazepines and cocaine are associated with increased risks of being responsible for an accident and that the risk is higher for a combination of alcohol and benzodiazepines than that for benzodiazepines alone.

The association between the use of benzodiazepines and the risk of road traffic crashes has now been documented with consistent results in several studies, but the effect of other medicines has been less assessed and the results of available studies are often inconsistent. A recent French study investigated the association between prescription medicines and the risk of road traffic crashes and estimated the attributable fraction. Medicines were grouped according to the four risk levels of the French classification system (from 0 (no risk) to 3 (high risk)). The study showed that users of level 2 (odds ratio = 1.31) and level 3 (odds ratio = 1.25) prescription medicines were at higher risk of being responsible for a crash. The fraction of road traffic crashes attributable to level 2 and 3 medicines was 3.3% (2.7–3.9%).

Legislation

Each developed country has its specific legislation to deal with DUID. There is a lack of uniformity in the way in which nations approach the drugged driving problem. Generally, there are two major types of DUID legislation, namely, "impairment" legislation and "per se" legislation.

Impairment Legislation

In impairment legislation, the prosecution must demonstrate that the driver was impaired, not fit to drive, or "under the influence." The analysis of drugs in body fluids only provides corroborating evidence as to the cause of the impairment. This kind of legislation is subjective and requires the assessment by a medical doctor or a specially trained police officer. As a consequence, many of the countries with this kind of legislation experience difficulties in obtaining convictions. For this reason, and in analogy with alcohol, many countries have introduced "per se" laws. Examples of countries with "impairment" legislation are Norway and the United Kingdom.

"Per Se" Legislation

A "per se" law prohibits driving if drugs are present in blood, serum, plasma, or OF above a certain threshold. Since the prosecution does not have to prove that the driver was impaired, this kind of legislation facilitates the enforcement process. The threshold concentrations, or cutoffs, used are analytical detection limits, meaning that any detectable concentration of a drug constitutes an offense. Therefore, these laws are sometimes called *zero-tolerance* laws. Presently, Germany, Belgium, Sweden, France, Finland, Luxembourg, Switzerland, Denmark, a number of Australian states, and 17 states of the United States have introduced "per se" legislation in addition to the "impairment" legislation. The analytical cutoffs in some European countries are given in **Table 2**.

There is no consensus on the analytical cutoffs between the different countries. This lack of consensus can be partially attributed to the use of different biological matrices (serum in Germany, plasma in Belgium, and whole blood in Australia, France, Sweden, and Switzerland) and the different consequences of a positive result: for example, in Belgium there is a criminal sanction, while in Germany there is an administrative sanction. The main challenge in establishing legal regulations combating drugged driving is to define clear rules for detecting and sanctioning an impaired driver. New (analytical) technologies are increasingly more sensitive and can detect very small quantities of substances. Positive results in per se laws do not necessarily prove impairment due to their presence, that is, when an illicit or medicinal drug was consumed many hours before and psychoactive effects are no longer present.

Two-Tier System

Per se limits are combined with an impairment approach. This system combines the advantages of the two legal regulations. For a limited list of drugs, the per se approach allows easy prosecution, and the impairment legislation is used to cover

Table 2   Matrix, legislation, and cutoffs ($\mu g\ l^{-1}$) per substance applied in each country.

Countries	BE	DK	FI	DE	LUX	PL	PT	SE	CH
Matrix	PL	WB	WB	Se	PL	WB	WB	WB	WB
Legislation	I + P	I + P	I + P	I + P	I + P	PER	PER	I + P	I + P
THC	1	1	1	1	2	2	3	0.3	1.5[a]
THC COOH				5		50	5		
Amphetamine	25	20	25	25	50	50	5	30	15[a]
Methamphetamine		20	25	25	50	50	5		15[a]
3,4-Methylenedioxymethamphetamine	25	20	25	25	50	50	5	20	15[a]
3,4-Methylenedioxyamphetamine		20	25	25	50	50	5	20	
3,4-Methylenedioxyethylamphetamine		20	25	25	50	50	5	20	15[a]
Cocaine	25	20	10	10	50	50	5	20	15[a]
Benzoylecgonine	25		10	75	50	50	5	20	
Morphine	10	10	2.5	10	20	20	5	5	15[a]

[a]+ 30%, in order to take into account the measurement uncertainty. Countries: BE, Belgium; DE, Germany; DK, Denmark; FI, Finland; LUX, Luxembourg; PL, Poland; PT, Portugal; SE, Sweden; CH, Switzerland; Matrix: PL, plasma; Se, serum; WB, whole blood; Type of legislation: I, impairment; P, per se; I + P, two-tier.

less frequently used drugs and other special cases like drug combinations and the effects of drug withdrawal.

Detection of Drugs in Drivers

Checklists for Impaired Driving

In many countries, checklists have been developed to standardize reporting of clinical signs of recent drug consumption, which are used by police officers (or physicians) to document that the driver is fit or not fit to drive. In the United States, the drug recognition evaluator (DRE) is a police officer trained to recognize impairment in drivers under the influence of drugs other than, or in addition to, alcohol. The Los Angeles Police Department originated the program in the early 1970s. DRE conducts a detailed, diagnostic examination of persons arrested or suspected of drug-impaired driving or similar offenses using a 12-step protocol. On the basis of the results of the evaluation, the DRE forms an expert opinion on the following: (1) Is the person impaired and, if so, is the person able to operate a vehicle safely? (2) Is the impairment due to an injury, illness, or other medical complication, or is it drug related? (3) Which category or combination of categories of drugs is the most likely source of the impairment? An example of a checklist is given in **Figure 1**.

Roadside Detection

For many years, police officers involved in road safety have expressed the need for a rapid and reliable roadside screening test for drugs, similar to an alcohol breathalyzer. This would help determine which drivers have to provide a blood sample or it would help take immediate administrative measures like confiscating the driver's license or impounding the vehicle. As illegal drugs are not released in measurable amounts in the breath, roadside drug testing must be based on other specimens. The use of OF as an alternative matrix for the detection of drugs of abuse has increased steadily over the last decade. Roadside OF testing to detect drug driving has already been introduced in the legislation of Belgium, France, Spain, and several Australian states.

The experience of the police has shown that performing on-site urine screening at the roadside is very complicated, often potentially intrusive or vulnerable to adulteration. In addition, a positive urine test may indicate exposure to a drug several days previously for long half-life drugs. Detection of drugs in OF indicates more recent drug use, and there is some correlation with impairment. On-site screening for drugs of abuse in OF provides a relatively quick and increasingly effective means of detecting if a motorist has consumed drugs or medicines. Nevertheless, a positive OF on-site screening result can only be interpreted as past use or exposure to drugs; it does not indicate impairment.

In the Rosita-2 study (performed between 2003 and 2005), the analytical evaluation of the cannabis tests showed a sensitivity and specificity in the range of 0–74% and 70–100%, respectively. In the DRUID project, eight on-site tests were evaluated but none of the devices performed well (above 80% for sensitivity, specificity, and accuracy) (**Figure 2**). Sensitivity and specificity in the range of 23–81% and 88–100%, respectively, for the different drug classes were found.

Despite the rather low sensitivity of the drug-testing devices, the experience in the state of Victoria in Australia shows that random roadside testing of OF of drivers for methamphetamine, ecstasy, and cannabis has a deterrent effect. The percentage of positive drug tests has decreased over the years

CHECKLIST DETECTION ILLEGAL DRUGS © SWOV, 2006

Survey session No. ..., Day ...., Date ...., Time span...............
Police observer: .... (police team ....) Subject No. .....

1. Subject gender: O male   O female

2. Signs of impairment
    Observation at some distance when subject enters and leaves mobile research unit:
        O unsteady on one's feet, swaggering (opiates)
        O uncoordinated movements (opiates)
        O drowsy, sleepy (opiates)
        O euphoria (opiates, XTC, amphetamine, cocaine)
        O not understanding instructions (opiates)
        O incoherent speech (opiates)
        O chattering (XTC, amphetamine, cocaine)
        O slurred speech (THC)
        O low, rasping voice (opiates)
        O scratching one's face (opiates)
        O trembling (XTC, amphetamine, cocaine)
        O shaking leg (XTC, amphetamine, cocaine)
        O excited, aggressive behaviour (amphetamine, cocaine)

    Observation at close range before and during breath test for alcohol:
        O bloodshot eyes (THC, XTC, amphetamine, cocaine)
        O red nostrils (cocaine)
        O trembling eyelids (XTC, amphetamine, cocaine)
        O sniffing (cocaine)
        O undue perspiring (opiates)
        O swallowing (THC, opiates, XTC, amphetamine, cocaine)
        O smell of hash (THC)
        O pinpoint pupils: <3.0 mm (opiates)
        O dilated pupils: >6.5 mm (XTC, amphetamine, cocaine, sometimes THC)

3. Breath test for alcohol; result (BAC) .... g/l (in two decimals)

4. Question (while waiting for breath test result):
    Did you during the past 24 hours use hash, weed or other illegal drugs?
        O no

        O yes, namely:...
        Name of medicine, if used:...(checklist
benzos!)

5. Test pupil reaction to light (only if pupils are dilated and BAC is below 0.2 g/l):
        O normal reaction

        O slowed reaction (XTC, amphetamine, cocaine, THC)

6. Police officer's final judgement about the use of impairing drugs other than alcohol
        O did not use

        O did use; substance: ....

        O in doubt between use or not, because:..

SEE OVERLEAF FOR SOME IMPORTANT REMARKS

Figure 1   An example of a checklist to detect illegal drug use.

2005–09 (from 2.6% in 2005 to 0.9% in 2009). Also, the prevalence of drugs found in killed drivers slightly decreased (2005: 40%; 2009: about 32%), but the target drugs decreased more rapidly (24% in 2005 to 16% in 2006).

It is possible that future developments could lead to on-site screening of capillary blood obtained by a finger prick and confirmation of the presence/absence of drugs by the analysis of dried blood spots. Possible advantages of this approach

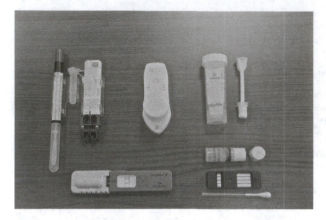

Figure 2 Some examples of on-site drug-testing devices; from the upper left corner and going clockwise: Mavand Rapid STAT, Innovacon OrAlert, Varian OraLab, Cozart DDS 806, and DrugWipe 6S.

would be the easy transportation (no need for refrigeration or shipping on dry ice), the stability of parent substances at ambient temperature, and less risk of loss of sample (e.g., breakage of glass tube of blood) or of infection.

Evidentiary Analysis

Blood is considered to be the best matrix for confirmation analysis because the presence of drugs in blood corresponds best to recent use and impairment. In many countries with per se legislation, the only legally allowed evidence for DUID is confirmation of the presence of drugs in blood. The most widely used method is gas chromatography–mass spectrometry (GC–MS) because of its sensitivity and specificity. However, the procedure is labor intensive and time-consuming, as extraction and derivatization are necessary for sample preparation. Therefore, liquid chromatography–(tandem) mass spectrometry (LC–MS/MS) procedures have been introduced for different classes of drugs for confirmatory analyses or even for screening and confirmation in one step. Several laboratories have developed methods that detect a large series of different drugs in one step in a small sample volume.

In Germany, Italy, and other countries, hair analysis is used for (re)granting license to drug-dependent persons. The hair samples are first screened by immunoassay and positives are confirmed by chromatographic techniques. The major practical advantage of hair testing is its longer detection window, which is weeks to months, depending on the length of hair shaft analyzed (hair grows at a rate of approximately 1 cm per month). Hair analysis can also be used for monitoring alcohol abstinence, by quantitating different markers like ethyl glucuronide and/or fatty acid ethyl esters. Other advantages of hair are its stability and ease of transportation.

Conclusion

There is an increasing knowledge regarding the influence of drugs on performance and the prevalence of drugs other than alcohol in road traffic. Experimental and epidemiological studies clearly show that many drugs can have a detrimental effect on driving performance. These negative effects are more pronounced when drugs are combined with alcohol. DUID is associated with increased crash risks and increased risk of being responsible for a traffic crash. These risks increase even more when drugs are taken in combination with alcohol compared to when drugs are taken alone.

There is a clear move toward "per se" legislation, although some countries at this time have decided to stay with impairment legislation. The detection of drivers under the influence of drugs can be done by the police by means of screening tests. The interest in OF screening tests has grown significantly. Studies, however, have shown that the currently available on-site devices lack sensitivity, but they are steadily improving. More recent methods developed for confirmation analysis use LC–MS/MS.

See also: **Forensic Medicine/Clinical:** Traffic Injuries and Deaths; **Investigations:** Collection and Chain of Evidence; **Legal:** Forensic Laboratory Reports; Legal Aspects of Forensic Science; Legal Systems: Adversarial and Inquisitorial; When Science Changes, How Does Law Respond; **Management/Quality in Forensic Science:** Certification; Principles of Quality Assurance; **Methods:** Gas Chromatography; Gas Chromatography–Mass Spectrometry; Liquid Chromatography–Mass Spectrometry; Mass Spectrometry; **Toxicology:** Behavioral Toxicology; Interpretation of Results; Methods of Analysis—Confirmatory Testing; Methods of Analysis—Initial Testing; Pharmacology and Mechanism of Action of Drugs; Postmortem Toxicology: Artifacts; Toxicology: Overview and Applications; **Toxicology/Alcohol:** Alcohol: Interpretation; Alcohol: Postmortem; Blood; Breath Alcohol; Urine and Other Body Fluids; **Toxicology/Drugs of Abuse:** Blood; Postmortem Blood; Validation of Twelve Chemical Spot Tests for the Detection of Drugs of Abuse.

Further Reading

Berghaus, G., Ramaekers, J.G., Drummer, O.H., 2007. Demands on scientific studies in different fields of forensic medicine and forensic sciences. Traffic medicine – impaired driver: alcohol, drugs, diseases. Forensic Science International 165 (2–3), 233–237.

Bolla, K.I., Brown, K., Eldreth, D., Tate, K., Cadet, J.L., 2002. Dose-related neurocognitive effects of marijuana use. Neurology 59, 1337–1343.

Bosker, W.M., Huestis, M.A., 2009. Oral fluid testing for drugs of abuse. Clinical Chemistry 55 (11), 1910–1931.

Bramness, J.G., Khiabani, H.Z., Mørland, J., 2010. Impairment due to cannabis and ethanol: clinical signs and additive effects. Addiction 105 (6), 1080–1087.

Chu, M., Gerostamoulos, D., Beyer, J., Rodda, L., Boorman, M., Drummer, O.H., 2010. The incidence of drugs of impairment in oral fluid from random roadside testing. Forensic Science International 2011 June 10 [Epub ahead of print].

Couper, F., Logan, P.B., n.d. Drugs and Human Performance Fact Sheets. National Highway Traffic Safety Administration. http://www.nhtsa.gov/people/injury/research/job185drugs/introduction.htm.

Gjerde, H., Normann, P.T., Christophersen, A.S., Samuelsen, S.O., Mørland, J., 2011. Alcohol, psychoactive drugs and fatal road traffic accidents in Norway: a case-control study. Accident Analysis and Prevention 43 (3), 1197–1203.

Gjerde, H., Normann, P.T., Pettersen, B.S., et al., 2008. Prevalence of alcohol and drugs among Norwegian motor vehicle drivers: A roadside survey. Accident Analysis and Prevention 40 (5), 1765–1772.

Jones, A.W., 2005. Driving under the influence of drugs in Sweden with zero concentration limits in blood for controlled substances. Traffic Injury Prevention 6 (4), 317–322.

Laumon, B., Gadegbeku, B., Martin, J.-L., Biecheler, M.-B., 2005. Cannabis intoxication and fatal road crashes in France: population based case- control study. BMJ: British Medical Journal 331 (7529), 1371–1377.

Maurer, H.H., 2009. Mass spectrometric approaches in impaired driving toxicology. Analytical and Bioanalytical Chemistry 393 (1), 97–107.

Orriols, L., Delorme, B., Gadegbeku, B., et al., 2010. Prescription medicines and the risk of road traffic crashes: A French registry-based study. Plos Medicine 7 (11), e1000366.

Polla, M., Stramesi, C., Pichini, S., Palmi, I., Vignali, C., Dall'Olio, G., 2009. Hair testing is superior to urine to disclose cocaine consumption in driver's licence regranting. Forensic Science International 189 (1–3), e41–e43.

Raes, E., Van den Neste, T., Verstraete, A.G., 2008. EMCDDA Insights: Drugs Use, Impaired Driving and Traffic Accidents. EMCDDA, Lisbon. http://www.emcdda.europa.eu/attachements.cfm/att_65871_EN_Insight8.pdf.

Walsh, J.M., Verstraete, A., Huestis, M.A., Morland, J., 2008. Guidelines for research on drugged driving. Addiction 103 (8), 1258–1268.

Relevant Websites

www.druid-project.eu—DRUID.

http://ec.europa.eu—European Commission, (Road Safety).

http://www.emcdda.europa.eu—European Monitoring Center for Drugs and Drug Addiction.

http://www.icadts.org—ICADTS, The International Council on Alcohol, Drugs, and Traffic Safety.

http://www.tiaft.org—TIAFT, The International Association of Forensic Toxicologists.

Drug Screening in Sport

L Rivier, Laurent Rivier Scientific Consulting, Lausanne, Switzerland

Introduction

The fight against drug abuse in sports started around 1960 and was forced to improve over time on each occasion when new and more sophisticated pharmacological products or forbidden practices were discovered. Doping using drugs is proven first by means of state-of-the-art sports drug-testing assays and was sometimes substantiated by confessions of convicted athletes and results of searches by regulatory authorities. When novel drugs or methods of doping and manipulation become evident, the development of new, complementary, and more comprehensive doping control strategies is required. These strategies need to comply with strict forensic requirements as penalties for athletes can be severe and some of the prominent athletes easily mount legal challenges to the evidence.

What Is Doping in Sport?

Besides stimulants and narcotics, anabolic agents, and peptide hormones, many substances are used and abused to improve the mental and/or physical performance of athletes. This is called doping and contradicts both sport and medical ethics. For the International Olympic Committee, the International Sport Federations, World Anti-Doping Agency (WADA), and all the national anti-doping organizations, doping is considered as cheating. The WADA Code defines precisely doping and its control in sport. The large majority of anti-doping testing programs endorse WADA regulations. Doping is considered an offense to the spirit of sport and is sanctioned by penalties as high as several years of suspension or exclusion to the practice of sport. The disciplinary authorities apply these important sanctions after the laboratory has reported an adverse analytical finding, that is, the presence of a forbidden substance, its metabolite(s), or marker(s) in the athlete's sample (usually urine) at any concentration, or the attempt to or the proof of using a forbidden method. The professional sports and National Collegiate Athletic Associations in the United States have their own prohibited lists, testing programs, and rules.

These sanctions restricted to the sport environment can have major economic, sportive, financial, or personal consequences and escape most of the time to the usual police and ordinary justice channels. One exception is doping agents' black market offenses that are assimilated to trafficking of drugs of abuse.

Some countries, however, have added to their own legislation specific laws that can also chase doping offenses directly.

Context of Adjudication of Anti-doping Rule Violations in Sport

The WADA Anti-Doping Program was developed in 2000 through an international consensus process involving athletes, sport leaders, and governments. More than 570 global sport organizations have now incorporated the WADA Code and its rules. The 158 governments (including the United States) who ratified the United Nations Education, Science and Cultural Organization (UNESCO) Anti-Doping Convention have also agreed to support the Program in their laws. So the Program truly represents an international consensus on how anti-doping rule violations should be addressed.

The burden of proof in anti-doping cases is not the criminal standard of beyond reasonable doubt, but rather the "comfortable satisfaction" standard used for violation of professional standards by many medical, legal, and scientific organizations. Athletes agree to abide by the anti-doping rules as part of the rules of their sport and as a precondition of their participation in the competition.

Anti-doping analyses are generally conducted in two steps. First, a screening is performed. In the case of a positive result, a selective confirmation is carried out. Results should be released rapidly. Therefore, high-throughput techniques are used to screen in a single method a large set of compounds with different physicochemical properties while avoiding false negatives and reducing false positive results ($\leq 10\%$). Advanced automated analytical methods are especially useful during important sport events, when reporting results are required within 24–48 h.

The List of Prohibited Compounds and Methods to Be Screened

The WADA has released six documents, three of which play a role in analytical method development:

1. The World Anti-Doping Code
2. The list of prohibited substances and methods
3. The International Standard for Laboratories

Forbidden compounds are placed on the list if they meet two of the following criteria:

1. The substance alone, or in combination with other substances, has the potential to enhance sport performance.
2. The substance represents an actual or potential health risk.
3. The substance violates the spirit of sport.

In addition, substances or methods that have the potential to mask the use of other prohibited substances are included. Currently, 209 substances are included in the list within several classes that include prohibitions effective at all times or in competition only. Examples of stimulants, narcotic analgesics, anabolic agents, diuretics, and peptide hormones are given for each class. The list's wordings include "… other substances with a similar chemical structure or similar biological effects." Therefore, one cannot claim to be not guilty because the detected drug that was used is not listed specifically by name. Only nine prohibited molecules (parent drugs and/or their metabolites) have a cutoff concentration in urine. For the others, any detectable amount will constitute an "adverse analytical finding," at least down to the specified minimum required performance level (MRPL) fixed for the laboratory by WADA. For example, MRPL is ranging from milligram per liter ($mg\ l^{-1}$) for stimulants down to the low microgram per liter ($\mu g\ l^{-1}$) level for anabolic steroids.

Accredited laboratories have to screen for substances with various polarities and volatilities, from simple stimulants to complex peptides. The choice of technology is determined primarily by chemical characteristics (e.g., solubility in water or organic solvents, volatility, thermic stability, and polarity). It is achieved routinely by more than one procedure or instrumental method. A way to improve cost-effectiveness of these analytical procedures is to maximize the number of analytes that can be determined in a single procedure (e.g., to use multicompound techniques).

Biological Sample Identity and Integrity

In doping controlled urine, it is important to collect an authentic urine sample from the correct person, get it properly sealed, and document it for shipment to the laboratory. Targeted athletes are properly identified before providing a urine specimen. A minimum of 70 ml required is collected in a cup under direct supervision (to avoid urine substitution or adulteration) by an official of the same gender. A chain of custody paperwork documents follow the samples until they are finally discarded.

Blood is collected more frequently within the newly developed drug-testing programs of specific international sport federations. The procedure for taking around 10 ml of venous blood is carefully described in one of the WADA technical documents and follows in a more precise standardized way what is applied daily in clinics.

Specific Procedures in Dedicated Laboratories

As doping accusations can have major consequences, the whole analytical process is based on forensic guidelines, for example, strictly controlled, validated, secured, and verified procedures. Hence, accredited laboratories only are allowed to conduct anti-doping analyses.

In practice, each sample entering the laboratory is first classified into in- or out-of-competition sampling, but for ease, the same screening procedures are applied to all of them. The analytical procedures for the small- (e.g., stimulants) and medium-sized molecules (e.g., derivatized steroids or glucocorticoids) are high-resolution gas chromatography (GC) with nitrogen-specific detection or high-pressure liquid chromatography (HPLC) with diode array detection, GC–mass spectrometry (GC–MS), and liquid chromatography–mass spectrometry (LC–MS) on the full scan mode or selected ion-monitoring mode. For larger molecules like the peptide hormones, immunoassays and isoelectrophoretic separation are preferred.

Statistics from WADA indicate that up to 280 000 samples have been analyzed around the world in 2009, out of which 1.1% have been declared as adverse analytical findings. Around 60% of these are anabolic steroids related to testosterone (**Table 1**).

In general, such a strictly controlled procedure for doping screening in sport is complex and includes the following key elements.

Chain of Custody

As far as the chain of custody is concerned, it starts well before the samples enter the laboratory after proper collection and tamper-proof transportation of the samples. Excessive

Table 1   Distribution of the 3 091 adverse analytical findings and 2 519 atypical findings reported by the WADA-accredited laboratories in 2009

Anabolic agents	64.8%
Cannabinoids	7.8%
Stimulants	6.4%
Beta-2 agonists	6.0%
Diuretics and other masking agents	5.4%
Glucocorticosteroids	5.2%
Hormones and related substances	2.0%
Hormones antagonists and modulators	1.0%
Beta-blockers	0.7%
Narcotics	0.5%
Chemical and physical manipulations	0.1%
Alcohol	0.1%
Enhancement of oxygen transfer	0.0%

temperature should be avoided for urines. It is known that a blood sample's composition changes rapidly over time and less stable doping parameters should be measured within a few hours after collection. Transportation at room temperature, or better around 4 °C, is preferred. This makes the handling of blood rather complex and expensive. In the laboratory, all processes including aliquots and extracts are recorded for the chain of custody requirements. This ensures the correct interpretation and reporting of the results and the appropriate disposal of the samples.

Validated Analytical Methodology

Analytical methods are implemented only if they have been correctly validated. The general procedure for method validation is defined in the International Organization for Standardization (ISO)/IEC 17025 companion documents. The accumulation of a vast body of analytical data is most often necessary to cover both intra- and interlaboratory variations. WADA is the ultimate body that allows the use of a newly developed procedure as was demonstrated for the introduction of the urine detection of erythropoietin (EPO) in 2002 or the biological passport (BP) in 2008.

Practical Analytical Approach

Only WADA-accredited laboratories are allowed to analyze official doping control samples in sport. The ISO/IEC 17025 requirements accreditation is the prerequisite condition to WADA accreditation. Mandatory requirements include, among others, quality assurance program, standard operating procedures for each assay, instrumental operation and maintenance, personal qualifications, restricted access to the laboratory's surfaces, computers, and electronic records, internal audit trails, and traceability of results obtained from reference standards or excretion studies.

To comply with forensic quality standards mandated by the WADA Code, several objectives must also be met during the development of a specific doping test. An important validation step is to demonstrate robustness, that is, small changes in the proposed procedure or the use of another instrument have no impact on the final interpretation of the test results. Thus, laboratories have agreed between them the common analytical procedures and interpretation criteria for the confirmation of identity of the compounds of interest.

The general strategy for handling and analyzing doping samples within the laboratory is schematized in **Figure 1**.

After registering each sample, the volume and the properties of the urine are recorded. The A-sample is then opened and the pH and density are measured together. Divided by groups of substances, the full screening can be covered by 8–12 separate analytical procedures (see **Table 2**) depending on the type of control (e.g., in- or out-of-competition).

For reasons of efficacy (highest sensitivity with best specificity), the most advanced analytical approaches are incorporated into doping controls. Today, mass spectrometry (MS), and particularly GC–MS, is so far considered the less likely technique to be challenged in court. Recently, liquid chromatography–tandem mass spectrometry (LC–MS/MS) has been

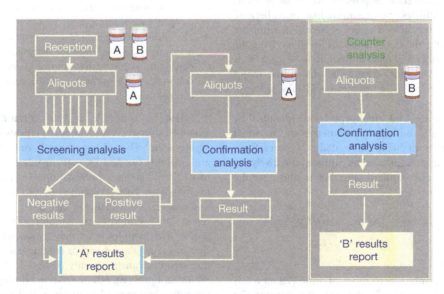

Figure 1 Place of the screening in the whole analytical process for doping controls. Before reporting an adverse finding, positives samples are always confirmed. For safety reasons, B-sample analysis—also called second confirmation or counteranalysis—is performed on the athlete's and/or sport authorities' request almost always in the same laboratory as the A-sample.

Table 2 Screening procedures in urine for the classes of prohibited substances and methods according to the WADA 2011 list

Prohibited substances/techniques	Immunoassay	GC	GC–MS	LC–MS or LC–MS/MS	Isoelectro focusing	Others
AAS			X	X		
Beta-2 agonists			X			
Diuretics and other masking agents				X		
Hormones	hCG, LH, hGH				EPO	
Antiestrogens			X			
Stimulants		X	X			
Narcotics		X	X			
Glucocorticosteroids				X		
Cannabinoids	X		X			
Alcohol		X				
Beta-blockers			X	X		
Chemical and physical manipulations						Various simple tests
Enhancement of oxygen transfer			HES, RSR-13		HBOCs	HES dextran by biochemical analyzer
Gene doping						No urine test

AAS, anabolic androgenic steroids; HBOCs, hemoglobin-based oxygen carriers; hCG, chorionic gonadotrophin; HES, hydroxyethyl starch; hGH, human growth hormone; LH, luteinizing hormone; RSR-13, Efaproxiral, a pharmaceutical hemoglobin modifier.

added to the extension of the panel of compounds already detected by GC–MS, including large, polar, and/or thermolabile substances. Over the last 5 years, the development of fast-switching MS/MS devices and smaller-diameter HPLC columns allows even more compounds to be screened from 2 ml of urine within less than 20 min of total analytical time.

Results are needed as soon as possible when the public is watching and when athletes compete more than once, because if they have used drugs, they should be removed from the competition. Typically, the time elapsed between receiving the samples at the laboratory and reporting results is 10 days, but it can be as short as 24 h for negative results during major international sport events. Confirmation will take a longer time.

For blood, most drugs and some peptides are identified by GC–MS or LC–MS and biological parameters are measured through the laboratory medicine-automated procedures. Standardization of the values is gathered by running repetitively the corresponding stabilized standards just before and after the samples.

The Specific Analytical Techniques Involved in Doping Controls

Sample preparation

In doping controls, minimum volumes of urine (70 ml total) and blood (3–10 ml total) samples are available for the detection of all listed drugs including their metabolites.

The use of urine is still considered as best sample for doping controls, in part due to the relative ease of collection and because of the higher levels found in urine over blood.

The analytical criteria for reporting adverse analytical findings in screening are the following:

- At a minimum, the analysis should consist of two steps, namely, screening the A-sample and performing an A-sample confirmation.
- The order recommended for injection into the analytical instrument for confirmation analysis is (1) reagent blank, if pertinent; (2) negative control urine; (3) sample being confirmed; (4) negative control urine; and (5) positive control urine.

When an A-sample analysis confirms the presence of a banned substance, the laboratory reports it to the anti-doping organization. The athlete—known only by the anti-doping authority—is notified by that organization and has the right to ask for a B-sample confirmation. He can witness the analysis himself or send a representative of his choice. After completion and conclusion, which may take up to 3 days, the laboratory reports the B-sample confirmation results. What remains from the positive samples is securely frozen for the length of time that meets regulatory and/or contractual requirements. Negative samples can be usually disposed of without delay. For critical samples (e.g., those collected during Olympic Games), the authorities may ask to preserve all the intact B-sample vials. WADA code allows retrospective analyses on these urines up to

8 years later. This is to take advantage of the development of new methods of detection during this time period.

Main Analytical Techniques

GC–MS detection

Automated GC–MS instrumentation is best suited to run many samples in a short period of time and to eliminate efficiently the many negatives. Modern MS instruments allow both automatic injection and treatment of the results. In general, total ion or selected ion current traces are generally very complex even at restricted time windows and targeted substances might be hidden behind the biological matrix background noise. A qualified laboratory technician will read the printed reports, with a second person, usually a senior scientist, verifying the findings. Because of so many true negative results ($>95\%$) even at low $\mu g \, l^{-1}$ concentration levels, the doping analyst should get best compromise between selectivity of the extraction and high recovery yield, speed, and low cost. Liquid–liquid partitioning or solid-phase extraction, either manual or automated, is most commonly used. Immunoaffinity chromatography and HPLC fraction collection have been recently introduced for improved reduction of the biological background to enable higher signal-to-noise ratios and improved detection limits.

GC–MS remains the technology of choice for the detection of anabolic steroids until the appearance in 2006 of tetrahydrogestrinone (THG) as a designer steroid, which was almost undetectable by the screening methods used at that time. The discovery of THG has led to the introduction of LC–MS/MS as an additional screening technology. As a result, GC–MS and LC–MS are now used as complementary techniques in doping control.

LC–MS detection

The high polarity of the conjugates eliminated in urine limits the use of GC–MS to hydrolyzed samples only. Such measurements offer targeted molecules with modified structure for identification and rather imprecise quantitative measurements of each individual moiety. One of the major advantages of liquid-based chromatography with MS is that the direct detection of thermolabile and polar compounds or metabolites involved in sport doping is possible. Now direct injection of diluted biological samples is even possible by ultra pressure LC–MS/MS provided sufficient resolving chromatographic power is obtained.

Developments in accurate mass detection

Conceptually achieved by the use of GC or LC in combination with full scan, accurate mass time-of-flight mass spectrometry (TOF-MS) or orbitrap MS, this new approach has gained popularity. The advantage of a full scan MS is its ability to

analyze a sample for a theoretically unlimited number of compounds. Furthermore, data can be acquired and reprocessed without prior knowledge about the presence of specific molecule (e.g., no analyte-specific information is required before injecting a sample and the presence of newly identified compounds can be confirmed in previously analyzed samples simply by reprocessing the data). As the number of forbidden doping agents is constantly expanding, the capability to identify compounds without reference standards is a clear advantage.

A general screening method for doping agents in human urine based on solid-phase extraction and LC–TOF-MS was developed and validated in 2007.

Discrimination between Endogenous and Exogenous Doping Agents

Pharmaceutical testosterone and natural testosterone mass spectra are identical when measured with ordinary MS detectors. In recent years, GC–carbon on-line combustion isotope ratio mass spectrometry (GC-C-IRMS) has been developed to make it possible to discriminate exogenous testosterone from endogenous testosterone by measuring $^{13}C/^{12}C$ ratio in these steroids and their metabolites. Since the 1998 Olympic Winter Games in Nagano, GC-C-IRMS has been an accepted method in doping controls. However, a relatively large volume of urine (~ 25 ml) is necessary and a time-consuming cleanup procedure is needed to obtain highly purified steroid fractions.

Criteria for Identification

Identification of a small molecule based on its mass spectrum is usually obtained by comparing spectra of the unknown sample by running on the same day the corresponding reference compound or standard through the same analytical procedure and instrumentation. In this way, the laboratory minimizes instrumental variations leading to slightly different MS to meet the required criteria of WADA for identification.

The Availability of Reference Doping Substances

Many doping substances are available at the requested purity for reference purpose through chemical manufacturers. However, most of the metabolites do not have readily available commercial sources and consequently no purity data are available. Consequently, all the laboratories prepare their own certified urines from controlled excretion studies. After the relevant permission from the medical ethics committee is granted, a small and unique dose of the doping agent is given to one volunteer. This healthy individual delivers several urine samples that allow the laboratory to trace and identify most relevant metabolites. After being analyzed, the remaining samples are mixed together. Aliquots are kept at a low temperature until used as reference samples.

Analytical Approach for Large Molecules and Peptide Detection

These screenings are basically performed by immunoassays directly on the urine or blood, or after specific manipulation of the samples (e.g., after ultrafiltration and concentration, blotting transfer, and electrophoretic separation). In principle, formal confirmation can be obtained by using other immunological tests acting on a different epitope of the targeted molecule.

The Biological Passport

The idea of a biological follow-up for athletes was first mentioned in 2002. The BP is based on the measurements of several key biological parameters (mainly in blood), the variation of which provides evidence of the use of banned substances.

First, it is necessary to establish the normal hematological profile of each individual athlete. All these parameters (e.g., hematocrit, hemoglobin content, etc.) are measured by standardized protocols in order to compare the values. To cover the forensic requirements, a statistical model based on the Bayesian approach is applied where the range of the normal variation of each parameter is defined on the same individual. Seven independent measurements are necessary before any prediction on the normal minimum and maximum values can be made. If these individual limit values are exceeded, doping sanctions can be made because such abnormality demonstrates manipulation of the blood parameters. The BP will possibly allow the detection of any kind of blood manipulation. The first case of abnormal hematological profile demonstrated by the BP passed successfully the Court for Arbitration in Sport (CAS) scrutiny in early 2011.

Developments for the Future

The continuous implementation of new analytical techniques to target a wider range of chemicals improves the deterrent effect of the controls. HPLC with matrix-assisted laser desorption ionization TOF-MS for determining protein molecular mass shows interesting promises for new applications, but requires additional development and validation before routine use in anti-doping laboratories. Against the recent outcome of new biotechnologies and new protocols for doping (e.g., EPO through micro doses, manipulation through blood autologous transfusions, use of growth factors, and cellular therapies), the present system should also find new strategies.

Targeted controls on suspicious athletes might also offer better yield for adverse analytical findings. The recent introduction of BP opens new possibilities. With high-quality intelligence information available, a more aggressive approach to catching cheating athletes can be developed. However, the high costs of such a program might restrict its implementation.

See also: **Toxicology:** Methods of Analysis—Confirmatory Testing; Methods of Analysis—Initial Testing.

Further Reading

Badoud, F., Grata, E., Perrenoud, L., et al., 2009. Fast analysis of doping agents in urine by ultra-high-pressure liquid chromatography-quadrupole time-of-flight mass spectrometry I. Screening analysis. Journal of Chromatography A 1216, 4423–4433.

Hatton, C.K., 2007. Beyond sport-doping headlines: the science of the laboratory tests for performance-enhancing drugs. Pediatric Clinics of North America 54, 713–733.

Rivier, L., 2003. Criteria for the identification of compounds by liquid chromatography-mass spectrometry and liquid chromatography-multiple mass spectrometry in forensic toxicology and doping analysis. Analytica Chimica Acta 492, 69–82.

Thevis, M., Kohler, M., Schaenzer, W., 2008. New drugs and methods of doping and manipulation. Drug Discovery Today 13, 59–66.

Van Eenoo, P., Van Gansbeke, W., De Brabanter, N., et al., 2011. A fast, comprehensive screening method for doping agents in urine by gas chromatography-triple quadrupole mass spectrometry. Journal of Chromatography A 1218, 3306–3316.

Relevant Websites

www.anado.org—Association of National Anti-doping Agencies.
www.tas-cas.org—Court for Arbitration in Sport.
www.olympic.org—International Olympic Committee.
http://portal.unesco.org—UNESCO. International Convention against doping in sport, 2007.
www.wada-ama.org—WADA. International Standard for Laboratories. Version 6: 1 January 2009 and The 2011 Prohibited List Internal Standard, Version September 2010.

Key Terms

Analytical strategy, Antemortem, Best evidence, Bias, Bile, Biological passport, Biological samples, Blood, Blood analysis, Bone, Brady material, Cerebrospinal fluid, Chain of custody, Chromatography, Collection site, Confrontation, Containers, Crash risk, Discovery, Driving performance, Drug detection, Drug-facilitated crime, Drug-facilitated sexual assault, Drugs, Embalming, Ethical considerations, Extraction, Flunitrazepam, Forensic, Forensic laboratory report, Forensic nurse, Gastric, GHB, Hair, Hair analysis,

Hazard, Health, Heart, Holistic approach, Identification requirement, Impairment, Instrumental analysis, Integrated case management, Investigations, Labeling, Legislation, Liver, Lung, Maggots, Mass spectrometry, Method validation, Muscle, Nail, Nonconsensual, Occupational health and safety (OHS), Oral fluid, Pericardial, Plasma, Pleural, Postmortem, Preservative, Prevalence, Putrefaction, Risk, Roadside detection, Safety, Screening, Serum, Spleen, Sport doping, Strategy, Submissions, Testimony, Toxicology, Urinalysis, Urine, Vitreous humor.

Review Questions

1. Are the models offered for forensic service provision suggested by Ramsey and Burton the only ones available? What other models might there be? Are toxicology laboratories more effective as for-profit businesses or as government services?
2. What is a "forensic strategy"? What questions are part of developing one? Why is it important to a case and to a laboratory?
3. Why is integration of forensic cases "the single biggest challenge to the forensic science community"?
4. What is currently in forensic reports? How do these differ from other scientific reports? How do they differ from published articles in peer-reviewed journals? What *should* be in forensic reports? Make a table listing each component and compare.
5. Who is the "audience" of forensic reports? Are the police using the technical information to investigate the case or other scientists who must review the technical information? Is it both? How does this affect the content of forensic reports? Should it?
6. How do the legal requirements of the contents of a forensic report differ between the UK and the US?
7. Can forensic reports stand on their own (that is, without an expert's testimony)? What determines this?
8. Are there ethical obligations to the format and content of a forensic report? If so, what are they?
9. What is "Brady material"?
10. What is "OHS"? What should this policy articulate?
11. What is a risk, in OHS terms? How is it prevented or mitigated? What is the hierarchy of control measures?
12. List some specific laboratory hazards. What are their risks, how are they managed?
13. Why is good housekeeping important in a forensic laboratory?
14. What is a drug-facilitated crime? List three types.
15. What types of drugs are used in DFCs?
16. Does the presence of a drug alone support a claim of DFC? Why or why not?
17. Why are vehicle crashes rarely attributable to only one cause?
18. What are some risks associated with driving under the influence of drugs (DUID)?
19. What does WADA stand for?
20. What is a biological passport?

Discussion Questions

1. How should forensic examinations and analyses be "integrated"? With laboratory specialization, how can cases move through a forensic laboratory in an integrated fashion? What are the benefits to doing this? What are the problems?
2. Why are forensic reports formatted the way they are? Is there a better way to present this information? Who are they written for and who should they be written for?
3. Are some types of forensic science more prone to hazards and health risks than others? If so, list them and explain why they are; if not, why not?
4. What are some of the issues relevant to toxicology in drug-facilitated crimes? Think in terms of time, sampling, matrices, and interpretation.
5. Is doping in sport a drug-facilitated crime? Why or why not? Is doping in sport *always* a crime? Given the fact that professional athletes will have significantly different metabolisms than nonathletes, what challenges are there for conducting toxicological investigations on the athletes?

Additional Readings

Boscia, C., 2014. Strengthening forensic alcohol analysis in California DUI cases: a prosecutor's perspective. Santa Clara Law Review 53. Available at: http://digitalcommons.law.scu.edu/lawreview/vol53/iss3/1.

Cole, S.A., 2014. History of Forensic Science in Policing. In Encyclopedia of Criminology and Criminal Justice. Springer, New York, pp. 2153–2158.

de Keijser, J., Elffers, H., 2012. Understanding of forensic expert reports by judges, defense lawyers and forensic professionals. Psychology, Crime & Law 18 (2), 191–207.

Holt, D., 2016. Forensic Toxicology: Drug Use and Misuse. Royal Society of Chemistry.

Howes, L., Kirkbride, K., Kelty, S., Julian, R., Kemp, N., 2014. Forensic scientists' conclusion: How readable are they for non-scientist report-users? Forensic Science International 231 (1–3), 102–112.

Roland, M.C., 2009. Quality and integrity in scientific writing: prerequisites for quality in science communication. Journal of Science Communications 8 (02), A04.

Siegel, J., King, M., Reed, W., 2013. The laboratory report project. Forensic Science Policy & Management 4 (3–4), 1–11.

Thevis, M., Geyer, H., Tretzel, L., Schänzer, W., 2016. Sports drug testing using complementary matrices: advantages and limitations. Journal of Pharmaceutical and Biomedical Analysis 130, 220–230.

Thevis, M., Kuuranne, T., Walpurgis, K., Geyer, H., Schänzer, W., 2016. Annual banned-substance review: analytical approaches in human sports drug testing. Drug Testing and Analysis 8 (1), 7–29.

Zamengo, L., Frison, G., Tedeschi, G., Frasson, S., Zancanaro, F., Sciarrone, R., 2014. Variability of blood alcohol content (BAC) determinations: the role of measurement uncertainty, significant figures, and decision rules for compliance assessment in the frame of a multiple BAC threshold law. Drug Testing and Analysis. http://dx.doi.org/10.1002/dta.1614.

INDEX

'Note: Page numbers followed by "f" indicate figures and "t" indicate tables.'